Bix

The Definitive Biography of
a Jazz Legend

Bix

The Definitive Biography of a Jazz Legend

Leon "Bix" Beiderbecke (1903–1931)

JEAN PIERRE LION

Translated from the French by
Gabriella Page-Fort
with the assistance of
Michael B. Heckman and Norman Field

continuum

NEW YORK • LONDON

2007

The Continuum International Publishing Group Inc
80 Maiden Lane, New York, NY 10038

The Continuum International Publishing Group Ltd
The Tower Building, 11 York Road, London SE1 7NX

www.continuumbooks.com

English edition of *Bix: Bix Beiderbecke, une biographie*
© Outre Mesure, Paris, 2004
Bix: The Definitive Biography of a Jazz Legend
Copyright © 2005 by Jean Pierre Lion
Foreword copyright © 2005 by Richard Sudhalter
Revised paperback edition 2007

Book design and composition by Susan Mark
Coghill Composition Company

Printed in the United States of America

Library of Congress Cataloging-in-Publication Data

Lion, Jean Pierre.
  [Bix. English]
  Bix : the definitive biography of a jazz legend / Jean Pierre Lion ; translated from
the French by Gabriella Page-Fort ; with the assistance of Michael B. Heckman and
Norman Field.
     p.   cm.
  Translation of: Bix : Bix Beiderbecke, une biographie. Paris : Outre Mesure, 2004.
    Includes bibliographical references (p.   ), discography (p.   ), and index.
    ISBN 0-8264-1699-3 (hardcover : alk. paper)
    ISBN 978-0-8264-2754-0 (paperback : alk. paper)
    1. Beiderbecke, Bix, 1903–1931.   2. Jazz musicians—United States—
Biography.   3. Cornet players—United States—Biography.   I. Title.
ML419.B25L5613   2005
788.9'6165'092—dc22

                                                                    2005010509

Contents

Foreword

Leon Bismark Beiderbecke lived a comparatively short life. Dead well before age thirty, he enjoyed a professional career, at least what the public saw of it, that lasted no more than seven years, woefully brief for a dance band musician. Still, Beiderbecke managed to leave a lasting impression. Even now, seventy-five years after his death, his approximately 250 records are constantly in circulation, with a partisan backing that is loud and passionate.

Writers can't stay away from him either: even Frederick Turner's *1929* was based on an author's comprehension of Bix and what he meant to his times. Others keep trying—Wareing and Garlick's *Bugles for Beiderbecke* failed only because of an over heavy reliance on secondary sources. Others, among them *The Bix Bands*, Phil Evans's various efforts, and long essays by Otis Ferguson, Benny Green, Burnett James, George Avakian, Digby Fairweather, Norman Gentieu, Albert Haim, Chip Deffaa, and my own modest efforts, added bits of understanding to an otherwise puzzling story.

The principals—among them most of the witnesses who either knew or even heard Bix—are gone, and with them the special memory which kept him and the sound he made alive. Bill Challis, Hoagy Carmichael, Artie Shaw, Eddie Condon, Andy Secrest, Joe Venuti—all departed—brought parts of a memory. Artie Shaw heard the Jean Goldkette Orchestra and spoke of Bix's tone quality with passion and eloquence. To Condon, it was "like a girl saying yes." Hoagy spoke of a mallet striking a chime. Others alluded to tone, attack, inevitability of phrases.

The essence is still lacking, but now a new scholar, working in far-off France, has drawn all elements of the story together. Jean Pierre Lion understands full well that the story of Bix Beiderbecke's brief, brilliant career is the story of jazz in the 1920s, its early and brilliant flowering as both an instrumental form and a way of life.

Carefully, scrupulously, he's gathered all the basic facts—from the details of Bix's life and music to the meaning and social significance of prohibition and the stock market crash—in shaping the story of the man known as jazz's anointed saint. No aspect of Bix's art goes unexamined: whether his reliance on unconventional fingerings or a virtually day-by-day tracking of the Jean Goldkette Orchestra on tour in 1927, Lion has done his homework thoroughly and excellently.

His narrative includes everything accomplished by Bix scholars throughout the years, shadowing his subject in every aspect of his musical and social life. He even includes a very perceptive essay on past Bix scholarship, examining closely and with sympathetic understanding the work of past cornetists, starting with the ill-fated Andy Secrest, devoted to Bix's way of playing.

Lion tells Bix's story in a straightforward style, neither too dry nor given over to the exaggeratedly sensational efforts of a pulp novelist. This is important, in that it allows the reader, not the biographer, to penetrate the curtain of neutrality and formulate his own conclusions about the man who emerges. Saint or sinner, innocent or guilty? Everything is here—the reader is only asked to decide for himself.

His handling of Bix's boyhood encounter with a morals charge, which may have led his parents to ship him off to Lake Forest Academy, is particularly good, in placing everybody's actions well within how people in the Beiderbeckes' social and economic bracket may have handled such matters.

In every way, this is the Bix book jazz fans have been awaiting. Three cheers for M. Lion in tackling a particularly difficult figure and handling the story so well. The book has my immediate and unqualified endorsement as a reading of the life and music of an irreplaceable and pivotal jazz figure.

—*Richard M. Sudhalter*

Acknowledgments

This biography is a continuation of the previous studies dealing with Bix Beiderbecke, and it would have never come to pass without them. Tribute must be paid in the first place to the gigantic work of Philip R. Evans—who unfortunately passed away while this book was being written—and his wife Linda; to the remarkable books and articles written by Richard M. Sudhalter, whose exhaustive research on white "early jazz" musicians was a primary source of inspiration; and to the historical Biographical Radio Series produced by James R. Grover.

Researching Bix's life and works led me to knock on many doors. Most of them opened widely, and I am greatly gratified by the impressive number of personal and essential contributions that were freely and zealously shared with me.

The first edition of *Bix* was published in Paris in 2004, thanks to Outre Mesure's indefatigable and meticulous editors, Claude Fabre and Vincent Cotro. The making of this new U.S. edition was actively supported by Michael B. Heckman and Norman Field: I am deeply indebted to the friendly way they shared with me their vast knowledge, to their patience and understanding, and to their comforting sense of humor. I will always keep vivid memories of the late Frank Powers, a true Bix aficionado who answered all my questions with a faultless science, until he, unfortunately, passed away before the French book was published. The city of Davenport has no more secrets for Rich Johnson, who most graciously drove me along its streets, in search of the many Bix related places he knows of: thanks a lot, Rich, for these most pleasant days and for your unlimited availability! Thanks to his helpful daughter, Vicki Wassenhowe, I was fortunate to be able to communicate with, and to finally meet, Leslie C. Swanson; the possibility of questioning this last personal friend of Bix Beiderbecke was a privilege and a great pleasure that I will not forget. Rick L. Kennedy wrote a fascinating history of the Gennett Studios, and he was also kind enough to accurately answer all the questions I sent him, and to show an interest in my work. Thanks for everything, Rick! Albert Haim runs an essential website, on which available information related to Bix is carefully gathered and preserved; he was extremely helpful and friendly during the writing of the French biography, for which I remain very thankful—may I hope that this American edition will seem more agreeable to him?

I am also extremely grateful for the effective assistance generously provided by Jim Arpy, Dave Bartholomew, Chris Beiderbecke, Scott Black, Vito Ciccone, Sue Fischer, David Geffen, Peter Hanley, James Kidd, Michael Kieffer, Steven Lewis, Joe Mosbrook, Bob Pecotich, Richard Raichelson, Don Rayno, Joe Showler, Allan Sutton, William Utter, William Trumbauer and Frank Youngwerth; I'm thankful to Brad Kay for his fascinating discoveries; and I want to express my appreciation to the archives and collections that provided valuable information, namely to Rita MacAyeal and Arthur Miller (Lake Forest); Sylvia Kennick Brown (Williamstown); Dan Morgenstern (Institute of Jazz Studies in Newark); Bruce Raeburn (Tulane University in New Orleans); Charles E. Brown (Saint Louis); Susan Sutton (Indiana Historical Society); Marisa Morigi (Princeton); Diane Schinnerer (San Francisco) and Cheryl Schnirring (Springfield).

Writing this book gave me the opportunity to meet Laurie Wright and his wife Peggie: thanks to both of you for the time and the attention granted to my work! Through *Storyville* and the many books you wrote and published, you have given us an invaluable source of information on the history of jazz.

I want also to deeply thank the many European contributors who tirelessly answered my questions and enquiries: William Dean-Myatt, Nick Dellow, Ray Mitchell, and Richard Warner in the U.K.; Victor Bronsgeest, Hans Eekhoff, and Frank van Nus in Holland; Helga Radau, Bernhard H. Behncke, and Karlheinz Drechsel in Germany; Enrico Borsetti, Fredrik Tersmeden, and the many participants to the "Bixian" Forum, whose communications were very often of high interest.

This book would have never come to light without the dedication and the intensive work of its publisher, Continuum-Books: thanks a lot to Gabriella Page-Fort and to her colleagues, who have been supporting this long-term project with amazing and smiling patience.

Many people were kind enough to share for this book the unique documents that were in their collections: I am most grateful to Liz Beiderbecke Hart, Dave Bartholomew, Bernhard Behncke, Hans Eekhoff, Albert Haim, Rich Johnson, James Kidd, Joe Mosbrook, Michael Neer, Frank van Nus, Michael Peters, William Trumbauer, and Vicki Wassenhowe; additional documents came from private collections or public libraries, and we want also to deeply thank for their assistance: Duncan Schiedt, Indiana University, Lake Forest Academy and Lake Forest College, Davenport Public Library, the Institute of Jazz Studies, Williams College, Tulane University, Saint Louis Mercantile Library, the Indiana Historical Society, the Eugene O'Neill Foundation, and Anne Legrand at the Bibliothèque Nationale de France.

BEIDERBECKE FAMILY TREE

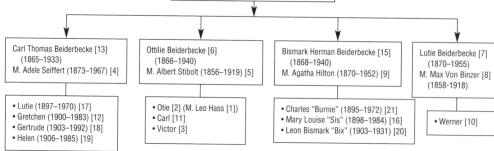

Carl "Charles" Beiderbecke (1836–1901)
M. Louisa "Louise" Piper (1840–1922) [14]

Carl Thomas Beiderbecke [13] (1865–1933) M. Adele Seiffert (1873–1967) [4]	Ottilie Beiderbecke [6] (1866–1940) M. Albert Stibolt (1856–1919) [5]	Bismark Herman Beiderbecke [15] (1868–1940) M. Agatha Hilton (1870–1952) [9]	Lutie Beiderbecke [7] (1870–1955) M. Max Von Binzer [8] (1858-1918)
• Lutie (1897–1970) [17] • Gretchen (1900–1983) [12] • Gertrude (1903–1992) [18] • Helen (1906–1985) [19]	• Otie [2] (M. Leo Hass [1]) • Carl [11] • Victor [3]	• Charles "Burnie" (1895–1972) [21] • Mary Louise "Sis" (1898–1984) [16] • Leon Bismark "Bix" (1903–1931) [20]	• Werner [10]

Introduction

Davenport, Iowa, September 21, 2002

An imposing mansion, now carefully restored to its late-nineteenth-century appearance, is proof of the Beiderbeckes' status in Davenport society. A huge home, suited for a large family. The clan was started in 1860 by the union of Charles Beiderbecke and Louise Piper. A picture remains, taken in the grand salon on Christmas day, 1912. Charles died in 1901, and Louise, who would survive her husband by twenty years, is surrounded by twenty of her descendants as she gazes proudly at the camera. Seated in the front row, a mischievous-looking nine-year-old grandson smiles. He is Leon "Bix," who would inscribe the Beiderbecke name in the history of jazz.

That big home was the setting for years of family celebrations and Sunday after-church gatherings. It is now a bed-and-breakfast, where I spent the night. The vast staircase that led down from my room trembled many times beneath the boisterous stampedes of the young prodigy and his many cousins. Two devoted Bixians met me on the sunny front porch: Rich Johnson, the musical director of the annual jazz festival, and Jim Arpy, a journalist for the *Quad City Times*.

It was a clear autumn day, bathed in deep blue light, as bright as a set in a movie studio. We drove along Ripley Street, which runs steeply downhill toward the Mississippi, and crossed the river on the first metal bridge to link Davenport to Rock Island, Illinois. Heading south, we soon arrived at the cozy country home where Leslie C. Swanson was awaiting our visit.

At ninety-seven, Les Swanson was, along with clarinetist Artie Shaw, one of only two surviving musicians who had played with Bix Beiderbecke.[1] He heard the tone of his cornet, vibrating a few feet away—a sound that, according to all who heard it, has never been adequately reproduced by any recording. Les and I exchanged several letters before this meeting. His, typed on a fifty-year-old Reming-

1. Both musicians passed away when this book was being written, Les Swanson on April 6, 2003, and Artie Shaw on December 30, 2004. In Russell Davies's *Quest for Perfection* (BBC Four, 2003), Artie Shaw recounted: "I bought a farm, a run-down . . . and went out there to, I thought, write a book. I don't know what—I must have been crazy— I must have thought you write a book and your fortune's made, I had no idea. I was gonna try to write a book about Bix. And . . . I couldn't. I couldn't make the writing live." (Thanks to Frank van Nus.)

ton, convinced me that he could easily resume his former occupation as journalist and writer, and that his fine-tuned memory remained accurate.

Les Swanson was an astonishing presence: alert, tall, his figure and health seemingly immune to the ravages of age. This grand old man showed a lively wit and a singular sense of humor. He had rubbed shoulders with Bix for several months, during the last two years of his friend's life, and played piano with him in dance halls throughout the region. He was immediately attracted by Bix Beiderbecke's unique personality, and by his musical abilities, the significance of which eluded the majority of the area's professional musicians.

Seated on a couch and regularly tapping his cane on the coffee table in front of him, the old pianist relived for us the years 1929 and 1930. I was familiar with many of the anecdotes he told: they had been included in his letters to me, or told to previous interviewers. But, as he let his memory lead him through the distant past, he related a story we had never heard before: "The proprietor of a speakeasy on Davenport's Skid Row was preparing to close up his restaurant," recounted Les Swanson, "when he noticed the disheveled look of a young man, crouched over at the end of the counter, staring at a cup of coffee. There was something familiar about the man, and he moved a little closer to get a better look at him. *'That can't be him,'* he muttered to himself as he reached the customer. He decided to venture a question: *'Do you happen to be Bix Beiderbecke?'* The sullen figure of the man remained motionless for a few seconds, then he turned slowly and nodded in agreement. *'This man is ill,'* the proprietor called out to the two girls who were busy cleaning the room. The girls really went to work on Bix, who sported a two- or three-day beard and rumpled clothes that looked like he had slept in them for a couple of nights. The proprietor didn't think Bix's condition warranted calling a doctor. After sleeping it off, Bix was reportedly returned to the family home on Grand Avenue. Joe Stroehle, one of Bix's classmates in high school, told me that story. He heard it from the owner of the bar."

Is this story authentic, or is it a new chapter in the legend that, since Beiderbecke's premature death, has been slowly built up around the musician's mythic figure? We will never know.

F. SCOTT FITZGERALD claimed to have coined the expression "the Jazz Age" with the September 1922 publication of his second collection of short stories, *Tales of the Jazz Age*. He would also write in 1931 that, in his opinion, this period started with the postwar May Day riots of 1919 and ended with the October crash of 1929—a decade that covered exactly the time between the American writer's first success and the moment when, his style being considered passé, his audience turned away from him.

Though Wall Street's collapse and Black Thursday, on October 24, 1929, did mark the end of an era, it seems more accurate to postpone by a few months the birth of the Roaring Twenties—this burgeoning age following the anguish of the war years—and to start them on January 17, 1920, the day the law banning the sale of alcoholic beverages all over the United States took effect. Prohibition was marching in, and it would give rise to an unexpected movement in defense of individual liberties, making consumption of alcohol an act of civic resistance—not exactly the desired end.

Thus began ten truly crazy years: a brief moment of abandon, a ray of light breaking through a rather somber century. The talents and the demons of youth took to the stage, filling the streets and shaking up life. Daring deeds were applauded, even encouraged; but a sickly dawn would follow a fiery night, leaving a bitter taste on the lips. The decade ended with no resolution. The curtain would fall on an economic crisis and the death of heroes. The background music for these sleepless nights followed the rhythms of the jazz band.

THE FIRST WORLD WAR brought about a marked increase in industrial production, but at the same time, the draft siphoned off large numbers of young men who would have filled the new factory jobs. Employers had to turn to two nontraditional sources for laborers: women and southern blacks. A flow of African-American migrants found in New York, Chicago, and other northern cities a degree of personal and creative freedom unheard of in the southern states they had moved from. As later recalled by the black poet Langston Hughes, the 1920s were a time "when the negro was in vogue." Fletcher Henderson, Louis Armstrong, Jelly Roll Morton, King Oliver, Sidney Bechet, and Clarence Williams had already recorded intensely during the first half of the decade, but their creations, labeled and promoted as "race records," were distributed only to a limited black audience. In the fall of 1923, the Cotton Club opened in Harlem, building its success on a simple business policy: entertainers were black; patrons, owners, and producers were white. And if an adventurous segment of the white audience dared to make its way to the exciting black Harlem and the South Side of Chicago, only a handful of "hot music" fanatics searched in black neighborhoods for the records of black orchestras—the players of a music that today we consider authentic, but that was generally qualified in the press of the 1920s as "primitive, noisy, discordant, and—because of the lascivious dances that often used to go with it—obscene."[2]

The indisputable King of Jazz was, for the white American audience, the dance bandleader Paul Whiteman, who sold records by the millions. "Whether we are playing the simple, suave theme of a pathetic Negro 'blues,' or the sharp, saucy, pepful rhythm of the jazz tune, we strive to make the effect as thoroughly musical as possible," wrote Whiteman in *The Étude* in August 1924. The recipe for such "musicality" was a combination of skillful multi-instrumental musicians, intricate written arrangements, and popular tunes . . . and it worked well! From "Whispering" in October 1920 to "My Angel" in June 1928, Paul Whiteman remained for

2. Blues was the exception, and in January 1921, "Crazy Blues," by black singer Mamie Smith, was a big hit for the Okeh label; in July 1923, "Down Hearted Blues," the first record made by Bessie Smith, sold more than a million copies. The word *hot*, which is no longer used, was mostly applied in the 1920s to improvised jazz executions, as opposed to the "straight music" played by dance bands reading a score.

eight years at the very top in record sales. Besides these "orchestral" performances, which included waltzes and semiclassical numbers, the category of "jazz" also encompassed the singing of Al Jolson and the novelty music of comedian-clarinetist Ted Lewis, as well as many popular white dance orchestras, bringing hit after hit to the music business. The best selling bands were directed by Isham Jones ("I'll See You in My Dreams," with the Ray Miller band in March 1925), Ben Selvin ("Dardanella" in January 1920), Fred Waring, and Ben Bernie, whose names were the only "jazz stars" known to the American public, those appearing in the national press.

3. Thanks to Frank Youngwerth's research, we know what Abbe Niles's "praise" consisted of. It was part of a review published in *Bookman* in August 1928, in which he wrote, "Fox trot records: 'Thou Swell' and 'Somebody Stole My Gal' by Bix Beiderbecke's (Okeh) are hard and brilliant." And that's all. Charles Edward Smith's article, included in the October 1930 issue of *The Symposium*, was titled "Jazz," and it covered fifteen pages. A few lines were dedicated to Bix's playing: the author alludes to his "ad-lib chorus" in the 1924 version of "Royal Garden Blues," and compares two recordings of "Jazz Me Blues," writing about the second (1927) that "the climax, reached in the chorus by Bix, is high poetry."

4. The first appreciation of Bix's music as a distinctly American art form came from Wilder Hobson, who wrote in October 1933 in *The Musical Record*: "Beiderbecke was a poet who took the materials at hand, the ragtime in the backroom of the ice cream parlor, the close harmonies of the negroes and their rhythms which diversify the heart beat and make of them an artistic entity. . . . His music was American, rooted in every accent. . . . Melody jetted from his cornet, his rhythms were varied and extremely agitating, his solos were shaped and cadenced with a fine instinct for style." Wilder Hobson is the author of other pioneering works, such as the first article dedicated to Duke Ellington in the August 1933 issue of *Fortune*, and the book *American Jazz Music* (1939).

5. Unfortunately, Edgar Jackson's lyricism was also used to denigrate the records made by black jazzmen. Speaking in the name of white "dance and jazz musicians," he dared to write, "We demand that the habit of associating our music with the primitive and barbarous negro derivation shall cease forthwith, in justice to the obvious fact that we have outgrown such comparison." (Thanks to Nick Dellow for the information related to early issues of *Melody Maker*.)

BIX BEIDERBECKE'S PROFESSIONAL CAREER lasted eight years, from 1923 to 1931, a period during which his name was known only within a limited circle formed by his colleagues, a few journalists, and some hot music fans in the U.S. and in Western Europe. On the cover of a 1961 RCA Victor LP, *The Bix Beiderbecke Legend*, jazz critic George Avakian wrote, "It is my fervent hope that every jazz musician of today will note Charles Edward Smith's observation that Bix Beiderbecke, in his lifetime, was praised perhaps twice in print, and then obscurely—for the record, the references were in magazine articles written by Abbe Niles in *Bookman* and Charles Edward Smith in *The Symposium*."[3] During his lifetime, Bix was actually mentioned several times in American newspapers and magazines. Aside from the Davenport local press, in which it's not surprising that Bix appeared from time to time, reviewers Billie Thomas and George Davis of the *Cleveland Press* also wrote articles about him published in 1927 and 1929. The Beiderbecke name appeared as well in national trade and music magazines, the first known reference to "Leon Beiderbecke" being found in an article written by Abel Green for *Variety* on September 24, 1924, when Bix's orchestra was featured at the Cinderella Ballroom on Broadway. With the sole exception of an article published by Charles Edward Smith in October 1930, whose critical approach was somehow more developed, the other texts devoted to Bix were in the style of a gossip column, emphasizing facts, events, and promotion, and ignoring the music.[4]

Bix's original and innovative playing seems to have received more appreciation in Europe, something he might have been aware of in the last years of his life. "Bix Bidlebeck [*sic*] is considered by Red Nichols himself, and every other trumpet player in the States for that matter, as the greatest trumpet player of all time," wrote the British bandleader Fred Elizalde in the April 1927 issue of *Melody Maker*, a magazine started sixteen months earlier. Its editor, Edgar Jackson, reviewed several of Bix's records, released in England by the Parlophone label a few months after being recorded in New York. Jackson used a lyrical style, writing for instance: "Bix has a heart as big as your head, which shines through his playing with the warmth of the sun's rays" (September 1927), and "The next sixteen bars are trumpet solo by Bix, and if this doesn't get you right in your heart, you'd better see the vet . . ." (April 1928).[5]

The general understanding at the end of the 1920s was, however, that the "musical jazz" played by Paul Whiteman or by the British bandleader Jack Hylton, with their white big bands and their *sweet* and sophisticated written arrangements, was a glorious pinnacle in the evolution of primitive black music. To our knowledge, the first author to clearly move away from that idea was a nineteen-year-old Frenchman, Hugues Panassié, who cleared the path to modern jazz criticism in two articles published in 1930. The second, included in the June 1930 issue of the prestigious *La Revue Musicale* and titled "Le Jazz Hot," is more detailed and elaborate. In the very first sentence—"Any new form of art doesn't fail to raise violent opposition . . ."—Panassié applies the word *art* to *hot* jazz music, which is considered "the real and unique form of jazz." The author emphasizes that its true creators are the musicians, improvising and thus composing new melodies from existing themes and chord progressions, and adding: "The biggest names in 'hot jazz' are, among black musicians: Louis Armstrong, Earl Hines, Coleman Hawkins; among the white: Bix Beiderbecke, Jack Teagarden, Pee Wee Russell, Bud Freeman, Frankie Trumbauer, Joe Sullivan, Tommy and Jimmy Dorsey. It would be a mistake to believe that white jazzmen are inferior to the black ones. They play actually so much in the style of the black players that one can easily be mistaken. . . . Louis Armstrong is generally considered as the master of 'hot jazz.' He plays trumpet with an outstanding technique. His unlimited imagination allows him to create the richest and most varied solos that can be heard, and to renew his inspiration permanently. . . . The most extraordinary 'hot' musician after Louis Armstrong is a white player, Bix Beiderbecke. He plays piano and cornet, and is equally brilliant on both instruments. . . . Bix plays cornet with a style which is less wild than Armstrong's, but he has the same spontaneity. His improvisations are miraculously well balanced. Never a lack of taste. His solos are played with a deep feeling of emotion." Immediately upon being informed of Bix's death, in the October 1931 issue of the French magazine *Jazz-Tango,* Hugues Panassié published a sensitive and penetrating article, which was the only scholarly work published at the time of the musician's demise.[6]

A similar approach to *hot* jazz was to be found in the work of a Belgian poet and writer, Robert Goffin. His book, *Aux Frontières du Jazz,* published in 1931, is imperfect and incomplete, but its distinctive warmth and resonance has the power to stir latent emotions in its readers, and thus it captures the essence of jazz. Hugues Panassié's first book, *Le Jazz Hot,* came three years later—a work disputable on some points, but of undeniable historic importance—with full chapters dedicated to Louis Armstrong and Duke Ellington, and with an analysis of the development of Bix Beiderbecke's unique style and main recordings. This French appraisal was confirmed with the publication in March 1935 of the bilingual first edition of a new jazz magazine, *Jazz Hot.* It included several pages dedicated to Bix, written by Charles Delaunay, who attempted—with amazing success, considering the few

6. A translation of this article is included in the "Documents" section.

firsthand sources that were available to him—to compile the first discography of the cornetist.[7]

At that time, the Beiderbecke name was still unknown to most American jazz aficionados, an audience buying hit records by Duke Ellington, Fats Waller, Louis Armstrong, Cab Calloway, Ethel Waters, and also by Bix's former partners Bing Crosby, Jimmy and Tommy Dorsey—and Benny Goodman, who had the first of his many best sellers with "Moon Glow" in June 1934. During a visit to Bix's hometown of Davenport in 1935, historian Marshall W. Stearns was surprised to hear Bix's parents admit that they were unaware of their son's reputation among Chicago and New York jazzmen.[8] Things started to change some months later, and five years after Bix's death, a more general interest focused on the musician's career and works. The December 1935 issue of *Down Beat* magazine included two pages written by Warren W. Scholl, who asserted: "I guess very few musicians will disagree with me if I say that I consider Bix to be the greatest white hot cornetist of all time." The California magazine *Tempo* released in June 1936 an article signed by Charles Edward Smith discussing the possible influences on Bix's style, from Nick La Rocca to King Oliver and Louis Armstrong. In July, Bix was voted "top trumpet of all time" by the musicians participating in the magazine *Down Beat*'s annual poll. On July 29, Otis Ferguson dedicated several pages to Bix in the *The New Republic*: titled "Young Man with a Horn," this lengthy and perceptive article concluded by asserting about a solo of Bix's that "One hears it, and is moved and made strangely proud; or one does not, and misses one of the fine natural resources of this American country." Ferguson's text was probably linked to the release, on the day it was published, of a six-record Victor set, *Bix Beiderbecke Memorial Album*, offering unpublished alternate takes by the cornetist, coupled with a highly documented booklet written by Scholl. This active summer celebration ended with a second article in *Tempo*, written by Charlie Preeble: "Bix as I Knew Him." November 1936 saw the publication of *Swing that Music*, the first autobiography of a jazz musician. It was written by Louis Amstrong, and its inscription read: "To the memory of the original 'Dixieland Five,' to King Oliver, to Bix Beiderbecke and Eddie Lang, now gone, and those other pioneers of a quarter of a century past, known and unknown, who created and carried to the world a native American music, who created Swing."

Supported by the memories of his friends, who claimed that Bix had changed their lives, the story of the cornetist who died when he was twenty-eight, reduced to silence by alcohol, started to take a posthumous place among the Fitzgeraldian heroes of the 1920s. A legend was growing up around the life of a highly talented jazzman. In the late 1930s, jazz—now called swing—was everywhere—and it had become, as John Paul Perhonis astutely puts it, "no less than the popular music of America," a part of the expression of the national American spirit.[9] Dorothy Baker borrowed from Otis Ferguson the title of her novel, *Young Man with a Horn*, a

7. Several important early articles about Bix were also published by the British magazine *Swing Music*: a tribute by Leonard Hibbs in August 1935; a two-part article by George Beall about the Jean Goldkette Orchestra, released between October and December 1935; "Bix—As I Knew Him," by Bix's drummer, Vic Moore, in March 1936; "Bix's Cornet" by Charles Delaunay the following month; and another Wolverine's memories, "Wolverine Days" by George Johnson, published in the Autumn 1936 issue.

8. Marshall W. Stearns, founder of the Institute of Jazz Studies in Newark, New Jersey—which is now directed by Dan Morgenstern—dedicated articles to Bix in *Down Beat* magazine in September and October 1935, as well as the two-page "Souvenirs," in the sixth issue of the French *Jazz Hot*, published in November 1935. The last sentence of this article reads, "A short while ago I asked Muggsy Spanier who he thought was the greatest trumpet player of all time. *'He's dead,'* replied Muggsy simply." Warren W. Scholl (1913–1992) was the U.S. correspondent for the British magazine *Melody Maker*, in which he published articles about Bix in March, April, and December 1934, as detailed in the bibliography. He also worked for the Victor label.

9. John Paul Perhonis, "The Bix Beiderbecke Story: The jazz musician in legend, fiction and fact," thesis submitted to the University of Minnesota, March 1978, p. 77.

book that was, according to its author, "inspired by the music, not by the life, of a great musician, Leon 'Bix' Beiderbecke." And it's true that the fictitious life of white jazz trumpeter Rick Martin does not follow the historic existence of Bix. However, for the first time in a best-selling novel "was stated the unconventional connection between jazz and art, and the jazz musician and creativity."[10] Dorothy Baker acknowledges the creative role of black musicians in jazz music and, through 250 pages of high literary value, she draws the vivid and "tougher portrait of the jazz musician as artist-hero."[11]

New recollections from Bix's friends were gathered in the November 1938 issue of *Metronome*, bringing a fond tribute to the vanished musician, and Edward J. Nichols wrote an article dedicated to Beiderbecke in the 1939 book *Jazzmen*, a collection of pioneering studies of jazz, edited by Frederic Ramsey and Charles Edward Smith. Bix had now taken his place in the American mythology. This young man, raised in a bourgeois midwestern family, comforted Americans with the idea that an original white jazz was possible, alongside the music of black musicians. But if Bix was "the first saint of jazz," this secular canonization was not devoid of a certain ambiguity.

TOWARD THE END OF 1938, Hugues Panassié directed three recording sessions for the French label Swing. Some big names of the golden age of New Orleans jazz gathered in the RCA Victor studios in New York: Sidney Bechet, Tommy Ladnier, James P. Johnson, Zutty Singleton, Pops Foster, and Milton "Mezz" Mezzrow. They were the half-forgotten heroes who, with these records, rekindled interest in their old music. Known as the Revival, the movement would call unemployed artists of this passé musical style to return to the studios and the international scene: Jelly Roll Morton, Bunk Johnson, and Kid Ory would be among them.

By the early 1940s, the swing era and its expensive big bands were coming to an end. Wishing to escape from the rigidity of playing intricate big-band scores, many musicians would find a freedom in smaller groups they lacked in large units. Bebop would be the innovative path followed by many young and highly talented jazzmen, while other "traditionalists"—mostly white bandleaders—would turn back to the "cradle of jazz" and reactivate a strong popular interest in the New Orleans style. Dixieland groups were formed, made up of young musicians longing to reproduce the original 1920s recordings: Lu Watters' *Yerba Buena Jazz Band* in San Francisco, Humphrey Lyttelton in England, and the French orchestras of Claude Luter and Claude Abadie would successfully emulate the manner of playing of the old masters.

The year 1946 was therefore the right time for Milton "Mezz" Mezzrow—with the assistance of Bernard Wolfe—to publish his autobiography, *Really the Blues*. Written in the jive talk of the time, the book has a punchy and catchy style. It walks its reader through the streetlife and smoky clubs, and drags him into the paradise

10. Perhonis, op. cit, p. 104.

11. Perhonis, op. cit, p. 132. In a letter to John Perhonis, dated February 1977, Howard Baker—who was Dorothy's husband, and was teaching in Cambridge, Massachusetts—related that "we were working at that time [1938] on a project for a musical version of *Young Man with a Horn* on Broadway, for Vinton Freedley. . . . Perhaps the best thing for Dorothy was the great Duke's composing a number called 'Young Man with a Horn' for her, and having her for his guest in Harlem when he played it for the first time. You can still hear it. It's called 'Boy Meets Horn.'" The number was recorded by the Ellington orchestra, with Rex Stewart on cornet, on September 2 and December 22, 1938, and it was part of the typical Ellington program of the time.

and the hell of drug addiction. Bix is very much present in the author's memoirs, which paint a touching image of the cornetist—that of an inspired and alcoholic vagabond, adding a new chapter to the legend.

A new generation of French jazz critics would, at about the same time, acknowledge the originality and the beauty of Bix's creations. Frank Ténot was the first, in the January 1947 issue of *Jazz Hot*, to credit Bix with true musical genius. He was followed in September 1951 by Michel Andrico, who wrote contradicting "the present popular opinion that Bix wouldn't have been more than a decent musician of the second or even third class."[12] Andrico's opinion was defended in the same magazine two years later by Lucien Malson and Jacques Hess, who dedicated several pages to a formal rehabilitation of the cornetist's image, emphasizing in their article that "Bix adds to the greatest melodic inspiration a harmonic understanding that is much ahead of its time and, lastly, a reliability of taste, an elegance that turns him into a prince among his contemporaries."[13]

THE FIRST BIOGRAPHY of Bix Beiderbecke was published in London in 1958: *Bugles for Beiderbecke* was written by Charles Wareing and George Garlick, unquestioning admirers of the musician who, despite living in England, had managed to assemble all the information about Bix available at that time. It was a time when several jazz scholars were working on research projects on both sides of the Atlantic. William Dean-Myatt was compiling a biodiscography in England, and he invited Americans Philip R. Evans and Robert Mantler to join him. George Hoefer, writer of the "Hot Box" articles in *Down Beat*, was gathering elements for a biography.[14] Richard M. Sudhalter, a journalist and excellent cornet player, would publish, in the September 1967 issue of the British magazine *Storyville*, a thirty-page article titled "Bixology," which gathered essays and interviews connected with Bix's life and work. Four major studies dealing with the musician came out in the early 1970s, more than forty years after Bix's death, at a time when the last surviving witnesses were growing scarce.

A series of radio programs, *Bix, A Biographical Radio Series*, was directed by James Robert Grover in 1971, and submitted as a "Creative Aural History Thesis" at Miami University, in Oxford, Ohio. Broadcast on the radio station WMUB, these nineteen programs covered the artist's short life with a combination of narration, interviews, and musical comments, offering a skillful and vivid homage to the musician.

Three books were published shortly after these programs were aired. The first, *The Bix Bands: A Bix Beiderbecke Discobiography*, was edited in Italy and attributed to three authors—two Italians and one Dutchman—who wished to present a complete discography of the cornetist's many recordings. The second was a book of "recollections," *Remembering Bix*, written by Ralph Berton, whose literary conceits overwhelm its historical value. The third and most important title, *Bix, Man and*

12. *Jazz Hot*, no. 58 (September 1951), p. 6.

13. "Regards sur le jazz de Bix," in *Jazz Hot*, no. 81 (October 1953), p. 10.

14. George Hoefer's files and the documentation gathered for his work are held by the Institute of Jazz Studies, Rutgers University, Newark, New Jersey.

Legend, published in 1974—as was Berton's—was the fruit of a collaboration between Philip Evans, Richard Sudhalter, and William Dean-Myatt. Philip R. Evans, who passed away in July 1999, dedicated more than forty years of his life to compiling and checking all available information related to Bix Beiderbecke. Richard M. Sudhalter had already been focusing his studies on the same subject for many years, and he brought his musical experience and literary talent to the completion of this pioneering work. This book met with great success. It included a discography that would remain, for almost three decades, an indispensable reference.

BIX IS NOT an underrated artist and his place among the "jazz giants" has never been disputed. His recordings have always been available, and the California editor of *Origin Jazz Library* released, between 2000 and 2004, a series of twelve discs compiling—with high sound quality—a practically complete collection of the recorded sides on which Bix was present. He remains nevertheless as little known by the general public as some of his fellow musical partners: Frank Trumbauer, Eddie Lang, and Joe Venuti, just to name a few. These young musicians, unrelenting in their disruption of the puritanical values of American society, don't deserve the silence in which they're still enshrouded and which surrounds much of the jazz music recorded by white artists during the 1920s. The centennial of Bix's birth, in March 2003, saw a limited number of celebrations, and a visit to his hometown clearly confirms that "No man is a prophet in his own country."

If no man is an island, every human being is guarded by his own personal mystery—but Bix really goes a bit too far! Unknown by his friends and misunderstood within his family circle, he met death as a youth, leaving our curiosity with a few photographs in which he ages quickly, forty-four letters—mostly written during his adolescence—and 200 recordings. The outstanding level of inspiration and the profound originality of some twenty sides make them true masterpieces, which would alone justify our study of their creator. To try to understand this musical angel, whose wings were clipped by thousands of pints of bootleg gin, lures us into a universe where, at the very end, darkness will prevail over light.

CHAPTER 1

Origins

The time of the pioneers: 1853–1903

arl T. Beiderbecke, grandfather of the American cornet player, was born in Benninghausen, near Lippstadt, in western Prussia.[1] He was eighteen when his father died, in 1851. His mother, Sophia Becker, passed away just a few months after her husband's death. Carl abandoned his study for the Lutheran ministry and joined the stream of emigrants who, with nothing to lose but hope, left a Prussia given over to chaos and set off for the New World. He arrived in New York in 1853.

He settled in Indianapolis, Indiana, and worked for ten months in a grocery store before spending two years with the United States Post Office. He was transferred to Dubuque, and didn't like this new assignment. He soon left government service and, in September 1856, moved to Davenport, Iowa, where he returned to his first profession by opening a grocery store with Frank Miller, another German immigrant. In this commercially deprived territory, a well-run new business was destined for quick success.

The Great Lakes region was developing rapidly. Pacification, which began in 1820, did not prevent the massacres of some conservative Indians who attempted to hinder progress, but it enabled Chicago to grow to 4,000 peaceful and industrious habitants by 1837. Railroads linked the city to New York in 1855, and a canal was constructed, connecting Lake Michigan and the Illinois River, giving Chicago easier

1. The Beiderbeckes' German roots were not in Mecklenburg, in northern Germany, as asserted by Joachim-Ernst Berendt in his book *Das Jazzbuch* (Frankfurt: S. Fischer Verlag). This false information was often repeated, and actually believed, by Louis Armstrong, who said in 1965 that he had been shown the house in Barth where Bix's grandparents used to live! (*Jazz Hot*, no. 481, September 1991, p. 18). Karlheinz Drechsel followed Louis Armstrong and His All Stars during their 1965 tour of Germany, and he explained that Louis had heard this story from local journalists during a stop at the Barth airport on April 9, 1965.

Beiderbecke and Miller, Wholesale Grocers, at 107–109 West Second Street, Davenport. The company shut down in 1902, but the building still stands. (Rich Johnson)

access to Saint Louis, the Mississippi River, and the port of New Orleans. The arrival of immigrants was accelerated by the Civil War, and the city counted 300,000 inhabitants when, in 1871, it was in large part destroyed by a fire. It was quickly reconstructed, and by 1893, a million Chicagoans greeted twenty-seven million visitors at the Chicago World's Fair. America was taking shape.

Carl Beiderbecke settled in a brand new city. During pacification, General Winfield Scott had, without much delay, driven the Fox Indians from their land, permitting Colonel Davenport to found "his" town in 1832, at the foot of a hill overlooking a bend of the Mississippi River. Iowa entered the Union in 1846, becoming the twenty-ninth state, and Davenport, built on the bank of the river and close to the Illinois frontier, was set to accommodate many immigrants. The newcomers gathered in communities of their own ethnic kind, and the influx of Prussians in 1857 gave rise to an essentially Germanic city.

In 1860, Carl Beiderbecke married Louisa Piper, a young German girl fresh off the boat from Hamburg. The development of Beiderbecke and Miller Grocers mirrored the growth of his own family, his wife bearing him four children. A contract with the Union Army during the Civil War enriched Beiderbecke and Miller, and their grocery store became the most important wholesale market west of the Mississippi. This economic success established the Beiderbecke family's social standing: in 1880 they built a large house on the heights of Davenport[2] and ten years later, Carl was named president of the bank he had founded with Heinrich Seiffert. The Germanic tradition, Carl's religious training, and the social life of his new urban community, concerned with the preservation of its European traditions, enhanced the importance of music in his life: Carl presided over the German Musical Society and directed the Maennerchor, a male choir destined for local fame.

2. This house is still standing at 532 West 7th Street. It was restored at the start of the 1990s, and now houses Pam and Dennis LaRoque's bed-and-breakfast, the Beiderbecke Inn (bbonline.com/ia/Beiderbecke). Much smaller, the house where Carl Thomas and his wife, Adele Seiffert, lived is located on the same street at 510 (506), close to the big Seiffert house at 532 West 6th Street.

Wishing to feel like full-fledged American citizens, many immigrants chose to anglicize their first and last names. Carl seems to have wavered over his decision: he changed his own first name to Charles, but retained Beiderbecke, which is not easy for an American to pronounce. However, he bestowed upon his children first names that were quite exotic for young Americans: the eldest was named Carl Thomas, the two girls Ottilie and Lutie, and the second son was anointed with a double Bismark Herman, which confirmed the familial faith in the budding chancellor's political

Home of Carl and Louise Beiderbecke (Bix's grandparents) in Davenport. (JPL, 2000)

The Beiderbecke family house on Grand Avenue in Daveport. (JPL, 2000)

3. Bix's family house, at 1934 Grand Avenue, is still there. Today it is painted white, though it was originally green. It is rather far from the homes of Bix's grandparents and uncle. Bedrooms were on second floor: the parents' on the left side, and the bedroom shared by Bix and Burnie on the right, opening on a false round balcony. This is the room where Bix stayed every time he came back to Davenport. His sister's bedroom was in the back. The house belongs today to Italian filmmaker Pupi Avati, creator of *Bix, an Interpretation of a Legend*. (All information related to Bix in Davenport was kindly supplied by Rich Johnson and Jim Arpy.)

future. Born in 1868, this second son joined his father's business at the age of twenty, and he was assigned bookkeeping duties. In June 1893, Bismark married Agatha Hilton, who, at age twenty-three, had gained an excellent local reputation as a pianist. The young couple moved into a two-story house that was newly built for them, at number 1934 Grand Avenue.[3] Three children were born within its green walls:

The Beiderbecke family in 1904. Left to right: Charles "Burnie," Bismark, Bix, Agatha, and Mary Louise "Sis." (Davenport Public Library Collection)

Charles Burnette "Burnie" in 1895, Mary Louise "Sis" in 1898, and Leon Bismark Beiderbecke on March 10, 1903.

Davenport, March 1903–December 1912

The nickname Bix quickly replaced the imposing Bismark within the family, and it was to become the everyday name of the youngest child. The family continued its social ascent. In 1905, Bix's father took over direction of the East Davenport Lumber & Fuel Company, an enterprise devoted to commerce in wood and coal.

A photograph taken in 1904 preserves the image of an ideal family: Agatha, pretty, with dark hair and in a severe dress, stands above the group; Sis dreams under her big white bow; Burnie, a fair-haired boy, smiles angelically; and resting on the knee of his visibly tense father, the infant Bix looks bored, enveloped in a scalloped dress, with a stubborn face, sullen lips, and protruding ears—ears that would soon awaken to music. The young Bix rapidly showed off his astonishing musical gifts. As early as five years old, reaching up to the piano on the tips of his toes, he could play with one finger the very melodies his older sister was persistently stumbling over. In 1908 he started kindergarten at Tyler School, located conveniently close to the family's home. His teacher, Miss Alice Robinson, would recall a remarkably talented child, capable of reproducing all the melodies taught to the pupils on the classroom piano.

Bix and friends, around 1908. Bix is third from the left. (Davenport Public Library Collection)

Bix in kindergarten, school year 1908–1909. (Davenport Public Library Collection)

Two years later, the family's youngest member caused the Beiderbecke name to appear in the columns of the local gazette, the *Davenport Daily Democrat*, which disclosed to its readers the exploits of the little prodigy: "Aged 7 years, Little 'Bickie,' as his parents call him, is the most unusual and the most remarkably talented child in music that there is in this city. He has never taken a music lesson and he does not know one key from another, but he can play in all completeness any selection, the air or tune of which he knows."[4]

4. *Davenport Daily Democrat*, 1910: "7-YEAR OLD BOY MUSICAL WONDER. Little Bickie Beiderbecke Plays Any Selection That He Hears," quoted in *The Leon Bix Beiderbecke Story*, by Philip R. and Linda K. Evans (Bakersfield, CA: Prelike Press), p. 24. This remarkable book, the last written by Phil Evans, offers an extensive chronology and database about the life and the work of Bix Beiderbecke.

Bix in 1911, age 8, with Nora Lasher, a neighbor. (Davenport Public Library Collection)

Davenport, bank of the Mississippi. (JPL, 2000)

Bix's strong attraction to music was accompanied by an aversion just as strong for any form of teaching. During 1912, while he was in the third grade, Bix's schooling was interrupted for several weeks by scarlet fever. His mother called for a music teacher, Charles Grade, who quickly gave up hope of taming the child's musical instincts and his predisposition to creative imagination, one that overcame his interest in undergoing the rigors of formal training. Without a professor who could keep his attention, Bix sought his own way and would always favor a path he had discovered himself to one already mapped.

He still hadn't returned to school when summer vacation arrived. Bix's mother showed him affection and involvement, which reinforced his feeling of difference and compensated for the absence of a father who was absorbed in his work. This period was important in the child's development because it marked a departure from normal daily activities and schoolwork, and gave him access to a personal universe in which the center was music. From this point on, Bix's short life would focus itself on his incomparably gratifying and infinitely painful relationship with his musical desires.

The family's Sunday afternoon walk would often lead the Beiderbeckes to the bank of the Mississippi, to enjoy the cool air by the river. Until World War II, Davenport served as a winter port for the Streckfus Line, whose huge paddleboats traveled up and down the river, over the several thousand miles between New Orleans and Saint Paul. The children couldn't take their eyes off the enormous steamboats, whose crews and personnel included more and more strange black men coming from the south.

Family parties and gatherings centered around the piano, a symbol of the European bourgeois culture and style that the new American middle class modeled itself on. Until the appearance of recorded music, and the radio broadcasts that followed, this instrument was the principal source of home entertainment and the central element of social life. Though Agatha took pleasure in interpreting popular melodies written for musicals, her personal taste carried her toward more ambitious works. She had a marked preference for *The Red Mill* by Victor Herbert (a composer remembered today only for some minor operettas) and for Claude Debussy's melodies. Bix discovered the harmonic universe of this French musician, his poetic visions, his diffuse emotion—a world that had already appealed to the ten-year-old boy and one where he felt comfortable.

Bix's ear refined itself. He remained unable to read music, but he could memorize more and more complex compositions and harmonies, repeating verbatim the errors of the performer he copied or, better still, correcting them. One of his childhood friends retained a memory of this exceptional talent: "His folks wanted him to be a concert pianist," he said. "And has that kid got an ear! He can tell you the pitch of a belch!"[5]

Bix in 1912, age 9, near his family home on Grand Avenue. (Davenport Public Library Collection)

At the start of the school year, in September 1912, the pupil's long absence resulted in his having to repeat the previous year. This pampered child, publicly designated as a prodigy, took the humiliation of his being left back badly, and he seems to have made a decision with ultimately serious consequences, subsequently regarding himself as outside a school system that refused him the sympathetic attention he thought he deserved.

New Orleans, December 1912

While Bix was celebrating Christmas in the bourgeois comfort of his family nest, 1912 ended tragically for a young New Orleans boy who had greeted the New Year by firing a pistol on Rampart Street. Arrested and locked up for the night, he was sentenced to a reformatory the next day. The name Louis Armstrong made its first appearance in the press, as the *Times-Picayune* informed its readers, "six white boys were arrested in Canal Street for disturbing the peace. The most serious case was that of Louis Armstrong, a twelve-year-old Negro, who discharged a revolver

5. George Johnson, as quoted by Hoagy Carmichael, *The Stardust Road* (New York: Da Capo Press, 1946 and 1999), p. 48.

at Rampart and Perdido streets. Being an old offender he was sent to the Negro Waif's Home."[6]

Louis was released from the reform school in June 1914, when he was thirteen years old. He had left his childhood behind those walls, but the training on the cornet he had received there and the experience gained in the reformatory's brass band allowed him, as soon as he was back in New Orleans, to attract the attention of Kid Ory and Joe "King" Oliver, two musicians who were the recognized masters of a musical style spreading within the limits of Louisiana and a few southern cities.

Recorded music: 1880–1920

At the start of the twentieth century, the American public was seduced by the allure of industrial progress. The exodus from the farms had begun, and cities grew with a population eager to enjoy the latest innovations. The Ford Model T was offered at the incredibly low price of $300, making it affordable to almost every salaried worker. At the same time, the appearance of recorded music made possible the wide distribution of high-quality interpretations of many different genres; the public, keen for novelties, took to it all.

In the U.S., the invention of a recording device and audio reproduction is credited to Thomas Edison in 1877. Its recording part consisted of a brass cylinder, covered with a piece of tinfoil. A steel point was mounted in a diaphragm, which sound waves could vibrate. Such vibrations moved the steel point—or stylus—vertically engraving the tinfoil it was pressing on. A motor operated by a battery maintained a steady rotation of the cylinder. It couldn't be any simpler. Edison's first practical machine was commercialized in 1888, using wax cylinders. However, this process had one important limitation: the cylinders were difficult to duplicate and to produce in large volume. Columbia, a concern affiliated with Edison's North American Phonograph Company, could produce only 300 to 500 units each day, and prices of the cylinders therefore remained high.

Edison would soon be confronted with the competition of a German immigrant named Emile Berliner, who in 1887 devised a system capable of recording and reproducing sounds on a flat disc. He called his machine the "gramophone." His patented process employed the lateral engraving of a wax-coated zinc disc, where sound vibrations were inscribed on the sides of the groove. In 1893, Berliner created the U.S. Gramophone Company. Disc records offered numerous advantages over cylinders: easier storage, improved listening quality, and above all, the possibility of large-scale reproduction on pressings derived from a metal matrix. Berliner's gramophones were equipped with spring motors, made exclusively in Camden, New Jersey, by Eldridge Johnson. The success of this co-

6. Laurence Bergreen, *Louis Armstrong, an Extravagant Life* (New York: Broadway Books, 1997), p. 69.

operation was rapid, and was followed just as rapidly by the severance of business between the two associates. On the basis of his own inventions, Johnson founded two companies, Victor Talking Machines and Victor Records. The American market of recorded sounds was soon to be dominated by two brands, Victor and Columbia, the latter gradually replacing its cylinders with lateral-cut discs. This dual monopoly would not be effectively broken until 1920, when the patents held by the pioneers of this new industry expired. One hundred million records were sold that year in the U.S., a sales number that speaks for itself. Records created a social phenomenon by introducing to the general public various musical forms, among which a new sound would appear and meet with surprising success—jazz!

New Orleans before 1915

By most accounts, jazz was born in the black quarter of New Orleans at the turn of the twentieth century. And it is true that the word "jazz" was made known by a band from Louisiana, who gave it its first big commercial success—but the five members of this orchestra were white. They were billed under the name of the Original Dixieland Jazz Band (ODJB).

Jazz is one hundred years old, and its vitality and longevity are now established. Its evolution coincided with the speedy expansion of twentieth-century society, and its turbulent and rich history places it among the major cultural phenomena of our era. Jazz could only be a bastard child: the offspring of noble blood don't enjoy such vigor.

It all started with the distressed song of the black slaves who realized they had been taken from Africa with no hope of return. The blues is the true expression of their anguished cry. It was influenced by spirituals, the African-American versions of the religious songs taught by the whites, and it also fed on the strongest components

Sketch of the Original Dixieland Jazz Band, Victor Talking Machine Company, 1920. (Enrico Borsetti)

of traditional African songs. Blues and spirituals are the true roots of all black American music. But New Orleans' development took place during the nineteenth century, amid a sparkling mixture of cultures and races: the French and Spanish, who disputed over Louisiana in the preceding century and from whose mélange Creole culture would rise; Acadians, the French settlers exiled from Canada by the British; Italian immigrants; newly arrived Americans who settled in the city's prosperous neighborhoods; and a black population that amounted to some 250,000 souls at the start of the twentieth century—souls that were liberated from slavery at the end of the Civil War, but kept under the control of the whites through legal segregation that covered every domain of public life. The Supreme Court ruled in 1896 that blacks were entitled to "separate but equal" facilities. They were happy enough to be equal, but had a hard time understanding why the places they were allocated were always the worst ones.

In this exceptional cultural melting pot, jazz was born as a result of fusing the power of traditional black music with elements borrowed from European traditions. Ragtime would find its inspiration in the popular dances of the old continent: gigues, minuets, polkas; and the famous brass bands of New Orleans derived from the military parades imported by French and German immigrants.

From this variety of musical forms, one in particular would emerge and spread toward the North of the country, due to its innate quality and versatility. It is still referred to today as "New Orleans style," or Dixieland, in reference to its southern origins. It consists of a small group of five to seven musicians. Four instruments are always present: a cornet, which generally plays the melody, a clarinet adding higher-pitched embellishments, a trombone used to provide the lower musical accompaniment, and a drum kit supplying the rhythm. When the job paid enough, a piano, a banjo, and a tuba could be added—these last two instruments often being replaced at the end of the '20s by a guitar and a string bass.[7]

Chicago, 1915

From 1915 on, the industrial development throughout the American Midwest, mostly in and around the cities of Chicago, Detroit, Cleveland, Indianapolis, and Cincinnati, generated a strong need for manual labor. Many of these workers came from the South. In New Orleans, the abundance of musicians made it difficult to find work there, so Chicago would welcome, on May 13, 1915, the first orchestra to have left New Orleans: it was led by Tom Brown, and it was engaged for six weeks at Lamb's Café. The band was made up of five white musicians, with Tom Brown on trombone and Ray Lopez on cornet. Their debut initially met with little success, but effective promotion soon attracted more spectators than the room

7. No recordings by black New Orleans musicians were made before 1922: the first side recorded was "Ory's Creole Trombone" (Kid Ory), cut in California on May 20, 1922.

could hold, and a line snaked every night along the sidewalk outside the entrance for the three months the orchestra played at the venue.

Black musicians were also playing in Chicago in 1915. Jelly Roll Morton was working on the South Side and in September 1915 his composition, "Jelly Roll Blues," became the first jazz music ever to be published, both as a written piano solo and as an orchestration. The Original Creole Orchestra played in February 1915 at the Grand Theater, including cornetist Freddie Keppard—one foot in legend and the other in the grave—and the amazing clarinetist Jimmy Noone. But segregation held fast, and these exceptional musicians, confined to the city's black South Side neighborhoods, couldn't reach a large enough audience to financially reward their unique talent.

The success of Tom Brown's band prompted Harry James, an able promoter, to send for a second orchestra from New Orleans. Driven by the aggressive horn of Nick La Rocca, five white musicians took the stage at Schiller's Café in March 1916. The orchestra was receiving a more than adequate welcome when, shortly after its debut, a controversial advertisement drew an even more sizable audience. Under the title "Sixty Women Rip Mask from Vice," an article in the *Chicago Herald* on May 1, 1916, described a raid led by "Leagues of Virtue" into the hell of Schiller's Café. The "turpitudes" of the drunken customers were smugly disclosed, and a titillated readership went on to learn details of the bedroom romps of these southern musicians of torrid reputation. The band was announced under the name of Stein's Dixie Jass Band, at a time when the word "jass"—as it was written then—had an undeniable sexual connotation: a "jass baby" was an easy girl. The orchestra's success was assured!

New York, 1917

Nick La Rocca well understood the power of publicity, and he engaged his quintet, which was now called the Original Dixieland Jazz Band (ODJB), at a prestigious New York restaurant, Reisenweber's. In January 1917, New York had never heard anything so dynamic, and the orchestra erupted with frenetic energy, propelled by extremely fast tempos. The burlesque effects were immediately successful. The music played by ODJB wasn't lacking in quality, but it sought to please the widest possible audience, and thus presented a simplified form, an attractive caricature of the New Orleans style. The band's Victor recording of "Livery Stable Blues," famous for its musical evocations of farm animals, reached an overwhelming popularity, surpassing Caruso's sales and swelling Victor's profits. It would even earn a million dollars for the ODJB! The historical first recording of "jazz music" had also given the young record industry its first commercial music success.

Davenport, 1917–1919

On December 21, 1916, Bix Beiderbecke made his stage debut, at age thirteen, in a Christmas cantata played and sung by the children of Tyler School. He had been enrolled in the seventh grade since September, and he was clearly behind his friends in his schooling, but that did not affect his charming smile and constant kindness. His father, however, did not mirror that smile while reading the grades on his son's report card.

As German submarines insisted on testing their torpedoes against the targets proffered by American ships, the United States declared war on Germany in April

Tyler Grade School, school year 1917–1918. Bix is at the far right in the middle row, with Larry Andrews on his side; Vera Cox is fourth from the right in the front row. (Davenport Public Library Collection)

1917. Burnie, Bix's older brother, immediately enlisted and was appointed as an instructor. He was ending his military training in Louisville, Kentucky, when the armistice was signed on November 11, 1918. He was released from the army a few days before Christmas, and on his way back to Davenport, he bought a Victrola phonograph and several records. Burnie had evidently chosen best-selling titles, among them the March 25, 1918, Victor recording by the Original Dixieland Jazz Band, of "Tiger Rag" and "Skeleton Jangle."

These records resulted in Bix's first encounter with jazz, and the adolescent was immediately fascinated by the discovery. His head plunged into the horn of the machine, he played the two sides over and over for hours, indifferent to anything else. Lea Ely, a neighbor, gave him an old dented cornet, and he spent weeks fiercely and relentlessly reproducing on the instrument notes that he had picked up, one by one, from listening to the record played at slow speed. "At first it was hard on the rest of us," remembered Burnie, "His playing consisted of short blasting notes, until he got a mute. The mute was a godsend and we were able to go on with our lives while the lad practiced. Every spare moment was spent in front of the phonograph, practicing, learning, and hearing what no one else heard. One day he suddenly seemed to know what he was doing, and he took off from there. The notes had changed and were coming through sweetly and quietly. It was startling how quickly he learned."[8]

8. *The Leon Bix Beiderbecke Story*, op. cit., p. 42.

In February 1919, at Davenport High School, where he was now enrolled, Bix met Fritz Putzier, who was playing cornet in a small ensemble of five or six musicians, and he was called upon to join the group on piano. On Friday nights, the musicians accompanied dance lessons in the gymnasium. Admission was ten cents, and Bix took to the piano for an hour or two, "faking" the songs by ear and performing quite decently.

At the start of school in September 1919, Fritz Putzier announced to Bix that he was thinking of quitting cornet and switching to saxophone, as his lips had been badly damaged by the long summer-night performances. For $35, Bix made a deal with his friend for the purchase of his horn, a Conn Victor model, and the two boys agreed on a long-term payment plan. Bix was given a few lessons by Albert Petersen, a relative of Agatha's, who directed the Davenport Brass Band, and also by Julius Paudiet, a German professor who, at more than seventy years of age, still held his spot in the city's orchestras. This double teaching doubtless brought him much precious advice, but Bix retained from his self-taught method a personal and unique fingering technique, very different from any orthodox playing of the instrument. His frequent use of the third valve alone, seldom employed by traditional musicians, would also contribute to the special sound that he made his own.

The adolescent's progress in learning cornet advanced quickly. In November 1919, he was able to integrate his new instrument into the band led by Fritz Putzier, who would look back on those first sessions with amusing and admiring recollection. Bix launched fearlessly into the construction of original passages, stumbling regularly over a tricky sequence, or letting out, just as regularly, a phrase of surprising grace.

Davenport High School. (JPL, 2003)

Play at Davenport High School in 1918. Bix is far right in the front row, his cousin Gertrude Beiderbecke is second from right in the middle row, and Vera Cox is far right in the back row. (Davenport Public Library Collection)

Prohibition, January 17, 1920

Prohibition took effect on January 17, 1920: America was officially "dry." The law was the outcome of a century-long fight against alcoholism led by temperance organizations. Their issue was well founded, as the annual consumption of alcohol in the United States in 1815 had reportedly reached in twenty-five million gallons, for a population of seven million! While the sale of alcohol to American Indians was forbidden, it had been freely permitted to the Union soldiers engaged in the Civil War, with the blessing of Abraham Lincoln.

The first success of the antialcohol organizations was gained in Maine, where the sale of alcohol became unlawful in 1840. The conclusive victory would, however, be driven by the massive engagement of women, united in 1874 in the WCTU (Women's Christian Temperance Union), a movement whose expansion was followed in 1893 by the creation of the powerful ASL (Anti-Saloon League), wherein the influence of the Protestant church was joined with that of "progressive" businessmen. The ASL was requesting national prohibition, and its members didn't hesitate to play up the anti-German feelings that arose with the First World War, campaigning against the owners of beer breweries, who were often of German origin. These crusades could backfire with unpredictable consequences, such as the unexpected publicity and the resultant popularity that the Original Dixieland Jazz Band had received during its debut in Chicago. The year 1919 was devoted to preparing the enforcement machinery, with the creation of a special police force, 1,500 agents strong, and of a Bureau of Prohibition, controlled by the ASL and which would subsequently become a hotbed of political-financial wheeling and dealing.

The law forbade the sale of alcohol to the public, but not its consumption. Only traffickers could be pursued, and as they were not few, the new legislation immediately gave rise to significant criminal activity. Counting speakeasy keepers, home distillers, bootleggers, and smugglers, the preventive policy created many jobs. The banning of alcohol had unexpected consequences: for instance, many Americans made it a point of honor to signify their rejection of Prohibition by markedly increasing their consumption. Hitherto sober people appeared in bars, while the unrepentant alcoholic was regarded as a national hero. For the young, drinking became a means of affirming independence and liberty. In 1927 an estimated 30,000 speakeasies were open in New York, twice as many bars as before Prohibition. Home production often resulted in awful-tasting alcoholic beverages, and the poisonous presence of methyl alcohol would kill several thousand consumers. Jazz was played primarily in bars, nightclubs, and dance halls, and jazz performers were not surprisingly major consumers of alcohol. Bix entered this world at a time when the floodgates of the traffic in illegal liquor were opening ever wider, and he would do his best to drink his full share of the resulting flood.

New Orleans, 1915–1920

Louis Armstrong had experienced hard times since his release from the Waif's Home in 1914. He was then thirteen—two years older than Bix—and worked all day long. He drove a coal cart during the day, and on nights and weekends picked up his horn and blew it in a dive haunted by prostitutes and shady characters from the local underworld. He toiled for sixteen or seventeen hours, and was given only $2 a day. The closing of Storyville's brothels, on November 12, 1917, dealt a significant blow to the nightlife in New Orleans, and a new wave of musicians emigrated to the North. The highly respected cornetist Joe "King" Oliver, who was Louis's musical father, left New Orleans for Chicago in June 1918. Louis Armstrong's musical reputation was growing, and Kid Ory offered him King Oliver's chair in the band that was playing at night at Pete Lala's. In the euphoria of the Armistice Day of November 1918, the young man gave up his coal cart and decided to devote himself exclusively to music.

By the end of the year, bassist George "Pops" Foster had asked Louis Armstrong and drummer Warren "Baby" Dodds to join him in the band of accomplished musician Fate Marable, who was leading the best of the riverboat bands, playing on the steam-powered paddleboats that so fascinated Bix as they passed by Davenport. In the nineteenth century, those boats carried merchandise and animals on their lower decks. The new railroad transportation provided tough competition for the riverboat companies' freight business. Many of them were obliged to modify their practices, adapting such vessels of their fleet as they could for passenger cruises. This policy was followed by the Streckfus Steamboat Line, which hired Fate Marable. In 1918 the band-

Fate Marable's New Orleans Band on the SS *Capitol*, 1920. Left to right: Henry Kimball (b), Fate Marable (p), Boyd Atkins (vln), Johnny St. Cyr (bjo), David Jones, Norman Mason (sax), Louis Armstrong (ct), Norman Brashear (tb), Warren "Baby" Dodds (dm); printed signs behind the band read MARABLE'S WALTZ REVIEW and MARABLE'S CAPITOL REVIEW. (Courtesy of the Hogan Jazz Archive, Tulane University)

leader agreed with its company to assemble an all-black orchestra. There were eleven musicians in his band, all able to read music and play tricky arrangements and intricate melodies.

It was on the *Dixie Bell* in 1919 that Fate Marable won his reputation: his band used to sit on the third deck and play from eight o'clock on to attract the public as the boat was leaving the dock for a three-hour trip. Fate would climb to the uppermost deck of the riverboat where there was a calliope—a steam-powered organ that he had fully mastered. The instrument was set up in the open air and, during rainstorms, the organist had to wear a slicker and a fisherman's hat. At the time, the sound of automobile traffic did not disturb the silence of the night. One could hear the approaching deep song of the calliope from far away and suddenly see, emerging from the fog, the shining boat and its musical attendants. After this waterlogged performance, Fate would put on his tuxedo and sit at the piano, directing his black band for an all-white clientele—for whom six nights per week were reserved, with Monday night's show the only one open to a black audience. This segregated schedule would be maintained on the Streckfus Line until 1969.

The SS *Capitol*, Streckfus Line Co. (Duncan Schiedt Collection)

Louis Armstrong started as second cornet in Fate Marable's "conservatory." With Baby Dodds, Pops Foster, and guitarist and banjoist Johnny St-Cyr, the band gathered some of the hottest shots around, but who, at Captain Streckfus's request, performed mostly *soft* music made of melodies borrowed from classical music, easy-listening dances, and waltzes, all played at very slow tempos. The band worked on Friday nights, Saturdays, and Sundays. At the end of a winter spent wandering around New Orleans, Fate asked Louis to follow him for the summer season on a several-month-long cruise, up north along the Mississippi. In May 1919, Louis left his hometown and took the long train ride to Rock Island, Illinois. With his old dented cornet, his little suitcase, a fish sandwich, and wondering eyes, Louis was the perfect picture of a traveling hick musician.

Fate Marable's band boarded the *St. Paul* and went on "tramping" along the Mississippi. "Tramping" meant that the riverboat spent just a night or two in each city, offering a short musical cruise on the river, and leaving in the morning for its next stop. "The first year we went up the river, we didn't do good at all," recalled Baby Dodds. "It was pitiful . . . I think people used to come on the boat more for curiosity than anything else."[9] For many Americans, however, the boat's stops would be their first contact with black music, and this trip through the northern part of the United States played a decisive role in the diffusion of jazz. It surely helped obliterate some racial prejudices.

9. Baby Dodds, as Told to Larry Gara, *The Baby Dodds Story* (Baton Rouge: Louisiana State University Press, 1959 and 1992 [revised edition]), p. 28.

Back in New Orleans by the end of September 1919, Baby Dodds and Louis Armstrong remained with the Marable band for the winter season. A photograph of the band was taken aboard a brand-new riverboat, the SS *Capitol*: the musicians are lined up in front of Fate's piano, all displaying expressions of happiness or devoted concentration. Louis is a fat boy, stuffed into his gray suit, and seated with a strange attitude. He holds his cornet in his left hand.

10. Louis Armstrong, *Ma Vie, Ma Nouvelle-Orléans* (Paris: Julliard, October 1952). This translation by Madeleine Gautier was published in France two years before the U.S. edition: *My Life in New Orleans* (New York: Prentice-Hall, 1954).

Davenport, summer and fall 1920

The *Capitol* and its band traveled up north and reached Davenport by the beginning of May. "It was there that I met the almighty Bix Beiderbecke, the great cornet genius," Louis Armstrong wrote in *My Life in New Orleans*. "Every musician in the world knew and admired Bix. He made the greatest reputation for himself, and we all respected him as though he had been a god."[10]

Concert—Vaudeville

· · · · · *Given by the* · · · · ·
MUSICAL ORGANIZATIONS
· · · · · · *of the* · · · · · ·
DAVENPORT HIGH SCHOOL

Under the General Direction of
MISS ALICE ROGER
· · · · · *Assisted by* · · · · ·
MISS IREN KIER, *Accompanist*
& MRS. ERNST JACOBSEN,
Stage Manager

GRAND · OPERA · HOUSE
Friday Evening, 8 o'clock, May 28th
1 · · · 9 · · · 2 · · · 0

BOYS' GLEE CLUB

FIRST TENOR	Hugh McGovern	LeRoy Evans
Francis Curley	Oscar Pries	George Summers
Victor Kloppenburg	Richard Petersberger	BASES
Paul Krasuski	Loring Pollock	Robert Hender
Raymond Moore	BARITONES	Vincent Klauer
SECOND TENORS	Earl Bertuliet	Richard Le Buhn
Boyd Ellis	Bix Beiderbecke	Erwin Sindt

BLACK JAZZ BABIES

Raymond Moore	Bix Beiderbecke	Earl Bertuleit
Hugh McGovern	Vincent Klauer	

Program from the Davenport Grand Opera House concert on May 28, 1920. (Davenport Public Library Collection)

(F)

Miss Kier and Her "Black Jazz Babies"

Far Away in the South.................................*Adams*
A Toast

Jazz Specialty

Moore and Beiderbecke
Ma Punkin Sue ....*Widener*

Boy's Glee Club, Davenport High School, 1920. Back row, Left to right: Raymond Moore, Boyd Ellis, Paul Krasuski, George Summers, Bix Beiderbecke; middle row: Erwin Sindt, Loring Pollock, Richard Petersberger, LeRoy Evans, Francis Curley; front row: Oscar Pries, Vincent Klauer, Victor Kloppenburg, Hugh McGovern. (Rich Johnson)

This is a nice story—two young jazz geniuses meeting on a boat cruising the Mississippi—and it would often be retold, varying with the imagination of each new author. The story is, in fact, probably incorrect. Louis has moved his first encounter with Bix back by a few years. Fate Marable's band toured around Davenport between May 6 and June 6, 1920, but Bix was then a novice musician, and though his presence one evening on the boat is quite possible, and even probable, an exchange at that moment between a young white and a black professional musician is difficult to imagine.[11]

Davenport High School celebrated the end of the school year by presenting a musical show, attended by the students' families and performed on May 28 in the Grand Opera House. Bix was first featured singing as a baritone in the Boy's Glee Club choir. He came back onstage for two more numbers: as a member of a vocal quintet, the Black Jazz Babies, that gave a spirited interpretation of "Far Away in the South," and then, picking up his cornet, he accompanied the tap dancing of a black classmate, Raymond Moore, on "Ma Punkin Sue." "It was the first time many of us had heard him play the cornet," recounts Vera Cox. "It stunned everybody—nobody realized how good Bix had become since he'd started playing. He was quiet, you know, never made much of a show about things. . . . He really thought he didn't have any real talent, and was honestly surprised when he got to be famous."[12]

11. The encounter between Bix and Louis Armstrong is placed on the *Capitol* in August 1919 in Richard M. Sudhalter, Philip R. Evans, and William Dean Myatt, *Bix, Man and Legend* (New York: Arlington House Publishers, 1974, and Schirmer Books, 1975), p. 39. In addition, *The Leon Bix Beiderbecke Story* (op. cit., p. 47—48), quotes Louis Armstrong answering in 1954, and gives the place as the Capitol, but between May and June 1920. For Laurence Bergreen (op. cit., p. 157—158), and for Gary Giddins, in his book *Satchmo*, it took place on the SS *Sidney* in 1920. James Lincoln Collier, in his biography *Louis Armstrong* (Oxford Univ. Press, 1983), doubts the event.

12. *Bix, Man and Legend*, op. cit., p. 42.

Linwood Inn in the 1920s. (Rich Johnson)

"Famous" he was three weeks later, when the *Davenport Daily Times* mentioned his name in its June 22 edition: "The fact that he was but 17 years old is all that saved L. B. Beiderbecke, a Davenport High School student, from being sent to jail by Police Magistrate Metcalf this morning." The young driver was arrested for speeding the night before, on West 4th Street, and got a $25 fine, which he paid "almost cheerfully," said the press. The summer vacation that followed was not too restful for Bix. Davenport's students got together for many parties, but Bix did not respond to the girls with the same attention he was often given. Vera Cox was an exception, and she seemed to have occupied a choice place among the bud-

TERRACE GARDENS

TUESDAY NIGHT

Club and Family Night

No charge for Dancing

25c Cover Charge

Every Night

6:30 P. M. 9 to 12 P. M.

ding young girls who surrounded Bix at these dancing parties. The Beiderbecke and Cox families were long acquainted, and the adolescent Bix used to follow Vera when she came back from school—but from a distance, and walking on the sidewalk across the street. Their first "official" date was under the watchful eyes of both their parents, who traded off their duties according to a prearranged schedule, and on this first encounter Bix's older sister, Mary Louise, chaperoned the two ardent but nervous youngsters. The young boy's priorities would, however, be set upon hearing the first note of music, and romantic feelings were immediately relegated to second place. "A lot of times Bix would take a date," Leon "Skis" Werentin recalled, "and just forget about her if someone let him play the trumpet or piano. It didn't really bother him to leave the girl alone all night. . . . And even then he'd want to have a drink, but I wouldn't call him a drunk. Everyone was always offering him drinks, but he held them very well. If I look back at Bix, I see him as a sloppy dresser. He just didn't give a damn how he looked."[13] This indifference didn't harm his charm: "Bix was so handsome," Vera Cox detailed, "with big brown eyes and clear complexion. He loved his family very much and they were terribly proud of him, particularly his mother."[14]

In July 1920, the girl received one of Bix's first known letters. She was staying with her grandmother in Vermont: "Received yours of the 8th with much satisfaction," he wrote, "as I feared that you would forget one so unimportant as I. Yes, I am working, but at an environment that I consider having a good time, playing for dances in a hot orchestra, making piles of jack, in preparation for a good time next fall, with you? . . . Tell your grandmother that old friendship is the best and that you've decided that I'm about as good as anyone, which I hope is true—tell her you're coming back to me."[15]

If his insistence is typical of a sixteen-year-old boy, his self-denigration is not surprising considering that, given his scholarly shortcomings, Bix's only strong suit would remain of a musical order. The band he mentioned in his letter was formed by pianist Neal Buckley, where Bix on cornet was joined by Fritz Putzier on C-melody sax,[16] Bob Struve on trombone, and Dick Woolsey on drums—all musicians with whom he had played the year before. Neal Buckley's Novelty Orchestra appeared twice at Linwood Park, at the end of July.[17] Within the circle of this small group, the cornet player was on a personal quest that often drove him beyond his technical capabilities. His partners' patience was put to the test, but fortuitous strokes of inspiration made them quickly forgive his many blunders.

Bix was not all smiles on the morning of August 30, as he entered eleventh grade at Davenport High School, but he found comfort in thinking of his parallel career on the cornet in the Neal Buckley Orchestra. The group got its first gig outside the city, and the musicians went to Sabula, Illinois, on November 5, where they performed as Billy Greer's Melody Jazz Band.

13. Jim Arpy, "Remembering Bix," article published on July 24, 1988, in the Davenport *Quad-City Times*.

14. "Davenport Day: Vera Cox Reminisces," in *Storyville*, no. 12 (August/September 1967). *Storyville* is the British jazz magazine published by Laurie Wright, an indispensable source of information.

15. *Bix, Man and Legend*, op. cit., p. 45.

16. The C-melody is a saxophone in the key of C, whose pitch is one step above the B-flat tenor sax. It is technically classified as a tenor, but with a somehow mellower sound. It was successful in the 1920s because it was easier for novice players, and could be played along with another C instrument, like piano, using the same music sheets. It went out of fashion, as players favored the tone of alto or tenor saxes.

17. Linwood Park was located in Linwood, a small town, now disappeared, on the Mississippi River, eight miles south of Davenport.

The American Federation of Musicians, a labor union that maintained local offices in each major town, regulated professional musical life in the U.S. Only registered musicians with union cards could take paid jobs. To join this organization, an examination, in which each candidate's ability to read music was tested, was compulsory, and had to be passed before a representative of the local chapter. Asked to participate in the opening of the Terrace Gardens in Davenport,[18] Neal Buckley's band could no longer avoid joining the union, and had to take the admission test. A group audition took place on December 21 before officials from the Union Local 67. "The musicians rehearsed one or two tunes, over and over, until they felt they had memorized the piece," Fritz Putzier remembered. "Roy Kautz held the testing. He suspected they had memorized their tune, so he asked each member to read a piece of sheet music he placed before them. All passed except Bix."[19] In support of their failed fellow musician, the other band members turned the engagement down.

Former entrance of the Terrace Gardens, Kahl Building, Davenport, present condition. (JPL)

If the newspapers in October 1920 were largely preoccupied with "Frenchie" Georges Carpentier's victory at Jersey City over light-heavyweight champion Battling LeVinsky, they evidently were unaware of one of Bix's inventions, made at the same time: the multiple acoustic recording. He correctly guessed that, with his hand-crank phonograph, and probably using a home-recording sound box, he could record more than once on one of the blank aluminum discs that came with the outfit. This was achieved by placing the cornet bell into the horn of the family phonograph, playing a short piece as the disc turned, resetting the recording machine at the beginning and playing into it again, letting the needle cut the same

18. Terrace Gardens was operating in the basement of the Kahl building, on Ripley and 3rd streets. The place is now used as a warehouse, but some parts of the mural decoration are still visible.

19. *The Leon Bix Beiderbecke Story*, op. cit., p. 53.

groove four times in a row. Unfortunately, such a recording could not stand many playings, and this historic moment is forever lost.[20] This experience underlined the adolescent's inventive spirit, as it illustrates his precocious musical abilities as a composer: he had been able to conceive, through instinct alone, a four-voice polyphonic piece.

20. Albert Haim runs a Web site dedicated to Bix's life and work, http://www.bixbeiderbecke.com, where information available about the musician is extensively gathered. Musician and researcher Brad Kay is among the participants in the forum linked to this Web site; in May 2000, he confirmed this technical possibility, explaining he had been able to record on similar equipment, blowing with his cornet into the horn of a phonograph. The disc was made of soft aluminium, and Kay asserted that he was able to record, by this "overdubbing," up to six different melodies, one after another.

CHAPTER 2

1921: At School in Chicago

Davenport, March–April 1921

Bix was destined to cross paths with a young cornetist, his shadowy double, who would die at the age of twenty-three without leaving a single recording. His name was Emmett Hardy, and he was born in 1903 in Gretna, Louisiana, across the Mississippi from New Orleans. He started playing cornet at age thirteen and progressed so quickly that he could perform in public after only one year of practice. He met Connie, Martha, and Helvetia Boswell, three sisters who were to form a singing trio, the Boswell Sisters, who would enjoy great success in New York during the 1930s. This friendly connection inspired Emmett to pursue a musical career, which he had to combine with a day job at a steelworks in nearby Algiers. This exhausting lifestyle was one of the probable causes of the tuberculosis he contracted a few years later. At the start of 1921, Emmett Hardy was part of the quintet playing with singer Beatrice "Bee" Palmer. Bee's husband, pianist Al Siegel, directed this group, which included clarinetist Leon Roppolo, who is ranked among the first jazz improvisers.

If Bee Palmer is completely forgotten today, her appearances in the 1920s as the Shimmy Queen drew a large audience. The success of her shimmy rested mainly on the voluptuous shaking of her shoulders and hips. The young woman was a cute little blonde, shapely as a pinup. She had curly hair, and her legs were advantageously displayed—she bore a saucy reputation and was always trailed by a coterie of male admirers.

Bee Palmer. (Albert Haim)

Bee Palmer's show, *Oh, Bee!*, appeared on the stage of Davenport's Columbia Theater[1] from February 27 through March 2. Bix and his friend Esten Spurrier rushed in and managed to attend every performance, equally attracted by the singer's seductive swaying, and by clarinetist Roppolo's brilliant choruses and Emmett Hardy's daring outbursts. They were wise to attend those first performances, for the scandal created in this puritanical city by the blonde siren's unbridled show soon put an end to the spectacle.

Emmett Hardy and Leon Roppolo spent several more days on tour with Bee Palmer but, by mid-March, had returned to Davenport and joined Carlisle Evans's orchestra at the Coliseum.[2] They played three months with this band, and they

had Bix as a devoted fan throughout their stay—his only limitation being the seventy-five cents required at the entrance. Emmett Hardy left his friends many memories, obviously magnified by his early death, but with the lack of recordings, appreciation of his playing and his possible influence on Bix relies on only a few contemporaries' accounts. However, he must have

1. The Columbia Theater was located at 406 West 3rd Street, right in front of the Kahl building. It is no longer standing.

2. The Coliseum Ballroom, the "Col," still stands at 1012 West 4th Street. It opened on November 4, 1914, and a great number of bands have played on its stage. The front of the building and its interior layout are practically unchanged today.

THE BEST IN VAUDEVILLE

PHONE 747

Columbia

Orpheum Circuit Junior Theatre

PHONE 746

SPECIAL ENGAGEMENT
CHICAGO SEASON'S BIG HIT
FOUR DAYS STARTING SUNDAY

BEE PALMER
AND COMPANY IN "OH BEE"
A Shivering Sketch by Herman Timberg
ASSISTING HER ARE DICK HUMBER, AL SIEGEL, "KINNEY" AND
HER WONDERFUL JAZZ BAND

Ad published in the Davenport *Daily Times* on March 2, 1921. (Rich Johnson)

shown a true artistic originality: he clearly contrasted with the brilliant and vivid style of New Orleans musicians, and he seems to have been among the first jazzmen to play solos. His mastery of his instrument was, at that time, far superior to Bix's, who in all likelihood benefited greatly from listening to Hardy during the three months he spent in Iowa. Bix often tried to sit in with the band, to the great irritation of Carlisle Evans, who considered with consternation this leechlike, stubborn boy approaching his band, the young man still capable of the worst clumsiness in his playing.[3]

Carlisle Evans's Jazz Band, at the Coliseum Ballroom in Davenport on March 1921. Left to right: Jack Willett (dm), Myron Neal (ts), Carlisle Evans (p), Emmett Hardy (ct), Leon Roppolo (cl), Lou Black (bjo), Tal Sexton (tb). (Duncan Schiedt Collection)

On April 22, 1921, police officers Len and Halligan came to the Beiderbecke house at 1934 Grand Avenue. Bix was arrested, driven to the station and interrogated on charges brought against him by Preston R. Ivens. Bix was accused of having taken this man's five-year-old daughter into a garage and committing on her an act qualified by the police report as "lewd and

Coliseum Ballroom, Davenport. (JPL, 2000)

3. The period when Bix tried to slip into Carlisle Evans's band was recalled in an article published in the March 21, 1952, issue of *Down Beat*. When the musicians saw Bix coming near the bandstand, a warning was sounded, "Here comes that Beiderbecke pest. Hide the horn!"

4. This incident was kept secret for years, and Richard M. Sudhalter wrote in *Lost Chords* (New York: Oxford University Press, 1999) p. 803n31: "But some documentation indeed exists: carefully husbanded, withheld from public view, it records an event deemed serious enough, at least in the context of the early '20s, to have kindled Bismarck Beiderbecke's indignation; prompted the family to ship the boy off to Lake Forest in disgrace; driven friends to circle the wagons when historical inquiry began to get too close; kept Bix, even as a grown man, desperately seeking parental approbation and forgiveness." Three documents have actually been archived in Davenport: two police blotters, dated April 22, 1921: (1) Name, Leon Beiderbecke; Arrested by, Len & Halligan; Crime, Lewd & lascivious act with child . . ."; (2) "He was accused by Sarah Ivens, 5 years old, 1703 Iowa Street, of putting his hands on her person outside her dress in Goddard's garage, Locust and Grand Avenue, where he took the girl out of the rain. They were in an auto in the garage and he closed the door on the girl and she hollered and attracted the attention of James L. Duncan, 1330 East 10th, and Mahlon Barley, 1105 Oneida Avenue, who were working across the street, and they went over and the girl went home. He waived preliminary hearing before Judge Scott and held to Y.J on $1500 bond"; (3) an affidavit handwritten by Preston R. Ivens, living at 3030 Grand Avenue, in which he declared: "On April 22, 1921, my little girl came home, told me that a man took her in the garage, said some awful things to her. I ran up to the garage, then called up the police but could get no clue. Next day I saw two boys whom I had seen when I went to the garage. I asked if they saw a man take a little girl into the garage the day before. They said yes, and told me it was the defendant. My little girl told her story to me and later to the Chief of police and the County Attorney. She said he asked to show herself. The little girl is five years old. In consideration of the child's age and the harm that would result to her in going over this case, I would request that no action be taken by the Grand Jury. I consulted with Dr. Eliot, and Dr. B.J. Palmer and Dr. Craven, and they all, besides with Mr. C.H. Murphy, thought it best to drop the case for the betterment of the child."

5. Lake Forest Academy still operates at 1500 West Kennedy Road, Lake Forest, Illinois 60045. Its archives still hold the following documents in relation to Bix:

(continued)

lascivious." Preston Ivens also lived on Grand Avenue, number 3030, and two boys who supposedly witnessed the scene had helped to identify the "seducer of little girls." The Beiderbecke's social position, the lack of serious charges—Bix had supposedly asked the girl to lift her skirt—and the reluctance of the girl's family to involve her in a court case led to the withdrawal of the complaint and the dismissal of the case. Bix was brought back home. The greatest discretion has protected this troublesome episode, omitted in all previous biographies of Bix.[4]

This humiliating incident would leave scars on a young man already discouraged by his school troubles. His family relations were irreversibly modified. The young prodigy, the brilliant child who had made his parents so proud, would henceforth feel abandoned and ashamed: he saw himself as suspect of perversion. How could his mother still love him, now that he had no faith in himself?

Davenport, summer 1921

The reaction of Bix's father at the end of this disastrous year in school will remain unknown, and we have no information regarding his behavior during the April incident. He apparently decided that his son had to be sent away from Davenport, and surprisingly, he left it to the women of the house to find a solution for his problem child. A request for an application form was sent on June 7 to the reputed Lake Forest Academy. Strangely, this letter was written by Bix's sister, Mary Louise. The young woman was then twenty-three, and she signed with her mother's name.[5]

The school year ended on June 17, and Bix was asked four days later to join the Plantation Jazz Orchestra on the steamer *Majestic*. He met up again with trombonist Bob Struve in this small band of six musicians. While he was traveling, his sister was exchanging letters with John Wayne Richards, headmaster of Lake Forest Academy, who sent the family an entry form on June 23. This document would sit for more than three weeks before being returned.

Bix was never involved in these administrative and scholastic negotiations. At the end of his fifteen-day engagement on the *Majestic*, on July 6 he was hired as a

I thoroughly understand the Word of Honor regarding the use of tobacco and remaining within limits at Lake Forest Academy and I fully and freely give my sacred Word of Honor as a gentleman to keep these rules.

(Signature of Applicant)

Word of Honor signed by Bix in July 1921. (Lake Forest Academy archives)

member of Doc Wrixon's band on the SS *Capitol*. This riverboat, which Fate Marable and Louis Armstrong had played on the year before, had just taken on Emmett Hardy for a few days, and Bix was replacing him. Bix's presence in this band of ten musicians, in which he alternated between cornet and piano, confirmed that he had reached a degree of musical maturity that qualified him for a structured ensemble. Strict discipline was the rule on the Streckfus Line, with frequent rehearsals and heavy workloads imposed by the management.

The *Capitol* left Davenport for a dozen days, and headed down the river for more than two hundred miles. On July 11, Bix wrote his mother from Quincy, Illinois, telling her that he was "having wonderful time—good food, etc—plenty of sleep—good band."[6] The boat was back in Davenport on July 15, where a union report took note that Bix was still not registered: he was forced to leave this professional orchestra.

Bix was never again to meet Emmett Hardy, who, after a summer spent in the orchestras performing on the Mississippi, returned to New Orleans in the fall. Starting in the autumn of 1922 and for several months thereafter, he played at the Friar's Inn in Chicago, but was forced to return to Louisiana in 1923 when his tuberculosis worsened. There he died on June 16, 1925, and his funeral procession was so huge that it took four ferry trips to carry all the participants across the river, from Jackson Avenue to Gretna. Emmett Hardy's mother would later confirm that she received from Bix, toward the end of 1925, a letter in which he reportedly asserted, "Emmett was the greatest musician that I have ever heard. If ever I can come near your son's greatness, I'll die happy."[7]

Agatha Beiderbecke had carefully filled out her son's admission form for Lake Forest Academy, and her husband signed it. She had made a point of adding several handwritten lines, in which she emphasized the terrible results Bix had achieved in high school, asking for "more individual attention," and confirming that he had "promised to apply himself." She explained that he was "very musical" and that "his mind was more on music than on any other study." This document awaited Bix's return to Davenport to be mailed, as the student was requested to sign an "honor agreement," committing himself to refrain from smoking and to remain on the school grounds—and Bix signed. The letter was sent to Lake Forest, together with a few nice words from the principal of Davenport High School, and a very accommodating attestation written by the Beiderbeckes' neighbor, W. F. Winecke.

The investigation on Bix's admission dragged on for a long time, as John W. Richards was hesitant to admit him. The headmaster wrote on August 3 to the Kimball family, who lived in Davenport, and whose children were in all likelihood his former students. The answer received from Mrs. Kimball was a convoluted one: "As near as I can learn, Bix is a bright boy," her letter read, "but who doesn't study. As I haven't heard anything to the contrary, I rather infer than know that his character is all right."

the 1922 *Caxy*, the school yearbook; copies of letters exchanged between the Beiderbecke family and Mr. John Wayne Richards, LFA headmaster (various excerpts of these letters are quoted in this chapter and the following one); Bix's registration file, with enclosed letters and documents; one six-page physiology exercise done by Bix. With the exception of the *Caxy*, above documents were unpublished.

6. *The Leon Bix Beiderbecke Story*, op. cit., p. 61.

7. This document has been lost.

Ad published in the *Davenport Democrat and Leader*, on August 5, 1921. (Rich Johnson)

Building where the Haynes Dancing School was located, on second floor. (JPL, 2000)

This diplomatic formulation seems to have prompted the decision, and on August 9, John W. Richards confirmed to Bix's parents that their son was admitted to Lake Forest Academy. For Bix, the one principally interested, this news was overshadowed by an event of far more significance: the birth of the first orchestra bearing the young cornetist's name, the Bix Beiderbecke Five. This band, which included Fritz Putzier, Bob Struve, Erkie Albright, and drummer Dick Woolsey, gave its first performance on August 5 at the Haynes Dancing School.[8]

At the end of the month, Bix and Fritz Putzier were asked to join the Ralph Miedke Society Orchestra for the grand opening of a bank in Moline, a city neighboring Davenport. On August 30, 1921, early in the afternoon and before their departure for Moline, Fritz Putzier led Bix into a photographer's shop, where the two musicians were immortalized in their rented tuxedos. Putzier would safely keep his romantic picture taken that day—a handsome young man, all done up and bending under the weight of an impressive saxophone. The photograph of Bix has been lost.

8. The Haynes Dancing School was located in the Hyberian Hall, a three-story building at 421½ Brady Street, which is now unchanged.

Lake Forest, September 1921

"Bix was a mystery to us," confessed cornetist Jimmy McPartland. "We all knew him, admired him, thought he was a great guy. But, in a way, we didn't know him at all. He wasn't really like us."[9] And Benny Goodman wondered from which moon this strange creature might have fallen.

Bix was eighteen. His clear innocent eyes were the shining surface of a dark and secret lake of unfathomable depths. His schoolwork failed, not for lack of intellectual abilities, but because of a mere lack of interest in his studies. Only music could hold his attention. Nevertheless, he would never have the true desire, or even the will, to gain technical musical knowledge. Out of necessity, he would learn to decipher a score—with great effort and the assistance of his friends—but his theoretical learning and his ability to write music would remain nonexistent. This deficiency would drastically hamper his creative aspirations, and he would suffer deeply from it.

Bix was a rebel. He was clearly aware of what he was turning down—the family "model" he had grown with—but living on the fringe of society was still painful. His choice of jazz, this "degenerate music born in the brothels of New Orleans," was a slap in the face for his parents: these bourgeois people, raised on rigid principles of Germanic rectitude, had obviously dreamed of a quite different future for their astonishing child.

Lake Forest "Lower Middle" Class, school year 1921–1922. Bix is far left in the middle row. (Lake Forest Academy archives)

The young musician did not attach any value to his art, which was still far distant from an ideal that he knew to be beyond his reach. He smoked constantly, and alcohol, which flowed abundantly in all the places where music led him, seemed to soothe his suffering and to dispel his permanent uneasiness. Bringing a bottle to his lips was a way of restoring his beneficial maternal imagos—and he became a boozer. The incident with the little girl had generated a new pain, that of shame. Bix was now the victim of a sustained anguish, magnified by a fear of rejection.

Several hours on the train brought him, at the start of September 1921, from Davenport to Lake Forest, Illinois, thirty miles north of Chicago. Lake Forest Academy was a boys' prep school, established in 1857, and its close neighbor, Ferry

9. *Lost Chords*, op. cit., p. 411.

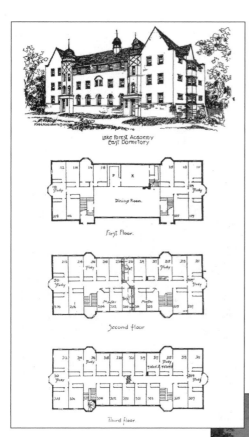

Lake Forest Academy
East Dormitory

First Floor.

Dining Room.

Second floor

Master

Third floor

East house Dormitory,
construction blue prints (from
around 1895). Bix's room is
said to have been number 105
or 107, on the first floor. (Lake
Forest Academy archives)

East house Dormitory.
(JPL, 2003)

10. Bix's lodging at Lake Forest
Academy was in the East House
Dormitory, which is still part of
the campus.

11. *The Leon Bix Beiderbecke
Story,* op. cit., p. 64.

Hall School, was the girls' equivalent.[10] These schools, catering to rich teenagers with learning difficulties, had built their reputations on their results, and on a military-style discipline that was meant to mold the students' lives. Exile this far from Davenport was a drastic measure, but it was expected to bring the lost cornetist back into the fold of his family life and its "normality." One may question the apparent delusion of parents who, concerned about releasing their son from his musical demons, were sending him to the gates of hell: Chicago.

This abrupt separation from his family led to Bix's most prolific period of writing: among the forty-four letters that we know of today, twenty-one were sent during the nine months he spent at Lake Forest. They are all addressed to his family, to whom he wished to convey only positive messages: truth was therefore altered, dressed up, and these letters do not tell it all.

The first letter postmarked in Lake Forest asserted that the exile was in good health, as he had just passed "a physical and medical exam . . . , was perfect in every respect, and there was about fifty respects."[11] This good news was tempered on September 12, when the student no longer wished to limit his activity to the classroom: "I forgot to say that I want my cornet P.D.Q. as I want to work-up a good lip, and as everyone else is practicing on various instruments, I may as well have mine here and besides there are chances for good jobs at Evanston or North Chi. Suburbs, as 'Wally' the drummer knows every dance manager around & on Sat nites, with Mr. Richards permission, we'll play some jobs & get some welcome dough." It was only in the musical field that Bix was mastering nuances. Trying to make this first part

Wabash Avenue, the Loop, Chicago. (JPL, 2003)

of his letter more acceptable, he couldn't resist inserting a moralizing proclamation, which should rather inspire a smile: "Mr. Dick made a talk on muckers who are low enough to hike out in the wds and shoot butts & believe me I felt like I'd never smoke or be bad again—it sure made some individuals creep. . . . Really folks I didn't know what the word of honor meant until I came to L.F.A. & heard Mr. Richards opinion of it."[12] The cornet would make the trip from Davenport to Lake Forest, before making, on a regular basis, the trip from Lake Forest to Chicago.

Chicago, 1921

Chicago, on the shores of Lake Michigan, had become the second city in the U.S., numbering a population of two million. Two hundred thousand blacks lived in the South Side, forming a community three times larger than New York's Harlem. They had come from Louisiana and the southern states to fill the need for laborers in a rapidly expanding industry. This flux in population hadn't been absorbed without incident, and in 1919, race riots exploded in several cities around the country: on one single night in July, thirty-eight black people were killed in Chicago.

Known as the Windy City, Chicago was a swarming and sprawling monster. Located at the heart of a vast transportation network, the largest city in Illinois was crossed by noisy railroads that wended their way between tall buildings, straight to the La Salle Street station and its huge and smoky steel dome, where, surrounded by a continuous din, extravagant luxury rubbed shoulders with the most abject

12. *The Leon Bix Beiderbecke Story,* op. cit., p. 65.

poverty. An elevated train, the "El," carried a million Chicagoans a day, packed morning and night into wooden cars or, for the less lucky ones, standing exposed to bad weather on uncovered platforms. This extensive rail line converged in the Loop downtown, running inches away from apartment windows, over streets, and plunging the population beneath it into darkness and noise. When the wind blew from the south, it brought the smell of blood, guts, and death from the vast slaughterhouses on the South Side, reminding the inhabitants that their prosperity was borne amid the cries of eviscerated cattle. This foul-smelling wind often reached as far as the shores of Lake Michigan, where miraculously preserved beaches, complete with crystal waves and seagulls, bordered the east side of the metropolis with an improbable vacation resort-like landscape.

Mayor "Big Bill" Thompson had reigned over this delirium since 1902, implementing a simple but efficient system: generalized corruption. He called himself "a friend to every citizen," but he was most friendly with the many gangsters, robbers, killers, pimps, and traffickers who nourished him and his political machine with their regular offerings within an organization that tolerated no losers, and that would allow Al Capone to reach his full potential.

Artistic creation also found its place in this hive of permanent turmoil. *Little Review*, a magazine situated at the forefront of the American avant-garde, would pride itself on the first publication of James Joyce's *Ulysses*, printed chapter by chapter over twenty-two consecutive issues between March 1918 and December 1920. Among the many contributors to this review were T. S. Eliot, Ezra Pound, Djuna Barnes, André Gide, Jean Cocteau, and Gertrude Stein. Mary Garden took over the direction of the Chicago Civic Opera in 1921. She was Claude Debussy's favorite performer, and swept away much of the old, mostly Germanic repertoire, introducing French and Russian creations: Debussy's *Pelléas and Mélisande*, in which she gave herself the main part, and *The Love of Three Oranges*, by Serge Prokofiev. Mary Garden was a redheaded whirlwind, respected for her talent but feared for her audacity—ever since she had informed the press, before the first production of Strauss's *Salomé* in Boston, that she would wear nothing beneath the seventh and last veil of the famous dance, and she kept her promise.

This urban hell and musical paradise, where the most talented black and white jazzmen were gathering, was only one hour by train from Lake Forest Academy, where Bix was now living. It took the young student little time to find his way to this appealing city.

Lake Forest, September–December 1921

For a while, Bix's parents were probably fooled by their son's solemn declarations. "I bought a fountain pen here," he wrote them on September 16, "I tried it and it's a wow. . . . I'm now fully supplied and have everything fixed on the table so cozy—it's really a pleasure to study when you are equipped with everything. You can't pay for it, they charge it & send bill home." But they were truly naive if they didn't hear, in the next part of the letter, the first rumbles of a coming storm. Bix was telling them that he had linked up with three new friends, a saxophonist, Sidney Stewart, a banjo player, and a drummer: "this orchestra is A-1 best I've ever play with & we will play in East House every night—the boys are hysterical with joy—same here, pretty lucky I claim. This place is sure beautiful I'll claim!"[13]—and this is where the Beiderbeckes should have started to ask questions.

Bix went even further with his confessions, reporting the next day to his brother his first tour of Chicago by night: "I sure had a wonderful time in Chi & in regard to the music you heard. That's Faite Maribores [Fate Marable's] bunch who used to be on the St. Paul [riverboat]—The talk of the river—why I tried to tell you about them—I heard them in Louisiana, Mo. But they can't carry water to Al Tearneys new nigger bunch at 35th & State, nor at the Sunset or Entertainer—boy theres some real jazz niggers. Don't think I'm getting hard Burnie, but I'd go to hell to hear a good band, so I made all these places in one nite with Kim Burr and his bunch."

Bix had claimed to his parents that he didn't know what working really meant before coming to Lake Forest, but his letters confirmed that he was experiencing great difficulties keeping up with his curriculum for the school year, which was doubtless due to his having fallen so far behind at Davenport High School. He told his mother, in a letter dated October 3: "Ill admit I was taken off my feet at first with assignments and Ill admit I had blue spells & I wasn't alone . . . , but now I'm used to it and I'm sure of success. The work is hard and you sure are tied up but I believe it will do me good & my absence will make you appreciate me the more." Bix was not deluding himself about the esteem his parents could hold for him, and this last line is an obvious cry out for love, for recognition that he can't seem to achieve, the lack of which affected him deeply. On the other hand, he knew he was appreciated for his athletic performance, at which he excelled. He had once won a tennis tournament in his native city, and at Lake Forest he had chosen to go out for basketball and baseball.

At the end of October, the school hired a band led by pianist Jimmie Caldwell for a weekend. Bix managed to sit in with the orchestra, where he met tenor saxophonist Don Murray, the brilliant young musician who would often sit beside him in later years.

A first incident was brought to the attention of Bix's father in October: his son had received a warning about unexcused absences. Bix took up his pen, elaborating explanations as confused as they were unconvincing, and concluded, "All I want to say is don't be worried because it doesn't mean anything as one will do no-one any harm and I swear it is my first and last censure & unintentional at that."

Halloween was the first party of the school year. Preparing for it gave Bix the

13. Bix's letters to his family have been preserved. They were published in *The Leon Bix Beiderbecke Story* (op. cit., pp. 66–106). Philip R. Evans wrote in his foreword, "We have been fortunate to be able to include in our text the complete set of the existing Bix letters" (page xiv). They are quoted throughout this book.

Bix with Sidney Stewart's family, Winnetka, Thanksgiving 1921. Left to right: Bix, Sid Stewart, and his father, (Davenport Public Library Collection)

opportunity to explore Chicago, and he managed to combine the purchase of decorations and paper chains with the discovery of two of the best dance bands in the city: the Benson Orchestra and the one led by Isham Jones. On October 29, the school gymnasium, adorned in autumn-colored leaves and bedecked with "pumpkins, cornstalks, lanterns festooned with witches and cats," accommodated a dance thrown for the students, and here Bix Beiderbecke played his first concert at Lake Forest. His band was announced as the Cy-Bix Orchestra, with drummer Walter "Cy" Welge sharing the bill; Cy couldn't come, and Bix led the musicians alone, with such energy that the headmaster had to stand up and "clamp an official soft pedal on the proceedings."

Mr. Richards received a letter dated November 15 from Agatha Beiderbecke, requesting that he permit her son to go to Chicago for Thanksgiving. "I am so pleased with the school," added Agatha, "and, by Leon's letters, I know he is very happy there."[14] The school only admitted children of a well-to-do background, and Bix was invited to visit the wealthy family of his sax player, Sid Stewart. The two young men traveled to Chicago on November 23, where they heard Isham Jones's band. Bix was able to get in touch with the star cornetist of the orchestra, Louis Panico, and to talk business with a professional musician.

In order to maintain an appropriate pose among these rich people, Bix had borrowed a dollar from his brother. He thanked him for sending it, adding in his letter, "I sure get in hard straights here due to the extravagant bunch of guys. As a matter of fact, though the folks have sure been acting great, financially and I really have been getting more than any guy would need if he weren't associating with a

14. Lake Forest Academy archives, unpublished.

bunch of millionaires." The Stewarts lived in a magnificent mansion in Winnetka, and the luxurious party he
attended dazzled Bix. "We ate until we were sick," he recounted to his parents, "then went in & they made us
play some more & then some more millionaires came
in with some port wine & Gordons gin, regular liquid
gold—we were given one thimble full a piece but no
more. I can't stand the stuff anyway." A huge and obvious lie!

Sid-Bix's Orchestra, formed with Sid Stewart, appeared on the Lake Forest Academy campus on November 26, and the performance created great
enthusiasm among its student audience, an audience
that approved of Bix's original music without reserva-
tion. "The last dance brought to an end one of the pep-
piest and best social events ever given at the 'Cad,'"
affirmed the *Caxy*, the school's yearbook.

Bix hadn't returned to Davenport since he had left
in September, and the last letter sent to his parents before his arrival was dated December 6: "I'm just dying
to get home, Folks. The only trouble is it will be like going to hell to come back & believe me I can't come back
unless I have my pockets loaded with 'do' made from

Bix in 1921 or 1922, Lake
Forest portrait. (Courtesy of
the Rutgers Institute of
Jazz Studies)

playing, so please think that over. . . . I've got to make some Do. I went to Ferry Hall
yesterday with a boy who went to see his sister & believe me I never saw so many
good looking girls in all my life. Well no use
going into detail I'll see you soon—just
think: 2 weeks & 2 days. Much Love. LB.B."

Lake Forest faculty,
1921–1922 school year.
R. P. Koepke (French,
Spanish, and Music) is at the
far right in the front row,
and John Wayne Richards
(Headmaster) is third from
the right. (Lake Forest
Academy archives)

CHAPTER 3

1922: Music Above All Else

Lake Forest, January–March 1922

I t is unfortunate that the letters Bix's parents wrote to him are missing. Were they resigned to their third child's scholastic failure, or did they still believe that he would finally come around? Bix's father seems to have reluctantly agreed to Bix's demand, on January 13, upon his return to Lake Forest: "I'm writing this during a test in English history which I know nothing about and am taking an incomplete as I had no time to study," wrote Bix, "I'm allowed 3 incompletes a month—(make ups.). . . . Dad, about the 26th, have you sent the permission for my absence? You see, I have a chance to play at the Edgewater Beach and make some easy dough, and in order to get out at night I'll have to have a permission from you people as they do not assume the responsibility—Stewart and Welge are going up and believe me I want to go as it will mean a little spending money and getting away from this confinement and being able to play for a few hours."

Authorization was granted, and on the set date, Bix took his place in a band directed by Jimmie Caldwell—whom he had met in October 1921, when the bandleader played at Lake Forest. Bix sat beside Don Murray, whom he befriended quickly as they were united by a shared passion for Dixieland music. The band performed on January 26 at the Edgewater Beach Hotel, a luxurious and outrageously pink-painted resort in northern Chicago. Bix arrived without a tuxedo, his cornet wrapped in a paper bag. Jimmie Caldwell tried to conceal Bix's gawkiness from the audience by asking him to sit behind the piano, but the quality and energy of his playing quickly brought him to center stage. "When a band of gypsies were on campus going about telling fortunes, Bix and Don had their palms read," recounted Jimmie Caldwell. "When the reading was completed, the gypsy refused to tell them what she saw! Only after pestering the woman were the two able to hear the findings. She predicted an early death for both youths. Bix and Don took it as a joke and laughed about it."[1]

The same orchestra appeared the next night at the Blackstone Hotel, a twenty-two-story tower erected in Chicago's Loop, and they also played on January 28 and February 10 for the students of the Evanston campus. Bix would immediately write to his brother about these concerts: "I had the best time I ever had and can safely say that it was the best orchestra I ever played with—sounded like Paul Whitman [Whiteman] on one piece and then like the Dixieland Band on another. God, they were good."

A school party, the Lake Forest Midwinter Weekend, reunited Bix with his parents on February 17 and 18. The Beiderbeckes were drawn as much by the thought of seeing the school campus for themselves as they

Blackstone Hotel, Chicago. (JPL, 2003)

Lake Forest Orchestra (1922). In the back row, Walter "Cy" Welge is at the far right, with Bix and Professor Koepke to his left; Sidney Stewart is at the far left in the front row. (Lake Forest Academy archives)

1. *The Leon Bix Beiderbecke Story,* op. cit., p. 97.

Lake Forest Academy Orchestra (1922). Bix is third from the right in the back row, and Professor Koepke is fifth; Sidney Stewart is sixth from right in the middle row; Walter "Cy" Welge is the far right in the front row. (Lake Forest Academy archives)

Lake Forest Academy baseball team (1922). Walter "Cy" Welge is at the far right in the front row, and Bix is front row center. (Lake Forest Academy archives)

were by their son's performance. The students put on a show, *The Academy Follies*, in which Bix took part in several sketches. He then accompanied Sid Stewart's saxophone on piano and led his own band during the dance that concluded the day.

Sid Stewart was a virtuoso on his C-melody sax, capable of working minor miracles and displaying flashy techniques to make his young admirers swoon. He was quite willing to admit, however, that he couldn't reach the level of emotion, the originality, the feeling that Bix had developed—that distinctive something that the cornet player could convey despite his still-limited means. Bix once responded subtly to a comment from his friend about the restraint in his playing: "Sid, the trouble with you is you play so many notes, but they mean so little." This self-imposed reserve, this refusal to show off, this search for a concise and emotionally charged expression, would essentially become a dominant part of the young musician's creativity. This introverted approach, which might have led to a self-effacing manner, didn't prevent Bix from attracting the attention of the pretty girls flitting about Ferry Hall School—and he wouldn't ignore them forever.

On the second day of the festivities, Bix managed to sit in with Bill Grimm's Varsity Five, a band hired to enliven the evening party. The addition, without preliminary rehearsals, of this young improviser to an orchestra limited to playing written orchestrations was quite a revelation for the group. Bix would be invited to repeat this experience the next weekend, at Northwestern University in Evanston, and he would regularly join this band over the course of the next two years.

So much music, so little studying. . . . It was hardly surprising that Bix's grades would be disastrous on all counts. Bix's parents were mystified when they exchanged the letters each had received one day in early March: Mr. Richards had written to Bismark Beiderbecke, and Bix to his mother. Mr. Richards's letter of February 28 detailed the difficulties Bix was experiencing. "We cannot have a boy continue here who is passing but one subject," wrote John W. Richards, "particularly if he has the ability to get his work. The faculty voted to put him on Special Probation." This severe measure forced the student to show "marked improvement in effort and attainment," without which he would be "reclassified or asked to withdraw." Bix's letter presented the situation in an entirely different light. After an introduction filled with smart wheedling, he told Agatha about the summons that had brought him before Mr. Richards: "We had a good talk—he sure is a peach," wrote Bix, "he told me that I had guts and brains and that I had done much

Friars' Inn Orchestra, end of 1921/beginning of 1922. Left to right: George Brunies (tb), Frank Snyder (dm), Paul Mares (ct), Arnold Loyacano (sb), Elmer Schoebel (p), Jack Pettis (sax), Leon Roppolo (cl). (Duncan Schiedt Collection)

better in my studies and holding myself down than he had expected I would due to my handicap in being a musician. He said that he thought I'd be a girl snip and a social butterfly judging from my D.H.S. record, but he said that it was a 'misled prejudice'; he said that if I came back next year I'd make something of myself athletically and scholastically, as he thought that this school had made me sit up & take notice, and was the place for me. I just thought I'd say this to convince you that I have something in me, which surprises me as much as it does you. He is supposed to know fellows." Bix ended his missive by trivializing being put on probation, something that evidently befell "nearly everyone," and swearing to make up for being considerably behind with two weeks of intense study.

Chicago, March–April 1922

During a stop-off in Evanston with Jimmie Caldwell's band sometime in early February, Bix had heard some musicians mentioning with great excitement an orchestra appearing at Chicago's Friar's Inn. He quickly managed to set up a plan to escape by night to the Windy City, in pursuit of this new musical temptation.

After 1915 many musicians followed the lead of Tom Brown and Nick La Rocca, and left New Orleans for Chicago. Trombonist George Brunies and trumpeter Paul Mares, ages seventeen and nineteen respectively, settled in Chicago in 1919. Some short-term engagements enabled them to meet up with drummer

Frank Snyder, pianist Elmer Schoebel, and saxophonist Jack Pettis, with whom they shared a great musical affinity. The Mississippi steamboats offered them many work opportunities during the summer of 1921, and the Streckfus Line hired George Brunies, probably followed by Paul Mares, who had played on the SS *Capitol* together with Emmett Hardy and Leon Roppolo.

The riverboat season having ended, the musicians went back to Chicago, looking for jobs. Bee Palmer landed one from Mike Fritzel, owner of the Friar's Inn, a night-club located in the Loop at 343 South Wabash Street.[2] The singer asked Paul Mares to put together a band to accompany her and warm up the place on cold winter nights. The trumpeter gathered three old friends around him: Snyder, Schoebel, and Pettis, who were soon to be reunited with George Brunies and Leon Roppolo. The Friar's Society Orchestra was born. The group was completed when Lou Black, a banjo player from Rock Island, and Arnold Loyocano, a bassist who had come to Chicago in 1915 with Tom Brown, joined the band. In 1922 they took on the name that would be inscribed in jazz history: the New Orleans Rhythm Kings (NORK).

If the music Bix discovered at the Friar's Inn that night in March 1922 was deeply imbued with New Orleans style, it was, however, innovative enough to seduce a young cornetist, still in the beginning stages of his artistic development. Bix knew the sides recorded by the ODJB well: they were spirited, but also—in some aspects— "mechanical" and repetitive. Even though he couldn't read music, he had already played in bands that followed a written score—with Bill Grimm and Jimmie Caldwell, for instance, whose work was similar to that of many other white orchestras— but the music he heard at the Friar's Inn sounded different and revolutionary.

Paul Mares was an unreserved admirer of Joe "King" Oliver, the black cornet player whose powerful horn led his band with a sinewy, raucous, and typically New Orleans collective style. Oliver's musicians did not hesitate to search for unconventional harmonies, which did not always sound accurate, but which favored the expression of crude emotions. The group performing at the Friar's followed a different approach. Made up of eight jazzmen, its strength was balanced between the four frontline players and the four members of the rhythm section. Elmer Schoebel was the only one who could read music, and that made him the arranger. The band appeared at the Chicago club until the beginning of 1923, and modified its original composition over the course of months. The rhythm section improved when Ben Pollack took over from Frank Snyder on drums, and Steve Brown (Tom's brother) strengthened the ensemble with string bass playing that was brilliant and totally new. The place was small, and it didn't allow the band to blow too loud. Paul Mares, who used an old felt hat, cut on one side and held in front of his horn, as a mute, would describe it: "Friar's Inn was in a basement. It was a cabaret style, with tables and a dance floor. There was a post on one side of the bandstand, and 'Rapp' used to play with his clarinet against it for tone. He used to like to play into a corner, too. . . . Friar's was a hangout of the big money guys. Al Capone and Dion O'Bannion used

2. The Friar's Inn was a basement establishment in Chicago's Loop, located in a complex that also included the Canton Tea Garden and the Moulin Rouge Café. It had "an old marble floor and tables 'n chairs—no tablecloth, and the place packed with millionaires," recalled Volly DeFaut. The place was remembered as a gangster hangout, and it employed a strict whites-only policy. Three different bands played at night, the Friar's Orchestra working the last shift, from ten at night until six in the morning.

to come in. . . . We tried to hold rehearsals, but no one would show up. So we did our rehearsing on the job. The crowd never knew the difference."[3]

It would be hopeless to try to name the many young Americans who discovered in that cellar a form of jazz that would become a model, an ideal accomplishment, and the confirmation of their musical vocation. One of them, Hoagy Carmichael, then a law student at the University of Indiana and future author of "Star Dust" and "Georgia on My Mind," devoted a great portion of his studies to the Chicago nightlife. He came one night to the Friar's Inn, together with saxophonist George Johnson and Vic Moore, a young drummer, and the three musicians settled down at a table: "The place smelled just right—funky, rundown, sinister, and dusty," wrote Hoagy. "Leon Roppolo, the clarinet player, was wiggling into action in his seat. He started 'Sensation Rag.' It was the doodle-style George had taught me. Then George Brunies, the trombonist, picked it up and blasted his notes jerkily, with penetrating brassy tones. The notes surprised me at unexpected times and in unexpected places. They went right down through my gizzard and made my feet vibrate. . . . Vic Moore laughed like an idiot and drummed the tabletop with his hands: *'I'm modern now.'*"[4] By the end of the night, George Johnson introduced Bix to Hoagy, adding before leaving the young men, "You ought to hear that kid play; he's going to be tops some day. He's got ideas, but his lip is still weak."[5] The young players were soon to reunite, and Bix, George Johnson, Min Leibrook, and Vic Moore formed "a vague sort of semi-pro group we called the 'Ten Foot Band,' from its five members," as Moore recalled.[6]

If the music played by the NORK had the same affect on both Bix and Hoagy, the cornetist was above all appreciative of the attitude these musicians had toward their creation, something he had never seen before but that he recognized in himself: these young artists, capable of getting into mischief in the wings or after the show, approached their work with an astonishing seriousness and concentration. More than just an easily mastered technically perfect performance, they sought a "vibe," an emotion . . . giving each note such meaning that one could say that they were "really playing like Negroes," which, at that time, for these jazzmen, was the supreme achievement.

It's easy to imagine Bix on his way back to Lake Forest, in the middle of the night, with his brain on fire. Seated at the rear of an empty train car, his cornet in a paper bag, the young man vibrated to the rhythm of the most beautiful music in the world: that which, at this point, only he could hear.

Lake Forest, April–May 1922

And the time came when Bix gave up his schoolwork altogether, without the least hesitation, once he was convinced that he had no hope of passing the June exams.

3. Nat Shapiro and Nat Hentoff, *Hear Me Talkin' to Ya* (New York: Rinehart Co., 1955 and Dover, 1966), pp. 122–123.

4. Hoagy Carmichael, *Sometimes I Wonder* (New York: Farrar, Strauss & Giroux, 1965, and Da Capo Press, 1999), pp. 89–90.

5. Hoagy Carmichael, *The Stardust Road* (New York: Rinehart Co, 1946, and Da Capo Press, 1999), p. 47.

6. Vic Moore, "Bix—As I Knew Him," *Swing Music*, volume II, no. 1 (March 1936), p. 6.

He sat in with Jimmie Caldwell's band again during the last two weekends of April, but this playing didn't bring him the pleasure it used to. Now only in his own band could he open up and, in total freedom, explore uncharted territories with his cornet. The Cy-Bix Orchestra took on an engagement for Saturday, May 6, and performed at a party thrown in Gary, Indiana. This nocturnal adventure was discovered, and it resulted in a serious reprimand to all its participants from the student council. But this was not enough to stop Bix, who could not be found on the evening of May 17, after having been summoned to Mr. Richards's office during the day. He managed to get away the next day, and joined Jimmie Caldwell's band for the night at the Black Cat Room of the Edgewater Beach Hotel. Bix was again reported absent on the evening of May 19, which led the dormitory master to keep a close watch over him: Bix was caught the following night, returning to his room up the fire escape. On May 21, the faculty voted for his immediate expulsion.

On that same day, Mr. Richards sent a telegram to Agatha: "Bix leaving Chicago one o'clock today for home. Letter following. J. W. Richards." This letter was addressed to Bismark Beiderbecke, informing him of the decision to expel Bix, adding that the boy had made no effort at all while he was on probation, and that "his influence around the school has been felt to be very injurious in that his influence upon other boys has deterred them from work and has upset them in the matter of conduct. This is true to such an extent," continued Mr. Richards, "that certain parents have objected strenuously to their sons' association with him." The letter ended in saying that, in this particular instance, Bix might return to Lake Forest and "take the final examinations after Commencement," if he wished to do so. Unwilling to face his family, Bix decided to temporarily remain away from Davenport, and moved to Chicago in hopes of finding some work.

The young outlaw's parents were in shock—most probably more disorientated than furious. Writing on the morning of May 24 to Mr. Richards, Bismark Beiderbecke disclosed the state of utter confusion he was in, and asked the headmaster for the true reasons that had caused this sanction. "May I ask you to state the nature of his conduct which aroused the parents' objection?" Bix's father wrote. "Was it something to be ashamed of?" He had then taken the first train for Chicago, where it wouldn't be difficult to find his son.

Chicago, May–June 1922

Bix had accepted the first offer made to him: to rehearse with a big band called upon to take part in a thirty-five week tour across the U.S. This production, directed by Marty Bloom for the Orpheum Time organization, was to be sent on the road with singers and chorus girls dancing to jazz music. The cornet player's participation in this show was brought to an end by the appearance of a well-dressed man at the entrance to the hall: Bix's father was in Chicago. The young man was apparently able to talk his father out of making him return immediately to Davenport, and he was allowed to delay by a few days his trip back to his family.

Bix was not yet home when the response from Lake Forest Academy, mailed on May 29, was received by the Beiderbeckes. Mr. Richards was highly surprised that they were unaware of the facts for which their son had been reprimanded. "At the time he left," he wrote, "we were not absolutely dead sure as to his part with regard to liquor around the School. Since then we have definitely learned that he was drinking himself and was responsible, in part at least, in having liquor brought into the School. . . . The more we have found out concerning him since he left, the more we regret the things he did and are sorry that he was in the School at all. Bix is a very clever excuse-maker, and I think he sometimes fools even himself

Portrait of John Wayne Richards. (Lake Forest Academy archives)

Telegram from John W. Richards sent to Agatha Beiderbecke on May 21, 1922. (Lake Forest Academy archives)

in a way." The director added that if the former student should return in June, he should "take the examinations and leave at once without mixing or meddling around the School."

When his parents received this stern verdict, Bix was staying at the Sheridan Beach Hotel in Michigan City, Indiana, where his friend Sid Stewart had him working as a pianist: "I'll only stay two or three days then return to Chi, and try lake Forest again," he wrote to his mother on May 31. "And then home. . . . Boy, this is life—they are all so wonderful to one here. I play the piano & everyone in the hotel crowds around & sings and complements me. The piano is a wonder and really I'm playing over my head. . . . Your erring son, Leon." The musician was clearly enjoying recognition that he hadn't been able to find as a student.

Around Chicago, summer 1922

Bismark Herman Beiderbecke (1868–1940), Bix's father, at the end of the 1920s. (Courtesy of Liz Beiderbecke Hart)

Left to right: Bill Grimm, Don Murray, Bix, and Ray Landis in Michigan City, June 1922. (Duncan Schiedt Collection)

The Beiderbecke family was notified that Bix was asked to sit for his makeup examinations on June 19. An extra charge of $1 was required for each subject he would take. The family was saved the expense, as Bix had joined Bill Grimm's band on June 7. The orchestra was working aboard the Morton Lines steamer *Michigan City*, which offered one day dancing excursions while crossing the lake between Chicago and Michigan City. Don Murray had met up again with his favorite cornetist, and the two young men stayed on this boat for three weeks.

In July his friend Sid Stewart from Lake Forest asked Bix to play a gig at the White Lake Yacht Club. The place belonged to Sid's grandparents, and the small band was billed on Fridays and Saturdays only for formal dance parties. Photographs were taken during these summer days, showing Bix in a bathing suit with a cigarette in his mouth, canoeing on the lake, and, dressed in golf pants and a flat cap, sitting on a railing.

He returned to Chicago on July 30, and jumped at an offer made by Vic Moore, whom he had met at the Friar's Inn. This quartet was made up of Bix on cornet, Jules Van Gende on C-melody sax, Wilbur "Bud" Hatch on piano, and Vic Moore on drums, and it played every Saturday at Delavan Lake, Wisconsin. Bix always showed an unlimited capacity for invention and harmonic ideas that were far ahead of their time. "Bix sat bending over, facing the floor with his horn, his fingers curled around the keys instead of playing them with the tips," recalled Bill Blaufuss. "His style was legato and it made the hair on my forearms stand up straight. I sure liked that style!"[7] Bix stayed at that vacation resort until September 4, when a summertime of sleepless nights ended.

Bix and Ed Meikel, White Lake, Michigan, July 1922. (Duncan Schiedt Collection)

New Orleans, Tuesday, August 8, 1922

Louis Armstrong was playing at a New Orleans funeral when he received a telegram: Joe "King" Oliver was asking him to come to Chicago and join his Creole Jazz Band at the Lincoln Gardens. The reasons that might have led King Oliver to call for a second cornet at his side can only be guessed, but Louis hurried to the station, leaving his native Louisiana for nine years.

Syracuse, New York, September 1922

Bix set out on his first long trip by mid-September, when he became part of a group of seven musicians engaged to play in Syracuse. Not all of these Royal Harmonists of Indiana have been identified, but at the cornetist's side were Mervin "Pee Wee" Rank on drums, saxophonists Johnny Eberhardt and Wayne "Doc" Hostetter, and a guitarist who would be destined to play an important role on the New York scene: Eddie Condon. The five musicians gathered at the LaSalle Street Station in Chicago on the evening of September 19, and took a late-night train headed east. "With nothing to do but sit and stare at the scenery from there to Buffalo I began to wonder about the cornet," Eddie Condon would write in his autobiography. "I got out my banjo. Eberhardt dug up his saxophone and doodled

7. Norman P. Gentieu, "Memories of Bix, Part 3" (from Harrington Archive), in *IAJRC Journal* (summer 1994).

along with me. Finally Beiderbecke took up a silver cornet. He put it to his lips and blew a phrase. The sound came like a girl saying yes."[8]

The orchestra made its first appearance in Syracuse, at the Alhambra Dance Academy, on September 22, and received a favorable mention in the local newspaper. Bix learned of his grandmother's death during the trip, and he wrote to his father on November 1: "Pop on top of Oma's death, my sorrow was heighten by the fact that I couldn't be home, but even if I wasn't there personally, I was in thoughts because I didn't realize how much Oma meant in my young life until she died. . . . We've got to take it as it comes, but Dad I can see your part of it. Of all the troubles that I can imagine and that are bound to come in time, the trouble I dread worse is to have the time come when mother and you & all of course must go, and I sometimes feel I'd as soon not live to see the time. Well I'll check this as I know it isn't making you feel any better but, just between you and me Dad, I think that we can say that when Oma was living we had the best mothers in the world, am I right?" He really was a disconcerting boy, able to show the keenest thoughtfulness when it was needed, and a sense of premonition that would sadly be borne out: his father would survive him nine years, and his mother twenty-one. Such kindness, such gentleness, which portray Bix in the most faithful way, would always allow him to secure his parents' affection. Step by step, his father was resigning himself to having a jazz musician in the family, without, however, ever approving of his son's choice.

New York, November 1922

Bix went to Scranton, Pennsylvania, from November 7 to 9, to sit in for an absent musician. He then went to New York. The city had not yet become the country's jazz capital, but he spent his first week in Manhattan in a state of bedazzlement, which is easy to imagine, hearing the Original Dixieland Jazz Band live for the first time, and its cornet player, Nick La Rocca, the man who had been the origin of his musical vocation.

Davenport and Chicago, winter 1922

After a two-day stop in Chicago on his way home and an inevitable visit to the Friar's Inn in search of musicians sharing his passion, Bix took a train to Davenport on November 20. While en route, he wrote to Nick La Rocca: "I saw Mike Fritzel last night and he sure seemed impressed when I told him about you boys wanting to come to Chi, and that you would consider the Friar's Inn if everything—'Do' and hours—were satisfactory. . . . All I knew was that you were the best band in the country. Well he expects a letter from you Nick."[9]

8. Eddie Condon with Thomas Sugrue, *We Called It Music: A Generation of Jazz* (New York: Henry Holt, 1947, and Da Capo Press, 1992), p. 85.

9. This handwritten letter was reproduced in *Storyville*, no. 9 (February/March 1967), pp. 29–31. It is written on three pages of "Rock Island Lines, en route" letterhead.

Once in Davenport, his father put Bix to work at the East Davenport Fuel & Lumber Company, where his brother, Burnie, was already employed as an accountant. This would be Bismark Beiderbecke's final attempt at convincing his prodigal son of the benefits of a life dedicated to the sale of coal and wood. The young employee did manage to get permission to leave town a few times. Wilbur "Bud" Hatch, with whom he played in August at Delavan Lake, asked him to join his band for several gigs on the outskirts of Chicago, and Bix finished the year of 1922 performing with Bill Grimm in Dubuque for the Christmas festivities.

First page of Bix's letter dated November 20, 1922, and sent to "Mr. D. Jas LaRocca, 225 West 11th Street, NYC." (Published in *Storyville*, no. 9, February/March 1967, p. 29)

CHAPTER 4

1923: Birth of the Wolverines

Davenport and Chicago, January–April 1923

In January 1923, Bix was authorized by his father to take a few more short breaks in Chicago. He rehearsed with Dale Skinner's quintet, but his style was too original and he didn't get the job. Naturally, he went back to the Friar's Inn, where he ran into Hoagy Carmichael, George Johnson, and Vic Moore—all permanent fixtures of the place. A late-night visit to the Lincoln Gardens allowed these young white jazzmen to meet the budding genius on second cornet in King Oliver's band: Louis Armstrong, who was twenty-one at the time, while Bix was almost twenty. "We took two quarts of bathtub gin, a package of muggles, and headed for the black-and-tan joint where King Oliver's band was playing," wrote Hoagy. "As I sat down to light my first muggle, Bix gave the sign to a big black fellow, playing second trumpet for Oliver, and he slashed into 'Bugle Call Rag.' I dropped my cigarette and gulped my drink. Bix was on his feet, his eyes popping. For taking the first chorus was that second trumpet, Louis Armstrong. Louis was taking it fast. *'Why,'* I moaned, *'why isn't everybody in the world here to hear that?'* I meant it. . . . Every note Louis hit was perfection."[1]

At the start of 1923, Doris E. Peavey's orchestra at the Arcadia Ballroom in Saint Paul, Minnesota, had hired Eddie Condon. Tired of hearing Condon speaking endlessly in praise of Bix Beiderbecke, Doris Peavey resolved to send a letter to Davenport and offer a job to the cornetist. Bix's response arrived in the form of a

1. *The Stardust Road*, op. cit., p. 53.

postcard, on the back of which a few words had been written in pencil: "I will come to work for you for $75 a week." "Originally he had put down sixty-five," Eddie Condon recounted. "There was a smudge where he had erased the six, but it was still plainly visible under the seven. Peavey handed me the card and watched me fidget. '*I don't think I want him in my band*,' he said."[2]

Bix celebrated his twentieth birthday on March 10 with his family. He worked for his father until June, with a total lack of interest, as can well be imagined. He took his friend Esten Spurrier to the Coliseum Ballroom, on April 24 and 25, to hear the Benson Orchestra of Chicago during its two days performing in Davenport. Among the three saxophonists in this big band was Frank Trumbauer. This first encounter between Bix and the man who would become his major musical partner left no lasting impression on the sax player, but Esten Spurrier retained a vivid memory of that day. With Bix right behind him, he went up to the bandstand during a short intermission and approached Trumbauer: "One thing that we had to ask him about was the band-aids that all of the sax and brass men wore across the bridge of their noses," recalled Esten Spurrier. "Frank explained that this was a gimmick they used and told the dancers, when asked about the band-aids, that they played so 'hot' that it would break the blood vessels in their nose, and this was put on as a precaution."[3]

Richmond, Indiana, 1922–April 1923

After 1922, the writing of jazz history was markedly changed. The opening of the record market—the end of Victor and Columbia's monopoly—would allow outsiders to find a place in the shadow of the two giants, and to set up recording studios far away from New York. Because of the primitive nature of their technical equipment and the severe constraints to which the players were consequently subjected, recorded music did not sound at all like the music heard in cabarets and dance halls. Records captured only a faint reflection of this live creation, and the available oral or written accounts from that age give us additional insights into these preserved early sounds, helping us to better appreciate the revolution led by the jazz pioneers.

Thanks to the outstanding quality of its jazz catalog, a company from Richmond, Indiana, stands out from its contemporaries: the Starr Piano Company, whose records were sold under the Gennett label. Richmond was founded in 1806 by Quakers on both banks of the Whitewater River, east of Indianapolis. Georges Trayser, a pianomaker from the French Alsace, brought his knowledge to the Starr brothers in 1872, and the Starr Piano Company's first instruments soon hit the market. At the start of the twentieth century, Henry Gennett took control of a firm that, with 15,000 pianos built in 1915, was among America's most important piano

2. *We Called It Music*, op. cit., p. 90.

3. Philip Evans and Larry Kiner, *TRAM, The Frank Trumbauer Story, Studies in Jazz 18* (Lanham, NJ: Scarecrow Press, 1994), p. 37.

manufacturers. That same year, the company launched the Starr phonographs, machines that could play records with either vertical or lateral grooves. This brand was added to the fifty others already available to American consumers—two million machines were sold in 1920 in the U.S.—and this new product-line couldn't achieve success without a supply of newly released records to draw in the customers. A recording studio was opened in New York, at the company's main office on East 37th Street. In 1917, Starr built a six-story building in Richmond, dedicated to phonograph production and record pressing. A second studio was also opened on the factory's ground. The proximity to Chicago, with its many and varied musicians, made this a prime location.

Victor, which at the time shared with Columbia a crushing commercial and technical domination over the record markets, used all possible legal means to protect its rights to the lateral-cut recording technology. Their competitors could only survive with the support of a more profitable activity: the manufacture of pianos and organs for Aeolian-Vocalion, furniture for Paramount Wisconsin, and billiard tables and supplies for Brunswick.

After the First World War ended, Henry Gennett daringly challenged the Victor label, introducing lateral-cut discs at low prices, without paying a licensing fee for using its competitor's patented technology. This commercial strategy was a direct assault on the exclusive field of the American giant. Supported in its fight by other small brands, the Starr Piano Company won a complete victory on April 4, 1922, with the Court of Appeals' denial of the validity of the Victor patents. The record market was now legally open, but practically, Victor and Columbia continued to dominate the field because of the size of their distribution networks and the exclusive contracts they had signed with the most prestigious artists. Just to survive, the Gennett label needed to be innovative.

The Richmond recording studio had been set up in a small gray single-story wooden building alongside the Whitewater River. The factory was erected conveniently close to the main rail line, and was served by a spur that ran alongside the studio building, crossing just in front of its entrance. The passing of freight cars obviously generated noise likely to spoil the recordings, and the studio's working hours had to be adapted to this rail traffic. The main Chesapeake & Ohio line, with its powerful and noisy steam locomotives, crossed downtown Richmond and ran above the Starr Piano factory, about fifty yards from the studio, transmitting vibrations and noise at the most unexpected times, and inevitably ruining the recording in process. The size of the studio was about 125 by 30 feet, which included a control room from which the recording engineer could watch over the session through a double-glass window. The space between interior and exterior walls was filled with sawdust, and large draperies were hung along the partitions in an attempt to improve the soundproofing of the room.

Until 1925, when the first electronic recordings appeared on the market, all labels used an "acoustic" process. Many pictures were taken in Richmond's studio by William Dalbey, a local photographer contracted by Gennett: they show the musicians gathered around a couple of large conical "horns," with diameters as wide as two feet. In the studio, the wide ends of the horns were pointed toward the orchestra, and the narrow ends entered the control room through a small hole in the partition, soundproofed by a small dusty curtain. They were suspended from the ceiling by heavy strings and directly connected to the recording table. The movement of the turntable was operated by a pulley system, which lacked mechanical accuracy and was highly sensitive to variations in temperature. As the speed of the phonographs was equally inconsistent, the distortion when playing the recordings could be either exaggerated or even corrected during playback. A cutting stylus at the narrow end of the recording horns was caused to vibrate by the sounds of the instruments playing into the wide end of the horns. The movement of the stylus etched a groove onto a polished blank disc covered with carnauba wax—a material used in candle-making. The presence of impurities in the wax would cause a high spoilage rate in production. In order to keep the wax at the right softness, the recording was done in an overheated, airtight, unventilated room, where two small fans could only stir up the air, heavy with humidity from the nearby river. In the photographs that were taken during these recording sessions, the musicians always appear to be sitting in a sauna.

At the start of each session, chief engineer Ezra Wickemeyer established the sound balance of the ensemble by placing each musician at the right distance from the horns: the weak banjos at front, and the powerful brass farther away.[4] This operation required making numerous test records, which were destroyed after each disc was played back. There was obviously no possibility of correction or editing, and each side was recorded continuously, from the start to the end of the title. It was common to keep two or three complete takes of each number.

The performances were limited to the three-minute capacity of the 78-rpm discs, and jazzmen were consequently submitted to a discipline public performances had not prepared them for. Recording at Richmond was for the artists an intense physical and mental test, but the chance they were given of hearing themselves play, often for the first time, left many of them with a nostalgic and emotional memory. They couldn't, however, in these difficult and tense conditions, always come through with free and fresh musical expression. Each side cut without incident was the product of a miracle, or the result of meticulous professionalism.

A copper-plated master was cast from the wax-engraved disc, and a few test pressings sent to the management, which selected the final cuts to be released to the market. A metal stamper was produced from the selected take, and used for pressing the shellac records that would bear the Gennett label. The musicians were not granted any royalties on records sold, and they were paid a mere $15 to $50 cash per recording session. As might be expected, black musicians received even

4. A photograph, taken during a Bailey's Lucky Seven recording session in New York's Gennett studios shows the placement of the musicians required to reach the right balance: the piano is right at the recording horn; the saxophone, clarinet, and banjo are two yards away, with the trombone slightly behind them, facing the horn; the two trumpets are placed one and two yards, respectively, behind the trombone.

less. Gennett's records never made an artist's fortune, but naturally it was quite different for the company itself.

Henry Gennett passed away on June 2, 1922, when his company was at its peak, but his three sons continued his work. Fred, the youngest, took over direction of Gennett records at a time when sales were affected by the arrival on the market, in 1923, of the first cheap home radios, which directly competed with recorded music. The Gennett family had made the American motto their own: "Business is business," producing what could be sold without paying any consideration to their contracted artists' political beliefs or skin color. And this led to drastic extremes in the nature of the material recorded: the worst being racist hymns of the Ku Klux Klan, which was deeply rooted in Indiana, and the best the music of Chicago's most active jazzmen, from Louis Armstrong to Bix Beiderbecke.

Gennett's jazz catalog led off in New York in 1921 with the recordings of a group of highly talented white musicians, Ladd's Black Aces and Bailey's Lucky Seven, which included cornetist Phil Napoleon and trombonist Miff Mole. These records followed the ODJB's path, and they shared a similar success. French composer Darius Milhaud, on a visit to New York in 1922, was fascinated by this music and brought the first Ladd's Black Aces recordings to Europe—the first ever to cross the ocean. The so-called race records—which were discs cut by black musicians for a black audience—appeared on the scene in 1921, and the big hit the Okeh label had with Mamie Smith's "Crazy Blues," attracted the attention of other record companies. Following this new interest, the New York Gennett studio made numerous recordings of black singers starring in musicals or vaudeville shows.

In Chicago in 1922, Fred Wiggins was managing the Starr Piano store, where the company's pianos, gramophones, and records were sold. The shop was located on South Wabash Street, a few blocks from the Friar's Inn, a place where Fred Wiggins used to spend nights enjoying the music. His boss, Fred Gennett, was not really attracted to the Friar's Inn band, but his acute commercial sense led him to pay attention to novelty: after hearing Paul Mares's band once, he invited them to record a few sides in Richmond.

On the morning of August 29, 1922, a dusty car pulled into the Starr Piano lot and out came the eight musicians, tired from a long trip on bad roads. These first Gennett jazz recordings, cut in the Starr Piano Company's recording oven, gave the New Orleans Rhythm Kings their first access to a studio. At the end of the session, engineer Ezra Wickemeyer kept only twenty satisfactory takes from that day, seven of which were later released by Gennett under the name of the Friar's Society Orchestra. Leon Roppolo did outstanding work on his clarinet and he would be credited, on the released take of "Tiger Rag," with the first jazz solo to appear on a record, preceding even Louis Armstrong and Sidney Bechet by a few months. These records, destined for quick success, would be for Bix a rich source of inspiration, and a confirmation of the value of his own musical inclinations. Their versions of

"Farewell Blues" and "Bugle Call Blues" would also serve as a model for numerous young musicians who, by endlessly playing these brilliant modern sides, learned their choruses by heart. Slightly modified, the orchestra returned to the studio on March 12, 1923, and—as the New Orleans Rhythm Kings—recorded an additional eight new titles, which were released a few weeks later.

Richmond residents did not pay any attention to the group of black musicians present in their town on April 5 and 6, 1923, and the visitors kept an eye open for trouble in a city where acts of racist violence were not uncommon. King Oliver's Creole Jazz Band had arrived by train on the morning of April 5. For the first time in their lives, Joe Oliver, the Dodds brothers, and Louis Armstrong entered a recording studio. "Of course everybody was on edge," remembered drummer Baby Dodds. "We were all working hard and perspiration as big as a thumb dropped off us. Even Joe Oliver was nervous; Joe was no different from any of the rest. The only really smooth-working person there was Lil Armstrong. She was very unconcerned and much at ease."[5] The band's stay in Richmond resulted in twenty-seven completed takes. The musicians carefully avoided any hotel located downtown, and on the evening of the second day, they left by train for the five-hour ride back to Chicago.

5. *The Baby Dodds Story*, op. cit., p. 69.

Although marred by the studio's limited technical means, the nine titles released by Gennett after those two sessions did capture a true account of one of the New Orleans style's most outstanding achievements, of an authentic and *hot* collective creation, within which each performer could express his own personal feeling and talent. However, the first commercial success of King Oliver's band would come later on the Okeh label, which had better distribution than Gennett, with two sides recorded in Chicago on June 22 and 23: "High Society Rag" and "Dipper Mouth Blues." These recordings would shortly be among January 1924's best-sellers.

Chicago, July 1923

And while musical history was being made, Bix moped among the wood and coal of his father's business. By the end of June, his future looked brighter, with the promise of a new contract starting on July 2. He was invited to join clarinetist Dale Skinner's Band in Chicago. Bix would be seated next to George Brunies, the famous NORK trombonist, but the job lasted only a few days, and he was replaced on July 20.

Gennett Studio in Richmond, Indiana, in the 1940s; rail track is visible in front of the wood building.

Richmond, July 1923

Don Murray was asked to be a member of the NORK's third Gennett session, and he invited Bix to travel with him to Richmond. The label had developed a close collaboration with Melrose Brothers Music Company, an important publisher of sheet music and orchestral arrangements, among them those played on Gennett records. In spring 1923, Melrose Brothers hired an extraordinary character: Jelly Roll Morton. This Creole, whose birth in New Orleans can most probably be dated to September 20, 1890, had gone through many different jobs all over the U.S. and had gained more than twenty years' experience as a composer and arranger of jazz, a genre that he claimed to have "originated." This boast was not totally inaccurate: he had actually written the first orchestrations in jazz history, demonstrating a unique finesse as a composer and an original mastery of the keyboard. The Creole Jelly Roll Morton joined the NORK musicians in the Richmond studio on July 17 and 18, 1923, and Bix would thus attend the first interracial session in jazz history to have been recorded.[6]

Don Murray was a big part of Bix's life at that time. The two young men had followed similar paths. They were driven by the same passion for jazz and both possessed truly original musical talents. They also shared a strong thirst for alcoholic beverages, and a gypsy had predicted the same destiny for both. Don Murray was the son of a Methodist pastor. During his first year at Northwestern University in Evanston, in Chicago's northern outskirts, he had chosen a major: jazz. This unexpected vocation led his father to send him to the state university in Bloomington, Illinois, with the hope of pulling him away from Chicago and its musical temptations. It failed.

Bloomington, Illinois, July 1923

Bix and Don Murray traveled together to Bloomington, where they joined Peter Lowry's orchestra, the Shuffle Along Band, for a few days. They worked out a duet to be performed during dance intermissions. "It would start with Don sitting at the piano on a bench that was placed at right angles to the piano," explained historian Warren K. Plath. "With Bix sitting with his cornet at the other end of the bench, a duet of one of the popular songs of the day would be played. At the end of the first chorus, Bix would set down his horn, sidle up to and replace Don at the piano, and pick up where Don had left off. Don, in the meantime, would pick up his sax from the top of the piano, sit down on the bench where Bix had been previously, and another chorus would be started. Several choruses would be played, Don and Bix alternating at the piano and on their respective instruments, with the band joining in on the final chorus and providing a real 'showboat' finish."[7] Pete Lowry's band appeared on Saturday, July 28, at Cagles Park, a large rectangular

6. Saxophonist Harold Ragland, who played with Don Murray in Pete Lowry's band, met Bix and Don just after the recording session, and he remembered Bix raving about "that colored piano player," as quoted in Warren K. Plath, "Don Murray, the Early Years (1904—1923)," in *Storyville*, no. 122, op. cit., p. 59. In a 1939 interview, Paul Mares remembered, "Bix was all set to play on the recording of 'Angry,' but Brunies and Roppolo nixed it. Bix actually cried . . . but they wouldn't let him." (Thanks to Sue Fischer.)

7. Ibid., p. 59.

open-air dance hall located on Route 13, between Marion and Herrin, Illinois. A beauty contest was added to the orchestra's performance on that night. On July 29, the C&A Railroad brought Bix and Don back to Chicago.

Chicago, August 1923

Starting the next day, Bill Grimm offered Bix a new engagement, similar to that of June 1922. The *Michigan City* steamer was still touring across the lake, and Bill Grimm was still on piano, but the orchestra had been modified. Jimmy Hartwell had replaced Don Murray on clarinet, and Johnny Carsella, Frank Lehman, and Harry Gale were playing, respectively, trombone, banjo, and drums. One morning a young boy in short pants got up onstage and moved close to the clarinet. Bix shouted, "Get away from those instruments!" But the boy had just been hired to succeed Jimmy Hartwell, and at age fourteen, Benny Goodman was beginning a musical career destined for the greatest success. Bill Grimm did ask him, however, to wear long pants. Benny and Bix would spend a full month in the band, and the cornetist's reputation spread rapidly among the great number of young musicians who were working in the area that summer.

Jimmy McPartland was seventeen years old, and was playing cornet in a band directed by Al Haid. The boat on which this orchestra was performing also crossed Lake Michigan, often cruising the same route as the *Michigan City*. "As soon as I started," Jimmy McPartland remembered, "I was told about a band playing on another boat, which had Bix Beiderbecke on cornet.... Everyone was saying how terrific the music was on this other boat, and the rumor had it that Beiderbecke was the greatest yet."[8]

Davenport, September 1923

The summer season on the lakes ended on September 3, and Bix returned to his family for a month. While in his hometown, he finally obtained his union card in Local 67. He took the unavoidable examination on the piano and passed, after his mother spoke to a relative in the union to have her son's weakness at reading music disregarded. Bix's professional career was officially launched. He found a job in a Saint Louis theater for two weeks only, and was back in Chicago by mid-October.

Hamilton, November–December 1923

At the end of 1923, the illicit organization that sprang up from Prohibition had been growing and strengthening for three years, and the system was now fully operating.

8. *Hear Me Talkin' to Ya*, op. cit., pp. 124–125.

It had expanded under the weak and accommodating presidency of Warren G. Harding, who had died in August 1923. Some members of his administration had maintained merely casual relationships with gangsters; others were direct supporters of nationwide criminal activities. In this unwholesome atmosphere, bootlegging flourished. Craft production—"bathtub gin"[9] or home distilling—filled only a small part of a strongly increasing demand. For the most part, supply was secured from the industrial breweries and distilleries, which were legally limited to the production and exportation of medical alcohol—and this "therapeutic" use had a momentous increase. An underground market was developing, creating false permits to sell alcohol and bringing side income to a long line of politicians and bureaucrats. These "official" dealings, supplemented by a network of ever more efficient moonshiners, allowed bootleggers to become outrageously rich by supplying the ceaseless demands of speakeasies, bars, and cabarets for any kind of liquor. As the city of all excesses, Chicago was at the height of its reputation, and collusion among politicians and gangsters reached a remarkable level. None of the big cities of the Midwest were safe from these crime gangs and their extreme violence.

Existing at the lowest echelon of this criminal organization, the Stockton Club offered a perfect example of a Prohibition nightclub. Located south of Hamilton on Route 4, the road between Hamilton and Cincinnati, the club occupied a two-story wooden building. The management office was on the second floor, along with a few shabby rooms available for clandestine purposes. The ground floor was divided into two parts: a big room cluttered with gambling tables, and a smaller one where a band was packed in between a tiny dance floor, some more tables, and a bar. The club opened every night at nine. Dinner was served, to be washed down with alcoholic beverages pouring out from an inexhaustible source: the organization of George Remus, a lawyer who was head of the biggest "legal" booze racket in Cincinnati. The place closed with the departure of the last patron, never before four or five in the morning.

The Stockton Club had opened in 1923, hiring at first a girls' band to bring some excitement to the place. They did not really attract any enthusiasm, and they were soon replaced by an orchestra including trumpet player George "Red" Bird, pianist Dudley Mecum, and clarinetist Jimmy Hartwell. George Bird would leave after a few days, and Jimmy Hartwell contacted Bix, whom he had met in August on the *Michigan City*. The idle cornetist was hanging around Chicago and was more than happy to leave for Hamilton at the end of October. This new group was made up of seven musicians: Bix, Dudley Mecum, and Jimmy Hartwell, accompanied by Bob Gillette on banjo, Ole Vangsness on tuba, Bob Conzelman on drums, and saxophonist George Johnson—one of the most faithful regulars from the Friar's Inn, who was the last to be added to the ensemble.[10] The young men stayed at the Hamilton YMCA, to which they would return at daybreak. None of them could read music, and Bix was asked to build up an orchestration of sorts by per-

9. Bathtub gin earned its name because it was supposedly made at home in a bathtub. It was produced by trying to take the poisons out of a denaturated alcohol, and to recover the ethyl alcohol. The concoction was then flavored with juniper, diluted, and bottled. The purification process had to be done by skilled chemists; otherwise, the results could be deadly.

10. Saxophonist Abe Cholden played at the Stockton Club a few days before George Johnson's arrival. Cholden recalled that sometime in October, he had "rehearsed with a band on the second floor of a multi-storied building at the north-east corner of State and Randolph Streets in Chicago. The band consisted of Bix Beiderbecke and Wingy Manone on cornets, Cholden on tenor sax, and Dick Voynow, Bob Gillette and Bob Conzelman on piano, banjo and drums respectively. There was also a clarinetist and a tuba player, whose names Cholden could not recall," quoted in "Don Murray, the Early Years (1904–1923)" op. cit., p. 62. In reference to the Stockton Club engagement, George Johnson confirmed that "some time later, in November, Bob Conzelman left for a job in Chicago, and his place in the band was taken by a local drummer named Johnson." George Johnson, "Wolverine Days," *Swing Music* (autumn quarter 1936), p. 30.

forming each player's part on his cornet or on the piano. Their repertoire was highly limited, and the playing hours were long, from opening at nine until the club closed at four or five in the morning. The same titles were therefore repeated several times each night, which, thanks to the general alcoholic haze of the audience and the lack of attention paid to the music, went totally unnoticed. Because *Wolverine Blues*, a successful Jelly Roll Morton composition, was played frequently, the band took the name of the Wolverine Orchestra.

While nosing about a Hamilton music store during a free afternoon, Bix was attracted by an announcement hung near the register: "Qualified teacher with professional experience offering piano lessons. Please contact Miss Priscilla Holbrock, 322 No. 6th St., Hamilton." Bix had often felt the need to upgrade his musical education, but was never capable of pursuing this intellectual effort for more than a few days. He contacted Priscilla, who was a respected pianist, working in theaters and dance halls, but he would only take a few classes with her. This innocuous instruction gave the young teacher a chance to pass onto Bix her admiration for Eastwood Lane, thus revealing a composer who would be to the cornetist a significant source of inspiration and great musical enjoyment.

Sidney Eastwood Lane is completely forgotten today. He was born in 1879. Assistant to Alexander Russell at Princeton University, his first compositions for the piano were written in 1913, when he was thirty-three years old. At the start of the 1920s, while living in Greenwich Village, Eastwood Lane infiltrated a group of literary enthusiasts who used to gather at the Algonquin Hotel, and who became famous as the *Round Table*. Located on 44th Street two blocks from Broadway, the Algonquin's Rose Room brought together the New York avant-garde scene's most bubbling characters, including humorist Robert Benchley, the fat and celebrated *New York Times* critic Alexander Woollcott, dramatist George Kaufman, and the fearsome Dorothy Parker, whose articles and essays were rightly famed as never missing their targets.

One year before Bix met Priscilla, Eastwood Lane had published his most successful work, *Adirondack Sketches*. This suite of six piano pieces was inspired by the landscapes around the Adirondack Mountains, a region in northern New York State, and by childhood memories. Bix would fall for the charm of this simple—and often simplistic—music, for this poetic meditation on nature and its Indian population, highlighted by some faint and elusive sparkles. The influence of this piano suite on Bix's future compositions is obvious, and the atmosphere of pieces entitled "The Legend of Lonesome Lake" and "The Land of the Loon"—which were Bix's favorites—can be found in his own creations. However surprising the infatuation of one of the most inventive jazz artists of his era with one conventional and often trivial composer may be, it gives us a key to Bix Beiderbecke's enigmatic personality, one that would always seek a utopian synthesis, achieved between the blazing freedom of jazz and the sensual pleasure of a well-mastered harmonic structure.

The night of December 31, 1923, would mark the end of the Wolverine Orchestra's engagement. Two groups of rival gangsters, coming from Hamilton and Cincinnati, had selected the same place to celebrate New Year's Eve—the Stockton Club! They were careful to keep clear of each other until three o'clock in the morning, when a bloody fight broke out in the jam-packed rooms of the cabaret. Bix and his band mates managed to shelter themselves behind an overturned table and to escape with their instruments into the snowy night. The police closed the Stockton Club the next day: its orchestra was out of work.

CHAPTER 5

1924: In the Studio—and in New York

Cincinnati, January–February 1924

The Wolverines returned to Chicago on January 3, and probably scared off by the dangers of a life in music, Ole Vangsness left the orchestra to start his dental practice. The group's next job was at Doyle's Dancing Academy in Cincinnati, on the third floor of a building at the corner of Court and Central Avenue, in

Doyle's Dancing Academy, Cincinnati, in the 1970s. (Dave Bartholomew)

the heart of a business district where there were no residents to complain of noise at night. The Academy was open evenings and was patronized by young working people.

There were eight musicians in the Wolverine Orchestra at that time, four of whom were survivors of the Stockton Club: Bix, Jimmy Hartwell, George Johnson, and Bob Gillette. The newcomers were Vic Moore, a drummer Bix had met two years before at the Friar's Inn and played with at Delavan Lake, pianist Dick Voynow, and Wilford "Min" Leibrook, a tuba player they had used several times during their

stay in Hamilton. At Bix's request—he wanted to give more of a Dixieland touch to their music—Al Gandee on trombone was added to the group before its debut at Doyle's ballroom on January 14.

Pictures of the band were taken for promotional purposes, most likely during the first days of the engagement. Three of them have survived. In the first two photographs, the eight members of the band are assembled around a banner printed with the name WOLVERINE ORCHESTRA, CHICAGO. The third photograph is a portrait of Bix: it captures an idealized image of the young musician in a graceful moment of artistic perfection that would become one of the basic elements of his legend, the image of the *Young Man with a Horn*, a symbol of the F. Scott Fitzgerald Roaring Twenties. In a tuxedo, Bix is seated, his cornet held in his right hand with the bell resting on his right knee. His features are delicate and refined, his lips turned up at the corners in a tiny smile and, in the latest fashion, his hair heavily plastered and parted in the middle. But the true attraction of this image is his look: two shining eyes that stare at you with intensity and serenity, from which you can hardly escape. This portrait would be reproduced again and again on the covers of albums of Bix Beiderbecke's records and books about him. The photograph has its own magic . . . but it probably bears little resemblance to its model.[1]

Doyle's Dancing Academy, Cincinnati in the 1970s. (Dave Bartholomew)

Wolverine Orchestra, Doyle's Dancing Academy, January 1924. Left to right, front row: Vic Moore, George Johnson, Jimmy Hartwell, Bix, Al Gandee, Bob Gillette; back row: Dick Voynow and Min Leibrook (Davenport Public Library Collection)

1. Both *Bix, Man and Legend* (p. 58) and *The Leon Bix Beiderbecke Story* (pp. 62–63) give the date of this photograph as August 1921. According to Fritz Putzier, it was taken before the Moline concert on Tuesday, August 30, 1921. In comparison to the photo taken of Fritz Putzier on that day, the poses, background, and lighting are different. On the other hand, Bix's pose, appearance, and clothes are identical to those in the Wolverines' group pictures taken in January 1924—which strongly suggests that is when this famous individual portrait of the cornetist was taken.

The Wolverines' repertoire was adapted from New Orleans standards, more precisely from titles recorded or composed by the Original Dixieland Jazz Band. The Wolverines, however, were playing those tunes quite differently than their celebrated elders had. If Nick La Rocca had set New York and Chicago on fire in 1917, revealing to a huge audience a new sound born in the South, he was now—in 1923— shelved with the forgotten celebrities of the previous decade. Less than five years after its flashy New York debut, the music created by those glorious pioneers sounded dated to the new jazz fans.

This audience was mostly made of college students and professional musicians from the Midwest's middle class. Bix's music would attract the interest of those young enthusiasts with its sophistication, its coolness, and its intelligence: a strong bond would form, built on similarities of age, origin, and level of education, between the musicians and their audience. The students of Indiana and Ohio were at that time deeply immersed in jazz and dance music,

Bix in Cincinnati, January 1924.
(Indiana University Collection)

and each college had one or more student bands. The soul of their music came from its specific nature, mixing in a subtle way the impatient and fiery impulses of youth with the cool and loose attitude of those raised without the experience of poverty.

On two successive Fridays, January 18 and 25, the Wolverines appeared at Miami University in Oxford, Ohio. Arriving in the afternoon, they performed from evening until late into the night, warming up an enthusiastic audience quite different from the less receptive patrons on Doyle's dance floor. This students' celebration, the junior prom, "was a big social event of the entire year," remembered Francis Hannaford. "Two orchestras were hired, the Wolverines and another band, the Ohio Nine. A great reaction of the Miami students, there at the dance, was the amazement at the vitality and the energy that the Wolverines brought to their music. Oxford at that time and Miami University had never had access to any *hot* music. . . . So when the Wolverines came on with this terrifically new, vitalized, energetic music, our horizons of dance-music were expanded. The rest of the year, any fraternity-dance committee-chairman was begged to get a band that played like the Wolverines, and this was a near impossibility . . ."[2]

2. Excerpt from the third program of *Bix, a Biographical Radio Series*, a series of nineteen radio programs produced in 1971 by Miami University Radio, Oxford, Ohio. Director: Jim Grover. Narrator: Bill Utter. Consultants: Joseph Campbell, Phil Evans, and John Steiner. Musical commentary and recording: Frank Powers.

Richmond, Indiana, February 18, 1924

Wolverine Orchestra, Gennett Studios, Indiana, February 18, 1924. Left to right: Min Leibrook (tu), Jimmy Hartwell (cl), George Johnson (sax), Bob Gillette (bjo), Vic Moore (dm), Dick Voynow (p), Bix (ct), and Al Gandee (tb). (Davenport Public Library Collection)

The Wolverines, Doyle's Dancing Academy, January 1924. Left to right: Al Gandee, Vic Moore, Bob Gillette, Dick Voynow, Jimmy Hartwell, Bix, George Johnson, and Min Leibrook. (Davenport Public Library Collection)

This musical excitement had a double effect on the activities of Gennett studios: sales of their jazz records showed a developed interest in this music, and the success of this part of the catalog encouraged Gennett to enlarge it. Located halfway between Cincinnati and Indianapolis, close to Chicago, Richmond was an ideal place for attracting musicians performing in the area. Besides the college orchestras, made up of young white students, many black musicians were working in the Midwest. The city of Indianapolis, for instance, had a sizable black community.

During the first months of 1924, Fred Wiggins left his Chicago store to manage the Gennett label. It was now up to him to select the musicians, set up the recording sessions, and decide the takes and the titles that were to be published. The Richmond company had carried on with its distribution of race records, adding to its catalog during the fall of 1923 Lois Deppe's Serenaders, a black orchestra that would be remembered for one reason only: the first solo recorded on "Congaine" by its nineteen-year-old pianist, Earl "Fatha" Hines. On January 21, 1924, Doc Cook and his Dreamland Orchestra would also record at Gennett's: this Chicago band included the legendary cornetist Freddie Keppard and the clarinetist Jimmy Noone. Six sides were issued after the session, but they were unfortunately recorded at a time when excessive drinking had irreparably spoiled Keppard's powerful blowing.

On Monday, February 18, the Wolverines left Cincinnati at four o'clock in the morning, after their work at Doyle's ended, and drove 125 miles north to Richmond, where Jimmy Hartwell and Dick Voynow had set up their first recording date with Fred Wiggins. A photograph was taken inside the Gennett studio during the recording session. The eight musicians appear worn-out. The studio where the band is confined is obviously well protected against the cold Indiana winter—the boys are immersed in a stifling heat.

Jackets are off, vests are wide-open, and Min Leibrook, slumped in his chair and weighed down by his tuba, is the only one whose bow tie is still fastened: he probably lacked the strength to take it off. Bob Gillette and Al Gandee can barely hold the pose and keep their eyes open. Vic Moore had been deprived of his bass drum—it made the cutting stylus on the recording machine jump, which spoiled the takes—and his drum set is reduced to its snare drum and crash cymbal.[3] Bix is sitting down, legs crossed, sleeves rolled up, with a slightly loosened tie. He looks quite young: a fresh-faced, dreamy kid who has been dropped into a world of exhausted adults.

In addition to these rather special recording conditions, the band had a tough challenge. They were asked to keep their numbers within the three-minute time of the recording capacity of the discs, which meant giving up those free ad-lib parts that used to excite their young admirers. Four titles were recorded on that day, selected by Fred Wiggins, for obvious marketing reasons, from the catalog of hits of the Original Dixieland Jazz Band: "Fidgety Feet" and "Lazy Daddy," by Nick La Rocca and Larry Shields, "Sensation" by E. B. Edwards, and "Jazz Me Blues" by Tom Delaney. By the end of the session, thirteen takes had been recorded, of which only two would be issued: the second takes of "Fidgety Feet" and "Jazz Me Blues." They were released in May 1924 on a record bearing the blue Gennett label.

Playback of the numerous test records, set by Ezra Wickemeyer to achieve the optimal sound balance, allowed the musicians, for the first time, to hear themselves playing. George Johnson remembered this magic moment well, when each musician listened for his own voice in the melody bursting out of the big horn: "I honestly believe that at that moment, and not at any time before, was born in each of us the idea that as a unit, we had something different in the music line. . . . Coming to us out of that horn, the music sounded more like that of another band, and entirely different than it sounded on the job."[4] The difficult recording conditions cannot really be detected when one listens to the two takes selected from the many recorded on that day, as those young musicians were surprisingly able to control and overcome their fatigue and nervous tension.

It is interesting to compare these two sides with the versions of the same titles previously recorded by the ODJB for Victor to appreciate the long way jazz musicians had come over a short period. The 1918 ODJB version of "Fidgety Feet," played at a jumpy tempo, sounds mechanical, and the trombone's plaintive breaks are dated. The ODJB musicians stay within a strict collective ensemble style, and Nick La Rocca's chorus is repeated twice, with no variation.[5]

Played at a slower tempo, the Wolverines' "Fidgety Feet" recorded six years later is relaxed and varied, breaks are more sophisticated, and Jimmy Hartwell's solo, using the lower register of his instrument, is deeply original. Bix carefully avoids any repetition on his second time through the verse and inserts some graceful melodic lines within a rich harmony. This noticeable fluency, this natural feeling, was rarely found in musical productions of that time.

3. "Drums did not record in any sense of the word when those records were made and, as a result, the records of the Wolverines give only a half-picture of the true band, with the bed-rock solidity of the drum background entirely missing," wrote George Johnson in "Wolverine Days," op. cit., p. 31.

4. *Bix, Man and Legend*, op. cit., p. 101.

5. "Fidgety Feet" was recorded in June 1918, and "Jazz Me Blues" three years later. Only five musicians were in the ODJB at the time—they had no saxophone, banjo, or tuba—but the Victor facilities' technical conditions were far superior to Gennett's.

The 1921 rendition by the ODJB of the second title, "Jazz Me Blues," shows an appreciable evolution of the band: the ensemble playing has more structure, more variation, breaks are longer, and thanks to Victor's recording technique, the powerful sound of La Rocca's cornet is rendered with accuracy. The music itself, however, remains quite conventional, progressing without any surprises, phrases being repeated one after another and backed by an insistent unvarying rhythm. The same title, as recorded by the Wolverines in 1924, is far more significant: it breaks new ground in jazz music, and reveals an exceptionally original and inspired artist. This interpretation is spacious, elevated, and the use of harmonic changes keeps the listener's interest alive throughout the side. The take that was preserved captures the first solo recorded by Bix: twenty bars long, during which his cornet develops a logical, delicate, and unique melody.[6]

Breaking with the former rule of ensemble playing as dictated by the New Orleans style, solos were a welcome novelty for orchestral jazz music. The first were recorded in Richmond, with choruses played by Leon Roppolo on "Tiger Rag" in August 1922 and by Louis Armstrong on "Chimes Blues" in April 1923. These pioneers' works would soon be followed by Sidney Bechet's recording of "Wild Cat Blues," cut in New York in June 1923. Playing a solo is an intricate art: a moment of complete freedom given to a musician within a fixed harmonic framework. Conditions of such a practice were even harder in 1924: a player had to leave the location where he stood during ensemble passages to quietly come close to the recording horn for his solo, then move back within the cramped studio to his original place. He was allowed a very short time to express himself, limited by the space available for the full take on the record: for instance, only twenty-five seconds for Bix's twenty-bar solo on "Jazz Me Blues." During this short time, the artist was asked to build a coherent story, to follow a logical development, and to conclude it on time . . . while he was simultaneously expected to show off his emotion, his tenderness, or his passion. Many musicians worked out their solos in advance, preparing a melody that was written out and memorized, leaving some room for possible variations. Few jazzmen were really improvising, playing on each take, in every concert, a new melodic line: Bix Beiderbecke was of that small number.

The sound of Bix's cornet is muffled by Gennett's primitive equipment. It would be better reproduced on subsequent recordings—though many of Bix's contemporaries have stressed that no recording was ever able to capture his cornet's magical power.[7] This take of "Jazz Me Blues" reveals for the first time some characteristics of the cornetist's personal style. He plays within the medium register of the instrument, much like that of the human voice: Bix *sings* with his cornet. He favors simplicity as a means of creating emotion, giving up all artificial and sensational effects. Bix believes in the power of a pure line. He instinctively possesses a unique melodic talent, and the development of this first recorded chorus

6. In his book *Jazz Masters of the '20s* (New York: MacMillan, 1972), Richard Hadlock rightly highlights the influence of clarinet players on Bix's improvised solos: "However, 'Jazz Me Blues' has Bix in better form, contributing an ordered solo that seems more inspired by clarinetists Larry Shield of the ODJB and Leon Roppolo of the NORK than by other trumpet players. Bix's early interest in harmonic alterations in melodic lines . . . suggests that clarinetists, weaving inner harmonic-melodic parts, may have held more fascination for him than cornetists, many of whom, like LaRocca, were limited to simple rhythmic variations on straight melodies. In any event, 'Jazz Me Blues' is the first of many recorded performances in which Bix moves with the fleetness, grace, subtlety, and harmonic sophistication that had previously been heard in some reedmen but seldom in brass players" (pp. 79–80).

7. "Bix worked out the arrangements at the piano and the boys learned their part by ear," wrote trombone player Charlie Preble. "But rhythm was uppermost in every man's mind. They were in the groove on every number and the swing of that band has never been bettered by a white band since. Their records may not tell you this but to have heard them in person would have converted any skeptic," in *Tempo* (July 1936).

is already a model. Esten Spurrier, a friend of his Davenport youth, would recall that Bix considered Louis Armstrong the father of this method of composition, often used in his own solos: "Louis departed greatly from all cornet players in his ability to compose a close-knit individual 32 measures with all phrases compatible with each other . . . so Bix and I always credited Louis as being the father of the correlated chorus: play two measures, then two related, making four measures, on which you play another four measures related to the first four, and so on ad infinitum to the end of the chorus. So the secret was simple—a series of related phrases."[8] The model followed on "Jazz Me Blues" is unquestionably of that type, each of its elements a natural continuation of the preceding one: the second bar is therefore a slight variation on the first one, as the fourth bar is for the third one, and this logical sequence runs until the final note, held over two bars. This part is short, but perfectly accomplished.

Other characteristics of the style Bix was creating may also be briefly heard, even if they are used timidly at this stage: the two running triplets that open the tenth bar, or the rest inserted before the last note—which is therefore played on the second beat of the bar, after a short expectation created by this small void. "The overall impression we get from this solo," trumpeter Randy Sandke clearly summarizes, "as in all of Bix at his best, is that every note is spontaneous yet inevitable."[9] This feeling of effortless plenitude and natural evidence is one characteristic of a master at work: at only twenty years old, Bix was moving in the right direction.

Bix's contemporaries would immediately agree when the record became available in May 1924. Cornetist Red Nichols was among this generation of young musicians: "Bix made a tremendous impression on me," Nichols would confess, "and I'd be the last one to deny that his playing had an influence on me, but I did not imitate him. We were both 'evolving' our styles, and we took inspirations from many of the same sources."[10] The influence of the Wolverines' leader on Red Nichols was actually greater than the latter would ever acknowledge. Red Nichols could have hardly forgotten that, less than two months after the Wolverines' first record was on the market, he had copied Bix's "Jazz Me Blues" solo note for note in "You'll Never Get to Heaven with Those Eyes," a side recorded in New York on June 26, 1924. Who could think of a better tribute to the creative power of the young artist from Davenport?[11]

The Wolverines' success, however, would be limited to a circle of jazz fans and a local midwestern audience. The orchestra was not given much promotion by Gennett, and their records were not widely distributed. This small label could not offer the powerful marketing campaigns that the two majors of the business, Victor and Columbia, could afford. The Wolverines' best-sellers would not exceed a few thousand records, sold mostly in the Chicago area, around Indianapolis and Bloomington, all cities where the band was asked to play.

8. *Bix, Man and Legend*, op. cit., p. 100.

9. Randy Sandke, *Bix Beiderbecke, Observing a Genius at Work* (self-published, 1996).

10. *The Leon Bix Beiderbecke Story*, op. cit., p. 122.

11. Chip Deffaa points out, "Neither the Wolverines nor Beiderbecke were household words, but their style was certainly being noticed by other musicians. In New York, bandleader George Olsen's pianist/arranger Eddie Kilfeather was so impressed with the cornet solo on the Wolverines' recording of 'Jazz Me Blues' that he transcribed it and wrote it into an arrangement of 'You'll Never Get to Heaven with Those Eyes'—which Olsen's band recorded, with Red Nichols on trumpet, on June 26, 1924. When Kilfeather told Nichols that the solo had first been played by the Wolverines young cornetist, Nichols knew he wanted to meet Beiderbecke—which he did in July, when he crossed paths with the Wolverines in Indiana." Chip Deffaa, *Voices of the Jazz Age* (University of Illinois Press, 1992), pp. 63–64 (also quoted in *Bix, Man and Legend*, op. cit., p. 113).

New York, February 1924

While the Wolverines remained in the shadow, the spotlights of the musical world were focused on New York's Aeolian Hall, where, on February 12, 1924— six days before Bix's first recording date—the Paul Whiteman Orchestra presented the world premiere of George Gershwin's *Rhapsody in Blue.*[12] Paul Whiteman's success was no accident: it was the result of an organized and resolute will to give the audience exactly what it wanted. This man, who could have doubled for Oliver Hardy, was born in Denver on March 28, 1890. He studied violin, and in September 1915 was hired by the San Francisco Symphony Orchestra. Walking away from classical music by the end of World War I, he formed a five-piece dance orchestra under his own name and opened at the Belvedere Hotel in Santa Barbara. At the end of December 1919, his band, now enlarged to a nine-member group, was engaged to play at the famous Alexandria Hotel. But real success was only to be had in New York, and Paul Whiteman moved his men to the East Coast. He made his first appearance in June 1920 at the Ambassador Hotel in Atlantic City. This seaside resort, located less than sixty miles from Philadelphia, was the first to lay out a large boardwalk along the beach. At that time, Atlantic City was considered extremely vulgar; it was a place where questionable restaurants competed for business with shabby cabarets. Record manufacturers had, however, selected this New Jersey city for their annual convention, to be held between June 28 and July 2, 1920. Calvin Child, manager of the Victor Talking Machine Company, would leave the Ambassador Hotel on one of those nights with a contract signed by Paul Whiteman, thereby making Victor's best deal by far for the new decade.

The orchestra's first recording session took place in Camden, New Jersey, on August 8. The records were introduced to the audience by Victor as offering a "new type of dance music," which was not entirely wrong. The Whiteman Orchestra was larger than its competitors, and, in an original and subtle way, it blended the tones of its various sections: saxophones, brasses, strings, and drums. The band's pianist, Ferde Grofé, was writing the more sophisticated arrangements, and he played an important part in building the Whiteman sound.[13]

Among the first three records made by the orchestra, the one featuring "Whispering" and "The Japanese Sandman" achieved a huge success, and two million copies were sold within one year. The labels on those 78-rpm discs clearly indicated their use: "for dancing," the title of the number being generally explained with the indication "fox-trot"—the new dance that had displaced the old "one-step" at the beginning of the 1920s—or, occasionally, "waltz." Launched by the commercial success of his records, Paul Whiteman was at last able to take on New York. Starting in September 1920, and continuing for four years, his orchestra played regularly at the Palais Royal, "the largest café in New York City," located at the corner of Broadway

12. The Aeolian Hall was located at 34 West 43rd Street. Paul Whiteman made a first acoustic recording of the *Rhapsody in Blue*, with George Gershwin, on June 10, 1924, and a second one—electric— on April 21, 1927, also with the composer on piano. Paul Whiteman played violin on his recordings until June 1924.

13. Gus Mueller, a noted New Orleans musician, was present on these first Whiteman recordings. Together with his friends Ray Lopez and Tom Brown, he had been part of the first Dixieland front line to play New Orleans jazz in Chicago in 1915.

and 48th Street. Recordings for Victor followed one after another, the company's promotional strength ensuring the success of each new title and lending its considerable fame to the "Paul Whiteman and His Orchestra" brand. The outstanding sales of "Whispering" would be exceeded by a title recorded on August 22, 1922, "Three O'Clock in the Morning," of which Victor would proudly claim to have sold some three and a half million copies.

It is at this initial peak of his public career that Whiteman first met with George Gershwin. Born in Brooklyn to a family of Russian expatriates, the young pianist was only twenty-four years old in August 1922. His first song, "Swanee," had been released in 1916, and Al Jolson had made a hit out of it. Since 1920, Gershwin had been writing music for George White's famous show, *Scandals*. He contributed to the 1922 edition with "I'll Build a Stairway to Paradise" and an experimental one-act opera, *Blue Monday*. George White had hired the Whiteman Orchestra for this show, which opened on August 28, 1922, at the Globe Theatre in New York. *Blue Monday* would be performed only once, but that was sufficient to attract Whiteman's interest and to make possible an encounter with its composer.

A seven-month tour, from March to August 1923, would take Paul Whiteman and his men to England, only four years after the ODJB's mixed reception in that country. Upon his return to the U.S., and with the combined promotional support of the Victor and the Buescher Band Instrument companies, Paul Whiteman was crowned King of Jazz. Today it may seem surprising that such a title was given to an artist whose commercial music was at that time very far from jazz as we now understand it, but the same word was used for any "peppy" musical expressions. As explained in 1931 by F. Scott Fitzgerald, in an essay called "Echoes of the Jazz Age," "the word *jazz* in its progress towards respectability has meant first sex, then dancing, then music."[14] Paul Whiteman's coronation was justified mainly by the second meaning.

The new "King" and his orchestra joined the troupe of the Ziegfeld Follies at the New Amsterdam Theater, where they played from October 20, 1923, until May 10, 1924. During this engagement, Paul Whiteman took time off from the Follies to present an ambitious concert, offered to the audience as "An Experiment in Modern Music." For some "classical" numbers, his band added a string section, and George Gershwin was asked to write a short piece in a modern spirit. He came up with *Rhapsody in Blue*, which remains his most famous composition. It was performed, with its composer on piano, at the end of the concert given at Aeolian Hall on the afternoon of February 12, 1924. As the performance's program clearly specified, "Mr. Whiteman intends to point out the tremendous strides which have been made in popular music from the day of the discordant jazz . . . to the really melodious music of today, which—for no good reason—is still called Jazz."

14. F. Scott Fitzgerald, "Echoes of the Jazz Age," in *The Crack-Up*, ed. Edmund Wilson (New York: Charles Scribner's Sons, 1931), p. 16.

The Whiteman Orchestra, augmented with violins and French horns, in February 1924, just before the Aeolian Hall concert. (The Paul Whiteman Collection, Williams College)

This concert was well received by the critics and by the audience, and was recognized as an important musical event. Victor quickly took advantage of this increased popularity and, in the three months following this performance, released sixteen titles by Paul Whiteman and His Orchestra. A tour was immediately organized covering various major cities, making them the best-selling orchestra in American popular music. One could hardly believe, at that moment, that the royal road of the mighty Paul Whiteman would one day cross the path of Davenport's inspired cornetist.

Cincinnati, February 19–March 31, 1924

Back in Cincinnati after the Gennett recording session and highly excited by this first experience, the Wolverines were still not enthusiastically received by the sedate patrons at Doyle's Dancing Academy. A fresh start before an appreciative audience of students on March 25 at the Elks Temple in Hamilton was enough to stir up the boys' desire for a more rewarding engagement. They tried to get out of their contract with Doyle's, but the offer was rejected by the manager, as he was unable to find a replacement. The band was told it had to play until the end of its commitment, and in order to prevent any possible escape, their instruments were locked in the ballroom every night after closing.

On the night of March 31, a large tuba tied to a rope was lowered silently from a third-floor window, down into a convertible parked on the pavement. It was followed by a set of drums, a saxophone, and a banjo. Cornet and clarinet landed together, leaving behind a solitary piano in the large and deserted ballroom. Dick Voynow, who had managed to get locked in after the show, slid down the rope and joined the group on the street. Al Gande decided to stay in Cincinnati, and the seven escaped Wolverines left without a trombone in search of a new job.

Indiana, April–May 1924

They managed to find a few jobs actually, but all short-term. The first engagement brought them to Butler College in Indianapolis, where, on April 18, they were directed to the small ballroom. The main ballroom was occupied by the orchestra of

Charlie Davis. Bix and his friends had discovered his new composition, "Copenhagen,"[15] a few days before at the Ohio Theatre, and the tune had immediately aroused their interest.

As a way of thanking Charlie Davis for his interest in them, the Wolverines set up a recording session for his orchestra with Fred Wiggins at Gennett's. Davis's session was a disaster. Its appalling result emphasizes the quality of the Wolverines' earlier performance: they had been able to record four songs, one after another, while Charlie Davis's professional unit could not produce even one acceptable take: "That horn heard the band play our tune and the playback sounded like a mish-mash. It was tame, disoriented and godawful. The next try was more of the same only worse; everyone played the lead. Three more takes and the technician gave up."[16]

Hoagy Carmichael gave the Wolverines the audience they deserved by inviting them to come to the Bloomington campus of Indiana University at the end of April 1924, and he gave the students the music they were waiting for. Bix and Hoagy had met at the Friar's Inn two years before, and again in Chicago at the beginning of 1923, when they were enlightened by Louis Armstrong's revelations.

Hoagy was born in Bloomington, Indiana, on November 22, 1899. His mother, like Bix's, was a pianist: she used to play ragtime songs in movie theaters. Hoagy

Students' Building on the Indiana University campus in the 1920s. (Indiana University Collection)

would also share with his younger friend from Davenport a much stronger aptitude for rebellion than for studies. He moved with his family to Indianapolis in 1916, where he spent three difficult years. Uprooted, cut off from his landmarks, he found a job running a cement mixer, then—a terrifying experience for a born artist—he worked in a slaughterhouse, before the tragedy of his sister's death in 1918. The only light in this never-ending tunnel came from a black pianist, Reg DuValle, who taught him some ragtime techniques. Hoagy had paid no attention to the preachings of the powerful Ku Klux Klan in Indiana, and he could hear in black music an echo of his own wounds.

Hoagy Carmichael at the time of his first encounter with Bix. (Indiana University Collection)

15. This title was an informal composition of Charlie Davis's orchestra, characterized by a sousaphone solo played by Ole Olsen, a musician of Swedish origin who used Copenhagen brand tobacco. After the Wolverines' recording, this title was published as a song by Melrose Brothers in Chicago, and was recorded many times.

16. Charlie Davis, *That Band from Indiana*, (New York: Mathom, 1982; quoted in Rick L. Kennedy, *Jelly Roll, Bix and Hoagy*, Indiana University Press, 1994), p. 106.

THE BOOK NOOK

The Book Nook, Bloomington.
(Indiana University Collection)

By inhaling cement powder and wading through spilled blood, he saved enough money to resume his studies at Indiana University, and to pull himself up from despair. In January 1919, he was back in Bloomington, a university town, surrounded by gently sloping hills and deep quarries. Students used to flock to the Book Nook, a college hangout located on Indiana Avenue. An old piano stood in one corner of the room with some tables crowded around it, and Hoagy would sit there for hours, fumbling for notes and melodies. Those free improvisations soon attracted the interest of some of his friends; the young pianist was joined by a drummer, and, in the days that followed, other musicians. Hoagy's first orchestra was born.

That same year would hold important events in his life: his discovery of the first *hot* fiddler, Hank Wells, Howard Jordan's black band's visit to Bloomington, and his new passionate love for Kate Cameron. He was now a "jazz maniac"—a new breed of nutcase that was rapidly growing at that time in the Midwest. The young artist was traveling in a circle of dreamy poets and music freaks, always ready to chase after a new orchestra or a source of bootlegged booze. The law studies he had started in 1920 could hardly compete with his increasing musical activity. During 1922 and 1923, Hoagy and his musicians were regularly performing at meetings and dances at colleges, and those trips frequently ended in Chicago. Nights spent at the Friar's Inn gave him the chance to get acquainted with two future members of the Wolverines, George Johnson and Vic Moore, to discover the NORK's music, and to meet Bix Beiderbecke.

He got an engagement for the summer of 1923 in Ithaca, New York. This small city, adjacent to the Finger Lakes, not far from Syracuse, where Bix had played one year before, was famed for its wine cellars, its many waterfalls, and Cornell University. Hoagy's band included George Johnson on saxophone, but his presence could not overcome the audience's indifference toward his music: this tour was a complete failure. However, the young pianist went back home with a suitcase full of champagne, which he was able to sell in Bloomington for a profit of about $100—and pay for one year of his studies with his earnings.

George Johnson had joined the Wolverines after this less than glorious summer, but he remained in contact with Hoagy. Because of this friendship, the Wolverines were invited for several performances on the university campus in Bloomington. Their first concert was set for April 25, 1924, at the Booster Club.

For the first time, Hoagy would hear Bix's cornet: "Just four notes," as he would remember. "But he didn't blow them—he hit 'em like a mallet hits a chime—and his tone, the richness . . . "[17] "Yes, just four notes," he would confirm in 1979, "some little thing—and I 'knew' it was right. . . . It's just that those few notes sounded like something I might have been waiting for, searching for, all my life—without even knowing that they were what I was after."[18]

It was springtime in Indiana, a season smiling on the two young musicians, and Hoagy was stuck on his new friend, "he of the funny little mouth, the sad eyes that popped a little as if in surprise when those notes showered from his horn. . . . The air was thick and soft and pale purple. Grass was greener . . . moon was yellower," as he would write many years later. They were young, and after the Wolverines' concerts, they spent hours in Hoagy's room, "taking a drink of whiskey that tastes like kerosene in your mouth and a blowtorch going down . . . , lying in front of the phonograph early in the morning. We were playing the *Firebird* music of Stravinsky."[19]

The Wolverines outside Gennett Studios after the May 6, 1924, recording session. Left to right, standing in car: Min Leibrook, Jimmy Hartwell, Vic Moore, Bob Gillette, Bix, Dick Voynow. (Courtesy of the Rutgers Institute of Jazz Studies, and Sam Meier)

Bix and his band performed again on the campus on April 26, then on May 2 and 3. During this last afternoon, while the orchestra was rehearsing at the Kappa Sigma House, the fraternity house where Hoagy was living, the pianist shared his latest composition with his new friends: "Free Wheeling." Bix managed to conceive on the spot an arrangement for this number, whose title he would later change to "Riverboat Shuffle."

Richmond, Tuesday, May 6, 1924

At about the time the Starr Piano Company began a promotion campaign for the Wolverines' first releases, the band returned to Richmond for a second recording session. Four titles were recorded that day, all kept by Gennett and issued by the end of May. Al Gandee's departure had reduced the number of jazzmen to seven, leaving a lineup of one cornet, one clarinet, and one tenor saxophone, somewhat different from the traditional New Orleans frontline and, because of the missing trombone, offering possibly more flexibility. The band had reached a higher level of assurance and mastery, and Bix was now clearly its leader. His dominance was such that Ezra Wickemeyer, the studio engineer, moved Bix's cornet closer to the recording horn, to render his playing more distinct.

17. *The Stardust Road*, op. cit., p. 7.

18. *Lost Chords*, op. cit., p. 442.

19. *The Stardust Road*, op. cit., pp. 65–68.

The Wolverines outside Gennett Studios after the May 6, 1924, recording session. Left to right: Ezra Wickemeyer, Min Leibrook, Jimmy Hartwell, George Johnson, Vic Moore, Bob Gillette, Dick Voynow, and Bix. (Courtesy of the Rutgers Institute of Jazz Studies, and Sam Meier)

The first number, "Oh Baby!" is executed with high spirit, and Bix constructs a thirty-bar solo with accuracy, simplicity, and brightness at the beginning of the side. This session started with a high quality take, in which jazz researcher Frank Powers saw "a unique milestone in jazz, because this is the beginning of what we call 'Chicago jazz,' of what we might call orchestral development in jazz. . . . Between the solos, the ensemble work and the turned around modulation-figures . . . , we have a unique quality. We also have generally a more swinging sort of a sound."[20]

"Copenhagen," the Charlie Davis composition that had fascinated them, was the next number recorded. After a short introduction, Jimmy Hartwell and George Johnson take twelve-bar solos, both quite brilliant and inspired. Bix follows and shows that, even within a limited space of six measures, he could nevertheless be original. This record was very popular, and Melrose Music immediately had a transcription printed, in which the Wolverines' solos are faithfully reproduced. "Copenhagen" was to become a jazz standard, and George Johnson's chorus would be imitated by many saxophone players until the middle of the 1930s. According to Johnson, the musicians were highly inspired that day, and the three takes of that title showed marked differences: "This number was made up almost entirely of individual choruses, and we all used different melodies and ideas on the three masters."[21]

But the most interesting title of the session is without a doubt the third one: "Riverboat Shuffle." This original composition by Hoagy Carmichael was introduced to the musicians only three days before they recorded it, but their rendition is perfectly mastered. Bix is the only soloist, filling thirty bars and two breaks by himself. The four-note motif, as presented in the first bar, is repeated several times, but with a different introduction each time. In this chorus of amazing construction and invention, Bix makes use of two of his favorite effects: grace notes, which would become a sort of signature, and bending notes, with which he would bring color and emotion to the most insipid melodies he would be asked to deal with.

Gennett kept two takes of the last recorded number, "Susie." Its melody is quite ordinary, but it gives Bob Gillette the opportunity to play a typical banjo solo over a stop chorus, and one can also hear, on the last seconds of the side, Bix and Jimmy Hartwell playing two different lines simultaneously. Those two takes are evidence of the cornetist's outstanding gift for improvisation: he would never play the same thing twice.

20. Excerpt from the third program of *Bix, a Biographical Radio Series*, op. cit.

21. "Wolverine Days," op. cit., p. 86.

Bloomington, May 1924

Two new Wolverines 78s, stamped with the gold and blue Gennett label and collecting the four songs they just recorded, went on sale on May 31, 1924. Following the recording session, the Wolverines were back in Bloomington, where, on May 10, they helped promote their first release by playing at Ed Williams's music store. On the evening of that same day, they could be found performing for a dance organized by a women's association. A tuxedo was the required attire that evening, and Bix did not have one. He asked Eddie Condon to lend him one, and Condon, with the help of his brother, put together a mismatched suit. When it was returned to them a few days later, the outfit looked even stranger: none of the returned elements were the ones Bix had borrowed. "Did you have a good time?" asked Eddie Condon. "I don't know," said Bix.[22]

Musicians from the Wolverine Orchestra in Bloomington in April 1924. Left to right: Jimmy Hartwell (in the back of the car), George Johnson, unknown woman, Dick Voynow, Hoagy Carmichael (with hat), Vic Moore, and Min Leibrook. (Indiana University Collection)

With no other engagement ahead, the musicians remained on the Indiana University campus, where, at the end of the following week, they were invited to play with Hoagy Carmichael's band. The nights were long, full of music, smoke, and booze. The mornings were bright, but awakenings were hazy: "Who is that guy in the other bed sleeping in his underwear?" wrote Hoagy. "It was Bix. A pale blond galoot needing a shave, sleeping in his tattered underwear with his funny little mouth open, smelling like a distillery, his crumpled clothes piled on the dirty rug, the hole showing in the sole of his right shoe. . . . We went chugging down Indiana Avenue, our minds personally unoccupied, aware we were alive, surveying casually the small-town Sunday morning. People coming from church, smugly pious in their righteousness, dressed in their best, at peace with a world Bix and I never knew."[23]

Indianapolis, June 1924

On May 23, the Wolverines played their last performance on the Bloomington campus. Six days later, they opened at the Rainbow Casino Gardens, an outdoor dancing pavilion on the outskirts of Indianapolis, where the band had been booked thanks to a member of the Charlie Davis orchestra. "The orchestra played from a tiered platform under dim lights" remembered Hoagy. "I can still see this lovely scene. The smartly dressed boys and the white-clad girls, their big hats making ever-changing patterns as they moved to the music under the big

22. *We Called It Music*, op. cit., p. 122; also quoted in Bill Crow's *Jazz Anecdotes* (New York: Oxford University Press), p. 223.

23. *Sometimes I Wonder*, op. cit., pp. 128–129.

24. *The Stardust Road*, op. cit., pp. 80–81.

yellow moon. . . . And that band up there: the Wolverines. They were at their best playing lowdown and dirty but sometimes Bix would cock his head to one side and pop his eyes and then would come a shower of notes of such beauty they would send the dancers back to their tables as though they were sleepwalking."[24] On May 31, the Wolverines celebrated the release of their latest record by giving a performance in the Starr Piano Company's store in Indianapolis.

Richmond, Friday, June 20, 1924

The Wolverines, Palace Theater, Indianapolis, July 21–23, 1924. Left to right, standing: Jimmy Hartwell, Min Leibrook, Dick Voynow; on sofa: George Johnson, Bob Gillette, Bix (holding their "Tiger Rag" record) and Vic Berton. (Duncan Schiedt Collection)

25. In *Bix, Man and Legend* (op. cit., p. 112), Vic Berton is said to be the drummer for this session, which was repeated in all Bix discographies published thereafter. Based on Vic Moore's schedule, Phil Evans has decided that Moore was the drummer on the June 20, 1924, session (*The Leon Bix Beiderbecke Story*, op. cit.). This is somewhat confirmed in Ralph Berton's *Remembering Bix*, and also by George Johnson in the articles he wrote for *Swing Music* and *Downbeat* between 1936 and 1938. Listening to the records, no difference in the drum playing can be detected from the previous recording sessions: it appears truly to be Vic Moore.

26. Only one take of "Tiger Rag" was kept, Gennett number 11932. At the very end of the record, after a few seconds of silence, a faint voice can be heard saying something like "It sounds better!" or "Use that take." This voice was identified as Bix. A master of "Tiger Rag" was found in the Gennett family's files, and it has a very clear sound: it was issued in 2000 on Gennett Records, *Greatest Hits, Volume II*. Contact: www.starrgennett.org.

27. Alain Tercinet, "Voyage en Bixieland," *JazzMan*, no. 38, op. cit.

The band, with no change to its lineup, returned to Richmond for a third Gennett session paid for by the musicians for promotional purposes.[25] Three titles were recorded on that day. The first two would be issued in a very limited quantity—probably fewer than 200 copies—and seven test records made of the third title, "Tiger Rag," were given to the band members. This last side would not be released until 1936.[26]

"I Need Some Pettin'" opened the session. Bix's solo is placed in the first moments of the number, just after the intro. Spun out over thirty-two bars, it is supported by an exemplary structure and plays subtly with the melody, reproducing it in its original form, yet bringing it up to a higher level of musical composition. Highly enthusiastic about the quality of this improvised chorus, French jazz critic Alain Tercinet wrote that with this side Bix has created "one of those ageless choruses that illuminate the history of jazz."[27] Coming after these brilliant forty seconds, George Johnson's playing sounds pale and heavy, but Bix comes back for the finale, which he dominates completely, running rings around the rest of the band as he drives them with an irresistible swing.

Bix would record very few blues numbers in his career. The second title selected for that day was one of them: "Royal Garden Blues." It had been published in 1919 by Clarence and Spencer Williams and was recorded by the Original Dixieland Jazz Band two years later—a rather repetitive and sloppy version, which a painful vocal made even heavier. The Wolverines' version of this song is played at a slower tempo. Bix begins his solo on a high whole note, which leads into an ethereal phrase, floating above the rhythm with an unpredictable evolution, and which comes down, on the twelfth bar, on a eighth rest. With a deep sense of originality, Bix carefully avoided the use of the traditional vocabulary of the blues in this passage, like blue notes he frequently employed on other recordings. With an economy of means, he played a poetic solo, which had no equivalent in the recorded jazz music of that time.

This day of inspired recordings ended with "Tiger Rag." Written by Nick La Rocca and Larry Shields, it had been recorded for the first time by the Original Dixieland Jazz Band on March 25, 1918—and was the first jazz record Bix ever heard. The band played at a breakneck tempo and loaded it with burlesque effects—clarinets squealing, trombones burping—the reproduction of which is to be commended. The same title was played by the New Orleans Rhythm Kings during their first sojourn in Richmond in August 1922; the real gem of this excellent side was the solo left by clarinetist Leon Roppolo. The Original Dixieland Jazz Band would record a third version in New York, on April 23, 1923, reaching a more natural and flexible rendering than the 1918 version. Even if they are used less, the burlesque effects can still be heard on the sides cut in 1922 and 1923, inextricably linked to the number itself.

This title was already well-known, which is why the Wolverines chose it to conclude the recording session. The record was paid for by the orchestra itself and was intended to be used as promotional material for prospective employers. The band therefore made a point of showing themselves off to their best advantage. A technically faultless execution gave them the edge over their predecessors. Firmly tied to a spirited tempo, the band fluidly follows the thread of a surprisingly modern rendition. Backed by finely arranged riffs[28], Bix blows out a new solo with the originality and melodic conception exhibited in previous ones. The first eight bars seem to be freed from the rhythm, as they lazily stretch over the underlying accompaniment. Because of its freedom and imagination, this outstanding recorded side was far ahead of its time.

In breaking with the spirit of traditional Dixieland, Bix opened up new possibilities of development for himself and his future disciples. Within four months, the Wolverines had released eight sides. These records were not bestsellers, but they introduced many jazz fans to a cohesive and consistent new orchestra, clearly dominated by an inspired cornetist, who already showed dazzling musical talents. His tone was warm and colored with a natural vibrato. His attack was confident, precise, and his melodic phrases were supported by a communicative swing. The construction of his solos displays an assurance and ease that belongs to only a few exceptional artists. At twenty-one, Bix had created an original style, and in the musical wave that would break over the decade, he stood out as a unique and touching voice. Regardless of their skin color, jazz musicians would become the Wolverines' most enthusiastic audience. The Boston trumpet player Max Kaminsky, in his book, *My Life in Jazz*, recalls his rapture at discovering Bix Beiderbecke's work: "Bix's tone was so pure, so devoid of any tinge of sentimentality or personal ego, that is was the nearest thing to perfect beauty I have ever heard."[29]

ANOTHER BAND of young white jazzmen had visited Richmond in February 1924, and, under the name of the Bucktown Five, had recorded seven titles and eleven sides in just one day. The orchestra was driven by an eighteen-year-old cornet player from

28. A riff is a short musical phrase, two or four bars long, that is repeated several times. This effect creates a feeling of tension, which may be increased by a tempo in crescendo. The riff will be an important element of the Kansas City style in the '30s, and its use on the Wolverines' "Tiger Rag" in June 1924 was highly innovative.

29. Max Kaminsky, with V. E. Hughes, *My Life in Jazz* (New York: Harper & Row, 1963), p. 23.

Chicago, Muggsy Spanier. His admiration for King Oliver and Louis Armstrong can clearly be heard on these dynamic sides, which offer another possible adaptation of the New Orleans style by a white band from the Midwest. But, listening to these records makes one aware of the originality of the Wolverines and of their leader. "I met Bix at the Friar's Inn," recalled Muggsy Spanier in 1939. "We'd sit around and listen to the boys and then one day Bix said, *'I'm a cornet player.'* And I said, *'I'm one too.'* After that we went out to the south side together and there was one place we dropped in at where there was a piano and a drum, and we sat in with our two horns and we played together so well we decided we'd be a cornet team."[30]

Chicago, June–July 1924

The Wolverines remained at the Casino Gardens until June 24. Their contract was not extended: the owner was getting tired of this music he didn't understand, and he probably thought it was time to introduce a new show.

Once again unemployed, the band accepted an offer presented by one of their new admirers, drummer Vic Berton. Twenty-eight-year-old Berton had been living in Chicago for several years and was the sole supporter of a family made up of his mother and two brothers: Gene was a twenty-year-old professional singer, and Ralph, the youngest, was twelve when he met Bix Beiderbecke for the first time.[31]

Already an expert percussionist, Vic Berton had been picked by John Philip Sousa himself to play in Sousa's world-famous military orchestra during World War I. After the war, Josef Zettelmann, outstanding percussionist of the Chicago Symphony Orchestra, became his master, and Vic Berton was soon considered as his possible successor. But the orchestra did not pay much, and Vic Berton took other employment, as a drummer in a dance band where he could earn considerably more money. In 1924 he played at the Edgewater Beach Hotel, in the same ballroom where, two years prior, Bix had started his musical career. Freed from financial worries, Berton managed to dedicate some of his spare time to the music he loved best: jazz. He quickly became one of the best jazz drummers of his time, with a reputation based not only on his musical qualities—quite well preserved on some amazing Red Nichols recordings from 1926 and 1927—but also on the technical innovations he brought to the drum kit, an instrument born along with jazz music. Vic Berton was a pioneer in the use, and possibly in the design, of wire brushes (lighter and softer than sticks), in affixing the cymbal to an independent vertical rod, and in inventing the hi-hat or sock-cymbal, played with a pedal—all of which remain part of the modern drum set. He also introduced an innovative use of the tympani on jazz records. This rare example of a musician working in both a symphonic orchestra and a jazz band, having heard the Wolverines, discovered that he also wanted to become an impresario. He asked the young jazzmen to come to Chicago on June 27, 1924, and he started searching for work for his new group.

30. Muggsy Spanier, interviewed by Sam Ross on April 28, 1939, as kept in the files of the American Life Histories, Federal Writers' Project.

31. Ralph Berton published his "memories" about Bix Beiderbecke in 1974, in a much debated book: *Remembering Bix, a Memoir of the Jazz Age* (New York: Harper & Row, 1974).

Back in the Windy City after six months, Bix spent his first two nights rushing to listen to Isham Jones at the College Inn, King Oliver at the Lincoln Gardens—where his band had been performing since June 21—and Louis Armstrong, now separated from his musical father and starring in Ollie Powers's orchestra at the Dreamland Cafe. In order to enlarge the Wolverines' repertoire, Vic Berton set up some rehearsals with his promising and fiery young artists, and he took Vic Moore's seat at the drums during the few engagements he managed to book for the band around Indianapolis. At one of those short jobs, Red Nichols met Bix, the cornetist whose improvised solo on "Jazz Me Blues" Red had just played from an accurate transcription on a side recorded ten days earlier.

The Wolverines spent the first three weeks of July 1924 in Chicago. Bix was invited several times to the Berton family apartment, at 945 Argyle, in the northern

The Wolverines, Palace Theater, Indianapolis, July 21–23, 1924. Left to right: Vic Berton (dm), Dick Voynow (p), Bob Gillette (bjo), Min Leibrook (tu), Jimmy Hartwell (cl), Bix (ct), George Johnson (ts). (Duncan Schiedt Collection)

part of the city, a few blocks away from the lakeshore. This artistic household possessed a superb Mason & Hamlin baby grand piano, which had been given to Eugene Berton, second oldest son, by one of his rich admirers.

Awakened to music as a pupil at Chicago's Lewis Institute, Gene Berton had studied music intensely and had started a career as an opera singer at New York's Aeolian Hall in 1916, when he was twelve. Four years later, he traveled with his mother and younger brother to Paris, where he was taught by Lilli Lehmann for several months. The *soprano assoluta* was seventy-two years old and was dedicating her last years to passing her art on to a new generation. The young American's quality of voice and the sensitivity of his performances had attracted the attention of Nadia Boulanger, who introduced him into the circle of the Groupe des Six, at the heart of Parisian musical creativity. Back in America, Gene Berton was soon ranked among the few brilliant performers of the contemporary French composers. The works of Satie, Ravel, and Debussy formed the better part of his repertoire. Gene was homosexual, but moved within a society—opera and classical ballet—where this trait went unnoticed.[32]

From his first visit to the Berton house, Bix was drawn to the living room and its grand piano. Sitting on a leather-covered stool, he fumbled around with some melodic phrases of Eastwood Lane's *Adirondack Sketches*, before gradually shifting into an extended improvisation—something that had always been common practice for the young pianist. "Those improvisations would start invariably in the most hesitant, reticent, coolest, most classic style . . . and were marred by frequent errors, which he'd usually go back over and correct, ten times if need be," as Ralph Berton would write. "Then you would realize you were hearing the first theme being repeated, but it was now putting forth modest buds, natural and consistent as a green leaf opening; often, at that point, something else happened: a pulse developed in the left hand, perhaps 'walking' upward from the low bass, that soon hardened into an insistent swinging beat, and now the language had become jazz; the original theme would start to lose itself in little words and eddies of melody, cast in the slurred intervals of the blue scale, though deformed echoes of the original still clung to the new sound, more like reminders than literal references. . . . Now there was no pausing over mistakes or blurred figures, to hell with them, to hell with everything, his onward drive careened straight ahead, drove headlong over skipped notes and clinkers like a runaway truck pounding over potholes."[33]

Bix was always dissatisfied with his playing, whether at the piano or on cornet, alone or with an orchestra, and listening to his own recordings was for him irritating. Rejecting the young Ralph Berton's insistent encouragement, he would just say, "Shit, I don't even know what the hell I'm doing half the time."[34] The pleasure Bix could really experience was in listening to other artists' work, encountering interests different from his own. He experienced moments of pure ecstasy when Gene

32. Though homosexuality was not surprising in Gene Berton's circle of friends, it seems to have been unusual among jazz people. Ralph Berton indicates in his book, *Remembering Bix*, however, that Dick Voynow, the Wolverines' pianist, was "gay," and he wrote, "forgetting for the moment that Dick Voynow was obviously *that way* . . ." op. cit., p. 209.

33. *Remembering Bix*, op. cit., pp. 158, 170.

34. Ibid., p. 169.

Berton sang for him Pierre Louÿs' refined poem, "La Chevelure," set to music by Claude Debussy, and when he discovered other recordings of the French composer, like *Prélude à l'Après-midi d'un Faune* or *Ibéria*. "When the first side of *Iberia* ended," recalled Ralph Berton, "Bix said, '*Wait a second*,' went directly to the piano and began fishing for the themes and chords he had just heard. To my astonishment, he had practically the whole thing by heart—stumbling often, to be sure, but invariably going back and finding the right notes. . . . After getting all the way to the end of his rendition by ear, Bix began to improvise on one of the sequences. It wasn't exactly jazz, and it wasn't exactly Debussy; it was—Bix."[35]

The Wolverines, Palace Theater, Indianapolis, July 21–23, 1924. Left to right, standing: Min Leibrook, Dick Voynow, Jimmy Hartwell; seated: Bix, George Johnson, Bob Gillette; and Vic Berton on the floor. (Duncan Schiedt Collection)

One night Bix went with Gene and his young brother to a drag party, held in an apartment on 66th Street, on the South Side of Chicago, near Jackson Park. The smoky half-light heavy with smells of incense and perfumes, the astounding drag artists of both sexes, the homosexual couples embracing each other on the dance floor or lying down among large cushions left the young man from Iowa speechless; all night he kept repeating the same words: "Davenport was never like this!"[36]

In his *Memoir of the Jazz Age*, Ralph Berton tells of a chat he had one morning with his brother, shortly after Bix's death, in which Gene claimed to have had a "fling" with the young cornetist. But . . . "Let's face it," Gene is reported to have said, "it meant absolutely nothing to him one way or the other. I don't even know how much girls meant to him, if it comes to that—or let's say sex. You know his favorite phrase: '*What the hell.*' That was about where he stood, on nearly everything but his music."[37]

Indianapolis and Davenport, July 1924

The most important contract signed by the Wolverines during this month brought them to the stage of the Palace Theater in Indianapolis from July 21 to 23. They were billed as the "Vic Berton Orchestra, famous recorder for Gennett Records." Several photographs of the band were taken on the stage of the theater: the boys are lost in an incredible décor—a profusion of painted flowers, richly colored peacocks, and a frenzy of swirling scrollwork.

35. *Remembering Bix*, op. cit.

36. Ibid., pp. 156–157.

37. Ibid., p. 217. Ralph Berton has always supported his brother's story, as reported by Chip Deffaa in his book, *Voices of the Jazz Age*, where he wrote: "In a telephone conversation with me on March 2, 1989, [Ralph Berton] spoke of Beiderbecke's open personality and general willingness to try anything, and confirmed having attended a drag party with his brother Gene and Beiderbecke, and having learned from Gene, in a kitchen conversation shortly after Beiderbecke's death, that Gene had a brief homosexual involvement with Beiderbecke" (note 1 to chapter 3, p. 221).

Following this engagement, Bix went back to Davenport for a few days. At that time, pianist Jess Stacy was playing on a riverboat with Tony Catalano's orchestra. This was where he remembered meeting Bix for the first time, and hearing him play at the piano "the kind of stuff I'd always had in the back of my mind, but had never been able to express."[38] Stacy was surprised by Bix's timidity, by his firmly expressed negation of his own talent, and by the length of his solos, quite different from the short ones he had been allowed to record.

Gary, August 1924

The city of Gary was built in 1905 in Indiana, at the southern tip of Lake Michigan, just a few miles from the Illinois border. On the first days of summer 1924, the municipality had completed the building of a new dance hall, in the heart of Marquette Park by the lakeshore. Louis Glueck was a member of the town council, and he was also Vic Berton's uncle. He secured a one-month engagement for the Wolverines, who were asked to heat up the summer nights at this new Pavilion . . . and so they would.

When they arrived for their first rehearsal on Saturday afternoon, August 2, a few hours before the opening, the musicians discovered a large barn, open to the four winds, offering deplorable acoustics. A stage had been set up at one end of the dance floor, where an old battered piano with many missing keys rested, looking as if it had spent the winter on the beach. The shore was only a few hundred yards from the building and a damp haze would come up from the lake in the evenings. The musicians were to live in two bungalows. The first was shared by the two married couples: the Johnsons, and Vic Berton and his young wife, Gladys. The second accommodated the boisterous group of five bachelors.

After a few somewhat quiet evenings, the orchestra's fame started to grow and, they attracted several dozen dancers every night. Some danced traditional foxtrots or one-steps to the Wolverines' music. Others experimented with exhibitions of the "toddle," "eagle-rock," or "ballin' the jack." The exaggerated movements of the girls doing these wild new dances revealed items of clothing not usually seen in public, throwing the few adult witnesses into a state of shock.

The orchestra played six hours a night, taking breaks during which they emptied the alcoholic contents of many bottles labeled GINGER ALE, or smoking "funny cigarettes," stuffed with an exotic Mexican herb whose trade—unlike that of alcohol—was still totally legal. Bix rarely stood up while playing. He remained seated, legs crossed, his right ankle resting on his left knee. He would keep his eyes wide-open, focused on some invisible musical score far away, on which he could follow the development of an amazing and never repeated melody. "Although I played with Bix for more than a year and a half," wrote George Johnson, "I can honestly

38. *The Leon Bix Beiderbecke Story*, op. cit., p. 157.

say that I have never heard him make a mistake in playing. Knowing his style as thoroughly as we did, we could often detect, in one of his solos, that he had hit a note that he had not intended to hit, but by the time the phrase or passage was complete, he had angled and squirmed out that difficulty in a run of notes that was so brilliant it would leave us almost breathless."[39]

The Pavilion closed by midnight, and the musicians used to finish up their nights in one of the many cabarets where alcohol flowed until dawn. One night's drive led them to the Martinique Inn, where sax player Milton "Mezz" Mezzrow was appearing.

BORN IN CHICAGO in 1899, Mezz Mezzrow was sent to a reformatory when he was sixteen. The establishment held teenagers of all races within a system that alternated segregated and integrated learning. He would teach himself to play saxophone during his stay, and the presence of black musicians in the school's orchestra introduced Mezz to the blues and confirmed his musical vocation. Released when he was nineteen, he picked up temporary jobs with small bands appearing in some of the wretched clubs managed by Chicago mobsters. He had worked in 1924 in Burnham, a huge brothel town located on the Illinois border, where the sole function of the band was to be loud. Most of the town was ruled by Al Capone's organization and used as a warehouse by bootleggers. Since the beginning of the summer, Mezz had been working at the Martinique Inn, a cabaret located in Indiana Harbor, on the road from Gary to Chicago. He had become a *viper*, a smoker of marijuana, whose inhalation was leading him far off to a land of magical, free, and easy music.

Bix and his friends had turned up at the Martinique Inn one night in August. "Music was the one thing that really brought him to life," wrote Mezz Mezzrow. "Not even whiskey could do it, and he gave it every chance. The kid must have been born with a hollow leg, the way he gulped the stuff down."[40] When the band started to play "Royal Garden Blues," Bix jumped to this feet, "grabbed his horn and hopped on the bandstand. I have never heard a tone like he got before or since. He played mostly open horn, every note full, big, rich and round, standing out like a pearl, loud but never irritating or jangling, with a powerful drive that few white musicians had in those days. Bix was too young for the soulful tone, full of oppression and misery, that the great Negro trumpeters get—too young and, maybe, too disciplined. His attack was more on the militaristic side, powerful and energetic, every note packing a solid punch, with his head always in full control over his heart. The attack was as sure-footed as a mountain goat; every note was sharp as a rifle's crack, incisive as a bite. Bix was a natural-born leader. He set the pace and the idiom, defined the style, wherever he played, and the other musicians just naturally fell into step."[41]

INFORMED BY SOME irate churchgoers about the excesses at the lakeshore, the bungalows stuffed with booze, the dubious cigarettes, and the *hot* physical exercises

39. "Wolverine Days," op. cit., p. 32.

40. Milton "Mezz" Mezzrow, with Bernard Wolfe, *Really the Blues* (New York: Random House, 1946).

41. Ibid. Additional information comes from an unpublished document, "Bix at Indiana Harbor," by Mezz Mezzrow, as told to John Bright (the author's collection): "What struck me first were his half-valve inflections, similar to Joe Oliver's. Yet he played them with Freddie Keppard's hard drive, and some of his phrases, as inventiveness, reminded me of Louis. All in all, it was more a polished riverboat style than anything else. . . . Bix produced little quarter and three-quarter and eighth tones in glissandos that blended precisely the right harmonies. He felt his way into these harmonies, groped towards them, with unbelievedly good judgment. Bix had the most perfect instinct of all. . . . Playing with Bix was one of the great experiences of my life. He was inspiring. . . . Bix would acknowledge his debt to Oliver and Armstrong freely and in any company, usually without being asked. One night we were riding to the South Side to hear Jimmy Noone and he commented pensively, 'I wonder why white musicians are so corny'."

Cinderella Ballroom, on the
second floor of 1600 Broadway.
(Albert Haim)

in the dunes, the Gary city government decided to shut down the Pavilion. The evening of September 2 saw the last appearance of the Wolverines, but they had already secured a post for their immediate future. Thanks to one of his relatives, Min Leibrook had been able to book the band into the Cinderella Ballroom in New York.

On the morning of September 3, three cars loaded with instruments, musicians, and fuel, both for the cars and for the musicians, set out for the East Coast. They had to drive 900 miles—more than thirty hours—through Cleveland and Pittsburgh, on poorly maintained roads (the cause of many flat tires), stopping only to refuel the boys and the engine. The brave travelers who arrived in New York City on the evening of September 6 were not in the best shape.

New York, September 1924

Upon his arrival in New York, Bix spent several days with the Berton family at their new apartment at 119 West 71st Street. Busy with numerous recording dates, Vic Berton soon gave up managing the Wolverines, and Vic Moore again became the group's full-time drummer.

For someone living in Manhattan, the only way to avoid jazz music was to stay home at night. Since 1915 the black population of the city had been increased by many emigrants fleeing the South, its racial discrimination, and its poverty. These newcomers gathered in Harlem, forming a unique society held together by its common and original culture. At the beginning of the 1920s, development in the press, radio, and the recording industry had transformed art into a consumer product. African-American artists discovered to their surprise that they possessed an unexploited resource: their most powerful cultural expression, their music. Originally limited to a black audience, this music spread to a much larger public— first white America, and soon an international audience. This artistic movement, which began in New York, is known as the Harlem Renaissance, and writers, painters, and sculptors took part in this creative explosion.

There were two principal theaters in Harlem: the Lincoln Theatre, which featured black comedians as early as 1909, and the Lafayette Theatre, which, in 1913, brought a white audience to Harlem for the first time, to attend an all-black show, the *Darktown Follies*. The 1920s began with the New York's recognition of a black actor's talent. It was downtown, at the Provincetown Playhouse in the heart of Greenwich Village, that Charles Gilpin's performance in *The Emperor Jones* gave a young dramatic writer, Eugene O'Neill, his first popular success. This stunning performance—the play is actually a lengthy monologue of the title character—made Charles Gilpin an overnight success, and broke with the long tradition that had so far confined all black actors to comical, burlesque, and often pathetic parts.

At the same time, cabarets multiplied in Harlem. Prohibition ensured them prosperous years, as the law was even less respected north of Central Park than it was in the rest of Manhattan. While the inventors of stride piano—James P. Johnson, Willie "the Lion" Smith, and the young Thomas "Fats" Waller—were performing in shady and dingy clubs like Edmond's Cellar or the Wilkins Astoria Cafe, some big bands could be heard in places of much higher quality. The mixed clientele of Barron's witnessed the beginning of Duke Ellington's career, while the all-white and wealthy audience at Connie's Inn could hear the orchestras of Wilbur Sweatman and Fletcher Henderson. The atmosphere of this last club, on 132nd Street, matched its high prices. The patrons' privacy was secured by the arrangement of the booths, and the vault of a low ceiling descended to a romantic mural, with tiny lights sparkling inside the windows of painted houses. These nightclubs were often used as tryout grounds for acts or shows that would later be successful on Broadway. True success could only be achieved on Broadway—or, more precisely, somewhere within the area bounded roughly by Times Square and 8th Avenue, 42nd Street and Columbus Circle, home of the numerous theaters that made a nation's stars.

Eubie Blake and Noble Sissle were the authors of the first show written, produced, and performed by black artists, which would run for one year in a midtown theater. *Shuffle Along* opened at the 63rd Street Theatre on May 23, 1921, and the crowd flocking around the place was such that the street had to be converted to a one-way thoroughfare. The play made Florence Mills, the young woman "singing like a bird," famous, and it also gave Josephine Baker the chance to shine among a chorus line with girls as attractive as they were talented as dancers—an amazing novelty for an audience accustomed to the *Ziegfeld Follies'* motionless beauties.

While walking down Broadway in the fall of 1924, Bix could have encountered a stunning and unique set of artists. At 62nd Street, Blake and Sissle's new show, *The Chocolate Dandies*, had recently opened at the New Colonial Theater.[42] Josephine Baker, displaying the wide range of her talents on stage, was being paid $125 a week, and was advertised as "the highest-paid chorus girl in the world."

42. Located on 1887 Broadway, at 62nd Street, the theater opened in 1905 as the Colonial Music Hall. It was renamed New Colonial Theater in 1917. The opening of *Runnin' Wild* took place there on October 29, 1923—a show famous for having introduced the Charleston to a white audience—and *The Chocolate Dandies* on September 1, 1924. The building was taken down in 1977.

On the corner of 53rd Street, the Arcadia Ballroom featured the Mound City Blue Blowers. This popular trio, which had spent the summer in Atlantic City, had just added a fourth musician: Eddie Lang, a guitar player who would join Bix in 1927 on many outstanding recordings.

Two blocks down, at the corner of Broadway and 51st Street, the Roseland Ballroom was a popular place. Two orchestras were featured: Sam Lanin's band of white musicians—among them Red Nichols and Vic Berton—and the band directed by Fletcher Henderson, an atypical black musician.[43] Unlike other black jazzmen, Henderson was born of a well-to-do family. He was taught piano as a child and had studied science in school. He came to New York in 1920 with the hope of obtaining a higher education in chemistry, but the color of his skin kept him out of Columbia University. Jazz music had therefore gained an original innovator and an outstanding bandleader. In 1921 he was made musical director of the Black Swan label, a record company located in Harlem and dedicated to promoting black music. Leading his sextet, the Black Swan Troubadours, he accompanied singer Ethel Waters and, in 1922, toured with her through the southern states. The Fletcher Henderson Orchestra, billed in October 1924 at the Roseland Ballroom, consisted of ten musicians, including saxophone player Coleman Hawkins, then at the dawn of a dazzling career, and the highly talented Don Redman, who was writing the innovative arrangements that would help the band to become the true pioneer of orchestral jazz. The orchestra's repertoire blended *hot* numbers and more commercial titles—those which the many dancers crowding the floor expected to hear. Louis Armstrong's addition to the band—upon his arrival in New York on September 29, 1924—brought the group an inspiration and a swing so far unknown. Don Redman would admit that he was compelled to modify his arrangements after that time to keep up with the new cornetist's fiery style.

A little farther down Broadway, at the corner of 50th Street, was the entrance to Sam Salvin's Plantation Club. Florence Mills had been the star of its 1922 show, and Ethel Waters and Josephine Baker would share its stage during the summer of 1925. Ethel Waters, an inspired and sensual blues singer who is unfairly forgotten today, was at that time enjoying a well-deserved success. She had started recording in 1921, and Bix was among her numerous fervent admirers.[44]

At 49th Street, the name of the Kentucky Club flashed constantly over the door of the corner building. The place featured a sextet, the Washingtonians, made up of Bubber Miley on trumpet, Charlie Irvis on trombone, Otto Hardwick on saxophone, George Francis on banjo, Sonny Greer on drums, and a pianist who would soon give his name to the band: Edward "Duke" Ellington. The room was small and could hardly accommodate more than one hundred people. The musicians squeezed onto a tiny stage, and the few standing patrons danced on a miniature floor—but the dancers were generally more graceful about this lack of space than the members of the orchestra. Access to the club was restricted to a white audience.

43. This double booking didn't last long, as Sam Lanin soon refused to share the bill with a colored orchestra. The Fletcher Henderson Orchestra became the "official" Roseland Ballroom dance band, where it was featured for five years.

44. French critic Hugues Panassié wrote in his *Dictionnaire du Jazz* (Paris: Albin Michel, 1971), "Ethel Waters is the greatest of all jazz singers, the one who inspired, influenced almost all the others." In 1925, Ethel Waters turned down a contract that would have taken her to Paris. The same offer was made to Josephine Baker, who accepted and was among the cast of *La Revue Nègre*.

"The Kentucky Club definitely became the place to go, and the biggies and musicians used to drop in every night," recalled Duke Ellington. "Many of the boys with the Wolverines used to come by, Bix Beiderbecke with them. Then we were friendly with the fellows from Paul Whiteman's band, and from the California Ramblers, and we used to often see Jimmy and Tommy Dorsey."[45]

The Cinderella Ballroom, at Broadway and 48th Street, was where the Wolverines would open on September 12.[46] Five days before that, Bix and his friends had gone to the Hippodrome Theater[47] to hear the Ray Miller Orchestra. Two musicians in that group aroused the Wolverines' enthusiasm: trombonist Miff Mole, who, since the Bailey's Lucky Seven's sessions in 1922, had made numerous recordings, and saxophonist Frank Trumbauer, whom Bix had not seen for over a year—since his show at the Coliseum in Davenport. Miff Mole thought that the noisy outburst during the show by these young fellows was an expression of derision, and he greeted his excited fans coldly during the intermission, until they set him straight. The Ray Miller Orchestra was to open a few days later at the Arcadia Ballroom, only a short distance from Roseland.

Bix had left the Bertons' apartment, and was now living in one hotel room with Red Nichols and Alfie Evans, both of whom were employed by Sam Lanin at the Roseland Ballroom. Alfie Evans remembered the way Bix used to wake up: "In the morning, Bix would sit on the edge of the bed, swing his legs a few times. Then he would reach for a barrel-shaped glass that he had in his suitcase. He'd pour four healthy ounces of gin, drink it 'as is,' and say that he had drunk his daily 'orange juice.' He'd splash some water on his face, comb his hair, and was ready for the new day."[48]

September 12 was an important day for the Wolverines, who were anticipating their first appearance in New York with mixed feelings: they were proud to be invited onto such a famous stage on Broadway, less than a year after their band had been formed, but they were also intimidated by the prospect of satisfying the expert and demanding New York audience. "There were a few Dixieland combinations in the smaller dance halls and cafés but no combination similar to ours, nor any with a similar style, and for this reason we all looked forward with great anxiety to our opening," explained George Johnson. "Our contract at the Cinderella was for thirty days, with two options of ninety days and one year. From the very start we were well received, and the word got around Broadway that the Wolverines at the Cinderella were something new and different. Famous musicians came to listen and were eager to sit in, just as we had been in the days of Friar's Inn in Chicago."[49]

The trade press was enthusiastic, and Abel Green proclaimed in *Variety* on September 24, "As a torrid unit it need doff the mythical chapeau to no one. Their sense of rhythm and tempo is ultra for this type of dance music, and their unquestionable favor with the dance fans speaks for itself. . . . The band has struck favor from the start! Out west they recorded for the Gennett disks, but although less than a week on Broadway they have had 'dates' with a number of minor companies, with the

45. *Hear Me Talkin' To Ya*, op. cit., p. 231. Appreciations of Bix's musical qualities were seldom lukewarm, with one exception: the comments made by Sonny Greer, the drummer in Duke Ellington's orchestra, who recalled some nights at the Kentucky Club. "At three or four o'clock in the morning, you could find musicians like Bix Beiderbecke, Tommy Dorsey, Miff Mole, Paul Whiteman, and many other ones. Whiteman directed for some time his orchestra at the Palais Royal, not very far away. Our bandstand was very small; the six of us were already cramped, and when other musicians wanted to sit in, they had to stay with the audience and play from their chair, at their table. Bix and myself were good friends, and we used to go often from one club to another one, drinking whiskey, but I have to say that people who did not know him—and jazz critics—have created a picture of him which is too flattering. They say he was an outstanding cornet player, but he was not actually as stunning as it is said. Bix could not have competed with Louis Armstrong, Joe Smith and Bubber Miley when they were at their best. The battle would have been too tough. He was not a legend during his time." Stanley Dance, *The World of Duke Ellington* (New York: Scribner's Sons, 1970).

46. Address was 1600 Broadway Avenue, at the northeast corner of Broadway and 48th Street. The Cinderella Ballroom was located at the second floor of the old Studebaker Building, a ten-story building erected in 1902, and which came down in 2005.

47. Opened in 1905 and located on Sixth Avenue, between 43rd and 44th streets, the Hippodrome Theater was one of the larger theaters of its time. It could accommodate 6,000 people, and was demolished in 1939.

48. *The Leon Bix Beiderbecke Story*, op. cit., p. 161. Drinking alcohol immediately when getting up is characteristic of a state of withdrawal after a night of forced abstinence. It points out that Bix was already, at this early time in his life, addicted to alcohol.

49. George Johnson in "Wolverine Days," op. cit., p. 87.

Brunswick also interested."[50] A student at Yale, Richardson Turner came to Broadway with a group of friends to listen to the Wolverines. He would confirm the impact the band had on its knowledgeable audience and the shock prompted by this new music: "Bix played in an unorthodox way. He shook the horn with all his fingers up—and played, leaning over at the floor at about 45 degree angle.... They took about 10 'last choruses'—standing up around the drum—playing at the drummer. It was fantastic! On the same occasion Paul Whiteman was there in a Polo Coat and Nick La Rocca who I heard say after one wild set, '*I guess I'll have to go home and get my cornet.*'"[51]

The Wolverines at the Cinderella Ballroom, September 1924. Left to right: Dick Voynow, Bob Gillette, George Johnson, Min Leibrook, Vic Moore, Jimmy Hartwell, and Bix. (Charles Delaunay Collection, BNF, Paris)

Nick La Rocca symbolized Bix's past, the inspiration he found in the Original Dixieland Jazz Band and its now old-fashioned music. Paul Whiteman was a figure in Bix's distant future, but a third visitor to the Cinderella Ballroom would offer him his next job. Charlie Horvarth was the manager of Jean Goldkette's orchestras, and on that evening he made an offer Bix couldn't refuse. The cornetist had outdistanced the other Wolverines, and he now felt they held back his development.

Frank Trumbauer and Miff Mole came one night to listen to the Wolverines at the Cinderella. The saxophonist was delighted by Bix's playing, but, "Unfortunately, as we approached the bandstand to heap our praise on the band, we witnessed an incident between Bix and pianist Dick Voynow, the leader," explained Trumbauer. "We later found out that they had been feuding for some time and Bix had given his notice. The friction had now resulted in the name calling stages, and we clearly heard Bix say: '*Voynow, you're an old bastard! And, a lousy piano player to boot!*'— '*That goes for you, too, and just double it,*' Voynow replied, and now his voice trailed off with, '*But, unfortunately, you are the best cornet player in the world!*'"[52]

50. Joshua Berrett, *Louis Armstrong and Paul Whiteman: Two Kings of Jazz* (New Haven: Yale University Press, 2004), p. 80.

51. *The Leon Bix Beiderbecke Story*, op. cit., p. 162.

52. *TRAM: The Frank Trumbauer Story*, op. cit., p. 48.

New York, Thursday, September 18, 1924

This cold atmosphere did not spoil the group's last two recording sessions. They were held in Gennett's New York studio, at 9–11 East 37th Street, with equipment technically superior to that in Richmond.

Trombonist George Brunies, who had been a member of the New Orleans Rhythm Kings and was presently playing with the Ted Lewis's orchestra, joined the Wolverines for the session on September 18. Gennett wanted to play it safe, and the two titles selected for that day were again from the Original Dixieland Jazz Band's proven repertoire: these were the bouncing "Sensation" and "Lazy Daddy," of which two takes were kept. The Wolverines recorded brilliant and relaxed interpretations of both pieces.

Former location of the Starr Piano Company and Gennett Studios, on top floor of the existing building at 9–11 East 37th Street in New York. (James Kidd, 2005)

Bix's approaching departure put the Wolverines in need of a new cornet player. Several candidates were rejected, but a telegram sent by Dick Voynow to Jimmy McPartland in Chicago located the right musician. Jimmy McPartland, then seventeen, was the soloist with a group called the Blue Flyers. His discovery of Bix's solos on Gennett records had revealed to him a new way of playing. The message from Dick Voynow read: CAN YOU JOIN WOLVERINES IN NEW YORK REPLACING BIX BEIDERBECKE AT SALARY OF EIGHTY-SEVEN DOLLARS FIFTY PER WEEK QUERYMARK STOP ANSWER IMMEDIATELY STOP. After making sure that it was not a joke, and having accepted the $32.50 covering the exact cost of the train ticket to New York, McPartland arrived in Grand Central Station one October morning, with a leather bag and a secondhand cornet. Taking Bix's chair was for him an impossible dream, but his integration into the band was facilitated by his extensive knowledge of the Wolverines' recordings. "As we roomed together, Bix was able to show me the different tunes and arrangements the band had, coach me in certain little figures he used in his playing," McPartland told the British jazz critic Max Jones. "For about five nights we both played in the band. First Bix would take the lead, then he'd play second in with me to break in. He was an enormous help and encouragement, and I got to admire the man as much as the musician."[53]

New York, Wednesday, October 8, 1924

For the last time, the Wolverines gathered in a recording studio. The dominance of the cornet player had become obvious, as had the widening gulf between Bix and his partners. The highlight of the first title recorded, "Tia Juana," is a two-bar break Bix plays at the end of his solo: the four rising notes and the five falling ones that

53. *Hear Me Talkin' to Ya*, op. cit., pp. 144–147; also quoted in Max Jones, *Jazz Talking*, (New York: Da Capo Press, 2000), pp. 156–157.

follow "have almost no relation to the underlying harmony and yet somehow they fit perfectly; this is an example of the inexplicable genius and magic of Bix," wrote Randy Sandke.[54] Bix would also record on that number the only *growl* he is known to have played; this device, characteristic of the New Orleans style, would soon become the trademark of trumpet players like Bubber Miley and, later, Cootie Williams.

The second side recorded during the session, "Big Boy," would be even more stunning, amounting to a veritable tour de force by Bix. He had conceived a cornet duet with Fred Rollison, one of the candidates contacted to replace Bix in the Wolverines. They had rehearsed this part at length, but at the very last minute, Bix—dissatisfied with the way it sounded—decided to delete it. He began the title with a cornet solo, perfectly and determinedly constructed, leading the band with confidence and resolution. Next, George Johnson's saxophone solo gave Bix the opportunity to move to the piano and to record on this instrument a brilliant passage. Bix then went back to his cornet to conclude the side, which remains amazing today because of its coherence, its dynamism, and the multifaceted talents of its main soloist.[55]

54. *Bix Beiderbecke, Observing a Genius at Work,* op. cit., p. 8.

55. More on Bix's talents as a soloist: Fred Rollison, from Evanston, Indiana, was playing Bix-style cornet in Curt Hitch's Happy Harmonists. "The only reward I got was the honor of holding Bix's cornet while he recorded one of his very rare piano solos," wrote Rollison in the March/April 1956 issue of *The Second Line* (New Orleans Jazz Club). Australian musicologist Frank Murphy wrote a Ph.D. thesis on Bix Beiderbecke's music, and was awarded a degree in 1983. "This project involved transcribing all of the solos and leads on Beiderbecke recordings, comparing them to the sheet music copies and analysing the material so produced. The project is in the library at La Trobe University, and it is an extensive piece of work, totalling about 800 pages in four volumes," as Frank Murphy told the author (letter dated august 9, 2002). Excerpts from this thesis have been published in 1985 in the review *Musicology Australia,* and also in the Austrian publication *Jazz Forschung* (Jazz Research), between 1985 and 1989. Bix's recording of "Bix Boy" has been studied by Frank Murphy, along with "Wringin' an' Twistin' " (see chapter 8, note 43).

56. Rube Bloom (1902–1976) was a pianist and composer, highly praised on the New York stages. He wrote works combining an Impressionist style with some jazz influences, many of which were quite successful. They can be found in Mike Polad's Piano Deco series.

New York, Thursday, October 9, 1924

Before leaving New York, Bix took part in one last session. He was invited to the Gennett studio to join three musicians from the Ray Miller Orchestra: Frank Trumbauer, Miff Mole, and pianist Rube Bloom.[56] Bix brought with him the Wolverines' rhythm section, Min Leibrook and Vic Moore. Ray Miller's band was under an exclusive contract with the Brunswick label, and its members were forced to conceal their identities under a whimsical name: this record was issued as the Sioux City Six. Bix lays back on the two sides recorded on that day: a Rube Bloom composition, "Flock O' Blues," and one written by Frank Trumbauer, "I'm Glad." These titles sound a bit strange, the first played at a spirited and fast rhythm, while the second follows a slow and bluesy tempo. Even if these performances are faithful to the New Orleans style, their development flows smoothly and they offer a relaxation and an ensemble unity much ahead of its time.

This was a successful session, but the New York Gennett studio was not always such a happy place for Bix and his impetuous friends. Miff Mole remembered an evening when he went there in the company of Vic Berton, Bix, Jimmy Dorsey, and two bottles of gin, planning to record the jazz side of the century. After some untidy and fruitless attempts, they were kicked out into the cold New York night to seek solace in one of the many nearby speakeasies.

THE SHOW at the Cinderella on Saturday, October 11, was the last performance by Bix and the Wolverines. Two young musicians, Louis Armstrong and Bix Beiderbecke, had just sown the seeds that flowered in many forms in the future of jazz. Bix left New York by train on the evening of October 13, and arrived in Detroit the following morning.

Detroit, October–November 1924

Located a few miles away from the Canadian city of Windsor, where alcohol was legal and cheap, Detroit was, to a large extent, dedicated to smuggling. The police department, directly interested in the profitability of rum-running, was as unmotivated to hinder it as it was efficient in protecting the prostitutes' commerce. "Detroit was as wide-open as a politician's pocket on election day; the town was having itself a ball around the clock," wrote Mezz Mezzrow. "The girls would sit themselves at the windows in come-on poses and tap on the glass with Chinese chopsticks, to catch your eye—I guess it was what you might call drumming up trade. . . . It struck me funny how the top and bottom crusts of society were always getting together during the prohibition era."[57]

JEAN GOLDKETTE was born in Greece in 1893. His mother was an actress, and he never knew who his father was. He first studied at the Moscow Academy of Music. Emigrating to the United States at the age of seventeen, he continued his musical studies at the Lewis Institute in Chicago. He lost his first job as a pianist at Lamb's Cafe when Tom Brown's orchestra, newly arrived from New Orleans, was hired on May 15, 1915. He started his own band at the end of the war, and played at the Detroit Athletic Club. But he really made his name at the Graystone Ballroom[58], and his fame grew to the point that, in March 1924, he was signed to a contract with the Victor label. In October 1924, the Goldkette Orchestra was made up of twelve musicians: Fred "Fuzzy" Farrar on trumpet; Bill Rank and Tommy Dorsey on trombones; Stanley "Doc" Ryker, Don Murray, and George Williams on reeds; Sam Anflick and Joe Venuti on strings; Howard "Howdy" Quicksell playing banjo; Paul Mertz on piano; Irish Henry on bass; and drummer Charles Horvath as leader.

The members of this large orchestra were all experienced artists who could read music well. Bix knew only one of them, Don Murray, whom he hadn't seen since the summer of 1922. After having been the Wolverines' leader, the cornet player was suddenly a sideman in a large orchestra that played from written scores. The first days were difficult for him, and because he couldn't read music, Bix had to be replaced during some radio broadcasts. It was only by sitting at the piano, at the end of a rehearsal at the Graystone Ballroom, that he was able to demonstrate his unique musical abilities to his colleagues. Paul Mertz, who had let Bix take his place at the keyboard, could never forget this stunning demonstration, at the end of which "for a clincher, Bix played a classical number, 'Arabesque' by Debussy. His

57. *Really the Blues*, op. cit.

58. The Graystone Ballroom was located at 4237 Woodward Avenue, in a building bought by Jean Goldkette in 1923. It was demolished in 1960.

interpretation might not have made the grade at Carnegie Hall, but Bix's conception sure sounded fine to us. Bix loved that number, and he had laboriously worked it out: note by note, and phrase by phrase, until he could play the whole piece through by ear. It's my considered opinion that this number, 'Arabesque,' provided the musical seed which grew to flower later in his own piano compositions. . . . From two o'clock in the morning at the old Billinghurst Hotel," continued Paul Mertz in 1971, "to this day, there still lingers a ghostly echo of Bix's favorite symphonic work: Debussy's *Afternoon of a Faun*."[59]

The marriage of his sister, Mary Louise, gave Bix the opportunity to take a short break in Davenport, where he arrived on November 6. The two days of rest were most welcome during this difficult period of adjustment to the Goldkette band. After attending the ceremony celebrating the union of Ted Shoemaker and the Beiderbecke's only daughter, Bix returned to Detroit two days later and bravely resumed his duties.[60]

Detroit, November 24 and 25, 1924

For Bix's first recording date with the Goldkette Orchestra, an additional trumpet player was added to the band in order to compensate for the newcomer's possible weaknesses. Joe Venuti was the violinist, and this meeting with Bix would be the first of many—all of which were much more musically interesting.

Recorded on Victor's portable equipment, these two sessions would not be issued until 1960. The musical director was Edward T. King, a man who was responsible for selecting each title and instructing the band how to play it. Driven solely by commercial considerations, the record producers knew exactly what their audience wanted, and their artists were forced to comply with these supposed expectations, whatever their preferences might be. Paradoxically, this tyranny weighed heavier on the white bands than it did on the black musicians. Black groups' recordings were directed at a limited audience, of less commercial importance, with presumably different tastes, about which the executives were less certain, and their "race records" consequently enjoyed a greater artistic freedom.

The first title recorded on November 24, "I Didn't Know," gave Bix a sixteen-bar chorus. Backed by a clever but quaint arrangement, Bix succeeded in playing a striking solo—clean, fiery, and well balanced. Eddie King did not like it at all. He hated *hot* trumpet, and he immediately made sure that Bix understood that this kind of japery was totally out of place. The cornet player was excluded from the other numbers recorded that day, and he was given only a short appearance on one title recorded the following day: "Adoration," a syrupy side that no jazzman could have saved from disaster.[61]

59. Excerpt from the sixth program of *Bix, a Biographical Radio Series*, op. cit. The piece referred to is most likely the first of Claude Debussy's two *Arabesques*. These piano pieces were written during the composer's youth, in 1888, and released unsuccessfully in 1891.

60. Mary Louise's wedding was celebrated at the Davenport Outing Club, located at 2109 North Brady Street. This was a very exclusive place, and the building is unchanged. The ceremony was performed by Dr. L. M. Coffman of the First Presbyterian Church, at 1702 Iowa Street.

61. "Bix never learned to read music to any extent, though in the later days with Whiteman I believe he got so that he could learn a part from notes. For Goldkette's recording of 'Adoration,' George Crozier, the arranger, had to write a special part for Bix with fingering marked over each note," wrote Charlie Preble, in *Tempo* (July 1936). The saxophone solo on one of the titles recorded on November 25, "Play Me Slow," sounds very much like Frank Trumbauer, playing incognito under the name George Williams. This interesting possibility is discussed in the liner notes of Timeless CBC 1-084, a CD dedicated to Jean Goldkette bands.

Psychologically sensitive, Bix felt the need to be constantly reassured, and he could only express himself within a circle where he was held in esteem, inside a protective cocoon. It is therefore not surprising that his first contract with the Goldkette organization lasted less than two months, and that it came to an end, on December 8, as a mutual parting of the ways. Freed from this emotionally trying experience, Bix escaped to Indianapolis.

Indiana and Iowa, December 1924

Back in Indiana, Bix reconnected with the memory of happy days and with the warm friendship of Hoagy Carmichael. He met a young girl, Cornelia Marshall, and they joined Hoagy and his girlfriend for an evening dinner at the Severin Hotel's Roof Garden, where Charlie Davis's band was playing. Bix and Hoagy were, however, less interested in their dates than they were in a new song played that night by the orchestra, "I'll See You in my Dreams."

Bix probably spent the day of December 17 in Richmond, where Marion McKay and his orchestra were recording for Gennett.[62] Without any imminent job offers, Bix went back to Davenport a few days before Christmas. "Bix remained at the family home during Christmas and New Year's," remembered Burnie Beiderbecke, Bix's brother. "While Bix was home, he raved about the musicians he had met. He praised them all so highly that the family was concerned Bix would soon become lost in his new world of music."[63]

62. The attribution of some solos to Bix Beiderbecke is sometime questionable. In *Bix, Man and Legend*, the discography given by Philip Evans and William Dean-Myatt included Bix in one of Marion McKay and His Orchestra's recording sessions, cut in Richmond on December 17, 1924, and Bix was also attributed a solo on "Doo Wacka Doo." Interviewed by Rick Kennedy in 1991, Marion McKay—who was ninety-three at the time—confirmed that Bix was in Richmond on that day, and added, "[At the Gennett studio,] you used to do a lot of test pressings to get the sound just right, and I honestly don't know if Beiderbecke was on the take used to make the record. It seems I've been asked this question about Beiderbecke at the Gennett studio more than any other. I wish I could have put it to rest, but at the time, it wasn't something I was really thinking about" (*Jelly Roll, Bix and Hoagy*, op. cit., p. 117). Jazz scholars Warren Plath and Franklin Powers decided, through much research done in the '70s, that the solo on "Doo Wacka Doo" was played by a young cornet player, Leroy Morris.

63. *The Leon Bix Beiderbecke Story*, op. cit., p. 176.

CHAPTER 6

1925: Frank Trumbauer

Davenport, January 1925

Early in January, Bix introduced himself to Merton "Bromo" Sulser and his band, the Iowa Collegians, who were performing at the Garden Theater in Davenport.[1] He offered to join. They were astounded by his offer, and even more so when Bix, the famed cornetist of the Wolverines, agreed to their modest pay scale of $7 per night. He appeared with the band four times in Iowa City, between January 16 and 24: a charity ball on the Iowa University campus, and three nights at the Blue Goose Ballroom in the Burkley Hotel.

Richmond, Monday, January 26, 1925

At his own expense, Bix had arranged a recording session at Gennett. For these first records to be made under his name, he called on four old colleagues from the Goldkette Orchestra: Don Murray, Tommy Dorsey, Paul Mertz, and Howdy Quicksell. The drummer, Tommy Gargano, was also from Detroit. Upon arriving in Indianapolis on January 25, Bix contacted Hoagy Carmichael, asking for a ride to Richmond in his new Ford. They set out at four in the morning. Just before dawn, they stopped the car in the middle of a landscape of fields white with frost. The country was asleep and the silence absolute. Bix took out his horn, and

1. The Garden Theater was located at 121 West 3rd Street. It has been torn down.

let loose with a blast to warm his lips. "I remembered that my own horn, long unused, was lying in the back of the car. I got it out," wrote Hoagy. "'*Way Down Yonder in New Orleans*,' Bix said. He had hit one I knew pretty well and I was in my glory. And then Bix was off. Clean wonderful banners of melody filled the air, carved the countryside. Split the still night. The trees and the ground and the sky made the tones so right. I battled along to keep up a rhythmic lead while Bix laid it out for the tillers of the soil. He finally finished in one great blast of pyrotechnic improvisation, then took his horn down from his mouth. '*Hoagy*,' he said thoughtfully, '*you weren't bad*.' I had achieved greatness. We drove on into the night."[2]

Bix returned for the last time to the uncomfortable Gennett studio, where he found awaiting him the musicians on loan from his former employer—and three bottles of gin. Hoagy did not play that day, but the group made several attempts, all unsuccessful, to record one of his compositions, "Washboard Blues."[3] They had better luck with "Toddlin' Blues," an Original Dixieland Jazz Band number that they got on the first take. The gin bottles were considerably lighter by the time the band started to play "Davenport Blues." This was the first Bix Beiderbecke composition to be recorded, and it would also be the only one ever written in a strictly "jazz" spirit.

The Rhythm Jugglers at Gennett Studios in Indiana, January 26, 1925. Left to right: Don Murray, Howdy Quicksell, Tommy Gargano, Paul Mertz, Bix, Tommy Dorsey. (Davenport Public Library Collection)

Hoagy on trumpet, around 1925. (Indiana University Collection)

2. *The Stardust Road*, op. cit., p. 94.

3. As per Tommy Dorsey's recollections, reported in Richard Hadlock's *Jazz Masters of the '20s*, op. cit., p. 245.

The successful performance of a song requires a jazzman to seek a delicate balance between the concentration that enables him to remain coherent and stick closely to the development of a piece, and the relaxation that is needed to reach a smooth and free playing. Musicians proceed along a narrow path, and the space is even more cramped in the case of improvised ensemble work. The search for such freedom, for this carefree and "cool" attitude, led many artists to rely upon the use of substances that are able to create the "total disorder of all senses" recommended by Arthur Rimbaud, a French poet who diligently followed his own advice. Smoking marijuana, said Louis Armstrong, helped him blow notes of incredible melodic inspiration; Bix and many of his companions sought access to an unexplored musical universe by the consumption of alcohol—which is, for a musician, a double-edged sword. Two photographs were taken during this Gennett session: in the first shot, the group is playing into the recording horn, while the second shows Bix, glassy-eyed, one arm around an unsteady Don Murray, and slumping over Tommy Dorsey—a grand piano is, luckily, firmly supporting the trio. Their recording of "Davenport Blues" would mirror the haziness of their appearance—which is regrettable because Bix conceived in the issued take a brilliant and often luminous improvisation, unfortunately marred by an imprecise attack and a tempo dissolved by excessive drinking.

The group tried hard on two other sides, "Magic Blues" and "No One Knows What It's All About"—this last title bringing an appropriate end to a difficult session. A Gennett disc coupling "Toddlin' Blues" and "Davenport Blues" hit stores on March 7, credited to Bix Beiderbecke and His Rhythm Jugglers. In June the Richmond company would destroy the memory of the other alcoholic "jugglings" perpetrated on that day. Bix would not return to a recording studio until twenty-one months later.

Iowa, January–February 1925

Back in Davenport, Bix had trouble finding work, except for a one-night stint with Bromo Sulser's orchestra, on January 30 at the Blue Goose Ballroom in Iowa City. With no prospects and not much to do, he decided three days later to register at the University of Iowa, and moved onto the campus. A vague impulse led him to enroll in a program that included music history and theory, and piano lessons. But he was advised by the college administration that courses in religion and ethics, physical education, and military training were also strict requirements, which would put a quick end to his belated and irrelevant turn toward academic education.

On February 6 and 14, Bix left the university campus and joined the bands led by Jean Goldkette and Bromo Sulser, respectively, for one night each. He found himself a few days later, on February 19, in the midst of a fight that had broken out on campus, at Reichart's Café, among a group of drunken students. Once furniture began to fly, the troublemakers were promptly ejected. The next day, Bix quit the college with no regrets, and sat back in with Bromo Sulser's band at the Burkley Hotel for two consecutive Saturdays. He probably spent a few days in Davenport, with little desire of discussing with his family this final scholastic debacle, and still unemployed, he left for New York at the beginning of March.

New York, March 13–21, 1925

"Talk about a surprise! This was it. Through the mist, what we suddenly saw was so astonishing that, at first, we refused to believe our eyes—but then, at a second look, once in front of it, galley slaves as we were, we had to laugh. . . . Can you imagine? Right in front of us, their city stood up, totally erect. New York is a standing-up city."[4] The French writer Louis-Ferdinand Céline arrived in New York by ship, on a medical mission for the League of Nations, just a few days before Bix's third visit to Manhattan.

The madness of Broadway was amplified by President Calvin Coolidge's inaugural celebration. This stolid man, preserved from the scandals of his predecessor's administration, would become the champion of a liberal and private economy, summing up his politics in a clear slogan: "The business of America is business." But Bix's affairs, as he turned twenty-two, did not go too well. For a week, he shared a room with Red Nichols at the Pasadena Hotel, located at the corner of Broadway and 60th Street. Red had left Sam Lanin's band and, for a short while, joined the California Ramblers. The band was featured at the Ramblers Inn in Pelham, New York, a cabaret where it had been performing regularly since May 1923.[5] The group Bix would discover on the night of March 13 had already built an excellent reputation, and because of its continuing popularity, it remained prominent on the New York scene throughout the 1920s. Their manager, Ed Kirkeby, was an efficient promoter, inviting many stars from the Broadway revues to Pelham and booking the Ramblers in October 1924 for an engagement at the Monte-Carlo in New York City.[6]

Bix followed Red Nichols for several days, spending his nights at the Ramblers Inn and sitting in with the ten-piece band as often as he could. He already knew Tommy Dorsey, who took part in the Gennett recording at the end of January, but he played for the first time with Tommy's older brother, clarinetist Jimmy Dorsey, and with drummer Stanley King, two partners he would often call upon later in his short career. Adrian Rollini was the true spirit of the California Ramblers. He was born in 1904 into a family of French-Swiss origin. He was a child prodigy, giving a Chopin concert at age four and, at fourteen, forming a band in which he played piano and xylophone. For still unknown reasons, in 1922 he picked up an instrument

4. Louis-Ferdinand Céline, Voyage au bout de la nuit (Paris: Denoël and Steele, 1932), p. 231.

5. Pelham is located north of Manhattan, south of New Rochelle, and some thirty minutes from the Manhattan theater district.

6. The Monte-Carlo restaurant was on Broadway, under the Roseland Ballroom, where Fletcher Henderson and his cornet player, Louis Armstrong, were featured.

jazz had so far ignored, the bass saxophone in B-flat, one of the biggest models in the line conceived by Adolphe Sax. He taught himself in a few weeks and quickly managed to master this weighty instrument.

String bass was used quite early by New Orleans bands—as evidenced in several photographs: one of Buddy Bolden and his musicians, taken in 1906, and one of Kid Ory's Woodland Band in 1905—but, for a time, dance hall acoustics and the limited sensitivity of the recording equipment replaced this string instrument with the powerful tuba, used for maintaining a steady and firm foundation. On the recordings made by the California Ramblers in 1922, Adrian Rollini's playing on his bass saxophone was limited to the creation of an imperturbable pulse, carried over the first and third beats of the measure. A first solo on this instrument was heard in July 1923, charting a new territory for jazz instrumentation. Gunther Schuller was right in asserting that the band's music was "lightly spasmodic, dynamic, casual, full of Charleston syncopations, and was an incarnation of the first of the jazz era."[7] The orchestra, for the most part, read from stock arrangements, available to all, bland and quite common, but these young musicians were also capable of playing *hot* sides, exhibiting a highly professional and sparkling technique.

These artists did more than just play music together, and Bix found in Red Nichols a faithful and reliable companion on his drinking binges: "During that period, we were loaded pretty much all of the time," Red Nichols would confess, "but I remember I had record dates with Sam Lanin, also the Ramblers, and Joe Candullo. How I got through them in the condition I was in, I shall never know. Anyway, this one morning we hadn't been to bed and I was afraid I couldn't get through the date, so I asked Bix to go along with me and help me out. . . . He agreed. Who this was for I will probably never know because it was a case of the blind leading the blind."[8] After failing to find any steady work in New York, Bix left again for Chicago on March 21, slightly warmed by the pale sun of this first day of spring.

Chicago, March–June 1925

It was snowing when Bix arrived in Chicago. A few hours spent in cafés frequented by musicians helped him find a job: he was soon hired by Charley Straight's orchestra at the Rendez-Vous Café. The place was located at 622 West Diversey Avenue, at the intersection of Clark and Broadway avenues. The union local made problems for Bix with this engagement. He was new to Chicago, and therefore unable to conform to the ninety-day clause.[9] "Straight made a statement which probably sums up what musicians thought of Bix," explained Eddie Condon. "He said that Beiderbecke was a unique attraction, that he was not just a cornet player, and that if it were possible to find his equal anywhere in Chicago he, Straight, would

7. Gunther Schuller, *Early Jazz: Its Roots and Musical Development* (New York: Oxford University Press, 1968).

8. *The Leon Bix Beiderbecke Story,* op. cit., p. 185. During the period of March 13–21, Red Nichols is known to have made only one recording: with the Goofus Five, on March 16 (Okeh 40340). Was Bix present in the studio, or was Red Nichols mixing up dates?

9. The American Federation of Musicians required its members to register immediately with the local union upon their arrival in a city. They couldn't get a paid job in the area before waiting out a three-month residence period. This ninety-day clause was obviously intended to protect local musicians from outsiders.

hire the equal rather than Beiderbecke. The union agreed with him; Bix was allowed to take the job."[10]

In that band, Bix again met saxophonist Dale Skinner, for whom he had unsuccessfully auditioned in January 1923. The group's trumpet player was Joe "Wingy" Manone, who was twenty-five years old and had gotten the nickname Wingy after the loss of his right arm in childhood in a streetcar accident. Bix soon proved himself on the job: he was far more serious than his band mates, who were more greedy for girls and alcohol than they were for music. "When it came time for the last set," wrote Wingy Manone in his autobiography, "we hurried through it in order to get with our babes. Our raggedy playing made Bix mad. . . . He didn't realize that those chicks had been waiting for us for two hours, and we had to get them before they cooled off. We would run off with them and leave him alone, and this burned him up some more. Bix was a genius and

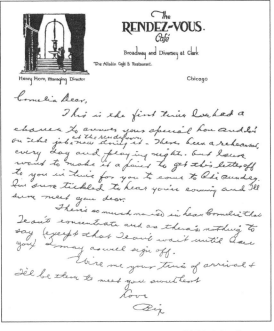

we just didn't understand him, I guess. He was always talking music, telling us, 'Let's play this chord,' or 'Let's figure out some three-way harmony for the trumpets after the job tonight.' It seemed to us he didn't want us to enjoy life."[11]

The Rendez-Vous Café attracted a young clientele, offering them dinner and dancing at a reasonable price. Bix's reading capabilities remained limited, but his presence in this ten-piece orchestra was justified by the *hot* choruses the cornetist could insert into an otherwise uneventful performance, enhancing it to unexpected brilliance. With no use for the sheet music in front of him, he opened a book on his stand and read Wild West novels in between his improvised solos. Bix also used to lead the small six-piece relief band that played during intermissions, and after the main band knocked off at one o'clock in the morning.

On Sunday, April 26, Bix invited Cornelia Marshall, the young girl he had met in early December in Indianapolis, to spend the day with him in Chicago. Cornelia would remember it as a pleasant day, begun at a Methodist church service and followed by a walk across the Windy City, a dinner at the Rendez-Vous Café, and a train ride home that concluded these "memorable and marvelous moments." It was an uneventful day—so much so that they would never see each other again.

Bix's letter to Cornelia Marshall, about April 20, 1925: "Cornelia Dear, This is the first time I've had a chance to answer your special hon and I'm on the job at the rendezvous now doing it. Theres been a rehearsal, every day and playing nights. But I sure want to make it a point to get this letter off to you in time for you to come to Chi Sunday. I'm sure tickled to hear you're coming and Ill sure meet you dear. Theres so much noise in hear [sic] Cornelia that I can't concentrate and as there's nothing to say (except that I can't wait until I see you) I may as well sign off. Wire me your time of arrival & I'll be there to meet you sweetheart. Love, Bix." (Courtesy of the Rutgers Institute of Jazz Studies)

10. Eddie Condon, *We Called It Music*, op. cit., p. 120.

11. Wingy Manone (with Paul Vandervoort II), *Trumpet on the Wing* (Garden City, NY: Doubleday, 1964).

Eddie Condon looked forward to school days, using them to recover from long nights spent playing banjo. "My school books stayed on the table, unopened," wrote the musician. "One day Bix saw them. *'What are these?'* he asked. I explained that I was getting an education. He looked perplexed. *'What are you going to do with it?'* he said. *'If you can't read music, why do you want to read books?'* He sat down at the piano. *'By the way,'* I said, *'Who is Proust?'* He hit a chord, listened to it, and then said, casually, *'A French writer who lived in a cork-lined room. His stuff is no good in translation.'* I leaned over the piano. *'How the hell did you find that out?'* I demanded. He gave me the seven veils look. *'I get around,'* he said."[12]

Bix had kept in touch with Charles Horvath, musical director of the Goldkette Orchestra in Detroit. Charley Straight agreed to release his cornetist for a day, on May 1, when the Goldkette band was invited to play at the annual Indiana University prom in Bloomington. "We sent the band by train, and this really impressed Bix," stated Horvath. "Russ Morgan, who was leading the band, said that Bix kept repeating, over and over, how impressed he was with riding a train to the date. Russ said they pulled into a depot, and after a minute or two, he looked out the window and saw Bix seated on a bench. Russ rushed off the train, grabbed Bix by the arm, and got back on the train just as it was pulling out. Morgan asked Bix what was he doing outside on the bench. Bix said that he was so thrilled with riding the train to the date that he had seen all that he wanted of the train inside, so he wanted to see how the train looked outside."[13] At the end of May, Bix met briefly with Red Nichols, who had come to Chicago to express his interest in Hannah Williams, the singer in Charley Straight's orchestra. Bix worked in the band for one more month, until July 2.

Lakeside Michigan, July 1925

The many resorts along the shores of Lake Michigan were busy in summertime. Being a wise businessman, Jean Goldkette knew how to respond to this seasonal demand. He controlled several small bands that he was able to book into various resort towns. Bix spent a few days at the New Casino Pavilion in Walled Lake, Michigan, with trumpeter Nat Natoli's orchestra. He was paid $60 a week—$15 less than the other musicians. He soon heard that Don Murray and Howdy Quicksell—with whom he had worked on his January recording—were members of the Breeze Blowers, a Goldkette unit that was featured at the Blue Lantern at Island Lake, only a few miles away. The young cornetist eagerly wished to rejoin his two friends; Charles Horvath agreed to the idea on the phone, and Bix spent the rest of the summer with the Blue Lantern group.

The musicians reunited on July 6 at Island Lake would become, one year later, the best band to ever record under the label of the Jean Goldkette Orchestra. Ray

12. *We Called It Music,* op. cit., p. 121.

13. *TRAM, The Frank Trumbauer Story,* op. cit., p. 56.

Lodwig, a renowned trumpeter, was its musical director. Several other members had played with Bix in Detroit at the end of the preceding year: they were trombonist Bill Rank, saxophonist Stanley "Doc" Ryker, banjoist Howdy Quicksell, and the cornetist's longtime friend, clarinetist Don Murray. Though Bix didn't know pianist Fred Bergin and drummer Enos "Doc" Cenardo, he was familiar with Steve Brown, whose playing he had enjoyed at the Chicago Friar's Inn, when Steve was part of the New Orleans Rhythm Kings. The brother of trombonist Tom Brown, Steve had quickly abandoned the tuba and become an outstanding string bass player, whose talent was admired and acknowledged as much by the audience as by his colleagues.

But the meeting that summer that would result in the greatest musical relationship was the one that paired Bix Beiderbecke and Orie Frank Trumbauer. Two years older than Bix, Frank Trumbauer was born in 1901 in Carbondale, a small mining village in southern Illinois. The nickname Tram quickly replaced his last name like the bellow of a cannon. Young Frank discovered the saxophone while listening to Ray Reynolds at the Arcadia Ballroom in Saint Louis one night in 1912, and he persuaded his mother to get him one of these superb shiny instruments, a C-melody sax. He closed himself into his room, and for an hour blew with all his might into the end of the horn. The saxophone remained mute. In de-

Frank "Tram" Trumbauer, photograph taken around 1920. (Courtesy of William Trumbauer)

spair, Tram threw the useless instrument onto his bed, which caused the protective cap to pop off, revealing the actual mouthpiece and its new reed. Learning to play this new instrument would come quickly and easily to him, and he soon formed a small band with a schoolmate, pianist Royal Howell. Within a few months, the band won local success and was earning some money. Frank enlisted in the navy during the last year of the war, and was discharged in January 1919. He found a job at Cicardi's Café in Saint Louis, one of the most beautiful dance halls in the Midwest. The dance floor was covered by a dome decorated with a romantic moon and myriad electric stars. At the end of one last wild party, during which the owners tried to drown their patrons in champagne, Cicardi's closed its doors on January 17, 1920, the morning of the first day of Prohibition.

Tram then joined drummer Joe Kayser's quartet, with which he traveled for a year, touring the local small ballrooms and playing the fox-trots, turkey-trots, waltzes, and other "Friscos" that were in style. His first steady job allowed him to settle down in Rockford, Illinois, in May 1921, where he met Mitzi, a pretty red-haired girl whom he married in September 1921, and who remained with him until the musician's death in 1956. Tram's admission into pianist Gene Rodemich's band led the saxophonist toward more jazzy interpretations, and toward his first success, "By the Pyramids," recorded in October 1921 in the New York Brunswick studios. Tram played history's first recorded saxophone break on that side, and the record sold fairly well.

The young musician could no longer resist the song of the jazz sirens, and he left for Chicago in September 1922. He signed with Edgar A. Benson, a retired bassist who directed the biggest music agency in the city, based in the Loop. Four months of waiting and inactivity would pass before Tram won his place among the eleven musicians hired in January 1923 to form the new Benson Orchestra. The band was called to the Victor studios in Camden, New Jersey, and the sax player recorded his first jazz solo on the song "Think of Me," cut on January 30.[14] Bix and Tram first met three months later, on April 24, when the Benson Orchestra's tour brought the band to Davenport Coliseum Ballroom. At the end of this journey, the musicians settled in Atlantic City for the summer of 1923. Between June 13 and 15, Tram took part in the band's second series of recordings. On the second day, he won an important victory, convincing the grouchy Eddie King to release "I Never Miss the Sunshine," a record including a historic sax chorus, played by Tram, that went on to inspire many musicians, including the young Benny Carter. The record sold well.

Though significant, their sales were overshadowed by a trio of amateur musicians, the Mound City Blue Blowers. William "Red" McKenzie, a former jockey from Saint Louis, was the creator of the "blue-blowing" technique, which involved humming into a comb wrapped in a sheet of tissue paper. He had quickly mastered this unusual instrument and was able to produce some truly *hot* choruses. With Jack Bland on banjo and Dick Slevin on the irritating kazoo, McKenzie created a show halfway between a gag and a music hall act. The joke ceased the day their first record, "Arkansas Blues," cut on February 23, 1924, sold more than a million copies. Three weeks later, Tram joined the Mound City Blue Blowers on two new titles, "Red Hot" and "San," recorded on March 13 and 14.

Tram's sax playing at this point was built on the surprising mix of primary progressions, straight from an exercise book, with elegant, perfectly constructed melodic lines. His intense musical activity and his commercial success attracted the attention of drummer Ray Miller, whose band had gained a good reputation in the eastern U.S., and was now looking to rise to the top. To spice up his band with a *hot* touch, he called upon two rising stars, Frank Trumbauer and Miff Mole, to complete a lineup of fourteen capable musicians. The Ray Miller Orchestra debuted at the Beaux Arts Café in Atlantic City on May 31, and moved to the Hippodrome Theater in New York at the start of September. The success of Miller's band was unquestionable, and as previously mentioned, their show aroused the Wolverines' enthusiasm on September 7. The recording session that reunited Bix and Tram at the New York

14. This title can be heard on the two-CD set, *Early Jazz*, produced by Daniel Nevers for the French label Frémeaux and Associés.

Gennett studios, on October 9, strengthened the friendship that already existed
between the two musicians.

In June 1925, Miff Mole left Ray
Miller's orchestra for Ross Gorman's,
where Red Nichols awaited him. At the
same time, Tram was contacted by the
management of the Arcadia Ballroom in
Saint Louis: he accepted an offer to form
an orchestra that would be ready to op-
erate in September, at the start of the new
season. Without hesitation, he decided
that Bix was the right man for the cornetist's chair: "I had heard Bix in the old
Wolverines Band," Trumbauer noted in
his journal, "and I said to myself, if I ever

The Frank Trumbauer Orchestra
at the Arcadia Ballroom in Saint
Louis at the end of 1925. Left to
right, front row: Ray Thurston
(tb), Marty Livingston (vln), Pee
Wee Russell (cl), Frank
Trumbauer (Cms), Damon
"Bud" Hassler (ts), Louis
Feldman (p); back row: Dee Orr (dm),
Wayne Jacobson
(bjo); back row: Dee Orr (dm),
Bix (ct), and Dan Gaebe (sb).
(Duncan Schiedt Collection)

had my own band again, that's my boy! When I tried to locate Bix, by asking
around, I always got the same answer, 'Look out, he's trouble. He drinks and you'll
have a hard time handling him.' That didn't stop me. I was determined. Finally I got
a lead that he was working with the Jean Goldkette office in Detroit."[15]

Bix's engaging nature won him the sympathy, as well as the sincere and faithful affection, of those around him. The young man's introverted character kept him from
getting too close to people, but many photographs seem to indicate that this reserved
and modest man could, through his gestures, express friendly feelings for which he
could not find words.[16] His friendships with Don Murray and Red Nichols stemmed
from a shared passion for music and alcohol. Bix's charm and his apparent fragility
also earned him the protective attachment of several "guardian angels," Hoagy
Carmichael and Frank Trumbauer among them. Tram was quite atypical in the jazz
world of the 1920s: this moderate man drank and spent little, and he organized his
professional activity in order to preserve his family life—a son was born in 1923—
and to make certain that the happy marriage he had with Mitzi would last.

Bix and Tram spent the full month of July 1925 with the Breeze Blowers, at Island Lake's Blue Lantern. Pianist Fred Bergin remembered these summertime
weeks as moments of pleasant and easy work, with nights doused in bootlegged
gin and the adulation of many charming girls—to whom Bix paid only limited attention. The cornetist lived in an abstract universe: flight of a sandpiper inspired
in him an original rhythmic structure, and hearing a record of *The Firebird* suggested new harmonic possibilities. Personal hygiene was not a significant factor in
his world, and his friends used to swear that "if Bix took off his socks, they would
stand by themselves . . ." "We frequented the Island Lake Hotel on the other side of
the lake, where most of the gals stayed," Fred Bergin recounted, "and some of our

15. TRAM, The Frank Trumbauer
Story, op. cit., pp. 51–52.

16. As noted by Albert Haim,
Bix often assumes an affectionate pose with his friends in existing photographs.

most memorable evenings were spent listening to Bix play an old pump organ in the hotel. We were—with the gals—the most consistent customers, so if we wanted to keep the place jumping until daylight, the few customers who wandered into the place could do very little about it. It is unfortunate that no recordings were ever made of Bix on the organ. It was sheer beauty, in spite of the fact that he had no particular knowledge of the instrument, and also that particular one must have been past the junk stage."[17]

The young musician's salary was fixed at $60, which was still less than his partners earned. Bix used to ask regularly for advances—in nickels, which he quickly slipped into the slot machine installed in the hotel lobby. It was not difficult for Jean Goldkette to convince Bix that granting him a raise would be useless: the machine was Goldkette's property, and its owner would get back all the money fed into it.

Saint Louis, August–December 1925

17. Norman P. Gentieu, "Memories of Bix, Part 2" (from Harrington Archive), in *IAJRC Journal* (summer 1993).

Bix arrived in Saint Louis on August 15, and settled at the Majestic Hotel. He was soon joined by Tram, and they played a few days together on the *J. S. DeLuxe*, one of the Streckfus Line riverboats cruising from the city. After several days of rehearsals, the Frank Trumbauer Orchestra started the Arcadia Ballroom's new season on September 8. The ballroom was open every evening from eight thirty to midnight, with an additional performance for young dancers on Sunday afternoons. Monday was the night off. The dance floor, which was one step below the level of the tables, was surrounded by a banister. A double stage accommodated two different groups. Frank Trumbauer Orchestra's ten musicians sat on the main stage, while the Kasback Band and the Arcadian Serenaders performed alternately on the smaller bandstand. Tram had complied with union rules and hired Saint Louis musicians. However, he was able to get permission from the union local for two exceptions: Bix Beiderbecke and sax player Karl Spaeth. As a bandleader, Tram was paid the highest salary, $125 per week, and Bix succeeded at last to get his raised to $90.

The Arcadia Ballroom, 3517 Olive Street in Saint Louis, photograph taken in the 1940s. The dance hall was originally called Dreamland, and it became Tune Town after World War II. (Saint Louis Mercantile Library Collection)

A third man stood out in this ensemble: Charles Ellsworth Russell, a nineteen-year-old clarinetist who entered jazz history under the name of Pee Wee Russell. Born in Saint Louis in 1906, he grew up in Muskogee, Oklahoma. His father worked as the steward of the local Elks lodge, serving as a bartender and supporting his son's interest in music by letting him slip backstage, where, over many long evenings, the boy dreamed of his future music career by playing along with the band on imaginary instruments. He discovered that the clarinet could have a magical power when, in 1918, he heard the Louisiana Five's leader, Alcide "Yellow" Nuñez.[18] The New Orleans jazzman's warm sound and improvising talent enthralled the young Pee Wee, who convinced his parents to let him take clarinet lessons from a local teacher, Charlie Merrill. At the end of this apprenticeship, Pee Wee got his first job and entered the Deep River Jazzband on a riverboat cruising the Arkansas River—but without telling his parents about his nightly occupation. He used to sneak out his bedroom window and, on the way to the job, change from his knickers to a pair of long trousers borrowed from his father.[19] He was fourteen—an ideal age for getting caught. He found himself enrolled at the Western Military School in Alton, Illinois, to obtain a formal education, something he had abandoned. He remained there for one year, and left in October 1921 for reasons that remain unknown. His parents moved back to Saint Louis, and at that time they accepted the fact that their son would be a musician. Pee Wee gained local fame, and in the summer of 1922, he was invited to join pianist Herbert Berger's orchestra at the Central Café in Ciudad Juarez. This frontier town, situated on the Mexican side of the Rio Grande, across from El Paso, benefitted immensely from the flood of American refugees from oppression—that is, prohibition in their homeland—and the town enjoyed a lively nightlife that proved to be more interesting to a sixteen-year-old boy than studying at a military school. The job was good training for Pee Wee's lips, which were soon able to adapt perfectly to the reed of his clarinet, just as they could fit the mouth of a bottle. The experience opened new doors for him, and during the summer of 1924, he was hired to play with Peck's Bad Boys, the band of pianist John "Peck" Kelley.[20] The orchestra—playing at Sylvan Beach, in LaPorte, Texas—included two former members of the Friars Society Orchestra, Leon Roppolo and bassist Arnold Loyocano, and Jack Teagarden, a young Texan trombonist who, at the age of nineteen, had already developed a very fluid style and an original technique.

These years spent in the southern states, coming in frequent touch with spirituals and black bands, made Russell and Teagarden familiar with the blues, a musical form they would feel close to, unlike musicians who remained in the north of the country, like Frank Trumbauer and Bix Beiderbecke.

Bix's encounter with Pee Wee Russell at the Arcadia Ballroom started an immediate friendship. "We hit it right off," confirmed Pee Wee. "We were never apart for a couple of years—day, night, good, bad, sick, well, broke, drunk."[21] This friendship was clearly founded on music, and Pee Wee Russell became aware of the cornetist's exceptional skills: "Among musicians, even at that time, Bix had a reputation. Very

18. This Creole, who got the nickname Yellow because of his skin color, was one of the first members of the Original Dixieland Jazz Band. He left the band three months before their first historic recording of "Livery Stable Blues," on February 26, 1917.

19. Up until World War II, American boys wore knickers, baggy knee-length trousers tied or buttoned at the bottoms to hold up knee-high socks. Graduating to long pants was a rite of passage to adulthood. Bix is wearing knickers in the photos on pages 5 and 7.

20. Kelley's band included: John "Peck" Kelley (piano), Leon Prima (trumpet), Jack Teagarden (trombone), Leon Roppolo and Pee Wee Russell (clarinet), Billy Watts (sax), Arnold Loyocano (bass), and Sammy Byrd (drums). They never recorded, which is too bad, because a lineup of these musicians would seem to indicate that the band might have sounded as good as the NORK or the Wolverines.

21. As quoted in Robert Hilbert, Pee Wee Russell: The Life of a Jazzman (New York: Oxford University Press, 1993), p. 34.

few of us understood what he was doing; even in Chicago only a limited number did . . . and as for the management, he wasn't even featured with the band! The thing about Bix's music is that he drove a band. He more or less made you play whether you wanted to or not. If you had any talent at all he made you play better. It had to do for one thing with the way he played lead. It had to do with his whole feeling for ensemble playing. He got a very large tone with a cornet. Records never quite reproduced his sound. Some come fairly close but the majority don't."[22]

The stability of the job, the free and idle afternoons, and Frank Trumbauer's friendly support allowed Bix to make noticeable progress in reading music. "We fixed up a book of regular trumpet parts and for hours on end, I would work with Bix," wrote Tram in his diary. "I would teach him a tune, note for note, and then hand him the part and we would follow it. Bix was a brilliant boy and it wasn't long before he could follow new parts. No one but Bix and I shall ever know the hard work and patience it took to accomplish this."[23]

The musical complicity that had developed between Bix and Pee Wee Russell grew night after night, and show after show, to a point where the two musicians often left their orchestra behind, bewildered by the originality of their creations. "We would do little things once in a while so drastic or rather so musically advanced that when we had a damn nice thing going the manager would come up and say, '*What in God's name are you doing?*'" added Pee Wee. "I remember on 'I Ain't Got Nobody' we had an arrangement with five-part harmony for the three saxes and the two brass. And the writing went down chromatically on a whole-tone scale basis. It was unheard of in those days. . . . That sort of music became more or less of a novelty with the people though. And they'd say at times, '*Play those awful things!*' Bix was instrumental in things like that."[24]

Bix drew some of his new ideas from listening to "serious" music, mostly that written by European composers. This taste originated in his childhood, with memories of his mother's piano playing, and of the choir directed by his grandfather at the Davenport church. His passion for jazz had not weakened the young man's interest in a different musical universe, where harmonic elements were obviously considered with a subtlety and a complexity quite different from the rudimentary approach of the early New Orleans musicians. Though the profundity of his research was hindered by his limited musical knowledge, Bix had found a poetic style in Eastwood Lane that aroused his sensitivity. He had shared the excitement of *The Firebird*'s luxurious sonority with Hoagy Carmichael, before being enchanted, some months later, by the discovery, at the Bertons' home, of Claude Debussy's Impressionist compositions. Piano was becoming Bix's favored means of exploring new harmonic possibilities, and the young musician, often reserved and introverted, knew how to share and communicate his enthusiasm. For Frank Trumbauer, "Bix didn't care much for other bands. Oh, we both loved Louis Armstrong. But, our favorites were: Delius, Debussy, Ravel and Stravinsky. . . . This was

22. *Hear Me Talkin' to Ya*, op. cit., p. 153.

23. TRAM, *The Frank Trumbauer Story*, op. cit., p. 54.

24. *Hear Me Talkin' to Ya*, op. cit., p. 154.

the happiest and healthiest period in our lives. I made Bix assistant leader of the band. We played golf, rode horses, and he didn't have a drink for months at a time. To my knowledge, it was here that Bix met the only girl that he ever loved. I have since read some of the letters he wrote to her, and they were beautiful. Her name is Ruth. We'll let it go at that!"[25]

Her name was Ruth Shaffner. She was nineteen and shared an apartment with her two sisters, Bess and Estelle. She had moved to Saint Louis in December 1924, and worked as a medical secretary. One of her friends brought her to the Arcadia Ballroom on September 18, and introduced her to Bix. The young girl fell under the spell of his laughing eyes, and she came back several times, dancing in front of a musician who could hardly miss the gracious swirl of her black velvet dress. Ruth was "as cute as a bug's ear," according to one of her assiduous admirers, and Bix invited her to share his Monday off. They went to see the Saint Louis Cardinals play at Sportsman's Park, and ended the night at Larry's, a restaurant that became a speakeasy after dinner, with a dark back room where Bix would sit at the piano. He played a few numbers, drank moderately, and then drove his dazzled companion home.

In early November, Bix left the Majestic Hotel and moved into room 608 at the Coronado. Located three blocks from the Arcadia Ballroom, and close to the Sheridan Apartments where the Shaffner sisters lived, this was where the early love between the musician and the secretary developed. Asked many years later about her relationship with Bix, Ruth would reluctantly share the privacy of these happy weeks of amorous discovery: "We were deeply attached to one another . . . he was deeply affectionate. No one could make love like he did. I could just sit and look at him . . . it was a feeling I can't explain. I had many dates with Bix before anything was discussed about sex. It was a feeling. No one could resist . . . it was a mutual decision. I was certain of Bix's love for me by the way he treated me, and the love he showed for me. What else can I say? He was so considerate, thoughtful . . . I know he loved me."[26]

Saxophonist Karl Spaeth was replaced at the Arcadia Ballroom by Damon "Bud" Hassler, formerly a violinist with the Saint Louis Symphony. Directed by Rudolph Ganz, the orchestra opened its winter season at the Odeon Theater Building on November 6. Bix took Bud Hassler to every Friday matinee. He bought the program of each concert and bombarded his companion with questions about the genesis and the meaning of each work. Beethoven, Dvorak, and Liszt were listed on the first day's menu. Bix faithfully attended a dozen of these weekly concerts, his enthusiasm reaching its highest point with the November 13 program, which presented Gabriel Fauré's *Pelléas et Mélisande* and *L'Enfant Prodigue* by Claude Debussy. "In the main only the Impressionists and modern tonal composers captured Bix's imagination," confirmed Bud Hassler, "especially harmonically. I tried to explain the classic masters, and what they were driving at, but he wasn't much impressed."[27] "Bix had a miraculous ear," added Pee Wee Russell. "There'd be certain things he would hear in some modern classical music, like whole tones, and he'd say, why not do it in a jazz

25. TRAM, *The Frank Trumbauer Story*, op. cit., pp. 54–55.

26. *Bix, Man and Legend*, op. cit., p. 150.

27. *The Leon Bix Beiderbecke Story*, op. cit., pp. 207–208.

band? What's the difference? Music doesn't have to be the sort of thing that's put in brackets? Then later it got to be like a fad and everybody did it, but they wouldn't know what the devil it was all about."[28]

Feeling more confident in his music-reading abilities, Bix contacted professional trumpeter Joseph Gustat, who, at age thirty-eight, had just been given the first trumpet chair in the Saint Louis Symphony Orchestra. Joseph Gustat's pedagogical skills had won him recognition as a teacher, and brought in many students. After listening to Bix's playing for a few minutes, and observing his peculiar fingering technique, the professor advised him to give up any idea of formal studies of the horn. He comforted Bix in his "faulty" playing—"erroneous" in regard to the playing taught in music schools—realizing it permitted the young man to express himself in a unique and surprising manner. Joe Gustat had the sense and the finesse to avoid "putting a wild animal in a cage," in his own words, and this validating encounter put a definitive end to Bix's vague desire for a "classical" apprenticeship.[29]

"Pee Wee Russell often told me that the greatest band he ever played in was the five piece intermission band at the Arcadia Ballroom in St. Louis in 1925," wrote producer Ernie Anderson. "This was Peck Kelley, Bix Beiderbecke, Jack Teagarden, and the drummer, who was probably Felix Guarino."[30] Pee Wee Russell had been able to convince Peck Kelley to leave Texas—an amazing decision for the pianist, who had left Houston only a couple of other times in his entire life. Dee Orr, who was the drummer in Frank Trumbauer's band, also remembered that Peck Kelley played piano at the Arcadia Ballroom, but for a few days only, sometime in October or November. "Peck scared Bix and Trumbauer," added Pee Wee Russell. "They went crazy over him, and we all agreed he had to be in the band. But we couldn't get past the union. We tried everything, even bribing the union man. The money wasn't as important as the music, and we were willing to pay Peck out of our own pockets. Nothing worked. We got a few club jobs for him to meet expenses, but it was a shame Peck wasn't allowed to work that Arcadia job. He was very advanced harmonically and was just what we wanted."[31]

SAINT LOUIS, the third-largest city in the U.S., was segregated, and the poorer part of the black population lived south of Olive Street, in a neighborhood of crowded, miserable wooden shacks. Josephine Baker was born there on June 3, 1906. She grew up in a dirty hut on Gratiot Street, where she had to fight off huge rats from her vermin-infested mattress. At age fourteen, she worked as a waitress at the Chauffeur's Club, a cabaret located on Pine Street, where black cornetist and saxophonist Charlie Creath was regularly featured. The American Federation of Musicians maintained two different, segregated locals, but a common passion for jazz music managed to beat down the high social barriers raised between black and white musicians. "We wouldn't have dared play in public with them," admitted Bud Hassler, "but after hours was another story."[32] Charlie Creath would introduce this

28. *Hear Me Talkin' to Ya*, op. cit., p. 155.

29. *Bix, Man and Legend*, op. cit., p. 148.

30. "Ernie Anderson talks about Pee Wee Russell," in *Storyville*, no. 154 (June 1993), p. 131. Felix Guarino was a member of the Arcadian Serenaders, the band playing opposite Tram's band on Wednesdays, Saturdays, and Sundays. The presence of Jack Teagarden in the small group playing during intermissions is more dubious, as he was at that time more probably featured in Doc Ross's orchestra in Albuquerque, New Mexico.

31. Richard B. Hadlock, "Peck Kelley: Jazz Legend," in *Down Beat* (January 14, 1965), p. 22.

32. *The Leon Bix Beiderbecke Story*, op. cit., p. 202.

audacious racial mixing in the Okeh studios on November 3, 1925, when he used white trombonist Thomas "Sonny" Lee—an old Texan friend and band mate of Pee Wee Russell, with whom he had sat in Herbert Berger's orchestra.

By the end of 1925, patrons of the Arcadia Ballroom were dancing to music that had reached a surprising level of quality. Night after night, the long hours Bix and Tram had worked together led to an exceptional partnership. The two musicians often ventured into an improvised dialogue: one would launch into a short musical statement, the other would respond, and they would continue to trade phrases, arousing the audience's enthusiasm for these innovative and virtuosic "chase choruses." On December 15, Bix wrote to his friend Hoagy Carmichael, who was still in Indiana: "We have absolutely the hottest band in the country. We're playing at the Arcadia here nightly and are panicking the town. . . . If that bunch at Indiana think the Wolverines & Goldkette were hot I'd like to see them when they hear this band."

Pee Wee was dating Ruth's sister, Estelle Shaffner. He used to take Bix and the two girls out to the West End, a cabaret in a hotel open to black people. These nighttime outings were frequent, and the boys did their very best to hear as much jazz as they could in Saint Louis. On December 23, Pee Wee Russell, Bix, and the Shaffner sisters celebrated Christmas one night early, at Joe's Club, across the street from the Arcadia. Ruth gave Bix cufflinks. The three sisters left Saint Louis the next day and went home to spend the holidays with their parents. The Frank Trumbauer Orchestra stayed at the Arcadia Ballroom to entertain the customers on Christmas Eve and New Year's.

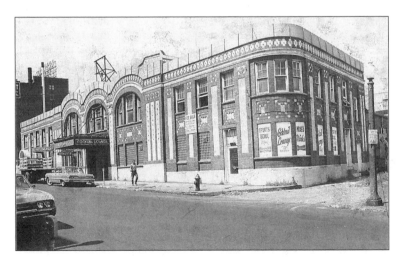

The Arcadia Ballroom in the 1960s; the Arcadia's owners were forced into bankruptcy in 1948, and the building was turned into a sports arena, with bowling as the main attraction. It was for sale when this picture was taken, and was torn down in 1966. The site became a parking lot. (Saint Louis Mercantile Library Collection)

CHAPTER 7

1926: The Happy Year

Saint Louis, January–May 1926

Bix spent the first week of 1926 in Davenport, and returned on January 7 to Saint Louis, where Ruth had been for several days. In December she had noticed an abnormal delay in her monthly cycle. Days went by with increasing anxiety, but nature was kind, and to the couple's great relief, Ruth was soon "freed" . . . and still very much in love. On January 29, the Frank Trumbauer Orchestra traveled to Carbondale—Tram's native city—where the band was featured at the Elks Club for one night. Bix and Ruth, no longer under the cloud that had temporarily cast a shadow on the happiest weeks of their lives, spent the following evening at Larry's Club in the company of Pee Wee Russell, Bud Hassler, and Ruth's sister, Estelle.

The band had a quick turnover in trombonists in February: Ray Thurston was replaced by Sonny Lee, who ceded his place to Vernon Brown on February 15, before permanently returning to the orchestra on March 29. On March 10, Bix celebrated his twenty-third birthday and checked into the Chase Hotel—probably having worn out his welcome at the Coronado with his boisterous activities and his hotheaded friends.

In response to Bix's December 15 letter, Hoagy Carmichael invited Tram and his group to Indiana University, to show off their talents at the 1926 junior prom. Hoagy was completing all the credits needed for a law degree, and was considering a possible career as a lawyer. Gennett studios had accidently destroyed the masters from his last session with his Collegians, two titles recorded in Richmond on February 2, for which Gennett had used new "electrical" recording equipment they had not yet fully mastered. Bix's return to Bloomington, on April 16, met his expectations. In addition to the thrill of seeing his friend Carmichael, he again met some of the old university "nuts." Dazzled by the event, Frank Trumbauer remembered in his diary, "In all my years in the music business, I have never found a school so sharp. We literally knocked each other out—the school and the band! The Music Corporation of America was just getting started and when we closed at the Arcadia on May 3, they offered us a job in Mansfield, Ohio. Somehow I felt that we should have taken the offer. But, about this time, Charles Horvath came to town and asked me to take over the leadership of the Jean Goldkette Orchestra in Detroit. Some of my men didn't want to go on the road, so I accepted the Goldkette offer, but only on one condition—that I take Bix with me!"[1] Jean Goldkette had mixed memories of Bix's stint in his orchestra in November 1924, and the cornetist's image as an irresponsible eccentric was persistent. The bandleader was reluctant to hire Bix. Frank Trumbauer had to step in, to the point of adding a condition to his agreement: "No Bix! No Tram!"

Bix and Ruth spent all day together on May 6, ending their night at Ethel's Club. They would part the next morning for an unknown period of time, and their promises to keep in touch could not minimize the distance that would keep them apart, or the difficulties that might arise from the trip. The orchestra was reaching the end of its long stay at the Arcadia Ballroom—eight months in Saint Louis—without having recorded a single side. This dearth is made even less explicable when one considers the number of local bands that passed through the city's recording studios during that period. The Arcadian Serenaders (who played at the Arcadia Ballroom with Tram's orchestra) recorded at that time, as did Charlie Creath, Dewey Jackson (an underrated trumpeter), and, on May 12, 1926, the Saint Louis Levee Band, whose only identifiable musician is pianist Jelly Roll Morton.

Detroit, May 1926

Bix left Saint Louis on May 7, in bassist Dan Gaebe's car. Their route passed through Chicago, where the two travelers probably stopped to hear some music, and it ended in Detroit. On May 12, Frank Trumbauer and Bix visited Jean Goldkette at the Graystone Ballroom. Goldkette had now cut back on his piano playing considerably, as managing a large musical organization and competing with Paul Whiteman took up most of his time. Frank Trumbauer could be a valuable figure in this commercial battle, and he was called to replace Russ Morgan at the head of one of Goldkette's orchestras.

1. TRAM, The Frank Trumbauer Story, op. cit., p. 56.

Within the form (as readable):

Davenport, Iowa — 78722 — Cornet — 5323 Parker — Beiderbecke, Leon B.

LOCAL NO. 67 — Oct. 15, 1924

TRANSFER RECORD IN LOCAL No. 5 A. F. OF M.

DATE		FOLIO	DEBIT	DATE		FOLIO	CREDIT
Apr	1	2nd nt	2.00	May 13			2.00

TRANSFER TO FULL MEMBERSHIP
TRANSFER REVOKED
TRANSFER WITHDRAWN — June 18-1926
NAME OF LOCAL — St. Louis, Mo
94407 — LOCAL NO. 2 — May 13, 1926
Cornet
Addison Hotel
Beiderbecke, L. B.

1. How long have you been in Detroit? One day
2. Have you ever had a transfer deposited in this Local before? Yes
3. If so, when? 1924
4. Were you ever a member of Local 5, A. F. of M.? No
5. Did you come in alone to solicit work, or with a combination? alone
6. Have you solicited a job prior to this time? Yes
7. Has anybody sent for or corresponded with you relative to securing working in this jurisdiction? No If so, who? ___
8. Have you been promised an engagement? No
9. Have you performed anywhere in this jurisdiction prior to depositing this transfer? No
10. I hereby affirm on my honor that I have answered the foregoing questions truthfully.

Signature: Leon B. Beiderbecke
Date ___

Bix's registration at Local 5 in Detroit (American Federation of Musicians) on June 18, 1926. (Rich Johnson)

2. The building of the Palais Royale has been restored. It is located in South Bend, over the storefronts, on the corner of Michigan Street and Colfax. This was probably Bix's first radio broadcast, as he seemed to have been excluded from the shows broadcast from the Graystone Ballroom between October and December 1924.

Bix joined the musicians' union, Detroit Local #5, giving the Addison Hotel as his address. Tram and the cornet player were reunited on May 13 in Terre Haute, Indiana, along with members of the Jean Goldkette Victor Recording Orchestra. They were booked for the junior prom at the Rose Polytechnic Institute, and the following day, the band played at a senior ball organized by Notre Dame University in South Bend, Indiana. "And now Radio Station WSBT in South Bend, is proud to bring you the exciting music of the Jean Goldkette Victor Orchestra! For you tonight, music is in the air ..." On the evening of May 14, as the band began to play, the radio announcer introduced the broadcast of a part of the concert given at the Palais Royale Ballroom[2], and Bix's music would ring out through hundreds of radio receivers.

Radio, at this time, was still a novelty. Before World War I, research into the possibilities of radio transmissions rested in the hands of a few scientists, such as Nikola Tesla, who built the first high-powered transmitting set in 1899 in Colorado Springs. The end of the war and the development of commercialized equipment gave birth in October 1919 to the giant RCA, a General Electric subsidiary. One year later, in Pittsburgh, Westinghouse—a manufacturer of receivers—launched the first commercial radio station to broadcast in America: KDKA. It was followed in May 1921 by New York's WJZ, which entered radio history with the first broadcast of a live show on February 19, 1922. The number of new stations grew quickly, and at the end of 1922, there were more than 500 radio stations operating in the U.S. The small South Bend station appeared on the air on June 29, 1922, and for four years broadcast to the American public musical offerings that competed directly with those available on record: in May 1926, at ten o'clock on a Friday night, Bix, Tram, Pee Wee, and the swing of the Goldkette Orchestra were part of its program.

Hudson Lake, May–August 1926

The orchestra was back in Detroit on May 15. After five days in the city, the musicians headed to Hudson Lake, in northern Indiana, where Jean Goldkette had engaged the band for the summer months. This small lake is close to South Bend, ninety miles east of Chicago and on the Chicago South Shore Electric's regular train route. In 1885 the Smith family had selected the place to settle down, and built a hotel near the train station. They spent several years establishing it as a popular vacation spot: the beach was equipped for watersports, and a dance hall, the Casino, was opened in 1922 alongside the lake. It soon became a bustling place on summer weekends. Having rented this location for his orchestra, Jean Goldkette decided to change its name: he had a blue lantern hung at

The Casino (Blue Lantern), Hudson Lake. (JPL, 2003)

the building's entrance, and for this season only, the ballroom became the Blue Lantern Inn. The space was huge—it could hold 2,000 people. It was sheltered by a gently sloping roof, and grand bay windows opened out over the lake. Many lamps hanging on boats shimmered in the night, and during the orchestra's breaks, the dancers could hear the waves lapping on the shore.

Jean Goldkette needed two different bands, one playing—as it had the summer before—at Island Lake, and another performing at Hudson Lake. The Graystone orchestra was therefore split in two parts, each half being reinforced by musicians picked up from Frank Trumbauer's for-

Interior of the Casino's ballroom, Hudson Lake. (JPL, 2003)

mer unit. The group assembled around Bix at Hudson Lake was made up of jazzmen

White City Amusement Park, Chicago, summer 1926. Left to right: Pee Wee Russell, Milton "Mezz" Mezzrow, Sonny Lee (standing), Bix, George Rilling, and Eddie Condon. (Duncan Schiedt Collection)

from the Arcadia Ballroom: Tram, Pee Wee, trombonist Sonny Lee, and drummer Dee Orr; plus two musicians the cornetist had played with at Goldkette's in November 1924—trumpeter Fred "Fuzzy" Farrar and saxophonist Stanley "Doc" Ryker—and three new associates: Frank DiPrima on banjo, Dan Gaebe on bass, and Irving "Itzy" Riskin on piano. The dance hall was open six nights a week, with an additional Sunday matinee, leaving Monday as the day off. The dance floor was impressive; it was surrounded on three sides by a railing separating it from the jam-packed dining space, the fourth side being closed by the stage. "The band at Hudson Lake wore uniforms," said Eddie Condon, "with fancy two-tone shoes. Bix was the last to arrive on the job, naturally; he got the last uniform and the last pair of shoes. The uniform was too small for him and the shoes were too big."[3] Business was bad all summer. A big audience from Chicago, South Bend, and Michigan City filled the room on the weekends, but the place was almost vacant on weeknights.

The musicians were housed in cottages. A group of three bungalows constructed alongside the lake had been assigned to married couples: the Farrars lived in the first, together with Frank and Mitzi Trumbauer; Charles Horvath, his wife Edith, and their two children were given the second one; while Doc and Norma Ryker were set up in the last bungalow. Behind the dance hall and the hotel, set back from the main buildings, two log cabins, painted yellow and surrounded by bushes and wild grass, accommodated the six single musicians. Two steps led to a narrow porch that opened onto the main room. Two small rooms, to the right, completed the tiny cottage. Irving Riskin, Dan Gaebe, Pee Wee Russell, Bix, and an old Knabe piano monopolized the first hut; Sonny Lee, Dee Orr, and Frank DiPrima romped about the second one. This rudimentary housing lacked bathrooms. All toileting needs were met in the neighboring hotel, at a cost of twenty-five cents per visit, which was more than enough to discourage any unlikely attempts at personal hygiene. The greatest disorder swept through this secluded spot in a few days: cans, empty bottles, and dirty laundry were strewn around the outsides of the two houses, but the places weren't any cleaner inside.

3. Eddie Condon, *We Called It Music*, op. cit., p. 138.

One payday evening, Bix and Pee Wee Russell came back from the neighboring city—by car! They had bought, for $80, a decaying 1916 Buick. The sole purpose of this purchase was to make the ten-mile journey to their main source of bootleg liquor. This fearsome hooch, totally homemade, was sold for $2 a jug by the decrepit female owners of a run-down farm. A few trips tired the car, and it died one night on the road. A farmer hitched his horse to the carcass and towed it to the cottage. "It never ran again," wrote Eddie Condon. "It had a fine mirror and the owners

Cottage occupied by Bix and his friends during the summer of 1926, present condition. (Rich Johnson)

used that while shaving. Ten years later Pee Wee was driving to the coast with the Louis Prima band; he took a detour to reminisce at Hudson Lake and found the cottage. The car was still in the backyard, on its wheels but groggy with rust. Pee Wee pointed it out to the Prima boys. *'I own half of that,'* he said."[4]

The local paper, the *South Bend Tribune*, regularly reviewed the music at the place, writing for instance in its June 11 edition, "A rare treat! A Double Orchestra attraction. Dance beginning Sat. June 12. Blue Lantern-Hudson Lake. The Indianans—under direction of Joe Dockstader, featuring Lola Trowbridge and her songs vs. Jean Goldkette's Orchestra under direction of Frank Trumbauer. Two orchestras!"[5] But the reports gathered leave no doubt about the winner: the quality of the music played by Bix and his partners completely escaped the audience. The crowd had a marked preference for the Indianans, a group that served a conventional show to the dancers, exactly what they were looking for. The music Jean Goldkette's jazzmen were exploring, night after night, was considered avant-garde, audacious, and innovative. It was out of place on a stage deep in the heart of America. Only a few readers, if any, of the *South Bend Tribune* would weep into their handkerchiefs when reading on August 29, "Art Haerens' Orchestra, under the direction of Myron Walz, will replace Goldkette's Orchestra on tomorrow's broadcast. The Goldkette organization is leaving the Blue Lantern due to a last-minute decision."[6]

THE DEPARTURE FROM Hudson Lake marked the end of an important year in Bix's short life, and it also concluded an essential phase of his musical development. For twelve months since his debut at the Arcadia Ballroom in September 1925, the cornetist had experienced a long working period, with brilliant partners, ending on a high point of several weeks of total freedom at Hudson Lake. Though it was not recorded, the music Bix composed day after day, on both piano and cornet, had reached a higher level, and henceforth shone with irresistible richness and

4. *We Called It Music*, op. cit., p. 139.

5. *The Leon Bix Beiderbecke Story*, op. cit., p. 215.

6. *The Leon Bix Beiderbecke Story*, op. cit., p. 217. The Casino building is still standing at Hudson Lake, and was reopened in May 2002. Bix's bungalow has been moved one mile from its original location: it is today painted in blue, and a kitchen and a bathroom have been added to it. (Information from Rich Johnson.)

brilliance. Musical creation was the jazzman's sole interest, and "sleep, food, and women were things he never allowed to interfere with music," as Eddie Condon understood it. Sax player Stanley "Doc" Ryker was well aware of this evolution: "What struck me most about Bix was his sweet-hot style. Although he played hot, it was his beautiful tone, everything sounded so sweet, although it was never schmaltzy or anything. I liked the harmony he would play. Very often, when he'd take a chorus, I'd be listening so intently I'd almost forget to come in. He was way ahead of all of us."[7]

The proximity of Chicago, only ninety miles away, made it possible for many musicians working there to travel on Saturday nights to the Blue Lantern, and to hear the Goldkette Orchestra. The most regular visitors were a group of very young men—between sixteen and twenty—who had neglected their studies at the Austin High School to concentrate their efforts on jazz and putting together a *hot* ensemble. Frank Teschemacher was a highly demanding clarinetist; Bud Freeman was trying to master his tenor saxophone; Jim Lannigan had given up piano for the string bass; and cornetist Jimmy McPartland had already advanced his career by taking Bix's place in the Wolverines in October 1924. These musicians, soon to be the creators of the "Chicago style"—an energetic and fierce adaptation of the New Orleans style—had found their model in Bix Beiderbecke, a man only slightly older than they were, who shared their social and cultural origins, but whose unique and bizarre musical expression was beyond their grasp. They were all impressed by his playing, and Bud Freeman expressed the general feeling when declaring in 1965 to British critic Max Jones, "I think Bix was the perfect player; he had the perfect, profound understanding of jazz."[8]

These innovative Chicagoans and their *hot* jazz music did not, however, meet with a favorable reception from the 1926 audience, and they were as under-appreciated by dancers as the Goldkette Orchestra was at Hudson Lake. The clientele that kept dance halls alive preferred waltzes, tangos, and rumbas, with an occasional Charleston. The popular taste of the Jazz Age was definitely for *sweet* music, and the best-selling titles reflected this musical inclination. After the amazing commercial success of his recording of "Whispering" in 1920, Paul Whiteman had cranked out hit record after hit record. The summer of 1926 brought him a new best-seller in America with "Valencia," at the very moment when he and the band were achieving international renown with a successful European tour, which concluded in France in early July. The Parisian public discovered "symphonic jazz" at the Théâtre des Champs-Elysées, at a show in which the orchestra was the only attraction. Following in the King of Jazz's wake, many bandleaders sought favor with the American public: violinist Ben Selvin, clarinetist Ted Lewis, and saxophonist Isham Jones, all of whom were outsold by Al Jolson, a singer completely untouched by jazz, who enjoyed unmatched commercial success and commensurate earnings. This music did not ruffle any feathers, but the opportunities offered to

7. On Albert Haim's web-site, under the general title "Bix's Fellow Musicians," an article is dedicated to Stanley "Doc" Ryker. This quote is taken from a letter to Brigitte Berman, dictated by Ryker to his wife in 1979.

8. Max Jones, *Jazz Talking* (New York: Da Capo Press, 2000), p. 34.

young innovators—whose music was more difficult to understand—were rare. Pianist Jess Stacy was right: "Chicago was really kind of a corny town. [Customers] went for people like Ace Brigode, Wayne King, Art Kassel. There was really no audience for what we were doing."[9]

Chicago, August 1926

Frank Teschemacher, Muggsy Spanier, and Jess Stacy had found a job for the summer at the Midway Gardens, a dance club in Cottage Grove, south of Chicago. Eddie Condon played his banjo in Art Cope's ensemble at the Vanity Faire Café, his interest for the job increased by the bass player in the band, the blonde and gorgeous Thelma Coombs.[10] Traditional theaters, restaurants, and movie houses remained closed to jazz music, as did "respectable" dance halls. *Hot* musicians, therefore, found their most secure and effective support from Jewish and Sicilian gangsters, who had taken full advantage of the opportunities presented to them by Prohibition. From these groups of recent immigrants, forming well-organized communities, came most of the owners of illegal restaurants and night clubs.

South of the Loop, on one block on 35th Street, three cabarets owned by bootleggers offered the public, in the summer of 1926, an outstanding "colored" lineup. At the corner of Prairie Avenue, the Apex Club featured one of the biggest names in Chicago jazz: Creole clarinetist Jimmy Noone. He had joined Freddie Keppard's Original Creole Band in 1917, and recorded with them twice: for Gennett in 1924 and in Chicago during the summer of 1926. He hardly ever left the Windy City. His impeccable technique and his hauntingly beautiful sound had brought him the fervid admiration of the young Chicagoans, regular visitors of the Apex Club. A few yards farther on, the Plantation Café Revue had, since February 1925, offered nightly musical entertainment from Joe "King" Oliver's Dixie Syncopators. The famous cornetist had gathered around him first-class musicians, among them trombonist Edward "Kid" Ory, saxophonist Barney Bigard, clarinetist Albert Nicholas, and pianist Luis Russell. They performed for an integrated audience, and their show included eight pretty chorus girls, whose enthusiastic swing matched that of the orchestra.

It was in the third place, the Sunset Café—on the corner of Calumet and 35th Street—that Bix, Tram, and Mitzi spent the evening of August 30. Passing through Chicago after the end of their contract at Hudson Lake, they wanted to hear Carroll Dickerson's orchestra, starring Louis Armstrong. The black cornetist had stayed with Fletcher Henderson until November 1925, recording one hundred titles during the fourteen months he was in New York. Forty of them were cut with the Fletcher Henderson Orchestra, including two sides that soon ranked among the best-selling records: "Sugar Foot Stomp," recorded for Columbia on May 26, 1925, and "Carolina

9. *Lost Chords*, op. cit., p. 193. The fame of Ace Brigode and His Virginians was limited to the Midwest. Wayne King, known as the Waltz King, was a midwestern dance band favorite, quite successful in the 1930s.

10. Thelma was not only a cute blonde, she was also an excellent string bass player, as evidenced by two recording sessions done in Chicago in 1928 and released under the name of Thelma Therry and Her Playboys. These records are available on the Dutch Timeless CD, *The Chicago Hot Bands, 1924–1928*, CBC 1-041.

Stomp," recorded on October 21. Armstrong, however, couldn't really show his worth in such a structured ensemble, and it is at the heart of a smaller band that his striking talent would burst forth. Louis had set Harlem on fire in April 1925, with the Okeh recording of "Everybody Loves My Baby" by the Clarence Williams' Blue Five. He renewed this success three months later when the record of "Cake Walking Babies from Home" went on sale. Armstrong's ringing breaks on this side were his response to the inspired creation of one of the few musicians able to match his genius: clarinetist Sidney Bechet. But the pinnacle of this New York series arose from a second dialogue, that between Armstrong and Bessie Smith, the Empress of Blues. Their best-selling items were a version of W. C. Handy's "Saint Louis Blues," recorded on January 14, and a beautiful take of "Careless Love Blues," a nuanced and haunting blues cut during the May 26 session.

The Okeh Record company and its musical director Tommy Rockwell were pioneers in recognizing Louis Armstrong's commercial power. They had been wise enough to realize that Clarence Williams' Blue Five best-selling titles were those featuring the cornetist, and that an identical success had met the Fletcher Henderson and Bessie Smith recordings where Louis was prominent. Okeh had therefore signed Armstrong to an exclusive contract during the autumn of 1925, and on November 12, upon his arrival in Chicago, had sent him to their studio as the leader of Louis Armstrong's Hot Five. The cornetist was backed by experienced musicians: Kid Ory, Johnny Dodds, Johnny St. Cyr on banjo, and Lil Armstrong on piano. Their record containing "Muskrat Ramble" and an incredible interpretation of "Heebie Jeebies" was a success. Recorded in February 1926 and available in stores in July, this second title was the first to feature scat singing—this singing without words. It also introduced Louis Armstrong's unique and husky voice, which would from then on be an essential counterpart to the luminous sound of his cornet. Earl Hines remembered the impact of this discovery, recounting, "the musicians spent their time with their heads out the window, trying to catch a cold in order to sing like Louis." The buyers of these records were, for the most part, urban black people and a handful of white jazz followers.

Bix and Tram were among these few impassioned citizens, and the evening of August 30 at the Sunset Café allowed them to hear an artist for whom the two shared the greatest admiration, although Tram had never met him before. The café, the property of Joe Glaser, a promoter with connections to the underworld, was known as the cream of the Chicago clubs, and its profitable trade in illegal business was carefully protected by continuous rounds of police patrolmen.[11] The Sunset revue was sumptuous, and it was displayed in a decor streaming with plants, with an enormous revolving glass ball that bathed the dancers in thousands of flashes of light. Louis Armstrong appeared onstage at about eleven o'clock, after finishing his show at the Dreamland or at the Vendome Theater. He could blow for eight hours straight, over the course of one night, and repeat this day after day.

11. Joe Glaser and Louis Armstrong did not know it at that time, but they would meet again. Glaser became a music business impresario and later a tycoon. He managed Louis Armstrong's career, ensuring his international fame.

Mitzi Trumbauer remembered that Louis had spotted Bix in the audience, and that he came down from the stage during the intermission to say hello: "Bix spoke to Louis, and nodded to Frank, and said, 'Louis, this is my good friend, Frank Trumbauer.' Tram reached out his hand to Louis for a handshake, but a quizzing Louis said, 'How's that? Frank Trrrr . . . what?'—'Trumbauer,' Bix repeated, 'Frank Trumbauer.' A giant smile crossed Louis' face. He reached for Tram's hand with both of his, gave Tram a warm grasp, and said 'Glad to know ya, Mr. Trambone.'"[12]

Detroit, September 1926

Arriving in Detroit at the beginning of September, Tram took over as director of a new Jean Goldkette "Victor" Recording Band, a group made up of twelve musicians from the two orchestras that had spent the summer at Hudson Lake and Island Lake. Since the two bands had had no contact with each other for weeks, several days of intense rehearsal were necessary to merge their styles. The success of this fusion would lead to the birth of one of the most explosive big bands of the 1920s. "To say that the band was a 'killer' would be putting it mildly," their leader affirmed.[13]

Banjoist Howard "Howdy" Quicksell had been with the Goldkette organization the longest: he had joined in 1922, when the band was formed. Originally from Indiana, he had been in a student orchestra with Stanley Ryker. Born in 1898, Ryker learned to play the saxophone during his military service, and in 1919, he was given a job in violinist Tade Dolan's band. He temporarily abandoned music to attend chiropractic school, obtaining a diploma in 1921 that served no purpose other than earning him the nickname Doc. In spring 1922 he accepted an offer to join Howdy Quicksell in the Goldkette band, and in 1923 he in turn called upon an old friend, trombonist Bill Rank. Ray Lodwig, the trumpeter with the quavering vibrato, came to Goldkette that same year, and in 1925 this experienced musician was given leadership of the group at Island Lake.

The year 1923 would also see the arrival in Detroit of several musicians from the brilliant Pennsylvania dance band the Scranton Sirens.[14] This unit supplied Jean Goldkette with some high quality musicians, three of whom would be part of Bix and Tram's new orchestra: trumpeter Fred "Fuzzy" Farrar, pianist Irving Riskin, and a key member whose arrival would be delayed by several days, arranger Bill Challis.

At the end of his engagement with the New Orleans Rhythm Kings, Don Murray also headed for Detroit. He was quite excited by the idea of replacing Pee Wee Russell at Frank Trumbauer's side, and reuniting, after a year of professional separation, with his friend and partner Beiderbecke. Bassist Steve Brown had been hired by Jean Goldkette in 1924. Born in New Orleans in 1890, this man with thinning hair and a drawling accent was the oldest of the group. He was fifteen

12. *TRAM, The Frank Trumbauer Story*, op. cit., p. 61.

13. *Hear Me Talkin' To Ya*, op. cit., pp. 150–151.

14. Based in Scranton, Pennsylvania, the Scranton Sirens started in 1920, directed by violinist Billy Lustig and counting many soon-to-be-famous musicians among their members: Russ Morgan (trombone), Fred Farrar (trumpet), Bill Challis (sax and arranger), Irving Riskin (piano), Alfie Evans (sax), Mike Trafficante (bass), and the Dorsey Brothers, Jimmy and Tommy.

when he started to follow his brother Tom in the brass bands led by Papa Jack Laine, before the two boys formed their own Brown's Band: Tom was trombonist, and Steve used to switch between tuba and string bass. He had given up music for seven years to work in a hospital in Jackson, Louisiana, and it wasn't until 1920 that he took his instrument out of the closet, when Tom asked him come to Chicago. His presence among the New Orleans Rhythm Kings in 1923 brought him renown, but Steve Brown always considered that his best years, musically speaking, were the ones spent with Goldkette. He had developed "slapping," a technique previously used by some New Orleans string bass players, and which he used in recordings of his instrument: "[Until then] I had used the bow, just like any legitimate bass player would," explained Steve Brown. "At one place the drummer failed to show up . . .

Bix, around the summer of 1926. (Indiana University Collection)

and left us without any rhythm, so I put the bow down and slapped the bass. Just slapped the strings against the fingerboard, which produced an afterbeat effect which gave a rhythmic effect to the band. And the boys liked it so well, even after we did get a drummer, they wanted me to continue. With the aid of the fingerboard, I used to make triple beats. You'll hear it on 'Dinah'—with Jean Goldkette. See, the string will hit the fingerboard and I'll catch it, catch it on the bounce, and it makes a sort of triple effect."[15]

The last four members of the orchestra had started with Goldkette in 1925: Bix, Tram, Chauncey Morehouse, and Newell "Spiegle" Willcox. Charlie Horvath's managerial duties were keeping him away from his drums, and Jean Goldkette called upon Chauncey Morehouse to replace him. Morehouse was twenty when he was hired by bandleader Paul Specht, a pioneer of broadcast dance music. Specht made up a small *hot* ensemble within his band, and gave it two thirty-minute sets each night. Chauncey Morehouse was its drummer. The band recorded for Columbia in 1922 and 1923 under the name of the Georgians. These sides preserved a nervous and incisive jazz style, with Morehouse performing the first recorded drum solo on "Land of Cotton Blues" in 1923.[16] Spiegle Willcox had followed his father as a trombonist, and had been selected to be part of the Big Four—an eight-piece band—which performed in Ithaca, New York. Discovered by Paul Whiteman in 1922, these young musicians had been engaged in New York City, billed as Paul Whiteman's Collegians. Spiegle Willcox was a member of his band until 1925. He had found a new job for the summertime in Auburn, New York, when Fred Farrar offered him the chair that Tommy Dorsey's departure had left empty. Willcox joined Goldkette in October. He was one of the *sweet* musicians who, possessing a good sound and a proven technique, helped

15. J. Lee Anderson, interview with Steve Brown, in *The Mississippi Rag* (November 1991), p. 6.

16. These Georgians, whose number varied between six and seven, featured trumpet player Frank Guarente and trombonist Russ Morgan. They traveled several times to Europe, and their recordings deserve better recognition.

build the solid foundation over which the *hot* elements of the orchestra could freely improvise.

The balance obtained in this *sweet*-and-spicy mix was particularly successful. Bix, Tram, Don Murray, and Bill Rank shared the *hot* improvisations, backed up by four *sweet* musicians: Fred Farrar, Ray Lodwig, Doc Ryker, and Spiegle Willcox, and a rhythm section that knew how to keep a rock-steady beat. Doc Ryker thought Bix had played a central part in this achievement: "It was hard not to like him. He always had something nice to say. Like, we'd play through a portion that gave him trouble, and instead of getting irritable or nasty he'd kind of laugh and say something like, '*I ain't got much technique, but I sure have a lousy tone.*' Things like that broke the ice and fostered a real spirit of cooperation in the band."[17]

Boston area, September 21–October 4, 1926

Being an astute organizer, Jean Goldkette sent his band on a several-day tour of New England to fine-tune their performance before opening in New York. A schedule of jobs had been arranged in the dance halls owned by Charlie and Sy Schribman, two brothers who ran many clubs in the Northeast and had hired, as early as 1924, a great number of jazz orchestras. The Goldkette group arrived by train on September 21 in Southborough, a small city west of Boston. J. A. Lyons, the tour director, awaited them, along with a green bus belonging to the Framingham Taxi Company, decked out with a large banner reading: JEAN GOLD-KETTE ORCHESTRA—NEW ENGLAND TOUR—J. A. LYONS, MGR. This vehicle, which lacked both elegance and comfort, would bring the band from the hotel to the dance halls they were playing in, rolling along for hours on the back roads of Massachusetts and jostling its tired passengers. The musicians were brought back every night after work to the Hillcrest Inn in Southborough, a big wooden house they had booked for the stay, and which they used for their afternoon rehearsals.

The Jean Goldkette Orchestra on tour in New England, September–October 1926. Left to right, front row: Ray Lodwig, Irving Riskin, Spiegle Willcox, Doc Ryker, Bill Rank, Chauncey Morehouse, Bix, Bill Challis, Steve Brown, Fred Farrar; back row: Don Murray, Howdy Quicksell, Frank Trumbauer. (Davenport Public Library Collection)

Hoping not to lose a single prospective customer, Charlie Schribman advertised the Jean Goldkette Orchestra as the "Paul Whiteman of the West"—for a Bostonian,

17. *Bix, Man and Legend*, op. cit., p. 172.

The Jean Goldkette Orchestra, Hillcrest Inn, Southborough, September 1926. Left to right, front row: Ray Lodwig, Bill Challis, Spiegle Willcox, Fred Farrar, Bill Rank, Bix (holding the neck of the bass); standing in back: Howdy Quicksell, Chauncey Morehouse, Irving Riskin, Doc Ryker, Don Murray, Frank Trumbauer, Steve Brown. (Duncan Schiedt Collection)

the West began at Niagara Falls—and, for the first night, he had booked the band into a dance hall in Newton (Waltham), the place then known as Nuttings-on-the-Charles. A large wooden building on the bank of the Charles River awaited the musicians. It was so dilapidated that, with each performance it seemed more likely that the vibrations of the dancing would cause it to collapse. Nonetheless, the ballroom was always busy. In order to guarantee the show's success, the promoter had also booked two local ensembles, setting up a "Triple Battle of the Bands" in which audience applause determined the winner. A seventeen-year-old spectator, Max Kaminsky, discovered Bix's music at this first concert of the tour, and it was a revelation to him. He had been playing trumpet since he was five, and was now leading a small jazz group formed

Former building of the Hillcrest Inn at 12 East Main Street, Southborough, Massachusetts, present condition. (JPL)

The Jean Goldkette Orchestra on tour in New England, September–October 1926. Left to right: Frank Trumbauer, Don Murray, Bill Challis, Irving Riskin, Chauncey Morehouse, Bix, Bill Rank, Ray Lodwig, Fred Farrar, Steve Brown, Spiegle Willcox, Doc Ryker, Howdy Quicksell. (Duncan Schiedt Collection)

The Jean Goldkette Orchestra on tour in New England, September–October 1926. Left to right: Bill Challis, Spiegle Willcox, Irving Riskin, Bix, Don Murray, Howdy Quicksell, Doc Ryker, Chauncey Morehouse, Fred Farrar, Ray Lodwig, Bill Rank, Frank Trumbauer, Steve Brown (on the hood). (Davenport Public Library Collection)

with a few classmates, the Six Novelty Syncopaters. Their fans were roughly of the same age as they were. "Mal Hallet's orchestra, a very popular local band that combined comedy routines with dance music, went on first and nearly knocked itself out putting on a whole big show," wrote Max Kaminsky. "Then Barney Rapp's band, which was just coming into prominence then, did all its acts; and finally the Jean Goldkette band came on. . . . They were such a stunning sensation that when the furor died down and it was time for Mal Hallet's band to play again, neither his musicians nor Barney Rapp's men would pick up their instruments. 'How can you follow that?' Mal Hallet asked plaintively, and the crowd wasn't bashful about letting him know they agreed with him. Nobody had heard anything like this music before."[18]

Though Bix's sound—"like a choirful of angels," according to Max Kaminsky—supported by the cohesion and dynamism of the ensemble, had enthralled the audience, the band's charts lacked originality. They were stock arrangements, available in any music store. Compared to the clever and commercial works Ferde Grofé brought to Paul Whiteman, to the jazzy scores Don Redman wrote for Fletcher Henderson, or to Duke Ellington's daring explorations, the Jean Goldkette Orchestra couldn't hope to make distinctive recordings without an innovative arranger. The missing piece was Bill Challis.

The son of a barber, Bill Challis was born in 1904 in Wilkes-Barre, Pennsylvania. His musical career began with his struggles with a violin whose strings seemed capable only of mouselike squeaks. He saw an advertisement for a C-melody sax, and eagerly abandoned fiddle and bow for a superb saxophone. The progress he made on his new instrument soon allowed him to enter his high school band, to join the musicians' union, and therefore to be able to sit in regularly with pianist Freddie Smalls's band. Smalls was hired by Billy Lustig to play in his band, the Scranton Sirens, and the young sax player was invited to join this ensemble, whose local reputation was growing rapidly. But Bill Challis wanted to finish college, and he refused the offer. He spent four years at Bucknell University, supplementing his classes with one-night gigs. He often crossed paths with the Scranton Sirens, a group regularly augmented by the addition of quality musicians such as Fred Farrar and Irving Riskin. After graduating in 1925, Challis decided to start his own band. His new duties as a bandleader led him to write arrangements. "I had a band and the guys didn't know what to do," said Challis. "We'd buy the sheet music, and I'd write parts for the fellows. Otherwise we'd all play the same thing. I wrote chords—symbols—for the piano and the guitar players, and the rest of the parts I wrote: the bass part, two trumpets and trombone, and our three saxophones."[19] Bill Challis jumped at an offer from singer Dave Harmon and went on tour with him and his accompanying band. Passing through Detroit, he visited friends from the Scranton Sirens, who were temporarily employed by Jean Goldkette at his Graystone Ballroom. He was introduced to Charlie Horvath and offered to supply him with orchestrations. The second set of scores he sent was accepted, and the Goldkette Orchestra added Challis's arrangements of "The Blue Room" and "Baby Face" to its repertoire. Charlie Horvath asked his new contributor to join the band. Certain he had been hired as a saxophonist, Bill Challis arrived at the Hillcrest Inn loaded with an impressive display of reed instruments: alto, C-melody sax, baritone sax, clarinet, and bass clarinet. Superfluous baggage . . . the band was waiting for just one person: the arranger.

The Goldkette Orchestra performed in the Boston area for two weeks. After

18. My Life in Jazz, op. cit., pp. 12–13.

19. Chip Deffaa, interview with Bill Challis, in The Mississippi Rag (December 1988).

their opening night at Nuttings-on-the-Charles, they played one night at the Lyonhurst Ballroom in Marlborough and twice at Boston's Music Box, a dance hall located on Huntington Avenue in the heart of the city. Max Kaminsky visited the Hillcrest Inn several times, where he could ask Bix about some of his musical ideas: "When I questioned him about a weird G-sharp that didn't look to me it had any business being there, he explained about the use of passing tones to give color and tonal accent to a phrase, and he went on to discuss anticipation—playing notes of the melody a hair-breadth before the strict time. The use of anticipation, without rushing, which is all a part of making the music swing, was just getting to be understood then." Talking with Bix was easy: he didn't feel the need to speak, and he could remain silent for hours, lost in his thoughts or ruminating over a phrase heard on an Ethel Waters record, until he could seize upon its true spirit and the way it was built. "Bix never tapped his foot to keep time," added Max Kaminsky. "The tempo and the swing that modeled his phrases funnelled out like steam rising from the spout of a boiling kettle. Another idiosyncrasy of Bix's was that as a further means of ensuring the mellow tone he loved he purposely kept his horn funky, never cleaning out the dried spittle that accumulates in the valves and mouthpiece. He had no use at all for a hard, brilliant sound."[20]

TELEPHONE BRYANT B-2500

44" Street Hotel

New York

On September 30, Max Kaminsky accompanied Bix to Lowell for the daily show. He was asked to make a detour through Boston, as Bix needed to get some gin and ginger ale. That night "he played like an angel," and when back at the hotel, Max shared Bix's room. "I went right off to sleep," said Kaminsky, "with my nose buried in the pillow to shut out the smell of his dirty socks steaming in the washbasin. . . . Bix is famous for his avoidance of water, internally and externally, but in spite of the dirt and the whiskey everybody loved Bix so much they just wanted to stick around him. I remarked to my sister Rose the next day, 'I love the way he plays, but I can't stand the way he lives.'"[21] The Goldkette Orchestra was billed in Methuen on October first and in Southborough on the second. Ending where they had started, the boys were back for their last concert of the tour, on October 4, in Nuttings-on-the-Charles, again facing the band led by Mal Hallet. The *Boston Post*'s readers were informed that "Following this appearance, Jean Goldkette's Orchestra will be appearing at Roseland, and Mal Hallet at the Million Dollar Arcade, both jobs in New York."[22]

20. *My Life in Jazz*, op. cit., pp. 15–16.
21. *My Life in Jazz*, op. cit., p. 19.
22. *The Leon Bix Beiderbecke Story*, op. cit. p. 227.

Location of former room 605 of the 44th Street Hotel, where Bix used to stay. Windows are on the right of the building, looking onto a backyard. (Walter Huerta, 2005)

New York, October 1926

A raucous group of musicians got off the train at Grand Central Station on October 5. Bix was back in New York, and the whole band checked in at the 44th Street Hotel, which had opened in a new building at 120 West 44th Street.[23] A desperate message from Joe Venuti awaited their arrival: Bix and Tram were asked to stand in for Red Nichols and Jimmy Dorsey, who were both ill. Venuti—who Bix had played with in Detroit in November 1924—was waiting for them at the Silver Slipper, a Broadway nightclub across from the Cinderella Ballroom. Reaching the place just a few minutes before the show, and quite anxious because they weren't prepared, Bix and Tram were quickly comforted by an uproarious Joe Venuti: "Fake it, boys, it'll sound better anyway."

The Goldkette Orchestra was awaited more seriously the next day for its opening at the Roseland Ballroom. Two small groups, led by Fats Waller and Miff Mole, were also on the bill. There were many musicians in atten-

23. The front of the sixteen-story building that housed the 44th Street Hotel is still visible at 120 West 44th Street, between Sixth Avenue and Broadway. It is today an office building. In New Orleans, the Jazz Collection of the Louisiana State Museum has a copy of a three-minute twenty-six-second home movie, which has recently been restored thanks to Hans Eekhoff. This movie was made at the end of 1926 during the Goldkette tour, and it shows the following sequences with Bix: in Boston, the musicians run in front of the camera; at a New York zoo (Central Park or Bronx?), the musicians play while a man holds a snake—then Bix comes through a door with his cornet-case in hand; the band plays in front of a bear cage; the last sequence—very dark—was shot on October 12 in the Victor studio: Eddie Lang and Bix are visible.

The Jean Goldkette Orchestra at a New York Zoo, October 1926. Left to right, front row: Charles Horvath, Howdy Quicksell, Bix, Fred Farrar, Bill Rank (behind the zoo attendant holding a snake); back row: Ray Lodwig, Irving Riskin, Don Murray, Steve Brown, Spiegle Willcox, Frank Trumbauer. (Indiana University Collection)

Bix and a fellow in a monkey suit; still from the restored Goldkette film, autumn 1926. (Courtesy of Hans Eekhoff)

dance, anxious to actually see and hear if the ensemble they had heard so much about could live up to its advance publicity. Frank Trumbauer had a sense of humor and a good feel for entertainment. He started their show with "Valencia," the syrupy Paul Whiteman hit from the summer of 1926. The audience, expecting a *hot* jazz band, was confounded. This mild opening number was immediately followed by an explosive "Tiger Rag," and by torrid renderings of the superb arrangements Bill Challis had done of "Baby Face," "Blue Room," and "My Pretty Girl." The audience's applause and the dancers' enthusiasm left no doubt: the ongoing battle for the position of top band in New York had a new entrant; the Jean Goldkette Victor Orchestra was now one of the big guys.

For several weeks, Bix regularly enlivened the show with an involuntary gag: the loss of his false tooth, which had a tendency to roll onto the floor in the middle of a piece. This denture, which was getting looser, replaced a tooth he had lost playing baseball, and when it fell, all the musicians got on their knees in search of the little white pearl. As this incident was frequently repeated, the management of the Roseland thought up a funny routine: a big wooden replica of a tooth, a foot tall, was ceremoniously presented to Bix at the end of the program. An inscription read, "to Bix, from the directors"—which always got a big laugh. Benny Davis, the author of "Baby Face," was invited to take part in the show and to sing his own version of the musical number played every night by the Goldkette Orches-

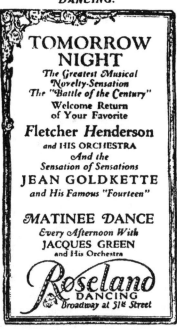

Ad published on October 12, 1926, in the *New York Daily News*. (Reproduced in Walter C. Allen, *Hendersonia, The Music of Fletcher Henderson*, 1973)

Spiegle Willcox, Frank Trumbauer, and Bill Rank on trombone (left to right); still from the restored Goldkette film, autumn 1926. (Courtesy of Hans Eekhoff)

Steve Brown, Bix (holding his cornet case), and Don Murray (left to right), leaving the building; still from the restored Goldkette film, autumn 1926. (Courtesy of Hans Eekhoff)

tra. Richardson Turner was there: "Benny Davis sang several wonderful choruses with lively animation—à la Eddie Cantor. Bix swung into three straight choruses after Benny and went crazy. I can state now, if I could turn back the clock to just one moment in Bix's life, I would rather hear that impromptu flight again than anything else I ever heard him do."[24]

On October 12, the Fletcher Henderson Orchestra was back at Roseland for the now legendary confrontation with Jean Goldkette's men. The ballroom management ran an ad in the *New York Daily News* to publicize the encounter: "The Greatest Musical Novelty-Sensation—The 'Battle of the Century'—Welcome Return of Your Favorite Fletcher Henderson and His Orchestra, and the Sensation of Sensations, Jean Goldkette and His Famous 'Fourteen.'" Since 1924, Fletcher Henderson had been regularly billed at Roseland, where his band was a kind of house band.[25] In November 1925, Louis Armstrong had been replaced in the group by Rex Stewart, a brilliant eighteen-year-old cornetist. The band's lineup included many talented jazzmen—Joe Smith, Coleman Hawkins, and clarinetist Buster Bailey among them—and its playing was enhanced by the skillful arrangements of Don Redman.[26] His orchestrations highlighted the soloists' work, and through a subtle play of opposition between the brass and wind sections, generated an irresistible swing. The band's recording of "The Stampede," on May 14, 1926, preserves a faithful example of such performances. Creator of the first *hot* big band of black musicians, Fletcher Henderson deserved better than his nickname, the Colored King of Jazz. Don Redman was absent when the band appeared opposite Goldkette on opening day, and Benny Carter replaced him. Rex Stewart would never forget this first encounter: "We in the Fletcher Henderson band were amazed, angry, morose, and bewildered as we sat on the opposite bandstand waiting our turn to go on, and it was a long wait—about forty-five minutes—because everything this band played prompted calls for encores from the crowd. This proved to be a most humiliating experience for us since, after all, we were supposed to be the world's greatest dance orchestra. . . . The facts were that we simply could not compete with Jean Goldkette's orchestra. Their arrangements were too imaginative and their rhythm too strong."[27] Stories of other witnesses have confirmed Rex Stewart's memories of that night: this "battle" was actually won by the Goldkette's men. Until the day of this concert, Rex Stewart's only idol had been Louis Armstrong, and all his efforts tended to emulate his illustrious model. The discovery of Bix's style would shake up that adoration: "All of a sudden, comes this white boy from out west, playin' stuff all his own. Didn't sound like Louis or anybody else. But just so pretty. And that *tone* he got. Knocked us all out."[28] "I felt very close to Bix," added Rex Stewart, "for we shared the same locker at Roseland, and we would hang out together at the speakeasy in the same building. Many is the time we had our private session in the band room after Broadway had settled down

24. *The Leon Bix Beiderbecke Story,* op. cit., pp. 230–231. If Benny Davis's success seems to have been limited to "Baby Face," things were quite different for Eddie Cantor, who became famous as a result of his appearance in the *Ziegfeld Follies of 1917,* and went on to become a "star of stage, screen, radio, and television" well into the 1950s.

25. Ad published on October 12, 1926, in the *New York Daily News.*

26. Trumpet player Joe Smith was often cited for his possible influence on Bix's playing. Because of his lyrical playing and mellow tone, Smith was in great demand with blues singers, and he recorded many sides with Bessie Smith and Ethel Waters, for whom Bix's interest is well established.

27. Rex Stewart, *Jazz Masters of the '30s* (New York: Da Capo Press, 1972), pp. 11–12.

28. *Bix, Man and Legend,* op. cit., p. 185.

for the evening. . . . In my book Bix was one-in-a-million artist. I doubt if what he played will ever be surpassed on the trumpet."[29]

In 1962—thirty-six years later—pianist Irving Riskin met Don Redman and Benny Carter in Hollywood, and he reminisced with them about those nights at the Roseland Ballroom: "*'Boy, that band was just great,'* said Redman, who had returned on October 13. *'It wasn't just great,'* said Carter, *'it was frightening.'* *'That made me feel,'* concluded Riskin, *'that we must have had a pretty good band.'* "[30]

New York, Tuesday, October 12, 1926

Unfortunately, the recordings cut by the Goldkette Orchestra during those days of October 1926 would not capture this astounding musical quality. The "twelve-piece" band numbered fifteen when it arrived at the New York Victor studios early in the afternoon of October 12. Singer Frank Bessinger would surely have improved the quality of the records by staying home, but the two other musicians added to the band for that session were of an altogether different caliber: their names were Joe Venuti and Eddie Lang.

Both born in Philadelphia, Eddie Lang on October 25, 1902, and Joe Venuti probably on September 16, 1903, the two men had been friends since childhood. They both came from big families that had left Italy at the end of the nineteenth century and settled on the East Coast. Baptized Salvatore Massaro, Eddie Lang was the eighth child born to a couple who emigrated to Philadelphia in 1891. His family included many musicians, playing banjo, mandolin, and guitar—instruments that Eddie's father made as a hobby. A photograph taken in 1915 of the James Campbell School Band shows both Eddie Lang and Joe Venuti playing violin. Venuti would stay with the violin his whole life, but Eddie Lang later took up the banjo for a few years before permanently settling on the guitar. He would soon develop a very personal style that influenced a generation of guitar players. The two men were drastically different characters. Eddie Lang was modest, helpful, and reserved, qualities that—when added to his musical talent—won him the respect and the affection of all his partners. Joe Venuti, on the other hand, was crude and rude, capable of anything—and often achieved the worst. Good taste didn't enter his domain of perception. He always managed to avoid being fired, choosing to escape the difficult situations he had created by breaking his violin over his victim's head and leaving the room cloaked in dignified outrage. Incredibly, this hoodlum played the violin like an angel, and in a recording career that lasted fifty-five years he never failed to extract beauty from the worst musical tripe he had to play. Fortunately, the remarkable professional artistry and the harmony between Joe and Eddie assured the durability of this unlikely duo.

From 1920 to 1923, Eddie Lang was a member of Charles Kerr's band, appearing in restaurants and cabarets in Philadelphia. Joe Venuti's activities during this period

29. *Jazz Masters of the '30s,* op. cit., p. 18.
30. *Bix, Man and Legend,* op. cit., p. 185.

remain uncertain, but it is likely that the two musicians often played together. It was not until 1923, upon the death of his mother, Carmela—a worrying and protective *mamma*—that Eddie Lang became free to leave Philadelphia and head for New York. In August the guitarist was part of the pit orchestra for a musical comedy, *Artists and Models*, and he spent the rest of the year in Al Burt's orchestra at the Blue Bird Dancing—the theater that would be renamed the Arcadia Ballroom. In January 1924, Eddie Lang was back in Philadelphia, where for six months he belonged to the Scranton Sirens, along with the Dorsey brothers, Alfie Evans, and Russ Morgan. On June 14, the ensemble made its debut at the Folies Bergères in Atlantic City. The Beaux Arts Café in the same city offered performances by the Mound City Blue Blowers—Red McKenzie's trio—who had already made three records that year (one with Frank Trumbauer), and was on the road to success. The addition of Eddie Lang enlarged it to a quartet, and the guitarist spent the winter with the group at the Arcadia Ballroom in New York. Joe Venuti had left for Detroit and the Goldkette organization, with which he stayed for eighteen months. Venuti was present in the Victor studio on November 24, 1924, when Eddie King ordered Bix Beiderbecke out of the recording session.

With Eddie Lang on board, the Mound City Blue Blowers sailed to England and, on April 7, 1925, gave their first concert at the Piccadilly Hotel in London.[31] They returned to New York on June 20. The guitarist would remain a member of the quartet until November, when he took a job in his hometown with the band of violinist Val Adley. At the same time, Joe Venuti was engaged in New York in a large orchestra directed by Roger Wolfe Kahn, son of millionaire banker Otto Kahn, which allowed Roger to recruit any musicians he wanted with offers they couldn't refuse. Venuti had not been too difficult to convince. He called upon Eddie Lang for a few gigs, and the guitarist was present on several of the orchestra's recordings made between January and May of 1926.

As Atlantic City was a corrupt, vulgar city, open to gambling and mobsters, it should be no surprise that Joe Venuti was numbered among its regular summer visitors. He was hired in August 1926 by the management of the Silver Slipper, one of the many cabarets operating in the town. On September 7, Venuti and Lang were in New York for the opening of the Playground, with a band that included Red Nichols, Jimmy Dorsey, and drummer Ray Bauduc. Joe and Eddie participated in a second opening a few days later, at the Perroquet de Paris, which featured Roger Wolfe Kahn's orchestra. September 29 would witness a historic event: the two musicians went to the Columbia studios in New York, and recorded the first jazz duet on guitar and violin. The three takes of "Stringin' the Blues" were rejected that day (the two that were mastered were cut on November 8) but the second take of "Black and Blue Bottom" would be released, bringing jazz a fascinating new concept that would lead, eight years later, to the first recordings of Django Reinhardt and Stéphane Grappelli.

The Victor studio called upon these two original and experienced players to enlarge

31. This hotel is today the Méridien Piccadilly.

the Goldkette band on October 12, 1926, which—as it would turn out—was a very good idea. Another good idea would have been to permit the band to record the titles they had the most success with at the Roseland Ballroom. Such, unfortunately, was not the case. Eddie King—again, sadly—was in charge of the sessions on October 12 and 15, and he had selected the numbers to be recorded. He gave the scores to Bill Challis only five days before the studio date. "I showed them to Charlie Horvath and we went directly to King to argue about the selections," explained the arranger. "King wouldn't budge. We thought maybe some song plugger had paid King to do these tunes. They certainly were not representative of our style. I arranged them and we had one rehearsal."[32] Victor's commercial policy was to grant the most promising titles to its two best-selling orchestras: those led by Paul Whiteman and Nat Shilkret. The other bands under contract with the label had to share the leftovers. Eddie King had produced hugely successful records with Paul Whiteman. He made the mistake of seeking to erase the Goldkette Orchestra's main characteristics, trying to cast it in a mold that didn't fit at all. He ignored the astonishing potential of its jazzmen for improvising, and hired singers whose names the band learned for the first time when they arrived at the studio. "This is where Joe and Eddie came in handy," added Bill Challis, "because they could do a quick job of working out those key modulations in and out of the vocals."[33] The Goldkette Orchestra was not allowed to record two of its best numbers: "Baby Face," which had already been recorded by Benny Davis with the Jan Garber Orchestra, and had been a best-seller since September 25, and "Blue Room," recorded by a vocal quartet, the Revelers, and successfully released on October 9.

Victor released two titles from this October 12 session: "Idolizing," of which two takes were kept, and "Hush-A-Bye." The issued sides are nothing but the work of good, industrious professionals. "Idolizing" is a pleasant melody, whose theme is delicately played by Bix, muffling the sound of his cornet by blowing into a hat.[34] Frank Bessinger's vocal interlude is disquieting. It offers one and only one positive element: it allows Eddie Lang to play an astonishing guitar accompaniment, in which chords and arpeggios played on a single string are blended in a very subtle way. Two eight-bar solos by Fred Farrar and Joe Venuti put a proper finish on this side of the record. They are played note by note, strictly following the sheet music—which musicians called a *straight execution*, radically different from a *hot* improvisation. "Hush-A-Bye" is still more insipid: it is a waltz, and Frank Bessinger drowns it in syrup. Lang and Venuti manage, however, to shine for a few seconds, skillfully enlivening the end of the piece.

New York, Friday, October 15, 1926

This was a busy day: seven hours in the recording studio, and four titles kept. It started well. Two takes of "Sunday"—a rather jazzy number—were retained. The

32. *The Leon Bix Beiderbecke Story*, op. cit., p. 231.

33. Warren W. Vaché, *Jazz Gentry, Aristocrats of the Music World* (New Jersey: The Scarecrow Press and Institute of Jazz Studies, 1999), p. 45.

34. "Idolizing" is among the titles analyzed by Frank Murphy in *Musicology Australia*, volume VIII (1985). Murphy compares Bix's solos on the two takes of "Idolizing" to the sheet music of the original tune. He notes that Bix's solos on both takes stay close to the original melody, with the sole innovation being the insertion of a syncopation where none previously existed.

band plays confidently. After a brief intro, Bill Rank takes a cheerful solo, followed by Eddie Lang, who plays a graceful modulation into the vocal by the Keller Sisters and their brother Frank Lynch ... and their thirty-two measure chorus could be from the soundtrack of a Betty Boop cartoon. Bix's solo, originally placed after the vocal, was rewritten as a sixteen-bar passage for three trumpets, which was the only way Challis could think of to introduce a bit of Bixian spirit into the side without having it vetoed by Eddie King, who was expected to be opposed to the very *idea* of a solo played by the cornetist. The chorus by the three trumpets is the highlight of the side, and it is followed by a short, remarkable solo by Don Murray. "Sunday," released in January 1927, would be the only title of this series to take its place among the best-sellers.

Building at 71 West Willis in Detroit that housed the Billinghurst Hotel, present condition. (The frame of the hotel sign is still visible.) (Troy)

The two sides that followed, "Cover Me Up with Sunshine" and "I'd Rather Be the Girl in Your Arms," saw the return of Frank Bessinger, which was hardly good news. The first title is a clear illustration of Bill Challis's talent in enhancing a banal melody, and the second one offers a beautiful duet between Lang and Venuti spirited and imaginative, concluding with a brilliant eight-bar finale by Tram. On the last selection of the day, "Just One More Kiss," the vocal was done by Frank Lynch. This singer was good at just one thing: clear articulation. Eddie Lang supported him as best as he could, but was unable to fend off the musical disaster that resulted. The lack of sales of this record restores one's faith in the public taste. There is an ironic postscript to this series of Goldkette recordings: five days later, Eddie King resigned from Victor, and went to work for Columbia.

BIX ENDED this long session quite frustrated, but he had responded very professionally to the producers' expectations, leading the ensemble parts with authority and precision, and giving his "heart and soul" to music that was in great need of it. His cornet's sound is reproduced here with much higher definition than on any previous record. Bix had been away from the studios for almost two years, during which time the technique of sound reproduction had evolved dramatically. Acoustic recording, with its technical demands and limitations, was history. The possibility of amplifying an electric signal, demonstrated in 1906 by Lee de Forest's invention of the electron tube, combined with the development of the electrostatic microphone by Bell Labs ten years later, paved the way for electrical recording. Musicians could forget the acrobatic arrangements in front of the old horn-shaped receiver, and they were now able to stand before the mike as they would onstage. With this new process, the size of the audio bandwidth that could be reproduced was doubled. In October 1925, the Victor company marketed its Orthophonic phonograph, a machine capable of reproducing the sound of the new electrically recorded discs.

Detroit, November–December 1926

The Goldkette Orchestra's contract with the Roseland Ballroom ended on October 17, and the musicians were back in Detroit on November 5. Bix, Bill Rank, and Don Murray found accommodation at the Billinghurst Hotel, across from the Graystone Ballroom.[35] Don Murray brought to his room an old parlor organ, on which Bix practiced for hours. The Goldkette Orchestra was on the bill at the Graystone Ballroom from November 6 on, alternating with another orchestra—most probably the Orange Blossoms[36]—in order to provide a continuous show from four o'clock in the afternoon until midnight.

Bix took a brief vacation and went home to Davenport on November 8, and the next day, his brother Burnie married Mary Dennison Neelands in Maquoteka, Iowa. Bix stayed for two days with his family and took a train back to Detroit on November 11. The orchestra remained at the Graystone Ballroom until early 1927.

The Graystone Ballroom in Detroit during the 1920s.

35. The four-story building that housed the Billinghurst Hotel is still standing on West Willis, unchanged. It has been converted into apartments.

36. The Orange Blossoms Orchestra was also part of the Goldkette organization. They would change their name to the Casa Loma Orchestra in 1927.

Paul Mertz rejoined the band, replacing Irving Riskin on piano. At the end of November, the Graystone received a visit from Paul Whiteman, whose band was booked for a week at the Michigan Theater. The King of Jazz always offered his audience the combination that had built his reputation: a clever mix of dance numbers, hit songs, and symphonic orchestrations written by Ferde Grofé. Since the summer of 1925, and the addition to the band of trumpeter Teddy Bartell, Paul Whiteman had been introducing some jazzier pieces into his repertoire. This trend continued in 1926 with the hiring of three *hot* musicians: violinist Matty Malneck, sax player Max Farley, and Dixieland-style trombonist Vincent Grande. These musicians would bring a new, and surely *hot,* style of playing to the band. The bandleader was, above all, a businessman, and it is certain that hearing the Goldkette Orchestra influenced Whiteman's future recordings, and would lead him to wonder about the profitability of adding some of Goldkette's jazzmen to his large unit—but this possibility was not yet on his agenda.

While in Detroit, on November 22, Bix attended a performance of *Miss Calico* at the Garrick Theater. Ethel Waters was the star of the show, and she was one of the rare singers to have won the cornetist's unreserved admiration. Her recording of "Dinah," released in January 1926, was highly successful, becoming one of the timeless classics of jazz. Ethel Waters explained in her autobiography, *His Eye Is on the Sparrow*, the secret behind the genesis of her shows: "We had eight girls, seven musicians, two young dancers, two comedians, plus one star—me, in the show. This was for all the southern cities. In the bigger northern cities, we added some girls and two or three extra numbers so that the show would be reasonably long. And we named the shows for all the things we could imagine—not only *Miss Calico*, but *Follies, Scandals, Vanities*—everything that came into our heads."[37]

Several times after a stint at Graystone, at around one o'clock in the morning, Bix and Tram stormed into a cabaret enlivened by Joe Hooven's orchestra. They got onstage and joined the band, to the great surprise of young cornetist Wild Bill Davison: "I always thought that the reason Bix and Trumbauer used to come over and sit in with our band was that they didn't get to play enough jazz in their band; although they had jazz arrangements, and good ones, I don't think he and Trumbauer got enough playing in. They used to come over and play in our band because we went to six in the morning."[38]

A weekly radio broadcast called *The Night of the Waltz*, obviously targeted toward an older audience, aired the Goldkette Orchestra on station WJR in Detroit. All the musicians were on hand to provide the entertainment for the New Year's festivities at the Graystone Ballroom. Bix didn't know that the following year would be his musical apogee.

37. Ethel Waters's autobiography, with Charles Samuel, *His Eye is on the Sparrow* (New York: Doubleday, 1951), p. 249.

38. *Voices of the Jazz Age*, op. cit., p. 75.

CHAPTER 8

1927: "Singin' the Blues," the Consecration

In a complete break with the first twenty years of the century, the Roaring Twenties planted the seed of progress as virtue, with the advent of new economic and cultural phenomena that still, at the start of the twenty-first century, make up the often-contested "values" of our society of leisure and consumption. The parallel is truly disturbing.

In the U.S., the Republican Party's domination and its free-market doctrine created an apparent growth and economic prosperity over the decade. A regular rise in salaries and an even faster increase in the value of stocks and bonds augmented the buying power of the richer part of the population. Business was stimulated by the greater variety of consumer goods available and, for expensive purchases, the development of sales on credit. Advertising was eagerly picked up by radio, cinema, and the press. The dozens of Hearst newspapers and the new tabloids didn't hesitate to make use of scandalous stories to increase their circulation. In addition to juicy stories on government corruption, a new phenomenon appeared: the cult of celebrity. Movie stars—displaying the ideal of the consumer society, and a perfect reflection of the American dream—would share the limelight with unexpected newcomers: sports stars who became living legends, like Babe Ruth or boxer Jack Dempsey[1]; or even adventurers like Charles Lindbergh or Richard E. Byrd, the first pilot to fly over the North Pole.

The social disruptions caused by the First World War had weakened the moral code inherited from America's Pilgrim Fathers; the young woman of the '20s

1. The 1920s saw the invention of sports business: boxing champion Jack Dempsey was offered one million dollars by Universal to make twelve short movies, and Babe Ruth was granted $70,000 annually for the use of his name—at a time when the average American family lived on $2,000 per year.

invented a new persona to match her era: the flapper. Empowered by her recently won right to vote, this rebellious woman declared her independence from parental restrictions. In place of her mother's long flowing tresses, the flapper got a short bob hair cut. She wore a skirt above her knees, painted her lips scarlet, powdered her face perfectly pale, and smoked and drank in public places, adopting characteristics that until then were associated only with "loose" women. The swirls of the Charleston and the "black-bottom" revealed flashes of her underwear, likely to call boys over for a closer look. Closed automobiles offered privacy for shared caresses, a heated flirtation that rarely went all the way—but went far enough. More than one flapper's mother, in recalling her own sheltered youth, must have swooned at the thought of it! Two actresses would represent the image of this modern woman: Louise Brooks, the rebel with an androgynous body and a striking face, and the sweet and spicy Clara Bow, the first sex goddess of the cinema age. Her film *It* opened in New York on February 5, 1927, and she became the personification of the flapper, the young woman for whom Zelda Fitzgerald claimed "the right to try everything, knowing that our existence is intense and ephemeral, and that tomorrow we will die."

The music business received its share of economic grace: 140 million records were sold in the U.S. in 1927, setting a new record; and this was just part of a general euphoria, as music profits were boosted by the technical improvements of electrical recording and the benefit of advertising—in which radio promotion played an essential role. It would, however, be inaccurate to paint a completely sunny picture. These socioeconomic blessings only reached an essentially urban segment of the population. In the late 1920s, more than half of all Americans earned less than $2,000 per year, which placed them below the poverty line. Southern and midwestern farmers had experienced a difficult decade because of the collapse of foreign demand. A reactionary movement attempted to identify the cause of America's problems, and seized on one culprit: the "foreigner." This led to a closed-door policy on immigration, and the growth of racist and xenophobic organizations like the Ku Klux Klan. January 1927 saw the release of the film *Metropolis*, Fritz Lang's prophetic vision of an uncontrolled mechanical universe that was left to drift along aimlessly—possibly something more significant than just innovative special effects displayed in a movie.

New York, January–February 1927

The Goldkette Orchestra remained at the Graystone Ballroom in Detroit until January 21, when they left for New York. They again stayed at the 44th Street Hotel. Their return to the Roseland Ballroom had been organized during their previous visit with the club's manager, Louis Brecker. The band opened on January 24, without Don Murray, who was suffering from a toothache, and whose place was taken by Jimmy Dorsey. Pianist Paul Mertz spent some time in Bix's room, and he held onto a fond memory of those New York nights: "It was one of the greatest events of my life: the salvos of applause and cheering of our performance at Roseland. The place was jammed principally with musicians, often nobody dancing."[2] Fletcher Henderson's orchestra again shared the bill at the Roseland, but Jean Goldkette's men awaited the encounter with confidence this time. This feeling of self-assurance would clearly show in the recordings done between January 28 and February 3, 1927. Four half-days at Victor studios were dedicated to the production of eight sides of varied interest, issued under the name of Jean Goldkette and His Orchestra. Eddie King's absence softened the atmosphere for these four sessions, granting the group more freedom, as much in their tune selection as in the way they could play them.

The Roseland Ballroom, New York, photograph taken in the 1920s. The signs above the double bandstand reveal that one of the two bands was that of Fletcher Henderson, and the other is the Harvey Marburger Orchestra. (From Gene Fernett's *Swing Out*)

New York, Friday, January 28, 1927

The first session was directed by Leroy Shield. Eddie Lang did not figure among the several musicians and, for reasons that remain unknown, his presence on this series is episodic. The first title recorded, "I'm Proud of a Baby Like You," brings back the Keller Sisters and Frank Lynch, sadly unchanged since their appearance on "Sunday" in October 1926. The instrumental accompaniment seems to vanish during the vocal, which makes the outpouring from Bix's cornet on the last note emitted by the trio an astonishing relief. "One moment Bix sounds strong and confident, the next questioning and vulnerable," Randy Sandke noted. "The inner conflicts that tormented him are here transmuted into music of the most exquisite depth and subtlety. The range of emotions that Bix expresses within a solo, or even one phrase is, I think, unique among jazz musicians. It is one reason that his solos sound fresh and alive. There is always a poignancy to Bix's playing as if its beauty is too rare and refined, even too fragile, for this world. We almost held our breath through his solos as we would watching a fawn running loose in the streets of New York."[3]

Victor used a popular song for the second title recorded that morning, "I'm Looking over a Four Leaf Clover," and featured a singer who could not have fit in less with the Goldkette style: Billy Murray. Fifty years old, this artist had made

2. *The Leon Bix Beiderbecke Story*, op. cit., p. 243.
3. *Observing a Genius at Work*, op. cit., p. 16.

his mark in vaudeville before commencing, in 1903, an interminable series of recordings that, for fifteen years, had met with great success. Bill Challis tried to add some color to an insipid melody, but Billy Murray's style was hopelessly outdated in 1927. On the final bars, Bix bravely propels the brass section, brilliantly supported by Steve Brown slapping out a driving beat on his string bass.[4]

New York, Monday, January 31, 1927

The Goldkette men returned to the studio the following week and added six sides to their discography. These three new sessions were under Nat Shilkret's supervision. Formerly a classical clarinetist and a member of the New York Philharmonic, Shilkret was in charge of Victor's "Light Music" from 1915 to 1945, and he himself made a great number of recordings as director of the Victor Orchestra. Seven songs were cut during those three days. The version of "Stampede," a piece by Fletcher Henderson and Don Redman, was unfortunately destroyed, leaving us no possible comparison with the Henderson version. The vocalist present on "Hoosier Sweetheart," Ray Muerer, has justifiably been forgotten. The side gets interesting when, after the vocal, Tram solos over an impatient-sounding punctuation by the brass, which finally take over with another rousing chorus for the three trumpets over Steve Brown's spirited backing. Nat Shilkret's choice for the three instrumental numbers of this series was more inspired. "I'm Gonna Meet My Sweetie Now" highlights a sophisticated and perfectly mastered execution, in which the *hot* soloists in the band alternate with short and inventive interludes.

New York, Tuesday, February 1, 1927

Clarinetist Danny Polo had taken Jimmy Dorsey's place on these next titles, and Eddie Lang's guitar can be heard on "Look at the World and Smile." The Goldkette musicians had insisted on recording "My Pretty Girl," which would turn out to be the best side of the series. Its arrangement had been constructed bit by bit, over the course of many weeks, and it was always a high point in the band's show. The two takes that were kept allow us to hear the group at its peak, and to better understand the high esteem in which it was held. Taken at an extremely fast tempo, the piece opens with a solo by Danny Polo, who re-creates Don Murray's style. The *hot* three-trumpet chorus follows, driven by Steve Brown, whose power and originality carry the band along in an energetic way rarely matched in the jazz of the 1920s. "You know, Steve was even better known to more people at that time than Bix was," Doc Ryker said. "In a way he was the star of the band. At that time all the bands were using tuba. But when they heard Steve they all switched to string bass. None of them could equal him, though—he had a really distinctive style and an uncanny sense of rhythm."[5]

4. Steve Brown starts off at the end of a break played on cornet, and Bix plays this break in a totally different way on the two takes that were kept; his second version is really amazing.

5. Richard Sudhalter, *Bix Beiderbecke, Giants of Jazz*, insert booklet in three-LP set (Time-Life Books Inc., 1979), p. 34.

New York, Thursday, February 3, 1927

A very famous vocal quartet, the Revelers, was featured on the two sides cut that day: "A Lane in Spain" and "Sunny Disposish." Despite the musicians' goodwill, the wonders of Eddie Lang's accompaniment, and an original solo by Joe Venuti, played pizzicato, neither of these two pieces would really take off and go beyond a good level of quality.

With just one exception, this second series of Goldkette records is deceivingly unrepresentative of the band's potential. Victor's commercial goals were, however, being met: released in May 1927, "I'm Looking over a Four Leaf Clover" was listed among the best-sellers, as were in June the issues of "A Lane in Spain" and "Look at the World and Smile." "I'm Gonna Meet My Sweetie Now" would sell well upon its release in September, which makes all the more unaccountable the public's neglect of the other beautiful side of the same record, "My Pretty Girl."[6]

New York, Friday, February 4, 1927

"For some time Bix and I had plans to make some recordings, and here was our chance," wrote Frank Trumbauer in his diary. "Through Red McKenzie, we met Tommy Rockwell, then head of the Okeh Record Company. That was the beginning."[7] The label was an affiliate of the French-German company Odeon, and Rockwell—its musical director—was already the producer of the Chicago recordings of Louis Armstrong and His Hot Five. On February 4, Okeh would add another historic session to its prestigious catalog by inviting to its studios a group of seven musicians, all from the Goldkette band. Frank Trumbauer had called up Bill Rank, Jimmy Dorsey, Paul Mertz, Howdy Quicksell, Chauncey Morehouse, and obviously, Bix Beiderbecke.[8]

The session opened with one of Tram's compositions, "Trumbology," the whole point of which was a long saxophone solo, designed to show off the player's virtuosity. Bix stands by, backing up his friend with admirable restraint. Things went quite differently on the next title, "Clarinet Marmalade," which was carried along by the cornet player at a breathtaking tempo. Bix's precise articulation and his perfectly assured attack are the hallmarks of an outstanding player, which Richard Hadlock pertinently analyzed: "It showed Bix to be one of the most agile horn players on the scene in 1927. Few men could execute such clean, precise, fully formed notes while improvising at this pace, and probably only one or two (Armstrong and Jabbo Smith come to mind) would have been able to conceive original ideas rather than clichés while carrying it off."[9] The cornet player's unique performances should not overshadow the quality of those he recorded with: they were the best jazzmen available on the white side of the color line, as their choruses on "Clarinet Mar-

6. Victor's sales records need to be carefully analyzed. They are given as follows in *The Leon Bix Beiderbecke Story*: 9,353 copies for "I'm Proud of a Baby Like You," 179,929 copies for "I'm Gonna Meet My Sweetie Now" (!), and 38,869 copies for "My Pretty Girl." The Goldkette sides were coupled with a recording by another band on the same record. For instance, "I'm Gonna Meet My Sweetie Now" was coupled on Victor 20765 with Nat Shilkret's "Me and My Shadow," a big hit of the summer of 1927. Also "Hoosier Sweetheart" on Victor 20471 sold 110,995 copies because of another Nat Shilkret hit on the same record, "What Does It Matter."

7. *TRAM, The Frank Trumbauer Story*, op. cit., p. 70.

8. The lack of string bass is surprising, especially considering that Steve Brown was such an important figure on all the Goldkette recordings. Brown's age may explain his absence: he was thirty-seven, and clearly older than the Trumbauer band members, who were all about twenty-four.

9. *Jazz Masters of the '20s*, op. cit., p. 90.

malade" clearly demonstrate.[10] Above all, the sheer pleasure of playing together emanates from this side. "I think you can hear, listening to this, our high spirits that day," confirmed Paul Mertz. "We were happy as hell to be able to play in a freewheeling style, pretty much on our own, the way we wanted, and for Okeh at that."[11]

The last number cut on that day was "Singin' the Blues." It was written by C. Conrad and pianist J. Russel Robinson. This song had been briefly popular toward the end of 1920, and had been recorded several times.[12] Its melody was "introduced" in the middle of "Margie," a record cut by the Original Dixieland Jazz Band in December 1920. Bix and Tram had added "Singin' the Blues" to their repertoire during their stay in Saint Louis in 1926, and their February 1927 version was obviously the outcome of several months of intimate work on the piece. This side revealed a resolutely new approach to jazz music. For historian Frank Powers, "this is the first attempt by a jazz musician to play a ballad at slow tempo, to experiment with the chords of it and to conceive a melodic pair of phrases in the framework of something out of a stomp or a blues tune."[13] Bix's interest in classical music—Claude Debussy's Impressionist compositions or Eastwood Lane's reveries, for instance—may have inspired him to try to play with a moderated tempo. "'Singin' the Blues' may not seem very slow by today's ballad standards," Richard Hadlock pointed out, "but in 1927 it was about as slow as anyone dared to be without strings and *sweet* arrangements."[14]

For this third title, probably recorded during the afternoon session, Bill Rank was replaced on trombone by Miff Mole, and Howdy Quicksell on banjo stepped aside for Eddie Lang on guitar. "Singin' the Blues" is basically made up of two thirty-two-bar solos, successively executed by Tram and Bix, both accompanied by Eddie Lang. It would be more exact to speak of two duets, because the part played by the guitarist is so original and inspired: more than accompanying the two solos, it flows inside them. Max Kaminsky thought that Eddie Lang "was one of the rare two or three musicians with whom Beiderbecke recorded who was equal in musicianship to Bix,"[15] an opinion that is clearly supported by the finesse and the invention of the part played behind Bix's cornet. Tram and Bix's choruses on "Singin' the Blues" would be copied very often, sometimes even note for note. Tram introduces the title's theme with his fluid and relaxed style, remaining, however, within the harmonic and melodic conventions that were then in use. Bix's solo is of a whole different nature. "When a musician hears Bix's solo," wrote Benny Green, "he becomes aware after two bars that the soloist knows exactly what he is doing and that he has an exquisite sense of discord and resolution. He knows also that this player is endowed with the rarest jazz gift of all, a sense of form which lends to an improvised performance a coherence which no amount of teaching can produce. The listening musician, whatever his generation or his style, recognizes Bix as a modern, modernism being not a style but an attitude."[16]

Beyond these technical or harmonic performances, beyond the unquestionable

10. This segregation rule had some rare exceptions, for instance: Jelly Roll Morton's presence in the Gennett studios with the New Orleans Rhythm Kings in July 1923, and Sonny Lee's in the Charlie Creath Orchestra in Saint Louis in November 1925. On May 31, 1927, Eddie Lang started a parallel job, recording race records with clarinettist Wilton Crawley for the Okeh 8000 series, which were aimed exclusively at a black audience.

11. *Bix Beiderbecke, Giants of Jazz*, op. cit., p.34.

12. In 1920, "Singin' the Blues" had been recorded by two singers: Nora Bayes, a Broadway star, and Aileen Stanley, famous for her duets with Billy Murray. Two instrumental versions followed: one by saxophonist Bernie Krueger, and the one cut by the ODJB on December 1, 1920. Bernie Krueger and J. Russel Robinson were in the ODJB band on that date, which explains the "Singin' the Blues" quote in "Margie."

13. Excerpt from the eighth program of *Bix, a Biographical Radio Series*, Miami University Radio, Oxford, op. cit.

14. *Jazz Masters of the '20s*, op. cit., pp. 89–90.

15. *My Life in Jazz*, op. cit., p. 69.

16. Benny Green, *The Reluctant Art, Five Studies in the Growth of Jazz*, (New York: Da Capo Press, 1991), p. 34.

novelty of the form, the dominating perception upon hearing this solo is that of an extremely touching voice, intimate, reserved, and shadowed with a touch of delicate melancholy. This mood of the song, which aims for the heart, was clearly sensed by French jazz critic Lucien Malson, who wrote in *Jazz Hot* in December 1956, "Bix has a light gait. At a time when those capable of expressing swing are few, he does it wonderfully. This inexpressible wave permeates his music, as it does Armstrong's or Bechet's. He outclasses by far most of his contemporaries. At the same time, Bix creates something new in jazz: a feeling of relaxation. In his way of swinging, one can undoubtedly see the foundation of a style which—through Trumbauer—Lester Young would adopt ten years later. But this is not all. Bix's sound—dull, in the sense that gold is dull, round and polished, totally different from Armstrong's—foreshadows to some extent the aesthetics of 'cool.' Red Nichols, Bobby Hackett tried in vain to capture the tone of Bix's cornet. There is a Bixian sweetness that can't be imitated, a moon glow that can't be reproduced."[17]

Bix's sound is captured remarkably well by Okeh, and three takes of "Singin' the Blues" were cut. Paul Mertz remembered that, for the first take, all the musicians wanted to solo, bringing the length of the recording beyond the three-minute limit. The master of the second cut was rejected, and the variations Bix might have played around this theme remain unknown. Backed with "Clarinet Marmalade," the third take of "Singin' the Blues" was released in June 1927 as Okeh 40772, and it remained a best-seller for several weeks. Its impact on jazz musicians was enormous. "After that, you couldn't go anywhere in New York without hearing some guy trying to play like Bix," said Chauncey Morehouse. "They copied his tone, his attack, his figures. Some guys tried to take his stuff right off the records. Others just came and listened."[18] In his autobiography, Max Kaminsky would confess that the desire to possess this record had led him to steal it from a friend, who had previously refused to let it go.

Fletcher Henderson acknowledged the perfection of this work when his orchestra recorded it in October 1931. The saxophone section faithfully reproduced Tram's chorus, before Rex Stewart paid a tribute to Bix's creation. "Admiring Bix as I did, it was not difficult for me to attempt to copy his memorable solo on 'Singin' the Blues,'" wrote the trumpeter, "especially since the phonograph company for which Fletcher recorded the number wanted my solo as close to the original as possible."[19]

Louis Armstrong, for his part, always refused to record this title, judging Bix's version unbeatable. "Now that's a classic," Louis Armstrong clarified several weeks before he passed away. "They ain't nobody else could play it like he did. They tried . . . all them little beautiful notes that came out of that horn. But it's the way he played it. It's just an ordinary tune . . . anybody can play it! But the way he played it, and phrased it with his tone, and you know, phrasing is the greatest thing in the world . . . don't care what instrument you're playing . . . or singing . . . you know

17. Lucien Malson, *Les Sillons de l'Histoire (IV): Singin' the Blues*, in *Jazz Hot*, no. 116 (December 1956).

18. Jerry Kline, "Chauncey Morehouse," in *The Mississippi Rag* (May 1980). One characteristic of Bix's playing was this *rip* note, flaring up to a higher note, a technique often copied by his emulators. Bix's first recorded use of the rip is on "Proud of a Baby Like You" (master take), and he uses it twice on "Singin' the Blues," in his solo, following the break, and at the end of the side.

19. *Jazz Masters of the '30s*, op. cit., p. 18.

what I mean there. And his technique is still outstanding. Ain't nobody else ever cope with it. . . . They tried, but ain't none of them play like him yet."[20]

Tram's solo was also emulated often, and almost every New York saxophonist owned a copy of the disc, trying to reproduce that chorus. After at first being fascinated by the young Coleman Hawkins, Lester Young fell under the spell of Frank Trumbauer's "little music": "Trumbauer was my idol," said Lester Young. "When I just started to play, I used to buy all his records. I imagine I can still play all those solos off the records. He played the C-melody saxophone. I tried to get the sound of a C-melody on the tenor. That's why I don't sound like other people. Trumbauer always told a little story and I liked the way he slurred the notes. He'd play the melody first and then, after that, he'd play around the melody."[21]

Detroit, February 11–April 10, 1927

The Jean Goldkette Orchestra ended its stay at the Roseland Ballroom on February 6. The band spent two days at the Butterfly Ballroom in Springfield, Massachusetts, where their appearance was a complete failure, and they returned to Detroit on February 11. They played at the University of Michigan, Ann Arbor, where they again met Fletcher Henderson's band and crossed paths with a group just starting what would be a long successful career: Guy Lombardo's dance band, which had also made its first records in 1924 at the Gennett Studios in Richmond.

Jean Goldkette brought his men back to the Graystone Ballroom in Detroit. Don Murray returned at the end of February, and Paul Mertz left the orchestra to join Fred Waring's Pennsylvanians. He was temporarily replaced on piano by Marlin Skiles: "I was always startled at how quickly Bix would master the third trumpet part," related the new pianist. "He was not a music reader, but it would take only three or four rehearsals, during which time he would sort of feel his way through the part, until he would be playing right along with the rest of the section much as if he were able to read."[22] In March, Tram decided to give up his leadership of the orchestra, and Eddy Sheasby, a violinist who started with Goldkette at the beginning of the year, took over. Irving Riskin replaced the ephemeral Marlin Skiles, and at the Graystone Ballroom on April 10, the Goldkette Orchestra gave a farewell concert, during which they played George Gershwin's *Rhapsody in Blue*. A new tour was about to begin.

From Ohio to the East Coast, April 10–May 28, 1927

The band played in Dayton, Ohio, for the General Motors Convention, then moved on to Columbus, Ohio, and Terre Haute, Indiana. Indiana University in-

20. Excerpt from the first program of *Bix, a Biographical Radio Series*, op. cit.

21. Nat Hentoff, "Pres," in *Down Beat* (March 7, 1956), pp. 9–11, and *A Lester Young Reader,* edited by Lewis Porter (Washington, DC: Smithsonian Institution Press, 1991), pp. 158–159.

22. *The Leon Bix Beiderbecke Story,* op. cit., p. 252.

vited the musicians to play at the junior prom on April 22. Back in Bloomington, Bix revisited the old familiar places and was greeted as always by an enthusiastic crowd, led by his exuberant friend Hoagy Carmichael. "What a screwy person he was," said Doc Ryker, "and he had all those kids in the school copying the things he did. They were all crazy down there."[23] The band then moved on to Pennsylvania. At Penn State University on April 29, the students preferred the clowning of Jan Garber's band to the classier executions of the Goldkette group, but the shows in Reading and Allentown over the next few days were more warmly applauded.

Camden, Friday, May 6, 1927

The Goldkette Orchestra took advantage of the proximity of the Victor studios to record an instrumental piece arranged by Bill Challis, "Slow River." Neglected by critics, the two takes that were kept managed to capture the band in its best moments. The first take kept is of particular interest—although Victor originally issued the second one. It carries a short Bix solo, impressive in its construction, an excellent chorus by Frank Trumbauer, and a swinging ending in which Bix is prominent.[24]

New York, Monday, May 9, 1927

One last stop in Scranton, home of the Sirens, and the band headed for New York, where they arrived on May 8, 1927. A modified version of the Frank Trumbauer Orchestra visited the Okeh studios the following day: Irving Riskin was on piano, Don Murray was sitting next to Bix, with Doc Ryker on alto saxophone added to the reed section. The two titles for that session were selected by Bix. As might be expected, his taste led him to a standard of the New Orleans repertoire, "Ostrich Walk," which had been recorded by the Original Dixieland Jazz Band for Victor in 1918. Its orchestration was written quickly, as Bill Challis recalled: "We got that done pretty much in one night, and it turned out well. Bix liked the result, and so did the guys. I didn't even know the tune 'Ostrich Walk.' So Bix sat down and played it over first, on the piano. . . . He was the best, as far as I was concerned. He played everything, and what struck me was the way he played it—would be the way he wanted voices for the instruments . . . he had the whole introduction coming right out of his fingers, as he played it."[25] Bix flies over the side recorded on that day, and he fills in for the lack of string bass by carrying the ensemble along with an irresistible drive. The introduction he conceived is interspersed with several breaks and is followed by a chorus written for the three saxes. Bix's solo, constructed over sixteen bars, is intensely radiant, and it ends up on a phrase played softly—the musical equivalent of a smile.

23. *Bix, Man and Legend,* op. cit., p. 201.

24. The two takes of "Slow River" were analyzed by Frank Murphy in *Musicology Australia,* op. cit., pp. 29–30, who wrote that "the relationship of Beiderbecke's solo on *take 2* to the original melody is much more distant that might have been expected," and that "given the extent of the divergence from the original melody of Bix's solo on *take 2,* it is hardly surprising that his solo on *take 4* should reveal very little influence of the popular song at all."

25. Eighth program of *Bix, a Biographical Radio Series,* op. cit.

The band carries on with the same energy on "Riverboat Shuffle," the Hoagy Carmichael composition first cut by the Wolverines in Richmond in May 1924, exactly three years earlier. Eddie Lang livens up a somewhat hurried introduction with remarkable breaks, leading up to a dazzling thirty-measure cornet solo. In a departure from the usual practice of the time, Bix often started his solos on a strong high note and, from that opening, created a line descending both melodically and dynamically. Compared with the Wolverines' recording of "Riverboat Shuffle," this 1927 cut clearly demonstrates how far Bix had traveled in three years: in just over thirty seconds, he displays an astonishing palette of nuances and feelings, from the most vibrant colors to the tenderest reflection, while maintaining a pure sound and a faultless attack. Don Murray gracefully glides over thirty bars, before Bix flares to a high C—an unusual note for him—which begins the coda of the piece.

At the end of this day of recording in New York, the musicians rejoined the rest of the Goldkette Orchestra and performed at the Ritz Ballroom in Bridgeport, Connecticut. Clarinetist Artie Shaw was then seventeen, and he had traveled many hours to finally hear the creators of his favorite records. "And I stood in front of that band open-mouthed," confessed the musician.[26]

THE YEAR 1927 was a very fertile period for jazz music. Seemingly, Eddie Lang hardly left the studios, where he accompanied an astounding number of singers: he joined Red Nichols, Jimmy Dorsey, Miff Mole, and Vic Berton on some sessions released under the name of the Five Pennies; he recorded his first guitar solos; and he created historic duets with Joe Venuti. With "Doin' Things," the two partners added a remarkable work to the Okeh catalog on May 4, a boldly melodic and harmonic construction peppered with amazing innovations.[27] In Chicago, Louis Armstrong continued to record for the Okeh label. After "Muskrat Ramble" in July 1926, a second Hot Five number, "Big Butter and Egg Man," cut in November 1926, would feature a masterly solo by Louis, with the same artistic excellence and perfect construction that Bix Beiderbecke brought to his recordings during the first months of 1927.

Louis Armstrong was also going through a period of intense activity. With his Hot Seven—which included brothers Johnny and Baby Dodds—he cut eleven titles in five sessions in May, at the Chicago Okeh studios. Louis seeks his limits on these effervescent sides: he takes all the risks, stretching his solos out, extending his register from warm lower notes to a striking high C, doubling the tempo on his breaks. His stop chorus on "Potato Head Blues" is a wonderful achievement, a breathless solo that, until its unpredictable conclusion, keeps the listener in a highly emotional state of uncertainty. This exuberant musical approach was quite different from that of Bix, a more introverted player who avoided overly demonstrative displays and found his most personal expression in the middle register, the voice of confidence and implied emotions.

It was at the beginning of 1927 that pianist Jelly Roll Morton finally achieved

26. *Voices of the Jazz Age,* op. cit., p. 76.

27. . . . like a recurring phrase based on Debussy's *The Maid with the Flaxen Hair.*

well-deserved commercial recognition. Three sessions recorded in Chicago in September and December 1926 by his Red Hot Peppers would result in what may be considered both the New Orleans style's brightest development and its swan song. "Black Bottom Stomp," one of Jelly Roll Morton's most beautiful compositions, and a best-seller for him, revealed a virtuoso demonstration of Morton's imagination. This first success would be followed by two more from the December 1926 session, "Original Jelly Roll Blues" and "Grandpa's Spells," two perfect gems on which Morton manages, with a group of seven musicians, to build up a surprisingly high number of distinct orchestral combinations.

If these recordings brilliantly showcased the end of an era, Duke Ellington's first success announced the future of jazz. Three different cuts of "East St. Louis Toodle-Oo" were recorded in New York between November 1926 and March 1927, and the version Columbia released under the name of the Washingtonians would rank among the hits of July 1927. Trumpeter Bubber Miley's sound was the dominant element on this side. Bubber was the same age as Bix, and his use of various types of mutes forged a style made up of unexpected tones, such as growls and wa-wa inflections, characteristics of Ellington's "jungle" period. This intense playing, often violent, was—like Armstrong's—quite unlike the white cornetist's more nuanced touch. Bubber Miley did, however, share Bix's strong taste for alcohol, and he would only survive Beiderbecke by several months, dying in 1932 at the age of twenty-nine.

This exceptional blossoming of high quality jazz music over such a short period, and the commercial successes of some of these records, shouldn't leave the impression that the American public had drastically changed its taste. *Sweet* music, soothing little songs, and syrupy dance bands still held the top of the bill and brought the major labels their most profitable sales. The first months of 1927 saw the release of Paul Whiteman's "In a Little Spanish Town," Ted Lewis's "Some of These Days," Ben Bernie's "Ain't She Sweet"—and the number of copies sold of these titles relegated the jazz and *hot* music records to obscurity. Several versions of "I'm Looking over a Four-Leaf Clover" were published in 1927. The public's favorites were those recorded by Nick Lucas and Ben Bernie, the Goldkette version coming in a distant third.

New York, Friday, May 13, 1927

Frank Trumbauer brought the same group that had accompanied him five days earlier back to the Okeh studios. The three titles selected for this third recording ses-

1927: "Singin' the Blues," the Consecration 🎺 143

Union Square West at the corner of 14th Street. After April 1, 1927, the Okeh studios were located on top floor of 11 Union Square. "The Okeh recording laboratory is moving to new and larger quarters on April 1, in the old Tiffany Building at 14th Street and Union Square" (*The Talking Machine World*, April 1927). (Information from Allan Sutton and James Kidd; photo JPL, 2005)

sion of the Frank Trumbauer Orchestra would essentially be the work of a trio, so preeminent were Bix, Tram, and Eddie Lang. "I'm Coming Virginia," sung by Ethel Waters, had given Columbia a new successful record when it was issued in February 1927. Bix's interest in the singer had drawn him to the haunting song he used to open this session: a ballad, whose form and quality had similarities with "Singin' the Blues." Eddie Lang is ever-present on the side, weaving a remarkable accompaniment. Tram's sixteen-bar solo on the verse leads to the shining first bell-like notes struck by Bix. The cornetist recorded his longest solo on this title, a part that continues, without stopping, through to the quiet reprise of the ensemble. On this lyrical side, Bix left us one of his most personal and intense works, played in an unusually high register for him, which gives this execution a strong emotional power.

The second number of the session, "Way Down Yonder in New Orleans," a standard from the early '20s, is played at a rather slow tempo. Bix and Tram's choruses are once again the heart of the side, the saxophonist spreading out an elegant melodic line over twenty bars—whose impact on the young Lester Young is easy to imagine. Bix seems less inspired: his solo is skillful, but it sounds made up of already worked-out and proven elements, things the player could comfortably rely on. On this piece he blew a high C-sharp, the highest note he ever recorded—a technical feat that was not really important to him.

Three musicians, Bix, Tram, and Eddie Lang, remained in the studio for the last side recorded that day, "For No Reason at All in C," an improvisation based on the chord progression of "I'd Climb the Highest Mountain," a 1926 hit for Al Jolson. This "melodic diversion" would become a common practice during the bebop era—with Charlie Parker, for example—but in 1927 it was still a major innovation. Tram is at his best on this important recording, which marked the beginning of a new form of jazz destined to be widely exploited in the near future: "chamber jazz," a domain where a warm and intimate approach would be favored. Harmonically, Bix seems more at ease on piano than on his 1924 recording of "Big Boy"; he shows, however, a lack of experience as an accompanist, and his playing seems to hinder rather than help Eddie Lang in the progression of his solo. At the coda, Bix steps away from the piano, picks up his cornet and blows a two-bar phrase of astounding beauty and clarity.

"Singin' the Blues," "I'm Coming Virginia," and "For No Reason at All in C" represent, at this stage in history, the most significant contribution that white musicians had added to the black music of jazz, already rich with multiple influences. Bix's voice was unique, gracious, and delicate. It could sparkle with luminous accents and, one second later, be veiled with a mist of melancholy. The cornetist was the creator of an original style, and his influence could be detected, many years later, in the music played by Lester Young and Miles Davis.

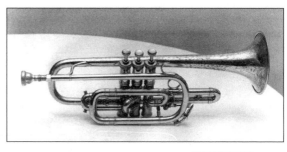

Vincent Bach cornet, Stradivarius model, number 620, bought by Bix in New York around May 1927. (Duncan Schiedt Collection)

While in New York, Bix bought two cornets at a store on West 48th Street owned by Vincent Bach's brother, Hans Bach. One of the two instruments was the "deluxe, gold-plated, elegantly engraved" model Bach Stradivarius, number 620, which today is in the collection of the Davenport Putnam Museum.[28]

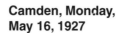

The Jean Goldkette Orchestra on tour, April–May 1927. Left to right, seated: Don Murray, Frank Trumbauer, Ray Lodwig, Bill Rank, Bix, Chauncey Morehouse, Eddy Sheasby; standing: unknown, Fred Farrar, Howdy Quicksell, Steve Brown, Irving Riskin, Spiegle Willcox, unknown, Doc Ryker. (Duncan Schiedt Collection)

Camden, Monday, May 16, 1927

The Goldkette Orchestra left New York that morning, and on the way to Philadelphia, stopped at the Victor studios in Camden, New Jersey. The musicians were worn out from their New York nights, and Bix's physical condition was

28. The two cornets purchased by Bix bore serial numbers 616 and 620, as confirmed by the shop cards of Hans Bach's store. Both cornets were large bore instruments (0.462"). These cards contain all the information available from the manufacturer. The dates "February 17, 1927" for 616 and "February 1927" on the card for 620, are the dates on which the instruments were completed in the factory, and not the time they were sold to Bix. The Goldkette band was in Detroit on February 17, and Bix was not likely to take a three-day round trip and miss work just to pick up a horn. Information about the cornets comes in a letter from Roy Hempley who has made an intensive study of the Bach Stradivarius line. He adds an intriguing bit of information: "The *Deluxe, goldplated, engraved* finish used on cornet #620 was called Finish #5." Mr. Hempley's research indicates that "an instrument in this finish cost $210, compared to the cost of a non-engraved instrument in raw brass at $125. It's possible that it cost more to have Bix's name added." (Thanks to Michael Heckman for pointing out this question.)

Bix and Ernest "Red" Ingle at Castle Farm in Cincinnati, June 1927. (Indiana University Collection)

particularly ravaged. He had stayed up late, drank a lot, and was exhausted. "I don't like to talk anything bad about him," explained Spiegle Willcox, "but he couldn't make it. He'd fluff the notes a little bit. Maybe history will tell you if there was anything produced that day, maybe there was, but he couldn't play."[29] The studio was set up in an old building that had previously been the Trinity Baptist Church, and—as in Richmond—long draperies lined the walls to improve the recording acoustics. Bix sat with the band for the first recorded title, "Lily," and his inability to keep time spoiled four successive takes. He left his chair at the start of the following number, "In My Merry Oldsmobile," whose swirling waltz rhythm quickly got the better of his sick stomach, and he went to sleep behind the dusty wall coverings until the end of the session.

Camden, Monday, May 23, 1927

At the end of a week of shows in the Philadelphia region, during which Charles Lindbergh made his historic first solo flight across the Atlantic, the orchestra returned to Camden and cut a more lively version of "In My Merry Oldsmobile." Bix was in great form, and—over a hopelessly old-fashioned tune—he added a fascinating countermelody to the ensemble part.[30] The disc, sponsored by General Motors, would be distributed by the car manufacturer to the participants at its annual convention.

29. Russ Tarby, "Spiegle Willcox: The Sweet Man," in *Syracuse New Times*, 1998.

30. In a station WKCR broadcast, Phil Schaap said he had noticed that Bix's entry after the vocal was delayed by four bars. The vocal is sung by four men: a leader and a trio. The names of Doc Ryker, Howdy Quicksell, and Ray Lodwig are generally accepted. One singer would therefore be missing: could it be the "late" Bix? (Information from Albert Haim.)

Shot of Bix taken in summer 1927 "outside a spot the Goldkette band played on the shores of Lake Erie at Fremont, Ohio." Photo published in the December 1, 1939, issue of *Downbeat*. (Courtesy of the Rutgers Institute of Jazz Studies)

Cincinnati, May 29–July 1, 1927

Their next engagement led the musicians to Cincinnati, where they appeared for more than a month at A. J. "Toots" Marshall's Castle Farm.[31] The audience response was enthusiastic, and their stay was extended until the end of June. The orchestra had been asked to back the show of a trio of French performers, stranded in Ohio and unable to speak English. Every evening, at the end of their act, the three Europeans indicated clearly through angry voices and agitated gestures their strong criticism of the music they had to perform with. But the band never understood what they were being reproached for, or what it was they were expected to do. The days were luxuriously long, with lazy warm afternoons stretching out in the heat of the summer before the nightly show. Bix had found an old gramophone, and repeatedly played a record of Rimski-Korsakov's *Scheherazade*, fascinated by the masterly orchestration and the diversity of its musical colorations. On Thursday, June 30, the Goldkette Orchestra was invited to play at the opening-night ball at the Mansfield-Leland Hotel in Mansfield, Ohio. The hotel manager, Edward Darvill, was a personal friend of Jean Goldkette's. On the following morning, the band left for Saint Louis, where they were on the bill at Loew's State Theater for a week.

Don Murray, Bix (on the floor). and Howdy Quicksell (on the stuffed horse) at Forest Highlands Park in Saint Louis, July 1927. (Duncan Schiedt Collection)

Saint Louis, July 2–8, 1927

Upon their arrival just a few hours before the show, they realized that Eddy Sheasby was missing. The musical director hadn't followed on to Saint Louis, and the large trunk containing all the orchestra's scores was with him. Frank Trumbauer was asked to quickly assemble a new program, made up of several old and easy numbers, known to all the musicians, while Jean Goldkette shortened the rest of the tour. Bix again met up with Ruth Shaffner, a regular spectator at Loew's Theater during those days. The young lovers shared a few nights, a few memories—they wouldn't see each other again for another two years.

Detroit, July–August 1927

Where the orchestra might have appeared for the four weeks that followed is not precisely known. Edward Darvill's business connections might have brought

31. The Castle Farm ballroom opened in the autumn of 1924 on Summit Road, in Cincinnati's northern suburbs. It was directed by Toots Marshall. The building was torn down during the 1970s. (Information from Frank Powers.)

Goldkette a few jobs in Ohio, as the band was announced at the Coliseum in Marion by mid-July, and at about that time Red Ingle took a photograph of Bix at Fremont, on the shores of Lake Erie, where Ingle remembered the band playing. The Goldkette men were back to their Detroit headquarters for the second part of the month, and Eddy Sheasby's return—he had fled in an attempt to escape divorce proceedings—brought back the long-awaited arrangements. This period was confusing and inactive. It weighed heavily on the Goldkette organization's finances, already weakened by the deficit accumulated by such a big orchestra, very costly in salaries and rooming expenses. Because of much lower operating costs, the three other Goldkette bands remained profitable: the McKinney's Cotton Pickers were booked for the summer at Island Lake, the Orange Blossom Orchestra—henceforth known as the Casa Loma—played at the Edgewater Park Ballroom, and a third group of musicians enlivened the evenings at the Book-Cadillac Hotel. Jean Goldkette was finally able to obtain a four-week contract for Bix's group at Young's Million Dollar Pier in Atlantic City. Their first appearance was set for August 8. Francis "Cork" O'Keefe, who had assisted Goldkette in booking the band, asked Bill Challis and Bix to drive his Jordan automobile to Atlantic City. Bill Challis wanted to put the car on a ferry boat in Detroit, and to head for Buffalo on the afternoon of August 5. But the boat left the dock long before Bix's arrival. "Finally, he came around, late," remembered Challis. "We couldn't get on the boat. He told me, 'Somebody rolled me for my money.' He had to go back to the office and get another check. We were all paid so we'd have the money to go to Atlantic City."[32]

Bix and Don Murray, Boardwalk,
Atlantic City, August 1927.
(Duncan Schiedt Collection)

Atlantic City, August–September 1927

They managed to catch another ferry leaving for Cleveland, where they arrived on the morning of August 6. Bill Challis drove, and Bix immersed himself in a book until they stopped for the night in Harrisburg. He remained sober throughout the journey, to his driver's great surprise: "The following morning we left and went the rest of the way," added Bill Challis. "Two guys driving to Atlantic City . . . and he made it! I think the guys thought that I'd have to take care of him, that he'd be drunk. . . . We were buddies. We got along well. We would have gotten along a whole lot better, but he could drink."[33]

The Goldkette Orchestra performed in Atlantic City from August 8 through September 5. At the same time, Paul Whiteman's men kept up a busy schedule, with shows in Philadelphia and a series of recordings at the Victor Studio, across the river

32. Chip Deffaa, "Bill Challis:
The Goldkette Years," in *The
Mississippi Rag* (December
1988), p. 4.

33. "Bill Challis: The Goldkette
Years," op. cit., p. 4.

in Camden. His orchestra had been significantly modified since its stay in Detroit in November 1926, one of the most remarkable events being the addition to the group the following month of a singer destined for a dazzling career: Bing Crosby.

Bix and Harry "Bing" Crosby had similar origins, and they had followed very similar paths. They were less than two months apart in age, and Bing had also grown up in a middle-class American family, with distant Irish roots. The Crosbys were, in 1850, among the first Americans to "emigrate" by sea—from New York around Cape Horn to Portland, reaching what would become in 1889 the state of Washington, next to the Canadian border. Bing's parents settled in Spokane in 1906. Their boy would stay in school longer than Bix did, but he did not earn any more diplomas. Bing Crosby would always acknowledge the virtues of the teachings of the Jesuits at Gonzaga University—his

Bing Crosby in Spokane, around 1925.

mother was Catholic and very religious—but the increasing amount of time he dedicated to his musical activities led him to quit the college in 1924, before getting a law degree. His friendship with pianist Al Rinker, and his presence in 1923 in a new band, the Musicaladers, inspired a new passion—to become a jazz singer. Russ Bailey's record shop was the "classroom" that he frequented most. Before buying a disc, Bing and Al Rinker would listen endlessly to twenty or thirty more, learning some by heart to build up their repertoire.

The two musicians formed a duet that appeared for several months at the Clemmer Theater in Spokane. They left for Los Angeles in October 1925 in an old Model T. Mildred Bailey, Al Rinker's sister, worked as a singer in a speakeasy just outside Hollywood, and she was helpful in getting the two boys hired for a thirteen-week tour with a vaudeville revue, *The Syncopation Idea*. The quality of their act would quickly be noticed, and they became part of Will Morrissey's *Music Hall Revue*. In October 1926, Paul Whiteman, then appearing at the Million Dollar Theater in Los Angeles, heard about the duo. He invited the two men to join his orchestra at a weekly salary of $150 each—an offer they couldn't, and didn't, refuse.

Bing Crosby and Al Rinker had their debut with the Whiteman Orchestra on December 6, 1926, at the Tivoli Theater in Chicago. On December 22, they made their first recording with the band, "Wistful and Blue." Their vocal on this side ends with a few bars of scat singing, a technique that appeared on record on Louis Armstrong's "Heebie Jeebies." This uninhibited vocal style was popular with the flappers, but when two handsome, elegantly dressed young men appeared onstage to indulge in some scat singing, their enthusiasm knew no bounds. Paul Whiteman now had two groups of vocalists at hand: a *sweet* trio, formed by Jack Fulton, Charles Gaylord, and

Austin Young, and a *hot* duo formed of his two newcomers. Al Rinker and Bing Crosby were, however, seriously disillusioned when, in January 1927, their act in Paul Whiteman's show at the Paramount Theater in New York was a complete failure. The reason for this fiasco was the result of the lack of electronic amplification in this vast concert hall; Bing Crosby's baritone voice was pretty, but weak. The singer would quickly make the microphone his true instrument and his trusty ally in his success.

The solution to the problem came from violinist Matty Malneck. He completed the duo with a third singer, the impetuous Harry Barris, and the result was magical. The Rhythm Boys were born. The complementary nature of the players in this new trio, the novelty of their natural, jazz-inflected vocal style, and the multitalented orchestra that was backing them helped Paul Whiteman secure his status at the top of American popular music. The first recording featuring the Rhythm Boys is "Side by Side," made in April 29 and released in June. It was very well received, and this side clearly emphasizes the *hot* evolution of a part of Paul Whiteman's repertoire.

The bandleader's success would always rest on his ability to offer to a varied audience a wide range of musical styles, each skillfully played. He therefore had to be surrounded by the best available musicians. As Bix Beiderbecke was under contract to Goldkette, Paul Whiteman approached Red Nichols. The cornet player had become omnipresent on the New York scene and in recording studios, and his reputation was growing. The offer made to Red extended to the other members of his Five Pennies—Miff Mole, Jimmy Dorsey, Arthur Schutt, Eddie Lang, and Vic Berton—but only Jimmy Dorsey and Vic Berton followed Red on April 18 to join the King of Jazz. The Whiteman records made on April 29 show the band with a new Goldkette-like sparkle. Vic Berton's stay in the Whiteman orchestra only lasted a few days, and

Red Nichols left at the end of May. Paul Whiteman was aware of Jean Goldkette's financial problems, and his search for new *hot* musicians led him to Atlantic City in the middle of August. He met the Goldkette Orchestra players and invited them to a party at Vince Martini's, a speakeasy where alcoholic beverages were readily available. He tried long and hard to convince Frank Trumbauer to join him, knowing that Bix and the others would follow the saxophonist, but Tram resolved to stay with Goldkette.

Photograph of Bix taken by Irving Riskin in Atlantic City, August 1927.

New York, August 23 and 25, 1927

On Tuesday, August 23, the Goldkette Orchestra arrived in New York for a three-day stay. They rehearsed several numbers in the Victor studios at Liederkranz Hall[34], but no takes were kept. Two days later, Frank Trumbauer brought his band together at Okeh, and three new titles were cut. The results were uneven, and none of the numbers would be fully convincing. "Three Blind Mice" was a pleasant composition by drummer Chauncey Morehouse, arranged by Bill Challis. The addition to the group of bass saxophonist Adrian Rollini, from the California Ramblers, supplied the foundation that the first Frank Trumbauer Orchestra recordings were lacking. Rollini's solo on the side emphasizes the player's amazing skill on his impossible instrument. Though it starts off well, Bix's chorus ends with a surprising silence, most probably caused by a lack of control of his breath; Eddie Lang follows with a harmonious but slightly stiff solo.

Bix was never a reliable accompanist, and his muted counterpoint on "Blue River" deliberately ignores Seger Ellis's vocal part, showing little respect for its progression or its pauses. It's difficult, however, to criticize the ill treatment of this insipid singer, as it was fully warranted. Bix was

Liederkranz Hall in New York at the beginning of the twentieth century. (Bernhard H. Behncke)

34. Liederkranz Hall was located at 111 East 58th Street, between Park and Lexington avenues. The place was famous for many historical recordings, of both classical and popular music (Frank Sinatra, Peggy Lee, etc.). The building was torn down in the 1950s.

Liederkranz Hall's interior
ballroom, which was later
converted into a recording
studio. (James Kidd).

Liederkranz Hall in New York,
around 1890. (James Kidd)

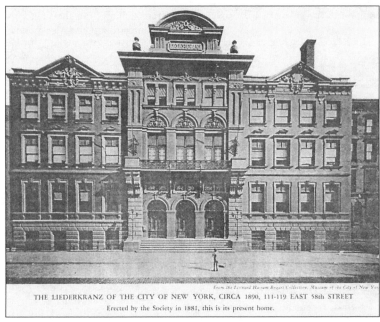

THE LIEDERKRANZ OF THE CITY OF NEW YORK, CIRCA 1890, 111-119 EAST 58th STREET
Erected by the Society in 1881, this is its present home.

152 1927: "Singin' the Blues," the Consecration

always, on the other hand, a remarkable leader, and this nice
tune inspires, at the end of the
side, a beautiful moment, both
emotional and radiant. The
third title of the session, "There's
a Cradle in Caroline," a song
with incomprehensible lyrics,
merits only derogatory comments; but because it sold well in
December 1927, its many buyers
were able to also hear "Blue
River," the other side of Okeh
record 40879.

New York, Thursday, September 1927

Leaving Atlantic City on September 6, the members of the Goldkette Orchestra
reached a new time of uncertainty. They could count on a third and last engagement at the Roseland Ballroom, from September 8 through 18, but their future beyond this contract seemed rather dark. The first to succumb to the siren song was
Bill Challis, who left Goldkette on August 28 and joined the large musical team
surrounding Paul Whiteman.

Members of the Jean Goldkette Orchestra autographed this picture after their final Roseland Ballroom performance, on September 18, 1927. Left to right, front row: Ray Lodwig, Fred Farrar, Bix, Chauncey Morehouse, Don Murray, Frank Trumbauer, Doc Ryker, Spiegle Willcox, Bill Rank; back row: Irving Riskin, Steve Brown, Howdy Quicksell. The photograph was taken several months earlier, as Spiegle Willcox had left the band on May 23, 1927, replaced by Lloyd Turner. (Duncan Schiedt Collection)

"Back in St. Louis, Bix used to play a piano solo for me and I suggested that he
record it on one of our dates," wrote Frank Trumbauer. "He just laughed and said
it wasn't good enough, but I was determined to get it on record, somehow, if only
for my own collection."[35] Bix fulfilled his friend's wish on September 8, when he sat
down in front of one of the pianos at Okeh studios. His playing on the first take
was too short, the next exceeded the record's limits, and Bix was ready to give up.
Tram convinced him to try again, but Bix was still unable to conclude his improvisation within the allotted time. The fourth attempt—in which a light tap on Bix's
shoulder allowed the pianist to wrap it up in less than three minutes—is the one
we know.

Okeh studios had just recorded a Bix Beiderbecke piano solo, something that
would never happen again. The hazy atmosphere surrounding its gestation suggested the title: "In a Mist." This work is among the rare Bix compositions; he
would create them on the keyboard, but his limited musical knowledge prevented
him from writing them down. Compared with Fats Waller or Earl Hines, Bix was
not an outstanding performer on piano; his left hand's playing is often limited to

35. TRAM, The Frank Trumbauer Story, op. cit., pp. 75–76.

an elementary accompaniment, supporting the notes hit by the right hand with simple bass harmonies. The conditions of this only recording offered but a faint idea of Bix's real ability at the keyboard. Such was Ralph Berton's feeling when discovering this recorded side: "There he was, Bix on piano, as I'd been listening to him since he first came to the house three years before. Oh, it was feeble, stiff, self-conscious, compared to what I'd heard him do hundreds of times in our living room—pale stuff for Bix, but still unlike anyone else; instantly, unmistakably Bix, nobody else in this world!"[36] Bix had used a proven composition for this take, created two or three years earlier, to which he often returned, elaborating continuously renewed variations. Milton "Mezz" Mezzrow heard the tune for the first time at Hudson Lake during the summer of 1926, and he was clearly not very interested in his friend's startling innovations. "Bix was already reaching out beyond the frontiers of jazz, into some strange musical jungle where he hoped to find Christ-knows-what. . . . Over and over he would play the peculiar 'modern' music that was like a signpost to him, showing him where he thought he had to go. These musical tangents, leading to a dozen different detours, were all scrambled up with the jazz in Bix's head, and that mess finally led him to compose 'In a Mist.' "[37]

Bix's recording has a great charm, and it immediately captures the ear. Though it resorts to composing techniques empirically learned by its author while listening to Debussy's works—such as the whole-tone scale, the phrase in "arabesque," and a selection of chords commonly used by the French master[38]— the piece is jazz, unquestionably. It's a melodious and cleverly constructed ragtime, broken up by tender moments, by delicate and vanishing sound pictures that were not heard in jazz music before that time. Its development maintains a strong coherence and a logical progression, which is surprising for a three-minute work that was partly improvised, and recorded under the conditions already stated. Upon its release in February 1928, "In a Mist" would briefly appear on the charts, allowing Bix Beiderbecke's name to be fleetingly listed among the best-selling artists. This title—along with "Singin' the Blues"—would above all assure the posthumous renown of its author. Albert Haim was able to identify more than fifty different versions of this composition, cut over the course of the last seventy years, by orchestral ensembles or by a single pianist. What better recognition could there be of the quality and seductive power of this timeless creation?

Tram had turned down Paul Whiteman's offer, but he and Bix agreed that, when the Goldkette band finished its Roseland run, they would join the band being put together by Adrian Rollini at the Club New Yorker. The place that had once been the Cinderella Ballroom—on the second floor of a building on the corner of Broadway and 48th Street—changed its name in February 1927 and became the Club Whiteman, a luxurious nightclub whose huge dance floor, aggressively decorated in black

36. *Remembering Bix*, op. cit. p. 353.

37. *Really the Blues*, op. cit.

38. Philippe Fourquet wrote a thesis dealing with the study of the influence of French musical language at the beginning of the twentieth century on American jazzmen, from Bix Beiderbecke to Bill Evans (Philippe Fourquet, *De l'Impressionnisme dans le Jazz*, Université de Paris-Sorbonne, 1993). "In a Mist" is extensively analyzed (pp. 90–95) in this excellent scholarly work. Philippe Fourquet wrote about the first fourteen bars of the piece: "One can find here Debussy's and Ravel's characteristic writing techniques, such as parallel seventh chords with the fifths in the bass, the use of eleventh augmented chords, the use of the whole-tone scale, and the preference for the root position . . . but also—rarer in jazz played at that time—a fondness for the phrase *en arabesque*, so characteristic of Debussy, as well as the thirteenth of the chord on top of one of these, which is a real tribute to the French master, and finally the use of the seventh degree chord which, with a jump from the G and the absence of the D sounds melodically like a defective whole-tone scale, before being played as an arpeggio in a position highly favored by the composer of *Pelléas*."

and gold colors, could hold a thousand patrons. The likelihood of turning a profit at such a vast place was not great, and Paul Whiteman soon withdrew his financial participation in the cabaret, which closed a short while later. For its reopening as the Club New Yorker, on September 22, the new management called upon Adrian Rollini.[39] The sax player was able to sign up ten musicians in a few days, and it would have been difficult—while remaining on the white side of the racial divide—to bring together higher-quality New York jazzmen.

Adrian Rollini's band at the Club New Yorker, September 1927. Left to right, front row: Sylvester Ahola, Bill Rank, Bix, Frank Trumbauer, Don Murray, Frank Signorelli; back row: Eddie Lang, Chauncey Morehouse, Adrian Rollini, Bobby Davis, Joe Venuti. (Duncan Schiedt Collection)

Bix, Tram, Bill Rank, Don Murray, and Chauncey Morehouse had a few more days to go with the Goldkette Orchestra. Eddie Lang, Joe Venuti, and Frank Signorelli were experienced partners, and two newcomers were added to the group: Bobby Davis, a saxophonist who had played with Rollini in the California Ramblers, and Sylvester Ahola, a trumpeter whose experience and musical abilities impressed Bix from the new band's first day of rehearsal, on the afternoon of September 9. "I met Bix," wrote Sylvester Ahola on his diary. "We shook hands, he apologized and said with a smile, '*I'm only a musical degenerate.*' He was embarrassed by his limited ability to read music. He was very modest and unassuming. Not a trace of egotism. Later he confided to me he wished he could play and read as well as I could."[40]

New York, Thursday, September 15, 1927

Sometimes fate smiles on you. Three days before its disbanding, the Goldkette Orchestra would, at Victor's Liederkranz Hall Studio, cut what would be a most remarkable swan song: "Clementine." Together with "My Pretty Girl," this side remains the best evidence on record of the band's notable value. The session opened with a mediocre take of "Blue River," into which the musicians couldn't breathe any life.[41] This unavoidable exercise was happily followed by a number on which the recording director, Leroy Shield, gave the players total freedom. From a stock score of "Clementine," the musicians worked out an arrangement for the tune themselves, section by section, under Doc Ryker's direction. "The idea was

39. "Frank Fay was the main attraction," wrote Frank Trumbauer in *Down Beat* (April 15, 1942), "Patsy Kelly was a stooge and Franklin was the piano player. Well, we all know where Fay is today . . . anyone who has ever been around the Paramount lot can tell you who he is. Needless to say, most of Frank's stuff was too fast for the public." Frank Fay became famous for routines sarcastically dismembering popular songs, and Patsy Kelly would come out to be insulted.

40. Dick Hill, *Sylvester Ahola, The Gloucester Gabriel* (New Jersey: The Scarecrow Press, 1993), p. 22.

41. "Blue River" is the last of the five Goldkette titles studied by Frank Murphy in *Musicology Australia*, op. cit. The author concludes on pp. 31–32, identifying the characteristic elements of Bix's musical creation, which are said to be: strong differences between Bix's solos and the original written melodies, a tendency to highlight the harmonic extensions of the original, a limited use of the jazz typical vocabulary (blue notes, rips), and a constant alteration of the rhythmic figures.

42. *Lost Chords*, op. cit., p. 316. This interview with Doc Ryker was published in *Storyville*, no. 12 (August/September 1967). In another interview with Jerry Kline, in the 1970s, Doc Ryker added that he had developed this method of working out arrangements as early as 1924, when the band started recording for Victor. (Information from Frank van Nus.)

43. Other excerpts from Frank Murphy's thesis were published in *Jazzforschung-Jazz Research*, edited by the Akademische Druck- u. Verlagsanstalt in Graz (Austria). Its issue no. 19, in 1987, offered an article by Frank Murphy, "Bix Beiderbecke as Jazz Pianist" (pp. 77–87) dedicated to three ensemble recordings made with Bix on piano: "Big Boy," "For No Reason at All in C," and "Wringin' an' Twistin'." Frank Murphy analyzes the main components of Bix's piano playing, comparing them to his cornet playing and to the original melody of the tunes. The author concludes with the similarity of the techniques used on piano and on cornet. Bix uses a rhythmic technique of paraphrasing the original melody, whose notes are extended or shortened, played with anticipation or delayed (syncopation). Melodically, Bix's characteristics are: repetition of notes, original note converted into blue note, transposition of a note to the higher or lower octave, inversion of two notes, and permutation. The author also studies the use of the correlated chorus, of harmonic extensions—mainly major sixth and ninth—as well as the use of musical motives, borrowed or created.

44. *Hear Me Talkin' To Ya*, op. cit., p. 151.

45. "Bix's close musical kinship with John Nesbitt (trumpet player and arranger) in McKinney's Cotton Pickers has also been commented on. The two bands did play together at the Graystone in 1926 and 1927, and according to Dave Wilborn: 'Bix and Nesbitt were exchanging ideas and they both had a bottle. They had a place out in the Graystone Gardens, a loose brick, where they could hide their bottle,' (interview with Jim Gallert, July 15, 1973). Since dancing in the Graystone Gardens did not start until the summer of 1928, the back of the Graystone was probably a better hiding place a year earlier." Lars Bjorn and Jim Gallert, *Before Motown, a History of Jazz in Detroit, 1920–1960* (Ann Arbor: The University of Michigan Press, 2001), p. 30.

that each section would work out part of the arrangement, and then we'd put it all together," explained Ryker. "That way, a part of everybody's style would be sure to get into the arrangement."[42] The result of this teamwork is striking, and the excellent studio acoustics captured the luster of a relaxed and warm interpretation, embodied with a natural feeling unprecedented in recorded jazz music. The climax of the side is a shining sixteen-bar solo by Bix, followed by Joe Venuti taking a Bix-like solo on the release, and turning it back to Bix for the final eight, creating an integrated and highly original melodic variation on the underlying theme.

New York, Saturday, September 17, 1927

The morning at Okeh studios was devoted to a second side by Tram, Bix, and Lang: "Wringin' an' Twistin'." The three men managed to reach a better balance on this new recording, Bix on piano paying more attention to ensemble playing, and again picking up his cornet for an amazing ending.[43] Years later, violinist Stéphane Grappelli told Italian writer Adriano Mazzoletti that he held the two sides cut by the American trio in great esteem, and that this intimate music had played an important role in his aesthetic development.

The next day, the Goldkette Orchestra gave its last performance at the Roseland Ballroom. The band's commercial success never lived up to Jean Goldkette's expectations, as the orchestra, conscious of its true musical worth, would never lower itself to participate in extra-musical spectacle, spiced with the burlesque numbers the audience liked so much. But it had built an immense reputation among professionals. The New York musicians who were in town on that night came to show their appreciation: "There are just no two ways about it—the old Jean Goldkette band was the greatest band ever brought together!" emphasized Russ Morgan. "I'll never forget our closing night in the Roseland. There were musicians from out of fifty-two different orchestras in the audience. After the last number was played, the people refused to leave the floor and the management had to call the cops in order to get the band off the bandstand."[44]

Tram and his companions didn't expect anything further from Jean Goldkette, who had opened the Graystone Ballroom's season on September 15 with the McKinney's Cotton Pickers.[45] In November he would put together a second Victor Recording Orchestra, featuring Hoagy Carmichael and Paul Mertz. Steve Brown would join Bill Challis with Whiteman. Fred Farrar entered Nat Shilkret's orchestra, and Irving Riskin joined B. A. Rolfe's. Doc Ryker would become part of the band accompanying Fred and Adele Astaire at Broadway's Alvin Theater, in George Gershwin's *Funny Face*. The orchestra that would inscribe the Goldkette name in jazz history was finished.

New York, Thursday, September 22, 1927

The Club New Yorker opened its doors in time for dinner. The band's program was drawn from the Goldkette repertoire, and Sylvester Ahola remembered, "Bix played his solos into a big megaphone, four or five feet long, which rested on the floor. Joe Venuti was the fellow who fronted the band with his violin, but it was Adrian who called the tunes."[46] The show given by this all-star band would have a brief run, as the club remained far from full on weekday evenings, and closed its doors on October 15, after only three weeks in business.

New York, Wednesday, September 28, 1927

The band appearing at the New Yorker would cut five sides for Okeh, as Frank Trumbauer and his Orchestra. Sylvester Ahola, whom Tram had forgotten to inform, missed the first day. This session has a curiosity value. On "Humpty Dumpty" and "Krazy Kat," the sophisticated arrangements dominated the sides, the players adopting a more intellectual than emotional approach, focused as they were on the execution. Bix's unerring instincts led him into daring harmonic explorations. Richard Hadlock offered an excellent analysis of these two pieces: "'Humpty Dumpty' contains an eight-bar gem by Bix in which the cornetist relates to the tonic scale of the composition rather than to the chord underlying his figures. The implications of this tactic are significant and extraordinary for 1927. The other experimental number is 'Krazy Kat,' utilizing fast and uncommon chord changes that Bix rides over with confidence and aplomb. His sixteen-bar solo stresses once more the reliability of that remarkable ear, which allowed him to anticipate an upcoming chord and, before reaching the harmonic root that would resolve his phrase, be off on an anticipation of the next chord. It is this practice that creates in much of Bix's work a sense of floating and searching, in lines that almost seem to begin and end in some other song."[47] The cornetist's infallible intuition always led him to bring his solo to an end firmly within the underlying chord—for the comfort of the listener.

Because of its simplicity and its unsurprising melodic progression, the third number recorded at the end of the session, "Baltimore," has been largely ignored by jazz critics, which is a shame. It is clearly dated, but the song is charming nonetheless.

New York, Thursday, September 29, 1927

This session is another that belongs to the realm of curiosities. In the 1920s, several chains of stores developed offering end-of-line stock and low-price articles. These ancestors of our "discount stores" were known as five- and ten-cent stores.

46. *Sylvester Ahola, The Gloucester Gabriel,* op. cit., p. 23.
47. *Jazz Masters of the '20s,* op. cit., p. 94.

A few weeks before the arrival of electronic recording, Columbia Records had unwittingly bought some impressive acoustical equipment—an unlucky investment that had to be justified. Columbia therefore used this brand-new, yet already obsolete, material for the production of discs sold exclusively in the cut-priced chain stores. New labels came to the market—Harmony, Velvet Tone, Diva—which offered records for thirty-five cents each—a third of the normal price. The orchestras also used made-up names on these sides, such as Fletcher Henderson's unit recording as the Dixie Stompers. Bix recorded for Harmony on September 29, with a group called, for this occasion, the Broadway Bell-Hops. Tram, Bill Rank, Don Murray, Bobby Davis, Frank Signorelli, Joe Venuti, and Vic Berton were part of the band, together with an astonishing tuba player, Joe Tarto.

The vocal part was done by the very prolific Irving Kaufman. The singer had been extremely active since 1914, and his performances under his various pseudonyms were more numerous than those recorded under his own name. His powerful voice and faultless articulation met the requirements of acoustic recording. His vocal style today seems dated, but it is not ridiculous, as is the case for most of his contemporaries. If crooner Bing Crosby opened the art of singing to a new and electronically amplified era, Irving Kaufman represented the preceding generation with panache. Under Sam Lanin's direction, the Broadway Bell-Hops cut two titles with Bix. Irving Kaufman fervently championed the charms of the Old South on "There Ain't No Land Like Dixieland to Me," but he was unable to save from disaster the second song, "There's a Cradle in Caroline." Bix played with elegance on these good-natured sides. As Eddie Condon used to say, "He could make lemonade out of any old lemon."[48]

New York, Friday, September 30, 1927

Two last titles were recorded on this day by the orchestra billed at the Club New Yorker. Sylvester Ahola missed the call a second time, but he must have consoled himself for this absence upon listening to the two lightweight songs this session added to the Okeh recording catalog, two sides whose interest is almost limited to an enjoyable exchange between Bix and Tram on "Just an Hour of Love."

The cornetist went to the movies with Tram and Ahola on the afternoon of October 4 to see the new Clara Bow film, *Wings*, showing at the Criterion Theatre on Broadway, close to their hotel.

New York, Wednesday, October 5, 1927

This session marked for Bix the beginning of a series of recordings released under his own name, on which he would create the most inspired works of this

48. *Bix Beiderbecke, Giants of Jazz*, op. cit., p. 41.

prolific fall. The first three sides cut by Bix Beiderbecke and his Gang stem from the New Orleans style. The five Gang members—Bill Rank, Don Murray, Adrian Rollini, Frank Signorelli, and Chauncey Morehouse[49]—were chosen by Bix, who felt confident with such a friendly entourage, and led these recordings with grace and authority. His partners would, however, remember a difficult session, though the result—a surprisingly natural performance—doesn't show a trace of it. The three titles cut that day were, once again, numbers played by the Original Dixieland Jazz Band, and two of them, "Royal Garden Blues" and "Jazz Me Blues," had already been recorded by the Wolverines in 1924. Bix's dedication to such New Orleans tunes was singular at a time when jazz was moving away from this repertoire—as clearly emphasized by the sides just cut by the Frank Trumbauer Orchestra—but the cornetist had a marked preference for these proven pieces, offering him a familiar territory in which he could freely create musical lines of original melodic and harmonic invention. More than a nostalgic reverence for his musical past, the choice of these Dixieland standards would allow Bix to redefine them, to masterfully build a perfect model of each one to be left for the studies of several generations of musicians that came after him.

"At the Jazz Band Ball" was Bill Rank's favorite—an opinion shared by the public, as this record would be the only one from the series to enter the best-seller list in February 1928. The enthusiasm that marked the session is faithfully captured on this side, whose sole weakness—relative as it may be—lies in the sixteen bars given over to Frank Signorelli's piano solo. Bix leads the ensemble parts with great confidence, firing the ending of the piece with blazing sparkles, blown with boldness and virtuosity. Adrian Rollini and Don Murray's solos maintain the high level of intensity running through the piece. "Royal Garden Blues" is by no means inferior. It gives Bill Rank the opportunity to blow one of his most imaginative choruses, and Bix's solo that follows it glides over twelve short bars, played far beyond the melody, far beyond the tempo, a few seconds of weightlessness, floating freely in the midst of a radiant eternity. "Jazz Me Blues" is a third miracle, ending this remarkable day. The ensemble parts come together in a perfect balance and cohesion, and the number conceals two gems: a solo by Don Murray, attacked on a very high note—a part of virtuosity and dazzling grace—and one played by Bix, started conversely with blurred tones and culminating in a sparkling break—eight notes strongly hit—before returning to an emotionally rich melodic line.

The Club New Yorker's closing down, on October 15, didn't surprise anyone, but it put eleven musicians out of work. They found a job for one night only in Jack Benny's show at the Audubon Theater. Before deciding to disband, they agreed to give Adrian Rollini a week to seek a new contract for a group that wished to remain united.

49. Frank Trumbauer's absence on the records released by Bix Beiderbecke under his own name is complete, as is Bix's presence in the Trumbauer's bands. This may sound surprising. Two reasons may explain Tram's absence on the records made by Bix Beiderbecke and His Gang: Bix's selection of Dixieland titles, which were not Tram's favorites, and the fact that it was probably easier for Bix to be a real *leader* outside the presence of his friend.

New York, Thursday, October 20, 1927

Composer Willard Robison was, for two years, the musical director of Pathé's Perfect Records.[50] Wishing to add a new series of jazz records to his company's catalog, he called for Bix and Tram, temporarily unemployed, who were joined by Don Murray, Frank Signorelli, Vic Berton, and an unidentified guitarist. Three sides were cut and released under two different names: Willard Robison and His Orchestra, and the Chicago Loopers. The intrusive presence of a male vocal quintet on the first two titles, "I'm More than Satisfied" and "Clorinda," seriously mars the already technically limited recording. The wide range of effects that Vic Berton could obtain from his various percussion instruments is one of the few pleasant surprises on these sides. Without the five singers, the musicians recorded "Three Blind Mice," the Chauncey Morehouse composition previously cut in August. This second version is played at a more flowing tempo, and its relaxed attitude, its limited ambitions, raise it—with no visible effort—to a level of high musical quality.

New York, Tuesday, October 25, 1927

A trying day awaited Bix, during which five titles would be recorded, selected from the eleven takes cut at the Okeh studios. The cornetist maintained a remarkable level of inspiration throughout the whole session. The personnel of the Gang was unchanged, but the three numbers chosen for this second series were more modern than the Original Dixieland Jazz Band standards. They would, however, be tackled in the Dixieland style.

"Goose Pimples" was written by Fletcher Henderson. The piece is taken at a rather slow tempo, almost a blues, and it offers Don Murray another opportunity to create an extremely beautiful chorus. On the take that was kept, Bix started to play over Frank Signorelli's solo. He instantly stopped and, making light of his blunder, pinned two brief and perfectly placed notes in the middle of the pianist's chorus. This harebrained interjection reveals the easygoing atmosphere that reigned in the studio, a smiling mood that the recorded music would faithfully reflect. Bix was more relaxed with his own group than he was as a member of Trumbauer's, and this lends a charm to the Gang's sides that helped make them successful. Bix energetically hammers out a resounding finale to "Goose Pimples," a sudden flare to the high register that brings a blazing ending to the piece. The Okeh company had the idea of coupling "Royal Garden Blues" and "Goose Pimples" on the same record, and releasing it under the name of the New Orleans Lucky Seven on its race-record label, to see if the black community would be interested in it. Sales, however, were scarcely more rewarding than those of other titles

50. Born in Kansas, Willard Robison (1894–1968) was a great American composer and songwriter. He is the author of "A Cottage for Sale"—a best-seller for Guy Lombardo and the Revelers in 1930—and a hundred other songs, many of which he recorded himself, singing, playing piano, and arranging the tunes. Some of Bix and Tram's records were released under the name of the Chicago Loopers. Started in 1922, Perfect was originally marketed as a low-priced record line by the Pathé Frères Phonograph Corporation. By late 1925, it had emerged as the most popular label in Pathé's lineup.

by Bix and His Gang, which, with the sole exception of "At the Jazz Band Ball," would not exceed 3,000 copies.

On the second title of the session, "Sorry," all the qualities of the preceding sides can be found again to an astonishing degree of perfection. The piece opens with a radiant chorus by Don Murray who, in thirty-two bars, builds up one of his most graceful melodic lines. From this point, Bix takes over brilliantly. Hearing this record, the feeling that prevails is the pleasure the players took in making it. The subtle accelerations, the harmonic richness, Bix's admirable solo floating over the tempo with astonishing authority, Adrian Rollini and Don Murray's outstanding support . . . these are among the elements that leave in the listener's ear an intense feeling of musical fullness. Bix told Esten Spurrier about "Sorry" that he "had never felt better on any recording date." This can clearly be heard, and the feeling is contagious.

Tram, Eddie Lang, Joe Venuti, and Pee Wee Russell—a clarinetist with whom Bix hadn't played since the summer of 1926—arrived in the studio by midday, gathering the members of the Frank Trumbauer Orchestra for two recordings. Tom Rockwell, the Okeh director, hoped to re-create the success of "Singin' the Blues." Tram and Chauncey Morehouse had composed "Cryin' All Day" with this in mind. The result, less spontaneous than its celebrated model, remains of a very high caliber. Bix's solo is absolutely faultless, but it seems to be constructed with a skillful assemblage of proven routines that erase some of its freshness. Pee Wee Russell's chorus, which immediately follows Bix's, achieves the marvel of maintaining the flow of Bix's solo without copying the cornetist and his ideas. The second title, "A Good Man is Hard to Find," doesn't really take off, in spite of two abrupt shifts into double time that try, at the end of the side, to artificially create an effect of surprise. Okeh record 40966, compiling these two last titles, wouldn't have the commercial and artistic impact of "Singin' the Blues."

This extended session would end for Bix, now back with his Gang, with two takes of "Since My Best Gal Turned Me Down." Taken at a fast tempo, this piece leaves the cornetist few opportunities to remove his horn from his lips and enjoy some rest. The tricky execution made the game still more perilous, and the ensemble's synchronization on the slower passages needed to be rehearsed. Bix does show signs of fatigue on the second part of the side, which doesn't detract from a work that remains quite impressive for its vitality and invention.

New York, Wednesday, October 26, 1927

Red Nichols left the Whiteman Orchestra at the end of May to return to his Five Pennies. At the end of June, he recorded two beautiful sides for Brunswick,

"Cornfed" and "Mean Dog Blues," and in August "Ida, Sweet as Apple Cider," which, upon its release in November 1927, sold more than a million copies. On the morning of October 26, Victor studios recorded two sides by Red Nichols and his Stompers, consisting of Bill Rank, Glenn Miller, Pee Wee Russell, Frank Trumbauer, Adrian Rollini, and Chauncey Morehouse, thus forming a variation on the Frank Trumbauer Orchestra, without Bix. An agreement had been made between Tram and Red Nichols: the two musicians would cut the same tune, "Sugar," under the name of the Stompers in the morning, then under Frank Trumbauer's in the afternoon, for the Okeh label. "Tommy Rockwell would not go along with the idea," remembered Red Nichols, "and nixed using me on this recording date, insisting that Tram use Bix. Tram found Bix in Plunkett's, and not in too good of shape, but Tommy insisted that he use Bix and that was that!"[51] Thinking he could enjoy a free day, Bix had been drinking to excess, and as in May, the unsteady man who was finally pushed into the studios had no control of his playing. As the cornetist who solos on the released side shows an obvious lack of elementary skill, it has often been suggested that this musician was Bix, under the influence of alcohol; this is at least what Bill Rank and Chauncey Morehouse, who were both present on that day, have always asserted. But no witness is infallible, and it is almost impossible to accept as an original such a clumsy copy of the Bixian style. Randy Sandke has offered a possible answer: "On the final eight bars, a second cornet briefly appears and plays two barely audible phrases. This must be a rather incapacitated Bix, located far enough from the microphone so that any fluffs wouldn't spoil a take."[52] There is little doubt that the identity of the soloist on "Sugar" will remain the object of future speculation.

Bix was at Plunkett's, celebrating his musical marathon of the previous day, but he had a second reason to raise his glass: an agreement had just been made with Paul Whiteman. Bix Beiderbecke and Frank Trumbauer were expected in Indianapolis on October 27, where they would join the big band of the King of Jazz.

Stage of the Indiana Theater in Indianapolis, 1927. (Indiana Historical Society Collection)

51. *The Leon Bix Beiderbecke Story*, op. cit., p. 297.

52. *Observing a Genius at Work*, op. cit., p. 30. Bill Rank and Chauncey Morehouse, who were both present on that date, have always asserted that this clumsy solo was played by a highly intoxicated Bix. During one visit in England, and opposing John R. T. Davies and Laurie Wright's incredulity, Bill Rank tried to put an end to this discussion by saying: "I know it: I was there!" (Information from Laurie Wright.)

Indianapolis, October 27–29, 1927

The contract had been agreed to by October 20 between Tram, Bix, and Jimmy Gillespie, in the Whiteman office in New York, at 33 West 42nd Street. Since September 1927, Paul Whiteman had been leading his band on a tour of the Paramount-Publix theaters, a contract covering a period of forty weeks, due to end in July 1928. Bix and Tram took a plane to Indianapolis, and were driven to the Indiana Theater, where the band was performing.[53] The show had already begun; the newcomers were dressed and thrown onstage. Tram found himself seated next to Jimmy Dorsey, with Bix just behind him. All smiles, the fat Paul Whiteman was facing them, beating time, leading his musicians—and directing from now on the rhythm of life for his two new employees. "Back in the hotel room, we had a few drinks and just sat and watched the sun come up," wrote Frank Trumbauer. "I have often wondered what would have happened if we had been able to look into the

Indiana Theater, East Washington Street, Indianapolis. (Duncan Schiedt Collection)

future. Bix just sat there, with the toes of his shoes turned up, looking out the window, saying over and over, 'Boy, that Whiteman! What a guy! What a guy!'"[54]

Bix was twenty-four. He was now part of the number one orchestra in American popular music, a band of international renown. This engagement could legitimately be considered as a major professional achievement, one to which many American musicians aspired.

Life led Bix more than he led life, and the decision to accept Paul Whiteman's offer was actually Frank Trumbauer's. Bix followed, as he doubtless would have followed any other suggestion from his friend. He should have been happy, but contrasting feelings gnawed at him: his satisfaction at seeing his art acknowledged was tempered by fears of being unable to respond to the high expectations of his new employer and band mates.

Compared to the uncertain situation Bix and Tram were facing in October 1927, Paul Whiteman's proposal offered them a substantial paycheck and a job as secure as they could hope for—lucky for them, as the times were becoming more difficult for musicians. When Milton "Mezz" Mezzrow moved to New York to join his friends, who had left Chicago in the first days of 1928 in search of a possible musical paradise, he had discovered a bitter reality: they were all parked in a seedy room, without work. "There wasn't a gas-meter between them all, and

53. The Whiteman Orchestra was appearing in movie theaters, in which their concert alternated with the showing of a movie. At the Indiana Theater, the film was *Three's a Crowd*, directed by and starring Harry Langdon.

54. TRAM, *The Frank Trumbauer Story*, op. cit., pp. 80–83.

they couldn't remember when they'd greased their chops last," recalled Mezz Mezzrow.[55]

Bix's dependence on alcohol made a regular income compulsory, since a significant part of it went to the acquisition of his indispensable beverages. Things had changed drastically for Bix since his stay in the Goldkette Orchestra, where he earned, at most, $125 per week. The weekly salary Whiteman offered him was $200, which put him at the middle of the orchestra's payscale.[56] Under Jimmy Gillespie's direction, the group numbered thirty-four people in November 1927: twenty eight musicians, four singers, and two staff arrangers—Ferde Grofé and Bill Challis—which brought the amount of the weekly payroll up to $10,000. This sizable sum—three times higher than that which had caused Jean Goldkette to fold his greatest band—could only be supported by intense activity, onstage and in the recording studios. The consequent workload on the musicians was intense.

Times were quite profitable for Paul Whiteman, who dominated the record market. Eighteen titles made by the King of Jazz were among the best-sellers of 1927. The audience's taste was not for the more jazzy tunes, but rather for *sweet* dance music. After "In a Little Spanish Town" at the beginning of the year, Jack Fulton's falsetto voice was back on the band's autumn best-seller: a flashy version of "My Blue Heaven"—a song that would give Gene Austin a big hit two months later. Bix knew the Whiteman repertoire perfectly well, and he was familiar with this resolutely commercial aspect of the bandleader's production. The cornetist's interest in his new job went far beyond simple economic considerations.

Bix regretted his lack of musical education. He saw himself as a "musical degenerate," able to shine on the surface, but missing the theoretical background that would have allowed him—or so he thought—to fully take advantage of his creative gifts. He was shoulder to shoulder in the Whiteman Orchestra with faultless professionals, like trumpeter Charles Margulis and clarinetist Chester Hazlett. All were capable of reading scores with one eye closed, and upside down if necessary, but none would be remembered in jazz history, but for his presence at Bix's side. The cornetist saw in his daily contact with "confirmed" musicians an opportunity to further his apprenticeship and to realize his artistic ambition.

The quality of the orchestra's work fascinated Bix as well. It excited a deep—but not clearly formulated—attraction toward an ideal fusion between the spontaneity of jazz and a more complex and orderly harmonic universe, which he only found in his favorite classical composers. In this stage of his life, Paul Whiteman's band was for Bix, in a rather naive way, the embodiment of a hope for progress in his elusive quest. This hope wasn't entirely baseless: "Whiteman was a sociological phenomenon responding to a particular need in the society of his time, the 1920s," wrote Gunther Schuller in *Early Jazz*. "On purely musical terms, however, the Whiteman Orchestra achieved much that was admirable, and there is no question that it was admired (and envied) by many musicians, both black and white. . . . And

55. *Really the Blues*, op. cit., p. 177.

56. Some figures: the highest paid musicians in the Whiteman Orchestra received $350 per week: they were reknowned professionals like Henry Busse, Wilbur Hall, Chester Hazlett, and the band director, Jimmy Gillespie. Harry Perella and Mike Pingitore were given $300. At $200 per week were Bix, Tram, Jimmy Dorsey, Charles Strickfaden, Charles Gaynor, and singer Austin Young. Bill Challis and Steve Brown were only paid $175, and Bing Crosby got $150, the lowest level in the Whiteman salary scale. Bix and Tram were also among the top musicians who were granted a special bonus of $50 per recorded side: the eighty sides recorded in 1928 brought them an additional income of $80 per week. As the average weekly salary was $40, the Whiteman employees were well paid. Compared with the movie industry, however, their incomes were quite modest. In 1926, *Motion Picture Classic* reported the following numbers: Harold Lloyd was making $40,000 a week, Charlie Chaplin $30,000, and Buster Keaton $4,000. In Hollywood, a cameraman could earn between $250 and $300 a week.

often enough to make the point worth making—the arrangements were marvels of orchestrational ingenuity. They were designed to make people listen to music, not to dance."[57] Reality would, unfortunately, be much more prosaic. Bix didn't know it, but he had reached his peak at the end of 1927. To maintain his amazing technical skill and to keep his rank in a highly demanding group would require from him a concerted effort, made more and more difficult by the deterioration of his health. He was well accepted by his new musical family, and—surrounded by Tram, the Dorsey brothers, Steve Brown, and Bill Challis—he would be at the center of a core of *hot* musicians with whom he was familiar.

Jimmy (left) and Tommy Dorsey. (Indiana University Collection)

On his arrival at the Indiana Theater the following day, Bix had the pleasant surprise of bumping into Hoagy Carmichael. His friend was planning a recording date in Richmond, with the Dorsey brothers, and he wanted to meet Bill Challis for possible work on the arrangements. "Bix was much bigger than when I had last seen him," wrote Hoagy, "and he looked well, exuding an atmosphere of jovial success and prosperity, from his neat bow tie to his shiny shoes. He had grown quite handsome and for a moment I was playing third base to him. But the feeling of remoteness vanished almost immediately when he took us in and introduced us to Paul Whiteman himself."[58] The bandleader knew the composer of "Riverboat Shuffle" by reputation, and was willing to hear one of his works. Hoagy sat at the piano, sang "Washboard Blues," and thought it was a joke or an excessive courtesy when Whiteman, after a careful listening, told him that he might consider recording this tune with his band. This was actually a serious offer, and the orchestration was entrusted to Bill Challis.

Saint Louis, October 29–November 4, 1927

The Whiteman Orchestra appeared for one disappointing week at the Ambassador Theater in Saint Louis, and Bix resumed his episodic relationship with Ruth Shaffner.[59] Bix and Bing Crosby had immediately become good friends, and Ruth fixed Bing up with her sister, Estelle, for double dates. "Bing was the most wonderful person I've ever known," confessed Estelle. "He was so much fun."[60] After the departure of the band, Bix stayed for two more days in Saint Louis, where he spent

57. *Early Jazz*, op. cit.

58. *The Stardust Road*, op. cit., p. 118.

59. The movie shown along with the concert was Joseph Henabery's *Lonesome Ladies* (1927), with Lewis Stone.

60. *The Leon Bix Beiderbecke Story*, op. cit., p. 300.

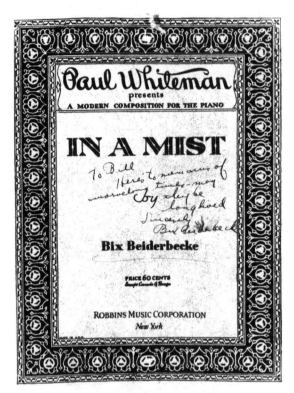

the last hours of an amorous relationship that he would never seek to revive.

Chicago, November 7–27, 1927

The next stop on Paul Whiteman's tour was the beautiful Chicago Theater.[61] Upon his arrival, Bix realized that, distracted by his separation from Ruth, he had forgotten his stage uniform in Saint Louis. A solution was found after several telephone calls: Jimmy McPartland was ready to help out for one piece, and Eddie Condon, once again, was asked to complete the outfit: "Jimmy contributed the jacket and pants," recalled the guitarist, "and I dug up the fixtures: studs, shirt, and tie. When Bix stood up to take his chorus on 'Sugar,' Jimmy's pants hit him halfway to the knees. He was wearing white socks."[62]

One night after the show, the musicians gathered in the speakeasy at 222 North State Street. It was given the name the Three Deuces, an ironic allusion to the most celebrated whorehouse in the city, the Four Deuces. Run by gangsters and frequented by the underworld, the place was hardly conducive to a romantic dinner, but alcohol flowed profusely and there was an old piano in the cellar. The presence of some of the finest jazz musicians in Chicago in this warm and cozy place couldn't fail to inspire some musical creation. "We all tore out for the piano," wrote Mezz Mezzrow, "lugging our instruments with us, and in no time at all one of history's greatest jam sessions was under way. Bing Crosby had the spirit too. He beat time all night with his hands, like he was at a Holy Rollers meeting. Under Bix's spell, everybody was a genius that night. I think the term *jam session* originated right in that cellar."[63]

One afternoon Bix would need to quickly hide the traces of his nights on the town when an unexpected impending visit was announced: his mother was coming to see him. His uncombed hair, rumpled clothes, and badly shaven cheeks left little doubt as to his nocturnal activities. Bix left the afternoon rehearsal and went to his hotel room to try to restore the neat appearance his mother would expect.

Cover to the "In a Mist" sheet music, copy signed "to Bill (Challis or Priestley)." (Duncan Schiedt Collection)

61. Opened in 1921 at 175 North State Street, in the Loop, this luxurious movie theater was decorated in the style of seventeenth-century European palaces. It contained 5,000 upholstered seats, and white-only jazz bands were its top attraction during the 1920s. The movie shown with the Whiteman concert was Edward Sutherland's *Figures Don't Lie* (1927). The theater was restored and reopened in 1986.

62. *We Called it Music*, op. cit., p. 149.

63. *Really the Blues*, op. cit., p. 148.

Hoagy Carmichael at the piano, around 1929. (Indiana University Collection)

"His mother was very pleased that he had—in her own words—made it to the top," confirmed Charles Margulis, "She felt her son had reached the height of his career."[64] The Whiteman Orchestra moved on November 14 to the northern part of the Windy City, and opened at the Uptown Theater.[65] Four days later, the copyright for "In a Mist" was registered in the name of Robbins Music Corporation. The title page of the sheet music contained the heading "Paul Whiteman presents a modern composition for the piano." It had been worked out by Bix with Bill Challis. Week after week, Bix would play four to six measures, and seated to the pianist's right,

64. *The Leon Bix Beiderbecke Story*, op. cit. p. 302.

65. The Uptown Theater was located at 4614 North Broadway, just north of Lawrence Avenue. Opened in 1925, it was one of the most spectacular buildings on Chicago's North Side. This movie palace enabled 5,000 people to attend "legitimate theater" at an affordable price, and the film shown that week was Harry D'Arrast's *A Gentleman of Paris* (1927), with Adolphe Menjou.

Bill Challis transcribed what he heard, trying to give a fixed form to musical material that sounded different each time its author played it.

Chicago, Friday, November 18, 1927

The Victor studios were located at 952 North Michigan Avenue. They played host this day to a cut-down version of the Whiteman band. The sides made were the first featuring Bix Beiderbecke and the Paul Whiteman Orchestra. The three titles were undeniably jazz music. The series started with the recording of "Washboard Blues," which had been arranged for Hoagy Carmichael three weeks earlier. The young composer, impressed by such a quick achievement, had been intensely rehearsing over the preceding days, without being able to quell his anxiety. "I was so nervous I ruined a half-dozen master records and the best of a double-time trio arrangement," confessed Hoagy. "I had a lot of vocalizing to do and a piano solo . . . was included in the arrangement. It was, for me, nerve-racking, jumping from one act to another. Whiteman remained calm. . . . Finally we got a master that was approved. When Leroy Shield came out of the control, I thought I saw a tear on his face. We were emotional slobs about music in those days."[66] Bill Challis's orchestration gave Bix the lead of the trumpet section for a part of the piece. Trumpeter Henry Busse, a Whiteman veteran, reluctantly accepted Bix's rapid promotion, but not without clearly expressing his frustration. "Washboard Blues" was a success, and Bix carries the ensemble over a sudden speeding up of the tempo that gives this side a lively touch. Upon its release, the tune would be briefly listed among the best-sellers of March 1928, and it sold a great number of copies: the other side of this Victor 35877 record featured Paul Whiteman's first big hit for the year 1928, "Among My Souvenirs," a sentimental Hollywood-style song, whispered by the sickly *sweet* voices of the Sweet Trio. On November 21, the band moved to a third location, the Tivoli Theater, ending its stay on the South Side of Chicago.[67]

Chicago, Wednesday, November 23, 1927

The first number recorded on this date, "Changes," allowed Bill Challis to display his remarkable ability in building over an attractive melody the harmonic framework within which the various talents assembled by Paul Whiteman could shine. The vocal part is skillfully constructed: the astute blending of the voices of the two trios—the Sweet Trio alternating with the *hot* Rhythm Boys—and the astonishing ease of Bing Crosby's singing brings an innovative sound to the vocal part of the tune—a much needed advance over the singing styles common at the time. The scores that have survived are written with only the melody line of the song in the

66. *Sometimes I Wonder*, op. cit., p. 180.

67. The Tivoli Theater, opened at 6325 South Cottage Grove—south of Washington Park—was, together with the Chicago and the Uptown Theaters, part of the Balaban and Katz Company, and was decorated in the same flamboyant style. The film shown was Edward Segwick's *Spring Fever* with Joan Crawford. The Tivoli was closed in 1963 and torn down shortly after.

measures where Bix was asked to play a solo, and Bill Challis just added above the upper line "solo improvisation." "When we finished the first take," recalled Challis, "Tommy Dorsey was all excited over what Bix had played. He rushed up to him and begged him not to change a note on any subsequent take, but to keep the solo intact. Well, Bix couldn't remember exactly what he'd played, but he did try to play as closely as he could to what he remembered in the takes that followed—just to keep Tommy happy."[68] The first take was destroyed, but the following two remain. Though the general conception of the solo is consistent, noticeable variations can be heard on the two recordings, giving new evidence of the cornetist's inspiration and of the abundance of his ideas. While the solo on the second take is simply excellent, the one played on the third ventures into complex harmonies, reaching a surprising degree of conciseness and melodic perfection. Take three was selected for release and went on sale in January 1928, rising to the ranks of the best-sellers for the next eight weeks.

Chicago, Friday, November 25, 1927

Matty Malneck's orchestration for "Mary" doesn't have the delicacy and invention of the works arranged by Bill Challis, but it gracefully alternates between two very different styles: Henry Busse's, a traditional dance band trumpeter who delivers a faultless and emotionless execution on the two takes that were kept, and Bix's. The cornetist leads the ensemble energetically, and he inserts, at the end of the side on the two different recordings, two brief solos as dissimilar as they are brilliant. The vocal part is sung by Bing Crosby solo, with a modern and natural feeling.

Bix Beiderbecke would spend two years with the Paul Whiteman Orchestra. His first three sessions with the band had already fixed the role he would be given during this period, a role that, for the most part, would be limited to the insertion of a few *hot* measures into an ensemble of variable inspiration and skill. "The smart boys in the business realized early that [the 'pure' musician] was an 'asset,' and liked to inject him into a mechanical no-spirit big band for his hypodermic value," wrote Mezz Mezzrow. "And they were right. A hot man gave any orchestra, and the dancers as well, a new spirit and a stimulating pulse. His tone would stand out clear, full and firm, and his hard attack and phrasing added new inspiration to the saggy-souled men around him. As soon as he took off on a solo the whole band seemed to scramble out of its stupor, shook off the sleeping sickness, snapped back into alertness and showed some real sparkle for once."[69]

During the orchestra's appearance in the Windy City, the *Chicago Daily News* published a series of interviews with its bandleader: "I can emphatically state one thing," said Paul Whiteman. "There is no future in orchestra music for the untrained boy. The day when the youth could learn to 'fake' his music, play wholly by

68. *Bix Beiderbecke, Giants of Jazz*, op. cit., p. 45. The Whiteman Collection at Williams College in Williamstown, Massachusetts keeps hundreds of original music scores written and used by the Whiteman Orchestra.

69. Mezz Mezzrow, *Really the Blues*, op. cit., p. 141.

Sketch published in the December 9, 1927, issue of the *Cleveland Press*. (Joe Mosbrook)

ear and get a job is gone. Neither myself nor any other leader can afford to have a man who is not highly trained in music: he must be able to read music, and read it with skill. . . . Playing in a jazz orchestra is the hardest work a musician can do. . . . If you get into a dance orchestra you play until the small hours of the morning, you're likely to play five times a day and rehearse in between. You must play whether you feel well or not. You must go anywhere the orchestra goes. You must be ready to toil in the recording room of your phonograph company up to show time, then rehearse between shows. Furthermore, you must practice by yourself in other hours. . . . Jazz musicianship requires not only talented men; it requires physically fit men."[70] Such a speech could only reinforce Bix's doubts regarding his own ability to ever become fully integrated in the Whiteman's unit.

Cleveland, December 4–11, 1927

The end of the Whiteman Orchestra's engagement at the Tivoli Theater coincided with Tommy Dorsey's departure. The trombone player, always a difficult person to get along with, had developed conflicting relationships with several members of the band, and frequently fought with his brother, Jimmy—to a point that the two musicians were known as the Battling Dorseys. The band went back on the road across Ohio. They spent the day of December 2 in Lansing, Michigan, and settled for a week at the Allen Theater in Cleveland, Ohio. Bix sent his family an article published on Friday, December 9, in the *Cleveland Press*: "Bix Beiderbecke and Frank Trumbauer known wherever musicians gather as leading exponents in the field of ultra-modern dance music. They are with Paul Whiteman, now appearing at the Allen. Bix has only one recognized rival as a trumpet or cornet player: Red Nichols. . . . To our way of thinking, no child should be started in life without being brought up on this kind of music."[71] And Bix had written in the margin of these last lines: "Get a load of this!"[72]

A photograph taken at about that time was featured on the cover of the January 4, 1928, issue of the music magazine *Variety*. Bix's portrait is one of the thirty-four pictures presenting the musicians of Paul Whiteman's "Greater Orchestra." A young and smiling man, strangling Don Murray or pinching Joe Venuti's neck, was shown in the photographs taken in August 1927 in Atlantic City. The studio portrait done four months later discloses the image of a suddenly older man, with an aged face and thinning hair. The shadow of a tiny mustache, grown at the advice of trumpeters Henry Busse and Charlie Margulis for obscure musical reasons, emphasizes the severity of the crease around the mouth, while his gaze, intense as always, is veiled by an elusive melancholy. Looking at the astonishing image of the somber and prematurely aged twenty-four-year-old man, one understands that the fiery

70. Don Rayno, *Paul Whiteman, Pioneer in American Music, Volume 1: 1980–1930* (Latham, NJ: Scarecrow Press, 2003), pp. 175–176.

71. Copy of the original article sent by Joe Mosbrook. In November 1927, Red Nichols's record, "Ida, Sweet as Apple Cider," stayed for 3 weeks at the top of the charts, and sold more than one million copies. This success made Red Nichols famous in Europe, where he was very often better known than Bix at the end of the 1920s.

72. *The Leon Bix Beiderbecke Story*, op. cit., p. 308.

leader of the Wolverines, the radiant player with the Goldkette Orchestra, and the deeply moving soloist of Frank Trumbauer's bands is, by the end of 1927, on the verge of becoming nothing more than an imperishable memory, existing only in the grooves of a 78-rpm record.

The seventy sides Bix recorded before 1928 would amount to only one-third of those on which he would be featured over the course of his career. However, all has already been said—or nearly all. Bix's moments of grace would return here and there; he would keep a remarkable musical instinct and a perfect mastery of the difficult art of expressing much in a short solo, but he would never regain the freshness, the spontaneity, and—for once the word is justified—the genius that drives most of the recordings he cut in 1927.

The Whiteman Orchestra left Cleveland on December 11, and toured the East Coast until the end of the year. They spent a week on the bill at Loew's Penn Theater in Pittsburgh, where Bill Rank came to take the chair Tommy Dorsey had vacated. From December 19 to 24, the band performed at the Century Theater in Baltimore, staying in the city for Christmas Day. They were in York, Pennsylvania, on December 26 and played the following day at a party held at the Ritz-Carlton in New York. The Town Hall in Scranton billed the band on December 28, and on the next day they played at the Armory in Wilkes-Barre, Bill Challis's hometown. They finished the year with a quick stay in Binghamton, New York State, and a New Year's Eve job at the Belle-vue-Stratford Hotel in Philadelphia, which had booked two renowned orchestras: Sam Lanin's, with Joe Venuti and Eddie Lang, to play for the dancing party, and Paul Whiteman's, which was hired to insure that the year-end celebration would be a success.[73]

Bix at the end of 1927. This portrait was reproduced on the cover of the January 4, 1928, issue of *Variety*. (Courtesy Liz Beiderbecke Hart)

73. Record production in the U.S. reached the incredible number of 140 million copies sold in 1927. This historic sales performance gave some in-demand jazzmen incredible working schedules. For instance, Eddie Lang took part in eighty-three recording sessions during the year, and he has been identified on some 170 titles.

CHAPTER **9**

1928: The Crack-Up

New York, January 1928

On January 1, the orchestra took a train to New York and settled in at their usual residence at the 44th Street Hotel. Whiteman had no work lined up for the band until January 14, except for a radio broadcast and four recording sessions for Victor. Over the next four months, the band would be called on to make an extraordinary number of recordings, as Paul Whiteman had decided to end his eight-year association with Victor, whose contract was to expire in May, and to sign with the rival label, Columbia Records.[1] Before the end, the Victor Company wanted to wring the greatest number of records out of its star orchestra, and its biggest moneymaker.

After a six-day ocean voyage onboard the *France*, celebrated French composer Maurice Ravel landed in New York on January 4 to begin a four-month tour of the United States. The recent deaths of Debussy, Saint-Saëns, Gabriel Fauré, and Erik Satie had left Ravel as the most important French composer living. This modest man, who had always refused decorations and honors, was none too happy about the duties attached to his status. Nevertheless, he enthusiastically agreed to make the American tour. His interest in jazz music was born in the supercharged atmosphere of the Gaya, a cramped club where Jean Cocteau amused and was amused by his illustrious friends in the early 1920s. Fascinated by the possibilities offered by this "astonishing musical frenzy," Ravel had introduced some elements of jazz into

1. Financial and marketing incentives helped make this decision, but according to Don Rayno, the internal competition that had developed at Victor between Whiteman and Nat Shilkret—the two men were fighting to get the "cream of the crop"—was a decisive factor.

his works. He confirmed his interest during an interview with Olin Downs, the *New York Times* music critic: "I think that you don't fulfill yourselves sufficiently and that you still peer too far across the ocean. An artist should be worldwide in his thinking, but implacably national once he begins to create. I think you know that I admire enormously and hold in high esteem—doubtless more still than most American composers—your jazz. But (even using this style in my *Sonata for Violin*) my musical mode remains obviously French, even to the least informed listener. I look forward to more Americans focusing on their popular sources."[2] Bix, who already admired Maurice Ravel's music, could only have been heartened by such words, but he would have to wait until March, when Ravel returned to New York from his cross-country journey, to meet him.

Ravel's arrival in the U.S. coincided with the start of an impressive musical marathon for Bix. In less than four months, he would participate in thirty recording sessions for Victor and appear, with varying degrees of participation, on some fifty sides cut by the Paul Whiteman Orchestra.

Former building of the 44th Street Hotel. (JPL)

New York, Wednesday, January 4, 1928

Whiteman's first recording session of the new year opened with "Ramona," a flashy waltz with a Spanish tinge, about as far away from jazz as musically possible. It became a huge success in America and Europe. Bix was more interested in the next song, "Smile," which had been arranged by Bill Challis. Victor kept one take of the song, but scheduled it for rerecording on January 24. The afternoon session was much more rewarding, with the band turning out two successful takes of "Lonely Melody." Henry Busse was only reluctantly accepting of the dominant part that Bill Challis's arrangements had assigned to Bix. In an attempt to soothe the veteran's feelings, the arranger kept on "Lonely Melody" a diplomatic balance among the three trumpeters, with Bix being given a twenty-five-bar solo. The two takes afford us a rare opportunity to observe how Bix varied his interpretations of a given theme. Most jazzmen of the time worked out their "improvised" solos beforehand, and repeated them with only minor alterations on succeeding takes. Though they could sometimes modify the details of the solo, they never changed its structure.

2. Marcel Marnat, *Maurice Ravel* (Paris: Fayard, 1986), p. 609.

But Bix was not among that number, and the abundance of his musical ideas allowed him to conceive and execute within a few minutes choruses offering quite distinct forms and feelings. "Lonely Melody" is a good example of his talent. The solo on the first take—the one released in 1928—progresses with confidence and clarity over a moderate tempo, ably supported by Steve Brown's string bass. The solo on the third take follows a more fluid line, more developed and musically richer, with an ending radically different from that of take one.

The session ended, but the day did not. The Whiteman Orchestra regrouped at ten o'clock that evening in the studio of WEAF, the NBC station in New York, for a radio premiere: a coast-to-coast broadcast over a network of thirty-three stations, linked by the wires of the American Telephone and Telegraph Company. From a studio in Hollywood, Will Rogers led off the broadcast, which was sponsored by Dodge Brothers, the car manufacturer. Then the Whiteman Orchestra in New York played an extract from *Rhapsody in Blue*, followed by a show from the Erlanger Theater in Chicago, a speech from the president of Dodge from his home in Detroit, and an Al Jolson recital transmitted from New Orleans.[3] The show concluded with Paul Whiteman's band playing "Among My Souvenirs"—his great success at the beginning of the year—and a version of "Changes" that allowed a cornet solo by Bix to be heard in millions of American homes.

New York, Thursday, January 5, and Monday, January 9, 1928

Bix was part of the brass section on the two titles Whiteman recorded on January 5, "O Ya Ya" and "Dolly Dimples," which rank with "Ramona" for jazzlessness. He returned to the Okeh studios with a greatly modified Frank Trumbauer Orchestra the next Monday. Only four of its members—Bix, Tram, Bill Rank, and Jimmy Dorsey—had been part of the group that had recorded the famous sides of the previous year. Whiteman's contracts with his musicians specified that independent recordings had to include the greatest possible number of Whiteman musicians. Chet Hazlett, Rube Crozier, Lennie Hayton, and drummer Hal McDonald were therefore added to the new Frank Trumbauer Orchestra. Bix was reunited with an old friend: Min Leibrook, who had given up his tuba of the Wolverine days for a bass saxophone—though he could not match Adrian Rollini's lightness and rhythmic power on this instrument. Eddie Lang was notably absent, and was replaced by a twenty-year old guitarist, Carl Kress, a talented and active accompanist during the 1930s. This new group certainly consisted of excellent professionals, but they would not be able to re-create the cohesion and level of inspiration reached by the 1927 Frank Trumbauer Orchestra.

The songs selected for this session did not help inspire the band. The Okeh label had been sold to Columbia on October 15, 1926. To some degree, Okeh managed

3. Al Jolson was starring in *The Jazz Singer*, a Warner Brothers movie, released in New York on October 6, 1927. Its success was immediate—even if the first "talking" movies, which were Lee de Forest's Phonofilms, had been shown at the New York Rivoli in 1923. *The Jazz Singer* was different because of the "natural" quality of its soundtrack, which was due to the Vitaphone system—using synchronized records made by Bell Telephone Labs' Orthophonic process—and to the sound amplification achieved by Western Electric's new equipment, one powerful enough to satisfactorily "fill" a large theater room.

until the early 1930s to keep its independence, its private studios, and its own catalog, but the commercial pressure put on it by its powerful owner became more and
more evident. The choice of titles recorded on that day is a consequence of this policy: they were standard pop items. The first tune cut was a very pleasant arrangement
of "There'll Come a Time." Bix plays gracefully throughout the side. Tram takes a full
chorus solo, and on the two-bar break in the release, unleashes a flurry of notes. As
a sly comment on Tram's prolixity, Bix's answer consists of only two notes. Another
measure goes by before Tram is heard again: was Tram laughing too hard to play?
"Jubilee" closed the session, and its intricate written score left no room for personal
breakouts.

New York, Wednesday, January 11, 1928

Bix was back at Victor two days later, seated in the brass section of the Whiteman
Orchestra. A rerecording of "Parade of the Wooden Soldiers"—a big hit from
1923—would not match the success of the original version, but the next title, "Ol'
Man River," from the musical *Show Boat*, hit the top of the charts by the end of
March. Written by Oscar Hammerstein II and composer Jerome Kern, *Show Boat*
had debuted two weeks earlier at the new Ziegfeld Theater, on 54th Street. For the
first time, a Broadway musical was based on a coherent dramatic plot and
broached serious themes, such as racial segregation. *Show Boat* was a revolution,
and the quality of its melodies proved a lasting success. White and black actors
shared the stage, and black singer Jules Bledsoe suggested to the heroine that she
directly ask the Mississippi, as only the river may know the answers we seek; he
then sang "Ol' Man River," an emotionally powerful song that still raises goose
bumps. The interpretation of this masterpiece by Paul Whiteman leaves the listener with dry eyes, but it swings enough to make him tap his feet. Bing Crosby fills
thirty-two bars with a perilous but well executed vocal—"I just barely made it,"
commented Bing Crosby, "and I think I busted my shoelaces or something trying
to hit those high notes"[4]—and Tram, magnificently backed by Steve Brown's bass,
ends this high quality side with an ethereal solo.

New York, Thursday, January 12, 1928

The same studio in the Liederkranz Hall ballroom was used the next day by a
group of ten members of the Whiteman Orchestra. The pianist was Bill Challis.
"Whoever it was that was supposed to play piano on this record showed up late,"
confirmed the arranger, "and I played piano in my simple 'oom-cha' style. They set
me off as far as they could from the microphones so I wouldn't bother anybody."[5]

4. *Paul Whiteman, Pioneer in
American Music,* op. cit., p. 184.
This first recording of "Ol' Man
River" by the Whiteman Orches-
tra, released in March 1928, was
followed by an Al Jolson version
for Brunswick, and a few days
later, by a second more "theatri-
cal," Whiteman recording cut on
March 1, 1928, with singer Paul
Robeson (who played Joe in
Show Boat, the 1936 movie by
James Whale).

5. *Storyville,* no. 12 (August/
September, 1967), p. 31.

Ad published in *The Talking Machine World*, April 1928.

There is little difference between this band and the Frank Trumbauer Orchestra of a few days earlier, and the piece recorded was "San." Bill Challis tried to re-create, in an orchestrated version, the spirit of Bix's 1927 small-band masterpieces, and he asked his friend to compose an introduction: "Bix played it over on the piano for me, right there at the studio," explained Challis. "Bix was great at those things, stretching his fingers out over the keys. I asked him to do it, and that's what he came up with, right there at the date. So I scored right there, on the spot."[6] The two surviving takes, driven by the cornetist's biting lead, are superb jazz records. Violinist Matty Malneck and guitarist Carl Kress play a duet, à la Venuti and Lang, after which Bix once again dominates a chorus scored by Challis for the three trumpets. On January 14, the Whiteman Orchestra began a run of seven nights at the Mosque Theater in Newark, New Jersey, which gave Bix a short break in this concentrated series of recordings.

New York, Friday, January 20, 1928

Following the last show of the Newark engagement, Frank Trumbauer returned to the Okeh studios with the group he had formed at the beginning of the month. Surprisingly, singer Bing Crosby was added to the band. The two songs selected, both to become big hits, were written by Harry Barris, Crosby's fellow Rhythm

6. *Paul Whiteman, Pioneer in American Music*, p. 185.

Boy. No test pressing of the first title, "From Monday On," was ever found, but rumors that one exists continue, after more than seventy years, to tantalize collectors. From the same session, we have the first and outstanding take of "Mississippi Mud." Bix was in great form and flies over the side masterfully. The vocal duet between Tram and Bing Crosby, in the tradition of the playful banter in minstrel shows, did not reach a similar degree of inspiration. When asked in November 1969, Crosby was certain he never sang with Tram, and it is only after hearing the record that he remembered the event: "I had a lot of nerve in those days," commented Bing Crosby. "Me, singing with Tram. I should have been arrested. . . . There was a pub, a bistro, on 48th or 49th, just off Broadway, where all the guys went. The one quality the place had was a piano on the balcony. Bix and all the rest would play and exchange ideas on the piano. With all the noise going on, I don't know how they heard themselves, but they did. I didn't contribute anything, but I listened and I learned. . . . I was now being influenced by these musicians, particularly horn men. I could hum and sing all of the jazz choruses from the recordings made by Bix, Phil Napoleon, and the rest. Bix, Bill Challis, even Frank Trumbauer, would make suggestions to me for my vocalizing and I'd give a try. After all, these were the giants of our day, and they knew their music."[7] The singer's vocal cords were tired. This temporary huskiness adds an emotional power to his voice, which skillfully plays with a pitch difficult for his range. Bix's solo that follows the vocal ventures alternately into light and shadow—an amazing exploration around the melody, which led Tram to write in his diary: "One of the greatest records I ever made with Bix was 'Mississippi Mud.' Bix played a chorus that just won't quit! The collectors and record enthusiasts never said much about it, but I always felt it was one of Bix's best!"[8]

Around Philadelphia, end of January and beginning of February, 1928

For several weeks, the recording marathon resumed in Camden, New Jersey, while the band played for five nights at the Stanley Theater in Philadelphia, across the Delaware River. Many sides follow the same pattern: after a slow opening and a languid vocal by Jack Fulton or the Sweet Trio, the last part of the number perks up and features a jazz solo over the irresistible rhythm of Steve Brown's bass. Victor record 35883, featuring "Together" and "My Heart Stood Still," cut on January 21 and 24 respectively, is made on this model. "Together" was a big hit, and the fifth take of "Smile," recorded on January 24, was released in March.

Something from the January 26 recording session should have been kept. At the Church Studio in Camden, the Whiteman Orchestra rehearsed a new version of "Whispering," its first big commercial success at the end of 1920. The surprise of

7. *TRAM, The Frank Trumbauer Story*, op. cit., pp. 92–93.

8. *TRAM, The Frank Trumbauer Story*, op. cit., p. 92. Some believed that Bix's solo was played muted. In the booklet included in the 2001 Mosaic Records CD box-set, *The Complete Okeh and Brunswick Bix Beiderbecke, Frank Trumbauer and Jack Teagarden Sessions (1924–36)*, Richard Sudhalter explains (p. 13): "Though the chorus is played open, some listeners have commented that the tone has a pinched quality, as if Bix were working in a mute. This can be the result of a small room and/or close miking: given the microphones of the time, a trumpet or cornet tone would have needed between 12 and 15 inches to coalesce. Anything closer would have introduced an element of distortion."

the day was the young black musician who sat at the organ: the dazzling Thomas "Fats" Waller. But Paul Whiteman did not like what he heard, and no recording was made, depriving us of an encounter between Bix and Fats Waller that would undoubtedly have been of great interest. Bill Challis's arrangement and Bix's two short solos could do little to help the recording of "Back in Your Own Backyard" cut two days later. The band then set off on a four-day tour in Pennsylvania, and they were back in New York on February 4.

New York, Wednesday, February 8, and Thursday, February 9, 1928

Bix shines on the recording of "There Ain't No Sweet Man That's Worth the Salt of My Tears," with Tram and Bing Crosby's talented backing. The three men were able to lift the "Whiteman machine" off the ground, and to force it into jazz music. The same alchemy occurs on "Dardanella," recorded the next day. This new version of Ben Selvin's 1920 huge hit sat for eight years in the Victor company's vault, and was not released until January 1936, when interest in unissued cuts by Bix led the company to search its archives. Bix's solo, once again backed by Steve Brown, plays subtly with the melody, taking off from the written score just enough to make the venture fascinating. His rhythmic approach is entirely new, and his irregular progression floats over the soft orchestral accompaniment. The innovative character of this side probably explains why it was not released in 1928.

New York, Friday, February 10, and Monday, February 13, 1928

Bix's eight-bar solo at the conclusion of "The Love Nest" is more suggested than stated, yet it bears the mysterious evidence of great achievements. On "Sunshine," Bing Crosby again confirms his mastery of his art and frees himself from the bouncing rhythm of the arrangement. The session reached its peak with "From Monday On." Victor kept the third take of this Bing Crosby and Harry Barris composition, but did not release it until December 1941. Though the version put on sale in 1928—which was recorded several days later—has a more polished form, the three minutes of this first take offer a pure and spontaneous moment of jazz creation. Bix begins with an energetic thirty-two-bar chorus, and Bing Crosby sings his own composition with remarkable ease. Bix leads the ensemble over the last part of the side, supported by Jimmy Dorsey on cornet, and for the last time, by the inimitable slapping of Steve Brown's bass.

Significant changes in the band's membership occurred this month. The departure of Steve Brown was a blow to the rhythm section: "When I joined Whiteman," said Steve Brown, "the music was a little different. It was a little symphonic in conjunction with rhythmically played pieces. That seemed to worry me quite a bit, and I never enjoyed myself playing as much as I did with the Goldkette outfit."[9] Mike Trafficante took over on string bass on February 15, and his place on tuba was taken by Min Leibrook. Jimmy Dorsey gave his notice and left to join his brother, Tommy; he was replaced by Irving "Izzy" Friedman, an experienced clarinet and saxophone player. Finally, Roy Bargy, bandleader, arranger, and composer, who had worked with Ed Benson in Chicago and played in the Isham Jones Orchestra, took over for pianist Harry Perella.

Bix had been part of Paul Whiteman's orchestra for more than three months, and the recordings achieved during this period gave him a place in the first rank, a more valuable position than the one he enjoyed the year before with the Jean Goldkette Orchestra. "He was more appreciated, you might say," confirmed Bill Challis. "He had more freedom to play his solos. They made a soloist out of him, actually. He still played the third and fourth parts in the band. But then I always had a chorus for him, here and there. On every tune I did, I think I had a chorus for Bix, or at least a half a chorus. Jeez, I was lucky enough to be thrown in with Bix—who I thought was, naturally, the greatest. He was a drawing card for the band, as far as musicians were concerned. I think every musician in the country wanted to play like him—tried anyway. Same way with Trumbauer. Saxophone players—they wanted to play like Frankie. At that time, it was either Frankie Trumbauer or Jimmy Dorsey, and they were both in the Whiteman band."[10]

New York, Tuesday, February 14–Thursday, February 16, 1928

This professional recognition helped Bix to put up with the band's "symphonic" recordings. Because of his limitations in reading music, these performances were difficult for the cornetist, and they were made still more painful by the need to be at the studio by 9:30 a.m.—an exhausting exercise for a man who never returned to his hotel before three or four in the morning. The titles cut during these three days—"Grand Fantasia from Wagneriana," "A Shady Tree," and "Three Shades of Blue"—undoubtedly responded to some demand of the market.

New York, Saturday, February 18, 1928

The Whiteman version of "Mississippi Mud" cut during this session does not have the charm and inventiveness of the Okeh recording made a month earlier—which

9. J. Lee Anderson, "Steve Brown's Story," in *The Mississippi Rag* (November 1991), p. 7.

10. Chip Deffaa, "Bill Challis: The Whiteman Years," in *The Mississippi Rag* (January 1989), p. 19.

did not prevent it from outselling Tram's record in May 1928. The reasons that led Whiteman to include on this side the nasal voice of Irene Taylor, wife of singer Seger Ellis, remain forever mysterious.

Ben Pollack's orchestra had left Chicago and its job at the Blackhawk for an engagement at the New York Little Club, a nightclub on 44th Street. The band formed by the drummer included some of the best hopes of white Chicago jazz: Glenn Miller, Bud Freeman, Jimmy McPartland, and the young Benny Goodman—he was nineteen—who, in January, had cut his first record under his own name, a side with a deep Bixian touch. "When I was playing with Ben Pollack at the Little Club," recalled Bud Freeman, "Beiderbecke came down to tell me that John Barrymore was back from England with the English company that had been playing *Hamlet*. He told me they were going to do *Hamlet* on the radio that night, and I went with him to hear it. I remember being gone an hour and a half or more, and missing the next set. Pollack was furious, but Bix and I were great friends from then on."[11] Bill Rank remembered the nights Bix ended up in Harlem. He was well accepted by black musicians, and was invited several times to sit in with the band at the Cotton Club in December 1927, the Duke Ellington Orchestra.

A quick one-week tour in Pennsylvania, Ohio, and Virginia gave the band a break in this grueling recording marathon, which, however, resumed with the same frenzy as soon as they returned to New York on February 26.

New York, Monday, February 27, and Tuesday, February 28, 1928

The Ferde Grofé arrangement of "Chloe," recorded on February 27, is difficult to listen to today. Such was not the case upon its release in June 1928, and the title lasted five weeks on the charts. The next day, three sides were cut in less than five hours. Bing Crosby faced a daunting task with the recording of "High Water: A Spiritual," one of his first titles to be geared toward listening rather than dancing. The Whiteman Orchestra then recorded three new takes of "From Monday On": two of them have been kept, on which Bix retains the very high level of inspiration reached during the February 13 session. The day ended with a recording of "Sugar," a song introduced by Ethel Waters in 1926, something that could arouse the cornetist's imagination. "'Sugar' is a composition by Maceo Pinkard," commented Frank Powers, "who is a composer best remembered for having written 'Sweet Georgia Brown.' An interesting thing takes place on this particular recording. Bix plays a trumpet counterpoint solo to the tenor saxophone. The saxophone plays straight melody, and this permits Bix to play something entirely different."[12] The choruses played by Bill Rank and Tram are identical on the two surviving takes of "Sugar," while the two counterpoints created by Bix are extremely different. This

11. *Jazz Talking*, op. cit., p. 34–35.

12. From the thirteenth program of *Bix, a Biographical Radio Series*, op. cit. Three different tunes were entitled "Sugar" in the 1920s. This one is different from the "Sugar" recorded during the mysterious session on October 26, 1927.

confirms, once again, the abundance of Bix's ideas, giving him ability to venture on each take into a new musical adventure.[13]

New York, Wednesday, February 29–Friday, March 2, 1928

1928 was a leap year, and February 29 added one more day to the contract linking Paul Whiteman to the Victor label—a day that might have been better employed. Ferde Grofé had orchestrated "Sea Burial," a piano piece by Eastwood Lane—the composer Bix admired so much—and the arranger's work was able to preserve a dominant element of the original score: the tediousness that assaults the listener after a few seconds and doesn't let up. Bill Challis's orchestration on "When You're with Somebody Else" is not much more exciting, and the interest to be found in the selections from *Show Boat*, recorded the next day, is limited to twelve measures of "Can't Help Lovin' Dat Man," which Bix springs upon. Roy Bargy's technique was displayed on "A Study in Blue"—a *Rhapsody in Blue* spin-off—and Bill Challis wrote for Bix the lead of the *hot* trumpet trio chorus on "Coquette," a piece that leaves a strong impression of déjà vu. The week off that followed was welcome.

New York, Saturday, March 3, 1928

Columbia recorded this day, for their mid-priced Harmony label, three sides by Lou Raderman and his Pelham Heath Inn Orchestra, and the bandleader asserted that Bix was present. This acoustic recording was made in conditions similar to those on the Broadway Bell-Hops session of September 1927, and the sound reproduction offers the same weaknesses. Two titles, "Why Do I Love You?" and "Ol' Man River," include a seventeen-bar cornet solo. Within the limitations imposed by such poor sound quality, the Bixian touch can be heard on these short passages. The presence in the orchestra of a young and gifted trumpeter, Mannie Klein,

Maurice Ravel and Paul Whiteman in New York, March 12, 1928. (Whiteman Collection, Williams College)

13. Comparison of alternate takes recorded by Louis Armstrong, Frank Trumbauer, Coleman Hawkins, Red Nichols, and other jazzmen of the 1920s, shows that "improvised" solos were almost always prepared and worked out before the recording session, the soloist following closely in the studio, on the different recorded takes, the plan he had previously developed. To compare two different takes, musician and researcher Brad Kay disclosed during the March 2000 *Tribute to Bix* in Kenosha, Wisconsin, a brilliant concept he had conceived: the two takes were simultaneously recorded, one dubbed to minidisc and the other on a turntable whose speed could be precisely adjusted up or down, enabling him to keep the two parts exactly synchronized. On the alternate takes played by most musicians, there is "close musical correlation: the notes tend to double up in unison, the phrasing is similar, the overall conception of the solo is the same for every take," wrote Brad Kay. Bix's solos are different. "His synchronized alternates are something else altogether. Instead of unison notes, there are harmonies. Instead of the same phrases in lockstep with each other, there are different phrasings that dovetail and chase about in crazy counterpoint. Bix does this consistently, on take after take, record after record" (Brad Kay on *Bix's Web site Forum*, February 19, 2005).

who repeatedly claimed to have played these solos, leaves some doubt as to Bix's participation—a topic for the experts to argue passionately about.[14]

MAURICE RAVEL'S AMERICAN TOUR had taken him as far as the West Coast, from Los Angeles to Vancouver, before returning him to New York at the end of February. He had crossed the continent in trains whose slowness was rivaled only by their luxury, the latter quality making the former more acceptable. Bix and Roy Bargy attended a concert directed by Ravel at Carnegie Hall on the afternoon of Thursday, March 8. Though he greatly appreciated Ravel as composer and pianist, *New York Times* critic Olin Downs was rather reserved in regard to Ravel's effectiveness as a conductor: "He directs simply, with a clear and demonstrative beat, though without great authority, or efficiency. . . . The execution of *Spanish Rhapsody* was trembling and uncertain, most of all in the final part where for an instant disaster threatened."[15] The *New York Times* review was, however, much more positive on the repeat of this concert at Mecca Temple on Sunday, March 11, the French composer being in outstanding form that day. In New York, Maurice Ravel happened to meet the great Hungarian composer Bela Bartok, who was likewise on his first visit to the U.S., and he also met George Gershwin at a party given by singer Eva Gauthier.

New York, Monday, March 12, 1928

Paul Whiteman's international renown explained the visit that Maurice Ravel made to Liederkranz Hall Victor studios. The King of Jazz's orchestra was working on the recording of "When," a side on which Bix's cornet insouciantly answers Harry Barris's breathless scat. "We played 'Metropolis' and the 'Suite of Serenades' by Victor Herbert for Maurice Ravel," recalled Roy Bargy. "He was politely interested but not overly enthusiastic about either composition, but seemed to appreciate the musicianship of the players." "Yes, Ravel was interested in the musicianship of the band," added Al Rinker, "and extremely interested in what Bix was playing."[16]

New York, Tuesday, March 13–Saturday, March 17, 1928

One single listening to the fifteen-minute "Metropolis" is enough to understand Ravel's lack of interest. Ferde Grofé did not limit himself to orchestrating other musicians' works, he also wrote his own compositions. In July 1927, Paul Whiteman had recorded Grofé's blurred "Mississippi Suite," and he dedicated three recording sessions to "Metropolis," announced as a "musical picture of the sounds

14. Are we to believe Lou Raderman or Mannie Klein? Experts' opinions differ on this attribution. I have decided on Bix, because the soloist's confidence hardly seems compatible with Mannie Klein's age—he was only twenty at that time.

15. Marcel Marnat, *Maurice Ravel*, op.cit., p. 610.

16. *The Leon Bix Beiderbecke Story*, op. cit., p. 340.

of New York." A vocal group featuring Bing Crosby hums a short passage on the third part, which is followed by several measures of solos in which Bix passes briefly before the microphone. On March 15, the recording of "Lovable" introduced a more jazzy mood into this "symphonic" week, and Bill Challis's arrangement saved a space for a short solo by Bix at the end of this pleasant side.

The last part of the month was dedicated to rehearsing a show at the Paramount Theater.[17] Opened the year before in Times Square, at the corner of 43rd Street, this hall was noted for its luxury and size. Whiteman's premiere was set for March 31. Two days before, the collaboration between Dodge and the NBC radio network went through a second episode. The advertising campaign of a new Dodge model, the Standard Six, planned to feature the speaking voices of some top stars of the silent screen, until then only faces to the American public. The program would be transmitted, on the radio and, simultaneously, in fifty-five movie theaters across the U.S. Paul Whiteman was invited to participate with his band in this broadcast. Broadcasting a radio show in a theater had never been tried—and the ten-minute opening by the president of Dodge, singing the praises of his new vehicle, quickly irritated the audience. The broadcast sound was partly broken up by strong rains and hailstorms, which didn't help the audience's mood. The most celebrated United Artists stars could not save the show, and the voices of John Barrymore, doing his *Hamlet* monologue, and of Douglas Fairbanks and Charlie Chaplin were soon drowned out by the public's boos and hisses. *Variety* magazine concluded of this never-to-be-repeated experiment: "Movie stars should be screened, and not heard."

Paul Whiteman was featured for three weeks at the Paramount Theater, accompanying three different shows. This heavy schedule and the numerous rehearsals forced by the weekly changes kept the orchestra away from the recording studios.

New York, Tuesday, April 3, and Tuesday, April 10, 1928

Momentarily freed from Victor's importuning, the Frank Trumbauer Orchestra accepted Okeh's offer and recorded six titles in three sessions. Irving Friedman replaced Jimmy Dorsey, and Eddie Lang was back on the guitar. The commercial choices made by the record label brought a selection of titles that would have subdued the most cheerful jazzmen: "Our Bungalow of Dreams" and "Lila" are distressing inanities, worsened by a vocal sung by Irving Kaufman.[18] The two sides recorded on April 10 are much better, featuring singer Harold "Scrappy" Lambert's more spirited delivery and Bill Challis's imaginative arrangements. "Borneo" contains, over thirty measures, the first recorded *chase chorus* played by Bix and Tram. During the several months spent at the Arcadia Ballroom in Saint Louis, the two friends had developed this exchange—a dialogue in which each musician blows a

17. The building is still standing at 1501 Broadway. It was for a long time known as the Paramount Building.

18. On the issued record, the singer was "Noel Taylor." It would be more than sixty years before someone realized that "Noel" was really the reliable old Irving Kaufman, who, taking advantage of the electric recording equipment at Okeh, adopted a more languid style, making him hardly recognizable.

short phrase whose theme is played back in modified form by his partner. The like-mindedness between the two jazzmen made the fluent execution of their new concept possible. "My Pet" is a pleasant title, in which the vocal does not totally cover the very subtle accompaniment of Eddie Lang's guitar.

New York, Tuesday, April 17, 1928

One Okeh record by Bix Beiderbecke and His Gang came out from this session, and the two sides cut that day were harshly commented on by jazz critics: "Bix tries desperately to swing his Whiteman colleagues," wrote Richard Hadlock, "but they remain rigid and uninspired. Even Bix plays stiffly and without real enthusiasm on these dates. Ironically, his short solos with the full Whiteman Orchestra sound less contrived than his contributions to his own final small-band recordings made at the same time."[19] It is true that these recordings have lost the inspiration of the sides cut in 1927; it is, however, possible to come down somewhat from a peak but remain at a high level. "Somebody Stole My Gal" and "Thou Swell" offer the listener a quality and original harmonic idea that can still be appreciated today.

New York, Saturday, April 21–Wednesday, April 25, 1928

This four-month musical marathon ended in a sprint. Following the last Whiteman show at the Paramount Theater, the orchestra returned to the Victor studios, where twelve titles would be cut in five consecutive days—and this home stretch started over a weekend. The three songs recorded on Saturday, April 21, lack any artistic interest, which didn't stop the public from making them successful: "My Angel," a catchy tune with Spanish echoes, was a big hit. The nine pieces cut during the Sunday session and the three following days are of varied quality. Bix was very much present on "My Pet," and Tram takes an excellent solo on the melody of "Do I Hear You Saying 'I Love You'?" by Rodgers and Hart. "It Was the Dawn of Love" and "Louisiana" give Bing Crosby the opportunity to show off his growing talent, and Bix creates on this second title a hybrid sound, halfway between a cornet and a mellower reed instrument, by playing into a hat. The arrangement Bill Challis wrote for "Forget-Me-Not" allowed Bix to develop a truly original melody over seventeen measures, and to do it in a different way on each of the two surviving takes. The last title the band cut for Victor, "You Took Advantage of Me," was ironically the biggest hit of this series. It was also written by Rodgers and Hart for the Broadway revue *Present Arms*. The Whiteman Orchestra cut a remarkable version of this piece, highlighted by the perfect ease of Bing Crosby's vocal solo, and by Bix and Tram's second recorded chase chorus. The symbiosis between the two

19. *Jazz Masters of the '20s,* op. cit., p. 100.

musicians reaches a peak on this new duet, the conciseness, wit, and invention of the phrases exchanged between the two instruments bringing these thirty-two bars to an extremely high level of creation.

The night before this last session, the Whiteman Orchestra could be heard at midnight on the Davenport radio station WOC. Broadcast from New York on the national network, the program included a "new composition of symphonic jazz" by Ferde Grofé, "Blue Fantasy"—which was merely another name for the fifteen-minute-long "Metropolis." This orchestral piece was followed, for the listeners who had not yet fallen asleep, by a much more interesting moment during which Bix played "In a Mist" on the piano. The April 25, 1928 *Davenport Democrat* dedicated two columns to this event. Bix's mother was interviewed in this article, disclosing a pertinent opinion about her son's talents: "We can always tell when Bix's horn comes in," she said. "We know everytime Paul Whiteman's orchestra is on the air, and Leon knows we'll be listening in. The air is carried out by the other cornetist but the sudden perky blare and the unexpected trills—those are the jazz parts, and they are Leon's."

At the end of eight years with Victor, Paul Whiteman switched over to Columbia and, on the morning of April 26, left New York with his men for a two-week engagement in Boston.

Boston, April 27–May, 10, 1928

The band that got onstage at Loew's Metropolitan Theater on the night of April 27 was made up of tired musicians, pleased with the change a two-week show would offer. The program was composed of numbers they knew well, freeing them from tedious afternoon rehearsals. Trumpeter Henry Busse's friendship with Paul Whiteman dated back to 1918, and he had played a key role in the orchestra since that time, always at its forefront. Wishing to form his own band, Busse took advantage of the move to Columbia to give his notice. He was replaced by Harry "Goldie" Goldfield, a skillful technician who was quickly able to reproduce Busse's solos exactly as they were featured on Whiteman's records, and as the audience expected to hear them. Harold McDonald followed Busse out of the band. He was replaced on the drums by George Marsh, a change that had no perceptible effect on a rhythm section. The band stayed in Boston until May 10, taking part in two broadcasts on the radio station WBET.

Bix's portrait in 1928, taken as an advertisement for Holton brass instruments.

Photograph taken in 1928 for a Holton brass instruments ad. Left to right: Eddie Pinder, Bix, Charles Margulis, and Harry Goldfield. (Duncan Schiedt Collection)

The Columbia Phonograph Company impatiently awaited Whiteman's return to New York. A subsidiary of the British holding company Columbia International, the American group had established its main offices and recording studios on the top floors of the Gotham National Bank Building, at Columbus Circle, in 1921.[20] As a long Whiteman tour was scheduled for the autumn, Columbia had not much time available to record the titles that would have to compete with Victor's flood of Whiteman releases, which were inundating the market.

A new long and intensive recording schedule began. In the next two weeks, the band would record fifteen titles, rehearse five others, and appear six nights in a row at the Metropolitan Theater in Brooklyn. This first series of records for Columbia was obviously conceived in a hurry, and the lack of character of the selected titles makes this haste even more evident. The band was filmed on the night of Tuesday, May 15, by Fox Movietone for its newsreel: the Columbia studio clock appears on-screen, marking the twelve strokes of midnight, the very minute the contract between Paul Whiteman and Victor ended. The bandleader enters the screen, faces his tuning-up musicians, and tears up what is supposedly the old contract. He then starts conducting "My Ohio Home." Fox Movietone has earned the eternal gratitude of jazz lovers with this two-minute film: this surviving reel has preserved the sole sound-film images of Bix Beiderbecke that we know of. He appears on the left of the screen for a few seconds, lifts his horn to his lips, blows while glancing to the right and left, and then sits back down. Fifteen inches farther to the left, and Bix would have found himself entirely off-camera.[21]

Bix was included on these first Columbia recordings, but his opportunities to stand out from a collective interpretation were rare. On "Melancholy Baby," he brightened Austin Young's dismal vocal with a brilliant countermelody; he was given a leading role on "Is It Gonna Be Long?" and "Oh! You Have No Idea," but the solos on these two sides, dully arranged by Bill Challis, were played by Henry Busse and Izzy Friedman; the overdone mewing on the fourth title, "Felix the Cat," conferred an anecdotal character to the choruses tossed off without conviction by Bix and Tram. The other selections sought to appeal to the varied tastes of the con-

20. The address of Columbia offices at Columbus Circle was 1819 Broadway. According to Don Rayno, most of the Columbia files for the Whiteman Orchestra's recording sessions over the period 1928–1929 indicate "Union Square" as the studio's location. A Columbia studio at Union Square could not be identified. Were these recordings made in the Okeh studios, at 9–11 Union Square, as Okeh was at that time a Columbia subsidiary?

21. The part of this Fox Movietone newsreel featuring Bix can be seen, together with other remarkable shorts, on the Yazoo 514 DVD, *At the Jazz Band Ball*. Two shorter parts of the same film are included in Brigitte Berman's documentary, *Bix, Ain't None of Them Play Like Him Yet*.

sumers: two waltzes, two Spanish-style compositions—"La Paloma" and "La Golondrina"—and some easy pieces that were expected to gain success. Such a policy, with clear commercial intent, was not fruitless. Released shortly after their recording dates, four sides were listed among the best-sellers in the summer of 1928: "C-O-N-S-T-A-N-T-I-N-O-P-L-E," a novelty tune, "Get Out and Get Under the Moon," "Last Night I Dreamed You Kissed Me," and "Evening Star." A fifth title in this series likewise had a good reception in September, "The Man I Love," featuring the passable radio singer Vaughn DeLeath, and an original Tram solo.

Professionally speaking, Bix could not find much satisfaction in these dates. His limited abilities to read music gave him the third or fourth trumpet part—the least important one in the orchestral ensembles. This routine work was scarcely exciting. "He's got to sit up there," recalled Bill Challis, "with his trumpet, and what's more natural than maybe have a drink, or something like that. [Onstage], you only had to sit up there to be seen—or if they gonna play a couple of dance numbers which were part of our latest records, and Bix was on it, he had to sit there all night waiting for these two spots. That can be very frustrating working with the band."[22]

Worried by the extremely high operating expenses of this large orchestra, Whiteman used the move to Columbia as an excuse to put an end to the $50 that he paid his *hot* and most valuable musicians for each side they cut—and Bix was among that number. Such a decision deprived him of a significant portion of his revenue. The Whiteman Orchestra was featured for one week at the Capitol Theater in Detroit, opening on May 26, and the next week at Shea's Buffalo Theater in Buffalo, New York. They returned to Manhattan on Saturday, June 9. Though the workload of the preceding months had been intense, Paul Whiteman was sure his musicians could do even better: they would record on Sundays, and appear onstage on weekdays.

New York, Sunday, June 10, 1928

Five titles were cut on this "day of rest." Three of them: "Japanese Mammy," "Chiquita"—a silly little song that stayed among the best-sellers for six weeks—and "In the Evening" are all forgettable, but the two others have a certain interest. "I'd Rather Cry Over You" has a pleasant melody, and Bill Challis had left some open space in his orchestration for Bix and Tram to insert a short improvisation. The gestation of "'Tain't So, Honey, 'Tain't So" was difficult: four takes were rejected on May 21, followed by three more attempts, also destroyed, on May 23. The ninth try made it, and this record was a well-deserved success. Roy Bargy as-

22. Thirteenth program of *Bix, a Biographical Radio Series*, op. cit.

The Whiteman Orchestra at the Capitol Theater in Detroit at the end of May 1928. Left to right, onstage: Roy Bargy (p), George Marsh (dm), Paul Whiteman, Lennie Hayton (p); front row: Harry Goldfield, Charles Margulis (tp), Chester Hazlett, Frank Trumbauer, Irving Friedman, Charles Strickfaden, Roy Maier, Rube Crozier (reeds); second row: Eddie Pinder, Bix (tp), Mike Trafficante, Min Leibrook (tu), Mike Pingitore, Austin Young (bjo), Kurt Dieterle (vln); back row: Boyce Cullen, Wilbur Hall, Bill Rank, Jack Fulton (tb), John Bouman, Charles Gaylord, Matty Malneck, Mischa Russell (vln). (Whiteman Collection, Williams College)

serted that these many failures were Bix's fault, but Bill Challis's arrangement was highly demanding for both the singer and the cornet player. Bix's first solo fills eight measures, played with a mute and following a most graceful development. His second solo, played with an open horn, combines a remarkable melodic creation with an amazing rhythmic exploration, one that led Randy Sandke to write that "Bix stretches the rhythm further than anything he'd done up to this point. Only five of the sixteen bars contain downbeats. This solo is a wonderful example of how Bix's playing can be both simple and complex at the same time."[23]

Bix met up with Jimmy McPartland on the evening of one of these hardworking days. The young Chicago musicians had abruptly lost their engagement at the Little Club. Out of work, they all lived crammed into suite 1411 at the Whitby Apartments. They crashed parties they were able to slip into, cadging at least a few drinks when they couldn't get hold of more substantial items. One night they managed to attend a reception on Park Avenue, to which Bix and several of his friends had been invited. Jimmy McPartland told Bix of their financial difficulties: "Bix brought out his wallet," recalled McPartland, "and from a bunch of cheques and notes picked out two 100-dollar bills. '*Take this,*' he said. I explained that I didn't want so much, just twenty bucks or so to save myself from starving, but he insisted."[24] The musicians took off on Monday, June 11, for Trenton, New Jersey, a few miles from Philadelphia, and set up for a week at the Lincoln Theater. They were billed for four daily shows, at three, six, eight, and ten o'clock at night.

23. *Observing a Genius at Work,* op. cit., p. 35.

24. *Jazz Talking,* op. cit., p. 163.

188 — *1928: The Crack-Up*

New York, June 17–20, 1928

As could be expected, their return to New York on Saturday, June 16, brought the band to a new three-day imprisonment in the Columbia studios. Five pieces were cut on Sunday, four more the next day, and two titles on Tuesday. "I'm on a Crest of a Wave" was recorded, ironically, on the same day that Amelia Earhart was celebrated as the first woman to fly across the Atlantic—and Norwegian explorer Roald Amundsen's plane disappeared at sea. Three titles arranged by Bill Challis gave Bix a new chance to be heard. "Georgie Porgie" and "Out o' Town Gal" were of decent quality, but Bing Crosby and Bix Beiderbecke gave a particular luster to "Because My Baby Don't Mean 'Maybe' Now." The cornet player was given two parts: an inventive seventeen-bar jaunt around the melody, interrupted by the orchestra playing the bridge, followed by six spirited measures from Bix, attacked *forte* in a high register, and gradually descending both melodically and dynamically with a

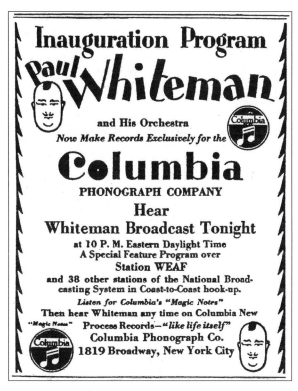

Ad published on June 19, 1928, in the *New York Times*. (from Franz Hoffmann documentation)

consummate artistry. Bix's fire was not shared by the rest of the band. "Indeed there are Whiteman records of this period where even Bix, with all his energy and sparkle, must struggle to lift the ponderous ensembles and leaden rhythm," wrote Richard M. Sudhalter. "'Because My Baby Don't Mean "Maybe" Now' is one of them. The arrangement by Challis is cheerful enough, but the orchestra is slow to move. It is here that Steve Brown's loss is most acutely felt: tuba and bowed string bass, keeping oompah time in octaves, weigh the rhythm down with a leaden rigidity even Bix has trouble overcoming."[25]

Tom Satterfield's arrangement of "That's My Weakness Now" cleverly creates a call-and-response scheme between the Rhythm Boys and different instruments. The realization is superb: the vocalists sing a one-bar phrase, answered, in turn, by Irving Friedman, Bill Rank, Tram, and Bix, the cornetist once again demonstrating his ability to make the most of the shortest possible space. June 19 and 20 were dedicated to two valueless records: "American Tune," a patriotic anthology by

25. *Bix Beiderbecke, Giants of Jazz*, op. cit., p. 50.

Ferde Grofé, and "Tchaikowskiana," a medley of different Tchaikowsky themes—an ill-chosen record in which Paul Whiteman leads his orchestra into territory where it does not belong.

The musicians left New York on June 21 for a long train trip, as it took two days and one night to get to Minneapolis, where they played at the Minnesota Theater between June 23 and 29. They arrived in Chicago on the evening of June 30.

Chicago, end of 1927–July 1928

The end of Louis Armstrong's engagement at the Sunset Café, in the autumn of 1927, and his departure from the Clarence Jones Orchestra had put the trumpeter temporarily out of work.[26] This period of inactivity allowed him to record one last time with his original Hot Five, at the Okeh studios. Six titles were cut in three days. This high-quality series was dominated by "Hotter than That," which was recorded on December 13 and appeared for three weeks among the best-sellers of May 1928. Louis Armstrong's success was beginning to sneak across the racial barrier. Then Louis had a pretty bad idea: to form his own band and rent a theater to accommodate the vast audience that would certainly flock to hear him play. Drummer Zutty Singleton and pianist Earl Hines were involved in this enterprise, and the Hot Six opened in January 1928 at Warwick Hall, near Forestville Avenue. A never-ending week in a nearly empty theater was enough to end the dream; then as now, publicity was necessary to complement talent. The debut of Louis Armstrong's group was hurt even more by the opening of a huge dance hall on 47th Street and Parkway Boulevard, only two blocks away: the Savoy Ballroom. The engagement of Caroll Dickerson in this new place brought Louis, in March 1928, back into the orchestra of his former employer. Zutty Singleton was still at the trumpeter's side, but Earl Hines joined Jimmy Noone at the Apex Club.

Three days before Bix's arrival in Chicago, Louis Armstrong had formed a new Hot Five and cut eight sides for the Okeh label. These sessions of uneven quality displayed Earl Hines's outstanding talent and produced one of the greatest records in the history of jazz, "West End Blues." Composed and recorded by King Oliver in New York a few days earlier, this number inspired Louis to an astonishing creation: the fame of its trumpet introduction is truly warranted, but Louis's vocal part—alternating phrases with the clarinet—and his ecstatic solo chorus that concludes the side are in no way inferior. The people loved these qualities, and "West End Blues" was a bestseller for two months, in September and October 1928.

The Whiteman Orchestra made its debut at the Chicago Theater on July 2. The band was expected to play four shows a day during the week . . . and five shows on

26. While Bix would always remain a cornet player, Louis Armstrong switched from the Harry B. Jay Columbia cornet he had used in King Oliver's band to a Buescher trumpet. This change seems to have taken place on the Hot Five recordings made after 1927.

Saturday and Sunday. The promotional campaign directed by Paul Whiteman emphasized the size of the company: "The traveling organization carries thirty-three players, twenty-four wives, four babies, nine dogs, two property men, two nurses, one manager, three arrangers, one macaw, one valet, and two stage directors." Bix Beiderbecke and Louis Armstrong had not seen each other since the end of August 1926. The success of "Singin' the Blues" had awakened Louis to the musical qualities of someone he had until then merely considered a "white cat." "The first time I heard Bix," said Louis, "I said these words to myself: there's a man as serious about his music as I am. . . . Bix did not let anything at all detract his mind from that cornet, and his heart was with it all the time."[27]

After a sleepless night, Louis Armstrong attended the first matinee of the Whiteman show, on July 2. Hearing "From Monday On" left the trumpeter with unforgettable memories: "They swung it all the way, and all of a sudden Bix stood up and took a solo," Louis

Louis Armstrong around 1930, portrait autographed to Hoagy Carmichael: "Hello 'Hoag' You 'Rascal' from Louis Armstrong, February 27, 1932." (Indiana University Collection)

added. "And I'm tellin' you, those pretty notes went all through me. . . . Then Mr. Whiteman went into the Overture by the name of '1812' . . . and he had those trumpets way up into the air, justa' blowing like mad, but good . . . and my man Bix was reading those dots and blowing beautifully . . . and just before the ending of the overture, they started to shooting cannons, ringing bells, sirens were howling like mad, and in fact everything was happening in that overture. But you could still hear Bix . . . the reason why I said through all those different effects that were going on, at the ending you could still hear Bix. Well, you take a man with a pure tone like Bix's and no matter how loud the other fellows may be blowing, that pure cornet or trumpet tone will cut through it all. . . . Bix sounded so good. I had to go back stage and say hello to him, and that's something I don't usually do. Some people don't act the same, oh, I don't know, maybe it's the nervous tension, or . . . . Anyway, Bix received me with open arms. We hugged

27. *Hear Me Talkin' To Ya*, op. cit., pp. 158–159, and *The Leon Bix Beiderbecke Story*, op. cit., p. 384. Louis said he was "playing for Joe Glaser at the Sunset at Thirty-fifth and Calumet Streets," which cannot be exact: he was at that time working at the Savoy Ballroom.

and kissed something wonderful." The two men met again, later in the evening, at the Savoy Ballroom: "When Bix finished work that night at the theatre," recalled Louis Armstrong, "he came directly to the place where I worked. He stayed there until the customers left. That's when we locked all the doors. My band stayed, Bix and his friends remained, and you're talking about a jam session that was priceless! Hmmm! I've never heard such good music since. Bix had a way of expressing himself. His music would make you want to go right up to the bandstand, shake his hand and make yourself known. . . . Everyone was feeling each other's note or chord . . . and blend with each other instead of trying to cut each other . . . we did not think of such a mess . . . we tried to see how good we could make music sound which was an inspiration within itself."[28] Bill Rank, Izzy Friedman, and Roy Bargy had followed Bix. They also remembered that night as a moment of great musical creation, of a true fusion between the different styles of Louis Armstrong and Bix Beiderbecke. It is almost certain that the latter could be in top form on such occasions, something that, unfortunately, no recording was ever able to preserve.

Chicago, Thursday, July 5, and Saturday, July 7, 1928

On July 5, Bix and Louis were both at the Okeh studios, at 227–229 West Washington Street, on the top floor of the Consolidating Talking Machine Company building, but, alas, they didn't record in the same room. Louis cut a title with his Hot Five and two with the eleven-piece group directed by Caroll Dickerson, recordings that the trumpeter and Earl Hines dominated. The other group recording that day was the Frank Trumbauer Orchestra, the band being nearly identical to the one formed three months before. Eddie Lang was in New York, and was replaced by George Rose. Two of Bix's old friends sat in with the group: drummer Harry Gale, with whom the cornetist had first played in January 1922; and Dee Orr, a second drummer, from the Arcadia Ballroom, who was part of the vocal trio. Bix's playing is of good quality, and it is difficult to decide whether the small imperfections that are perceptible on these sides originate from tired lips or from a lack of practice on the tunes chosen by Okeh. The two songs, which supposedly responded to the taste of the audience, use a half-sung, half-spoken minstrel show dialogue that was then popular. Tram's strange voice can be heard on "Bless You! Sister," singing in a gospel style. "Dusky Stevedore" was selected for its commercial potential—and this title would shortly be featured on the October 1928 charts.

Two sides were recorded two days later, in the same studio, by Bix Beiderbecke and His Gang. "I was present in the studio when 'Ol' Man River' was being

28. Hear He Talkin' to Ya, op. cit., p. 159.

recorded," recounted Burnie, Bix's brother. "All the musicians were in their shirt sleeves as it was hotter than hell. . . . I was surprised no one knew before they started recording what numbers were to be recorded. All from scratch."[29] The truth is that it can be heard, if only through the lack of precision in the musicians' entries. They could hardly feel uneasy with "Ol' Man River," a song they had played many times since the beginning of the year. They also knew the second title well, "Wa-Da-Da," cut in New York on June 19 by the Rhythm Boys. The band executes this Harry Barris composition with spirit, but the initial pressing of the record featuring these two numbers didn't sell more than 3,000 copies—ten times fewer than the worst-selling Paul Whiteman releases.

The orchestra remained at the Chicago Theater until July 8. They moved for one week to the Uptown Theater, and ended their stay in the Windy City with a last week spent at the Tivoli Theater. Gene Krupa was one of the young Chicagoans, and he remembered a visit Bix made one night to the club where he was playing drums: "Bix came over, between or after the last show, and sat in with us. Up to that point, the greatest thrill in my life was to play in the same group, to jam with Bix. . . . If you couldn't get along with him, you couldn't get along with anybody. I remember being hungry a lot of times . . . and Bix would come and get us in . . . he put in the bill for the meal, and not for one, but for the whole band."[30]

Davenport, July–August 1928

Paul Whiteman's musicians were generously granted three weeks of vacation, except for the Rhythm Boys, who were sent on tour on the Radio-Keith-Orpheum circuit. Bix returned to Davenport, with hundreds of hours of lost sleep to make up. He met old friends in his hometown, some of whom were musicians, and Bix noticed that things weren't as easy for him as they used to be: he had become a star, and his presence could intimidate his one-night partners. Herbert Ross Reaver, for example, remembered, "Bix came 'home' for a vacation. It was between July 22 and August 15. Eagles Hall was a dance hall in the Fraternal Order of Eagles Building. I was playing a public dance job there and Bix sat in for a few tunes. It was thrilling to feed him the banjo chords and the beat, and listen to him take off."[31]

The Whiteman Orchestra would spend the second part of the year on the road. The band gathered in New York on August 15, facing a heavy schedule. They were expected in a different city and a different dance hall every night, the company moving by train from one place to the next during the day. The band crossed Pennsylvania, stopped in Atlantic City, went up to Massachusetts, Rhode Island, and New Hampshire, and returned to New York on September 3.

29. *The Leon Bix Beiderbecke Story*, op. cit. p. 387.

30. Twelfth program of *Bix, a Biographical Radio Series*, op. cit.

31. *The Leon Bix Beiderbecke Story*, op. cit., p. 388. The Eagles building is still visible at 1404 Sixth Avenue in Moline, a town built on the left bank of the Mississippi, across the river from Davenport.

New York, Tuesday, September 4–Thursday, September 6, 1928

A single side was released from the many takes recorded during the first day in the studio, an Irving Berlin composition, "Roses of Yesterday." From the next day on, Paul Whiteman engaged in a long and difficult challenge: the recording of George Gershwin's *Concerto in F*. The sessions on September 5 and 6 were fruitless. *Rhapsody in Blue* had been a spontaneous work, hastily written on a whim by Gershwin, and orchestrated by Ferde Grofé in 1924 for performance by the Whiteman Orchestra. Gershwin took up the writing of his *Concerto in F* in a different way. He worked on this composition over a long period, doing the orchestration by himself. These efforts resulted in a more reflective and subtle piece, in which the composer exhibited obvious technical improvement. The harmonic and melodic complexities of this music represent a significant move on the path Gershwin followed toward a fusion between certain elements of jazz and the composition methods of Debussy and Ravel. Premiered in 1925 at the New York Symphony So-

ciety, with its composer on piano, the *Concerto in F* was the fruit of a long labor. Similar efforts, and many hours in the studio, were necessary to complete the six recorded sides that contain this twenty-four-minute work.

The Paul Whiteman Orchestra, September 1928. Left to right, front row: Matty Malneck, Chester Hazlett, Mike Pingitore, Lennie Hayton, Paul Whiteman, Roy Bargy (on piano), Kurt Dieterle, Mischa Russell, Charles Margulis, Irving Friedman, Roy Maier, George Marsh, Mike Trafficante, Wilbur Hall; second row: Charles Gaylord, Eddie Pinder, Austin Young, Rube Crozier, Charles Strickfaden, Min Leibrook, Frank Trumbauer, Bill Rank, Jack Fulton, Bix, Boyce Cullen, Harry Goldfield. (Duncan Schiedt Collection)

New York, Friday, September 14–Tuesday, September 18, 1928

The Columbia recordings resumed on September 14, after the band returned from a week at Boston's Metropolitan Theater. Two musical compilations, unsuccessfully attempted ten days earlier, were successfully recorded: "In the Good Old Summertime" and "On the Sidewalks of New York" made up the two sides of a superfluous record. Two more days were dedicated to the *Concerto in F*. The first part of the second movement, *Andante Con Moto*, was recorded at the end of the session, on Saturday the fifteenth. It opened on two trumpet solos: the first was executed by Charles Margulis, and the second, played with a mute, was probably by

Bix.[32] The cornetist was able to handle this short and tricky part, an achievement that might have brought a proud and brilliant smile to the lips of the "musical degenerate."

On September 17, Columbia also asked Paul Whiteman to record "Jeannine, I Dream of Lilac Time," a tune written after the silent film *Lilac Time*. This was a strange decision. Gene Austin's version was already a big hit in September 1928, and a Nat Shilkret record of the same song also ranked high in sales at very time when Whiteman recorded it. Paul Whiteman could not expect much from this overexposed hit. Larger twelve-inch 78-rpm records, which could hold up to nearly five minutes of music, had already been used for some Whiteman recordings since the end of 1927: "Washboard Blues," "The Man I Love," "My Melancholy Baby," and the *Concerto in F*. The two titles cut on September 18 were also released on these large records. Comparing these two sides gives a good opportunity to appreciate the quality of Bill Challis's work. The two orchestrations are constructed on the same model: three and a half minutes of singing and "musical variations," played at a rather slow tempo, followed by thirty seconds of a "rhythmic part"—focused in both cases on a *hot* solo by Bix—and a short "symphonic" conclusion. Ferde Grofé had written the arrangement for "Gypsy," and Bill Challis the arrangement of "Sweet Sue." Good taste is a missing element in Ferde Grofé's work: his score is turgid and pompous, crammed with several measures of accordion, a part for a gypsy violin, and a quote from Liszt's second *Hungarian Rhapsody*. At the end of this chaotic display, Bix's solo falls like a pearl into a broth, a high-priced gem packed in a paper bag.

"Sweet Sue" had been Ben Pollack's first big hit in the summer of 1928. Despite some Hollywood effects, Bill Challis's orchestration is interesting, as wisely summed up by Marc Richard, "The scoring written for 'Sweet Sue' is similar to the one for 'Gypsy,' less the accordion and the cimbalom, but with a more subtle range of sound colors: a beautiful quartet of muted trombones (cup mutes) can be heard, probably for the first time. The vocal part is firmly supported by an accompaniment on celeste which enhances Jack Fulton's ultra-tenor voice, preceding Tino Rossi and Michael Jackson. Bix's chorus seems to have been expected for a long time, as if the first part of the side was nothing more than a three minute and a half introduction."[33] Bix's solo is a true jewel, developed with a gripping melodic and dramatic sense, and masterfully brought to its peak. It is played with a "derby" mute, according to Bill Challis's instruction. Bix would, however, make more and more frequent use of a mute, this accessory providing resistance to the flow of air blown into the instrument, thus reducing the effort required to create the desired sound.

32. Richard Hadlock wrote: "When a cornet soloist was called for in the Whiteman recording of George Gershwin's *Concerto in F*, Bix was assigned the part. His moody, muted opening statement, sounding curiously like Miles Davis in the late fifties, comes off without hitch or hesitation" (*Jazz Masters of the '20s*, op. cit. p. 100). Randy Sandke does not agree, writing, "It has often been reported, by pianist Roy Bargy and others, that Bix played the solo on the first part of the second movement. Nevertheless, the aural evidence confirms that this is not the case. The sound and phrasing of the soloist is nowhere near Bix's." (*Observing a Genius at Work*, op. cit., p. 38).

33. Booklet of the French Masters of Jazz CD: *Bix Beiderbecke, Volume 7, Complete Edition, 1928–1929*, pp. 1–2.

New York, Wednesday, September 19–Friday,

September 21, 1928

After being featured on September 18 on another radio broadcast from the Astor Hotel in New York, the next day the Whiteman Orchestra carried on with its interminable series of recordings. The end of the year was getting closer, and two sides were devoted to Christmas carols. Bix left the studio during the session, which seems understandable and forgivable. Quickly released, the record reached a good place in the December sales. It offers an effective remedy for the most incurable insomniacs, but this peaceful aspect escaped the musicians during their difficult day's work, as Bill Challis recalled: "Eddie King, the fellow who didn't like the bands to do any improvising, had decided that we would make a record of 'Silent Night, Holy Night' and another side, both Christmas records. Nobody felt like making things like that, but King wanted to put them out, and he went right ahead . . . started off the record with sleigh-bells, then an organ, the whole works. Well, here he is . . . playing the organ himself, then turns around and the band is supposed to start playing. But nothing worked right, and the boys were losing their patience. You know there's a point where you get almost to exhaustion, where you can't go any further . . . and just before King is ready to give the down beat for 'Silent Night,' Chet Hazlett breaks everything up with a great big horse whinny."[34]

Bix was in good form during the September 20 and 21 sessions in the Okeh studios. He played with an open horn on both days. On September 20, the Frank Trumbauer Orchestra recorded two high-quality sides: "Take Your Tomorrow" and "Love Affairs." The next day, Bix recorded with his Gang for the last time. A strange decision had relegated pianist Lennie Hayton to the drums, and the lack of finesse of the rhythm section is the only negative element of a session that generated "Rhythm Kings," "Louisiana," and "Margie," three good numbers, although they do not reach the standard of the sides cut one year before by the same group. Bix was obviously not aware that he had begun an inexorable descent.

Paul Whiteman had organized a new tour, and the band traveled from September 22 through 29 in western New York, with stops in Pennsylvania, West Virginia, and Ohio. Sunday the twenty-third was a day of rest in Harrisburg, Pennsylvania. Bix spent the day with a trumpeter friend, Richardson Turner. The two men shared a great admiration for British humorist P. G. Wodehouse. "Around noon I dropped down to Bix's room," said Turner. "He got to talking about the Original Dixieland Jazz Band, and how it had been his original inspiration. Talk drifted to Larry Shields, and Bix slowly picked up his horn and started fooling around with some of Larry's clarinet breaks. He warmed to the idea and, oblivious to my presence for about a half an hour, worked out many of the difficult Shields breaks and riffs—on his cornet! I don't know why I was so impressed, but I've never forgotten that not only did he remember so many of them, but he could play them on a cornet. I mentioned what the Gennett

34. "Bill Challis Speaks Out, An Interview," in *Storyville*, no. 12 (August/September 1967), pp. 29–30.

Wolverines meant to me, and he said with embarrassment, *'They were so corny that I'm ashamed of them!'*"

The two men played a game of golf that afternoon, a sport at which Bix managed to be worse than his partner—"which is pretty bad," added Turner. "We halved many holes at ten. He insisted on betting every hole, and never had a penny to pay up." Playing sports is indispensable to maintaining good physical condition, but golf can be boring. Bix and Tram found a way to spice it up, developing a new game they called "drink and sniff." Irving Friedman recalled its rules: "One day we decided to have a tournament amongst ourselves. Each foursome would start at the first hole with two quarts of whiskey. The two low men on each hole would take a drink, the two losers would get to 'smell' the bottle. Needless to say, it wasn't too long before the winners were losers and vice versa. However, the winner was Bix—no one could compete with him. While we somehow staggered in after losing golf balls and clubs all over the course, Bix was just as fresh as when we started. We never tried that again."[35]

The band's return to New York on October 2 was the occasion for a lavish celebration: the tenth anniversary of Paul Whiteman's arrival in the city where he achieved success. Six hundred fifty guests gathered that night at a gala dinner at the Astor Hotel.

New York, Friday and Saturday, October 5 and 6, 1928

Neither Columbia nor Paul Whiteman was satisfied with the recording the previous month of the last part of the *Concerto in F*, a four-minute *allegro brio* that was tricky to perform. George Gershwin was present at the new session, directed by William Daly, the conductor who had led the premiere of the work, and the last side of the three-record set was satisfactorily completed.

In the afternoon of the same day, Frank Trumbauer recorded four new titles under his name for Okeh. The musicians assembled were an odd lot, and according to Richard M. Sudhalter's analysis, nothing good could be expected from its rhythm section: "Trumbauer apparently persuaded Whiteman reed man Rupert 'Rube' Crozier to use his bassoon, heavily miked, as a wind bass. Whiteman trombonist Wilbur Hall, if a competent guitarist, was no substitute for Eddie Lang. . . . The identity of the drummer is lost to history. Suffice to say only that his banging and clattering is even more jarring than that on the September 'Gang' sessions. It all adds up to musical ruination."[36] It should be added that commercial considerations had dictated the selection of titles: "The Love Nest" and "The Japanese Sandman" had been big hits—back in 1920. Guy Lombardo was somehow more successful than Tram with "High Up on a Hill Top," introducing his record briefly in the charts of January 1929, and the musical value of "Sentimental Baby" is near zero. The singer called on

35. *The Leon Bix Beiderbecke Story,* op. cit., p. 403.

36. Booklet of the Mosaic Records CD box set, *The Complete Okeh and Brunswick Bix Beiderbecke,* op. cit., p. 15.

for that date, Charles Gaylord, amplifies the disaster by inflicting on these sides the worst vocals that Frank Trumbauer ever had to endure—a difficult feat, as possible candidates for that distinction were many. Bix seems mysteriously indifferent to his devitalizing environment. He added a solo to "The Love Nest" that is not without its qualities, and he limits his participation on the other sides to a minimum. "On the very first take," recalled Charles Margulis, "our recording engineer, Peter Decker, motioned to me that Bix was too far away from the microphone. I reached and gave him a shove. I have big hands and it must have jarred him a bit. Bix stopped playing and quietly said, '*Don't shove. Push politely.*' For weeks thereafter, those four words were the standing joke throughout the Whiteman band."[37]

"Where Is the Song of Songs for Me?"—a waltz recorded on October 6—concluded this first series of Whiteman recordings for Columbia. The band would not return to a studio until December, and they would be engaged for two months on a grand tour, giving eighty concerts throughout twenty-two states, and even crossing into Canada.

New York, Sunday, October 7, 1928

The first show of the tour had a prestigious location: Carnegie Hall in New York.[38] Seven thousand spectators attended a program that, with only a few modifications, would be given on each stop. Sergey Rachmaninoff was in the hall, seated in the first row. The show opened with "Yes, Jazz Is Savage," a reprise by a small combo of old Whiteman tunes, covering the history of jazz from the jungle drums to the Dixieland orchestras, which permitted Bix, Bill Rank, and Izzy Friedman to shine. With the exception of "Tiger Rag," a version arranged for a large orchestra, the titles that followed were not selected from the *hottest* ones in the Whiteman repertoire: "Sugar," "Just Like a Melody Out of the Sky," "Valse Inspiration," and "My Melancholy Baby" were played with twelve violins added to the orchestra. George Gershwin and Ferde Grofé were credited with two of their compositions, the *Concerto in F* and "Metropolis." At the end of this symphonic section, three Steinway grand pianos were brought onstage. Roy Bargy and Lennie Hayton came to the instruments placed on the sides, and Bix left his chair in the brass section, walked to the piano in the center and played his own composition, "In a Mist."

This night at Carnegie Hall was a peak in Bix's professional career, an achievement he could not have believed possible when Tram, one year earlier, had convinced him to record this piece for Okeh. Generous applause greeted the end of the number, and Paul Whiteman had to stop Bix from returning too quickly to his chair: nervous and embarrassed, Bix bowed awkwardly before retreating behind his music stand. The show ended with Wilbur Hall's demonstration of the many sounds a bicycle pump could produce, followed by an acrobatic violin rendition of

37. *The Leon Bix Beiderbecke Story*, op. cit., p. 406.

38. Opened in 1891 on the corner of Seventh Avenue and 57th Street, the theater named for steel magnate Andrew Carnegie became internationally famous. The Carnegie Hall audience was introduced to "jazz" in 1912 with James Reese Europe's appearance. On April 27, 1928, six months before the Whiteman concert, the orchestra of W. C. Handy and the Jubilee Singers gave a blues and spirituals concert there: Thomas "Fats" Waller played organ and Steinway piano.

"Pop Goes the Weasel," a lowbrow vaudeville turn that Whiteman apparently felt no need to omit merely because he was playing in Carnegie Hall before Rachmaninoff. With "Chiquita" and the patriotic "American Tune" as a finale, and *Rhapsody in Blue* as an encore, the audience left the concert hall after a five-minute ovation.

Tour of the eastern and southern U.S., October–November 1928

The Whiteman Orchestra left New York on October 8 and appeared that night in Norfolk, Virginia. They would perform daily for two months—weekends included—and the days would follow one another in a similar way: departure by train in the morning for a trip of a few hours, one or two shows in the destination city, one night in a hotel, and another train waiting for them the next morning. Bix could barely stand this endless traveling, and in turn increased his alcohol consumption. The band's itinerary crossed Virginia, North and South Carolina, Georgia[39], and Tennessee, and stopped in New Orleans on October 28, where two concerts were scheduled. During the intermission of the first concert, while the musicians walked around outside the St. Charles Theater, Bix and Tram were approached by Paul Mares, the former trumpeter with the New Orleans Rhythm Kings, saxophonist Eddie Miller, and a nineteen-year-old pianist, Armand Hug. These jazzmen had come to hear *hot* music, and they asked Paul Whiteman to give Bix a more prominent part in the second part of the show. "When Whiteman got back on the floor," said Armand Hug, "he made an announcement that he had to give the floor over to Bix, or the local New Orleans musicians would tear the place

39. The Whiteman Orchestra appeared at the City Auditorium in Atlanta, Georgia, on October 23: "We were living in Atlanta," recalled Mary Louise Shoemaker, Bix's sister. "My husband and I gave a party for the whole orchestra at the Ansley Hotel. Bix and the rest of them played and played. I especially remembered 'I Can't Give You Anything but Love, Baby.' . . . It was the last time I went to bed at the break of dawn. And it was the last time I saw Bix" (*Boston Traveler*, Friday, January 17, 1958).

down. With that introduction, Bix took a solo on 'Dinah' and the place was electrified. He then went on to play his celebrated 'Singin' the Blues.' After about fifteen or twenty minutes of hearing Bix and some of the other guys trading solos, the audience was satisfied."[40] Some of the musicians met at Paul Mares's home between the two shows, where they were joined by a young guitarist, Edwin "Snoozer" Quinn, a new member of the band whom Whiteman had heard backstage and engaged on the spot. "I asked Bix how he went about working out his solos," added Armand Hug. "He told me he liked to work alone. He would be playing a few chords and then he would jot them down. He worked a lot of things out on paper. He could write

New Orleans train station on October 28, 1928. Left to right: Irving Friedman, Bix, and Paul Whiteman. (Courtesy Liz Beiderbecke Hart)

things down, you know. He worked a lot of cornet solos out on piano first. He thought things out through the piano. That's where he got many of his harmonic ideas. . . . I don't think he knew the names of the chords he was playing. He just played them through his mind and heart. It was amazing. You can hardly hear anyone outside of Armstrong that had solos that stayed with you so that you couldn't forget them." Before leaving New Orleans, Bix met for the last time with Nick La Rocca. The voyage continued on to Texas, where the orchestra spent eight days before heading north for Oklahoma.

The stop in Ponca City on November 11 left the musicians with an amusing memory. Bix could not get to the station before the train's departure. The only way he could join the band for the evening concert was to hire a private plane. A telegram reached Paul Whiteman during his trip: Bix was announcing arrival by air. Irving Friedman was among the small group that met him. "A few of us were at the 'airport'—a field that had recently been a cornfield—to witness his arrival. A converted 'Jenny,' of 1919 vintage, came in for a landing and made a very good one. We rushed up to the plane, an open cockpit type, as Bix and the pilot climbed out. As they both hit the ground, Bix put his arms around the pilot and shouted to us, '*He's the best damned pilot in the world.*' With that the pilot took two steps towards us and fell flat on his face. He was so drunk we had to support him to our cars and take them both to the hotel."[41]

Bix did not only drink on airplanes . . . and the quantity of alcohol he was swallowing during the trip began to affect his professional activities more and more often, which had not previously been the case. Paul Whiteman shared his

40. In 1976, Armand Hug recorded in New Orleans a double-LP set entitled *Bix-Hug*, released by Jazzology Records, Atlanta, Georgia. Hug's reported memories are taken from the cover of this LP set, in which the pianist plays twenty-two titles—numbers recorded by Bix, as well as four Bix piano compositions, Eastwood Lane's "Legend of Lonesome Lake," and the solo played by Bix on cornet on "Dinah," as Armand Hug remembered having heard it on October 28, 1928. (Information from Albert Haim.)

41. *The Leon Bix Beiderbecke Story*, op. cit., p. 416.

concern with Frank Trumbauer, who had a serious talk with his friend. Bix tried to calm Tram's worries, asserting that he had the situation perfectly under control, and that he could stop drinking at any moment. Bix was soon given a chance to demonstrate his ability to do so: the orchestra was going to stop on November 23 in Clinton, Iowa, a few miles north of Davenport, where the cornetist's family and numerous residents of his hometown were expected. Four days before this concert, Bix greatly reduced his consumption of alcohol, and his parents met a musician close to sobriety, doubtless somewhat nervous, but perfectly presentable. They were honored with a visit backstage after the show, where they blushingly heard Paul Whiteman emphasize the importance of their son in his orchestra.

The Hotel Cleveland on Public Square, next to the Terminal Tower in Cleveland. (Joe Mosbrook)

The day of rest granted to the musicians five days later was a disaster for Bix and his brave resolutions, and he shared his hours of idleness with a bottle of gin. The sudden resumption of excessive drinking had devastating effects on his tired body. On November 30, the orchestra was featured at the New Music Hall in Cleveland. Charles Margulis had a precise recollection of that evening: "Bix had too much to drink before the concert, and he ended up passing out as we were playing. He was seated on my right, and I am normally left-handed, so I was able to play the trumpet with my left hand and hold him upright with my right. Bix sort of snapped out of it, for a moment, and was uncertain of where he was and what was happening. . . . He took a poke at me, missed, and sort of settled back into his haze. Paul witnessed the incident and immediately had him hustled back to the hotel."[42]

When he reached his room at the Hotel Cleveland, Bix suffered a severe nervous crisis: his face and his body were streaming with sweat, and he was trembling, agitated, and delirious. A doctor was called. The tour had to resume, and the band left Cleveland the next morning, leaving Bix under the care of the doctor and a nurse.

The events of the following weeks in the life of Bix Beiderbecke are mostly lost in the shadows, and because of the lack of recollections and documentation, dates are still not cleared up. Frank Trumbauer sadly noted in his diary on the date of December 2: "Bix still gone. Stayed in Cleveland with DTs. I spent four years with him to no avail."[43]

42. The Leon Bix Beiderbecke Story, op. cit., p. 418.

43. The Leon Bix Beiderbecke Story, op. cit., p. 419. "DT," delirium tremens, as used here by Frank Trumbauer, is not medically correct, as Bix was suffering from the consequences of an excess of alcohol, and not of a withdrawal.

New York, Monday, December 10–Friday, December 14, 1928

The cornetist was in his 44th Street Hotel room on December 10, the day Paul Whiteman and his men returned to New York. Bix may have participated passively in one or two recording sessions, in a disquieting state of fatigue. "At one of these dates, Bix was trying to get a nap between numbers," wrote Frank Trumbauer. "Someone gave him a 'hot foot.' Bix jumped up and said, *'Okay, school boy, pass me a clam,'*"[44] On December 14, Bill Challis signed the orchestration of "How About Me?," a tune that was to be recorded that same day. Bix's name is not listed among the musicians selected to play this piece. This absence gives an indication, within a few days, of the date on which Bix was admitted to the River Crest Sanitarium across the East River in Astoria, where Paul Whiteman had him hospitalized. The doctors diagnosed him with pneumonia. The hospital imposed an abrupt stop of Bix's consumption of alcohol. As could be expected, this withdrawal brought on, after the third or fourth day of abstinence, a case of delirium tremens: added to the effects of the pneumonia, this crisis resulted in severe physical trauma. The gravity of this illness kept Bix in the hospital for about two weeks. "I had no trouble getting in," remembered Bill Challis. "Bix was in a top bunk bed. He said that he'd had DT's. And he said, *'I'm never going to have another drink.'* I said, *'Well, I don't think that I would either if I were you.'* He was getting out that day. He talked to me very normally, but he didn't look so hot. Not that he'd been beaten up, but his eyes were dark. He looked like a guy who had been drinking and was suffering a horrible hangover."[45]

Reading newspapers allowed Bix to keep up with the excitement of the holidays and the end-of-year celebrations. Paul Whiteman filled Carnegie Hall for a second time on December 23, participating in a concert given to benefit the fight against tuberculosis. Six days later, he opened two new shows: an evening performance at the Palace Theater, followed by a late after-show revue at the New Amsterdam Roof Garden.[46] Located on the top floor of the New Amsterdam Theater, the Roof Garden was a prestigious nightclub. Irritated at seeing the wealthy spectators of the *Ziegfeld Follies* leaving the theater at the end of the show to spend their money in the neighborhood cabarets, Florenz Ziegfeld had managed to keep a part of this clientele by opening his own club in the upper part of his theater. A late supper show regaled the night owls: the *Midnight Follies*. Joseph Urban designed a luxurious decor, with a mobile stage that slid back to provide a dance floor, and a glass mezzanine where the chorus girls could display their charms above the diners. After eight successful years, the club closed in 1923 because Prohibition had eliminated the profitable sale of alcohol. In December 1928, with Prohibition having become somewhat irrelevant in the Times Square area, Florenz Ziegfeld decided to give this nocturnal show a second try, and he called on Helen Morgan, the Duncan Sisters, and above all the Paul Whiteman Orchestra to liven up the revival of the *Midnight Follies*.

44. *TRAM, The Frank Trumbauer Story*, op. cit., p. 103. The expression "Pass me a clam" was said to have become popular among Whiteman musicians, for whom a recording session was soon known as a "clambake."

45. *Paul Whiteman, Pioneer in American Music*, op. cit., p. 218.

46. The Palace Theater was built in 1913 at 1564 Broadway, between 46th and 47th Streets. It was converted into a movie theater in 1930, and reconverted to theater for plays in 1965. The New Amsterdam Theater opened in 1903 at 214 West 42nd Street, offering a beautiful room and a huge stage, where the Ziegfeld Follies were presented for the first time in 1913. It was converted into a movie theater in 1936, and back into a theater for plays in 1997.

The monthly review *The Talking Machine World* confirmed the presence of Paul Whiteman's records among the greatest hits of the year. The band had five tunes listed among the top sellers: "My Angel," "Among My Souvenirs," "Ramona," "Together," and "Ol' Man River"—the version recorded with Bing Crosby and Bix. Whiteman's dominance was only disputed, in a minor way, by Al Jolson—with "Sonny Boy"—and by Gene Austin—with "Ramona" and "Jeannine, I Dream of Lilac Times." If he was aware of them, these December sales figures must have delighted Bix. The American public had not only rewarded "his" Whiteman records, but also several other jazz discs. The duet between Louis Armstrong and Earl Hines on "A Monday Date," Duke Ellington with "Diga Diga Doo" and "The Mooche," Fletcher Henderson and his "King Porter Stomp," King Oliver with "Four or Five Times," all had reached significant sales levels. Two Paul Whiteman recordings featuring Bix were also present on the list of hits of the last month of the year: "Out of Town Gal" and . . . "Silent Night, Holy Night."

CHAPTER 10

1929: Toward the Fall

New York, January 1929

The Whiteman Orchestra ended its stay at the Palace Theater on January 5, and two days later, took part in the premiere of *Whoopee* at the New Amsterdam Theater. Eddie Cantor, the star of this new revue produced by Florenz Ziegfeld, introduced a song that became a huge hit, "Makin' Whoopee."

The exact day on which Bix left the River Crest Sanitarium remains unknown, and his whereabouts during the month of January still raise many questions. The official discographies have Bix listed on two titles cut by the Whiteman band: "Liebestraum," a Liszt composition transcribed by Roy Bargy, recorded on December 13, 1928; and "Chinese Lullaby," cut on January 10, 1929. Bix, if present, is inaudible on these two sides, and Columbia's files do not list the names of the participating musicians. The cornetist's name does appear, however, on the related musical scores—now held in the Whiteman collection at Williams College in Williamstown, Massachusetts—and that seems to be the only "evidence" upon which Bix's presence on these two sides was assumed. But, as the "Liebestraum" score is dated March 29, 1928, and the second "autumn 1928," these documents do not prove whether or not Bix participated in the session during which these titles were recorded.

Two clues, however, allow us to name in all likelihood some of Bix's activities at the start of 1929. On January 10, following the Whiteman recording session, several musicians from the big band remained in the studio to record with singer Beatrice "Bee" Palmer. Guitarist Snoozer Quinn repeatedly insisted that Bix was present at the session. The Shimmy Queen had been performing regularly onstage since her boisterous 1921 tour of the Midwest, but her voice had never been recorded. Frank Trumbauer was a true admirer of her original vocal style: "Bee Palmer, one of the Ziegfeld girls, was a beautiful blonde who possessed a most unusual voice. Her phrasing and interpretation of a song was just about fifteen years ahead of the times. Strange as it may seem, Bee turned down various offers to record, and sang in her own apartment among friends. Lenny Hayton was always there to play piano for Bee. Ted Koehler . . . wrote two choruses of special lyrics to 'Singin' the Blues' for Bee. Lyrics for Bix's chorus and my chorus."[1] It is rather difficult to understand what Tram heard in her: the two titles she recorded that day, "Don't Leave Me, Daddy" and "Singin' the Blues," reveal a forced and piercing voice, perhaps adapted to the needs of a live performance with no stage miking, but unsuited to the microphone's intimacy.[2] But this vocal "improvisation," constructed over a recorded instrumental chorus, would have its followers.

A second piece of the puzzle can be found in Max Kaminsky's autobiography, in which the trumpeter wrote that his last encounter with Bix took place during this period. "Milt 'Mezz' Mezzrow, who was very popular in Harlem in those days," wrote Kaminsky, "had a booking for a band at the Renaissance Ballroom, and he put together a pickup group composed of Bix, who had just come out of the sanitarium after one of his alcoholic breakdowns, Bud Freeman, Tommy Dorsey, Jimmy Dorsey, Joe Sullivan, Gene Krupa and myself. It was quite an unusual thing in those days to have white musicians play for a colored dance, but it was a dreadful night for me. It was bad enough that the other musicians were older and more experienced, but the thought of playing with Bix had me so nervous I couldn't even speak. . . . I don't remember Bix playing much that night; it was so mixed up with all the different styles of playing."[3]

The Paul Whiteman Orchestra went back on the road. They were billed at Cincinnati's Music Hall from January 13 through 19, and scheduled to play in Cleveland the next week. Bix Beiderbecke's health remained precarious, and it was most likely agreed that he would skip this new tour. He probably stayed in New York for a few days, building up his strength before setting out for Davenport for some much-needed rest. His route passed through Chicago, where he had to change trains at the LaSalle Street station.

Chicago, Thursday, January 24, 1929

New York and Chicago were ruled by a law of terror and violence dictated by gangsters who acted without restraint, corrupting politicians, magistrates, and policemen

1. TRAM, *The Frank Trumbauer Story*, op. cit., p. 106. Bee Palmer had been an added attraction at the charity concert given at Carnegie Hall on December 23, 1928, and the recording session was probably agreed upon at that time.

2. The Bee Palmer recording was published on CD: '*TRAM!*' *Volume 1*, MB 107, released by the Old Masters, San Mateo, California, and also on the Mosaic set, *The Complete Okeh and Brunswick Bix Beiderbecke*, op. cit. The sound quality of the recording is average, but it's important to realize that Bee's voice was "received" better onstage than on record.

3. *My Life in Jazz*, op. cit., p. 22.

to ensure their impunity. On February 14, 1929, Alphonse "Scarface" Capone celebrated Valentine's Day by murdering seven members of George "Bugs" Moran's gang. The wild slaughter of these men, lined up and killed in a garage, at 2122 North Clark Street, would mark the beginning of the decline of Al Capone's foul empire, as he was soon implicated in the homicide. Chicago's residents had to awaken to the horrifying activities of a "syndicate" that, until this point, had managed to present a rather favorable public image. The election of Herbert Hoover as president in November 1928 accelerated the fall of Capone. Born into a family of Iowa farmers, and a strong believer in the virtues of Prohibition, the liberal Republican Hoover came to power with a designated target: Al Capone and organized crime.

"Four blocks from the LaSalle Street station, a ten-minute walk, or a two-minute cab ride, at the corner of Randolph and LaSalle, was the Hotel Sherman, one of Bix's old haunts. The Sherman's in-house night spot was the College Inn, where, in January 1929, the resident band was Ray Miller and his Orchestra," wrote Brad Kay, who suggests the possibility that Bix spent some time in Chicago during the last days of January.[4] Bix had known bandleader Ray Miller for many years. Muggsy Spanier, the cornet player in Miller's band, was also one of Bix's old acquaintances, and meeting him again brought back memories of bygone days, of an easy and happy period of his youth, spent at the Friar's Inn and on Chicago's South Side. Seven years had passed, as short and endless as a dream.

Ray Miller's orchestra had a recording session for the Brunswick Company on the afternoon of January 24. The studios were located on the sixth floor of the Brunswick building, at 623–633 South Wabash Avenue, near the train station. Bix's contract with Paul Whiteman prohibited him from appearing on records made by any of Columbia's competitors, but Muggsy Spanier knew how to convince his friend to join in, and Bix showed up in the studio on condition that his presence would remain anonymous. Ray Miller's orchestra was ready to record "Cradle of Love." Bix knew the piece—Paul Whiteman had recorded it in New York a few days earlier—and it would have been easy for him to disguise his playing, already weakened by his poor physical condition, to make sure that he would not be identified. The record has two solos, by two different trumpeters, which was uncommon.

Three takes of "Cradle of Love" were kept. Muggsy Spanier appears first with a sixteen-bar solo, and plays it identically on all takes. Singer Bob Nolan follows with a dismal vocal chorus, and a second cornet solo can be heard after the vocal, over sixteen measures. The player is obviously weak and lacks confidence, but the attack of notes and the sweet vibrato can be identified with Bix. The three recorded solos develop an original melodic line and offer significant differences, a typical Beiderbecke feature. The first take is an inspired draft, whose ideas are completed on the other two. Whether Bix was present in the Brunswick studios on January 24 remains unknown, but it is a tantalizing possibility.[5]

Such breach of contract was common practice at that time, and Irving Friedman

4. Brad Kay's article in the booklet included with the Timeless CD CBC-1-066, *Ray Miller and his Brunswick Orchestra, 1924–1929*.

5. The process of synchronized takes developed by Brad Kay (see chapter 9, note 13), applied to the first two takes of "Cradle of Love," brings a complementary element in favor of Bix: the two different solos (on the "vocal" takes) complete each other, as if Bix was answering the first one when recording the second.

readily acknowledged his participation in such "wildcat recordings." He named himself, in addition to Bix, Tram, Eddie Lang, and Joe Venuti: "We would not let them use our names for the 'Old Man' would really raise hell. Besides, our contracts were exclusive to Whiteman. But to recall time, names, place, etc., I have no recall. On most of these dates, we were paid immediately after the session and mostly in cash."[6] During the last week of January 1929, Bing Crosby also played with fire—and he got burned. Back from a tour in the Radio Keith Orpheum circuit, on January 25 he took part in a recording session with Sam Lanin's orchestra in New York. It was followed the next day by a second recording, with the Dorsey Brothers' band. Paul Whiteman immediately fired the singer, who was ultimately kept in the band thanks to Bill Challis's diplomatic intercession.

On Sunday, January 27, the Whiteman Orchestra traveled from Cleveland to Detroit, where they were featured for a week at the General Motors Research building. Whiteman found a substitute for Bix in Jean Goldkette's orchestra: Andy Secrest. Born in 1907 in Muncie, Indiana, Secrest had already established a solid reputation as a trained ensemble musician and as a soloist. Bix was his idol, and Andy Secrest's playing did not seek to minimize the strong link with his model, "I don't want anyone to say that I copied Bix," explained Secrest. "I didn't. That is, I didn't take his solos off note for note, or anything like that. You could say I was a pupil of his. . . . I sounded a good deal like him."[7] At first Paul Whiteman "borrowed" Andy Secrest from Jean Goldkette for the duration of his stay in Detroit, then—convinced by the high quality of this replacement—he hired the young man and took him away with his band to New York.

New York, February 1929

The popular Saturday night *Lucky Strike* radio broadcast promoted sales of Lucky Strike cigarettes. Lucky's competitor, P. Lorillard Company—the maker of Old Gold cigarettes—called upon Paul Whiteman's orchestra to strengthen its new musical radio program. On the evening of Tuesday, February 5, the New York radio station WABC broadcast the first *Old Gold* program in which the Whiteman Orchestra appeared.[8] It was a national broadcast, carried by forty-three stations. The contract Paul Whiteman had signed hired the band for a series of nine weekly appearances, at $5,000 each. Bix missed the first four broadcasts. According to Bill Challis, these different working conditions marked the time when the band began going downhill. "We just played the chorus and got out two and a half minutes of it to satisfy the producers," recalled Bill Challis. "Play the chorus, and always have a vocal in there—you have to. Then they got to like Bing's masculine voice. Bing became so popular. He could sing almost anything. . . . When we started to do the radio music, you got new tunes that came out as often as once a week. And you had

6. *The Leon Bix Beiderbecke Story*, op. cit., p. 427.

7. *Bix, Man and Legend*, op. cit., p. 265.

8. The radio program was broadcast from studios located in the Steinway building, which was built in 1925 at 111 West 57th Street, across from Carnegie Hall.

to play them. We had sixteen of these tunes. We couldn't concentrate on them, like we could on a recording, where we'd have a few weeks to make a nice arrangement. The band began to lose its appeal by playing radio music. It wasn't the dance music that we used to try to do at first."[9]

On the evening of February 6, the orchestra returned to the New Amsterdam Theater, where they accompanied the young talents who Florenz Ziegfeld was trying out in his *Midnight Frolics*. The singer who joined the band on February 18 was no longer a young hopeful: at forty-one, Maurice Chevalier made his true debut on a Broadway stage, after a failed attempt during his first visit to the U.S. in 1922. "Three young men were featured in an act as the Rhythm Boys," wrote Maurice Chevalier in his memoirs. "The third one, quietly leaning on the piano, looked melancholic. A pleasant voice, but slightly veiled, husky, and yet strangely captivating. I asked for his name: Bing Crosby. The truth is that the audience at the Ziegfeld Roof paid little attention to the Rhythm Boys. Their act was short—six minutes only—and it went on to marked indifference."[10]

Davenport, February 1929

Bix was in Davenport. He had left Chicago during the last days of January and returned to his childhood home, and to his mother's care. He sent Tom Rockwell, director of the Okeh recording department, a letter dated Tuesday, February 5: "Dear Tom: Guess you know that I've been through quite a siege and I thought I'd write you and tell you that I'm practically over it and will be in N.Y. in a couple of weeks, so be prepared for some bigger and better Okeh records. . . . Here's hoping I see you in a week or so."[11]

Several days later, Bix sat with a reporter from the *Davenport Sunday Democrat*, and on February 10, the musician's interview took up four columns of the Sunday paper. The paper informed its readers that "the world's hottest cornetist" was recovering at his parents' house after a recent illness, and recalled Bix's presence in Paul Whiteman's orchestra for the past year and a half. "Jazz is musical humor," Bix is quoted as saying. "The noun jazz describes a modern American technique for the playing of any music. It also describes music exhibiting influence of that technique which has as its traditional object to secure the effects of surprise, or in the broadest sense, humor."[12]

Bix then supposedly emphasized the importance of the "first jazz concert" given by Paul Whiteman in New York on February 12, 1924, at the Aeolian Hall, and he added, "The jazz band's chief stimulus, of course, was the rise of the negro 'blues' and their exploitation by the negro song-writer, W.C. Handy. They at once were melancholic and humorous, and dealt exclusively with the singer's own emotion and philosophy. . . . The visual effect of comic instruments and bodily contortions

9. "Bill Challis: The Whiteman Years," op. cit., p. 19.

10. Maurice Chevalier, *Ma route et mes chansons, tome 2: Londres, Hollywood, Paris* (Paris: Julliard, 1947), p. 152–154. During the last days of his appearance, on March 14 and 15, 1929, Chevalier recorded three songs for Victor from his movie *Innocents of Paris*: "Louise," "Wait Till You See 'Ma Chérie,'" and "Les Ananas."

11. *The Leon Bix Beiderbecke Story*, op. cit., pp. 432–433.

12. "'Jazz Is Musical Humor,' Says Davenport Composer and Cornetist of Whiteman's Band," article published in the *Davenport Sunday Democrat* on February 10, 1929.

of the musicians is, though dispensable, a part of jazz itself." Bix classified jazz as *sweet* or *hot*, clearly confirming that his heart favored the freshness of *hot* music, rather than the purring respectability of *sweet* executions whose "muffled throb" is only to be heard at debutante dances. "The humor of jazz is rich and many-sided," continued Bix. "Some of it is obvious enough to make a dog laugh. Some is subtle, wry-mouthed, or back-handed. It is by turns bitter, agonized, and grotesque. Even in the hands of white composers it involuntarily reflects the half-forgotten suffering of the negro. Jazz has both white and black elements, and each in some respects has influenced the other. Its recent phase seems to throw the light of the white race's sophistication upon the anguish of the black."

The article then recalled the musical environment in which "Bixie" had grown up, explaining that "at the Beiderbeckes', music was in the air." Bix relived for the newspaper the early days of his cornet practice, when he had taught his instrument to "live" and to express an extended range of emotions. At the end, the paper summed up Bix's career, from the Wolverines to the recent days with Paul Whiteman's orchestra, and the cornetist concluded his interview with false enthusiasm for touring across the country. "We have great times traveling about," said Bix. "The 'boys' are airplane crazy and movie-shy. We have a new Travelair plane and several are learning to pilot. Might come in handy sometimes . . . in case we oversleep and miss the train, but we're generally on time." This long interview gives, at the end, a faithful image of the young musician: once again, the mirror is empty. Bix had managed to limit his words to general considerations, shying away from any personal or intimate question.

Bix stayed in Davenport for a month. The resolution shown in the letter to Tom Rockwell was intended to delude its reader—and possibly its writer as well. Bix was facing a brutal and solitary battle with his alcoholism, and under the distraught watch of his parents, he was living in purgatory. The sense of isolation and alienation that dwells in serious alcoholics when they stop drinking often results in feelings of guilt when they relapse, which is taken as a personal failure. Bix experienced the intense physical symptoms that are caused by sudden stop of a regular ingestion of ethanol. This withdrawal causes trembling, nausea, asthenia, and acute anxiety. To a greater degree, it may also create serious distress, painful nightmares, and hallucinations. The nervous crisis that had brought him down in Cleveland and the delirium tremens attack he had suffered during his hospitalization in Astoria had reached an alarming intensity. The possibility of a recurrence could only add to his anxiety.

New York, March 1929

Somewhat comforted by a month of rest, Bix took a train for New York on March 2, placing beside him his cornet, which had remained silent for several long weeks. His mother was concerned about sending him off to his friends and his music—but she loved and accepted her son's talent, his fragility, and his weakness. Two days later, he resumed his place in Paul Whiteman's orchestra, replacing Eddie Pinder—but not Andy Secrest, who had expected to lose his job when Bix returned. On March 5, Bix participated for the first time in an *Old Gold* radio program. The Whiteman Orchestra returned to WABC's New York studios every Tuesday, and performed every evening at the New Amsterdam Theater, where Bix shared the stage with Maurice Chevalier until the French singer's departure on March 16.

Jimmy McPartland was still in New York, working in Ben Pollack's orchestra together with Benny Goodman, Bud Freeman, and a new trombonist, Jack Teagarden. The band played at the Park Central Hotel, and was featured later in the evening in the musical show at Lew Fields's Mansfield Theater.[13] These incessant and separate nocturnal activities did not prevent the musicians from getting together: "Bix didn't talk much," recalled Jimmy McPartland, "and there was certainly no conversation when a record was on. After it was over, we'd talk about how the chords resolved and, in Stravinsky or Holst, how different and interesting the harmony was. . . . We used to talk about writing a jazz symphony. The plan was to give the soloists a terrific background, with a good beat, and let them take off. Nothing ever came of the idea, but, as you know, he was very interested in writing"—a vague desire which would remain a dream. Bix managed to read music, but rather slowly, and the night before a recording, he had to go over by himself the parts that were given to him. "One thing we talked about a lot was the freedom of jazz," added Jimmy McPartland. "People used to ask Bix to play a chorus just as he had recorded it. He couldn't do it. *'It's impossible,'* he told me once. *'I don't feel the same way twice. That's one of the things I like about jazz, kid, I don't know what's going to happen next.'*"[14]

New York, Friday, March 8, 1929

Bix returned on that morning to the Okeh studios and to the Frank Trumbauer Orchestra. The band's last recording, on October 5 of the preceding year, could easily be forgotten. Tram had learned his lesson, and he supported his new ensemble with a strong rhythm section, formed with drummer Stan King, Min Leibrook on bass saxophone, and guitarist Snoozer Quinn. Tram also added Chet Hazlett on alto saxophone, as well as violinist Matty Malneck. The surprising element of the date is the presence of two cornet players: Andy Secrest was actually seated next to Bix Beiderbecke. This doubled trumpet chair has to be considered as an indication of a lack in confidence in Bix, who was known by his employers to now be fragile and unpredictable. This feeling of doubt was already felt by Bix himself, and the young understudy at his side could only inhibit the convalescent

13. Located at 256 West 47th Street, Lew Fields's Mansfield Theater is today known as the Brooks Atkinson Theater.

14. *Hear Me Talkin' To Ya,* op. cit., pp. 157–158.

musician's return. The two songs cut that day are part of the commercial repertoire that the Okeh Records catalog was increasingly leaning toward. "Futuristic
Rhythm" was one of the hit songs from the Broadway musical *Hello Daddy*—the
show that featured Ben Pollack's orchestra—and "Raisin' the Roof" was by the
same authors. Tram sings on the first title, and his vocal is followed by two Bix solos: sixteen bars, then eight more, between which Bill Rank adds a short trombone
solo. The imperfections of the cornet chorus have led certain critics to attribute all
or part of this solo to Andy Secrest.
However, the degree of inspiration of
the melodic development by the
soloist suggests it has to be Bix Beiderbecke, something Richard Sudhalter urged as early as 1967: "The
muffled notes—every one of them
attributable to the ravages of sickness
and inactivity on his lip—do little to
detract from the essential beauty of
the improvisation." Sudhalter went
on to explain that the lack of regular
practice quickly affects a trumpet
player's technique: "Bix's accuracy
had dropped off. In the seventh bar
of the chorus, he misses the culmi-

Red Nichols's band on tour in
the spring of 1929. Left to right,
front row: Tommy Thunen (cut
off on the left, only his collar is
visible), Max Kaminsky, Joe
Sullivan, Pee Wee Russell,
Red Nichols, Herb Taylor; back
row: Mezz Mezzrow, Bud
Freeman, Dave Tough, Eddie
Condon. (Duncan Schiedt
Collection)

nating note of one of those arpeggiated triplet figures he had tossed off with ease
on such earlier discs as 'Riverboat Shuffle' with Trumbauer. After a thoroughly
lack-lustre release by Bill Rank—not one of his better days, either—Bix enters
forcefully, a la 'Goose Pimples,' but his chops betray him and the result is an ugly
'clam' in the second bar. But the cadence of the same passage, only two bars later,
is a definitive study in the kind of pure-toned lyricism which stamps Leon Beiderbecke to all who hear him and marvel."[15] Bix is much less present on the second ti-

15. Richard Sudhalter [Art
Napoleon], "Heresy, Hearsay
and Humbug: Bix and the
Discographers," in *Storyville*,
no. 12 (August/September
1967), pp. 13–14.

16. "Louise" was one of Maurice
Chevalier's most famous songs.
His recording was preceded by a
few days by Ben Pollack and His
Park Central Orchestra, which
recorded the tune on March 1,
1929. It was followed by Bing
Crosby's first version, cut with
the Whiteman band on March 15,
then by a second Crosby recording, with the Rhythm Boys on
April 10, and finally by a Frank
Trumbauer Orchestra recording
dated April 17.

tle cut, "Raisin' the Roof," which is a weaker piece. March 10 was Bix's twenty-sixth
birthday, a date he was probably not in the mood to celebrate.

The March 12 *Old Gold* program featured Bix's solo on "Singin' the Blues," and
it also treated its listeners to Bing Crosby's interpretation of the soon-to-be hit
"Louise."[16] The song had been written for Maurice Chevalier's first American film,
Innocents of Paris, and it gave the French singer his first American success, remain-
ing ten weeks among the best-sellers of the summer of 1929. Bing Crosby first
heard this attractive tune during Maurice Chevalier's act in the Ziegfeld *Midnight
Frolics*, and he recorded it on March 15, the day Bix returned to Columbia studios.
Playing the fourth part in Whiteman trumpet section—which also included
Charles Margulis, Harry Goldfield, and Andy Secrest—the cornetist can hardly be

heard on either of the two titles cut that day, "Louise" and "Blue Hawaii." These songs were released on the same Columbia record, and both became hits during the summer of 1929.

Until the end of April, the Whiteman Orchestra appeared daily at the New Amsterdam Theater in the musical *Whoopee* and played late-night shows on the Roof in the *Midnight Frolics* revue. Monday afternoons were dedicated to rehearsals for the *Old Gold* broadcast, which was aired live the next day. The rehearsal on Monday, April 1, was attended by Ray Ventura, a twenty-one-year-old French dance band leader who, with several of his musician friends, had just arrived in New York on the liner *Ile de France*.[17]

A few months after his return to France, Ventura contributed two articles to the *Revue du Jazz* recounting the impressions of a French musician landed in New York. "In New York, jazz is boiling all over," Ventura wrote. "In any hotel worthy of the name, a renowned jazz band plays during meals. In the dance halls, two bands. In movie theaters, as a show between two films, you hear jazz. At the theater, in the pit, for revues and operettas, still more jazz. As an attraction, billed at the top, in any music hall, always and everywhere, jazz follows you like an obsession. Jazz without any doubt is America's popular music . . . but a popular music of quality that has nothing in common with our working-class little waltzes." Ray Ventura was driven to the Harlem night clubs, where he heard black jazzmen, the true "jazz apostles," and the creators of a music of which "Armstrong's records give only a vague idea. You must see with your eyes and hear with your ears to believe it."[18]

Ray Ventura and his friends were invited by a Columbia employee to attend the April 1 rehearsal of the Whiteman Orchestra. "For a one-hour radio concert, the musicians practice all of Monday afternoon, from around one o'clock to six o'clock," continued Ventura. "Each has a set place. Paul listens to his band through loudspeakers and, from a room next to the studio, makes suggestions." The European visitors were enthusiastic spectators at the creation of an imaginative and inventive musical presentation: they heard a Bix improvisation on "Sleepy Time Gal," and "a few measures of unequalled sweetness and tone" played by Frank Trumbauer. A medley of French songs—"La Madelon," "On the Boulevard," and "Ça c'est Paris"—were on the afternoon's program. Directed by Ferde Grofé, the band broke down chaotically after the first few measures: "An uproar begins that no one tries to stop . . . all of a sudden, an extraordinary calm. Paul himself, although ill, had just entered the studio. We look at each other, very surprised by the way he impresses his men, who resume rehearsing the 'French Medley.' But things are not going well . . . the tempo, the rhythm aren't there. Paul then takes over the direction and conducts with an energy that one would scarcely expect him to show at first sight. He knows very well at which tempo these French pieces are to be played, and they are soon finalized."[19] At the end of the session, Ray Ventura man-

17. The steamer *Ile de France* sailed from Le Havre to New York in six days. A number of entertainers sailed on her: Florence Mills in September 1927; Maurice Chevalier in October 1928; Milton "Mezz" Mezzrow took the ship to go back to France on March 2, 1929.

18. Ray Ventura's article published in *La Revue du Jazz*, no. 5 (November 1929). This magazine, one of the very first dedicated solely to jazz, was created in July 1929 by a French bandleader, Krikor Kélénian, known as Grégor (his band was Grégor et ses Grégoriens). The magazine was discontinued in March 1930.

19. Ray Ventura's article in *La Revue du Jazz*, no. 6–7 (January 7, 1930).

aged to get Paul Whiteman and his main soloists to autograph a $20 bill, and he kept this collector's item in his wallet until the end of his life.[20]

New York, Friday, April 5, 1929

With amazing consistency, Al Jolson created huge hits for the Brunswick label. Two of his songs, "There's a Rainbow Round My Shoulder" and "Sonny Boy," remained among the best-sellers for three months at the end of 1928, and Jolson renewed this success in the summer of 1929 with "Little Pal" and "I'm in Seventh Heaven," both from his new film *Say It with Songs*. The Whiteman Orchestra devoted its April 5 recording date to versions of these two last songs. Four takes of "Little Pal" were rejected, but Columbia released a version of "I'm in Seventh Heaven," featuring the Rhythm Boys and Jack Fulton. Bill Challis's arrangement reused an idea that had worked well on "Sugar" in February 1928, with Charles Strickfaden playing the "straight" melody on baritone saxophone, accompanied by a countermelody improvised by Bix. The lack of confidence of the cornetist is obvious on the first part of his sixteen bars, and the repeated emission of high notes that opens the last eight measures seems forced. His performance on "Sugar," a year earlier, was of an entirely different caliber.

New York, Wednesday, April 17, 1929

The ensemble that Frank Trumbauer led to the Okeh studios was similar to the one at his previous recording. Two cornet players were again present: Bix and Andy Secrest, and Roy Bargy replaced Lennie Hayton on piano. The titles required a singer, and the studio called upon one of its up-and-coming talents, Smith Ballew, a twenty-seven-year-old Texan. He had learned to play banjo and guitar, and in 1920, he entered the University of Texas, where he met Jimmie Maloney; the two formed a small student band, Jimmie's Joys. After leaving the university, Smith Ballew gradually gave up the banjo and focused on singing. His first significant record was made with the Dorsey Brothers Concert Orchestra, recording "Was It a Dream?" on July 16, 1928. "It was a tremendous recording," said Smith Ballew, "with all the top musicians in New York. It filled both sides of a 10-inch record and it turned out beautifully. . . . After making that record, Okeh gave me a contract, and it was easier sailing. Also, about that time, I started recording with Frank Trumbauer. He usually asked for me on his dates, except when he wanted to sing the number himself. . . . I wish you might have sat in on some of those dates with Frankie. They would all sit around for the first hour, just noodling and entertaining each other. Then they would get around to making a test and, by the time the

20. Daniel Nevers, to whom Ray Ventura had shown this document, was able to confirm the existence of this autographed bank note. Bix added on a card a few words for Danny Polo, who had been playing in France since 1928, taking part in Ray Ventura's first Columbia recording session. Unfortunately, these documents could not be found in Ventura's personal papers after the bandleader's death. (Information from Ventura's nephew Sacha Distel.)

morning session was over, they hadn't accomplished very much. They had not even made a master in that three hours. In the afternoon, they would play around some more and finally get maybe one master. While Okeh wanted to give them ample leeway for a fine recording, the way they went at it made the recording master crazy."[21]

Smith Ballew was exaggerating. Though they did not churn out take after take, Frank Trumbauer's men were generally able to record two sides on the same date. This April session was even more productive, and they raised the number of sides cut to three. Okeh's commercial orientation is again confirmed by the artistic choices made for the session. The first two selected titles, "Louise" and "Wait Till You See 'Ma Chérie,'" were both successes from Maurice Chevalier's film *Innocents of Paris*. Smith Ballew knew them well, having recorded them six weeks earlier with Ben Pollack's orchestra. On "Louise," the confidence shown on the theme's exposition leads us to attribute this part to Andy Secrest, while Bix tries again to insert a series of high notes on the end of the piece, as he had done on "I'm In Seventh Heaven" a few days before . . . and he does not do any better this time. The impression is shifted, and the notes played don't fit with the key of the passage. Smith Ballew's vocals are sung with the sugary style that was in fashion, but the band had suffered even worse vocalists in the past.

Bix played muted on the following two titles, with the hope that limiting the air blown into his cornet would make playing easier. Though subtleties are missing in the eight bars played on "Wait Till You See 'Ma Chérie,'" the result achieved on the third number, "Baby, Won't You Please Come Home!"—a song recorded in a blues style by Bessie Smith in April 1923—is much more convincing. Bix blows a skillful and delicate countermelody behind Tram's vocal, and he is able to develop, without technical mishap, a solo whose melody approaches his old high standard.[22] Frank Trumbauer was in great form throughout the session. His saxophone chorus on "Baby, Won't You Please Come Home?" is elegant, and it displays, over sixteen measures, a surprising sweetness and delicacy. Guitarist Snoozer Quinn left the Whiteman Orchestra after this last date, and returned to New Orleans.

The reopening of the *Midnight Follies* in December 1928 turned out to be a financial failure for Florenz Ziegfeld, who ended the ignoble experiment on April 25 and closed this Mecca of New York nightclubs for the second time. That same day, Paul Whiteman recorded two sides for Columbia, on which Bix is silent. After having stumbled over "Little Pal" on April 5, the orchestra finally succeeded in getting it right on the fifth take. The record had honorable sales, though they were not warranted from a musical point of view. Having already done battle with Liszt in December, Roy Bargy was emboldened to assault Rimsky-Korsakov's "Song of India." His arrangement gave the recording session its second title, and a side that loses nothing by remaining in obscurity.

21. "A Visit to Smith Ballew," with Reagan Houston and Roger Ringo, in *Storyville*, no. 59 (June/July 1975), pp. 164–165.

22. Lacking any precise historical information, the human ear remains today the only available instrument able to decide whether a cornet solo was played on certain sides by Andy Secrest or Bix. Secrest had reached at the time a very high technical level, bringing him close to Bix, who was physically weak. The difference between the two musicians became subtle. The attribution of the cornet solos on "Baby Won't You Please Come Home?" generated different expert opinions. First solo is (almost) always given to Secrest. Some listeners believed that the two players shared the muted part, played behind Tram's vocal, which is not possible. Bix plays muted. The muted cornet solo that gracefully follows Tram's is also played by Bix. Andy Secrest, on open horn, leads the ensemble on the end of the side, with a few notes played by Bix over the last bars.

New York, Thursday, April 30, 1929

Eddie Lang returned to Frank Trumbauer's ensemble and to the Okeh studios. The band had added a trio of violins for the first title recorded, "No One Can Take Your Place." The insipidity of the melody, worsened by the woolliness of Smith Ballew's singing, paralyzed Bix, who limits himself to blowing into a hat, creating a finale lacking in dynamism and invention. The second number from this date, "I Like That," an entertaining and pleasant tune, could have offered an effective springboard for one of the lyrical flights Bix was famous for. Such was not the case, and none of the three choruses he plays on this side takes off. Bix struggles through the octave jumps that end his solo, and this physical effort can be heard.

This side marked the end of Bix Beiderbecke's presence on recordings directed by Frank Trumbauer. During the eighteen months that followed, the saxophonist would arrange ten more recording sessions under his own name, in which only Andy Secrest participated. "Months after Bix decided, in his own mind, that he was not playing up to his standard, we tried, again and again, to get him to record on some of our dates," explained Tram. "He did not want to record with prominent names because he felt that he wasn't playing well. That alone shows how intelligent he was. He decided, after April 1929, not to make any more recordings with Okeh Records until he felt that he was returning to his old form.... Even though Bix and I went on different paths at the end of 1928, we were still closer than most people thought. Whenever there was trouble, he always found me, and I tried to help in every way possible. And, that went for Whiteman, too! But when Bix departed on that voyage that was to take him out of this world, neither Whiteman nor I could have helped him!"[23]

Such a renunciation could not have motivated Bix to improve his health. Since the end of 1928, he had been reducing his drinking, which, in the absence of medical supervision and a modified diet, had degenerated his physical condition considerably. This prematurely broken health affected his playing, eroded his inspiration, and carried him away from his only purpose in life: music. "As a result, he generally felt pretty rough," recalled Bing Crosby, "so much so that if anybody asked him, *'How do you feel?'* he answered, *'I don't ask you how you feel. Why do you ask me how I feel? You know I feel bad. Just leave me alone.'* He wasn't bellicose about it, it was just that it annoyed him when anyone asked him how he felt. Anyone who's ever had a 'black-dog-riding-on-the-shoulder' type of hang-over will understand his mood. He slept fitfully, and he liked a room equipped with twin beds, so that he could move back and forth from one to the other if he became restless. Every once in a while he'd wake me up in the middle of the night and make me change beds with him. He never exercised. He didn't believe in it."[24]

23. *TRAM, the Frank Trumbauer Story,* op. cit., pp. 111–112.

24. Bing Crosby, *Call Me Lucky,* as told to Pete Martin (New York: Simon and Schuster, 1953), p. 42.

New York, Friday, May 3, and Saturday, May 4, 1929

Bix was in better form for these two Whiteman Orchestra recording sessions. Two or three calmer nights, a bright spring sun over New York, or even a smile picked up in the street might have helped restore a self-confidence that could still momentarily shine through the black mood. Jack Fulton's old-fashioned vocal makes mush out of Irving Berlin's title "When My Dreams Come True," which ruthlessly pervaded the soundtrack of *The Cocoanuts*, the first Marx Brothers film.[25] For many years, Groucho Marx would tease Berlin by reminding him that, for their debut on-screen, he had not been able to write them a single hit song. Bix was spared from this take, and Andy Secrest and Tram were the two called on to support this musically desperate side. Bill Challis's arrangement of "Reachin' for Someone" gave Frank Trumbauer room to spin out a winding melodic line, loaded with glissandos. Bing Crosby continued in the same spirit in a thirty-two-bar solo—something that he would never try again in the Whiteman band. At the end of the side, Bix plays an open horn chorus whose dexterity and precision are surprisingly and unexpectedly welcome.

The last number recorded that day, "China Boy," was the best side, and over a lively tempo, it offered three of Paul Whiteman's jazzmen the opportunity to shine. Clarinetist Irving Friedman goes off brilliantly over twenty-two measures, followed by gracefully drawn arabesques by Frank Trumbauer, and by sixteen measures in which Bix regains the inspiration of his best moments. Richard Hadlock emphasized that "in sixteen bars Bix steps in from his private musical world, creates an engaging new melody, makes use of sixths, ninths, and augmented chords that were never there in the first place, changes the mood and quality of the entire arrangement for the better, and quickly vanishes into the musical ferment that follows. It is a cool, modern solo, a little like the way Lester Young played ten years later. But these flashes were rare now."[26] Rare, but still possible—as Bix proved it the next day on "Oh! Miss Hannah." Bill Challis's orchestration demonstrates one more time the way in which Bing, Tram, and Bix could enhance a charming melody with unexpected emotional power. Bing Crosby colors his vocal with southern accents, inspired by the lyrics of the song, and Bix, blowing with a cup mute that gives his cornet a romantic tone,[27] improvises a sixteen-bar chorus of moving simplicity. "Orange Blossom Time" concluded the date, giving Bing Crosby the opportunity for a new masterful vocal.

"Louise," "Little Pal," and "When My Dreams Come True" spent several weeks among the best-sellers, reaching sales of twelve to fifteen thousand units. These figures represent a sharp decline when compared to Paul Whiteman's commercial results over the course of the previous years, but they are still four to five times higher than the sales figures of the Okeh records released under the name of the Frank Trumbauer Orchestra.

25. During the shooting of their first movie *The Cocoanuts* in spring 1929, the Marx Brothers were performing their third successful play every night on Broadway, *Animal Crackers*. Opening night was on October 23, 1928, at the 44th Street Theater, 216 West 44th Street, and it was played more than two hundred times. The theater was very close to Bix's hotel. It seems unlikely that a fan of P. G. Wodehouse would ignore the Marx Brothers devastating humor . . .

26. *Jazz Masters of the '20s*, op. cit., pp. 100–101.

27. Bix was using a mute more and more often. Placed in front of the bell of the horn, this accessory modifies the sound of the instrument, which could have helped disguise a coarsening of his tone, and the resistence it gives to the air flow makes the control of the air tone easier, which was helpful to Bix in his weakened condition. Bix used mostly two types of mutes: the *derby*, which looks like a derby hat and is held with the hand in front of the horn, and the *cup mute*, shaped like a cone with the narrow end jammed into the bell of the horn, and the wide end covered with a cup, with its top facing the bell.

The evening of May 4, the Paul Whiteman Orchestra opened at the Pavillon Royal, a fancy cabaret on Merrick Road, in Valley Stream, Long Island, where the band appeared for two weeks. Bix participated in a single title cut during the May 16 session, "Your Mother and Mine," a trivial tune sung by a duet formed with Bing Crosby and, most likely, Jack Fulton—a side that doesn't help anyone's reputation. On May 19, 1929, the Whiteman Orchestra added two prestigious new members: Joe Venuti and Eddie Lang, who remained with the band for several months. "In my eyes, Lang was the one of the greatest musical geniuses we ever had in the orchestra," said Paul Whiteman. "I never saw him look at a note of

The Whiteman Orchestra on the road to California at the end of May/beginning of June 1929. Left to right, front row: Paul Whiteman, Chester Hazlett, Kurt Dieterle, Wilbur Hall (with guitar), Mischa Russell, Bix, Jack Fulton, Lennie Hayton, John Bouman, unknown, Boyce Cullen (with hat), George Marsh, Fred Hass (far right); back row: Roy Bargy, Charles Margulis, Roy Maier (on top), Bill Rank, Irving Friedman, and on the right: Mario Perry and Harry Goldfield. (Duncan Schiedt Collection)

music. I don't even know whether he could read or not. It made no difference. What's the use of bothering with those pesky black blotches when you can anticipate the next chord change five bars in advance? No matter how intricate the arrangement was, Eddie played it flawlessly the first time without having heard it before, and without looking at a sheet of music. It was as if his musically intuitive spirit had read the arranger's mind, and knew in advance everything that was going to happen."[28] After a final *Old Gold* program, broadcast from WABC studios on May 21, Paul Whiteman gathered a huge company at New York's Penn Station for the start of a long voyage to the West Coast and the Mecca of the movies, Hollywood.

Movies with sound, or "talkies," as they were known, which had been around for less than five years, had been immediately accepted by audiences as the new standard. The big winner in this new generation of films was the musical drama released in 1928, *The Singing Fool*, which introduced one of Al Jolson's biggest hits: "Sonny Boy." In three years, the movie brought Warner $5 million. Such a lucrative source of income was highly appealing, and in July 1928, the same producers contracted Ted Lewis on an exclusive basis. Since the early 1920s, the singer-clarinetist had been constantly turning out hit records for the Columbia label. His first film, *Is Everybody Happy?*, was shot in Hollywood in the spring of 1929. This second-rate movie, afflicted with a distressing plot, justifiably drew the sustained fire of the critics. Only Don Murray's presence in the Ted Lewis Orchestra would save this insipid work from obscurity, and give it a place in jazz history.

28. *Paul Whiteman, Pioneer in American Music*, p. 224.

Universal Studios also wanted to get its share of the money generated by musical films. Its president, Carl Laemmle, approached Paul Whiteman in November 1928, and the two men agreed to unite their talents and capitals to produce the biggest musical movie ever, *The King of Jazz*. Scriptwriter Paul Schofield went to New York to run his preliminary ideas by Whiteman, who was given a comfortable advance of $50,000.

From New York to San Francisco, May 24–June 6, 1929

On the morning of Friday, May 24, some fifty people boarded the Old Gold Special, a six-car luxury train assembled by Union Pacific. Most of the passengers reunited at Penn Station were members of the orchestra: musicians, singers, and arrangers; the others were the management team, a few technicians, a chef, three waiters, and a photographer. E. G. Weymouth, the vice president of the P. Lorillard Company, represented the sponsor in the caravan, and *Variety* reporter Abel Green represented the press. At each stop, he wired informative dispatches to his readers, who got weekly reports on the many episodes of the trek to Los Angeles. The main news of the show-business world had become the story of a railroad and an orchestra.

On the evening of May 24, the first show of the tour was performed at the Philadelphia Metropolitan Opera House. The musicians dived into their bunks immediately after the show, and the train rolled through the night—as it would every night and every day—to another town, and another theater. An *Old Gold* broadcast was transmitted the next evening on the CBS network, from the Syria Mosque in Pittsburgh. Bing Crosby's growing popularity was proved by the increasing number of titles that he was given, which he sang either solo or as part of the Rhythm Boys.

Sunday, May 26, was no day of rest for the group. The morning was spent in the studios of station WHK in Cleveland, a city of dark memories for Bix Beiderbecke. It was followed by an early afternoon performance at the Toledo Armory, and ended with an evening concert broadcast from the Olympia in Detroit. The next day, at the station in Fort Wayne, Indiana, the show was cut short by heavy rains. The band reached Chicago on May 28, and appeared at the Auditorium Theater. As it was a Tuesday, the *Old Gold* radio program was broadcast from the studios of the local station. The voyage continued with the same intensity, with stops in Springfield on May 29, Indianapolis on May 30, and Saint Louis on May 31. These long train voyages were disastrous for Bix, whose drinking increased as the journey wore on. The Paul Whiteman collection at Williams College contains a page of sheet music, the first trumpet part of "Sunrise to Sunset," used from May 25 through May 29. On the page, Harry Goldfield had written himself a reminder: "Wake up Bix."

Before playing a concert at the Washington University Field House in Saint Louis, the orchestra had taken a few hours rest at the Mayfield Hotel. This was where Ruth Shaffner met Bix Beiderbecke for the last time: "He had called me," recalled Ruth, "and I remember there were several musicians in his room when I arrived. He looked bad, but said he was not indulging. I didn't go to the concert but, afterwards, we went to the train together. . . . He wasn't the same Bix that he used to be. I was surprised at the way he looked. As I recall, he was weak or looked like he was. He had a slight limp. . . . He didn't seem unhappy, particularly, but he looked very bad. I was terribly worried about him and told him so. He just smiled—the way he always did when you tried to tell him something—and said it'd be all right, not to worry."[29] Bix limped; he had been feeling sharp pains in his lower limbs for several months, and was having trouble walking. This reduced mobility was followed by strong nocturnal cramps, convulsive movements, and shakes that disturbed his sleep. The doctors at the River Crest Sanitarium had quickly diagnosed a case of alcoholic polyneuritis, and had informed their patient of the origins of the illness: excessive consumption of alcohol, a progressive poisoning by products derived from faulty distillations, and a deficiency in vitamins resulting from a poor diet. Bix had clearly concentrated the risks. As his walk became more hesitant, he made use of a cane more and more often. When his friends asked why he needed this support, Bix explained that his thigh had been cut in a brawl at a New York speakeasy. This fiction—which only Bill Challis, who knew Bix well, seems to have doubted—would be told again and again in every book or article about the cornetist's life, based solely on the stories of band members who believed what Bix had told them.[30]

On June 1, the band gave a three-hour concert at the Convention Hall in Kansas City. Torrential rains had slowed down the train's progression during the night, and brakemen had to walk ahead of the train to check the railway. Running slowly along the banks of the Missouri River, the Old Gold Special managed to reach Omaha just in time for the afternoon show at the Civic Auditorium. All of Paul Whiteman's persuasive powers were needed to convince the reluctant train crew to resume the journey over flooded tracks in order to reach Lincoln, Nebraska, by 6:30 p.m., where an

29. *The Leon Bix Beiderbecke Story*, op. cit., p. 461, and *Bix, Man and Legend*, op. cit., p. 273.

30. Besides the fact that Bix's limping was undoubtedly caused by polyneuritis, three elements support the hypothesis of an invented story: first, the story of the brawl remains highly confused, and it was never possible to really know what might have happened; second, the two witnesses, Izzy Friedman and Bill Challis, later denied making the statements attributed to them; and third, a medical examination of Bix's body on October 14, 1929, showed "no scar of importance."

enormous crowd awaited them. The endless heavy rain, which obliged the orchestra to perform inside the station, and the intimacy of the setting seem to have fired the audience's enthusiasm: "The crowd surged after the musicians. Several women fainted in the jam. . . . Inside the building every inch of standing space was taken. Very few could see Whiteman because of the jam," the *Lincoln Star* reported the next day.[31]

Another night on the train brought the band to Denver on the morning of June 3. Paul Whiteman's parents were still living in the capital of Colorado, where his father had been the director of the city's musical education pro-

Musicians of the Whiteman Orchestra on the train to California. From left to right, front row: Mischa Russell, Mario Perry, Roy Maier, Joe Venuti, Eddie Lang; second row: George Marsh, Mike Trafficante, Roy Bargy, Charles Margulis. (Michael Peters)

grams. The day was dedicated to numerous official receptions for the band, although several less sociable members of the orchestra slipped away to the nearby golf courses. They all regathered that evening at the Whiteman family farm for a copious feast prepared by the bandleader's mother. This wholesome treatment appeared to benefit Bix, and he was in top form during the next day's rehearsal at the Shirley-Savoy Hotel. He managed to revive the spark of his best days for the weekly radio broadcast of the *Old Gold* program. Bix and Tram vigorously launched off on a chase chorus on "Glad Rag Doll," and Bix laid down two magnificent solos on the next two numbers, "Sweet Georgia Brown" and "Runnin' Wild." His spirit and determination were high, as was the surprise of the other musicians present.

En route to Salt Lake City, the train crossed the Utah Desert the next morning. As was now usual for him, Bix slept deeply, and his torpor inspired a practical joke from Joe Venuti that, for once, was funny: "At the end of each passenger car was a bucket of sand to be used in case of fire. This was long before fire extinguishers," said the violinist. "I went through the cars, gathering up as many as I could, and carefully dumped the sand onto Bix, the seat next to him, and all around the floor. Then I sat back and waited for him to awake. Finally, Bix awoke, noticed all of the sand around him, and was startled by it! *'What happened?'* Bix shouted. *'Where did all this sand come from?'* I rushed over to calm him. *'Don't worry, Bix,'* I assured him, *'we've got most of it cleaned up. I don't know how you do it. The conductor said it was the worst sand storm that he'd ever seen, and you slept right through it all!' 'Why didn't someone wake me up?'* panicked Bix. *'I could have suffocated.'* "[32]

The band played at Salt Lake City's Granada Theater that evening, got back on the train, and resumed the journey toward Los Angeles. At a stop on the morning of June 6, Bill Rank stepped off the train to buy a newspaper. Under the headline "Death of a Musician," a short article announced the death of Don Murray, four

31. *Bix, Man and Legend,* op. cit., p. 274.

32. *TRAM, the Frank Trumbauer Story,* op. cit., pp. 114–115.

days before. The shooting of the movie *Is Everybody Happy?* had just ended, and Murray had gone out on the night of Thursday, May 30, probably looking for some alcohol—which could have exacerbated his already critical state of inebriation. He met some friends in a car, and stopped to talk. He fainted—maybe an alcoholic epileptic seizure—and fell back off the running board, and his skull hit the sidewalk violently. Transported to the Dickey and Camp Hospital, Don Murray regained consciousness briefly before dying from his injuries on June 2. Bix received the news without noticeable emotion. His stare became more distant, more somber. . . . Was he thinking of the gypsy woman's prediction in January 1922 that had linked his destiny to his friend's, when she asserted that both would die a premature death? Without saying a word, he went to close the car's window; he was suddenly cold.

The train reached Los Angeles at three o'clock in the afternoon. It stopped in San Bernardino, east of the city, to board Paul Fejos, the director of the forthcoming motion picture, and made a short stop downtown, at Santa Fe's La Grande Station, before heading north for San Francisco.[33]

San Francisco, June 7–14, 1929

The musicians were surrounded by journalists upon their arrival at the San Francisco station, and were escorted to their hotel by a press contingent dying for answers to such essential questions as the evolution of Paul Whiteman's waist size. Questioned about the presence of jazz in the shooting that was about to start, the bandleader responded to the reporter from the *Los Angeles Examiner*: "I haven't seen the script yet, but I can tell you one thing. Jazz is losing out to the slower rhythms. You might print that and quote me!"[34]

The band performed for a week at the Pantages Theater in San Francisco. The June 11 *Old Gold* program once again gave Bing Crosby an important part, which the singer proudly announced to his mother, "My name is being prominently featured in the newspapers and in the broadcasts, and considerable invaluable publicity thus redounds on me," wrote the singer. "What awaits us on the Coast is as yet problematical and whether we get much of a break in the picture or not, I can't tell now."[35] The last show at the Pantages Theater in San Francisco was performed on June 13. After a day of rest, the members of the band boarded the train that, during the night, traveled back to Los Angeles, the last stop on their long journey.

Los Angeles, June 15–August 28, 1929

On the morning of June 15, Alexander Pantages welcomed the orchestra at the Southern Pacific Central Station, and they paraded in cars through Los Angeles to

33. La Grande Station was opened by the Sante Fe Railway Company on July 29, 1893, in downtown Los Angeles at the corner of Santa Fe Avenue and 2nd Street. The building of the station, with its amazing Spanish Moore style, had cost $50,000. In San Francisco, the train stopped at the Central Station, located at Townsend and 3rd streets.

34. *Tram, the Frank Trumbauer Story*, op. cit., p. 115.

35. Gary Giddins, *Bing Crosby: A Pocketful of Dreams, The Early Years, 1903–1940* (New York: Little, Brown and Co., 2001), p. 194.

the L.A. Pantages Theater, where the band was booked for a week of concerts.[36] At the end of one show, Bix was visited by one of his oldest friends, Fritz Putzier, a companion from his first music groups in Davenport, who was on a business trip and met Bix backstage: "He was still nervous," recalled Putzier, "chain-smoking cigarettes one after the other. He didn't look at all good—he had this terrible pallor about him. But he said he was happy about the trip—looked on it as a vacation, a chance to soak up the sunshine and the rest. I told him I thought that was the right idea, that relaxation and fresh air would do wonders for him and his health."[37] On Tuesday, June 18, Paul Whiteman's big band rehearsed for the first time in studio A in the Don Lee Building, at 7th and Bixel streets. For the duration of the band's stay in California, the weekly *Old Gold* program would be broadcast from station KMTR, over the CBS network.

Los Angeles is built over a depression, bordered on the south by the Pacific Ocean and closed on the north by a sprawling and high rocky barrier: the Santa Monica and San Gabriel mountains. Hollywood is in the northern part of the city, overhung by the eastern end of the Santa Monica Mountains, known by every movie lover as the Hollywood Hills. Thomas Edison, inventor of the phonograph, was intimately familiar with the development of Hollywood's cinematographic industry. He was also the owner of patents related to moviemaking, and he had tried at the beginning of the century to legally control the production of silent films. The movie industry was then centered in New York, Chicago, and Philadelphia. Carl Laemmle was one of the most active opponents of Edison's "trust," and he set up as an independent producer in Los Angeles, which, he judged, was beyond Edison's reach. He founded Universal Studio in Hollywood in 1912, and three years later he built a monumental movie production facility in the San Fernando Valley, east of the Hollywood Hills, known as Universal City.

Protected by a wall and tightly guarded, Universal City spread over 250 acres. The enclosure housed the management offices and their countless employees, stages, recording studios, workshops where the film sets and costumes were made, locations for outdoor shooting, and a zoo. Erich von Stroheim had reigned over the place for a year, from July 1920 through June 1921, for the filming of his extraordinary and extravagant masterpiece *Foolish Wives*. By June 19, 1929, when Carl Laemmle Jr., son of the founder, guided Paul Whiteman and his orchestra around for a visit of the family kingdom, the company's cultural ambitions were less lofty. The production team of *The King of Jazz* had built a large wooden cottage inside the studio, the "Whiteman Lodge," for the private use of the musicians. It was fully equipped with rehearsal space, a library, a billiard room, and an immense dining table laid out in front of a giant chimney—leisure facilities that the band members would not really benefit from . . .

Paul Whiteman ordered thirty-five new cars from a local Ford dealer, and each musician was offered his own at the affordable price of $900, with payments to be

36. The Southern Pacific Central Station was located between Central Avenue and Alameda Street, and 3rd and 6th streets, close to La Grande Station. The L.A. Pantages Theater was, in 1929, at 401 West 7th Street, downtown Los Angeles. Alexander Pantages was the perfect model of a self-made man. Born in Greece, he joined in 1896 the numerous adventurers who flocked to Alaska, attracted by gold. The money he earned managing a small joint was invested in a theater, opened on the frozen ground of the Arctic Circle. The place soon met with success, and he settled down in Seattle in 1902. Within a few years, he was managing the first theater network in the U.S.: in 1926, he directly owned thirty theaters and controlled forty-two others scattered along the West Coast. At the time of Paul Whiteman's arrival in San Francisco, he was finalizing the sale, for $24 million, of his entire organization to Radio Keith Orpheum—a wise decision, made just a few weeks before the stock market crash.

37. *Bix, Man and Legend,* op. cit., p. 278.

deducted from his salary. The spare tire cover, very visible at the rear of the vehicles, sported a caricature of the bandleader, the famous "potato head." "That tire cover was easily spotted by the local gendarmes, who immediately began to follow us, knowing that sooner or later we would get into some kind of trouble," explained Frank Trumbauer.[38]

The orchestra's appearance at the Pantages Theater ended on Saturday, June 22. Six days later, Paul Whiteman and his men arrived at Universal City, ready to cope with the intense working schedule that the Hollywood studios were known for. An unpleasant surprise awaited the future stars of the screen: the screenwriters, Paul Schofield and Edward T. Lowe, had worked up a trivial romantic story, which was immediately rejected by the bandleader, and none of the numbers to be played on the soundtrack had been composed yet. Paul Whiteman's contract with Universal granted him a weekly salary of $8,000, plus $4,500 for his band. During their eight-week stay in Los Angeles, the musicians were each given $200 every Friday, in addition to the $50 they received for each broadcast of the *Old Gold* radio show. These few hours of rehearsal and broadcasting had become the musicians' only activity: in Hollywood, idleness was royally paid. Checks were collected weekly at Universal Studios, where Paul Whiteman greeted his prodigal sons with a short pep talk.

The band members were dispersed all over the city. Bing Crosby, Kurt Dieterle, and Mischa Russell had rented a house on Fairfax Avenue. Frank Trumbauer lived in a bungalow on Highland Avenue, close to Bill Rank's. Others favored solitude in the Hills. Bix and trombonist Boyce Cullen were of that kind, and they shared a villa far up Laurel Canyon. This odd house, in the style of a Spanish hacienda, was losing the test of time. The way to this crumbling place was a dangerous, narrow, tree-filled, windy road. Andy Secrest made the journey once, at the risk of his life. Bix, who no longer drove, played it safe, limiting the number of his outings to a bare minimum. The days stretched out, and the heat of the California summer drained the energy of the few ambitious musicians. Tram was regularly flying above the city, continuing the pilot training he had started a few months earlier. Bing Crosby, Al Rinker, Roy Bargy, and Kurt Dieterle became members of the Lakeside Golf Club, a prestigious place north of Universal City where they mingled with luminaries such as Oliver Hardy and Johnny Weissmuller. Bix's activities were limited to carrying bottles and refilling glasses. He was carefully following Fritz Putzier's advice: rest and sunshine—he slept on the terrace most of the day, sedated by alcohol. Smuggled beverages flowed in from the Mexican city of Tijuana, ensuring an abundant supply. "Bix was drinking pretty heavily again," said Andy Secrest. "We really thought he'd taken the cure at home, but he'd apparently just rested or something, because it didn't slow him down."[39] Andy Secrest shared an apartment and an upright piano

Paul Whiteman's "Potato Head"; ad published in *The Talking Machine World*, September 1928.

38. *TRAM, the Frank Trumbauer Story, op. cit.*, p. 117.
39. *Bix, Man and Legend,* op. cit., p. 283.

with an old friend from Indiana, freshly arrived in Los Angeles: Hoagy Carmichael. The composer was convinced that the development of sound movies would open the doors of the studios to him, as the producers had to be desperately waiting for the dozens of songs he could offer them. His hopes quickly vanished, as the jobs had already been given to known New York composers. Hoagy met once again with Bix, but his joy of reuniting after such a long separation was spoiled by what he saw: a drifting man, losing control of his wrecked life.

In July, Bix's mother arrived in Los Angeles: "She stayed a week," wrote Hoagy, "but I know she only saw Bix once during this visit. It wasn't something Bix wanted to talk about, and I didn't want to bring it up. There was a conflict between them, although they were very attached to each other. The visit was not a success. It may have been partly because Bix knew he wasn't very presentable and didn't want his mother to see him in that rancid castle up there in all its rustling Spanish decor, with him most likely in his cups most of the time. . . . Bix's mother went back home, and Bix continued to burrow into his Spanish hill. It didn't do him any good to add this guilt about not seeing his mother to his other problems. The drinking continued."[40]

During these long summer holidays, only the Rhythm Boys had steady work: they were engaged on July 3, for several weeks, at the Montmartre Café. Situated on the second floor of 6757 Hollywood Boulevard, this very expensive restaurant attracted customers who were not shy about being seen, as mobs of fans gathered outside the front door every night to watch the Hollywood stars coming and going. The place offered musical attractions at dinner, and a dance floor allowed couples to spin around between the tables. "The Montmartre was *the* place," confirmed drummer and future bandleader Phil Harris, "that and the Cocoanut Grove. And that's the first time I heard Bing Crosby do a ballad, 'I Kiss Your Hand, Madame,' and he knocked the roof in with it. When Bing finished, I mean, I never heard anything like it, you could hear a pin drop."[41] Among the women who succumbed to the singer's charm was actress Dixie Lee, a cute blonde and a daily spectator at the Montmartre Café. Dixie and Bing married in September 1930, and Dixie Lee remained Mrs. Crosby for twenty-two years, until her death from cancer in November, 1951.

Bix emerged from his aerie on the Fourth of July. The Paul Whiteman Orchestra had been invited to play at a party given by actor Richard Barthelmess, a star of the silent film era. Hoagy Carmichael recalled a beautiful interpretation of *Rhapsody in Blue*, and how Bix was inspired that evening: "Bix was there and he had his moments when they played "Clementine" and "Sweet Sue." . . . He was right that night. Boy, was he right! You know how you sometimes say you wish the whole world was here to hear or witness such and such. This was the case. I wanted the whole world to hear Bix this night."[42]

Joe Venuti's encounter on July 31 was not as pleasant. As he drove on Roosevelt

40. *Sometimes I Wonder*, op. cit., pp. 201–202. "There was a story that Bix's mother visited him at this time," wrote Phil Evans in *The Leon Bix Beiderbecke Story*, (op. cit., p. 474), "but none of the former Whiteman musicians could remember seeing her there." The reason for this is given by Hoagy, who specified that Bix's mother met her son only once. And this meeting had a witness, Ernie McKay, who was Marion McKay's brother. Interviewed by Warren K. Plath, Ernie McKay, who was playing in his brother's band at Roscoe "Fatty" Arbuckle's Plantation, recalled "talking with Bix—with whom he had briefly roomed at the Billinghurst in Detroit—walking with a cane, in the company of his [Bix's] mother," in "Marion McKay and His Orchestra" by Warren K. Plath, *Storyville*, no. 60 (August/September 1975), p. 207.

41. *Bing Crosby: A Pocketful of Dreams*, op. cit., p. 199.

42. *Sometimes I Wonder*, op. cit., p. 205 and *The Leon Bix Beiderbecke Story*, op. cit., p. 475.

Highway, his "Whiteman model" Ford struck a car containing two ladies on vacation from Springfield, Illinois. Violinist Mario Perry, Venuti's passenger, was critically injured on impact. Eddie Lang and his wife, Kitty, were following Venuti's car: "I tried to comfort Mario who was screaming," remembered Kitty Lang. "I was trying to help him as well as I could, wiping the blood pouring out of his nose. Two doctors came and rushed him to the operating room. Poor Mario, he died a few hours later because of internal lesions. Joe had several bad cuts on his face, but his wrist looked the worst: two broken bones were sticking right out from the flesh. I thought he'd never play again."[43] The two lady tourists brought suit against Joe Venuti. Paul Whiteman's lawyers defended Venuti, and the case was settled out of court for $600. The violinist regained the use of his right arm in a few weeks, but Mario Perry's death threw the members of the band into great dismay. Joe Venuti had managed to be even less funny than usual.

In October 1925, when Bing Crosby and Al Rinker had arrived impoverished and unknown in Los Angeles, they had been helped out by Rinker's sister, singer Mildred Bailey. Born in 1903, the eldest of four children, she was thirteen when her mother died. Two years later, she left home when her father remarried. A brief marriage to Ted Bailey left her nothing but his name, and at the start of the 1920s the young woman moved to Los Angeles, where she married Benny Stafford, a purveyor of illegal alcoholic beverages to the city's speakeasies. Mildred had always sung, endlessly listening to records and quickly memorizing the songs' lyrics and melodies. Following her amazing musical instinct, she lent a personal touch to the tunes she worked on, her clear and fluid voice endowing her performances with a truly natural feeling. Her tastes tended toward jazz and blues singers. Self-taught, Mildred Bailey developed an art of spontaneous singing in an original way. She could give the illusion of "creating" her song on the spot, of always interpreting it as if for the first time, and of addressing herself to a single person: her listener. Louis Armstrong was a pioneer of this direct and intimate relationship with the audience, of this often exuberant spontaneity that constitutes the dominant spirit of jazz. Bing Crosby had found inspiration in Mildred Bailey's personal style, and he bore a grateful admiration for her. In 1929, however, she was out of work, and she dedicated much time to her second passion: cooking—with disastrous effects on her naturally curvy figure.

Mildred also made beer, which gave Bing Crosby and Al Rinker an idea of how to repay her for her support of their professional beginnings, and bring her back into music, where she belonged. Paul Whiteman was constantly bombarded with requests to listen to the allegedly talented brothers, cousins, and relatives of his musicians, and obstinately closed his ears to all such pleas. But, Bing and Al reasoned, quality beer was difficult to find, and they let Whiteman overhear them praising Mildred's domestic production and mentioning a party she was throwing, at which her marvelous home brew would doubtless be served. Whiteman came to

43. Adriano Mazzoletti, *Eddie Lang, Stringin' the Blues* (Rome: Editoriale Pantheon), p. 186–187.

the party, and on the evening of August 3, as he enjoyed a beer in the kitchen, Mildred, in the living room, sang "(What Can I Say, Dear) After I Say I'm Sorry?" Paul Whiteman came out of the kitchen and asked to hear more. To say he was impressed would be an understatement: on August 5, he signed her to a contract, making Mildred Bailey the first female singer to headline a big jazz band.[44] She made her debut with the orchestra on Tuesday, August 6, on an *Old Gold* broadcast, singing a chorus of "Moanin' Low" between solos played by Tram and Bix. Success was immediate, and one year later, Mildred was receiving the highest salary in the band. This vehement young woman was not very feminine, or very delicate, and she could at times have the mouth of a sailor. These qualities facilitated her integration into an orchestral ensemble that had already accommodated Joe Venuti—an accurate measure of its level of refinement. Musicians in the band confirmed that Mildred used to drop her "tomboy" behavior when Bix was around. Her maternal instincts were aroused by his haunted and moving presence, and Mildred became sweet and thoughtful. She scolded Bix when his appearance left something to be desired, she grumbled when he was drunk, and rewarded him with a caress on the head or a kiss when he played well.

During the start of the month of August, only Bing Crosby and Paul Whiteman still frequented Universal Studios. They had distinct motives. Bing Crosby had introduced himself to James Ryan, the casting director from Fox Studios on Western Avenue, and he was offered a screen test. Ryan was favorably impressed by Bing Crosby's performance, but he declared with no uncertainty that the size of Bing's ears, two protruding wings, definitively compromised his cinematographic future. He added that "a camera pointed straight at Bing would make him look like a taxi with both doors open."[45] Hindsight is always clearer than foresight: with the same ears, Bing Crosby appeared in sixty-four films between 1930 and 1972!

Paul Whiteman's regular presence on the Universal film sets was not entirely of a professional order: he flitted around actress Margaret Livingston in an attempt at courtship. One tries, vainly, to imagine the corpulent bandleader flitting, but it must have had some effect, as the pretty and distinguished Margaret could come up with only two obstacles to their possible union: Paul Whiteman's portliness, which a severe diet could hope to modify, and the fact that he was legally married. These bagatelles were eventually overcome, and the happy pair wed in 1931.[46] Mixing business with pleasure in the offices at Universal, Whiteman frequently asked the producers about the status of the script for *The King of Jazz*. By the end of August, Carl Laemmle presented him the much-awaited fruit of weeks of labor: "Paul read the script," reported Frank Trumbauer, "and flatly refused to have any part of it. It was a love story with 'Pops' [Whiteman] as the romantic hero. The whole concept was so wrong for Paul and the boys. After much consideration, it was decided that a big mistake had been made! We decided to return to New York to fulfill previous engagements."[47] Universal added up the cost of the error: $350,000 had been spent

44. As accurately pointed out by Richard M. Sudhalter in *Lost Chords* (op. cit., p. 830n10), Paul Whiteman did play an important part in discovering and supporting new talents. Many are the names of the artists to whom he brought effective and often conclusive support at the beginning of their career: Red Norvo, Mildred Bailey, Bing Crosby, Bix, Frank Trumbauer, Joe Venuti, Tommy and Jimmy Dorsey, Hoagy Carmichael, Willard Robison, Jack and Charlie Teagarden, and George Gershwin. According to James T. Maher, Whiteman was also instrumental in securing Earl "Fatha" Hines a ten-year residency at the Grand Terrace in Chicago, but the black pianist added: "Paul Whiteman loved my playing, and he would have liked me to join him, but he always had to qualify his admiration by saying, 'If you were only white . . .'" (quoted in Joshua Berrett, *Louis Armstrong and Paul Whiteman*, op. cit., p. 149).

45. *Call Me Lucky*, op. cit., p. 121.

46. Margaret Livingston was "The Woman from the City" in F. W. Murnau's *Sunrise*. She was asked to lend her voice to Louise Brooks, who had left for Europe and G. W. Pabst, who post-synchronized *The Canary Murder*. During the summer of 1929, she was playing in Universal's *Tonight at Twelve*. She married Paul Whiteman in 1931, a marriage that lasted until the bandleader's death in 1967.

47. *TRAM, the Frank Trumbauer Story*, op. cit., p. 120. Several discographies list Eddie Lang and Joe Venuti as present on Okeh recording sessions that took place in New York during the second half of August 1929: with the Justin Ring and His Okeh Orchestra on August 16 (just Eddie Lang), for instance, or with Seger Ellis and Louis Armstrong on August 23 (Lang and Venuti). Aural evidence does not confirm their presence. Because of his broken arm, Venuti could hardly have been playing so early after the accident, but did Eddie travel back to New York with his wounded friend before the end of the month?

Musicians of the Whiteman Orchestra attending a party in Los Angeles in August 1929. Left to right, back row: unknown, Bill Rank, Roy Bargy, Mildred Bailey, unknown, Al Rinker, Wilbur Hall (in front of Rinker), unknown, Mike Trafficante (drinking), Mike Pingitore; front row: Mischa Russell, Charles Strickfaden, Joe Venuti (with bandaged arm), Kurt Dieterle, George Marsh (at front), Irving Friedman (behind Marsh), Eddie Lang (behind Friedman), three unknown men and two women, Chester Hazlett (Mildred Bailey is the only identified woman). (Michael Peters).

in a few months, with no result. It was decided that the orchestra would remain at the studio's disposal, and that a new script would be immediately started.

On Wednesday, August 28, the musicians got back onto the Old Gold Special—this time with an extra passenger, Hoagy Carmichael, who was returning to New York with his rejected tunes. Fritz Putzier came to the station to greet his friend Bix before the train left. "Finally Bix came down the walkway, heading for the train—and he was using a cane. I was shocked," recalled Putzier. "He seemed intent on making certain that he boarded the train. His only conversation was a mumbled greeting—not at all like him—and a quick handshake. Then he said something like *I've gotta get on the train,*' and disappeared. He looked awful, and was clearly embarrassed to meet me in that shape."[48] A strange photograph was taken during the voyage at a stop at an unknown location: Bix and Frank Trumbauer, shown in profile, stand a few yards from the railroad tracks, in the midst of a flat and empty countryside. Bix, slightly below Tram, stands in ankle-deep grass, a newspaper in his hand and a handkerchief in his breast pocket. They are shaking hands. This hazy portrait is the last known picture of Bix.

Frank Trumbauer and Bix, August 29 or 30, 1929. (Indiana University Collection)

48. *Bix, Man and Legend,* op. cit., p. 286.

228 ⟅ *1929: Toward the Fall*

New York, August 31–September 15, 1929

On August 31, the very night of their arrival back in New York, the musicians were expected at the Pavillon Royal in Long Island, a place where they had played in May before leaving for California. Warren Scholl, who had listened to all of the *Old Gold* broadcasts, rushed to the club on September 1 to hear his favorite band. Bix was not in the brass section, but was seated at a table near the stage. He was dressed in his tuxedo, with a vacant stare, apparently unable to play. Bix seems, however, to have taken short solos during the radio broadcasts on September 3 and 10, but he fared worse upon his return to the Columbia studios. The September 6 session opened with the recording of "At Twilight," a lovely melody sung by Bing Crosby, Al Rinker, and Jack Fulton. Eddie Lang's guitar brought valuable support to the rhythm section, and Frank Trumbauer concluded this pleasant side with a short solo. The second tune of the date was an Irving Berlin composition, "Waiting at the End of the Road," written for the soundtrack of King Vidor's brilliant film, *Hallelujah*. The number was to end with an eight-bar solo played by Bix Beiderbecke. The cornetist stumbled four times in a row, over four successive takes, which forced a postponement of the recording of this title to the next week.

It was on Friday the thirteenth that Bix reached "the end of the road" he had been traveling on for two years with Paul Whiteman's orchestra. As planned, the recording session began with the reprise of "Waiting at the End of the Road." Four more attempts were necessary before a worn-out Bix finally reached a result that no one expected anymore: on his eighth attempt he blew a nuanced solo with strong emotional content and a level of melodic invention that remains his most reliable mark.[49]

Bill Challis's arrangement for the next title, "When You're Counting the Stars Alone," gave Tram and Bix a chorus apiece and a vocal to Bing Crosby. At the end of the first take, which was rejected, Bix fainted and was laid on several folding chairs, set up side by side in the back of the studio. He was unable to continue and was driven back to his room at the 44th Street Hotel. Andy Secrest took the cornet solo on the two next takes, and the third was released.

Bix remained in his room all the next day, Saturday the fourteenth. Paul Whiteman and Kurt Dieterle visited him in the afternoon. "Bix was in bed," recalled Kurt Dieterle. "Paul took a step towards him and kicked an empty liquor bottle that was under the bed. Paul sat down on the bed and put his head in his hands and said, *'Bix, we've got to get you straightened out, things can't go on this way.'* He told him to get a good night's sleep and that we would be back for him in the morning to put him on a train. Paul had decided to send him to Davenport to recuperate."[50] On Sunday morning, Paul Whiteman and Kurt Dieterle escorted Bix to nearby Grand Central Station, where the cornetist set off on the first train to Chicago. As he was used to doing in such cases, his boss generously "kept him on with full pay for a

49. The attribution of the cornet solo in "Waiting at the End of the Road" has been and continues to be endlessly discussed. Musicians' memories are contradictory. Andy Secrest asserted different things to different people, and we lack conclusive evidence. "The simple yet solid melodic construction is definitively Bix's," wrote Randy Sandke, "but it is possible that Secrest is repeating phrases that Bix had played on an earlier take." (*Observing a Genius at Work,* op. cit., p. 42). Richard Sudhalter noticed that on "My Sweeter than Sweet," recorded with Frank Trumbauer on October 19, 1929, Andy Secrest "plays a seven-note figure that almost exactly replicates one that occurs in the same place and harmonic circumstances on Whiteman's 'Waiting at the End of the Road.'" Sudhalter concludes therefore that the similarity between these two incidents, "the fact that they are both played against a B-minor chord, and the atypicality of the latter solo among other Bix efforts prompt speculation that Secrest may have been the soloist in both instances." (*Lost Chords,* op. cit., p. 806n16). Agreeing with Lucien Malson and other Bixophiles that "there is a Bixian sweetness that can't be imitated, a moon glow that can't be reproduced," we feel that this solo recorded with the Whiteman Orchestra offers the emotional quality we attribute to Bix.

50. *The Leon Bix Beiderbecke Story,* op. cit., pp. 490–491.

couple of months, then on half pay for about four or five," as Whiteman recalled later.[51] Bix arrived in Davenport on Monday, September 16, and settled in at his parents' house. In November his work with Paul Whiteman would give him one last professional reward when "Waiting at the End of the Road" spent three weeks among the best-selling records.[52]

Bill Challis had written the orchestration for a Vincent Youmans composition, "Great Day." Youmans had little regard for the "symphonic jazz" played by Paul Whiteman, but Bill Challis had wrested an agreement from the composer, allowing Whiteman to record the song with the promise that the only improvisation would be played by Bix Beiderbecke, which assured Youmans that his work would be treated with respect. The recording session was scheduled for October 9, and Bix was no longer there. Bill Challis, citing his commitment to have Bix, tried to postpone the date, but finally gave in to Paul Whiteman's demand, and assigned the cornet solo to Andy Secrest. Vincent Youmans tried to prohibit the release of the record when he heard the "horse whinny" and squeals coming from the horn of the "replacement" soloist. The public was apparently not deterred by this tasteless display, and in December, "Great Day" reached first place among the best-sellers, giving Paul Whiteman his only big hit of the year.

Davenport, September 16–October 14, 1929

Bix was doing terribly. He isolated himself at home, asking his mother to keep visitors away. Cooped up in his childhood bedroom, he suffered in body and soul. Added to his psychological torments, exacerbated by the trial of his last recording session, a permanent pain in his legs was becoming unbearable. The Beiderbecke family's doctor had no trouble confirming the diagnosis of alcoholic polyneuritis that Bix had been suffering from for almost a year, emphasizing that the only cure to this grave illness, which could lead to paralysis, was complete abstinence from alcohol. This medical advice put a definitive word on a reality that Bix's parents now reluctantly had to face: their twenty-six-year-old son was a drunk. Treatment was needed immediately. The choice of the Keeley Institute in Dwight, Illinois, was almost inevitable, as the place had long enjoyed an excellent reputation, and was located less than five hours by car from Davenport.

If Prohibition effectively increased alcohol consumption in big cities, it was more effective in medium-sized towns and in the countryside, where supplies were more difficult to obtain, but not impossible, and the knowledge of a few "good addresses" sufficed, in a city like Davenport, to avoid the shortage. The indifference of gangsters to the effects their products might have on customers, and the consequent lack of sanitary controls, increased the risk of toxicity in the drinks available, and bootlegged alcohol was frequently charged with toxins like methyl alcohol,

51. *The Leon Bix Beiderbecke Story*, op. cit., p. 491.

52. During his short stay in New York, Bix made another record before leaving for Davenport. Edgar Jackson, from the British magazine *Melody Maker*, traveled to New York with the bandleader Jack Hylton in August 1929. He attended one Whiteman performance, at the end of which he recorded on portable equipment (using an aluminum record) the voices of the main musicians of the band. Bix's voice was recorded. This unique disc was destroyed in 1941, together with Edgar Jackson's collections during the bombing of his house. (Information from Nick Dellow and Brian Rust.)

which is a vicious poison. Conventional medicine and hospitals were generally not called upon until the victims had little chance of surviving more than a few weeks.

The huge quantity of alcohol imbibed in the country had led some American politicians, as early as the end of the eighteenth century, to question the dangers that such excessive consumption might represent for the young democracy. Dr. Benjamin Rush, born in 1746, had been the first to consider alcoholism an illness, to define its symptoms and to work on possible therapeutic methods, both medical and psychological. Dr. Leslie E. Keeley was born a century later, in 1832. He studied medicine at Rush Medical College in Chicago, where he learned of his brilliant predecessor's research. He served in the army as an assistant surgeon during the American Civil War. He was appalled by the magnitude of the devastation created by alcoholism among the soldiers, and he sought a remedy for this national scourge. Working in Dwight, he made public in 1879 the result of his collaboration with a young Irish chemist, John Oughton, announcing it had led to a major discovery. A few months later, he opened in this small city, located less than a hundred miles south of Chicago, the first clinic bearing his name, the Keeley Institute.

Until then, the possible treatments offered to heavy drinkers were limited to various "miracle cures," ads for them flooding the newspapers with the most shameless quackery, or to the salvation promised by religions to the penitent sinners. The clinic Dr. Keeley opened claimed to make use of a "scientific" treatment, though limited by its high price to the most wealthy patients. An astute and effective promotional campaign quickly brought the establishment success. The *Chicago Tribune* relayed to its readers the "prodigious" results obtained in three days with six "drunkards," qualified for the study by an extreme state of intoxication. The Keeley Institute promoted itself with a surprisingly modern media campaign. The large buildings erected in Dwight over the next few years were immediately filled with desperate patients. In 1893, 118 Keeley Institutes operated in the United States, under the license of the founders at Dwight, and several European subsidiaries cropped up as well.

Dr. Keeley kept the formula of his cure secret. This decision brought him harsh criticism from his peers, shocked by his absence of scientific spirit. The patients were accommodated in spacious rooms, where a relaxed and informal atmosphere reigned and direct supervision was kept to a minimum. The cure took four weeks, during which medical attention was focused on four daily injections of a colored solution. Dr. Keeley's advertisements

Ad for the Keeley Institute at the end of the nineteenth century. (Dwight Historical Society)

U. S. Veterans' Hospital, Dwight, Illinois

Postcard from the 1940s showing the former buildings of the Keeley Institute. (Dwight Historical Society)

revealed only that the solution was a "double chloride of gold." The effectiveness of this mysterious medication was obviously questioned by medical authorities, and after Keeley's death in 1900, the public's confidence in the miraculous medicine started to erode. John Oughton took over the management of the network of franchised clinics, but he could not hold off an irreversible decline: only eleven institutes bearing Dr. Keeley's name were still operating at the start of the 1920s. The doctor's only new and positive contribution may well have been the extensive camaraderie that developed among former patients of the institute: "graduates" of the institution organized Keeley Leagues, a group therapy idea that would take off after 1935 under Dr. Robert H. Smith, founder of Alcoholics Anonymous.

Two of Bix's signatures on the Keeley Institute medical file, as completed and signed during admission on October 14, 1929 (left) and on final examination on November 18 (right). (Keeley Institute archives, Springfield)

Former buildings of the Keeley Institute in Dwight, present condition. (JPL)

Former buildings of the Keeley Institute: entrance to the Livingston Hotel, present condition. (JPL)

Dwight, October 14–November 18, 1929

Just as Bix's sister had started the process of registering him at Lake Forest Academy, it was Bix's brother, Burnie, who made the first contact with the Keeley Institute. The response from the clinic, dated October 8, not surprisingly sang the praises of a treatment that was said to have cured several thousand people in the last fifty years, and confirmed that they could accept a new patient immediately. Burnie drove his younger brother to Dwight on Monday, October 14, and dropped him at the admissions center of the Keeley Institute. The set of buildings was imposing, and the high columned facades retained the arrogance of a faded prestige. Most patients resided in the Livingston Hotel, next to the building housing the laboratories and offices.[53] The clinic offered several levels of accommodation, ranging in cost between $16 and $20 per week. Bix and his family had chosen an intermediate option, which was billed at the rate of $18 per week.

The day of his arrival, at four o'clock in the afternoon, Bix was admitted and a pre-printed form was filled in by the receiving physician. Bix stated he suffered from a loss of appetite, lapses of memory, dizziness, accelerated heart rate, and shortness of breath, and also insomnia for the past two weeks. His pneumonia and delirium tremens crisis from December 1928 were noted, as well as the pain in his feet that had appeared at the same time. Bix admitted to having used liquor "in excess" for the past nine years, his daily dose over the last three years amounting to three pints of "whiskey" and twenty cigarettes. The patient's signature, at the bottom of the document, underlines the gravity of his condition: this chaotic autograph is that of a truly ill man.

The following day, an extensive examination confirmed the devastating effects of Bix's chronic alcoholism. A hepatic dullness was obvious, "knee jerks could not be obtained"—which confirmed the spread of the polyneuritis, and Bix was "swaying in Romberg position"—standing up with his eyes closed. The practitioner also noticed that "breath sounds were very harsh," and he noted that his patient had a "marked coarse tremor in hand." He concluded that Bix's mental condition was bad, showing "a mild delirium at times," and that he might "overlap DT's or convulsions at any time."[54] This probability called for the constant presence of an attendant, during four days and four nights, the treatment beginning with an inevitable and painful withdrawal. There is no existing information on Bix's stay at the clinic. Without music, his days must have felt long. Burnie visited his brother on November 4, bringing with him the additional money the institution had been insistently asking for. For unknown reasons, Bix's parents requested an extra week of treatment for their son—making his stay five weeks long.

On November 18, Burnie drove to Dwight for the last time, and brought his brother back to Davenport. The Keeley Institute mailed the final medical report to Agatha the same day. Her son had been examined upon his exit, and his condition

53. The first buildings of the Keeley Institute were destroyed in a fire in 1902. The ensemble, which is still visible today, was erected in 1903. The former offices, laboratories and the Livingston Hotel are used by the William W. Fox Developmental Center, a State of Illinois institution for handicapped children. They are all located on Main Street. (Information from Carol Ohlendorf.)

54. Bix's medical file, filled during his stay at the Keeley Institute, is kept in the archives of the Illinois State Historical Library in Springfield, Illinois. It includes several letters exchanged between the Institute, Phil Evans, and Charles Wareing in 1964. Copies of the letters sent by the Keeley Institute to the Beiderbecke family are classified in two big files, under references D-27 and D-28. All these documents are unpublished.

was judged to be satisfactory. The patient had claimed to no longer feel "a craving for liquor," but he still showed "a considerable tremor in extended fingers" and a lack of stability. Bix's cure was invoiced for $332.80, which was less than two weeks of his salary. His bank account, fed for the past two years by the large revenues coming from Whiteman, had in a few days, however, become as blank as his face. The cost of his stay at the Keeley Institute was not responsible for this financial rout, and Bix had millions of companions in his misfortune: a tornado had just devastated the New York Stock Exchange.

THE COUNTRY'S ECONOMIC PROSPERITY had naturally led to an increase in stock values. The consistency of this ascension had attracted more and more investors into the stock market, fascinated by the ease and speed with which they could earn money. A strong demand had consequently increased the value of a supply that had become rarer. This frenetic acquisition of stock shares was logical in the context of a society that held wealth and success as primary targets. A sophisticated and perverse system allowed employees, whose weekly salaries did not exceed $50, access to this promised fortune: the shares were paid for only ten to twenty-five percent of their market price, the stockbroker fronting the difference to his client and holding the stocks for securing the loan. Six billion dollars would thus be loaned out in 1929, inflating a speculative bubble, the reliability of which few people were actually questioning. A stick of a pin would suffice to pop the balloon, and economist Roger Babson's announcement of an inevitable and terrible financial disaster accelerated the transfer of shares. Only massive purchases organized by a bank cartel could prevent the total collapse of the stock market on October 24, 1929, a day known as Black Thursday. Wall Street quotations were not suspended upon Monday's opening calls, and professionals stood powerless to the crashing of prices during the Tuesday session: sixteen million securities were traded during this full panic day, and $30 billion in shares vanished within several hours. "Some of the people I knew lost millions. I was luckier," recalled Groucho Marx. "All I lost was two hundred and forty thousand dollars—or one hundred and twenty weeks of work at two thousand per. I would have lost more, but that was all the money I had."[55] The stock market crash was, however, progressive, and for certain shares, its effect spread over several years into the Depression.

Davenport, November 18–December 31, 1929

The extent of Bix's losses is unknown, but it had obviously nothing in common with these breathtaking amounts. His income during the two years he spent with Paul Whiteman can be estimated at about $25,000. This was really big money at the time, and adjusted for inflation, it would amount today to approximately

55. Groucho Marx, *Groucho and Me* (New York: Bernard Geis Associates, 1959).

$600,000. His financial predicament created a double blow for Bix, as in his family's eyes, this vanished money was the only possible justification for a career that they did not approve of. Notice of the return of the "Beiderbecke boy," after a detoxification cure, soon reached Esten Spurrier.[56] He called Bix, and the two friends happily got back together. Bix had remained secluded at his house for almost three weeks, playing the piano, smoking his pipe—a habit he had picked up at the Keeley Institute—and playing the same records over and over again, a number of which were his own recordings. "He never got tired of recounting the little occurrences during recordings," recalled Spurrier, "where someone got mixed up—wrong downbeats or something, or Frank Trumbauer's foibles and little persnickety introductions, interludes and endings. Soup to nuts."[57]

Since the beginning of December, Esten Spurrier had been playing cornet in Jimmy Hicks's orchestra several nights a week at the Dancehall, a newly opened ballroom in downtown Davenport at Scott and 4th streets.[58] Trombonist Bob Struve, another friend from Bix's childhood, was also among the musicians, and this welcoming environment prompted Bix to sit in with the band. "Union scale was $6 per night," added Esten Spurrier. "We got Bix $15."[59] An ad in the December 18 issue of the Davenport *Daily Times* informed its readers that the Jimmy Hicks orchestra would offer a "big surprise and a special added attraction": Bix Beiderbecke was on cornet that night, and again three days later. A twenty-three-year-old pianist, Les Swanson, discovered Bix's playing during these evenings, and seventy-two years later, when he was interviewed for this book, he remained under the spell of this encounter: "I spent many nights just listening to his fascinating style of playing," remembered Les Swanson, "and we forgot all about dancing when he was playing."[60]

Bix often used to go for walks in downtown Davenport, where he ran into another childhood friend, Larry Andrews, who had become a banjo player. They met in a cigar shop, and the two friends shared memories of Vera Cox and their high school years: "One of our local orchestra leaders, by the name of Trave O'Hearn, came into the store and asked us both if we would like to play a job," wrote Larry Andrews. "I thought he had a lot of guts to ask Bix, but I was even more surprised when Bix said '*Sure, if Larry can play too.*' . . . As far as the money was concerned, he didn't seem tremendously interested in what he would receive. We got on the platform and Bix told Trave right off the reel that he expected to sit next to me, so we sat together right in front of the piano. . . . I mentioned that there were several pretty good looking girls there that evening for the dance, and he said, '*Well, I'll tell you Larry, after you play behind the Follies where they pick the most beautiful girls out of thousands of them, and then ride on a train from New York to California with them, you get so the girls don't interest you much.*'"[61] This show took place on December 23 at the Blackhawk Hotel.[62] The musician seated at the piano, in front of which Bix and Larry Andrews were cheerfully conversing, was Les Swanson. "The

56. The stories told by Esten Spurrier were often intended to support the idea that the Beiderbecke family rejected Bix's activity, his music, and his friends. One of these stories was endlessly repeated: back in Davenport, Bix found all his records unopened in a closet— the records he had proudly sent home over the years! Because of Bix's way of living, it's almost impossible to think of him packing and mailing to Davenport these fragile 78-rpm discs, which Charles "Burnie" Beiderbecke clearly confirmed in 1959: "Bix never did send home any test pressings or recordings," in *The Leon Bix Beiderbecke Story*, op. cit., p. 491.

57. *Bix, Man and Legend*, op. cit., p. 291.

58. The Danceland was located downtown in the Davenport Eagles Building at 501 West 4th Street, where it still stands.

59. *The Leon Bix Beiderbecke Story*, op. cit., p. 493.

60. Sixteenth program of *Bix, a Biographical Radio Series*, op. cit. Les Swanson was born in 1906. He died on April 6, 2003, a few days after having played piano on March 10, at the Davenport Blackhawk Hotel, for Bix's 100th birthday celebration.

61. Larry Andrews's letters, addressed to the jazz critic Otis Ferguson, author of the article *Young Man with a Horn.* Andrews's letters were quoted in *Storyville*, no. 12 (August/September 1967), pp. 16–17.

62. Located in downtown Davenport, at 200 East 3rd Street, the hotel is today known as the President Casino Blackhawk Hotel. The building is practically unchanged.

surprising part was that Bix didn't even bother to come to our rehearsal," recalled the pianist. "Trave O'Hearn wasn't bothered a bit either as he said, '*Oh, he gets by some way and he'll have a lot of solos.*' . . . Bix showed up with his horn and sat right there on the second trumpet chair. We didn't use any arrangements and he'd never heard us play before, but I was really amazed at how he could just

Danceland Ballroom, Davenport, present condition. (JPL)

follow along. . . . He only had to play one chorus and he had it."[63]

Trave O'Hearn's orchestra returned to the Blackhawk Hotel on December 27, as the band's agenda became booked by the New Year's holidays. Bix appeared at the Danceland in Jimmy Hicks's band on December 28 and 29; he then played with Trave O'Hearn on New Year's Eve at the Elks Club in Rock Island, Illinois.[64] Together with Larry Andrews, Bix sat in back with the drummer who had taken him to Syracuse in September 1922, Mervin "Pee Wee" Rank. "Bix rode with me to

Leslie C. Swanson at the time of his encounter with Bix. (Vicki Swanson Wassenhove)

and from the dance," recalled Larry Andrews. "During intermission, he stayed on the bandstand because he wasn't drinking, and the place was loaded with drinkers. I decided to stay with him."[65]

The Whiteman Orchestra spent New Year's in Los Angeles. Universal Studios had called the bandleader on October 15 to inform him that John Murray Anderson, a Broadway stage producer, had been hired to replace director Paul Fejos, and that the former "romantic scenario" had been dropped and would simply be

63. "Remembering Bix," op. cit., and Les Swanson's letter to the author, dated January 21, 2002.

64. Rock Island is the town next to Moline, across the Mississippi from Davenport. The Elks Club was located at the corner of 3rd Avenue and 17th Street. It no longer exists. (Information from Rich Johnson.)

65. *The Leon Bix Beiderbecke Story*, op. cit., p. 495.

replaced with a series of musical numbers. Paul Whiteman agreed, and the band left for Los Angeles at the end of October. The sound-track was carefully worked out, and the first two months in California were dedicated to recording the sixteen titles forming the musical portion of the movie. The shooting began at the end of the year, filming on silent Technicolor film.[66] Dialogue and the prere-corded music numbers were post-synchronized in a studio, which permitted optimal sound quality. Some last retakes were shot at the beginning of March, and the set of the *King of Jazz* closed down for good on March 20, 1930. The shooting was finally over, leaving a film of which Bix Beiderbecke would be only a spectator.

Blackhawk Hotel, Davenport, present condition. (JPL)

66. *The King of Jazz* was filmed in two-strip (two-color) early Technicolor, a process that bathed *Rhapsody in Blue* in turquoise. The first movie-musical in color was *On With the Show*, filmed in 1929, with Ethel Waters singing "Am I Blue?"

CHAPTER 11

1930: Final Recordings

The stock market crash did not immediately affect the entire country—just the city dwellers who were well-off enough to dabble in stocks. Gradually, however, the effects of the collapse spread as the financial institutions, which had also invested a considerable portion of their assets in stocks, had their resources seriously depleted. Not only were the banks unable to fuel the economy with loans of money they no longer had, but they were also forced to call in as many outstanding loans as they could. Some banks even went bankrupt. Businesses that would have borrowed to buy equipment and inventory had to cancel their orders. The manufacturers with no customers laid off workers. Workers with no income cut spending to the bare essentials. Four million U.S. workers were without jobs at the end of 1929. Lines of the unemployed outside relief agencies grew, as the lines outside Broadway theaters disappeared. In Davenport, far from New York and Chicago, at the beginning of 1930, the import of the crash was still just a rumor in the local papers and on the radio.

Davenport, January 1930

On January 1, Bix asked Esten Spurrier to join him and see a movie at the Garden Theater[1]: it was *Is Everybody Happy?*, the film Ted Lewis had made in Los Angeles the previous summer. Bix did not want to be alone when he saw the posthumous images of his old friend Don Murray.

Vera Cox, with her husband and her fourteen-month-old child, was visiting her

1. The Garden Theater was located downtown, at 121 West 3rd Street. The building has been torn down.

parents for the holidays. Bix was invited to this home he knew well, where he saw for the last time the young woman he had probably once loved. Vera Cox was often asked about the conversation she had with Bix on that day. During World War II, she confided in Belgian critic Robert Goffin, who wrote in his *Histoire du Jazz*, "Vera told me that Bix, on one of his last stays in Davenport, shortly before his death, came to see her. He was melancholy, and he complained at length about the hard life he led. He confessed to her that he had achieved, in improvised jazz, everything syncopated music could bring to a man, and that he was tired. He was also bitter and, as he left, he murmured with a sigh that perhaps he would have been better off if he had been simply a husband, with family obligations."[2]

Vera Cox's house at 1709 Bridge Avenue, Davenport. (Rich Johnson)

"DANCING TONIGHT—Danceland—Jimmy Hicks and his Orchestra, featuring 'Bix' Beiderbecke—Hottest Trumpet Player in the Country—Gentleman, 50c.— Ladies, 25c." This ad appeared in the Davenport *Daily Times* during the weekend of January 4 and 5. Bix's trumpet was mentioned again on January 19, but never again after that date, although Jimmy Hicks's orchestra performed in the same ballroom until the end of January. On Sunday, January 12, the Danceland bandstand was occupied by Ray Miller's orchestra, but whether Bix was present is unknown.

New York, end of January 1930

Sultry actress and singer Libby Holman came to the public's attention on April 30, 1929, at the Music Box Theater, during the premiere of the Broadway revue *The Little Show*.[3] Her song "Moanin' Low" brought her a dozen curtain calls on opening night, and raves from critics on the days that followed. In July 1929, she recorded it twice for Brunswick, both times with bands including the Dorsey Brothers and trumpeter Phil Napoleon, and the first of the two became a bestseller by September. *The Little Show* ran for more than three hundred performances, and was coming to the end of its run when, on January 22, 1930, Brunswick set up a new recording session for Libby Holman. Two new songs were selected for the date, "Cooking Breakfast for the One I Love" and "When a Woman Loves a Man." They were recorded with an unidentified studio group, labeled as the Roger Wolfe Kahn Orchestra and probably partly made up of members of Kahn's band. On the two sides of Brunswick record 4699, Libby Holman's vocals are followed by

2. Robert Goffin, *Histoire du Jazz* (Montreal: Lucien Parizeau and Cie, 1945), pp. 182–183. Robert Goffin completed the story of this part of his stay in the U.S. in his memoirs, *Souvenirs avant l'Adieu* (1980): "From Leadville we went to Denver and from there to Moline where we were hosted by Fred Flick, the banjo player with the Georgians, who told me about the history of jazz in the Midwest. . . . One day, in a hotel downtown, Fred Flick introduced me to a beautiful woman, who had been for a time Bix's fiancée. I had a long talk with her but, as she was afraid of her jealous husband, she mentioned in veiled terms her engagement with the boy who had promised he would give up jazz and to continue his studies" (p. 21).

3. The Music Box Theater opened in 1921 at 239 West 45th Street, and is still in existence. Murder, millionaires, sex, scandals, and death were recurrent themes in the life of Libby Holman, who committed suicide in 1971.

a solo played on muted cornet. The cornetist on "Cooking Breakfast for the One I Love" is the same one who, five days later, recorded the same tune with Annette Hanshaw: he is probably Muggsy Spanier. Surprisingly, the *hot* soloist on the second number, "When a Woman Loves a Man," is a different musician, and one who doesn't appear on any other Roger Wolfe Kahn recording. His muted cornet solo sounds highly Bixian, but with a tone and a melodic inspiration that reminds one of solos recorded by Bix later in 1930—something that one of Bix's many emulators could hardly have copied in January 1930.[4]

The last questionable element related to this side is that there is a second take, also with Libby's vocal, but with a totally different sixteen-bar cornet solo. This second version shows improvement, and it offers quite a distinct construction. At this point, one must wonder which jazz cornetist would have been invited to share solos with Muggsy Spanier, to record two drastically different takes in a row, to sound like a "1930" Bix . . . and to remain anonymous. Obviously, the first name that comes to mind is none other than Bix Beiderbecke. It is possible that Bix left Davenport on the morning of Monday, January 20, boarded a train in Chicago in the afternoon, and after a sixteen-hour trip, reached New York on the morning of January 21. He could have met Muggsy Spanier later in the day, and agreed to make a few bucks by joining the group at the Brunswick studios, at 799 Seventh Avenue. Because of his exclusive contract with Paul Whiteman, Bix's presence on any non-Columbia record had to remain secret—a mystery that endures today, as does the one surrounding the Brunswick recording of "Cradle of Love," exactly one year before.

BIX SPENT LITTLE TIME in New York. He paid a short visit to Bill Challis at his Riverside Drive apartment. "He looked good. My God, he looked good," said Challis. "He made you want to hope it would all work out well for him."[5] His meeting with Jimmy Gillespie was equally brief. Paul Whiteman and his men were working full-time in Los Angeles on *The King of Jazz*, and a tour of the West Coast awaited the orchestra at the end of shooting. Jimmy Gillespie had little to say, but Bix was just happy to have been able to show him that he was overcoming his personal problems, and recovering his health and his musical abilities. He was sure that this information would make it back to the boss, which was the unstated goal of this brief journey to the Big Apple.

Chicago, February 1930

On his way back home, Bix stopped for several days in Chicago, and stayed at the Hotel Sherman.[6] On one evening, Bix visited the Three Deuces, now renamed My Cellar, the North State Street speakeasy where he had taken part in memorable jam

4. We don't know how Bix might have sounded in January 1930. His last recording was cut on September 1929, and the next official one not until May 1930, leaving an eight-month silent gap. Bix had suffered a strong physical and psychological shock in October 1929, and he stayed on the wagon for several months. He suffered from nervous problems during this period, as his health was going up and down. This physical condition might explain the tiny variations of tone, vibrato, and breath control that can be heard on the side, and that are not to be found on other recordings by Bix.

5. *Bix, Man and Legend*, op. cit., p. 296.

6. The Hotel Sherman was located on Randolph Street, between Clark and LaSalle streets. His restaurant-cabaret, the College Inn, featured the Isham Jones Orchestra and hosted many celebrities staying in the Windy City. The building no longer exists.

sessions in November 1927. Bix's friends from that carefree period had moved to New York, and the management of My Cellar had hired Wingy Manone's orchestra. At closing time, a small group of fascinated musicians surrounded Bix Beiderbecke, who was improvising endlessly on the piano—to the great despair of the restaurant employees who were waiting to clean the place and get home.

Ted Weems's orchestra had been playing for a few months at the Granada Café, and Bix had heard their Challis-inspired arrangements on the radio, beautifully backed by an effective rhythm section. Ted Weems had brought many hits to the Victor label since the start of the 1920s, and his recent recording of "The Man from the South" was at the top of national sales. Joe Haymes, the band's arranger, received a telephone call announcing Bix would be at the Granada Café that night. The musicians thought it was a joke . . . until dinnertime, when the cornetist sat in with the band. Joe Haymes was impressed by Bix's somewhat revived playing and inspiration, and he invited him to join the first rehearsals of an orchestra hired to play in Tulsa, Oklahoma. Bix accepted. "He told me he wanted to get himself back in shape to rejoin the old man [Paul Whiteman], and welcomed the chance to play," recalled Joe Haymes. "He went along a time or two—but he kept having nervous spells, during which it was sometimes hard for him to finish a chorus, especially on piano. He'd just stop—you know, drop his hands and say, 'I'm too nervous, I can't go on.'"[7]

Former building of the LeClaire Hotel in Moline, present condition (the ballroom was located on top floor). (JPL)

Davenport, February 14–April 17, 1930

Bix was back in Davenport by mid-February, playing on Valentine's Day at the Elks Club of Rock Island. He called his friend Esten Spurrier one morning: "To my surprise, Bix said he wanted to pick me up and bring me to his house. . . . When we arrived, he immediately sat down at the piano and played through a complete composition and told me it was 'Candlelights.' He had composed three bridges and couldn't decide on which one to use, I had to select the best! I listened to all three, liked all three. Bix was adamant, the bridge had to be picked up by me. Finally I selected one."[8]

During the first week of March, Bix played in drummer Bob Tyldesley's orchestra, which appeared for eight days at the Roof Garden, the restaurant and cabaret of the LeClaire Hotel in Moline.[9] Bix's health was still unsteady, and he had a very rough time on the night of March 6. He felt bad enough to send an urgent message

7. *Bix, Man and Legend*, op. cit., p. 298.

8. *The Leon Bix Beiderbecke Story*, op. cit., p. 497.

9. Located on Route 6 in Moline, the tall building that was once the LeClaire Hotel has been converted into apartments. Its large ballroom was located on the top floor.

to one of his old friends, Wayne Rohlf, who was playing that night at the Capitol Theater. Wayne Rohlf did not take the emergency note seriously, as it asked him to run to the Roof Garden as soon as his work was over: he ignored the message. When he ran into Rohlf in downtown Davenport a few days later, Bix informed him, in the ironic tone that he often used, of his disappointment with this breach of their old friendship.

The small group thrown together for the night of March 17 at the Fraternal Hall in Rock Island had no drummer. Upon their arrival at the dance hall, Esten Spurrier, Bob Struve, clarinetist Ed Anderson, and Les Swanson were surprised to find Bix fighting to assemble a drum kit. Several hours earlier, he had accepted Jimmy Hicks's urgent request, and he managed to provide the band with an acceptable rhythmic support, as steady as a metronome. "Bix certainly enjoyed getting out and playing with the local boys," confirmed Les Swanson. "He wasn't anything like what we had expected. He just wanted to be one of the local guys when he played here. There was no air of superiority or aloofness, which you might expect from somebody who had been playing in the big times. I recalled he insisted on being paid whatever the other men and the band received, and in those days—in the mist of the terrible Depression era—we were getting $6 a night for a job going to 1:00 a.m., and $9 if it went to 2:00 a.m."[10]

On March 18, Bix wrote a belated answer to a letter that Ruth Shaffner had sent him from Saint Louis: "I could kick myself all over the place for not having written to you before, you old sweet thing, but honestly I've been out of town, and sort of taking advantage of the first vacation I've had in eight years. . . . I'm joining Paul again in two weeks in Chicago, from where we go to New York, and then possibly London, England, for a few weeks to be present at the premiere of the picture King of Jazz Revue. . . . I'm entirely well again and haven't had a drink of anything intoxicating for over six months and it looks like I'm going to lay off for good. I made a promise to the folks and that goes—imagine me a teetotaler. It's a fact . . ."[11]

Bix and Les Swanson met frequently during the second half of March, an idle period for the two musicians, who weren't able to find a job. The young pianist used to pick up Bix at his parents' house after dinner, and they would go to the movies, hear a band playing at the Danceland, or attend a boxing match. One night stood out in Les Swanson's memory: "We were going to the movies together. I got to his house early and Bix wasn't ready, so I talked to his mother who was the essence of culture and refinement. Bix called from upstairs and said, 'Play something on the piano, Les.' I played 'In a Mist.' Just about the time I finished, he came down and muttered something like 'very good,' but I don't think he was too impressed with my rendition. . . . I said to Bix, 'Now let's see you play it the way it's supposed to be.' And he played right away, without any coaxing. I noticed he was inserting a lot of new wrinkles to the whole thing. When he finished, I said to Bix:

10. Sixteenth program of Bix, a Biographical Radio Series, op. cit.

11. Bix, Man and Legend, op. cit., pp. 298–299.

'It seemed that you were straying a little from the script in spots.' He laughed and replied, 'That's me, I never play anything the same way twice.'"[12]

Days passed. Bix had learned that the shooting of *The King of Jazz* had ended on March 20, and that the Whiteman band was preparing to leave California on April 1 for a tour up the West Coast and into Canada. Bix was to meet up with Paul Whiteman in Chicago by mid-April, to take back his chair in the band and follow them to New York. In a few days he would face the intense and demanding professional activity that had broken him down—and the anxiety that he had managed to master for some months came flooding back. The devils that had so often led him into the false comfort of alcohol were back—and again they won. "One night we went to Danceland to see Krazy Katz and his Kittens, a big name band in those days," recalled Les Swanson. "Of all times I'd been with Bix, I'd never heard him mention anything about drinking, but that night some of his friends brought us a couple of drinks. I think that triggered what happened later. I was driving Bix home, and when we were about even with the Blackhawk Hotel, he started shivering and grabbing out and yelling, '*I have to have it! I have to have it! Pull over. I'll tell you in a minute,*' Bix said. There was a bootleg joint in the next block. In about five minutes, he was back with a sack. Bix pulled out a half pint of alcohol, and said he was going to take it to bed with him."[13]

Paul Whiteman and his men had left the Canadian city of Vancouver, moved south along the Pacific coast over 150 miles, and set up in Seattle for a week. The band was successfully featured for five days at the Olympic Hotel, and left Seattle on April 14, moving farther south to play in Portland, Oregon.

On April 17, Bix checked into the Sherman Hotel in Chicago, waiting for Paul Whiteman's arrival. The encounter did not take place as planned. The bandleader had wished to return to New York as fast as possible, and his train crossed the country from west to east, nonstop, in four days and four nights. The musicians arrived in Manhattan on April 21.[14]

New York, April–October 1930

Bix learned too late of Whiteman's decision, and he could not reach New York before April 23. He set up for a few days in an apartment located on the third floor of a building on Seventh Avenue, where Hoagy Carmichael was one of his first visitors. The Depression was now badly affecting show business, but it had not yet slowed down Paul Whiteman, who was still fulfilling existing contracts. The *Old Gold* program remained on the airwaves every Tuesday, Columbia was preparing a new series of recordings, and starting in early May, the band was hired to play five daily shows at the Roxy Theater, alternating with the first showings of *The King of Jazz*.[15]

12. Les Swanson's letter to the author, dated January 21, 2002.

13. Les Swanson's recollections in "Remembering Bix," op. cit. The cornet player in Al Katz's band was Fred Rollison, the musician with whom Bix almost recorded "Big Boy" in New York in 1924. The Coon-Sanders Nighthawks Orchestra was widely popularized by their NBC broadcast, performed at the Blackhawk Hotel in Chicago. Two members of the band, Bob Pope (trumpet) and Rex Downing (trombone), recalled visiting Bix at his home in Davenport. They remembered his personal record collection, quite large and "all classic. No jazz." This visit probably took place on April 10, 1930, the day the band was playing in Davenport. (Information from Frank van Nus and Scott Black.)

14. Train schedules for 1930 lead to the following itinerary: the band boarded in Portland on "Oregon–Washington Ltd" on April 16 at 10:00 am, and arrived on April 20 at 11:00 am at Chicago Station on Madison Street; they had a two-hour transfer to Union Station (the "Pennsylvania Railroad") or La Salle Street Station (the "New York Central"), where they boarded at about 3:00 pm: in either case, they arrived in New York City on April 21 by noon time. The short connecting time in Chicago explains why Bix missed them.

15. Located at the corner of Seventh Avenue and 50th Street, the Roxy Theater opened in March 1927. It was called the Movie Cathedral because of its flamboyant decoration. It was razed in 1960.

The Roxy Theater, New York.

Bix Beiderbecke felt faint when Paul Whiteman laid out for him, upon their first encounter, the calendar for the coming weeks. The intensity of this busy schedule would have meant quite a test for the cornetist's precarious health, and it was made still more difficult by Bix's need to learn the new titles written for the film's soundtrack, all recorded in his absence. "Paul had kept him on full salary while he was out of the band," confirmed Andy Secrest. "I'm positive Paul kept that place for him. He loved Bix. I honestly think that when Bix talked to Paul, and Paul asked him if he was ready to return, Bix decided that his nerves just weren't up to the daily routine and that he didn't feel he could handle it. He didn't have the stamina. . . . But even then, Paul always said the spot was his any time he wanted it."[16] A sentimental element also affected Bix's decision: taking back his chair in the orchestra would have led to Andy Secrest's departure, in a difficult economic situation—and Bix was a very kind man, unacquainted with any idea of competition. He hemmed and hawed, asked for a few days to think it over—when his mind had already been made up. He would never take back his chair in the Paul Whiteman Orchestra.

On April 28, Bix returned to the 44th Street Hotel, his New York residence, and moved into room 605. His neighbor was a young trumpeter, Pasquale "Pat" Ciricillo, who devoted his days to music studies, financed by nocturnal gigs in the nightclubs of the area. He owned an upright piano, a Wurlitzer model purchased a few months earlier for $300. Bix was immediately attracted to the piano: "I lived in the 44th Street Hotel until June," recalled Pat Ciricillo in 1973, "and then again from September 1930 to June 1931. I lived in room #606 and Bix lived in #605. Bix loved poetry, especially Byron, Shelley and Keats. . . . He lived 20 years too soon. He hated to play for peo-

Pat Ciricillo's piano, played by Bix in New York. (On display at the Louisiana State Museum, the Old U.S. Mint, 400 Esplanade Ave., New Orleans.) (JPL)

16. *Bix, Man and Legend,* op. cit., p. 302.

ple who were dancing and not listening to the music. Today he would have been happier. During 1930 he used to be 'on the wagon,' off and on. At 3:00 in the morning his musician friends, such as the Dorseys, Bill Moore, Stan King, Rollini and the like, would bang on my hotel room with gin bottles and they'd bring Bix in to improvise on my piano for them."[17]

The New York premiere of *The King of Jazz* took place on May 2 at the Roxy Theater. The Whiteman Orchestra's presence on stage, along with the 125-piece Roxy Symphony Orchestra and George Gershwin on piano, offered a live continuation of the images projected on the screen. The stage was crowded, but the audience was sparse. The first week was so disappointing that the Roxy management cancelled Paul Whiteman's contract after only ten days, when he had been hired for two more weeks. Critics had shown little enthusiasm for the Universal Studios film, whose unreal sequences, bathed in the Technicolor blues and pinks of a glittery cardboard universe, were as appropriate in the midst of the Depression as a comic act in a funeral parlor.[18] But the public's indifference to Paul Whiteman was not limited to his film. His orchestra's records had met with only rare success over the past months, with three exceptions: "Great Day," "Nobody's Sweetheart," and a song from *The King of Jazz*, "It Happened in Monterey." The consumers' tastes were changing, favoring younger bands. Rudy Vallee and His Connecticut Yankees had recorded the hit of the year, "Stein Song," based on a Brahms Hungarian dance, and the records released by Guy Lombardo's Royal Canadians were regularly among the best sellers. "The picture was a flop and the business was, by this time, pretty flat. There was nothing much to do for a band," remembered Bill Challis. "I think Paul told me one time that he had forty-four weeks a year that he could do theaters. And that's what he did for three years! But when they came back to New York . . . Paul made up his mind that he couldn't go any further. . . . When I first saw him, I knew what was going to happen. He pointed his finger and said, '*You're fired!*' He was just showing off. But he then said, '*Yeah, I'm sorry, Bill, but we got to cut the band down.*' So that was the time that I got out."[19] The number of musicians was reduced to eighteen, after the departure of ten band members, among whom were Joe Venuti, Eddie Lang, Lennie Hayton, Bill Challis, Min Leibrook—and the Rhythm Boys, who took off for California. The salaries of the remaining musicians were reduced by fifteen percent.

Bix was henceforth deprived of any income, and in great need of a job. The first offer came from the Dorsey Brothers, who were playing on the first weekend of May at Princeton University, in New Jersey, midway between New York and Philadelphia. A shortage of adequate dining within the university grounds had led groups of wealthy students to organize Eating Clubs at the end of the nineteenth century. They were housed in luxury buildings erected on Prospect Avenue, and offered lodging and food service. These clubs had quickly become powerful social organizations, with access limited to the students whose families were of the upper crust. Such elitism was often criticized, but those bothered most were those who

17. *The Leon Bix Beiderbecke Story*, op. cit., p. 502. Pat Ciricillo confirmed that Bix composed "Flashes" and "In the Dark" on this piano, which is today on display at Louisiana State Museum Jazz Collection in New Orleans, at 400 Esplanade Avenue.

18. *The King of Jazz* is available on video from MCA Universal. The title of the movie is deceptive: it is nothing more than an average Broadway musical revue. However, a few sequences are worth preserving: Eddie Lang and Joe Venuti playing "Wild Cat"; the Rhythm Boys singing "Mississippi Mud," "So the Bluebirds and the Blackbirds Got Together," and the excellent "Happy Feet"; Roy Bargy (who looks like Gershwin) playing *Rhapsody in Blue*—in total, material for a very good short musical movie. It is also intriguing to see the band Bix played with, and to recognize many of the players and their routines.

19. "Bill Challis: The Whiteman Years," op. cit., p. 19.

Colonial Club, Princeton, present condition. (JPL)

remained outside. The Dorsey Brothers' band performed on May 2 and 3 at private parties organized by the Colonial Club, the Ivy Club, and the Tiger Inn, three of the oldest and most influential Eating Clubs in the Princeton hierarchy.[20] Two weeks later, Bix, Tommy Dorsey, and guitarist Carl Kress were part of an ensemble hired to play on May 16 and 17 at Williams College in Williamstown, Massachusetts.[21] The warm reception the three musicians were given induced them to stay over for two more days, and they returned to New York on May 19.

Ivy Club, Princeton, present condition. (JPL)

20. The Eating Clubs buildings where Bix played in 1930 and 1931 are still visible on Prospect Avenue, on the magnificent campus of Princeton University. They can be found at the following numbers: the Colonial Club at no. 40, the Ivy Club at no. 43, and the Tiger Inn at no. 48.

21. Williams College houses the Paul Whiteman Collection, comprising 4,000 manuscripts of orchestral scores, contemporary recordings, files of clippings, and some photographs.

Tiger Inn, Princeton, present condition. (JPL)

New York, Wednesday, May 21, 1930

Hoagy Carmichael's stay in New York worked out much better for him than his time in California. He had found a job at S. W. Strauss and Company, one of New York's leading investment houses, and since the end of 1929, his compositions were becoming in demand. Eddie Lang's orchestra had recorded one of Hoagy's tunes on October 5, 1929, "What Kind O' Man Is You?," beautifully sung by Mildred Bailey. Two months later, Hoagy was invited to the Okeh studios by Louis Armstrong, where together they sang another Carmichael tune, "Rockin' Chair," cutting a record that would sell well—in the summer of 1932. In January 1930, a version of "Star Dust," recorded by Irving Mills and His Hotsy Totsy Gang—a gang that featured Hoagy, Jimmy Dorsey, Pee Wee Russell, Miff Mole, Mannie Klein, and others—reached an acceptable level of sales, but it was a record cut on May 16 by Isham Jones that established "Star Dust" as a classic, and gave Hoagy Carmichael his first of an impressive series of hits.

This growing reputation won Hoagy a Victor studios recording session under his own name. It was scheduled for May 21, and the composer was permitted to call upon any musicians of his choosing. This was a dream offer, and he assembled some of the best white jazzmen working in New York at the time, among them Tommy Dorsey, Benny Goodman, Bud Freeman, Joe Venuti, Eddie Lang, Gene Krupa, and Bix Beiderbecke. The night before the recording, the selected musicians met in Hoagy's apartment. Critic Bob Kumm remembered hearing Tommy Dorsey, in a 1945 radio interview, mention the name of pianist Thomas "Fats" Waller among the jazzmen invited by Hoagy for this evening jam session. This information was worth confirming, and Bob Kumm asked Hoagy Carmichael about it. "The party you mentioned was actually held on 31st Street at my apartment, just off Park Avenue," answered Hoagy. "It was supposed to have been a rehearsal for a recording session we were to make the following day. As usual, it turned into a jam session and my hoarded supply of liquor was totally consumed. Fats was not in on the recording date, but since everybody wanted to hear him play and play with him, my rehearsal went to pot. We were warned about our loudness by neighbors several times, and finally a policeman closed us up around 3:00 a.m. We all left the apartment and boarded a trolley-car, with some of the boys still blowing on their instruments. We wound up the session on the trolley as dawn was breaking over Jackson Heights!"[22]

A black musician was, however, present in the Leiderkranz Hall Studios on the morning of May 21: trumpeter James "Bubber" Miley.[23] Seated at his side, Bix Beiderbecke was officially back for the first time in a recording studio after the tragically interrupted September 13, 1929, session. The undisputed master of the *wa-wa* style and specialist in the use of mutes, the trumpeter had brought Duke Ellington his husky and speech-like sounds, his growl, and his colorful style, becoming one of

22. Bob Kumm, "Further Facets of Fats," in *Storyville*, no. 23 (June/July 1969), p. 180. Jackson Heights is in northern Queens.

23. Two reasons have been suggested to explain Miley's presence on Bix's only racially integrated record date: either a request from Loren Watson, one of the RCA-Victor executives, for whom Miley had recorded five days before; or the intervention of Irving Mills, who was— or had been—managing both Duke Ellington's band and Hoagy Carmichael. The Victor label had been sold on January 4, 1929, to Radio Corporation of America (RCA). RCA-Victor did survive the 1929 Depression, but not without suffering deeply from it: its sales went down from 34 million records in 1927 to only 1.6 million in 1933. These figures give a fair appreciation of the severity of the economic crisis.

the dominant figures of the orchestra's jungle period. He had left Duke's band in January 1929, and was now doing some freelance recordings and playing in Leo Reisman's white orchestra, usually hidden behind a screen. The first title of the session was "Rockin' Chair," which Hoagy had recorded with Louis Armstrong several months earlier. Bubber Miley dominates the first part of the side, even if his harsh and insistent playing hardly fits with the melancholic tone of the piece. After a vocal duet sung by Hoagy with himself—the singer makes use of two different registers[24]—Bix improvises an eight-bar solo, hindered as much by Miley's exuberant style as by his own apprehensions. Bix's tone has lost part of its former brightness, but he confidently turns in a sensitive chorus. The side ends on three measures played by Bix and Joe Venuti: "Bix had just returned from Davenport where he had been convalescing, and I did not give him a lot to do," explained Hoagy. "Actually, I did not want to press him. . . . I wrote one specific part for him to play on the ending of a tune we recorded for Victor, 'Rockin' Chair.' I needed a certain type of ending, to finish it . . . so Joe Venuti could come in, and finish the record with a couple of sweet little notes of his, and the two phrases would tighten together. . . . That, I believe, is the only time I ever, out of the two or three records we made, tried to write something for Bix. I'd just say, 'Bix, go!' What else could you say?"[25]

The next song, "Barnacle Bill, the Sailor" was a humorous tune in march tempo, with which the prolific band vocalist Frank Luther had achieved some success in October 1929. Asking such a remarkable studio band to record such a hokey number was unthinkable, and Bix told Esten Spurrier that he had played on this side without restraint, as he could not imagine that this "joke" record would ever be released—and it's just unfortunate that Bix was not given more unrestrained opportunities in front of a microphone. Played at a very fast tempo, his twenty-bar solo on "Barnacle Bill, the Sailor" is carried over with an irresistible spirit and a totally unexpected vitality. For a man in his condition, it is an amazing achievement.

The *Old Gold* radio program was discontinued at the beginning of May, depriving Paul Whiteman of a regular and lucrative job. Judging that the time was right, the Camel cigarette brand asked Nat Shilkret to form an orchestra to be featured on a new weekly broadcast on NBC, *The Camel Pleasure Hour*. Nat Shilkret entrusted its production to John Wiggin and its musical direction to Charles Previn, and he asked Bill Challis's advice for the selection of musicians. The producers contacted some of the men Paul Whiteman had dismissed a few days before, like Min Leibrook and Lennie Hayton, and even Charles Margulis, who had left Whiteman in February 1930. John Wiggin visited the 44th Street Hotel by end of May to talk to Bix and explore the possibility of an engagement. The cornetist was surrounded by friends when John Wiggin entered his room. He was relaxing with Ray Lodwig, Bud Freeman, and Mildred Bailey, and he seemed to be in peak form. The producer's last hesitations were allayed when he learned that Ray Lodwig would

24. This vocal was generally described as a duet between Hoagy and pianist Irving Brodsky, which is not aurally confirmed.

25. *The Leon Bix Beiderbecke Story*, op. cit., p. 505, and the sixteenth program of *Bix, a Biographical Radio Series*, op. cit.

share room 605 with Bix, which would insure the frail musician's presence at rehearsals and broadcasting sessions.

The band assembled by Charles Previn during the first rehearsals was of a considerable size—it boasted nearly forty musicians. Troubled by this turbulent activity, Bix sat next to one of his longtime fans, trumpeter Leo McConville, a former musician with the Roger Wolfe Kahn, Sam Lanin, and Red Nichols orchestras. McConville found Bix physically changed. He had memories of a young and attractive face, which was difficult to detect under the extremely pale mask of this prematurely aged man, putting on unhealthy weight. Bix's life seemed to have accelerated over the course of the last few years. His appearance was altered, but Bix was still the same pleasant companion, and a true music nut: "Sure Bix loved his horn," recalled Leo McConville, "and it took up many of his thoughts. But Bix always seemed to me a serious minded fellow, somewhat apart from the rest of us. When he came back, he was essentially the same quiet fellow—just seemed to be minding his own business, but who sometimes became quite witty in his remarks, and of course always ready for fun when surrounded by people who understood him. I believe he was in the same good spirits as before his illness."[26]

The first show was broadcast on June 4 at 8:30 p.m. on the NBC network from New York, station WJZ.[27] The *Camel Hour* was a variety program, in which musical numbers alternated with the most popular songs of the week. The star invited for the first night was Helen Kane, the spicy and plump singer who had created "I Wanna Be Loved By You" in 1928, and whose curly hair and squeaky voice would be borrowed by Betty Boop.

New York, Friday, June 6, 1930

Irving Mills was born in 1894, in the Jewish neighborhood of New York's Lower East Side. He started his musical career as a "demonstrator," hollering into a megaphone the songs he was expected to sell to the customers of a big Philadelphia store. His success came from music publishing, a less tiring activity for his vocal cords, and the Mills Music Company, created in 1919, soon made a name for itself on Tin Pan Alley, exclusively promoting some young and talented songwriters. Dorothy Fields, Gene Austin, Harry Barris—of the Rhythm Boys—and Hoagy Carmichael were among the house's protégés. However, Irving Mills's greatest accomplishment was gained as the impresario of the Duke Ellington Orchestra. He had discovered the band in 1926 at the Kentucky Club, and put it under contract immediately. He was the one who booked the orchestra at the Cotton Club in December 1927, affording Duke Ellington access to international renown. As a record producer, Mills gave his name to the various studio groups he booked, whose records were released between 1928 and 1930 under the generic identity of Irving

26. As quoted in Thurman and Mary Grove, "Some Notes on the Fallacy of Bix Beiderbecke's Declining Years," in *Bix, a Discographical Society's Pamphlets*, published by R. G. V. Venables and Clifford Jones.

27. Station WJZ was broadcasting from the NBC studios at 711 Fifth Avenue.

Mills and His Hotsy Totsy Gang. The best white jazzmen of the New York scene participated in these sessions, and Irving Mills had called Bix Beiderbecke for his June 6 date. Ray Lodwig and Bix probably took a cab to cover the short distance between their hotel on 44th Street and the Brunswick studios, at 52nd Street and Seventh Avenue, where they were joined by nine musicians: Jack Teagarden, Benny Goodman, Joe Venuti, Min Leibrook, Gene Krupa, and pianist Frank Signorelli were among this "all-star" band. Sadly, this session did not reach the high level that could legitimately be expected from such an impressive cast.

Tram and Bix had recorded "Loved One" one year earlier under another title, "I Like That." This melody, composed by Frank Trumbauer and Lennie Hayton, is pleasant and catchy, but the all-star band could not make it take off and escape cliché. Two takes of "Loved One" have been preserved. Bix's solo on the first take—the one that was released—loses its unity and dissolves after a few bars, while that cut on the second take seems to progress toward a better and elaborate conclusion. "Deep Harlem" is a blues number in which Bix's sixteen measures, played in a linear and repetitive way, introduce a Benny Goodman solo that is not lacking in skill and originality. The last song of the session was "Strut Miss Lizzie," a hit song released by Billy Murray and the highly popular American Quartet—back in November 1921. Dick Robertson, the vocalist, would have to wait until the end of the 1930s for a personal success; in the meantime, he shared with Smith Ballew, Irving Kaufman, Scrappy Lambert, and others the interchangeable role of "studio singer," filling records with mundane vocal choruses, conventional work of which "Strut Miss Lizzie" is a good example. The soloists on the second part of the side do not escape convention either, with one exception: the "fart chorus" perpetrated for four measures by Joe Venuti, an artist who truly knew bad taste. Bix's lack of inspiration has led several critics to question his presence on these Brunswick sides, but this is the Bix of 1930. The discrepancy between our expectations and the realization of these recordings justifies a feeling of disappointment, but it is not difficult to find much worse in the "current production, most often insipid, of this era."[28]

During the summer, Bix was from time to time a member of Plunkett's All Stars, a baseball team put together by jazzmen like Red Nichols and the Dorsey Brothers, competing with teams of other musicians from Duke Ellington's orchestra or Fred Waring's band. Bix seems to have been relatively inactive musically in June and July 1930, with the radio broadcast of *The Camel Pleasure Hour*, every Wednesday night as his only income. The cornetist's regularity and professional conscientiousness were indisputable: "Bix was very anxious to receive this chance to play regularly in a band again," confirmed Nat Shilkret, "and he took full advantage of it. He would often arrive as much as an hour early to make certain he wouldn't miss a program. He detested rehearsals but would make an early appearance here too. A regular arranger was not assigned to the show, but many of the arrangements were made by Bill Challis . . . who featured Bix as much as possible."[29] This behavior reveals Bix's

28. Marc Richard, in the booklet included with the Masters of Jazz CD, *Bix Beiderbecke, Volume 8, 1929–1930*, 1995, p. 5.
29. *The Leon Bix Beiderbecke Story*, op. cit., p. 506.

feelings of anxiety: could he return to his best level, or would he fail to do so? Deep still were the scars caused by recent memories.

"It's behind can number three," Bix whispered into Leo McConville's ear, upon returning to his seat during a morning rehearsal. The cornetist's breath left no doubt as to the nature of the hidden object: Bix was again seeking bottled relief for the stress generated by this new job and its professional demands. Removed from the environment of bars and speakeasies, and from the stress stemming from his musical activities, Bix had managed, not without effort, to stay dry for the most part during the few months spent in Davenport. A return to New York and to regular work in the *Camel Hour* orchestra was a threat for Bix, and a true test. He was able to sight-read his cornet part, or improvise a solo in the space Bill Challis had left for him, but following the arrangement remained difficult, even impossible. He could not hope to follow the band without the friendly assistance of Leo McConville, who helped him determine where his solo began and ended with one kick to Bix's shin for the start, and two for the ending. Bix could then put on a good show, and even cope with the intricate orchestrations of the eccentric Arthur Schutt.

This stressful situation pushed the cornet player, inexorably, toward the only tranquilizer he knew of that was able to sooth his anxiety and to dispel for a few moments the fear of a new public failure.[30] Temporary and illusory, this promised relief would lead to disaster. On Bix's already weakened body, large quantities of alcohol would quickly have a destructive effect, worsened by the chemicals that increased the liquor's toxicity.

The ravages of alcohol were amplified by the lack of sleep the cornetist also suffered from, generating an irreversible state of chronic fatigue. Pee Wee Russell remembered precisely how Bix was often deprived of much needed rest: "Everybody likes privacy," said he, "privacy enough to sleep and eat, but it was impossible for him to get any. There were always people in his room. They would knock on the door even at six a.m., and it was impossible for him because of the kind person he was to insult anybody, to say get out of there. . . . He even had a piano in the room, and, when he had a spare moment, he'd try to get a composition started, but with all those people always hanging around he didn't have a chance. In a sense, Bix was killed by his friends. But I think the term is being used loosely . . . because they weren't his friends. They were the kind of people who liked to be able to say, '*Last night I was up at Bix's and oh, he was drunk. Gee, you should have seen his room!*' You know that type of people . . ."[31]

One of the favorite New York locations for musicians to gather at the end of the 1920s was Jimmy Plunkett's speakeasy at 205½ West 53rd Street. The place was known as the Trombone Club, as Tommy Dorsey was seemingly its maître d', bringing in its most faithful and exuberant patrons. Bud Freeman, Pee Wee Russell, pianist Joe Sullivan, and Bix Beiderbecke were among the regulars, standing between an old upright piano and the bar. Vague ideas of forming a band were tossed about

30. This new "relapse" will have very serious consequences. Bix had been medically informed of the potential dangers of his drinking habits. Until the end, he kept alternating between days of abstinence—an answer to his profound demand for ideals—and periods of heavy drinking in an attempt to relieve his anxiety. The origin of alcoholism is always complex, and it involves physiological, psychological, and social elements. An interesting theory, known as "autohandicap," was developed in the 1970s. "According to Berglas and Jones, the reputation of alcohol to be able to reduce human performances can be used with profit by people willing to limit the incidence of failures, and to take advantage of success. This is an 'always winning' strategy, and the person who uses it wants to protect his image and his professional recognition: for instance, someone who is afraid of a possible failure in public, in a performance during which he is not certain to shine at his best, may decide to drink conspicuously. If he is successful, he will be highly credited as being also able to overcome the handicap of alcohol; but if he fails, he will have the excuse of excessive drinking. Autohandicapped drinkers are not 'losers,' but rather people who suffer an excessive fear of evaluative situations, and who are looking to protect a favorable but frail image of their talent," in Alain Cerclé, *L'Alcoolisme* (Flammarion, 1998), pp. 95–96.

31. *Hear Me Talkin' To Ya*, op. cit., pp. 162–163.

in the course of endless conversations, spurred by the lack of work that grew more worrying each day. The customers at Plunkett's were all possible candidates for the band. With Bix as the leader, this project included Tommy and Jimmy Dorsey, Bud Freeman, Cass Hagan, and Gene Krupa, and it reached a level of credibility strong enough to prompt a few lines in the August 6 issue of *Variety*: "Bix Beiderbecke starting his own band. Formerly with the Whiteman Orchestra and wants Whiteman to manage him." A few rehearsals took place on the bandstand at the Roseland Ballroom, but the dire economic situation and Bix's lack of fame prevented the band from finding any engagements.

New York, Monday, September 8, 1930

The Victor Studios did, however, invite Bix and this band for a recording session. It was to be the last date bearing the name of Bix Beiderbecke. The ensemble gathered for the day was fairly large: it consisted of twelve musicians, among them three clarinetists, and the reason for such an abundance was not only musical. "Bix couldn't say no," recalled Pee Wee Russell. "He couldn't say no to anybody. I remember this Victor date we did. . . . He had hired me for the date but, rather than hurt anybody's feelings, he also hired Jimmy Dorsey and Benny Goodman and Tommy Dorsey and everybody. Every time somebody would walk into the door at Plunkett's, the bar we hung out at, Bix would say, *'Gee, what am I going to do?'* So he'd go up to the guy and hire him for the date. . . . He went way over his budget and we had to scrape cab fare to get back from the date."[32] The band sat in one of the many studios used in New York by the new RCA-Victor Corporation, which was studio 2 on 24th Street. Ray Lodwig was present on trumpet and Boyce Cullen on trombone; Bud Freeman added his alto saxophone to the three selected clarinets; Joe Venuti and Eddie Lang played on the first two titles; and a rhythm section made up of Min Leibrook on bass, Irving Brodsky on piano, and Gene Krupa on drums completed this quite imposing Bix Beiderbecke Orchestra.

This was a big day for the cornetist, who hoped that high-quality records would help bring him the jobs he and the band needed. He trained for the date, and regular practice had restored his lips and usual technical mastery. His physical condition was up to his artistic ambitions, but he had to surmount two real obstacles, two anti-jazz barriers thrown in his way by the studios: the choice of three commercial tunes of little musical interest, and the hiring of a most dismal singer, Wes Vaughan. The two takes of "Deep Down South" gave Benny Goodman and Bix the chance to improvise inspired and well-structured solos. Effectively backed up by Gene Krupa's drumming, the cornetist moves forward easily and naturally. He blows with power and confidence, and after an amazing break by Gene Krupa, concludes the side with great freedom. The musical weakness of the next title, "I Don't Mind

32. *Hear Me Talkin' To Ya*, op. cit., p. 163.

Walkin' in the Rain," incited Bix to limit his appearance to a short eight-bar exposition of the theme. A duet played by Pee Wee Russell and Joe Venuti ends an easy and uninteresting side; the first take was accepted and released by Victor.

Joe Venuti, Eddie Lang, and Min Leibrook left the studio at lunchtime. The Frank Trumbauer Orchestra was recording on the same day for the Okeh label, with Andy Secrest replacing Bix on cornet, and Eddie Lang and Min Leibrook were expected by Tram in the early afternoon. They cut two sides in less than two hours, while Bix and his group dragged out their break, awaiting the return of Min Leibrook and his string bass to start recording the last side of the date, "I'll Be a Friend with Pleasure." The authors of the orchestrations used for this session are unknown, but it makes sense to follow Randy Sandke's opinion and to believe that Bix was instrumental in arranging this last title. The vocal is worth forgetting, but the four introductory measures, assigned to four different instruments, are quite original. The passages written for Ray Lodwig and Boyce Cullen lead to the peak of this melancholic side: the two choruses played by Bix and Jimmy Dorsey. It would be excessive to call these few bars the swan song of a condemned artist—a step that some critics did not hesitate to take—but Bix's remarkable solo is clearly filled with emotion. The first of the two remaining takes is the more accomplished. Its melodic line is very pure, sparkled with tiny modulations and delicate breaks that create, in a very simple way, an intense feeling of solemnity and tenderness. In the state of anxiety he was in, Bix's solo on "I'll Be a Friend with Pleasure" is probably his most personally expressive. The best way to compliment the solo played by Jimmy Dorsey is to say that it is in total harmony with Bix's.

"I'll Be a Friend with Pleasure" sheet music. (Duncan Schiedt Collection)

Bix told Esten Spurrier that he remained unsatisfied with these Victor records. We will never know if he was prouder of his second piano composition, "Candlelights," released by the publisher Robbins Music Corporation at the end of August. Bill Challis had again been instrumental in writing down the new piece, finding its author this time less restrained by the indecision that had delayed the scoring of "In a Mist": "When Bix returned to New York," confirmed Bill Challis, "he declared himself ready with another composition he had already titled 'Candlelights.' I had much less difficulty with the notation since it was practically set in his mind and thus it was just a matter of getting together and getting the work done. 'In a Mist' was done while he was working, whenever and wherever I could find him. . . . He had a lot of ideas in 'Candlelights,' and his interest in the whole-tone scale comes out quite a bit there. His music and his harmonies were pretty simple, pretty modal. They didn't particularly entangle chords as they're today. They were much simpler, more pianistic, you know."[33]

Out of the four pieces Bix Beiderbecke wrote for piano, "In a Mist" would remain the only one recorded by its author. With its style, its ragtime-inspired phrasings, and Bix's added improvisations, it is undoubtedly a jazz composition. "Candlelights" is different: when played from the published score, it sounds like one of the many "modern music" works that blossomed on the music rests of American high society's pianos.[34] Moving near the boundaries of classical music, popular art, folklore, and jazz, these highly popular piano scores were written by authors whose names have faded with the passing of time: Zez Confrey, Rube Bloom, and Eastwood Lane, for whom Bix held a somewhat inexplicable admiration.

Eastwood Lane's wife confirmed several encounters between Bix and her husband during the summer of 1930. The two musicians met in Lane's Manhattan apartment or in his workplace, the Wanamaker Auditorium. Bix had still not exhausted the charms—rather meager in our eyes—of a seemingly limited repertoire, and hearing the "Adirondack Sketches" or the "Five American Dances," interpreted on piano by Eastwood Lane, plunged him into perfect bliss for hours. Marty Bloom, who had fleetingly engaged Bix in May 1922, after he was kicked out of Lake Forest Academy, attended one of these reunions: "Bix and I went down to Wanamaker's in downtown New York and had a long visit with the composer," recalled Marty Bloom. "Upon returning to Times Square, and at my insistence, Bix and I went up to the Nola Recording Studios—they recorded those large aluminum disks—and Bix cut and gave me the three large recordings of 'Adirondack'! I know what you're thinking—NO! I haven't got them. I treasured them for years, but lost them in a 3rd Avenue storage fire."[35]

New York, Monday, September 15, 1930

This late-summer day remains the last Bix Beiderbecke recording date, and also a failed meeting with jazz history. The RCA-Victor studio on 24th Street accommodated a session organized by Hoagy Carmichael, who had gathered an excellent ensemble, not too different from the one formed by Bix the week before. Ray Lodwig, Boyce Cullen, Jimmy Dorsey, Bud Freeman, Pee Wee Russell, Irving Brodsky, Joe Venuti, and Eddie Lang were, not surprisingly, among the selected musicians.

33. *The Leon Bix Beiderbecke Story*, op. cit., p. 516, and the eighteenth program of *Bix, a Biographical Radio Series*, op. cit.

34. Jazz music is characterized by the way it is played. As it is written, the "Candlelights" sheet music can be played jazzy. This is the case for the recordings of this number by Bunny Berigan and His Men (1938), or by pianist Jess Stacy in January 1939. Other interpretations of this composition emphasize its relation with Eastwood Lane's works, and the tribute paid by Bix Beiderbecke to the feeling of "floating time" dear to Claude Debussy. "Yet for all their melodic and harmonic richness," wrote Randy Sandke, "these pieces seem to be more related to the semi-classical piano music of their day than concert classical music or later developments in jazz. They seem to be closer in spirit to the less ambitious works of Gershwin, or Eastwood Lane, than Ravel or Bill Evans." Randy Sandke, *Observing a Genius at Work*, op. cit.

35. *The Leon Bix Beiderbecke Story*, op. cit., pp. 511–512.

Jack Teagarden had been added, and drummer Chauncey Morehouse—Bix's regular partner during the summer of 1927—replaced Gene Krupa. Though no one could have known it at the time, Min Leibrook's presence brought Bix's recording career full circle, from the first Wolverine recordings in 1924 to Bix's last record just six and a half years later.

Eastwood Lane at his piano. "I shall continue to attempt little tunes for the great fun of it." (Lane's letter to Norman Gentieu, 1941)

Three songs were cut between 1:00 and 5:00 p.m. Bix Beiderbecke was not featured on "One Night in Havana," which, according to Hoagy, did not match the cornetist's style. Answering questions raised by Richard M. Sudhalter in 1979, Hoagy Carmichael recalled the memories he had of that day: "I really wish I'd given him more. I'm sorry now, because when he did play he was the old Bix, beautiful, as if nothing had ever happened. And just listen to that rideout on 'Bessie': you can hear what a lift he gave the band."[36] This is, however, questionable and partly contradicted by Jack Teagarden's version: "After a few minutes, I noticed Bix was sitting towards the back of the studio, against a dark covered drape. He was seated on a stool, and as I looked at him, I could see him repeatedly pushing the valves of his horn. I swear he was talking to the cornet, saying things like, *'Don't let me down.'*"[37]

The first song of the session was a recent Hoagy composition, "Georgia on My Mind," whose arrangement seems rather weird: a sixteen-bar chorus is assigned to Ray Lodwig's quavering trumpet, while Joe Venuti, Jack Teagarden, and Bix are all given much less time. Had Hoagy wanted at first to have his vocal followed by a full cornet solo, something that his friend's weakness had convinced him to forget about? Bix's appearance is at the end of the side, limited to ten measures. He blows a chorus through a derby mute of amazing intensity and melodic conception, but the last seconds of this short part reveal an obvious lack of breath. On the last song of the day, "Bessie Couldn't Help It," Bix plays a strong introduction, and comes back to lead the ensemble to the conclusion. We remain hungry for more—even though the two takes kept, for the most part identical, display an even mastery, and a precise attack of notes.

The disappointment prompted by these last recordings by Bix is justified, but our disappointment should not blind us to the qualities of these two Victor sides. Marc Richard was right in pointing out that "the main interest in Bix's last two numbers lies in the skillful arrangement of the first recording of a top 20th century

36. Richard M. Sudhalter, *Stardust Melody, The Life and Music of Hoagy Carmichael* (New York: Oxford University Press, 2002), p. 143.
37. *The Leon Bix Beiderbecke Story*, op. cit., p. 521.

hit, 'Georgia on My Mind,' and the beautiful choruses played by Teagarden and Freeman on 'Bessie Couldn't Help It.' "[38]

As the summer was coming to its end, Bix's regularity in attending *The Camel Pleasure Hour* rehearsals began to decline. A lack of preparation could not but increase his difficulties in playing at sight the scores he was given. Bix had gotten tired of this weekly commercial performance, and his musical interest was focused on a vague project, that of a European tour, as Bud Freeman recalled: "After those recording sessions, we soon found ourselves rehearsing a band to go to Europe. We had Bix on cornet, and he was to lead the group. We also had Tommy Dorsey on trombone, Jimmy Dorsey on clarinet, me on tenor, Joe Sullivan on piano, Gene Krupa on

Beiderbecke family's house on Grand Avenue in Davenport. (JPL, 2000)

drums, Dick MacDonough on guitar, and Adrian Rollini on bass saxophone. We were rehearsing at the Roseland Ballroom in New York to do a ten-week tour of Europe when Bix became ill. . . . What a tour that would have been, because we were famous there. We were not known in America, except to music people around New York, where we did a lot of recording."[39] The illness that Bud Freeman alludes to was pneumonia once again, easily developed in a body weakened by excessive alcohol consumption. Ray Lodwig had detected that the cornetist's physical condition was approaching a breaking point. He explained that Bix "was seeing things, designs and all"—which could medically be interpreted as hallucinations linked to an alcoholic delirium, or vision troubles caused by optical neuritis.

At Paul Whiteman's request, Bix consulted a doctor, but that precaution could not avoid the inevitable disaster, and *The Camel Pleasure Hour* broadcast on Wednesday, October 8, brought a definitive end to the musician's contract. "Bix had an eight-bar take-off to play," recalled Frankie Cush, a former trumpeter with the California Ramblers. "He stood up to take his solo, but his mind went blank and nothing happened. As I heard the story, he was not drinking at the time, but excessive drinking was the source of this sudden mental lapse; it finished him in radio."[40] Bix took a train to Davenport the next day. On October 10, he spent a day in Chicago, seeking in vain to join one of his friends, and he arrived the following day at Davenport, back for the last time to the refuge of his family's nest.

BIX BEIDERBECKE'S DEATH would give rise to a cult that is not dissimilar to the one in France surrounding the figure of poet Arthur Rimbaud, who also died young. Legends have grown up about both "accursed artists," who shared a similar precocity, the same difficulties of communication, a secluded life in search of an ideal creation,

38. Marc Richard, in the booklet included with the Masters of Jazz CD, *Bix Beiderbecke, Volume 8, 1929–1930*, 1995, pp. 5–6.

39. Bud Freeman, *Crazeology: The Autobiography of a Chicago Jazzman, as told to Robert Wolf* (Chicago: University of Illinois Press, 1989).

40. *The Leon Bix Beiderbecke Story*, op. cit., p. 525.

and—as a result—the same disdain for their "always imperfect" works. Both went back to their childhood homes when faced with unmanageable personal problems.

Davenport, October 11–December 31, 1930

Once more, the large house on calm and shady Grand Avenue offered its asylum to Bix's recovery. His physical condition was hardly enviable those days of October and November 1930. Laid up in his childhood bedroom, he was fighting a pulmonary infection that kept him in an extremely weak state. A return to complete sobriety was mandated, his recent abuses having stimulated the polyneuritis he had been suffering from for more than a year, aggravating the pains that burned his legs and kept his nights sleepless. Lilian Leonard, who was working as a maid for the Beiderbecke family, recalled the difficulties Bix experienced every morning: "He came home during the last year of his life, and I felt so sorry for him. He'd had pneumonia in New York and he'd have to lift his legs up with his hands when he first got up, and then he'd just shuffle along."[41]

Bix's bedroom window at the Beiderbecke family's house. (JPL, 2000)

The musician's financial situation was not faring any better. The collapse of the stock market had wiped out his savings, his living expenses in New York had devoured the rest, and a total absence of income since his return to Davenport, had accelerated his ruin. Toward the end of the year, Bix reluctantly decided to send his friend Frank Trumbauer a letter in which his distress speaks for itself. "I've been having a hell of a time," wrote Bix. "I am writing this flat on my back as I have been since my arrival home. The rest is sure making a new man of me, I'm in good shape, all but my knees. . . . Here at home, [our doctor] noticed a slight infection in the lower right lobe of my lung. It seems that after all this trouble, the poison in my system has settled in my knees and legs—I guess I am a minus quality. I have never suffered so continually without a letup in my life. The doctor says the heart and everything is okay, but I am not worth a dime. My knees don't work. I try to stand and fall right on my face. I am taking walking lessons and I am improving every day, but with great pain." Bix continued his letter emphasizing that he had stopped drinking, and that his financial situation was critical: "After going through a grand of my own, I am really broke and now is when I need money the most. So I wonder if you could see fit to send me some money. Try like hell, boy. 'Itzy' [Izzy Friedman] said in a wire that Paul said to hurry and come back when I am able . . ."[42] Tram's answer remains unknown. The saxophonist had gone with the Paul Whiteman Orchestra from New York to Chicago, where they were hired in October 1930 to play at the Casa Granada Café, a

41. "Remembering Bix," op. cit.

42. *TRAM: The Frank Trumbauer Story*, op. cit., pp. 134–135. This letter is not dated, and Phil Evans indicates: "Just before Christmas, 1930, Tram received the following letter . . ." Izzy Friedman was living in Los Angeles, where Paul Whiteman was regularly visiting his fiancée, Margaret Livingston.

South Side cabaret located in Woodlawn and run by Al Capone's organization.[43] The nearby huge Tivoli movie theater and White City amusement park helped keep business at an acceptable level, in spite of the economic crisis. In this strictly white part of the town, Paul Whiteman's show lived up to the audience's expectations, and the orchestra's contract was extended until the end of the year.

At the beginning of December, Bix finally got to see the Whiteman Orchestra musicians again: they were on screen at the Uptown Theater in Davenport, where *The King of Jazz* had been playing since November 23. Bix probably viewed these images with mixed emotions, feeling at the same time the bitterness of being absent from the screen and also, most likely, relief at not being involved in certain scenes that can only be described as mawkish.

Eagles Club, Moline.
(JPL, 2000)

Upon his arrival at the Moline Eagles Club, on the night of December 10, Les Swanson was surprised to discover Bix, seated next to Merwyn "Bus" Howe in the brass section of Trave O'Hearn's orchestra. Bix was pale, emaciated, and still weak, but he managed to acquit himself honorably. "The local musicians weren't always impressed when Bix sat in with them," remembered Cy Churchill. "He played a very different style and didn't read music as most of them did. He'd just suddenly appear and sit in. That story about him carrying his horn in a paper sack is true. I saw him do it a couple of times, even into LeClaire Hotel ballroom. . . . Local bands did know that he'd played with some pretty good musicians like Hoagy Carmichael, and with Paul Whiteman's orchestra

43. The address of the Casa Granada Cafe was at 6800 South Cottage Grove.

for a while. But none of us ever imagined that Bix would become a legend. Such a thing never entered our heads."[44]

Bix was back in the orchestra the next Wednesday, playing for a show that would be Trave O'Hearn's last appearance at the Eagles Club. The dance floor was deserted, and job offers became more and more rare, making this popular group the last jazz band to maintain regular activity in the area. It survived by reducing its size from eleven to eight members, which excluded Bix from any further engagements.

44. "Remembering Bix," op. cit

CHAPTER 12

1931: Final Days

Davenport, January 1931

As he had the year before, Bix spent the Christmas holidays with his family. The traditional wishes for a Happy New Year were particularly heartfelt as the country's economic crisis showed no sign of letting up. More than twenty million unemployed workers shivered in endless lines outside employment offices and Salvation Army soup kitchens. Workers in the cities had been the first and most strongly affected, but the economic slowdown had now reached rural America.

Iowa's farmers were not spared, and in the middle of winter, Bismark Beiderbecke had to advertise in the Davenport *Daily Times* that his coal was for sale at a twenty percent discount. It is easy to imagine what must have been the concerns of Bix's parents at the threshold of the new year, faced with the fragile health of their second son and the difficulties he would contend with in his search for employment.

Davenport, Saturday, January 17, 1931

Fortune seemed to smile on them for a few days, when they read the announcement that the Paul Whiteman Orchestra would be coming to Davenport. At the beginning of January, the bandleader had given his musicians two weeks off and had left for California, where he reached an agreement with Universal to turn out several musical shorts. While in Los Angeles, he officially announced his upcoming marriage to actress Margaret Livingston. A tour of several days had then been organized, which included a show at Davenport's Danceland on the evening of January 17. This special event never faded from Andy Secrest's memory: "Our train pulled into the station, and we didn't know if we'd see Bix at the dance or even if he was still in town. Our doubts were quickly put to rest when a familiar figure awaited us at the depot. It was Bix. He looked like a million dollars to all of us. Tram threw his arms around Bix and hugged him as someone would a long lost son who had just returned home. They didn't say a word. They didn't have to, you could see their feelings in their eyes."[1] This emotion was shared by all the band members who, upon getting off the train, came to greet their friend with a slap on the back and a warm welcome. Paul Whiteman was no less exuberant—but he had to insist before Bix reluctantly agreed to join the band for a few numbers during the evening concert.

Danceland Ballroom, Davenport. (JPL, 2000)

The appearance of the famous orchestra at the Danceland was a success. Bix was dancing with sax player Leo Bahr's pretty wife when Paul Whiteman approached the microphone to announce that Bix was present, and that he was going to take his old place in the band. Bix waited until the end of the number before he slowly walked toward the stage. "I didn't know what we expected," continued Andy Secrest. "We knew that Bix had been ill, but because he looked so well, I guess we expected the old fire to be in his cornet. It wasn't! We played one of the tunes that would give Bix some solo spot, and when he stood and played, you could see the hurt in Paul's eyes. Pops didn't let on, nor did any of us." At the end of the show, Whiteman renewed his offer to Bix to return to the band any time, but the cornetist insisted that he needed two more months of rest. He was standing on the platform when the train departed; some last embraces and good-byes were exchanged as the musicians climbed into the cars, and dozens of hands waved from the windows as the voyagers were carried away from the Davenport station. "Paul turned to Frank and asked if Tram thought Bix would be back," recalled Andy Secrest. "Frank told Paul that he was uncertain. He didn't know what to think, but he hoped that he would be back, very soon. Paul said, '*You know that I love Bix like a son, but, deep down inside, I don't think Bix will ever be with us again.*'"[2]

Bix shuffled along for three more weeks in Davenport, during which only one public appearance has been identified. He performed around January 20 with the band of saxophonist Neil Whiteside, apologizing for his out-of-shape lip, and explaining that he had not played much recently. He was always realistic about his

1. *TRAM: the Frank Trumbauer Story, op. cit.,* p. 137-138.
2. Ibid., p. 138.

playing abilities, as he had shown in April 1929 when withdrawing from the Frank Trumbauer Orchestra's recording activities. In the span of three days, two disheartening experiences had confronted him with the terrible reality that he was losing his grip on the only way he knew to make money: his ability to play the cornet. What other job could he expect to find? Bix's latest bender, as recounted by Les Swanson at the beginning of this book, took place during the last days of January: once again drowning himself in alcohol, he disappeared for two or three days, wandering into Davenport's skid row, between 2nd and 3rd streets. Following this incident, Bix decided it was time to leave, and most likely with the help of loans from his family and several friends, he got on a train for Chicago in the first days of February.

He checked into the Hotel Sherman on February 6 and contacted Paul Whiteman, who was starting a new season at the Casa Granada Café. He confirmed to the bandleader that any possible return had to be delayed by several months. Whiteman was not surprised by the decision, and was probably somewhat dubious when Bix announced that he was going to New York to discuss several job offers. Andy Secrest could not forget this moment: "Bix turned to Tram, half kidding, and said, *'And you, Frank, all I have to do is give a call and you'll be there for me. Right?'* Bix flashed a big smile at Tram. Tram reached out, grabbed Bix, gave him a hug, and said, *'You know it.'* That was the last time we ever saw Bix."[3]

New York, February–August 1931

On February 11, Bix returned to New York and to room 605 of the 44th Street Hotel. The terrible cold that paralyzed the city added to the omnipresent misery. Thousands of families lived on the $2.39 they were given weekly by the city. Evicted from apartments for non-payment of rent, they gathered on Manhattan's West Side, between Central Park and the Hudson River, and crammed into shacks built out of debris and scraps. Men sold apples on street corners at the feet of dozens of unfinished buildings whose metallic frames, beaten by the wind, symbolized the shattered American dream. Faithful to his principles and the American tradition of social Darwinism, President Herbert Hoover waited for better days.

Movie houses, theaters, and hotels were practically deserted, and show business was going through hard times. The recording industry would come close to completely disappearing in 1932. About six million records in total were sold during the year, which could be compared to the 1927 peak, when the American public bought 140 million discs. Though record sales were devastated, there were still some leaders, and several veteran performers held their own against the aggressive push of young talents. Faced with the astonishing success of Don Azpiazu's "Peanut Vendor," Paul Whiteman managed to survive. The release of "Body and Soul" in October 1930

3. Ibid., p. 139.

brought him back to the top of the charts for six weeks where, ironically, he was competing with Bing Crosby and the Rhythm Boys, singing with Duke Ellington's band. Their recording of "Three Little Words" helped establish Duke's fame, and gave his orchestra its first major hit. The most popular titles were often covered by several different artists. In December 1930, Guy Lombardo's Royal Canadians and Rudy Vallee's Connecticut Yankees both had successful releases with "You're Driving Me Crazy," and one month later, the bands of Ted Lewis and Ben Bernie vied for the top of the sales charts with their versions of the new song "Just a Gigolo."

Glen Gray and the Casa Loma Orchestra, featuring Kenny Sargent (as), Pee Wee Hunt (tb, voc), and Sunny Dunham (tp), at the beginning of the 1930s. (Indiana University Collection)

In his critical condition, Bix Beiderbecke could not help but be aware of the achievements of Red Nichols, his fortunate rival, who, at the end of the year, had released a successful new title, "Embraceable You." Upon his arrival in New York, Bix would also witness the flowering of a band he knew well, the Casa Loma Orchestra. Under the name of the Orange Blossoms, they had shared the Graystone Ballroom's stage with Jean Goldkette's orchestra at the end of 1926. The financial difficulties of the Goldkette organization had forced its musicians to survive independently and to become a cooperative venture. Under the direction of Spike "Glen Gray" Knoblauch, the members of the band, which had become known in 1927 the Casa Loma Orchestra[4], agreed to share the financial risks of their artistic adventure—and they succeeded. The originality of the orchestrations written by guitarist Harold "Gene" Gifford, and several years of hard training, would assure, between 1930 and 1935, the Casa Loma Orchestra's supremacy over other dance music ensembles. Their amazing savoir-faire reached a peak with "Casa Loma Stomp," recorded for the Okeh label on December 6, 1930. With its exchanges between the brass and the reed sections, its haunting riffs, and the faultless execution of intricate arrangements, the band gradually moved toward the more relaxed style of the Swing era, which it predated. In January 1931, their recording of "Casa Loma Stomp" was among the best sellers, or more exactly, in the small-group-at-the-top-of-the-least-bad sales.

The intricate Casa Loma arrangements would not tolerate the sloppy performance of players plunged into an alcoholic fog. It was unanimously agreed that the consumption of booze was to be limited to the hotel rooms and to post-concert

4. The band was named after the Casa Loma Hotel in Toronto, a venue where they were booked, but that never opened.

parties. One musician used to break this rule: a fervent admirer of Bix, trumpet player Dub Shoffner, whose performances became progressively more wavering and uncertain each night. His dismissal had been decided upon. Bill Challis knew the orchestra's manager, Cork O'Keefe, and the two men considered Bix as a possible replacement for Dub Shoffner—which was a truly optimistic idea. Bix was reluctant, as the precise Casa Loma arrangements seemed to him rather incompatible with his weak reading abilities. Bill Challis almost managed to convince his friend. "I picked him up and we set off, driving through the traffic up Fifth Avenue," recalled Bill Challis. "The Casa Loma Band was playing somewhere in Connecticut. Well, we're stopping for traffic and things, and Bix has a chance to think. I could feel the tension, as he thinks, *'Where the hell am I going, what am I going for, what am I going to do, what's this all about?'* We got as far as Central Park. He said, all of a sudden, *'I don't think I want to go out tonight.'* So out of the car he got. That was that. But I was sure he'd be interested."[5]

During the weekend of February 14 and 15, Bix put up Jack Teagarden in his room at the 44th Street Hotel. The trombonist was to join Red Nichols's band for several days, to play at the Hotel New Yorker's Terrace Restaurant.[6] Bix had started composing a new piece on Pat Ciricillo's piano. "He was working on 'In the Dark,'" said Jack Teagarden, "and had only a beginning and an ending, being unable to connect the two. I whistled a bridge that I felt would fit. Bix was delighted and kept it in the composition that Challis scored. He wanted to go down to the Bellevue morgue. I figure it's the most gruesome morgue in the world, because it's where they hold unidentified bodies as long as they can. We went down there and he gave the night caretaker a five-dollar bill to take us through. After the first couple of cases I was doing pretty good, it hadn't bothered me too bad. But Bix was starting to get sick, so we left, and that was all that was said about it."[7]

Boston, Monday, February 16–Thursday, February 19, 1931

On Monday morning, Bix's hesitation about joining the Casa Loma Orchestra gave way to his need for money. He took the train to Boston, and met the fourteen members of the big band at the Metropolitan Hotel. He attended the afternoon rehearsal, and was reinforced in his doubts by the repetitive and wearisome nature of the game. "He went alone this time," recalled Bill Challis, "because I couldn't make it. He had no self-control. . . . They had a bunch of real tough drinkers in that band. Bix, well . . . a couple of sniffs of gin, and he was on his way—then there goes the whole bottle. After those first few had gone, the rest didn't make any difference. Those guys, the Casa Lomans, just rehearsed and rehearsed. After full rehearsals, they'd get off by themselves and rehearse. Bix couldn't take this."[8]

The band performed the next evening in Taunton, Massachusetts, two hours

5. "Bill Challis Speaks Out, An Interview," p. 32.

6. Located at the corner of 34th Street and Eighth Avenue, the New Yorker Hotel was then, with 2,500 rooms and 43 stories, the largest hotel in Manhattan. It was closed between 1972 and 1994.

7. *The Leon Bix Beiderbecke Story*, op. cit., p. 531, and Bill Crow, *Jazz Anecdotes* (New York: Oxford University Press, 1990, p. 226).

8. "Bill Challis Speaks Out, An Interview," pp. 32–33.

south of Boston by car. Dub Shoffner had brought a bottle to while away the hours of the journey, and Bix was not in a state for playing by the time they reached the theater. The two men remained cooped up all Wednesday. Bottles brought to their room spared Bix from having to make any perilous sorties into the winter cold that reigned over the city. This three-day trial period ended with a mutual rejection, as could have been expected: neither the musician nor the orchestra was willing to work with the other. "Bix was despondent," said Gene Gifford. "Obviously we had had our doubts. He wasn't really a section man, and we as a cooperative couldn't afford—as had Whiteman—an extra trumpet player for solo work alone. Bix said himself that his heart wasn't really inclined toward big band work. But the thing he kept emphasizing was his conviction by now that his was a hopeless condition, that he was apparently simply unable to reconcile his alcoholic problems."[9]

Bix was back in New York on Thursday, February 19. His physical condition had quickly followed the declining curve of his morale, and the benefit of several months' abstinence had vanished with a few pints of bootleg gin. Bix remained cloistered in his room until the end of the month. Hoagy Carmichael was his sole visitor during these somber days. "Bix in the semi-darkness was lying on the bed, partly dressed," wrote Hoagy. "He looked bad; there was something wrong, as if part of him were detached, indifferent to life in the dark. *'Hi, Bix.'* I sat down on a rickety chair, pushing soiled shirts off it. *'How's it going, fella?'* Bix smiled with a waxy grimace. . . . Then he said, *'Hey, that new tune of yours is pretty good.'* I smiled at Bix. It was the second time he had ever given me a compliment. The first time was back in Indiana, when we were on our way to record 'Davenport Blues.'"[10] Isham Jones's recording of "Star Dust" had just been released. It climbed to the top of the charts in early March, and remained for twenty weeks among the best-sellers, establishing the song as a classic. Hoagy would now be able to concentrate his professional activities on writing music.

Bix was drowning in despair, a mood that was reflected exactly in the letter he addressed to his parents in February. The first lines alluded to the drinking incident that had preceded his departure from Davenport, and his less than glorious return to the family home: "You probably will tear this up before you read it because you must be disgusted with me, but I'll take a chance and write anyway. You can believe me or not but I was sick. I had that yearly attack of toncilitus [sic] and it was terrible lying here, thinking of you. I had to cancel three dates." Bix continued with a personal version of his missed entry into the Casa Loma Orchestra, ascribing his failure to his illness, and his healing to the efficiency of Christian Science, which was dear to his uncle Carl Thomas.[11] "I would have died if I hadn't talked myself out of it," he wrote. The effects of the current economic crisis weighed heavily on his parents' financial situation, and Bismarck Beiderbecke had told his son what a burden he was. "If I'd known that it was so tough for dad to send that, I wouldn't have asked for it," continued Bix. "Another thing that I'm

9. *Bix, Man and Legend*, op. cit., p. 319.

10. *Sometimes I Wonder*, op. cit., pp. 210–212.

11. Christian Science was founded by Mary Baker Eddy (1821–1910). Religiously inspired, she considered illness as a mental illusion, and healing as the revelation of a "true vision" of God and of the human condition.

sorry about is not sending mom anything for her birthday but March 1st was my sickest day. *I swear this wasn't from drinking.* I'm all right now and have booked several jobs—(college parties) with my band, Friday night Princeton—the 14th Amherst and others. I may go back on the Camel Hour or synchronize movies—I don't think I'll rejoin the Casa Loma band because there's more 'do' here, doing club dates—radio, etc . . . I'll do my best to send you the money that you very kindly (and timely) sent me as soon as I can, also the income money."[12] The man who wrote these pitiful and deeply moving lines was going to turn twenty-eight six days later. The number of job possibilities he was actually offered was nothing like what his letter suggested.

Amherst, Saturday, March 14–Monday, March 16, 1931

Bix's presence at a Princeton engagement on Friday, March 6, cannot be confirmed, but he was a member of the group led by the Dorsey Brothers that performed on March 14 at Amherst University in Massachusetts. That night, the cornetist on his way downhill crossed the rising path of a new rival, trumpeter Roland "Bunny" Berigan. He was born in November 1908 in Wisconsin. An engagement in violinist Frank Cornwell's orchestra brought him to the East Coast. In 1928 he moved to Philadelphia, close enough to New York to bring him to the attention of Rex Stewart and the Dorsey Brothers, who could hardly fail to notice the amazing spirit and power of this young musician. In September 1929, Berigan went with Frank Cornwell's orchestra to Manhattan. For almost two years, destiny prevented him from meeting Bix. Berigan had left with Hal Kemp's band on a European tour on May 15, 1930, a few days after Bix's arrival in New York—and Bunny's return at the end of September had coincided with Bix's retreat to Davenport. Launched by his European voyage and by several remarkable recordings, Bunny Berigan's activity intensified: at the beginning of 1931, he was present on radio broadcasts and in recording studios, and was playing in jam sessions in New York nightclubs, drawn out to the early morning. The trumpeter's style offered a fascinating amalgam of the colorful and virtuoso exuberance of Louis Armstrong—with whom he shared a breathtaking range—and Bix Beiderbecke's lyrical, finely shaded, and intimate poetry. Berigan's irresistible power could drive a unique vibration into an orchestra, and his mastery of low-register notes allowed him to bring sweetness and emotion to a ballad.

The additional challenge just added to Bix's reluctance to attend the engagement in Amherst on March 14. Besides Jimmy and Tommy Dorsey, he was among friendly partners: trombonist Glenn Miller, pianist Arthur Schutt, and guitarist Carl Kress, but Bix's morose expression had not escaped the group's drummer, Johnny Morris: "Bix was very moody and despondent on this date, but the stu-

12. *The Leon Bix Beiderbecke Story*, op. cit., pp. 532–533.

dents recognized his talent. . . . Bix played all his old tunes—the Okeh recordings that made him famous—and was so tremendous! The crowd gave him a great ovation. At this point in Bix's career, his lip was going and the peak of his fame had passed . . . Tommy had brought Bix along on the date to help him make a few dollars."[13] Bix spent the weekend in Amherst. On Monday morning, before leaving the city, he took care to send a birthday telegram and a money order to his father: "Spend this any way you like so long as you turn it into birthday gladness. Warmest congratulations. Bix."[14]

During the following weeks, Bix seems to have spent most of his time in his hotel room. The Depression was only one of the obstacles he had to face in his search for a job. His precarious health was known, and the lack of reliability that went along with it closed the doors to any long-term engagement. The cornetist's name also remained linked, in the views of show promoters, to the New Orleans style, a musical genre that had now gone out of fashion. Its biggest stars were disappearing from the New York and Chicago stages: King Oliver left New York in March 1931, launching his orchestra on an endless tour of Middle America; Jelly Roll Morton vanished after a final Victor recording in October 1930, and his musical activity would be limited to sporadic appearances; upon his return from Europe in December 1930, Sidney Bechet vegetated for several months in New York in Noble Sissle's band before returning to France in May 1931; Kid Ory was featured in lackluster orchestras, before giving up music in 1933; and Bessie Smith, the Empress of the Blues, was left with only fleeting contacts with her crown and her empire.

At the start of the 1930s, Hoagy Carmichael expressed his nostalgia of a bygone era in *Jazzbanders*, his first memoir: "I was tiring of jazz, and I could see that other musicians were tiring of it as well . . . with the result that music lost much of the rich spontaneity and color it had in the days when the record business was booming. Even songs were being constructed in a monotonous pattern to satisfy the musical tastes of the average radio audience."[15] Jazz lovers' interest was now focused on a style of music different from that of Hoagy's youth. The public loved big bands, such as McKinney's Cotton Pickers, Duke Ellington, and his successor at the Cotton Club, singer Cab Calloway, who enjoyed a big hit in March 1931 with "Minnie the Moocher."

Bix never truly felt that he was "of his time." But music was his life, and playing the cornet had become a test for him: he was quickly running out of breath, and was losing his lip from lack of practice. Pat Ciricillo's piano was friendlier, and Bix composed his last two pieces on this instrument, in the cramped quarters of room 605. The writing of "In the Dark" was finished shortly after Jack Teagarden's visit, and once again, Bix called on Bill Challis for its transcription. " 'In the Dark' had the same formula, main part rhythmic with a melodic middle," said Bill Challis. " 'Flashes,' Bix did it in a hurry. He wasn't working and he did the composition because he needed the money. Jack Robbins was willing to accept almost anything.

13. *The Leon Bix Beiderbecke Story*, op. cit., p. 533, and *Bix, Man and Legend*, op. cit., p. 314.

14. *The Leon Bix Beiderbecke Story*, op. cit., p. 533.

15. *Stardust Melody, the Life and Music of Hoagy Carmichael*, op. cit., p. 147.

Bix would say, '*I have another one.*' It was the only income he had going. 'Flashes' was done in the same format as the others but required too much musical knowledge, too much musicianship to understand it. If Bix had lived, he would have changed the formula . . . and come up with something different."[16] "In the Dark" and "Flashes" were published by Robbins Music Corporation. Their copyright is dated April 18, 1931.[17]

Pianist Fred Bergin had played with Bix in Goldkette's Breeze Blowers in the summer of 1925. He met the cornetist again in the spring of 1931. "It was evident that he wasn't going to be around very long, and yet he was the same nice guy that I had always known," said Bergin. "He never blamed anyone for any of his problems and, as far as I can remember, he always had nice things to say about everyone. . . . I have often felt that his life came to such a premature end because of frustration. His ear heard things that he was unable to execute on either the cornet or the piano, and it drove him to excesses in many things."[18] Bix's art was at a standstill. He could not hope to recover the subtle cornet playing, the sound that his public expected to hear from him, and his lack of theoretical music knowledge precluded the career as a composer that he doubtless aspired to. This feeling of professional loss can be seen in a conversation reported by Richardson Turner. Bix told him during this period that "he'd only go across the street to hear two horns— Louis and La Rocca," who had left the music business several years before. "Bix felt abandoned by the musicians. '*Where are they when I need them?*' he asked."[19]

New York, Thursday, April 16, 1931

Charles "Sunny" Clapp was a trombonist, bandleader, and composer. He had written "Come Easy, Go Easy, Love" with Hoagy Carmichael, and was to record it for Victor. Eli Oberstein, one of the label's directors, suggested that he call Bix, probably as a mark of sympathy for the broke artist, but also because of the cornetist's familiarity with Hoagy's work. The session took place on April 16, and Sunny Clapp and His Band O'Sunshine cut two takes. They were never released, and to this day, they have not been found. Sunny Clapp asserted that Bix was present—an affirmation that, in the absence of the two sides, remains hypothetical.

Princeton, Friday, May 1–Monday, May 4, 1931

One year exactly after his first appearance at Princeton University, Bix was called back by a student group to perform during a "house party" weekend, starting on May 1. He came with Benny Goodman, saxophonist Bud Freeman, and pianist Joe Sullivan. Trumpeter Charlie Teagarden, Jack's brother, was also present, ready at

16. "Bill Challis speaks out, an interview," op. cit. p. 29, and *The Leon Bix Beiderbecke Story*, op. cit., p. 534.

17. The 1989 issue of *Jazzforschung-Jazz Research*, no. 21, offers Frank Murphy's final article, "Bix Beiderbecke, Composer for the Pianoforte" (pp. 71–81). The author analyzes the five published Beiderbecke compositions for the piano (which include Bill Challis's transcription of "Davenport Blues"), in order to verify the conventional view that "they consist of a combination of jazz and impressionist techniques, mostly the latter." Murphy concludes that all these works are based "upon a clear and reasonably consistent model," that they are all in rondo form, using a rather simple pianistic technique. "There are the left-hand figurations, the consistent use of the same rhythmic motif, syncopations, and blue notes that give the works their jazz flavor, while the harmonic language owes much to the Impressionists, even if the accent is American rather than French," adds Frank Murphy. He also concludes that "the works of Eastwood Lane and Edward MacDowell probably influenced Beiderbecke's style, but only in a general way," and that "the markings with regard to tempo and dynamics in Bix's works are simpler and fewer in number than in the compositions of either of the other composers."

18. "Memories of Bix (from the Harrington Archive), Part 2," edited by Norman P. Gentieu, in *IAJRC Journal* (summer 1993), pp. 65–66.

19. *The Leon Bix Beiderbecke Story*, op. cit., p. 530.

every moment to support Bix in case he faltered. The first concert was given at the Cottage Club, the most prestigious of the Eating Clubs—the one that had counted F. Scott Fitzgerald among its members in 1915. The evening went by without mishap, and, as before, Bix's performance was warmly received by the Princeton audience. A difficult morning followed a boisterous night of drinking. Suffering from a hangover and having trouble walking, Bix was "mean, sarcastic, and ornery," according to Richardson Turner. His pitiful musical attempts on Saturday afternoon resulted in his remaining silent for much of the job. The effects of alcohol, too, shall pass, and Bix was able to participate in the evening performance at the Charter Club. Jimmy Dorsey had replaced Benny Goodman on clarinet. Two young organizers of the evening were then focusing their artistic ambitions on the music business, with no inkling of the fame that would soon be theirs in Hollywood: their names were Jose Ferrer and James Stewart.

After the show, the band was invited to the Morgan House, a huge mansion where Byrnes McDonald, a Charter Club member, was living.[20] The musicians' abilities diminished in direct proportion to the number of gin bottles opened that night. Several strings of drunken "clams" forced Bix to put down his cornet. He clumsily disassembled his instrument, seeking the origin of his incongruous blunders in the pieces of the horn. Giving up his search, he left

Cottage Club, Princeton. (JPL, 2003)

Charter Club, Princeton. (JPL, 2003)

Morgan House on Constitution Hill East, Princeton. (JPL, 2003)

20. Both clubs were on Prospect Avenue: the Cottage Club at number 51 and the Charter Club at 79. A telephone directory for the year 1931 indicates that Byrnes McDonald lived on Constitution Hill East, in a large mansion built at the end of the nineteenth century by the Morgan family. The house is now divided into apartments and the building is unchanged. (Information from the Princeton Historical Society.)

the parts of his cornet on top of the piano, and sat at the keyboard next to Joe Sullivan. "Bix sober was a fine pianist," recalled Johnny Powell, the band's drummer, "but he was playing very badly in his potted condition. Sullivan became progressively angrier with him. Finally, Sullivan became so enraged, he pulled his hair over his face and began pounding his fists on the piano keys. He demanded that Bix leave the piano. Bix, with his feelings hurt, got up and left. When it came time to leave, Bix could not be found. We searched from the attic to the cellar. We decided to go back to town, and Bix would have to fend for himself."[21]

Charlie Teagarden had thrown the dismantled cornet's parts into a paper bag, and he returned this metallic jigsaw puzzle to its negligent owner several days later.

After his dispute with Joe Sullivan, Bix had spent the night laid out on the sofa in the library. The sun woke him up, and he was in fairly good form. Several of Bix's friends in Princeton were playing with two local groups, the Princeton Triangle Jazz Band and the Equinox Orchestra.[22] Cornet player Bill Priestley was a fervent Bix admirer, as were other members of the bands: Richardson Turner, Edwin "Squirrel" Ashcraft, Doug MacNamee, and Charles L. Smith—who recalled that morning for a weekly Princeton review, "At twenty-eight, Bix was completely bald on top, had a light-colored little mustache, and looked something like the elderly Ernest Truex. After the all-night session, Bix and Bill Priestley, along with several of the rest of us, went down to Doug MacNamee's house. . . . Just as I reached the porch of Doug's house, out came Bix, who stood on the porch and casually pulled a bottle from his hip pocket and took several swigs. Since this was Sunday morning, many of the good burghers of the village and their families were walking by, on their way to church. My brother Shelly rushed in to get MacNamee and, between the two of them, persuaded Bix to do his drinking indoors. Bix's lip was shot as a result of his playing the night before, so instead he played one of his piano compositions which I have never heard again since that time. He called it 'Brooklets,' and said it was named by a friend of his, a New York bartender."[23] Bix was escorted to the station and, in the afternoon, he took a train back to New York.

Sobered up and smiling, on Monday the cornetist presented himself to the receptionist of the Belvedere Hotel, asking for Johnny Powell.[24] Bix took a fat roll

Doug McNamee's house at 32 Vandeventer, Princeton, present condition. (Mike Neer)

21. *The Leon Bix Beiderbecke Story*, op. cit., pp. 536–537.

22. The Princeton Triangle Jazz Band was recorded by Columbia in May 1924. At the end of the 1920s, many members of that band were Bix's admirers and emulators (Frank Norris and Herb Sanford can be added to the list). Doug MacNamee lived at 32 Vandeventer Avenue, where his house is still visible. His daughter keeps the chair that Bix used on that day.

23. Charles L. Smith's letter, in *Princeton Alumni Weekly* (April 23, 1974), p. 7.

24. Opened in 1926, the Belvedere Hotel is still in operation at 319 West 48th Street.

of bills from his pocket, his comfortable reward for the weekend escapade. The two men became friends, and spent hours talking together in the hotel room. "Bix impressed me, he had a fine mind and was very intelligent," recalled Johnny Powell. "We sometimes played recordings of Ethel Waters. I had a few classical records by Jasha Heifetz and they were something of a favorite of ours. Other times, Bix would arrive early and we would go to Loew's New York theater and attend the 8:30 a.m. movie. We would sit in the balcony with a jug of gin under the seat. Whenever someone in the film took a drink, we would join in. Some of those 'society' films featured considerable drinking and it got a bit hard on us to stumble out of the theatre at 11 a.m., drunk, into the bright sun, with the press of the crowded sidewalk."[25]

Princeton, Friday, May 8, 1931

Bix went once more to Princeton. The Dorsey Brothers had called upon him for another university party, for which they had also hired Bunny Berigan, saxophonists Artie Shaw and Eddie Miller, guitarist Carl Kress, and bassist Min Leibrook, a faithful partner from Bix's musical debuts. That night, the cornetist's physical degradation reached a disquieting new stage. During the trip back to New York, he lost all feeling in his legs, and upon arriving in front of the 44th Street Hotel, he was unable to get out of the car. Eddie Miller and Carl Kress waited a few minutes before deciding to help Bix out of the car, and then carried him slowly toward his room. This crisis marked a new episode of the neuropathy that, for several years, had been following the evolution of his alcoholism.

New Haven, Friday, May 15, 1931

The same band was hired for the night by Yale University in New Haven, Connecticut. The Dorsey Brothers' band was one of many orchestras performing for the Derby Day festivities, and Red Nichols's musicians were also present on campus. Bix's physical weakness was obvious, as was his limited musical ability. "Bix hadn't been well," said saxophonist Eddie Miller. "He didn't look well and was playing far from his best. It was so sad: here was my idol Bix, and he was clearly on the way down. And here was Bunny Berigan, a young guy full of piss and vinegar—he had the technique, the chops, the heart and warmth going for him."[26]

In June, Bix tried to win forgiveness for his long silence by writing to his parents, explaining that he was returning from a three-week tour with his own orchestra. In all his research, Phil Evans could not identify a single tour stop, and the archives of the cities in New England that might have hosted the group were silent

25. *The Leon Bix Beiderbecke Story*, op. cit., p. 537.

26. *Lost Chords*, op. cit., p. 492.

on the subject. This "tour" was most probably Bix's invention, aimed at masking an inactivity that became each day more difficult to justify.

These long idle weeks made the musician's financial situation more precarious, and his hopes of returning to the stage or a recording studio more hypothetical. Bix's morale was as deflated as his purse. His partner in the *Camel Hour,* trumpeter Leo McConville, managed to bring him to an audition by the end of May. Pianist Arthur Schutt had written the arrangement used for the session, a complex score that didn't allow the cornetist to shine. Bix failed to get the job, darkening an already somber outlook with a new disappointment. Unemployment offered increased opportunities to drink that a regular working schedule would have limited. Any excuse for gathering around a few bottles was awaited, created, provoked—and Bix was invited on Saturday, June 6, to celebrate the return to New York of Squirrel Ashcraft, one of his friends from Princeton. Eddie Condon, Joe Sullivan, and Bix reunited at a party given in one luxurious apartment in the Dakota building.[27] The place belonged to Richardson Turner's uncle. The music room—decorated in a flamboyant Victorian style, with polar bear rugs competing in bad taste with huge Chinese vases—contained a Steinway piano. Joe Sullivan took to the keys, and Bix took care, this time, to keep out of it. He tried Richardson Turner's Buescher trumpet, and slipped over a few notes before returning to the mouthpiece he now mastered best, the mouth of a gin bottle. The night stretched on. On Sunday morning, Bix had the strange idea of loading seventeen night owls into three taxis, and driving to Bill Challis's place at the corner of 81st Street and Riverside Drive. "Bill Challis was there," recalled Richardson Turner, "and he was pretty burned up about a recording that had just come out. That was his whole topic for about two hours and by that time we were pretty loaded. We carried Bix to the twin bed in the bedroom and gently laid him down, clothes and all. Bix slept there all night. Poor Bix, he was going fast by then, but we didn't realize it. He had a slight fuzz on his lower lip and a tiny fuzz on his upper lip to help his embouchure. His face had gotten sort of puffy and his eyes slightly popped."[28]

Bix's entourage, at this point in his life, was of no help to him—quite the contrary. Bill Challis clearly felt no esteem for this group of heavy drinkers, who remained for the most part anonymous, and among whom Eddie Condon played a leading role: "Eddie was always hanging around Bix—a real Bix fan, fanatic even. It was laughs, that's Condon's style, everything for laughs. He figured Bix was a real character, although Condon himself was as much a character as anybody. He was an operator. Bix shouldn't have been around with guys like that. . . . Bix was well liked by most people, but these guys made fun of his drinking, they made fun of his remarks—everything was funny to them."[29] Red Nichols's critical opinion in regard to this bunch of false friends and hypocritical admirers was even more severe: "I lost respect for certain jealous musicians that made fun of Bix when he was in a drunken state. First they'd get him so loaded that he didn't know where he was

27. The Dakota Apartments building was built in 1884 at 1 West 72nd Street, across the street from Central Park. It was the first luxury apartment residence in New York. It's a square building, enclosing an interior yard and offering four fifteen-room apartments per floor. Lauren Bacall, Leonard Bernstein, and Judy Garland lived there. It was also used as the venue of Roman Polanski's *Rosemary's Baby* in 1968. The apartment occupied by Richardson Turner's uncle was said to be John Lennon's residence in New York: the rock star was killed at the side entrance of the building on December 8, 1980.

28. *The Leon Bix Beiderbecke Story,* op. cit., p. 539.

29. "Bill Challis Speaks Out," op. cit., p. 31.

or what he was doing. In their jealousy they tried to destroy Bix's reputation by laughing at him when they'd stand him up and force him to play. Then they'd make fun of his mistakes. I told one of them off and tried to put a stop to it. Bix didn't deserve that."[30]

Williamstown, Wednesday, June 10, and Thursday, June 11, 1931

Bix still had a few good friends, who held enough faith in his artistic abilities to ask him to work with them. Benny Goodman was one. He had been hired for two days by students of Williams College in Williamstown, Massachusetts, and he had asked Tommy Dorsey and Bix to be part of his band. While still in New York on the morning of the show, the two musicians realized that neither the car nor the train would get them there in time for the evening performance. "So they finally decided to fly up," remembered Benny Goodman. "They sent us a wire about the situation, and chartered a plane out on Long Island and started out. Everything went fine— except that Bix, whose health was pretty low, got sick. . . . The plane came roaring over the campus, and we all ran out to watch them, and waved and shouted, but it was no go. There was no place to land there, either. Finally, they went over in the direction of Pittsfield, and put the plane down there."[31] Exhausted, indisposed by the voyage, Bix offered a weak performance on the first evening, and didn't do much better the next day. This concert would be the last he shared with Benny Goodman.

Bix returned to New York and to a life lived on tenterhooks, haunted by his financial situation, which barely skirted complete downfall. The anxiety was relieved only by nightly binges that brought him the illusion of a sunnier future. Jimmy McPartland ran into him one night, lost among the crowd at Plunkett's: "Bix was there, looking bad. He was all run down and miserable, had been drinking excessively and not eating much. We talked about it, I remember, and he said he didn't feel like eating anything. I told him he should at least swallow some silver fizzes to get something nutritious inside him. Fizzes were concocted out of gin and the whites of eggs and they sure set you up. So we both had about six of these, with a little sugar, and I gave Bix some dough because he was clean out."[32]

Singer Smith Ballew, who had recorded with Frank Trumbauer's Orchestra in April 1929, was gaining popularity. His last recording for Columbia, "Say a Little Prayer for Me," was selling well. He had his own band and was billed at Saltzman's, a restaurant in the Lincoln building.[33] The place was a short walk away from Bix's hotel. On the night of June 12, Smith Ballew ran into Bix leaning on the bar at Saltzman's, a glass in his hand. He invited him to come onstage and to accompany him for a few minutes. George Van Eps, the band's guitarist, remembered the night: "It

30. *The Leon Bix Beiderbecke Story*, op. cit., p. 539.

31. Benny Goodman quoted in Charles H. Wareing and George Garlick, *Bugles for Beiderbecke* (London: Sigwick and Jackson Ltd., 1958), p. 192.

32. *Jazz Talking*, op. cit., pp. 165–166. The official recipe for a Silver Fizz is one cup of vodka, one raw egg, half-cup of cream, sugar, and crushed ice.

33. This tower was built by the end of the 1920s at 60 East 42nd Street, right across from Grand Central Station.

Portrait of "Alice O'Connell," as kept by the Beiderbecke family; the woman's identity is uncertain. (Courtesy Liz Beiderbecke Hart)

was kinda sad. Bix'd stand up to play a solo, and it just wouldn't come out any good. He'd take the horn away from his mouth, fiddle with the valves, then hand it to J. D. Wade, our first trumpet player, and J. D. would check it over and hand it back to him, saying there was nothing wrong with it. But the funny thing is that during intermissions he'd sit at the piano and play beautifully. I mean impeccably. Of course it didn't involve anything as variable as embouchure, and his coordination at the keyboard was unimpaired."[34] The cornetist's obvious degradation alarmed Rex Gavitte, the band's bassist, who offered to let Bix stay at his apartment in Astoria. Bix accepted with relief. The discouraging exhibition at Saltzman's did not deter Smith Ballew from inviting Bix to join him in Princeton on June 15, where some students were organizing a dance party in the university gymnasium.

The next day, Bix wrote his parents an unbelievable letter: "This time I have a pretty legitimate excuse for not having written. I had a sudden offer to take my own musicians on the road—the fellows I used on records. I was in pretty much of a sweat—Burnie will tell you what one-nighters are. I stood up part of the time in swallow-tails and directed. 3 weeks around New England and the P.A. coal regions—of course I played too." Bix was trying to conceal a painful reality, and various witnesses have confirmed that his physical condition would not have allowed him to lead a "three-week tour." The following part of the letter is even more troubling, when Bix introduces his "future wife," Alice O'Connell, a young Irish girl born in New York twenty years before, and a "staunch catholic—something I've been dreading to say because of mother," wrote Bix. She was said to have two brothers and three sisters, and to have lost her mother and father "when she was quite young." This disappearance had deprived her of the love of her parents, but she had inherited a sizeable estate. "I told Alice that I wouldn't get married until I had a couple thousand," added Bix. "She winked at me and said '*you've got it*' and showed me a bank book—I almost swooned—she's got bonds, bank stocks, etc, and plenty in the bank—I promise you that I fell in love with her before I knew that. . . . I think Alice is worth $ 10,000 at least with her bonds, etc & I didn't know it." Bix ended his letter by mentioning some professional projects and giving his address as Rex Gavitte's. A photograph of the young woman was said to have been sent to Davenport, but the portrait that is today in the Beiderbecke family's possession hardly looks like the "enlarged picture" taken "in a Photomaton on B'way," that Bix described.[35]

Hoagy met Bix several days after the letter was written, most likely around June 20. "I ran into Bix in a speak-easy," wrote Hoagy, "and he had a beer. I proposed again that he come out to the Shackefords with me for dinner. Of all surprising things, he accepted. . . . Harry Shackelford and Bix sat back in a bedroom while I

34. *Lost Chords*, op. cit., p. 524.
35. *The Leon Bix Beiderbecke Story*, op. cit., pp. 540–541.

was doing a few songs for the girls in the living room. Bix intimated to 'Shack' that his style was a passing phase and that he was 'through.' He also used the expression 'has-been,' and Shack told me that Bix's manner was that of a melancholy boy.... Bix came back into the living room and said, *'Ran into a girl the other day. She's going to fix me up in a flat out in Sunnyside.'* *'Great, how's for bringing her over to my kip some night?' 'Any time,'* and we made a firm date."[36] Rex Gavitte had probably initiated this encounter. The young woman lived in Sunnyside, Queens. Its urbanization occurred rapidly in 1909, after the con-

Outside of the building at 43–30 46th Street in Sunnyside, Queens, present condition. (James Kidd)

struction of the Queensboro Bridge connecting this vast borough to the heart of New York. With the bridge and the elevated train line running over it, residents of Sunnyside working in midtown or downtown Manhattan could be home in thirty minutes.

Sunnyside, end of June–August 7, 1931

Toward the end of June, Bix moved into a small apartment on the first floor of a brand new building. This small flat, 1-G, at 43–30 46th Street—less than one hundred yards from Queens Boulevard and the subway station—was quite empty.[37] Its only furnishings were a desk, a bed, and a piano, still on loan from Pat Ciricillo and brought from the 44th Street Hotel. "I never did learn the identity of the girl who was with him the day he picked out the apartment," explained George Kraslow, rental agent for the building. "Extremely attractive—she came once or twice afterwards, maybe more, but I just caught glimpses of her. Bix lived alone. There was only a small bed: it would have been impossible for someone to share the bed with him."[38]

Around July 15, Bix and his young girlfriend visited Hoagy Carmichael in his apartment at 114 East 57th Street, near Park Avenue. The musician's appearance was neater, and he was more talkative than he had been on their last visit. "She was Bix's kind of girl," wrote Hoagy. "A bit mothery, maybe lost herself, but neat, willing to put up with Bix's habits. I liked her. We didn't have a drink. We didn't talk much music, and it became apparent that this girl had no idea who Bix was and why he was the way he was. It was just two strangers meeting. Perhaps she knew he was a musician, but that was all. The thought struck me—later—I didn't know Bix either. He was my

36. *Sometimes I Wonder,* op. cit., p. 224.

37. Phil Pospychala, the organizer of the annual Tribute to Bix, visited the apartment on September 11, 2001, at 12:20 a.m., a visit he reported in the September 2002 issue of *The Mississippi Rag.* So did Albert Haim one year later: the door opens onto a small hall; a living room is just inside, with a window opening onto the courtyard of the church next door. A narrow corridor to the left of the entrance gives access to three doors: kitchen, bathroom, and a small bedroom. (Information from Albert Haim.)

38. *Bix, Man and Legend,* op. cit., p. 328.

Interior hall of Bix's building in Sunnyside, present condition. (James Kidd)

friend, yet intimately, deeply, warmly, I didn't know him. He was unfathomable, the bit on the surface hiding the deep-lying man."[39] The girl's name is not mentioned in either of the two books that Hoagy Carmichael wrote. When asked about it in 1959, the composer answered with the name of Helen Weiss, information he later repeated. Hoagy's memory is hardly a model of precision, but he was quite positive about not being aware of any other girl in Bix's entourage at this time.

Various jazz historians have searched for one Helen Weiss or an Alice O'Connell—to no avail. In the 1970s, Joe Giordano, writer of technical manuals for the U.S. Army, tried in vain to trace Alice by contacting some 500 O'Connells living in the New York area. But Helen and Alice have vanished with Bix's death.[40] One of these two girls remained in a few memories as a kind and thoughtful presence around Bix at a time when he was a lost and lonely man. A passenger during the last hour of an already-derailed life, Alice/Helen has kept her memories of the summer of 1931 private. With his letter, and the announcement of an impending wedding, which, like the three-week tour he supposedly led, was probably more fantasy than reality, Bix hoped to soothe his parents' anxiety about his unpromising future.

Bix seems to have quickly realized that such a tricky game was of little use. A few days after the letter dated June 16 was sent, he began to write a second one to his family, and stopped it after only a few lines: "Dearest Folks:—By now you have Alice's picture— what do you think of her? We're together constantly—I dragged her in one of those photomatons on B'way & for a buck we had that made & enlarged. The little sweetheart framed it, packed it, and sent it to you when she knew you wanted it."[41] This

Interior hall of Bix's building in Sunnyside (back door leading to Bix's former apartment), present condition. (James Kidd)

39. *Sometimes I Wonder*, op. cit., p. 225.

40. When *Bix, Man and Legend* was written in 1974, this letter was unknown. Based on Hoagy's recollections, the name of the young woman seen with Bix several times was given as Helen Weiss. Burnie was certain that they did not meet this woman during their short stay in New York: "It all happened so fast," he said, "I'm sure that we were told that Bix wanted Miss Weiss to have his Weber grand piano. It is, however, still in our family" (*Bix, Man and Legend*, op. cit., p. 334). Bix's letters written in June 1931 were mentioned for the first time by Curtis Prendergast in the insert booklet for the *Giants of Jazz* LP set (Time-Life, 1979), in which Helen Weiss disappeared to the advantage of Alice O'Connell, who became the young woman Hoagy met. This version was followed in 1990 by Chip Deffaa in *Voices of the Jazz Age*. Finally, Philip and Linda Evans in *The Leon Bix Beiderbecke Story*, published in 1998, mention the two women, confirming their double existence. However, Helen Weiss is the only girl to be identified by witnesses of that time: Stephen Ickes, Hoagy Carmichael, and Charles "Burnie" Beiderbecke. During this last part of Bix's life, nobody ever met "Alice."

41. *Bix Beiderbecke, Giants of Jazz*, op. cit., p. 30.

unfinished letter was found by Bix's mother among her son's personal papers on the day following his death.

Summer in New York is usually hot and humid, and 1931 was no exception. Because of the temperature outside and his chronic weakness, Bix remained secluded in his new apartment. "Bix seldom went out," said George Kraslow, "except to buy gin. He seemed to be struggling with himself and drank almost continuously. It wasn't until a few people living in the apartment house complained to me, half-heartedly I would say, about someone playing the piano around 2 a.m. that I discovered Bix was working on musical arrangements during the wee hours of the morning. . . . I became friendly with him and tried to stop him drinking so heavily, but it seemed to be an obsession with him. He just couldn't stop. . . . He seemed dreamy, far away, a lot of time. He usually talked about his previous connections with different top musicians. There were times when he wasn't entirely coherent. But even then, his love for jazz was the basic theme of any conversations I had with him."[42]

Bix and Red Nichols ran into each other at Plunkett's bar on the evening of Monday, August 3. Bix's health had significantly degraded, and he succumbed to frequent and worrisome coughing fits. Red Nichols could hardly forget this last encounter with his friend: "Bix, between a hacking cough, related his feelings to me. He was really down in the dumps, feeling sorry for himself. He felt the world had deserted him. At a time when he really needed a friend, he didn't seem to have one. *'None of the guys in this place would give me a quarter if I asked for it,'* he commented. I asked why he didn't try going back with Paul Whiteman, and all he said was, *'Sure, Paul would take me back if . . .'*—and then his voice trailed off. I strongly suggested he come home with me but he shrugged it off, saying he'd be better in a few days."[43]

A dry cough was the first clinical sign of the lobar pneumonia that, three days later, would come upon the musician. This infectious disease originates from the proliferation of bacteria—a pneumococcus—in one or several lobes of the lung: the infected part of the organ is filled with a fibrillated fluid, which reduces the breathing capacity of the inflamed lung. The patient feels intense pain in the chest, an accelerated breathing rhythm, a shortness of breath, and a high fever. Tachycardia accompanies these symptoms. Since the 1940s and the availability of antibiotics, this

Last letter from Bix to his family, unfinished and probably written by end of June 1931; Bix's mother added the supposed date of its writing to the top of the letter, "July 30/31," and she wrote at the bottom: "Bixie's letter, never finished." (Lake Forest Academy archives hold a copy of this letter)

42. *Bix, Man and Legend*, op. cit., pp. 327–328. In 1931, Saxophonist Charlie Barnet worked in New York in Frank Winegar's orchestra. Barnet wrote in his autobiography, "Bix and I were rehearsing in Huston Ray's orchestra at the Jane Grey Studios in New York, a place where a lot of bands rehearsed. We made the one rehearsal and were supposed to return the next day, but Bix never showed up. He didn't look well and he had been playing badly. A few days later I heard he had died" (Charlie Barnet, with Stanley Dance, *Those Swinging Years*, Louisiana State University Press, 1984). The last sentence would place this rehearsal somewhere in June, which would therefore have been Bix's last professional appearance.

43. *The Leon Bix Beiderbecke Story*, op. cit., p. 546.

disease can be cured within a few days, but until 1936, pneumonia was the leading cause of death in the U.S. Bix's general weakness could only lead to a very somber prognosis: his immune system, ruined by twelve years of excessive drinking—and the use of often-dubious alcohols—could not fight off the development of such a virulent infection.

On August 4, Bix consulted Dr. John H. Haberski, whose office was in the same building as his patient's apartment. The diagnosis came quickly. Bix called Red Nichols in the evening. The trumpeter was performing at the Park Central Hotel, and his wife, Bobbi answered the phone. Bix was coughing badly. He was alone and wanted to talk. For long minutes, he unloaded his bitterness and desperation on his petrified listener. His respiratory tract being obstructed, talking was difficult for Bix, and he insisted that Red Nichols be informed of his call. Dr. Haberski visited his patient on the morning of Wednesday, August 5, and decided that the development of the illness required immediate hospitalization. Bix firmly refused. The practitioner then asked George Kraslow about the possibility of contacting a close relative of his extremely ill neighbor. The first name that Kraslow could think of was Paul Whiteman's. The orchestra was playing at the Edgewater Beach Hotel in Chicago, where the bandleader was easily contacted. "Whiteman came rushing over," remembered Andy Secrest, "and he called for Tram. 'Come quickly, Tram,' he said. 'It's Bix!' Bix was in need of immediate medical care and refused to enter a hospital. Tram put a call to the Beiderbecke home in Davenport, and advised them of the seriousness of the situation: Bix's brother and mother caught the first train to New York. Then we waited for word."[44]

On Thursday, August 6, at three fifteen in the afternoon, Burnie and Agatha Beiderbecke got on a train for Chicago. They had departed as quickly as possible. Bix's wishes were respected: he would not be hospitalized. The day in New York had been extremely hot. At around nine thirty that night, George Kraslow heard cries coming from the musician's flat. "His hysterical shouts brought me to his apartment on the run," said Kraslow. "He pulled me in and pointed to the bed. His whole body was trembling violently. He was screaming there were two Mexicans hiding under his bed with long daggers. To humor him, I looked under the bed and when I rose to assure him there was no one hiding there, he staggered and fell, a dead weight, in my arms. I ran across the hall and called Dr. Haberski's wife to examine him. She pronounced him dead."[45] Mrs. Haberski served as a nurse to her husband, who was apparently absent that night. The doctor wrote out the death certificate the next morning, stating that a lobar pneumonia had caused the death.[46]

AT THE TIME of her youngest son's death, Agatha Beiderbecke and her eldest child were changing trains in Englewood station—a connecting hub south of Chicago. They arrived at Grand Central Station the next evening at 9:20 p.m., twenty-four hours after the death of their "Bixie." From the station, Burnie called

44. *TRAM, the Frank Trumbauer Story*, op. cit., pp. 142–143.

45. *The Leon Bix Beiderbecke Story*, op. cit., p. 546.

46. The cause of Bix's death was analyzed in *Bix, Man and Legend* (1974) and *The Leon Bix Beiderbecke Story* (1998), and the other books or articles following their conclusions. The first book said: "Cause of death: lobar pneumonia, with edema of the brain. From the account of his death given by George Kraslow . . . and by Haberski himself, it is easily inferred that Bix died in a seizure of delirium tremens" (p. 399). The same main cause, "lobar pneumonia," is given in *The Leon Bix Beiderbecke Story* (p. 546), which adds on the following page: "the conclusion is that Bix died in a seizure of delirium tremens." There is no scientific link between these two lethal factors. Delirium tremens is the most serious consequence of alcoholic withdrawal, and it appears two or three days after drinking has been totally stopped, the crisis reaching its peak after three or four days. There is no evidence that Bix stopped drinking around August 3. The high fever generated by pneumonia itself explains the hallucinations Bix suffered. Bix died from lobar pneumonia, and this is all we can say. Frederick J. Spencer gives a serious medical analysis of Bix Beiderbecke's health problems in his book *Jazz and Death* (University Press of Mississippi, 2002, pp. 97–106).

the Sunnyside apartment and learned of his brother's death. He was given the address of the funeral parlor where the body had been transferred. They met with Dr. Haberski, George Kraslow, and Michael J. Kimmel, the funeral home director who was to arrange for the transport of the body. When asked in 1967, Burnie declared himself "certain that Miss Weiss had made all the arrangements to have Bix's body shown."[47] This mysterious

Agatha Beiderbecke at home in 1935, Grand Avenue, Davenport. (Photo: Marshall Stearns, Courtesy of the Rutgers Institute of Jazz Studies)

young woman also called Hoagy Carmichael to inform him of his friend's passing. "I asked her why she hadn't called," recounted Hoagy. "She said that it all happened too fast. A few days later when she came by I was still in shock. I know we talked about Bix, but I don't remember a thing we said. . . . How could it have happened? She gave me some of Bix's effects: cuff links, a couple of handkerchiefs, and his mouthpiece."

It was most likely Burnie who called Paul Whiteman in Chicago. Andy Secrest was present: "Finally the telephone call came," said Secrest. "The one that we never wanted to receive. . . . When Paul gave us the news, Tram went out back. I didn't know whether to leave him alone, or whether he needed comfort, but I elected to go out and see if he was all right. All Tram could do was ask, *'Andy, why didn't Bix call? I've always been there for him. Why didn't he call?'* Of course, I did not have any answer. No one did."[48]

Davenport, Sunday, August 9–Tuesday, August 11, 1931

Agatha and her two sons returned to Davenport. Daughter of pioneers and raised in the uncompromising heart of the American Midwest, Agatha was a courageous woman, but what words could express the pain of a mother who has just lost her son? She had stayed in New York for only a few hours, discovering the few rooms where her son had lived on Saturday morning, and returning to Grand Central Station on the afternoon of August 8. The next evening at Davenport station, the casket was removed from the baggage car and driven to the Hill

47. *The Leon Bix Beiderbecke Story*, op. cit., p. 549.

48. *TRAM, the Frank Trumbauer Story*, op. cit., p. 143.

Former building of the Hill and Fredericks Mortuary, Brady Street at 13th, Davenport. (JPL, 2000)

49. The two buildings of the former Hill and Fredericks funeral house are still standing, but are now occupied by a radio station. When his coffin was opened in Davenport, Bix was dressed in his tuxedo—perhaps that was the only presentable attire that could be found in his New York closet. His parents asked that he be changed, and for the Iowa wake Bix was dressed in a grey plaid suitcoat, a white shirt, and a colorful tie. "He was the first corpse I saw that wasn't dressed in black," remembered a witness. (Information from Rich Johnson.)

50. Les Swanson's letter to the author dated August 14, 2002. This recollection contradicts what was written in *Bix, Man and Legend*, where it was said that Bix was buried "after the largest funeral in the city's memory" (p. 334).

51. Pages of the register opened on August 10, 1931, at Hill and Fredericks Mortuary are reproduced in *The Leon Bix Beiderbecke Story*, op. cit., pp. 550-551. The first page was signed by the nine "friends who called," and the three following pages list the names of the forty-one persons who sent flowers or telegrams. Among the names written are: "Alice O. Connell, N.Y." on the fourth line, and "Weiss Family, N.Y." on the fifth. The list was handwritten by one person after the ceremony was over. The Weiss/O'Connell family had sent something (Bix wrote that Weiss was the name of Alice O'Connell's mother), but Alice's name might have been dictated by Bix's mother, who had learned it from her son's two letters.

and Fredericks Mortuary, at the corner of Brady and 13th streets.[49] Bix's body was on display on Monday 10, and was visited by few people; there were only nine signatures in the register of condolences, among them Esten Spurrier, Trave O'Hearn, and Tal Sexton. The religious ceremony was held in the funeral chapel on Thursday, August 11. Les Swanson came by himself. He arrived late and sat at the back. "The fifty to sixty people crowded into the small room were all men," remembered the pianist, "and the casket was closed. The family was seated in a side room of the chapel. Ceremony was like a Masonic ritual, with many readings of the Bible and no sermon. I was expecting to meet up with a number of local musicians, but I didn't see any of them, not even Esten Spurrier. I didn't talk to anyone, and left as soon as the ceremony was over."[50] Bix's remains were buried at noon at the Oakdale Cemetery, with only his immediate family present.[51]

Ceno Petersen, the son of Albert Petersen and a relative of Agatha's, had employed Bix in his Harrison Street Drug Store when the adolescent was attending Davenport High School. Ceno was present the day of the burial and he remembered a distraught young woman. She was pretty, dressed carefully, and she left town after the ceremony. A member of the Beiderbecke family may have told him that she had come from New York. Could Alice/Helen have been in Davenport on that day?

The local radio station paid a quick homage to the "boy from our City" by including several trivial comments about the musician into a dance music broadcast, and by asking pianist Bert Sloan to play "In a Mist." Bix's 1924 photograph was printed on the first page of the August 7 edition of the *Davenport Democrat*, which dedicated two columns to the event. And that was it. Neither the *Chicago Tribune* nor the *New York Times* saw fit to report the information.

Oakdale Cemetery is a vast hilly place, not far from the Beiderbecke home. In accordance with custom, remains are buried "six feet under," and a small, simple stone marker emerges several inches above the grass. The stone contains the following inscription: "Leon Bix Beiderbecke—Born March 10, 1903—Died August 6, 1931."

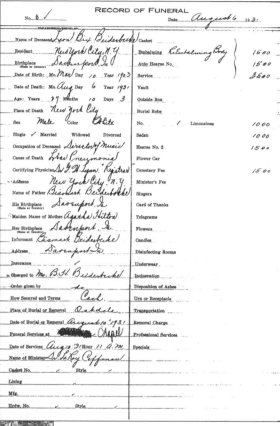

Invoice for Bix's funeral issued by the Hill and Fredericks Mortuary, Davenport. (Rich Johnson)

Bix's grave at Oakdale Cemetery in Davenport. (JPL, 2000)

Epilogue

At the end of 1929, Bix's boyhood friend Larry Andrews had left Davenport, employed by an insurance company that sent him to a remote part of Iowa. The article published on August 7, 1931, in the *Davenport Democrat* informed him of his friend's death. Some years later, answering questions raised by jazz critic Otis Ferguson, Larry Andrews gathered recollections of his early life in Davenport into several letters. A strange story, repeatedly confirmed as authentic, gave these letters an unexpected conclusion. "I had eighteen agents under me and several collecting agents," wrote Larry Andrews. "There was a spiritualist medium who was a member of our organization, who chanced to be at the collector's house one day when I called her in Strom Lake, Iowa. I dodge such things myself . . . but this woman told me she had something to tell me. She said there was a young fellow who had recently passed on and told me to tell 'Helen' that he couldn't understand why that had to happen now. I laughed and said, '*Well, I don't know any young fellow and right offhand I don't know any Helen to which he might refer.*' Imagine my utter astonishment when she told me this young fellow says his name is Dix—no, he shakes his head and writes the letter 'B,' and what could he mean by that? In my astonishment I said '*Bix*' and she informed me that that was correct, and that he also wanted me to tell his folks the same message as Helen."[1] True or not, this posthumous appearance has never been repeated. Would that it had been: it would have been of great help to Bix's biographers.

Though the medical causes of Bix's death are well established, the reason behind the lethal drive that accelerated his demise remains unclear. Alcohol abuse does not inspire happiness—it generates sadness and anxiety, and drowns drinkers into a hell of unfathomable depression. Paul Whiteman did not lack intelligence or insight. In 1938 he shared his personal view of the battle Bix fought and lost with himself with the readers of *Metronome* magazine: "Somehow or other," said Whiteman, "he gave you the impression that he was constantly striving for something that was just out of his reach. His continual searching for some sort of ultimate created almost a mystic halo about him—it gave you the feeling that here was

1. "Larry Andrews' Letters," in *Storyville*, no. 12 (August/September 1967), pp. 17–18.

a genius who knew of something beautiful to strive for and that, even though he might never reach it, he was far above you merely because he could sense that beauty for which he was reaching. . . . Sure, Bix drank, and I'll bet you he got far more out of imbibing the stuff than any of us ever did or will. Drinking to him was an emotional release . . . he was getting further away from our reality. He had a terribly fatalistic attitude about our world: he couldn't see any future in it. It even got to the point when he was convinced that everything wrong had to happen to him."[2] For the bandleader, this painful separation was the unfortunate privilege of great artists, called forth to the creation of an inaccessible beauty and living at a height from which the triviality of our daily life seemed unbearable.

Bix died completely unaware of the importance of his work; the focus on his suffering blinded him to his exemplary destiny. Plunged into alcohol, each day more deeply removed from the surface of a reality to which he instinctively knew he was a stranger, Bix understood very early on that his literal dissolution would be his deliverance. Freed from his earthly trappings, he could hope to reach an ideal music, liberated from the weakness of the lips and the shortness of the breath, a music that only he could hear and to which we will have never access.

"Of course all life is a process of breaking down," wrote F. Scott Fitzgerald in 1936, at the opening of a deeply moving confession, "The Crack-Up."[3] Fitzgerald wished to die at thirty . . . and Bix only made it to twenty-eight. By dying young, he had secured an eternal youth. For his aging companions and for a constantly renewed audience, his figure would become, over the course of the years, the symbol of a bygone golden age. America had added a new hero to its mythology. Bix preceded Robert Johnson, Charlie Parker, Clifford Brown, and Charlie Christian in the pantheon of jazzmen; all prematurely vanished, and joined in musical talent—with no talent for living—by Jim Morrison, Brian Jones, and Jimi Hendrix, their spiritual and boisterous sons. Apart from the legend of Bix as the doomed artist, and the image of him as a young, well-brought-up man, hiding his bottle under the piano lid, his recordings have preserved a unique voice, a pure tone so fresh that, still today, it speaks to us and moves us.

This angelic demon possessed me for five years. Musical genius, despair, and tenderness are timeless. Bix remains a long-lost, pain-burdened friend, as elusive today as he was for his contemporaries, among whom he passed like a dream.

2. Paul Whiteman, "The Greatest Gent I've Ever Known," in *Metronome: A Tribute to Bix* (November 1938), p. 16, 21.

3. F. Scott Fitzgerald, "The Crack-Up," in *The Crack-Up*, edited by Edmund Wilson (New York: Charles Scribner's Sons, 1931), p. 69.

Appendix 1: Texts and Documents

"Bix has been my big influence. I don't think anybody playing
today has not been influenced by Bix."

George Barnes, in *American Life Histories:*
Manuscripts from the Federal Writers' Project (May 1939)

1—Posthumous joys

Rudi Blesh is one of the few American jazz critics to offer a negative assessment of
Bix's playing. In *Shining Trumpets* (1946), he wrote, "Beiderbecke was and is a per-
vasive influence. A whole school of white playing, which pretends to be jazz, stems
from him; but real jazz is a strong music. Objectively considered, Beiderbecke's
playing is weak, and weakness characterized his life." Notwithstanding his "virile"
and obtuse view that jazz needs to be "strong," Rudi Blesh does admit the importance of Bix's influence.

Two models were offered to jazz trumpet players during the second half of the
1920s: Louis Armstrong and Bix Beiderbecke. The historical supremacy of the
black musician is obvious, and the first years of his long career established, in an
outpouring of daring and perfectly mastered inventions, the canon of African
American jazz music. "The first third of his recordings appear like a laboratory in
full activity," wrote Alain Gerber, "a work in progress in which an unprecedented
language and a new way of transposing or arousing primitive emotions are built
with method, precision and perseverance."[1]

Bix Beiderbecke's approach was clearly different, and the regret expressed by
Hugues Panassié that "Bix could never completely assimilate the black musicians'
style" makes no sense. The main characteristic of Bix's music is its sincerity: he created a personal and original style, which was a faithful reflection of the sensitivity
and imagination of a white American born a thousand miles north of New Orleans, far from the Delta and the origins of the blues. Louis Armstrong's playing
dazzled with its virtuosity, its blazing energy, and the incredible risks the soloist
was taking. Bix, an introverted artist, expressed himself with restraint. He favored

1. Alain Gerber, "Bix Beiderbecke: Des garçons sages et
plutôt bien élevés," *Fiesta in
Blue(1)* (Éditions Alive 1998).

nuance, preferring to suggest rather than to assert, and focusing his art on the achievement of pure melodic constructions or original harmonies. "The white players of the twenties and early thirties brought a particular lyric sensibility to jazz," wrote Martin Williams, "and this sensibility has had an effect on its subsequent development. Bix Beiderbecke was the most gifted and important of those players, important not only because his work was the most influential, but also because he was intrinsically an exceptional, original soloist."[2]

Bix had many emulators, but his short career and his evanescent personality prevented him from becoming the leader of a school of white jazzmen, a position that his true musical genius did deserve. And creation in which subtlety wins over effect is obviously more difficult to emulate. "Bix did not play second-hand Negro jazz but authentic white jazz," wrote Burnett James. "Had he lived longer he might have led the way to a decisive complementary white jazz that would have saved his successors from a great deal of vain floundering."[3] His influence, however, is strong and unquestionable.

As might be expected, Bix's influence was strongest among his white trumpet-playing contemporaries. But their names—Sylvester Ahola, Sterling Bose, Chelsea Quealey, Johnny Wiggs, and Mannie Klein—are known today to only a limited number of jazz aficionados. But these forgotten musicians participated in hundreds of recording sessions; Bix inspired them all, and all have recorded very Bixian solos. The cornetist had three closer emulators, and they are well represented in this book: Red Nichols and Jimmy McPartland came to Bix when he was a member of the Wolverines, and Andy Secrest was called on by Paul Whiteman by the end of 1928. They remained faithful to this first inspiration, intensely reflected in their music for many years. Bunny Berigan is one of the top trumpeters of the 1930s. He played with Bix in 1931, and followed him so closely that he died at thirty-four after years of excessive drinking. Bunny Berigan had also listened to black musicians, and like Max Kaminsky, Wingy Manone, Muggsy Spanier, or Wild Bill Davison, who were directly inspired by King Oliver and Louis Armstrong, the playing of these white musicians never freed itself from the Bixian influence that had marked their youth.

Bix is one of the few white jazzmen of the 1920s who influenced black musicians: John Nesbitt, soloist with McKinney's Cotton Pickers, was the first trumpet player whose style blended, across the racial boundary, characteristics of Bix and Louis's playing; the warmth of playing shown by Joe Smith, a short-lived accompanist of Bessie Smith and Ethel Waters, echoes Bix Beiderbecke's tenderness[4]; and cornetist Rex Stewart, one of the leading brassmen in Fletcher Henderson and Duke Ellington's groups, wrote about the admiration inspired by his "opponent" in the Jean Goldkette Orchestra. "Rex Stewart's playing unexpectedly merges Louis Armstrong's virile power with Bix's self-effacing lyricism," wrote French critic Alain Pailler.[5] European musicians were also inspired by Bix's timeless creation: the Frank

2. Martin Williams, "Bix Beiderbecke and the White Man's Burden," *Jazz,* (May/June 1964).

3. Burnett James, *Bix Beiderbercke* (London: Cassell, 1959), p. 63.

4. Bix's influence on Joe Smith is analyzed in Edward Brooks's *The Young Louis Armstrong on Records* (Lanham, MD: The Scarecrow Press, 2002). Smith's solo on "Memphis Bound," recorded by the Fletcher Henderson Orchestra on April 18, 1925, is viewed as "a fair imitation of Bix Beiderbecke in tone and phrase construction." Edward Brooks also studies a possible Bix's influence on Armstrong playing in *Influence and Assimilation in Louis Armstrong's Cornet and Trumpet Work* (Lewiston, NY: The Edwin Mellen Press, 2000), concluding actually that there was none.

5. Alain Pailler, *Plaisir d'Ellington* (Arles: Actes Sud, 1998).

Trumbauer Orchestra's recordings were issued in Europe from 1927 on, and French trumpet player Philippe Brun, soloist with Grégor, Ray Ventura, and Jack Hylton's orchestras, was first in a long line of Beiderbecke's European emulators.

Bix's influence reached a second circle of musicians who did not play trumpet. Bix was an outstanding leader. Thanks to the precision of his attack and his mastery of accentuation, he could drive the brass section of a big band—and the recordings he made with the Jean Goldkette and Paul Whiteman Orchestras preserve many examples of this irresistible swing. This creative energy also allowed him to inspire amazing performances from jazzmen who, once thrown back on their own personal talent, showed nothing more than a true skill. It is of course impossible to imagine what Don Murray would have done in the 1930s, but the recordings cut by Bill Rank—and even Frank Trumbauer—after Bix was gone would only occasionally come near the quality of their sparkling achievements of 1927 and 1928. Bill Challis asserted to have written some of his arrangements based on ideas or musical phrases that Bix had created. Similar constructions were used in big band arrangements during the swing era, and even in the accompaniment of popular songs.

Bing Crosby is the only American jazz artist to have stayed at the high end of the charts for two decades, from 1930 to 1950. The singer willingly acknowledged having learned his art by listening to his first band mates, among whom Bix was prominent. It is of course significant that, during the 1930s, musicians whose careers started in Bix's shadow dominated the music business. Their names are those of the stars of the swing era: Tommy and Jimmy Dorsey, who, whether together or leading separate bands, achieved great success after 1935; Benny Goodman, the King of Swing, who managed to combine the recording of best sellers with the creations of small combos in which the presence of black musicians—Teddy Wilson, Lionel Hampton, Charlie Christian—was a daring and most welcome innovation; Artie Shaw and Glenn Miller, whose big bands in 1938 and 1939 joined the group of best-selling orchestras. There are few bands or singers who have not recorded "Star Dust," a song that has been endlessly interpreted. The music was written by Hoagy Carmichael, and it is, for Richard Sudhalter, "a jazz composition whose shape and overall flavor are heavily indebted to Beiderbecke's phrasing."[6]

As mentioned in the introduction of this book, the revival movement of the early 1940s reactivated a popular interest for the New Orleans jazz style. Not surprisingly, it led many young musicians to discover Bix's music, creating another wide field of posthumous influence for the cornet player. Benny Goodman reached consecration after a concert given at Carnegie Hall on January 16, 1938. During the performance, a twenty-three-year-old cornetist played Bix's solo on "I'm Coming Virginia" note for note: his name was Bobby Hackett. For writer and jazz musician Boris Vian—one of Bix's French emulators on trumpet—he was "the only successor of Bix worthy of the name." Hackett became popular with a personal style that

6. *Stardust Melody, The Life and Music of Hoagy Carmichael,* op. cit., p. 109.

was both sweet and powerful, both innovative and faithful to the spirit of Dixieland. Recorded versions of "In a Mist" followed one after another, and in March 1959, Billy Butterfield released an LP containing eleven titles from Bix's repertoire. Even today, significant trumpet players mine a musical vein that finds its obvious origin in Bix's original creation. Among these musicians is Ruby Braff who, according to Burnett James, "plays not so much like Bix (for that is most times mere imitation) but in the direct line of succession stemming from Bix"[7]; Randy Sandke and Richard Sudhalter, who are both musicians and writers of important books and essays dedicated to Bix; and Tom Pletcher, who is considered by many amateurs to be the cornetist who has come the closest to reproducing Bix Beiderbecke's style and tone. In France in 2004, Patrick Artero, a notable member in the 1970s of the Anachronic Jazz Band, released a tribute to Bix, which was named the "best jazz recording by a French musician" by the Académie du Jazz.

Bix wrote the first chapter of a poetical art in jazz music: ethereal music, at once joyous and melancholic, a definition that clearly applies to Debussy and Ravel's creations. Such a poetic warmth was unknown in jazz music, until the records cut by Bix Beiderbecke were released. "Some musicians, as early as the end of the 1920s, decided that jazz did not always have to be red hot," wrote Alain Tercinet. "Sweetness was also rich with many possibilities, and this new approach was mainly the one of white jazzmen, such as Joe Venuti and Eddie Lang, or the association of Bix Beiderbecke and Frank Trumbauer."[8]

This school of lightness would lead to Lester Young. Asked by François Postif about the saxophone player who had been his major influence, Lester Young answered: "Frankie Trumbauer. . . . There was no other musician who told me little stories I liked so much . . . Frank Trumbauer was my master. Did you ever hear his 'Singin' the Blues'? It got me worked up, that was what I wanted to do."[9] Lester Young's path led to Chet Baker—"As with Bix's, Chet's playing is sweet, light, but also direct and honest," said Charlie Parker[10]—and to Miles Davis, masters of silence, the broken phrase, and delicacy as a strength.

2—Listening to Louis Armstrong

After feeling dizzy one night in 1959 and having had to cancel a scheduled concert in Spoleto, Italy, Louis said smilingly to the press: "Bix tried to get a job for me to play solos in Gabriel's band, but it didn't work out . . . because of problems with Joe Glaser or the Union, or even with the State Department." When gathering stories for his broadcast series, *Bix, A Biographical Radio Series*, Jim Grover contacted Louis Armstrong, and by the end of 1970, he recorded a phone interview with the trumpet player: more than eight minutes of a continuous monologue that was used as the conclusion of the

7. *Bix Beiderbecke*, op. cit., p. 47. Ruby Braff passed away on February 9, 2003.

8. Alain Tercinet, *West Coast Jazz*, (Marseille: Parenthèses, 1986), p. 131.

9. François Postif, *Jazz Me Blues*, (Paris: Editions Outre Mesure, 1999), p. 88.

10. William Claxton, *Young Chet*, (Schirmer: Gitanes Jazz Productions, 1993).

radio broadcast. Louis Armstrong passed away at his house in Corona, New York, on July 6, 1971: Gabriel finally had the soloist he'd been waiting for.

Louis Armstrong's monologue appears in three parts, two in the first program and the longest part in the final broadcast.

Louis Armstrong in PROGRAM 1:

Every note he blew was so beautiful. I like that "Singin' the Blues" record, and things like that. Nobody else could blow like he did. I never did play that tune because of Bix . . . I didn't want nobody to mess with it . . . Yeah, but now that's a classic. They ain't nobody else could play it like he did. They tried . . . pa-dooby-dooby-doo [*Louis sings a portion of the chorus*]. All them little beautiful notes that came out that horn . . . and in those days, he wasn't listening to things like that. But it's the way he played it. It's just an ordinary tune . . . anybody can play it! But the way he played it, and phrased it with his tone, and, you know, phrasing is the greatest thing in the world . . . Don't care what instrument you're playing . . . or singing . . . you know what I mean there. And in certain ways people have their techniques, and his technique is still outstanding. Ain't nobody else ever cope with it . . . They tried. I've heard a lot of cats try to play like Bix . . . Ain't none of them play like him yet!

You can tell the whole world: there'll never be another Bix Beiderbecke. Take that from Satchmo! He was a born genius, but they crowded him too much with love. You know, even when he played "In a Mist" on the piano . . . He was an artist without appreciation in all times. Nobody could play the piano like Bix played "In a Mist" . . . and he had another tune he played there . . . and right now, ain't nobody could play that tune . . . ain't nobody could duplicate it yet.

AND WE ALL (were on) the Steamer *St. Paul*, on the Streckfus Line. They had four steamboats, you know, and I came up from New Orleans where I played for Fate Marable on the steamer *Sidney* in New Orleans. So we came up to Saint Louis to get on the big boat, and that's when we went up the river, and . . . that big boat out of that chute . . . and who was standing there? This young kid: Bix Beiderbecke!

Louis Armstrong in PROGRAM 19: **BIX, The Final Chorus:**

Well, what actually could a man get with a fellow like Bix . . . "Jesus!" or "Thank God!" . . . you know what I mean . . . Don't know what to say . . . Oh God! If there is anything I could do just to bring him back, it would have been beautiful and I would have been . . .

Take over, you know, one of them things but you couldn't do that . . . it all happens, you know . . . death is, who knows when it hits you to the extent, and now all the cats that was around him . . . and right now they just regret that incident when they talk about it, you know. Man, they lost a genius . . . I ain't just trying to pull your leg, man . . . they lost a genius when they lost Bix because . . . he didn't even have a chance to really explore the world, his ability and his musical genius and Bix. . . . he didn't go to Europe, he didn't do a lot of things. He didn't make the records he should have been making, like he was coming up . . . you know, and things like that, and all of a sudden he was stricken . . . we never did get over it. Like today, every time I go to Davenport, the whole family comes to the occasion, concert or wherever I play, and such a-boo-hooin' . . . and, you know, sad incidents.

It's so beautiful. All he wanted was a horn in his hand . . . that's all he wanted, to play that horn, and every time he picked it up, he played it . . . and there ain't a musician that played with him won't tell you the same thing I'm telling you right now: he's the model of all the musicians that played with him. With tears in their eyes, they'll tell it . . . we miss him. Most of the bands he played with, they wasn't good . . . but pretty near all the bands . . . Paul Whiteman was the best band to the extent what they was playin' a lot of music . . . you know what I mean . . . but when Bix got his part, I mean, he played his solos . . . what he had on the program, but it came out different . . . ah-ah-ah . . . He couldn't play like "tattattatta," things like that, you know . . . he had sixteen bars, and you could tell the difference.

Nowadays if he could play the music he wanted . . . he had the band and his arrangers and, oh, it would be a great difference . . . you understand? Every band he played, he was better than all the musicians. Ain't a man yet that was equal to him, or superior . . . it's impossible to be superior . . . even Trumbauer and all them boys he played with, they were all good but he was the best thing among them . . . A record didn't even mean nothin' till he picked up that horn and come in . . . you know that!

If he'd a-been living today, we don't know what his standards or his salary or whatever, uh . . . it might been telephone numbers by now, you know . . . he was such a genius.

But I don't know, sometimes the environment "makes" you, you know . . . They loved him so well . . . and the boy would say, "Well I don't feel so good tonight"— "Oh, come on, man, we'll go to this party!" He never would say "no" and things like that . . . you know . . . and I used to talk to him . . . I'd say, "Well, man, you got to have your own mind sometimes, man. Them cats, they don't mean you no harm or nothing like that." But Bix, he never would say "no," and that's what hurt him.

Bix, he had so much beautiful technique and beautiful things like that he did. Well, I come up from the old rough and tumble days. Probably I had to blow a little louder and a little stronger . . . He didn't have to do that. He just played nice, fine, technical and beautiful notes at all times . . . you know what I mean . . . he was outstanding tone and everything like that . . . but I mean, he was a kind of timid kind of fellow, you know . . . I don't know what would have happen if he was blowing with all these rough characters today, you know . . . but in those days, there

wasn't any finer notes come out of a horn. I don't care who was blowing it. To me, believe it, take it from me, he was a born genius, but they crowded him too much with love . . . wrong cats, you know . . . they didn't say: "Well, why don't you go and get a little sleep tonight?" . . . you know, and they keep going that . . . that . . . we call it "Ignorant Oil" . . . and stuff like that. They wouldn't say, "Well, clean out again." Half the time he didn't eat properly and a whole lot of things like that. He was a very little fellow at that.

How much could you stand in those days? . . . and even right now, you know . . . but if he was with the right cats . . . he would be living right today. It's his friends that killed him.

And certain cats . . . I won't call their names . . . Oh come on, man, they loved him so much, you know . . . they killed him with love. No privacy at all. No privacy at all.

Man, he didn't have a chance to even go home one night and go to sleep. And if he'd go to sleep, they wouldn't say: "Well, why don't you get undressed . . . kind of cool it, and take a shower, bla-bla . . ." You know what I mean, them good old things . . . Oh man, they just get stoned and the boy didn't even have a chance to even live his own life . . . I always say his friends did him wrong, and they killed the goose that laid the golden egg.

But poor Bix, he never would say "no" . . . It's a drag! The boy just "lived" his horn! The environment, could have had him right here today, but they weren't much good themselves. They didn't know what to do with him, how to act . . . they were wild minded characters . . . we wouldn't go into that, but still all they meant well . . . that's one thing you want to realize: they meant well . . . But they didn't know what to do for a fine man like Bix, and I don't care how many styles come up today and all that. There'll never be another Bix Beiderbecke . . . and you take that from Satchmo!

LOUIS ARMSTRONG
© 1971 Miami University, Oxford, Ohio, and Jim Grover
transcription: Albert Haim and Jean Pierre Lion (June 2002)
revised: Dave Bartholomew (July 2002)

3—Duke Ellington on Paul Whiteman:

Paul Whiteman was known as the King of Jazz, and no one as yet has come near carrying that title with more certainty and dignity. He gave up his position with the Denver Symphony to organize and lead a class jazz band. Despite his classical background, he didn't have a snooty bone in his body.

Now there have been those who have come on the scene, grabbed the money, and run off to a plush life of boredom, but nobody held on to his band like Paul Whiteman did. He was always adding interesting musicians to the payroll, without regard to their behavior. All he wanted was to have those giant cats blow, and they blew a storm. He brought them in from all over the country, stars of the years that followed, like Tommy and Jimmy Dorsey, Jack and Charlie Teagarden, Red Nichols, Bix Beiderbecke, Miff Mole, Eddie Lang, Joe Venuti, Roy Bargy, Chester Hazlett, Bill Challis, Ferdie Grofé, and Red Norvo, not to mention singers like Bing Crosby and Mildred Bailey. As we said in *A Drum Is a Woman,* he "dressed her in woodwinds and strings" and made a lady out of jazz.

We knew him way back when we were at the Kentucky Club, which stayed open as long as the cash register rang. It was the after-hours hangout for all the musicians who played in the plushier Broadway places. Paul Whiteman came often as a genuine enthusiast, listened respectfully, said his words of encouragement, very discreetly slipped the piano player a fifty-dollar bill, and very loudly proclaimed our musical merit. . . .

In 1939, Paul Whiteman organized what I think was considered his most successful concert. He had a forty-three-piece orchestra, all hand-picked musicians, none but the best. And he chose several people—Roy Bargy was one, I remember—to write original compositions connected thematically or otherwise with bells. I was honored to be included among them, and my work was "The Blue Belles of Harlem."[1]

EDWARD KENNEDY "DUKE" ELLINGTON
Music Is My Mistress
Doubleday, New York, 1973

4—An obituary by Hugues Panassié:

Grégor's historical magazine *La Revue du Jazz* started in Paris in 1929, and its ninth and last issue was published in March 1930. One month prior, the February issue included the first article of an eighteen-year-old critic: Hugues Panassié. In October 1931, Panassié wrote for *Jazz-Tango* the only serious and analytical obituary to have been published in the months that followed Bix's death.

The announcement of Bix Beiderbecke's death plunged all jazz musicians into despair. We first believed it was a false alarm, as we had heard so often before about Bix. Unfortunately, precise information has been forthcoming, and we even know the day—August 7—when he passed away.

It is impossible to lament this tragic event enough. Bix was not only one of the greatest jazz musicians, an outstanding cornetist and pianist, but also one of the

1. *The Eighth Experiment in Modern American Music* concert at Carnegie Hall in New York on December 25, 1938. "The Blue Belle of Harlem," the second number, was arranged by Fred Van Epps. This concert, featuring Louis Armstrong as a guest-star, is available on a 2-CD set by Nostalgia Arts, no. 303 3025 (2005), www.storyville-records.com.

key players in the development and recognition of *hot* jazz. We are indebted to him more than to any other musician. Without Bix, jazz wouldn't have followed the salutary path on which it is moving today.

His death was accelerated by his own carelessness. In his last years, his robust health was ruined by excessive drinking—and what excess! He sometimes used to drink almost two liters of gin per day. Sent several times to a sanatorium, he resumed his drinking habits as soon as he was left to himself. He reached such a bad physical condition that he was not able to play consistently any more, and he could never, during the last two years, get back to work.

Only twenty-six years [*sic*] of age at the time of his death, he could have still been active for many years and led the most part of jazz musicians, even the greatest ones. We are happy to possess a great number of records he played on, and they must be preserved with care.

Bix was, at the beginning, a miracle of intuition. At a time when all *hot* white musicians hated the way black jazzmen played and despised those who liked it, Bix had the courage—both in will and judgment—to move away from this general feeling, and to go with his friend Muggsy[1]—another great pioneer of the *hot* style—to the Chicago night-clubs, listening to Louis Armstrong, becoming imbued with his playing, and following his way. Like all innovators, they were both scandalously perceived among white musicians. But it did not last. Within two years, all musicians followed their example.

And Bix became famous. He was hired by Jean Goldkette, then by Paul Whiteman. He took part in a huge number of recordings, and was soon compared with Red Nichols, who, until that time, was considered to be the best white cornetist.

Such a comparison was a joke. It was like drawing a parallel between a skillful writer of verse and a poet of genius. One phrase played by Bix on cornet is enough to put all of Red Nichols' choruses in the shade. The former was making *hot* jazz in a natural way, something the latter was desperately trying to give the illusion of. Red Nichols would actually soon copy Bix's playing as much as he could, but with no better results.

It has often been said in Europe that the revelation of Louis Armstrong overshadowed Bix's creation. It was even said that black style made Bix's outdated. No bigger mistake could be made. Bix never wanted to find inspiration in the letter of Louis's playing, but rather in its spirit. He assimilated the pathos in the sound of the great black trumpeter, and he filtered it through his own personality. It is not because he doesn't make use of a "black" vibrato, or of certain typical phrases, that he remains separated from the black style. He is closer to it than Jack Purvis, or Phil Napoleon, even if it's not obvious. . . .

Bix possessed a finely shaded personality which could reflect his sweetness and his vehemence with great precision: in his tone, both strong and extremely pure (I have never heard a cornet played with such a beautiful tone); in his vibrato, both subtle and

1. Hugues Panassié was able to meet Muggsy Spanier in Paris in 1930. The trumpet player was, together with Jimmy Dorsey, a member of the Ted Lewis Orchestra during its European tour.

quivering, and which is so delicate that no one could ever copy it—it seems to be produced not so much with the lips but rather with the heart's beating; and also in his ideas, amazingly clear, that the development of his phrases—which could be powerful or of an almost transparent delicacy—expressed with the highest accuracy.

This outstanding personality was also reflected in Bix's piano playing, but with different means. On this instrument, Bix played on one level only, and the nuance of his feelings was less perceptible, but not less deep. The true Bix can be found in his famous piano solo, "In a Mist." This short piano piece . . . is remarkable by its elusive atmosphere, and also by its compact style, tough, without any compromise. It is undoubtedly one of the finest *hot* jazz creations, and a basic composition. Together with Earl Hines and Joë O'Sullivan [*sic*][2], Bix is certainly the most original pianist, and one worthy of close study.

BIX MADE VERY FEW records on piano, but many on cornet, most of them with Frankie Trumbauer, or with Paul Whiteman, or even leading his own group.

His most famous solos can be heard on "Singin' the Blues," "Riverboat Shuffle," "I'm Coming Virginia," "Mississippi Mud," and "Sweet Sue." Their construction is a model of balance and good taste, subordinated to an inspiration that carries all before it. The records Bix cut with his own band give a more truthful reflection of his idea of *hot* jazz. Ideas of genius, with pure improvisation, in solo or in ensemble, and a very different tone between the ensemble playing at the beginning of the record, very even, and that at the end of the side, driving, with full force, with great heart, to a seemingly impossible climax in which a "totality" is finally achieved.

Unfortunately, Bix was not surrounded by musicians worthy of his talent, and capable of following his example. . . . It is, however, worth noticing that Don Murray and Bill Rank, who might well be quite ordinary musicians, were transformed when playing with Bix. Bill Rank recorded his best solo on "Somebody Stole My Girl" [*sic*] and, with Bix at his side, Don Murray got flashes of inspiration that can't be found in his other recordings. They were both obviously stimulated by the cornetist's generous ardor and unfailing inspiration, and they transcended themselves. Can we imagine records made with more talented musicians? For instance, those Bix used to play with before he got sick: Eddie Condon, on Banjo; Piwie Russel [*sic*] on clarinet; Milton Mesirow on tenor saxophone.[3] Americans who have heard such a group told me it was staggering, which I'm ready to believe.

On top of his talent as a soloist, Bix could lead a *hot* improvisation with a very rare intelligence. To "lead" meaning here, for the one who plays the main part, to orientate the other players, to unite them around him, and to set up, thanks to a given drive, a mysterious communal inspiration. One must listen to Bix's records to appreciate the dominant power which his playing radiates: the tremendous surge at the end of "Goose Pimples," which lifts up the band from the pattern it was in the second before, these phrases sweetly played—but filled with a continuous tension,

2. Original spellings are kept: he is Chicagoan pianist Joe Sullivan.

3. Mesirow is the real family name of Milton "Mezz" Mezzrow.

bursting out suddenly in a deeply moving cry, as in the last chorus of "At the Jazz Band Ball" or in "Ol' Man River," falling away after the break and raising up again eight bars later.

Bix was incredibly gifted to play *hot*, which means: to improvise naturally—but with a deep spiritual work—phrases that inspired an undefinable emotion in the listener. . . . And he was *hot* in a very personal way. It is impossible not to identify his presence on a record from the very first bars. His best emulators, among whom Andy Secrest comes first, are able to copy Bix's familiar phrases, but they are not able to reproduce his emotion, and this is so true that we may wonder whether it is not easier to imitate Louis Armstrong. It is impossible to equal the black trumpet player, but we know from experience that some musicians are able, on an inferior level, to play faithfully in Louis's way. Such a thing never happened with Bix. No one came near, and this is because Bix played, as it were, isolated from other musicians. He didn't care about any existing style, which allowed his already well-defined personality to follow its own development. At a lower level, the white cornetist Jimmy McPartland is another example of a natural and inimitable originality.

In each note played, Bix strongly imparts the mark of his character. Even when he plays badly, because of ideas less brilliant than usual, or because of a declining technique (like on "Futuristic Rhythm," for instance), his characteristic tone remains intact. This is why one can't write off a single bar of his many choruses. Each one, in the shortest quarter rest, truly reflects his talent. The deficiencies can only emphasize the power of his talent.

Among his many qualities, Bix had a most uncommon musical taste, and the way he used the harmony of a tune to create his own melody was often admirable. His outstanding chorus on "Sweet Sue"—apparently simple—is a brilliant example. One question remains: how did Bix manage to link together so beautifully the different elements of his solos? He seemed to be able, without effort, to transmute melodies into much more beautiful phrases, which did not evolve by accident, but which were as tightly linked together as the original tune. The solos played on "Singin' the Blues" and "Mississippi Mud" strongly support this comment. Bix's developments seem to have been traced out in advance, skillfully, but the sound is full of spontaneity. At first hearing, phrases come out and merge together easily, but one sublty feels Bix's high concentration, enjoying his natural ease, but always looking for a step forward, surpassing his usual possibilities. To move ahead is his continuous effort, and it is a true heroism. He could have just enjoyed his talent, and been satisfied with his achievements . . . but he decided to fight, to search for a very painful unity, and to give of his best. This pain makes him so poignant—but without any self-indulgence—and generates these exclamatory phrases, played with such an impressive intensity. He is fully involved in each of his choruses. I used to imagine him blowing beside himself, with a tense, strained expression. Americans visitors later told me it was like that.

In Bix's tone there is a real background of optimism which, blended with his pain, brings to all his recordings a touch that is melancholic, but never in despair. A remaining elation can always be heard, even through his nostalgia, with a surprising strength, as in the final and vehement phrase of his chorus on "Somebody Stole My Girl."

Bix's voice had fallen silent much too early.

Hugues Panassié
Jazz-Tango, no. 13
October 1931

5—A few keys to a very special tone

> "Bix's sound—dull, in the sense that gold is dull, round and polished, totally different from Armstrong's—foreshadows to some extent the aesthetics of 'cool.' Red Nichols, Bobby Hackett tried in vain to capture the tone of Bix's cornet. There is a Bixian sweetness that can't be imitated, a moon glow that can't be reproduced."
>
> Lucien Malson,
> *Des Musiques de Jazz*

The main characteristic of Bix's playing is its originality. In the past, the poor quality of some pressings and the inferior sound reproduction on many 78-rpm and 33-rpm record players led to a loss of much of the sound information contained on the original matrix. High quality digital transfers—made by John R. T. Davies, Michael Kieffer, or Doug Pomeroy—make faithful reproduction of Bix's recordings possible today. They allow us to listen, under great conditions, to the cornetist's melodic daring, and they preserve the particular tone of his instrument in all its fullness.

In his lifetime, Bix played several cornets, but his personal taste led him to pick up an instrument in the catalogue of the two best American brands: Vincent Bach and C. G. Conn.[1] The condition of the Bach Stradivarius no. 620 in the Davenport museum's collections and bought in New York during the spring of 1927, seems to indicate that this cornet was not played much. Bix had a marked preference for the Conn Victor (New Wonder) models produced by C. G. Conn & Co. in Elkhart, Indiana. In photographs of the Wolverine Orchestra (1924), Bix is playing a model Conn Victor 80A—most likely the one he bought from Fritz Putzier in September 1919—while he is holding a model 81A in the picture of the New Yorker band taken three years later, in September 1927.[2]

As its etymology indicates, the cornet is a remote descendant of the primitive horns made out of an animal's horn (*cornu* in Latin), of which it keeps the conic shape. Cornets are based on a slightly conical tube that increases in diameter from its

1. Although these American cornets are longer than European instruments, they are otherwise identical.

2. Bix owned other instruments: he plays a Martin cornet in photographs of the Rhythm Jugglers (Richmond, January 26, 1925), a horn he had probably borrowed for the session; in a promotional photograph taken in May 1928, Bix holds a Herbert Clark cornet made by Holton & Co.—which he may never have used. The origin of the Triumph cornet, which is on display in New Orleans, is not clearly traced.

beginning, and which ends with a bell. They have a mellow, velvety, warm tone, less bright than the trumpet's (based on cylindrical tubing, trumpets have a purer and cleaner tone, and fire across greater distance). The Conn Victor models Bix selected offered a very large bore (.484")—the term *bore* referring to the average inside diameter of the conical tubing. Such instruments did have the warm and veiled tone of cornets, but no woolliness, which went very well with Bix's precise and clear attacks.

The player's lips, pressed against the circular rim of a mouthpiece, vibrate the column of air enclosed in the tube. At the beginning of the twentieth century, the cup of these metal parts was curved in a deep funnel shape, which accentuated the dark and dull tone of the instrument.[3] Bix's famous portrait, taken in January 1924, indicates that he was using the funnel mouthpiece sold by C. G. Conn & Co. for their Victor models.

Bix used B-flat cornets. A metal tube about 53 inches long, either straight or bent at angles, produces a basic low-pitched B-flat tone when blown with a mouthpiece (as the cornet is a transposing instrument, this note is written on the trumpet part one whole step above: C [1]). An experienced player should be able to produce a series of harmonic notes with the same tube, which starts as follows:

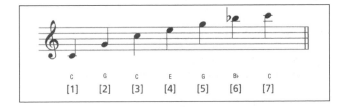

| C | G | C | E | G | B♭ | C |
| [1] | [2] | [3] | [4] | [5] | [6] | [7] |

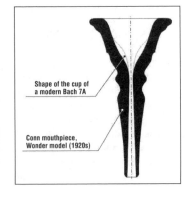

Shape of the cup of a modern Bach 7A

Conn mouthpiece, Wonder model (1920s)

The melodic possibilities offered using only these seven notes are obviously limited. A set of three valves was therefore conceived at the beginning of the nineteenth century: when the player presses a valve, the air blown into the horn is redirected through an extension that drops the overall pitch a fixed interval, allowing thus the production of all middle and missing notes. The first valve (closest to the player) drops the pitch a full step; the middle valve, half a step; and the third one, a step and a half. A traditional fingering technique was developed by music scholars to

3. At the end of the 1920s, brass instruments manufacturer Vincent Bach introduced new mouthpieces designed with bowl-shaped cups. They would quickly become the standard, as they accentuated the brightness of the horns and made it easier to play high—and very high—notes. When used with a cornet, such mouthpieces give the instrument a tone closer to the trumpet's.

allow for the most comfort and create the best-tuned intermediary tone. Starting from the note written C [1] (sound: B♭), this fingering is as follows:

Open			C [1]
2nd valve alone	–½ step	→	B
1st valve alone	–1 step	→	B-flat
1st and 2nd valves	–1½ step	→	A
2nd and 3rd valves	–2 steps	→	G-sharp
1st and 3rd valves	–2½ steps	→	G
1st, 2nd, and 3rd valves	–3 steps	→	F-sharp

The conventional range of the B♭-cornet goes from low-pitched F sharp to high C, and the fingering taught in music schools is indicated as "traditional" on the diagram below:

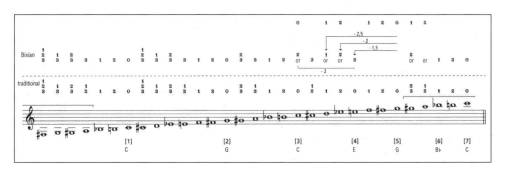

Bix was self-taught. In 1919, he had learned cornet by reproducing Nick La Rocca's playing on the ODJB records by ear, note for note, searching for each one to combine the control of the air blown with a certain position of the valves. This method led to a personal system—whose main characteristic was a lack of system. According to the traditional fingering, A and E are played by depressing valves 1 and 2 together, which drops the pitch a step and a half. A similar result can be achieved by pressing only the third valve. "Bix thought only in terms of concert pitch," said Ray Thurston, a member of the Frank Trumbauer Orchestra at the Arcadia Ballroom in Saint Louis. "He thought of his horn as a concert instrument, with valves 1 and 3 as 'C' instead of 'D' the way most trumpet players think of them. Partially because of this, he rarely played open tones; instead he'd rely to a marked degree on the first and third [valves] together and third alone. This produced a sort of 'jug tone' effect, and gave his phrasing and articulation a different effect from the orthodox players, and it was beautiful to hear. He had no range at all. High 'G' concert—played, by the way, with third valve rather than the standard 1 and 2—was about the limit and not too many of them. But his playing was remarkably accurate. He never sounded strained or lost. He could play anything that he could think."[4]

Bix used the third valve alone to produce even less expected notes. He played an E [4] with valve 3 alone, lowering G [5] a step and a half. E-flat could be played the classic way or with valves 2 and 3, lowering G [5] two steps. The same note, lowered two and a half steps with valves 1 and 3, allowed him to play a D. Finally, E [4] lowered two steps with valves 2 and 3 created a C. While the traditional fingering makes use of the third valve to play a quarter of the notes of the chromatic scale, Bix was using it to produce half of all the notes he played. This peculiarity "often allowed him to bring off with ease passages which might have daunted technically more polished players," as wrote Richard Sudhalter.[5] Randy Sandke added that "these fingerings lend a unique coloring to Bix's phrases, and also result in a less legato flow between notes that we normally hear in jazz trumpet and cornet players. . . . Bix was also adept at using his tongue, and combined with his unique fingerings, his playing takes on a unique sharpness and definition."[6]

The cornet Bix had selected, his personal fingerings, and the characteristics of the mouthpieces sold at that time combined to create his original and moving tone. They have, however, a minor influence. Bix's melodic and harmonic genius blossomed due to two outstanding technical factors: total control of the tonal response he had reached, and his remarkable ear. "He had perfect pitch," clarified Richard Sudhalter, "the ability not only to identify or reproduce a given tone without aid of an instrument, but to relate pitch to key, harmony and timbre in ways beyond the hearing of normal persons."[5]

Sources:

Randy Sandke, *Observing a Genius at Work*, op. cit., pp. 21–23
Richard M. Sudhalter (Art Napoleon), "The Music Goes Down and Around" (*Storyville*, no. 37, October/November 1971, pp. 18–27)
R. Sudhalter, P. Evans, *Bix, Man and Legend*, op. cit. pp. 473–478

Thanks to Patrick Artero, Enrico Borsetti, Marc Richard and Frank van Nus for their effective assistance.

---

4. *Bix, Man and Legend*, op. cit.,
p. 149.

5. *Bix, Man and Legend*, op. cit.,
p. 476.

6. *Observing a Genius at Work*,
op. cit., p. 23.

Appendix 2:
Bix's solo on "Singin' the Blues"

Transcribed by Vincent Cotro in concert pitch.

Appendix 3: Bibliography

References quoted in the text

BOOKS

ARMSTRONG (Louis), *Swing That Music*, introduction by Rudy VALLEE and new foreword by Dan MORGENSTERN, Da Capo Press, New York, 1936, 1993.

ARMSTRONG (Louis), *Ma Vie, Ma Nouvelle-Orléans*, Paris, Julliard, 1952; this translation by Madeleine Gautier was published two years before the American edition: *My Life in New Orleans*, Prentice-Hall, New York, 1954.

ARMSTRONG (Louis), *The Life and Thoughts of Louis Armstrong, a Self-portrait: An Interview by Richard Meryman*, Eakins Press, New York, 1971.

BAKER (Dorothy), *Young Man with a Horn*, Houghton Mifflin, Boston, 1938.

BERGREEN (Laurence), *Louis Armstrong: An Extravagant Life*, Broadway Books, New York, 1997.

BERRETT (Joshua), *Louis Armstrong & Paul Whiteman, Two Kings of Jazz*, Yale University Press, New Haven, CT, 2004.

BERTON (Ralph), *Remembering Bix: A Memoir of the Jazz Age*, Harper & Row, New York, 1974.

BJORN (Lars), GALLERT (Jim), *Before Motown, a History of Jazz in Detroit, 1920–1960*, University of Michigan Press, Ann Arbor, 2001.

BLESH (Rudi), *Shining Trumpets: A History of Jazz*, Alfred A. Knopf, New York, 1946 & 1958 (revised).

CARMICHAEL (Hoagy), *Sometimes I Wonder*, Farrar, Strauss & Giroux, 1965, and Da Capo Press, New York, 1999.

CARMICHAEL (Hoagy), *The Stardust Road*, Rinehart Co., 1946, and Da Capo Press, New York, 1999.

CASTELLI (Vittorio), KALEVELD (Evert, Ted), PUSATERI (Liborio), *The Bix Bands: A Bix Beiderbecke Discobiography*, Raretone, Milan, 1972.

CELINE (Louis-Ferdinand), *Voyage au bout de la nuit*, Denoël et Steele, Paris, 1932.

CHEVALIER (Maurice), *Ma route et mes chansons, tome 2: Londres, Hollywood, Paris*, Julliard, Paris, 1947.

CHILTON (John), *Who's Who of Jazz, Storyville to Swing Street*, Time-Life Records Special Edition, New York, 1978.

CLAXTON (William), *Young Chet*, Gitanes Jazz Productions, Schirmer, 1993.

COLLIER (James Lincoln), *Louis Armstrong*, Oxford University Press, New York, 1983.

CONDON (Eddie), with SUGRUE (Thomas), *We Called It Music: A Generation of Jazz*, H. Holt, 1947, and Da Capo Press, New York, 1992.

CROSBY (Bing), *Call Me Lucky, as told to Pete Martin*, Simon and Schuster, 1953, Da Capo Press, New York, 1993.

CROW (Bill), *Jazz Anecdotes*, Oxford University Press, New York, 1990.

DANCE (Stanley), *The World of Duke Ellington*, Charles Scribner's Sons, New York, 1970.

DAVIS (Charlie), *That Band from Indiana*, Mathom Publishing, New York, 1982.

DEFFAA (Chip), *Voices of the Jazz Age*, University of Illinois Press, Chicago, 1992.

DELAUNAY (Charles), *Hot Discography, 1938 Edition*, Jazz Hot, Paris, 1938.

EVANS (Philip R.), KINER (Larry), *TRAM, The Frank Trumbauer Story, Studies in Jazz no. 18*, Scarecrow Press, Lanham, NJ, 1994.

EVANS (Philip R. and Linda K.), *The Leon Bix Beiderbecke Story*, Prelike Press, Bakersfield, CA, 1998.

FREEMAN (Bud), *Crazeology: The Autobiography of a Chicago Jazzman, as told to Robert Wolf,* University of Illinois Press, Chicago, 1989.

GARA (Larry), *The Baby Dodds Story,* Louisiana State University Press, Baton Rouge, 1959.

GERBER (Alain), *Lester Young,* Fayard, Paris, 2000.

GIDDINS (Gary), *Satchmo,* Doubleday, New York, 1988.

GIDDINS (Gary), *Bing Crosby: A Pocketful of Dreams, The Early Years, 1903–1940,* Little, Brown and Co., New York, 2001.

GOFFIN (Robert), *Histoire du Jazz,* Lucien Parizeau et Cie, Montréal, 1945.

GOFFIN (Robert), *Souvenirs avant l'Adieu,* Institut Jules Destrée, Charleroi, 1980.

GREEN (Benny), *The Reluctant Art, Five Studies in the Growth of Jazz,* Da Capo Press (new edition), New York, 1991.

HADLOCK (Richard), *Jazz Masters of the '20s,* MacMillan Publishing Co., New York, 1972.

HILBERT (Robert), *"Pee Wee" Russell: The Life of a Jazzman,* Oxford University Press, New York, 1993.

HILL (Dick), *Sylvester Ahola, The Gloucester Gabriel,* Scarecrow Press, Lanham, NJ, 1993.

HODEIR (André), *Introduction à la musique de jazz,* Librairie Larousse, Paris, 1948.

Histoire de la Musique, vol. 2, Coll. "la Pléiade," Gallimard, Paris, 1963.

JAMES (Burnett), *Bix Beiderbecke,* Barnes & Co., New York, 1961.

JONES (Max), *Jazz Talking,* Da Capo Press Edition, New York, 2000.

KAMINSKY (Max), with V. E. HUGHES, *My Life in Jazz,* Harper & Row, New York, 1963.

KENNEDY (Rick L.), *Jelly Roll, Bix and Hoagy,* Indiana University Press, Chicago, 1994.

MANONE (Wingy), with Paul VANDERVOORT II, *Trumpet on the Wing,* Doubleday, Garden City, NY, 1964.

MARNAT (Marcel), *Maurice Ravel,* Fayard, 1986.

MARX (Groucho), *Groucho and Me,* Bernard Geis Associates, New York, 1959.

MAZZOLETTI (Adriano), *Eddie Lang, Stringin' the Blues,* Editoriale Pantheon, Rome, 1997.

MEZZROW (Milton "Mezz"), with Bernard WOLFE, *Really the Blues,* Random House, New York, 1946.

PAILLER (Alain), *Plaisir d'Ellington,* Actes Sud, Arles, 1998.

PANASSIÉ (Hugues), *Le Jazz Hot,* Éditions R.-A. Corrêa, Paris, 1934.

PANASSIÉ (Hugues), *Douze Années de Jazz, (1927–1938), Souvenirs,* Éditions Corrêa, Paris, 1946.

PANASSIÉ (Hugues), *La Véritable Musique de Jazz,* Robert Laffont, Paris, 1946.

PANASSIÉ (Hugues), *Dictionnaire du Jazz,* Albin Michel, Paris, 1971.

POSTIF (François), *Jazz Me Blues,* Éditions Outre Mesure, Paris, 1999.

RAYNO (Don), *Paul Whiteman, Pioneer in American Music, Volume I: 1890–1930,* Scarecrow Press, Lanham, NJ, 2003.

SANDKE (Randy), *Bix Beiderbecke, Observing a Genius at Work,* self-published, 1996.

SCHULLER (Gunther), *Early Jazz: It's Roots and Musical Development,* Oxford University Press, New York, 1968.

SHAPIRO (Nat), HENTOFF (Nat), *Hear Me Talkin' to Ya,* Rinehart Co., 1955, and Dover, New York, 1966.

SPENCER (Frederick J.), *Jazz and Death,* University Press of Mississippi, Jackson, 2002.

STEWART (Rex), *Jazz Masters of the '30s,* Da Capo Press Edition, New York, 1972.

SUDHALTER (Richard M.), EVANS (Philip R.), MYATT (William Dean), *Bix, Man and Legend,* Arlington House Publishers, London, 1974, and Schirmer Books, New York, 1975.

SUDHALTER (Richard M.), *Lost Chords,* Oxford University Press, New York, 1999.

SUDHALTER (Richard M.), *Stardust Melody, The Life and Music of Hoagy Carmichael,* Oxford University Press, New York, 2002.

TÉNOT (Frank), *Boris Vian, Jazz à Saint-Germain,* Editions du Layeur, Paris, 1999.

TERCINET (Alain), *West Coast Jazz,* Parenthèses, Marseille, 1986.

TOLEDANO (Ralph de), *Frontiers of Jazz,* Oliver Durrell, Inc., New York, 1947.

VACHÉ (Warren W.), *Jazz Gentry, Aristocrats of the Music World,* Scarecrow Press and Institute of Jazz Studies, Lanham, NJ, 1999.

WARD (Geoffrey C.), BURNS (Ken), *Jazz: A History of America's Music*, Alfred A. Knopf, New York, 2000.

WAREING (Charles H.), GARLICK (George), *Bugles for Beiderbecke*, Sidgwick and Jackson Limited, London, 1958.

WATERS (Ethel), with Charles SAMUEL, *His Eye is on the Sparrow*, Doubleday, New York, 1951.

STUDIES, ARTICLES, THESES

ARPY (Jim), "Remembering Bix," *Quad-City Times*, Davenport, IA, July 24, 1988.

BEALL (George), "Jean Goldkette," in *Swing Music*, October (part 1) and November 1935 (part 2).

Bix, a Discographical Society's Pamphlets, published by R. G. V. VENABLES and Clifford JONES; *Some Notes on the Fallacy of Bix Beiderbecke's Declining Years*, by GROVE (Thurman and Mary).

Davenport Sunday Democrat, February 10, 1929: "'Jazz Is Musical Humor,'" Says Davenport Composer and Cornetist of Whiteman's Band," an interview with Bix Beiderbecke.

DELAUNAY (Charles), "Bix's Cornet," in *Swing Music*, April 1936.

ESPOSITO (Bill), "Princeton U . . . ," *Princeton Alumni Weekly*, February 26, 1974; letter by Charles L. Smith in issue dated April 23, 1974.

FOURQUET (Philippe), *De l'Impressionnisme dans le Jazz*, thesis at the Paris-Sorbonne (Paris IV) University, 1993.

GENTIEU (Norman P.), "Memories of Bix (from Harrington Archive)," in *IAJRC Journal*: Part 1, no. 25/4 (autumn 1992); Part 2, no. 26/3 (summer 1993); Part 3, no. 27/3 (summer 1994).

GERBER (Alain), "Bix Beiderbecke: Des garçons sages et plutôt bien élevés," in *Fiesta in Blue(1)*, Éditions Alive, 1998.

HIBBS (Leonard), "A Poor Tribute to a Great Artist," in *Swing Music*, August 1935, pp. 146–147.

HOEFER (George), "Studies for a biography of Bix Beiderbecke: notes, correspondence, articles . . . ," a file kept at the Institute of Jazz Studies, Rutgers University, Newark, NJ.

Jazz Hot, no. 81, October 1953: MALSON (Lucien) and HESS (Jacques B.), "Regards sur le jazz de Bix," p. 10.

Jazz Hot, no. 86, March 1954: "Boris VIAN's Revue de Presse," in VIAN (Boris), *Oeuvres Complètes, VI*, Fayard, Paris, 1999, p. 411.

Jazz Hot, no. 107, February 1956: "Boris VIAN's Revue de Presse," in VIAN (Boris), *Oeuvres Complètes, VI*, Fayard , Paris, 1999, p. 496.

Jazz Hot, no. 116, December 1956: MALSON (Lucien), "Les Sillons de L'Histoire (IV): 'Singin' the Blues,'" in *Des Musiques de Jazz*, Parenthèses, 1988.

Jazzman no. 38, July-August 1998: TERCINET (Alain), "Voyage en Bixieland."

JOHNSON (George L.), "Wolverine Days," in *Swing Music*, autumn 1936.

KAY (Brad), "'Cradle of Love' and Bix Beiderbecke," booklet of the Timeless CD CBC-1-066: *Ray Miller and his Brunswick Orchestra, 1924–1929*.

La Revue du Jazz, no. 5, November 1929: VENTURA (Ray), "Ce que mes yeux ont vu . . ."; *La Revue du Jazz*, no. 6–7, January 1930: VENTURA (Ray), "Une heure avec Paul Whiteman."

Metronome, A Tribute to Bix, November 1938: "The Greatest Gent I've Ever Known," by WHITEMAN (Paul); "His Heart Was Ahead of His Lips!," by RISKIN (Irving); "The End, Not the Means interested Bix," by CONDON (Eddie); "High School Days with Bix," by ROHLF (Wayne H.); "Nutsy Musician," by CARMICHAEL (Hoagy); "Bix," by TRUMBAUER (Frank); "Bix, The White Pioneer of True Hot Style!," by PANASSIÉ (Hugues).

The Mississippi Rag, May 1980: KLINE (Jerry), "Chauncey Morehouse."

The Mississippi Rag, December 1988: DEFFAA (Chip), "Bill Challis: the Goldkette Years."

The Mississippi Rag, January 1989: DEFFAA (Chip), "Bill Challis: The Whiteman Years."

The Mississippi Rag, November 1991: "Steve Brown's Story," an interview with Steve Brown by J. Lee ANDERSON.

MOORE (Vic), "Bix—As I Knew Him," in *Swing Music*, March 1936.

MURPHY (Frank), "Bix Beiderbecke and the Jean Goldkette Orchestra," *Musicology Australia,* Volume VIII, 1985.

MURPHY (Frank), "The Recordings by Bix Beiderbecke and His Gang," *Jazzforschung-Jazz Research* 17 (1985), Institut für Jazzforschung, Graz, Austria.

MURPHY (Frank), "Bix Beiderbecke as a Jazz Pianist," *Jazzforschung-Jazz Research* 19 (1987), Institut für Jazzforschung, Graz, Austria.

MURPHY (Frank), "Bix Beiderbecke, Composer for the Pianoforte," *Jazzforschung-Jazz Research* 21 (1989), Institut für Jazzforschung, Graz, Austria.

PREBLE (Charlie), "Bix Beiderbecke as I knew him," in *Tempo,* August 1936.

SCHOLL (Warren W.), "Bix's Tragic Death Marred Brilliant Career," *Down Beat,* December 1935–January 1936.

Storyville no. 9, February/March 1967: "A Letter from Bix."

Storyville no. 12, August/September 1967: SUDHALTER (Richard M., as Art NAPOLEON), "Heresey, Hearsay & Humbug: Bix and the Discographers"; "Why Bix? An appraisal"; "Davenport Days: Vera Cox Reminisces"; "Larry Andrews' Letters"; "Bill Challis Speaks Out"; "Stanley 'Doc' Ryker: A band like nothing you ever heard (I)".

Storyville no. 13, October/November 1967: "Stanley 'Doc' Ryker: A band like nothing you ever heard(2)."

Storyville no. 23, June/July 1969: KUMM (Bob), "Further Facets of Fats."

Storyville no. 59, June/July 1975: HOUSTON (Reagan) and RINGO (Roger), "A Visit to Smith Ballew."

Storyville no. 60, August/September 1975: PLATH (Warren K.), "Marion McKay and his Orchestra."

Storyville no. 120, August/September 1985: BROWN (Lawrence), "Jimmie's Joys."

Storyville no. 122, December 1985–January 1986: PLATH (Warren K.), "Don Murray, The Early Years (1904–1923)."

SUDHALTER (Richard M.), *Bix Beiderbecke, Giants of Jazz,* booklet included in the 3-LP set, Time-Life Books Inc., 1979.

TARBY (Russ), "Spiegle Willcox: The Sweet Man," in *Syracuse New Times,* 1998.

WILLIAMS (Martin), "Bix Beiderbecke and the White Man's Burden," *Jazz,* May/June 1964.

Other published Bix references:

BOOKS

ALLEN (Walter C.), *Hendersonia: The Music of Fletcher Henderson,* self-published, 1973.

BALLIETT (Whitney), *Such Sweet Thunder,* The Bobbs-Merrill Company, 1966.

BARNHART (Scotty), *The World of Jazz Trumpet,* Hal Leonard, Milwaukee, 2005.

BERENDT (Joachim-Ernst), *Une Histoire du Jazz,* Fayard, Paris, 1976: *Chicago,* by Werner BURKHARDT.

BIGARD (Barney), *With Louis and the Duke,* Oxford University Press, New York, 1986.

BRUNN (H. O.), *The Story of the Original Dixieland Jazz Band,* Louisiana State University Press, 1960.

BÜCHMANN-MØLLER (Frank), *Is This to Be My Souvenir?—Photos from the Timme Rosenkrantz Collection,* Odense University Press, Denmark, 2000.

CARLES (Philippe), CLERGEAT (André), COMOLLI (Jean-Louis), *Dictionnaire du Jazz,* Bouquins, Robert Laffont, Paris, 2000/6; *Bix Beiderbecke* by Frank TÉNOT.

COLLIER (James Lincoln), *The Making of Jazz: A Comprehensive History,* Houghton Mifflin, London, 1978.

COLLINS (David R.), *Bix Beiderbecke, Jazz Age Genius, "Notable Americans,"* Morgan Reynolds Inc., Greensboro, NC, 1998.

COLLINS (David R.), JOHNSON (Rich), SPEER (Mary Louise), WILLARD (John), *Davenport: Jewel of the Mississippi,* Arcadia Publishing, 2000.

CONDON (Eddie), GEHMAN (Richard), *Eddie Condon's Treasury of Jazz,* Dial Press, NY, 1956; *Bix,* by George AVAKIAN, Otis FERGUSON, and Eddie CONDON.

CONDON (Eddie), O'NEAL (Hank), *Eddie Condon's Scrapbook of Jazz*, Galahad Books, New York, 1973.

DELONG (Thomas A.), *"Pops": Paul Whiteman, King of Jazz*, New Win Publishers, Piscataway, NJ, 1983.

DOUGLAS (Ann), *Terrible Honesty: Mongrel Manhattan in the 1920s*, Noonday Press, New York, 1995.

DRIGGS (Frank), LEWINE (Harris), *Black Beauty, White Heat*, William Morrow and Co., New York, 1982.

EGAN (Bill), *Florence Mills, Harlem Jazz Queen*, Scarecrow Press, Lanham, NJ, 2004.

ELLINGTON (Edward Kennedy "Duke"), *Music Is My Mistress*, Doubleday, New York, 1973.

FOSTER (Pops), *The Autobiography of a New Orleans Jazzman, as Told to Tom Stoddard*, University of California Press, Berkeley, 1971.

GOFFIN (Robert), *Aux Frontières du Jazz*, Éditions du Sagittaire, Paris, 1932.

GRACYK (Tim), *Popular American Recording Pioneers, 1895–1925*, Haworth Press, New York, 2000.

HARDIE (Daniel), *Exploring Early Jazz*, Writers Club Press, 2002.

JONES (LeRoi), *Blues People*, Morrow, New York, 1963.

KEEPNEWS (Orrin), GRAUER (Bill), *A Pictorial History of Jazz*, Spring Books, London, n. d.

KENNEY (William Holland), *Jazz on the River*, The University of Chicago Press, 2005.

KENNEY (William Howland), *Chicago Jazz: A Cultural History, 1904–1930*, Oxford University Press, New York, 1993.

LARKIN (Philip), *Reference Back: Uncollected Jazz Writings 1940–84*, University of Hull Press, 1999.

LASTELLA (Aldo), *La Vita, la leggenda di Bix Beiderbecke*, Nuovi Equilibri, Roma, 1991.

LEVIN (Floyd), *Classic Jazz*, University of California Press, Berkeley, 2000.

MAGEE (Jeffrey), *Fletcher Henderson, the Uncrowned King of Swing*, Oxford University Press, New York, 2005.

MALSON (Lucien), *Histoire du jazz et de la musique afro-américaine*, Union Générale d'Éditions, 1976.

MILLER (Mark), *Some Hustling This!*, The Mercury Press, Toronto, 2005.

MITCHELL (Raymond F.), *Feeling My Way: A Discography of Eddie Lang*, self-published, 2002.

MORGENSTERN (Dan), *Living with Jazz*, Pantheon Books, New York, 2004.

MORRIS (Ronald L.), *Wait Until Dark: Jazz and the Underworld, 1880–1940*, Bowling Green University Popular Press, Bowling Green, OH, 1980.

MOSBROOK (Joe), *Cleveland Jazz History*, Northeast Ohio Jazz Society, Cleveland, 2003.

PERETTI (Burton W.), *The Creation of Jazz*, University of Illinois Press, Chicago, 1992.

PRIDMORE (Jay), *Many Hearts and Many Hands: The History of Ferry Hall and Lake Forest Academy*, Lake Forest Academy,1994.

RAMSEY (Frederic, Jr.), SMITH (Charles Edward), *Jazzmen*, Harcourt, Brace & Cy, New York, 1939; *Bix Beiderbecke*, by Edward J. NICHOLS.

RÉDA (Jacques), *Autobiographie du Jazz*, Éditions Climats, 2002.

RUST (Brian), *Jazz and Ragtime Records, 1897–1942*, Mainspring Press, Denver, 2002.

RUST (Brian), LAIRD (Ross), *Discography of Okeh Records, 1918–1934*, Praeger Publishers, Westport, CT, 2004.

SHAPIRO (Nat), HENTOFF (Nat), *The Jazz Makers*, Holt, Rinehart and Winston, 1957; *Bix Beiderbecke*, by George HOEFER.

SHAW (Arnold), *52nd Street: The Street of Jazz*, Da Capo Press, New York, 1971.

SHAW (Arnold), *The Jazz Age: Popular Music in the 1920's*, Oxford University Press, New York, 1989.

SCHEUER (Klaus), *Bix Beiderbecke, Sein Leben, Seine Musik, Seine Schallplatten*, Oreos, Waakirchen-Schaftlach, 1995.

SCHIEDT (Duncan), *The Jazz State of Indiana*, Indiana Historical Society, 1999 (1st ed. 1977).

SCHIEDT (Duncan), *Twelve Lives in Jazz*, Delta Publishing, Parma, 1996.

SCHLEMAN (Hilton R.), *Rhythm on Record*, published by *Melody Maker*, London, 1936.

SHIPTON (Alan), *A New History of Jazz*, Continuum, London and New York, 2001.

SIMON (George T.), *Simon Says: The Sights and Sounds of the Swing Era, 1935–1955*, Arlington House, 1971.

SIMOSKO (Vladimir), *Artie Shaw: A Musical Biography and Discography*, Scarecrow Press, Lanham, NJ, 2000.

SMITH (Jay D.), GUTTRIDGE (Len), *Jack Teagarden: The Story of a Jazz Maverick*, Cassell, London, 1962.

STEARNS (Marshall), *The Story of Jazz*, Oxford University Press, New York, 1958.

SUTTON (Alan), NAUCK (Kurt), *American Record Labels and Companies, an Encyclopedia (1891–1943)*, Mainspring Press, Denver, 2000.

TEN HOVE ("Boy"), *Caricatures, Drawings of Jazz Musicians (1935–1940)*, Uitgeverij Aprilis, Holland, 2006.

TERKEL (Studs), *Giants of Jazz*, New Press, New York, 1957, 1975.

TRAVIS (Dempsey J.), *An autobiography of Black Jazz*, Urban Research Institute, Chicago, 1983.

TURNER (Frederick), *1929: A Novel of the Jazz Age*, Counterpoint, New York, 2003.

ULANOV (Barry), *The History of Jazz in America*, New York, 1957.

WATERS (Howard J.), *Jack Teagarden's Music* (foreword by Paul Whiteman), published by Walter C. Allen, New Jersey, 1960.

WHITBURN (Joel), *Pop Memories, 1890–1954*, Record Research Inc., 1986.

WHITBURN (Joel), *A Century of Pop Music*, Record Research Inc., 1999.

WHITE (John), *Artie Shaw: His Life and Music*, Continuum, London and New York, 1998, 2004.

WHYATT (Bert), *Muggsy Spanier, the Lonesome Road*, Jazzology Press, New Orleans, 1995.

YANOW (Scott), *Trumpet Kings: The Players Who Shaped the Sound of Jazz Trumpet*, Backbeat Books, San Francisco, 2001.

YANOW (Scott), *Classic Jazz: The Musicians and Recordings that Shaped Jazz*, Backbeat Books, San Francisco, 2001.

YANOW (Scott), *Jazz on Record: The First Sixty Years*, Backbeat Books, San Francisco, 2003.

STUDIES, ARTICLES, THESES

BESSOM (Malcolm E.), "The Davenport Legend, Bix Beiderbecke," in *Jazz*, (1963?).

CARMICHAEL (Hoagy), in *Metronome*: "The Boys Who Broke the Ground" (July 1933), "The Jazz Pioneers Are Passing" (August 1933).

Catfish Jazz Society, November 1989: "Omer Van Speybroeck: Jazz Man"; December 1990 and January 1991: "The Jazz Man's Memory Book" (Glenn SEARS).

Down Beat, May 1939: "Bernie Cummins Gave Bix the Push to Fame!," by Milton KARLE.

Down Beat, May 15, 1940: "Story of Emmet Hardy told by New Orleans Musicians," by Dave DEXTER, Jr.

Down Beat, April 15, 1942: "Frankie Trumbauer recalls the good old days . . . ," by Frankie TRUMBAUER.

Down Beat, June 24, 1956: "Trumbauer and the No. 1 Jazz Legend," by Russ WILSON.

Down Beat, August 1961: "The Happy Summer," by Gilbert M. ERSKINE.

EDEY (Mait), "Bix Beiderbecke," in *Jazz Panorama*, Collier Books, New York, 1964.

FERGUSON (Otis), "Hear Them Right: Young Man with a Horn," *The New Republic*, July 29, 1936.

FERGUSON (Otis), "Hear Them Right: Young Man with a Horn Again," *The New Republic*, November 18, 1940.

GOFFIN (Robert), "Bix at Lake Forest," in *Esquire*, March 1944.

HENTOFF (Nat), "Bix Beiderbecke's Pure Sound Cuts through Time," JVC Jazz Festival, 2003.

HOEFER (George), "The Hot Box: Frank Trumbauer," in *Down Beat*, July 25, 1956.

HUG (Armand), "The Bix Hardy Story," *Jazz Journal*, December 1950.

JACKSON (Robert E., Jr.), "Bix Beiderbecke: His influences and playing style with the Wolverines," *Jazz Research Papers*, NAJE, 1983.

JACKSON (Robert E., Jr.), "Bix: What made him unique?," *Jazz Research Papers*, NAJE, 1984.

Jazz Hot, no. 1, March 1935: "Leon 'Bix' Beiderbecke," by Charles DELAUNAY, pp. 17–21.

Jazz Hot, no. 6, November/December 1935: "Souvenirs de Bix Beiderbecke," by Marshall W. STEARNS.

Jazz Hot, no. 12 (2nd part), January 1947: "Quand les blancs jouent hot," by Franck TÉNOT.

Jazz Hot, no. 22 (2nd part), April 1948: "Propos sur une musique," by Lucien MALSON.

Jazz Hot, no. 42, Special issue 1950: "Regards en arrière," by Michel ANDRICO.

Jazz Hot, no. 58, September 1951: "Bix Beiderbecke," by Michel ANDRICO.

Jazz Hot, no. 69, September 1952: "Bix Beiderbecke de 1927 à 1929."

Jazz Magazine, no. 119, July/August 1956: "Leon Bix Beiderbecke, le premier génie blanc," by Frank TÉNOT.

Joslin's Jazz Journal, February 1998: "Remembering Bix at Lake Forest Academy," by Bill SAUNDERS; November 1998: "Bix at Lake Forest Academy, 1921–1922," by Bill SAUNDERS.

Joslin's Jazz Journal, November 1999: "Bix Beiderbecke, Hudson Lake, Indiana," by Bill SAUNDERS.

LANG (Eddie), "Hello, Rhythm Fiends!," in *Rhythm*, September 1932.

LEE (Amy), " 'Goldkette Band Greatest of Them All!' so Claim Graduates of Famed '20's Outfit," in *Metronome*, June 1940; "Goldkette Band Rocked Floors in Summer," in *Metronome*, July 1940; "Jan Garber Cut Jean Goldkette's Band!," in *Metronome*, August 1940.

Melody Maker, September 1931: "Sad News for Trumpet Players" (Bix's obituary).

The Mississippi Rag, June 1978: "Changes . . . Paul Whiteman," by William J. SCHAFER.

The Mississippi Rag, September 1978: "Doc Ryker's Story," by Jerry KLINE.

The Mississippi Rag, September 1979: "Bill Rank Plays Last Gig . . . ," by Bob HARRINGTON.

The Mississippi Rag, February 1982: "Hoagy Carmichael . . . Some Afterthoughts," by Duncan P. SCHIEDT.

The Mississippi Rag, July 1987: "Jimmy McPartland's Story (part 1)," by Chip DEFFAA; (part 2): August 1987.

The Mississippi Rag, April 1988: "Frank Trumbauer: Master Musician," by Jerry KLINE.

The Mississippi Rag, March 1992: "Joe Venuti: The Clown Prince of Jazz," by Bob PATRY.

The Mississippi Rag, July 1992: "Martha (Boswell) and Emmet, Louis and Bix," by J. Lee ANDERSON.

The Mississippi Rag, February 1994: "On the Road to Eastwood Lane," by William J. SCHAFER.

The Mississippi Rag, June 1995: "Spiegle (Willcox) at 92," by Ron Dean JOHNSON.

The Mississippi Rag, October 1997: "Bing Crosby and Jazz," by Arne FOGEL.

The Mississippi Rag, September 1998: "Conversations with George Brunies," by Dan HAVENS and Thomas B. GILMORE.

The Mississippi Rag, October 1999: "Farewell, Spiegle (Willcox) . . . ," by Jim LEIGH.

The Mississippi Rag, November 1999: "Hoagy (Carmichael) 100th Year," by Phillip D. ATTEBERRY.

The Mississippi Rag, September 2001: "Miff Mole's Final Notes," by Peter PEPKE.

The Mississippi Rag, September 2002: "Bix and the Day the NY Twins Died," by Phil POSPYCHALA.

The Mississippi Rag, March 2003: "Bix Beiderbecke: His Centennial Year," by Chip DEFFAA; "Of Bix and Bubber," by Mike SLACK.

The Mississippi Rag, June 2003: "Copying Bix: Cornet Solos from Bix Beiderbecke's First Three Recording Sessions," by Albert HAIM.

The Mississippi Rag, March 2005: "Bix at 1600 Broadway," by Albert HAIM.

PERHONIS (John Paul), *The Bix Beiderbecke Story: The jazz musician in legend, fiction and fact;* thesis from the University of Minnesota, March 1978.

QUICKSELL (Howdy), "Jean Goldkette, Pioneer of Swing," reprinted from June 1939 issue of *Swing*.

La Revue du Jazz, no. 2, August 1929: *Trois vedettes du phono: Red Nichols, Bix Beiderbeck et Lou Armstrong* (sic), by Philippe BRUN.

RIVELLI (Pauline), "What's in a Name," in *Jazz*, December 1962.

SCHEUER (Klaus), *Zur Improvisationweise des Kornettisten Bix Beiderbecke*, Darmstädter Jazzforum 89, pp. 67–84.

SCHOLL (Warren W.), in *Melody Maker:* "Frankie Trumbauer" (March 17, 1934), "Introducing Bill

Rank" (April 21, 1934), "Bix, the Irreplaceable" (December 1, 1934); in *Down Beat*: "Trumbauer Still Greatest White Alto Sax Man" (November 1935), "Bix's Tragic Death Marred Brilliant Career" (December 1935–January 1936), "Challis Recalls Bix Got Fed Up With Grofé" (July 1938), "What Broke up Goldkette's Band?" (August 1939); booklet for the *Bix Beiderbecke Memorial Album* (Victor & Co., July 1936); in *American Music Lover*: "Complete Discography of Bix Beiderbecke" (October 1937, part 1; November 1937, part 2).

The Second Line, Vol. 7, New Orleans Jazz Club, March/April 1956: "The Guy Who Held Bix's Horn: The Story of Fred Rollison," by George W. KAY.

The Second Line, Vol. 27, New Orleans Jazz Club, Spring 1975: "Everybody Loves My Baby, Bix and Louis, NYC, Fall 1924," by Gilbert M. ERSKINE.

SMITH (Charles Edward), "Source of Bix's Discussed: Oliver, Armstrong or La Rocca?," in *Tempo*, June 1936.

SMITH (Ernest), "The Bix Years," in *Record Research*, Vol. 2, no. 3, July/August 1956.

STEARNS (Marshall W.), "The Gods of Swing, an Essay in Memoriam" (1935?), on file at the Institute of Jazz Studies, Rutgers University, Newark, NJ; in *Down Beat*: "Fetch that Gin Son" (September 1935), "Swing Musicians Slightly Balmy" (October 1935); in *Jazz Hot,* no. 6: "Souvenirs de Bix Beiderbecke" (November/December 1935).

St. Louis Post-Dispatch, September 24, 1972: "Bix Beiderbecke: Updating the Legend," by Tom YARBROUGH.

Storyville, no. 19, October/November 1968: "Laurie Wright: Talking to Bill Rank."

Storyville, no. 20, December 1968–January 1969: "Laurie Wright: Talking to Bill Rank(2)."

Storyville, no. 27, February/March 1970: "Pee Wee Russell Writes on Sterling Base."

Storyville, no. 29, June/July 1970: "Did Bix Record with Sunny Clapp?," by Peter TANNER.

Storyville, no. 37, October 1971: "The Music Goes Down and Round," by Richard M. SUDHALTER (as Art Napoleon).

Storyville, no. 39, February/March 1972: "Aw, Get a Piccolo: Jazz Horns, Short and Long," by Richard M. SUDHALTER (as Art Napoleon).

Storyville, no. 159, September 1994: "Spiegle Willcox, Goldkette and All That Jazz," by Hans EEKHOFF.

Storyville, 2000–2001: "The New Orleans Rhythm Kings," by Tom BUHMANN.

VENABLES (R. G. V.), "Connoisseurs' Corner," in *Rhythm*, July 1939; "Bixology," in *Melody Maker*, August 5, 1939.

YOUNGREN (William H.), "Bix," *Hudson Review*, vol. 28, no. 1, Spring 1975.

ZENNI (Stefano), *Quando il grande Bix si offriva come amico* (study on "I'll Be a Friend with Pleasure), n.d.

Appendix 4: Discography

The main instruments are abbreviated as usual: (c): cornet—(tp): trumpet—(tb): trombone—(cl): clarinet—(as): alto saxophone—(Cms): C-melody saxophone—(ts): tenor saxophone—(bar): baritone saxophone—(bsx): bass saxophone—(reeds): reed section—(vln): violin—(bj): banjo—(g): guitar—(p): piano—(cel): celeste—(tu): tuba—(sb): string bass—(dm): drums—(perc): percussion—(voc): vocals; the names of instruments not listed here are not abbreviated.

The use of a cornet equipped with a mute has been specified in the case of Bix Beiderbecke:

—straight mute: *dry mute (most often in the shape of a cone and inserted in the bell)*;
—derby mute: *hat held in front of the bell*;
—Harmon mute: *developed in the early 1920s by Dave Harmon, owner of the Dreamland Ballroom, this closed mute attempted to reproduce the wa-wa sound achieved by King Oliver by combining a straight mute and a plunger.*

The number of bars in each solo is indicated in parentheses after the musician's name; the instrument played is given in some peculiar cases. Bix Beiderbecke playing open cornet is simply indicated as "Bix," and Frank Trumbauer playing C-melody sax is indicated as "Tram."

When more than one take of a number was issued, the matrix number of the original 78-RPM record is italicized, for example:

BVE 36829-2 Sunday: alternate take
BVE 36829-3 Sunday: master take

This discography is based on the works of Philip R. Evans and William Dean-Myatt (Bix, Man and Legend, 1974), Marc Richard and Philippe Baudoin (Intégrale Bix Beiderbecke, Masters of Jazz, 1991–1995), Philip R. and Linda K. Evans (The Leon Bix Beiderbecke Story, 1998), and Don Rayno (Paul Whiteman, Pioneer in American Music, 2003); the research done by Richard M. Sudhalter and Scott Wenzel and their team for the release of the Mosaic set, The Complete Okeh and Brunswick Bix Beiderbecke Sessions (2001), was of great help, as were Brad Kay's discoveries and the expertise of many participants on Albert Haim's internet Forum.

1: February 18, 1924   **GENNETT (IN)**

WOLVERINE ORCHESTRA

Bix Beiderbecke (c), Al Gandee (tb), Jimmy Hartwell (cl), George Johnson (ts), Dick Voynow (p), Bob Gillette (bj), Min Leibrook (tu), Vic Moore (dm)

11751-A   **Fidgety Feet** (La Rocca-Shields)
              solos: Hartwell (2)—Gandee (2)—Bix (2)—
              Hartwell (14)—Gillette (2)
11754-A   **Jazz Me Blues** (Delaney)
              solos: Hartwell (2+4)—Bix (20)—Gandee
              (2+4)—Gillette (2)—Johnson (4)

2: May 6, 1924   **GENNETT (IN)**

WOLVERINE ORCHESTRA

Bix Beiderbecke (c), Jimmy Hartwell (cl), George Johnson (ts), Dick Voynow (p), Bob Gillette (bj/g), Min Leibrook (tu), Vic Moore (dm)

11852   **Oh Baby!** (Donaldson-DeSylva)
              solos: Bix (30)—Gillette, bj (8)—Johnson (30)—
              Hartwell (16)
11853   **Copenhagen** (Davis-Melrose)
              solos: Hartwell (12)—Johnson (12)—Bix (6+8)—
              Hartwell (2)—Leibrook (4+4)—Gillette, g (2)
11854-C   **Riverboat Shuffle** (Carmichael-Voynow-Mills)
              solos: Voynow (2)—Bix (2+30+2)—Hartwell
              (2)—Gillette, g (2)—Johnson (2)
11855-A   **Susie** (Naset-Kahn)
11855-B   **Susie**
              solos: Johnson (30)—Gillette, bj (16)—Moore
              (8)—Bix, leads (32)

3: June 20, 1924   **GENNETT (IN)**

WOLVERINE ORCHESTRA

Bix Beiderbecke (c), Jimmy Hartwell (cl), George Johnson (ts), Dick Voynow (p), Bob Gillette (bj), Min Leibrook (tu), Vic Moore (dm)

11930-B   **I Need Some Pettin'** (King-Fiorito-Kahn)
              solos: Bix (32)—Johnson (30)
11931-C   **Royal Garden Blues** (Williams-Williams)
              solos: Bix (12)—Hartwell (12)
11932   **Tiger Rag** (La Rocca)
              solos: Hartwell (8+2+2+2)—Bix (2+32)—
              Johnson (2)

During the final seconds of the recording of "Tiger Rag" released by the Starr-Gennett Foundation (*Gennett Records Greatest Hits-Volume II*), one of the musicians (Bix?) says a few words, which might be "It sounds better" or "Use that take."

4: September 18, 1924   **GENNETT (NY)**

WOLVERINE ORCHESTRA

Bix Beiderbecke (c/p?), George Brunies (tb/kazoo or tb/mouthpiece), Jimmy Hartwell (cl), George Johnson (ts), Dick Voynow (p), Bob Gillette (bj), Min Leibrook (tu), Vic Moore (dm)

9079   **Sensation** (Edwards)
              solos: Bix (16+2)—Johnson (2)—Hartwell (16)
9080-A   **Lazy Daddy** (La Rocca-Shields-Ragas)
9080-B   **Lazy Daddy**
              solos: Leibrook (1)—Bix (2)—Hartwell (2)—
              Leibrook (2)—Johnson (2)—Brunies, kazoo
              (16)—Johnson (2)—Bix (2)

Philip R. Evans indicates that Bix plays piano during George Brunies's solo.

5: October 8, 1924   **GENNETT (NY)**

WOLVERINE ORCHESTRA

Bix Beiderbecke (c/p), Jimmy Hartwell (cl), George Johnson (ts), Dick Voynow (p), Bob Gillette (bj), Min Leibrook (tu), Vic Moore (dm)

9115-B   **Tia Juana** (Rodemich-Conley)
              solos: Hartwell (8)—Johnson (32)—Bix (30)—
              Hartwell (2)
9116   **Big Boy** (Ager-Yellen)
              solos: Bix, c (14+14)—Johnson (2+32)—Bix,
              p (32)—Bix, c (2)

6: October 9, 1924   **GENNETT (NY)**

SIOUX CITY SIX

Bix Beiderbecke (c), Miff Mole (tb), Frank Trumbauer (Cms), Rube Bloom (p), Min Leibrook (tu), Vic Moore (dm)

9119-A   **Flock O' Blues** (Bloom)
              solos: Bloom (2)—Mole (2)—Bix (2)—Tram
              (2)—Mole (1+1)—Leibrook (1)—Bloom (2)—
              Mole (2)
9120-C   **I'm Glad** (Trumbauer)
              solos: Mole (16)—Bloom (16)—Tram (2)

7: November 24, 1924 **VICTOR (Detroit)**

JEAN GOLDKETTE AND HIS ORCHESTRA
Fred "Fuzzy" Farrar, Tex Brusstar (tp); Bix Beiderbecke (c); Bill Rank, Tommy Dorsey (tb); Stanley "Doc" Ryker, Don Murray, George Williams (reeds); Joe Venuti (vln); Paul Mertz (p); Howdy Quicksell (bj); Irish Henry (tu); Charles Horvath (dm)

BVE 31206-2   **I Didn't Know** (Williams-Jones)
              solos: Dorsey, with cl trio (16)—Bix (16)—? tb
              (1)—Venuti (16)—Ryker (2)

8: November 25, 1924 **VICTOR (Detroit)**

JEAN GOLDKETTE AND HIS ORCHESTRA
Same personnel as previous session (7) with the addition of Gorner (vln) and a second unknown (vln).

BVE 31212-1   **Adoration** (Borowski-arr. George Crozier)
or -4

An article published in Davenport at the time these titles were recorded revealed that Bix also played on "Honest and Truly," the second title recorded on that day. It has been suggested (*Jean Goldkette Bands*, a Timeless CD, CBC 1-084) that Frank Trumbauer could be heard on "Play Me Slow," the first title recorded on that date, the name George Williams being "presumably a pseudonym to conceal Trumbauer's presence."

9: January 26, 1925 **GENNETT (IN)**

BIX BEIDERBECKE AND HIS RHYTHM JUGGLERS
Bix Beiderbecke (c), Don Murray (cl), Tommy Dorsey (tb), Paul Mertz (p), Tommy Gargano (dm)

12140   **Toddlin' Blues** (La Rocca-Shields)
         solo: Dorsey (2)
12141   **Davenport Blues** (Beiderbecke)
         solos: Bix & Murray (2)—Bix (32)—Dorsey
         (2)—Murray (4)

10: October 12, 1926 13:30–17:25 **VICTOR (NY)**

JEAN GOLDKETTE AND HIS ORCHESTRA
Fred Farrar, Ray Lodwig (tp); Bix (c); Bill Rank, Newell "Spiegle" Willcox (tb); Doc Ryker, Frank Trumbauer, Don Murray (reeds); Eddie Lang (g); Joe Venuti (vln); Irving Riskin (p); Howdy Quicksell (bj); Steve Brown (sb); Chauncey Morehouse (dm); Frank Bessinger (voc)

BVE 36813-1   **Idolizing** (Messenheimer-Abrahamson-West-
              arr. Bill Challis)
BVE 36813-2   **Idolizing**
              solos : Bix, derby mute (16)—Bessinger, voc + g
              (32)—Farrar (8)—Venuti (8)
BVE 36815-2   **Hush-a-Bye** (Galvin-Spencer-arr. Bill Challis)
              solos: Bessinger, voc + vln + g (32)—Venuti (8)

11: October 15, 1926 10:00–14:30 & 15:00–17:20 **VICTOR (NY)**

JEAN GOLDKETTE AND HIS ORCHESTRA
Same personnel as previous session (10), Eddie Lang was absent on 36830, as was Frank Bessinger (voc) on 36814 and 36830; addition of Nan and Taddy Keller (Keller Sisters) and Frank Lynch on 36929, Frank Lynch on 36831

BVE 36814-8   **I'd Rather Be the Girl in Your Arms**
              (Thompson-Archer-arr. Billl Challis)
              solos: Lang (8)—Venuti (2)—Venuti & Lang
              (16+7)—Bessinger, voc + g (32)—Tram (8)
BVE 36829-2   **Sunday** (Miller-Cohn-Stein-Kreuger-arr.
              Bill Challis)
BVE 36829-3   **Sunday**
              solos: Rank (16+6)—Lang (8)—Keller Sisters
              & Lynch, voc + g (32)—Bix, leads (14)—
              Murray (10)
BVE 36830-2   **Cover Me Up with Sunshine** (Dixon-
              Henderson-arr. Bill Challis)
              solos: Willcox & Venuti obbligato (8)—
              Bessinger (voc)
BVE 36831-2   **Just One More Kiss** (Owens-Montgomery-
              arr. Eddy Sheasby)
BVE 36831-4   **Just One More Kiss**
              solos : Farrar (8)—Lynch, voc + g (32)—
              Lodwig & Venuti (16)—Ryker (8)

12: January 28, 1927 9:30–13:40 **VICTOR (NY)**

JEAN GOLDKETTE AND HIS ORCHESTRA
Fred Farrar, Ray Lodwig (tp); Bix (c); Bill Rank, Spiegle Willcox (tb); Doc Ryker, Frank Trumbauer, Jimmy Dorsey (reeds); Joe Venuti (vln); Paul Mertz (p); Howdy Quicksell (bj); Steve Brown (sb); Chauncey Morehouse (dm); Nan and Taddy Keller (Keller Sisters) and Frank Lynch (voc) on 37579; Billy Murray (voc) on 37580

BVE 37579-1   **Proud of a Baby Like You** (Schonberg-
              Stevens-Helmick-arr. Bill Challis)

BVE 37579-4 **Proud of a Baby Like You**
solos: Ryker (16+6)—Farrar (4)—Keller
Sisters & Lynch, voc (4+32)—Bix (16)—
Willcox & orch (8)

BVE 37580-1 **I'm Looking Over a Four Leaf Clover**
(Dixon-Wood-arr. Bill Challis)

BVE 37580-4 **I'm Looking Over a Four Leaf Clover**
solos: Venuti (16)—Tram (8)—Venuti (8)—
Murray, voc (30)—Dorsey (2)—Bix & orch
(14+2+14)

13: January 31, 1927   13:45–17:20   VICTOR (NY)

JEAN GOLDKETTE AND HIS ORCHESTRA
Same personnel as previous session (12); Ray Muerer (voc)
on 37584

BVE 37583-2 **I'm Gonna Meet My Sweetie Now** (Davis-
Greer-arr. Challis)

BVE 37583-3 **I'm Gonna Meet My Sweetie Now**
solos: Tram (16)—Rank (8)—Bix, leads (8)—
Dorsey, bar (16)—Venuti (16)—Willcox (8)—
Venuti (8)—Dorsey & orch (16)—Bix & orch
(8)—Dorsey (8)

BVE 37584-2 **Hoosier Sweetheart** (Goodwin-Ash-Baskette-
arr. Bill Challis)
solos: Willcox (16+8)—Bix (4+2)—Muerer, voc
(32)—Tram (16+8)—Bix, leads (16)—Rank
(8)—Dorsey & orch (8)

14: February 1, 1927   13:45–17:00   VICTOR (NY)

JEAN GOLDKETTE AND HIS ORCHESTRA
Fred Farrar, Ray Lodwig (tp); Bix (c); Bill Rank, Spiegle Will-
cox (tb); Doc Ryker, Frank Trumbauer, Danny Polo (reeds);
Joe Venuti, Eddy Sheasby (vln); Paul Mertz (p); Howdy
Quicksell (bj); Steve Brown (sb); Chauncey Morehouse
(dm); Eddie Lang (g) only on 37586

BVE 37586-1 **Look at the World and Smile** (Caldwell-
Hubbell-arr. Sheasby)

BVE 37586-2 **Look at the World and Smile**

BVE 37586-3 **Look at the World and Smile**
solos: Willcox & Venuti & Sheasby (16+8)—
Venuti & Lang (16)—Bix & orch (16)

BVE 37587-1 **My Pretty Girl** (Fulcher-arr. Murray-Riskin-
Challis-Dorsey)

BVE 37587-2 **My Pretty Girl**

solos: Polo & Willcox (32)—Tram (2)—Bix &
tps (32)—Rank (2)—Venuti (8+8)—Tram (8)

15: February 3, 1927   13:45–17:00   VICTOR (NY)

JEAN GOLDKETTE AND HIS ORCHESTRA
Fred Farrar, Ray Lodwig (tp); Bix (c); Bill Rank, Spiegle Will-
cox (tb); Doc Ryker, Frank Trumbauer, Danny Polo (reeds);
Joe Venuti, (vln); Eddie Lang (g); Paul Mertz (p); Howdy
Quicksell (bj); Steve Brown (sb); Chauncey Morehouse (dm);
The Revelers (voc): James Melton (1st tenor), Lewis James
(2nd tenor), Elliot Shaw (baritone), Wilfred Glenn (bass)

BVE 37738-1 **A Lane in Spain** (Lewis-Lombardo-arr.
Bill Challis)

BVE 37738-3 **A Lane in Spain**
solos: Ryker (8)—Willcox (16+8)—The
Revelers, voc & Lang (4)—Lang, g—Lang (4)—Venuti
(16)—Farrar (8)—Polo (6)

BVE 37599-2 **Sunny Disposish** (Gershwin-Charig-arr.
Don Murray)

BVE 37599-3 **Sunny Disposish**
solos: The Revelers, voc & Lang, g (32)—Polo
& orch (10)—Farrar (8+8)

16: February 4, 1927   OKEH (NY)

FRANK TRUMBAUER AND HIS ORCHESTRA
Bix Beiderbecke (c); Frank Trumbauer (Cms); Jimmy Dorsey
(cl/as); Bill Rank (tb); Paul Mertz (p); Howdy Quicksell (bj);
Chauncey Morehouse (dm); on 80393 only, Eddie Lang (g)
replaces Quicksell, and Miff Mole (tb) replaces Bill Rank

W 80391-C **Trumbology** (Trumbauer-arr. Paul Mertz)
solos: Bix (4)—Tram (18)—Rank (4)—Tram
(16+16+22+14)—Mertz (2)—Tram (16)—Bix
(2+2)—Tram (8)

W 80392-A **Clarinet Marmalade** (Shields-Ragas)
solos: Rank (16)—Mertz (16)—Tram (16)—Bix
(16)—Dorsey (16)—Bix & Tram (2)

W 80393-C **Singin' the Blues** (Robinson-Conrad)
solos: Tram & Lang (32)—Bix & Lang (32)—
Dorsey (8)—Lang (1)

The label of the original Okeh 40772 record, which included
"Clarinet Marmalade" and "Singin' the Blues," was labelled:
"Frankie Trumbauer and His Orchestra with Bix and Lang";
the Mosaic edition of these Okeh recordings specifies that
on the metal part of "Singin' the Blues" "the matrix number

(80393) is located in the run-ON groove area with take-C being shown"; the only issued take of that title is therefore the third one. According to the April 1934 issue of *Melody Maker* (Warren Scholl) and the July 1939 *Rhythm* (interview with Tram), Bill Rank was replaced by Miff Mole on "Singin' the Blues."

17: May 6, 1927   VICTOR (Church Studio, Camden)

JEAN GOLDKETTE AND HIS ORCHESTRA
Fred Farrar, Ray Lodwig (tp); Bix (c); Bill Rank, Spiegle Willcox (tb); Doc Ryker, Frank Trumbauer, Don Murray (reeds); Irving Riskin (p); Howdy Quicksell (bj); Steve Brown (sb); Chauncey Morehouse (dm)

BVE 38607-2	**Slow River** (Myers-Schwab-arr. Bill Challis)
BVE 38607-4	**Slow River**
	solos: Bix (8)—Farrar (2)—Tram (16+6)—Bix & Murray & orch (16)—Willcox (8)

18: May 9, 1927   OKEH (NY)

FRANK TRUMBAUER AND HIS ORCHESTRA
Bix Beiderbecke (c), Frank Trumbauer (Cms), Don Murray (cl/ts), Bill Rank (tb), Doc Ryker (as), Irving Riskin (p), Eddie Lang (g/bj), Chauncey Morehouse (dm).

W 81071-B	**Ostrich Walk** (LaRocca-Shields-arr. Challis-Bix)
	solos: Tram (1)—Bix (1)—Rank & Murray (2)— Murray (2)—Tram (1)—Bix (1)—Rank & Murray (2)—Bix (16)—Rank (16)—Tram (1)— Bix (1)—Rank & Murray (2)—Tram (2)—Bix (2)
W 81072-B	**Riverboat Shuffle** (Carmichael-Voynow-Mills-arr. Challis)
	solos: Lang (1+1+1+2+2)—Riskin (2)—Murray (2)—Bix (2+30)—Rank (1+1+1)—Murray (30)—Bix (2)—Tram (2)—Lang (2)—Tram (2)

19: May 13, 1927   OKEH (NY)

FRANK TRUMBAUER AND HIS ORCHESTRA
Bix Beiderbecke (c), Frank Trumbauer (Cms), Don Murray (cl/bar), Bill Rank (tb), Doc Ryker (as), Irving Riskin (p), Eddie Lang (g/bj), Chauncey Morehouse (dm, harpophone)

| W 81083-B | **I'm Coming Virginia** (Heywood-arr. Riskin) |
| | solos: Lang (2+1+4)—Tram & Lang & Rank (16)—Bix (24 + leader: 22)—Lang (1)—Bix (1)—Lang (fin) |

| W 81084-B | **Way Down Yonder in New Orleans** (Creamer-Layton-arr. Murray) |
| | solos: Tram (2+2+20+4)—Bix (1+28)— Morehouse (1+1)—Murray (4) |

TRAM, BIX, AND EDDIE (IN THEIR THREE PIECE BAND)
Bix Beiderbecke (c/p), Frank Trumbauer (Cms), Eddie Lang (g)

| W 81085-B | **For No Reason at All in C** (Trumbauer-Beiderbecke) |
| | solos: Bix, p (4)—trio (32)—Lang & Bix, p (31)—trio (1+32)—Bix, p (32)—Tram (2)— Lang (2)—Bix, c (2)—Tram & Lang (coda) |

This side is a trio improvisation developed over the harmonic structure of "I'd Climb the Highest Mountain," a song written by Lew Brown and Sidney Clare.

20: May 16, 1927   10:00–12:00   VICTOR (Church Studio, Camden)

JEAN GOLDKETTE AND HIS ORCHESTRA
Fred Farrar, Ray Lodwig (tp); Bix (c); Bill Rank, Spiegle Willcox (tb); Doc Ryker, Frank Trumbauer, Don Murray (reeds); Irving Riskin (p); Joe Venuti (vln); Eddie Lang (g); Howdy Quicksell (bj); Steve Brown (sb); Chauncey Morehouse (dm).

| BVE 38264 | **In My Merry Oldsmobile** (Bryan-Edwards-arr. Eddy Sheasby) |
| | solo: Wilcox (8) |

Bix was present during the recording of the first number of this session, "Lily," of which no take was released, but he left the band before the second title, "In My Merry Oldsmobile," was recorded.

21: May 23, 1927   9:30–12:00   VICTOR (Church Studio, Camden)

JEAN GOLDKETTE AND HIS ORCHESTRA
Fred Farrar, Ray Lodwig (tp); Bix (c); Bill Rank, Spiegle Willcox (tb); Doc Ryker, Frank Trumbauer, Don Murray (reeds); Irving Riskin (p); Eddy Sheasby (vln); Howdy Quicksell (bj); Steve Brown (sb); Chauncey Morehouse (dm); Ray Lodwig, Howdy Quicksell, Doc Ryker, Bix? (voc)

BVE 38268-1	**In My Merry Oldsmobile** (Bryan-Edwards-arr.Bill Challis)
BVE 38268-2	**In My Merry Oldsmobile**
	solos: Willcox (16)—trio or quartet vocal (32)— Murray & orch & Bix, c, starting on 8th bar (30)

22: August 25, 1927   **OKEH (NY)**

FRANK TRUMBAUER AND HIS ORCHESTRA
Bix Beiderbecke (c), Frank Trumbauer (Cms), Don Murray
(cl/bar), Bill Rank (tb), Doc Ryker (as), Adrian Rollini (bsx),
Irving Riskin (p), Eddie Lang (g), Chauncey Morehouse
(dm); Seger Ellis (voc) on 81274 et 81275

W 81273-C **Three Blind Mice** (Morehouse-arr. Trumbauer
& Challis)
solos: Lang (2)—Tram (1)—Bix (16)—Lang
(16)—Rollini (16)—Murray, cl (1)—Tram (1)—
Rollini (1)—Bix (1)

W 81274 **Blue River** (Bryan-Meyer)
5 seconds of rehearsal (test groove)

W 81274-B **Blue River**
solos: Bix, straight mute (2)—Ellis, voc & Bix,
straight mute (32)—Bix, *leads* (24)

W 81275-D **There's a Cradle in Caroline** (Young-Ahlert)
solos: Murray, cl (20)—Rollini (3+4)—Tram
(3)—Ellis, voc (20)—Murray, bar (4)—Murray,
cl (6)

23: September 8, 1927   **OKEH (NY)**

BIX BEIDERBECKE
Bix Beiderbecke (p)

W 81426-B **In a Mist** (Beiderbecke)
piano solo

24: September 15, 1927 13:45–17:00 **VICTOR (LH, NY)**

JEAN GOLDKETTE AND HIS ORCHESTRA
Fred Farrar, Ray Lodwig (tp); Bix (c); Bill Rank, Lloyd Turner
(tb); Doc Ryker, Frank Trumbauer, Don Murray (reeds); Irving
Riskin (p); Joe Venuti (vln); Eddie Lang (g); Howdy Quicksell
(bj); Steve Brown (sb); Chauncey Morehouse (dm); Lewis
James (voc) on 40211

BVE 40211-3 **Blue River** (Bryan-Meyer-arr. Bill Challis)
solos: Murray, bar (16+6)—Farrar (8)—Lang
(2)—Venuti (2)—James, voc (30)—Tram (8)

BVE 40212-2 **Clementine (from New Orleans)** (Creamer-
Warren-arr:Murray-Quicksell-Trumbauer)
solos: Rank (8)—Lang (2+2)—Bix (1+16)—
Venuti (8)—Bix (1+6)—Lang (2)

25: September 17, 1927   **OKEH (NY)**

TRAM, BIX, AND LANG
Frank Trumbauer (Cms), Bix Beiderbecke (c/p), Eddie Lang (g)

W 81450 **Wringin' an' Twistin'**
4 seconds of rehearsal (test groove)

W 81450-A **Wringin' an' Twistin'** (Trumbauer-Waller)
solos: trio (4+16+16+16)—Lang & Bix, p (16)—
Bix, p (8)—trio (8)—Tram (2)—Bix, c (2)—Lang
(coda)

26: September 28, 1927   **OKEH (NY)**

FRANK TRUMBAUER AND HIS ORCHESTRA
Bix Beiderbecke (c), Frank Trumbauer (Cms), Don Murray
(cl/ts), Bill Rank (tb), Bobby Davis (as), Adrian Rollini (bsx),
Frank Signorelli (p), Eddie Lang (g), Joe Venuti (vln),
Chauncey Morehouse (dm, harpophone)

W 81488-A **Humpty Dumpty** (Livingston-arr. Fud
Livingston)
solos: Bix (2)—Tram (12)—Bix (2)—Tram (6)—
Signorelli (6)—Venuti (30)—Signorelli (6)—Bix
(10)—Rollini (4)

W 81489-B **Krazy Cat** (Morehouse-Trumbauer-arr.
Don Murray)
solos: Venuti (2)—Tram (2)—Bix (2+16)—
Venuti (16)—Tram (2)

W 81490-B **Baltimore** (Jimmy McHugh)
solos: Bix (2)—Rollini (2)—Morehouse (2)—
Venuti (16)—Bix (16)—Rollini (14)—Rank
(2)—Lang (16)—Venuti (1)

27: September 29, 1927   **HARMONY (NY)**

BROADWAY BELL-HOPS
Bix Beiderbecke (c), Herman "Hymie" Faberman (tp), Bill
Rank (tb), Don Murray (cl), Frank Trumbauer (Cms), Bobby
Davis (as), Frank Signorelli (p), John Cali (bj), Joe Tarto
(tu), Joe Venuti (vln), Vic Berton (dm), Sam Lanin (cymbal),
Irving Kaufman (voc)

144809-2 **There Ain't No Land Like Dixieland**
(Donaldson)
solos: Rank (1)—Faberman (1)—Venuti (14)—
Murray (4+4)—Kaufman (30)—Bix (2+16)—
Rank (8)—Bix (6)—Tram (16)—Murray (2)

144810-2   **There's a Cradle in Caroline** (Ahlert-Lewis-
             Young)
             solos: Faberman (8)—Tram (16)—Bix, straight
             mute (8)—Tram (8)—Kaufman (40)—Rank
             (16)—Bix (8)

For the third number of this session, "Rainbow of Love"
(144811), Bix and Bill Rank were replaced by Manny Klein
and Chuck Campbell.

28: September 30, 1927   OKEH (NY)

BENNY MEROFF AND HIS ORCHESTRA
(FRANK TRUMBAUER AND HIS ORCHESTRA)
Frank Cush? (tp), Bix Beiderbecke (c), Bill Rank (tb), Frank
Trumbauer (Cms/as), Don Murray (cl/ts), Bobby Davis (as),
Adrian Rollini (bsx), Frank Signorelli (p), Eddie Lang? (bj),
Joe Venuti (vln), Chauncey Morehouse (dm), Irving Kauf-
man (voc)

W 81499-A   **Just an Hour of Love** (Trent-deRose-von
             Tilser)
             solos: Kaufman, voc & vln (32)—Bix (8)—Tram
             (8)—Bix (8)—Tram (6)—Rollini (1)
W 81500-A   **I'm Wonderin' Who** (Trent-deRose-von Tilser)
             solos: Rollini (2)—Kaufman, voc & vln (32)—
             Murray (4+4)—Venuti (1)—Bix (1)

The Okeh 40912 78-rpm record, with both titles, was released under the name of bandleader Benny Meroff. Trumpeter Sylvester Ahola's diary indicates that Eddie Lang was
sick and away from the studios between September 30 and
October 20, 1927. Sylvester Ahola confirmed to his biographer Dick Hill that he never recorded with Bix.

29: October 5, 1927   OKEH (NY)

BIX BEIDERBECKE AND HIS GANG
Bix Beiderbecke (c), Bill Rank (tb), Don Murray (cl), Adrian
Rollini (bsx), Frank Signorelli (p), Chauncey Morehouse (dm)

W 81518-B   **At the Jazz Band Ball** (LaRocca-Shields)
             solos: Rollini (2+16)—Murray (16)—Signorelli
             (16)—Bix (1)—Rank (1)
W 81519-B   **Royal Garden Blues** (Williams-Williams)
             solos: [Bix (1)—Murray (1)—Rank (1)—Rollini
             (1)]—[same sequence repeated]—Murray
             (12)—Rollini (12)—Rank (12)—Bix (12)

W 81520-A   **Jazz Me Blues** (Delaney-arr. Adrian Rollini)
             solos: Rollini (2)—Rank (8)—Murray (12)—Bix
             (20)—Rollini (2+4)

Okeh 8544, with "Royal Garden Blues," was released under
the name of the New Orleans Lucky Seven.

30: October 20, 1927   PERFECT (NY)

WILLARD ROBISON AND HIS ORCHESTRA
Bix Beiderbecke (c), Frank Trumbauer (Cms), Don Murray
(cl), Frank Signorelli (p), Eddie Lang or unknown (bj), Vic
Berton (dm/harpophone), The Deep River Quintet (voc) on
the two first titles only

-1   **I'm More than Satisfied** (Klages-Waller)
-2 & -5   **I'm More than Satisfied**
             solos: ? , bj (2+1)—Berton, harpophone (2)—
             Deep River Quintet, voc (31)—Tram (2)—
             Murray (2) & Bix (2) & Tram (2)
-1 & -4   **Clorinda** (Heywood)
-2 & -5   **Clorinda**
             solos: Deep River Quintet (6)—Tram (2)—Deep
             River Quintet (24+31)—Tram (1+16)—Bix (8)
-1 & -3   **Three Blind Mice** (Morehouse)
-2   **Three Blind Mice**
             solos: Signorelli (1)—Murray (2)—Bix (2)—
             Tram (16)—Murray (2+4)—Bix (16)

"Clorinda" and "Three Blind Mice" were released on Perfect
record 14910 under the name of the Chicago Loopers. The
matrix numbers for these three titles were: 107854,
107855, and 107856, but the order in which they were
recorded is unknown. Identical takes were given different
numbers, and the whole session may appear a bit long for
just one day.

31: October 25, 1927   OKEH (NY)

BIX BEIDERBECKE AND HIS GANG
Bix Beiderbecke (c), Bill Rank (tb), Don Murray (cl), Adrian
Rollini (bsx), Frank Signorelli (p), Chauncey Morehouse
(dm)

W 81568-B   **Goose Pimples** (Trent-Henderson)
             solos: Rollini (1+1)—Murray (12)—Rank (8)—
             Signorelli (16, Bix, c, plays 2 notes on bar-
             12)—Bix (12)

W81569-A   **Sorry** (Quicksell-arr. Quicksell)
             solos: Murray (32)—Rank (16)—Bix (16).

"Goose Pimples" was released on Okeh 8544, together with "Royal Garden Blues," and also sold under the name of the New Orleans Lucky Seven.

FRANK TRUMBAUER AND HIS ORCHESTRA
Bix Beiderbecke (c), Bill Rank (tb), Frank Trumbauer (Cms), Don Murray (cl/ts), Charles "Pee Wee" Russell (cl/as), Adrian Rollini (bsx), Joe Venuti (vln), Eddie Lang (g), Frank Signorelli (p), Chauncey Morehouse (dm)

W 81570-C   **Cryin' All Day** (Trumbauer-Morehouse)
             solos: Venuti (2)—Rollini (2)—Bix (2+16)—
             Russell (14)—Tram (2)—Venuti (2)
W 81571-B   **A Good Man Is Hard to Find** (Green)
             solos: Tram (2)—Venuti & Lang (2)—Tram
             (20)—Bix (12)—Rank (7)—Russell or Murray?
             (15)—Venuti & Rollini (12)—Rollini (2)

BIX BEIDERBECKE AND HIS GANG
Bix Beiderbecke (c), Bill Rank (tb), Don Murray (cl), Adrian Rollini (bsx), Frank Signorelli (p), Chauncey Morehouse (dm)

W 81572-B   **Since My Best Gal Turned Me Down**
             (Lodwig-Quicksell-arr. Quicksell)
             solos: Rollini (16)—Bix (16)

32: October 26, 1927   OKEH (NY)

RUSSELL GRAY AND HIS ORCHESTRA
unknown (tp); Bix Beiderbecke (c); Bill Rank (tb); Frank Trumbauer (Cms); Don Murray or Bobby Davis? (reeds); Adrian Rollini (bsx); Joe Venuti (vln); Eddie Lang (g); Frank Signorelli (p); Chauncey Morehouse (dm); Ed Macy, John Ryan (voc)

W 81575-B   **Sugar** (Yellen-Ager-Crum-Nichols)
             solos: Venuti (14)—Lang (1)—Macy & Ryan,
             voc (32)—Rollini (2)—?, tp or ct (8, then 8
             bars with same musician leading the band)

A session full of questions: even if we believe that Bix might have intentionally wished to spoil the take (and if so, why was it kept and released?), he couldn't possibly have played the eight-bar solo, even if he was "under duress." But he has inspired it. Trumpet-player Boe Ashford is a possible candidate, as is Don Murray, who had started on trumpet his musical career on trumpet, and whose lack of practice on this

instrument could explain the soloist's amazing clumsiness. It has also been suggested that "Ed Macy" might be a pseudonym for Irving Kaufman. One thing is sure: Tram refused to put his name on this recording, and Okeh decided to sell it under the name of Russell Gray, a trombone player who had no link with the studio—and who was the first to be surprised by this decision.

33: November 18, 1927   9:30–12:15   VICTOR (CHI)

PAUL WHITEMAN AND HIS ORCHESTRA
Bix Beiderbecke (c); Tommy Dorsey, Boyce Cullen (tb); Jimmy Dorsey (cl/as); Charles Strickfaden (bar); Chester "Chet" Hazlett (bcl); Mischa Russell, Kurt Dieterle, Matty Malneck (vln); Hoagy Carmichael (p); Wilbur Hall (g); Steve Brown (sb); Hal McDonald (dm/vibraphone); Hoagy Carmichael (voc)

CVE 40901-1   **Washboard Blues** (Carmichael-Callahan-arr.
              Bill Challis)
CVE 40901-4   **Washboard Blues**
              solos: Carmichael, p (12)—Carmichael, p &
              voc (24+24)—Bix, leads (20, on fast tempo)

34: November 23, 1927   9:30–11:45   VICTOR (CHI)

PAUL WHITEMAN AND HIS ORCHESTRA
Charles Margulis, Bob Mayhew (tp); Bix Beiderbecke (c); Wilbur Hall, Tommy Dorsey (tb); Jimmy Dorsey, Nye Mayhew, Charles Strickfaden (bar/as); Chester Hazlett, Harold McLean (as); Kurt Dieterle, Mischa Russell, Matty Malneck, Mario Perry (vln); Harry Perrella (p); Steve Brown (sb); Mike Trafficante (tu); Mike Pingitore (bj); Hal McDonald (dm); Bing Crosby (voc); Jack Fulton, Charles Gaylord, Austin Young (Sweet Trio) and Harry Barris, Al Rinker, Bing Crosby (Rhythm Boys) (voc)

BVE 40937-2   **Changes** (Donaldson)
BVE 40937-3   **Changes**
              solos: Sweet Trio (16)—Rhythm Boys (8)—
              Sweet Trio (8)—Bing Crosby & Sweet Trio
              (16)—Bix, straight mute (16)

35: November 25, 1927   9:30–12:00   VICTOR (CHI)

PAUL WHITEMAN AND HIS ORCHESTRA
Henry Busse, Charles Margulis (tp); Bix Beiderbecke (c); Tommy Dorsey (tb); Wilbur Hall (tb/bj); Frank Trumbauer

(Cms); Jimmy Dorsey, Harold McLean, Chester Hazlett (cl/as); Charles Strickfaden (ts); Kurt Dieterle, Mischa Russell, Matty Malneck, Mario Perry (vln); Harry Perrella (p); Steve Brown (sb); Mike Trafficante (tu); Mike Pingitore (bj); Hal McDonald (dm); Bing Crosby (voc)

BVE 40945-2   **(What Are You Waiting For?) Mary**
                  (Donaldson-arr. Malneck)

BVE 40945-4   **(What Are You Waiting For?) Mary**
                  solos: Busse (8+16)—Bix (15)—Malneck (1+3)—Crosby, voc (32)—Malneck (1+3)—Bix (8)—Busse (8)—Tram (2+2)

36: January 4, 1928   VICTOR (LH, NY)

PAUL WHITEMAN AND HIS ORCHESTRA
Henry Busse, Charles Margulis (tp); Bix Beiderbecke (c); Wilbur Hall (tb/g); Boyce Cullen (tb); Frank Trumbauer, Harold McLean, Chester Hazlett, Rupert "Rube" Crozier, Charles Strickfaden (reeds); Kurt Dieterle, Mischa Russell, Matty Malneck, Mario Perry, Charles Gaylord (vln); Harry Perrella (p); Steve Brown (sb); Mike Trafficante (tu); Mike Pingitore (bj); Hal McDonald (dm); Austin Young, Jack Fulton (voc)

BVE 41293-3   **Ramona** (Gilbert-Wayne-arr. Ferde Grofé)
                  solos: Young, voc & Fulton on second part (intro + 32) (end 4)

PAUL WHITEMAN AND HIS ORCHESTRA
Henry Busse, Charles Margulis (tp); Bix Beiderbecke (c); Wilbur Hall, Bill Rank (tb); Jimmy Dorsey, Harold McLean, Chester Hazlett, Charles Strickfaden, Rube Crozier (reeds); Kurt Dieterle (vln); Harry Perrella (p); Steve Brown (sb); Mike Trafficante (tu); Mike Pingitore (bj); Hal McDonald (dm); Austin Young, Al Rinker, Jack Fulton, Charles Gaylord (voc)

BVE 41294-1   **Smile** (Heywood-arr. Bill Challis)
                  solos: Young, voc (16)—Young, Rinker, Fulton & Gaylord, voc (32)—Dorsey, cl (4)—Strickfaden, bar & Bix, leads tp-trio (16)—Dieterle (6)—Bix (4)

PAUL WHITEMAN AND HIS ORCHESTRA
Henry Busse, Charles Margulis (tp); Bix Beiderbecke (c); Wilbur Hall, Bill Rank (tb); Frank Trumbauer (Cms); Chester Hazlett, Harold McLean (as); Jimmy Dorsey (cl); Charles Strickfaden (ts); Kurt Dieterle, Mischa Russell, Matty Mal-

neck (vln); Harry Perrella (p); Steve Brown (sb); Mike Trafficante (tu); Mike Pingitore (bj); Hal McDonald (dm)

BVE 41295-1   **Lonely Melody** (Coslow-Meroff-Dyson-arr. Challis)

BVE 41295-3   **Lonely Melody**
                  solos : Bix (1+16) (1+8)—Strickfaden, ts (8)— Dorsey & orch (12)

37: January 5, 1928   9:30–13:00   VICTOR (NY)

PAUL WHITEMAN AND HIS ORCHESTRA
Henry Busse, Charles Margulis (tp); Bix Beiderbecke (c); Boyce Cullen, Wilbur Hall, Bill Rank, Jack Fulton (tb); Frank Trumbauer, Chester Hazlett, Harold McLean, Jimmy Dorsey, Rube Crozier, Charles Strickfaden (reeds); Kurt Dieterle, Mischa Russell, Matty Malneck, Mario Perry, John Bowman, Charles Gaylord (vln); Harry Perrella (p); Steve Brown (sb); Mike Trafficante (tu); Mike Pingitore (bj); Hal McDonald (dm)

BVE 41296-2   **O Ya Ya** (Klages-de Markoff-arr. Domenico Savino)

PAUL WHITEMAN AND HIS ORCHESTRA
Henry Busse, Charles Margulis (tp); Bix Beiderbecke (c); Boyce Cullen, Wilbur Hall, Bill Rank, Jack Fulton (tb); Chester Hazlett, Harold McLean, Rube Crozier, Charles Strickfaden (reeds); Kurt Dieterle, Mischa Russell, Matty Malneck (vln); Harry Perrella, Ferde Grofé (p); Mike Trafficante (tu); Mike Pingitore (bj); Hal McDonald (dm)

BVE 41297-4   **Dolly Dimples** (Alter-arr. Ferde Grofé)
                  solos: Pingitore (16)—Perrella & Grofé (16)— Hazlett (12+2)—?, vln (2)

38: January 9, 1928   OKEH (NY)

FRANK TRUMBAUER AND HIS ORCHESTRA
Bix Beiderbecke (c), Bill Rank (tb), Frank Trumbauer (Cms), Jimmy Dorsey (cl/as), Chester Hazlett (as), Rube Crozier (ts/bassoon), Min Leibrook (bsx), Lenny Hayton (p), Carl Kress (g), Hal McDonald (dm, harpophone), Charles Margulis (tp) only on 400004

W 400003-B   **There'll Come a Time** (Manone-Mole)
                  solos: Bix (2)—Dorsey (16)—Bix (8)—Dorsey (8)—Tram (16)—Tram & Bix (2, with Bix last 2 notes)

W 400004-C   **Jubilee** (Robison)
                  written arrangement; solo: Tram (2)

39: January 11, 1928   9:30–13:45   **VICTOR (LH, NY)**

PAUL WHITEMAN AND HIS ORCHESTRA
Henry Busse, Charles Margulis, Bob Mayhew (tp); Bix Beiderbecke (c); Boyce Cullen, Wilbur Hall, Bill Rank, Jack Fulton (tb); Frank Trumbauer, Chester Hazlett, Harold McLean, Rube Crozier, Charles Strickfaden (reeds); Kurt Dieterle, Mischa Russell, Matty Malneck, Mario Perry, John Bouman (vln); Harry Perrella (p); Mike Trafficante (tu); Mike Pingitore (bj); Tom Satterfield (cel); Hal McDonald (dm); unknown xylophonist

BVE 27268-11   **Parade of the Wooden Soldiers** (Jessel-arr. Ferde Grofé)
     written arrangement
BVE 41607-2   **Ol' Man River** (Hammerstein-Kern-arr. Bill Challis)
BVE 41607-3   *Ol' Man River*

PAUL WHITEMAN AND HIS ORCHESTRA
Henry Busse, Charles Margulis (tp); Bix Beiderbecke (c); Boyce Cullen, Wilbur Hall, Bill Rank, Jack Fulton (tb); Frank Trumbauer, Chester Hazlett, Harold McLean, Jimmy Dorsey, Charles Strickfaden (reeds); Kurt Dieterle, Mischa Russell, Matty Malneck, Mario Perry, John Bouman (vln); Harry Perrella (p); Steve Brown (sb); Mike Trafficante (tu); Mike Pingitore (bj); Hal McDonald (dm); Bing Crosby (voc)

BVE 41607-2   **Ol' Man River** (Hammerstein-Kern-arr. Bill Challis)
     solos: Malneck (2+2)—Crosby, voc & Malneck, vln (32)—Bix (2)—Tram (16)

40: January 12, 1928   10:00–13:20   **VICTOR (LH, NY)**

PAUL WHITEMAN AND HIS ORCHESTRA
Bix Beiderbecke (c), Charles Margulis (tp), Bill Rank (tb), Frank Trumbauer (Cms), Jimmy Dorsey (c/cl), Min Leibrook (bsx), Bill Challis (p), Matty Malneck (vln), Carl Kress (g), Hal McDonald (dm)

BVE 30172-6   **San** (McPhail-Michels-arr. Bill Challis)
BVE 30172-7   **San**
     solos: Leibrook (24)—Tram (2)—Malneck & Kress (32)—Bix, Margulis & Dorsey, c (32)—Rank (8)

41: January 20, 1928   **OKEH (NY)**

FRANK TRUMBAUER AND HIS ORCHESTRA
Bix Beiderbecke (c); Charlie Margulis (tp); Bill Rank (tb); Frank Trumbauer (Cms, as, voc); Jimmy Dorsey, Chet Hazlett (as); Matty Malneck (vln); Lennie Hayton (p); Carl Kress (g); Min Leibrook (bsx); Hal McDonald (dm); Bing Crosby (voc)

400034-A   **Mississippi Mud** (Barris)
     solos: Malneck (4)—Crosby & Tram, voc & Malneck, vln (10+22)—Bix (4+22)—Margulis (8)—Rank (2)—Crosby, voc (10)

42: January 21, 1928   9:30–12:30   **VICTOR (LH, NY)**

PAUL WHITEMAN AND HIS ORCHESTRA
Henry Busse, Charles Margulis, Bob Mayhew (tp); Bix Beiderbecke (c); Boyce Cullen, Wilbur Hall, Bill Rank, Jack Fulton (tb); Frank Trumbauer, Chester Hazlett, Harold McLean, Jimmy Dorsey, Charles Strickfaden, Rube Crozier, Jack & Nye Mayhew (reeds); Kurt Dieterle, Mischa Russell, Matty Malneck, Mario Perry, John Bouman (vln); Harry Perrella, Tommy Satterfield (p); Steve Brown (sb); Mike Trafficante (tu); Mike Pingitore (bj); Hal McDonald (dm); Jack Fulton (voc)

CVE 41635-3   **Together** (DeSylva-Henderson-Brown-arr. Ferde Grofé)
     solos: Fulton, voc (32)—Busse (32)

43: January 24, 1928   9:30–11:50   **VICTOR (Church Studio, Camden)**

PAUL WHITEMAN AND HIS ORCHESTRA
Same personnel as previous session (42), without Satterfield (p) and with Rube Crozier (flute) and Jack Fulton, Charles Gaylord, Austin Young, Al Rinker (voc)

CVE 41465-1   **My Heart Stood Still** (Rodgers-Hart-arr. Bill Challis)
CVE 41465-3   **My Heart Stood Still**
     solos: Hazlett, cl (16 + 8)—Young, voc (16)—Quartet, voc (32)—Perella (4)—Bix (4)—Tram & Brown, sb (32)—Crozier, flute (4)

PAUL WHITEMAN AND HIS ORCHESTRA
Henry Busse, Charles Margulis (tp); Bix Beiderbecke (c); Wilbur Hall, Bill Rank, (tb); Chester Hazlett, Harold McLean, Jimmy Dorsey, Charles Strickfaden, Rube Crozier, (reeds); Kurt Dieterle (vln); Harry Perrella (p); Steve Brown (sb); Mike Trafficante (tu); Mike Pingitore (bj); Hal McDonald

(dm/ vibraphone); Austin Young, Jack Fulton, Charles Gaylord, Al Rinker (voc)

BVE 41294-4   **Smile** (Heywood-arr. Bill Challis)
BVE 41294-5   *Smile*
        solos: Rank & brass (16)—Young, voc (16)—
        Quartet, voc (32)—Dorsey, cl (4)—Strickfaden,
        bar & Bix, leads tp-trio (16)—Dieterle (6)—
        Bix (4)

44: January 28, 1928   9:30–11:25   **VICTOR (Church Studio, Camden)**

PAUL WHITEMAN AND HIS ORCHESTRA
Henry Busse, Charles Margulis (tp); Bix Beiderbecke (c); Boyce Cullen, Wilbur Hall, Bill Rank, (tb); Frank Trumbauer, Chester Hazlett, Harold McLean, Jimmy Dorsey, Charles Strickfaden, Rube Crozier (reeds); Kurt Dieterle, Mischa Russell, Matty Malneck, Mario Perry, Charles Gaylord (vln); Ferde Grofé (p); Steve Brown (sb); Mike Trafficante (tu); Mike Pingitore (bj); Hal McDonald (dm)

BVE 41471-3   **Back in Your Own Backyard** (Jolson-Rose-Dreyer-arr. Bill Challis)
BVE 41471-4   **Back in Your Own Backyard**
        solos: Bix (4)—Dorsey (1+8)—Bix (8)
        [Bill Challis (p), on takes 1 and 2, destroyed.]

45: February 8, 1928   10:00–12:05 / 13:00–15:00   **VICTOR (LH, NY)**

PAUL WHITEMAN AND HIS ORCHESTRA
Henry Busse, Charles Margulis (tp); Bix Beiderbecke (c); Boyce Cullen, Wilbur Hall, Bill Rank, (tb); Frank Trumbauer, Chester Hazlett, Harold McLean, Jimmy Dorsey, Charles Strickfaden, Rube Crozier (reeds); Kurt Dieterle, Mischa Russell, Matty Malneck, Mario Perry, John Bouman (vln); Roy Bargy (p); Mike Trafficante (tu); Mike Pingitore (bj); Hal McDonald (dm); Bing Crosby, Jack Fulton, Austin Young, Charles Gaylord, Al Rinker, Harry Barris (voc)

BVE 41681-2   **There Ain't No Sweet Man that's Worth the Salt of My Tears** (Fisher-arr. Tommy Satterfield)
BVE 41681-3   **There Ain't No Sweet Man that's Worth the Salt of My Tears**
        solos: Tram (2)—Bix (8+32 with orch)—Hazlett, as (4)—Bargy (4)—Crosby, alone and with vocal background (8+18+8+10)—Dieterle (4)—Tram (16)—Bix (8+7 with orch)—Hazlett, as (4)

46: February 9, 1928   10:00–12:20 & 13:20–15:00   **VICTOR (LH, NY)**

PAUL WHITEMAN AND HIS ORCHESTRA
Henry Busse, Charles Margulis (tp/c); Bix Beiderbecke (c); Boyce Cullen, Wilbur Hall, Bill Rank, (tb); Frank Trumbauer, Chester Hazlett, Irving Friedman, Roy "Red" Maier, Charles Strickfaden (reeds); Kurt Dieterle, Mischa Russell, Matty Malneck (vln); Roy Bargy (p); Steve Brown (sb); Mike Trafficante (tu); Mike Pingitore (bj); Hal McDonald (dm)

BVE 41683-2   **Dardanella** (Bernard-Black-Fisher-arr. Bill Challis)
        solos: Tram (8)—Bix (1+32)—Tram (8+4)

47: February 10, 1928   **VICTOR (LH, NY)**

PAUL WHITEMAN AND HIS ORCHESTRA
Same personnel as previous session (46); Harold McLean replaces Irving Friedman; Jack Fulton, Charles Gaylord, Austin Young (voc)

BVE 41684-2   **The Love Nest** (Harbach-Hirsch-arr. Bill Challis)
        solos: Busse (32)—vocal trio (32)—Strickfaden, ts (7)—Bix (1+8)

48: February 13, 1928   13:15–16:00   **VICTOR (LH, NY)**

PAUL WHITEMAN AND HIS ORCHESTRA
Henry Busse, Charles Margulis (tp); Boyce Cullen, Wilbur Hall (tb/g); Chester Hazlett, Charles Strickfaden, Rube Crozier, Roy "Red" Maier (reeds); Kurt Dieterle, Mischa Russell, Matty Malneck, Mario Perry, John Bouman (vln); Roy Bargy (p); Mike Trafficante (tu); Mike Pingitore (bj); Hal McDonald (dm); Bing Crosby, Al Rinker, Jack Fulton, Charles Gaylord, Austin Young (voc)

BVE 41688-2   Sunshine (Berlin-arr. Ferde Grofé)
BVE 41688-3   Sunshine
        solos: Cullen (intro+16)—Bargy (8)—Cullen (8)—Crosby, voc (32)—vocal quartet (8)—Crosby & vocal quartet (8)

Previous discographies list Bix Beiderbecke in this session. According to Don Rayno, Ferde Grofé would always give the first and second trumpet parts to Busse and Margulis. This seems to be confirmed, as Bix is not audible.

PAUL WHITEMAN AND HIS ORCHESTRA

Charles Margulis (tp); Bix Beiderbecke (c); Bill Rank, (tb); Chester Hazlett, Rube Crozier, Roy Maier, Charles Strickfaden (reeds); Kurt Dieterle, Mischa Russell, Matty Malneck (vln); Harry Barris (p); Steve Brown (sb); Mike Trafficante (tu); Mike Pingitore (bj); Hal McDonald (dm); Bing Crosby, Charles Gaylord, Austin Young, Jack Fulton, Al Rinker (voc)

BVE 41689-3   **From Monday On** (Barris-Crosby-arr. Matty Malneck)
solos: Fulton-Gaylord-Young, voc (4)—Fulton (4)—Crosby-Rinker (6)—Bix (31)—Crosby & vocal quartet (31)—Bix, leads (30+6+14+4)—Malneck (3).

Jimmy Dorsey was listed on cornet in previous discographies. According to Don Rayno, he had already left the band. The Victor files list only two trumpets on the number.

49: February 14, 1928   9:30–12:00   VICTOR (LH, NY)

PAUL WHITEMAN AND HIS ORCHESTRA
Henry Busse, Charles Margulis, Eddie Pinder (tp); Bix Beiderbecke (c); Boyce Cullen, Wilbur Hall, Bill Rank, Jack Fulton (tb); Frank Trumbauer, Chester Hazlett, Irving Friedman, Rube Crozier, Roy Maier, Charles Strickfaden, Nye and Jack Mayhew? (reeds); Kurt Dieterle, Mischa Russell, Matty Malneck, Mario Perry, Charles Gaylord, John Bouman (vln); Roy Bargy (p); Steve Brown (sb); Mike Trafficante (tu); Mike Pingitore (bj); Hal McDonald and a second unknown percussionist (dm)

CVE 41690-2   **Grand Fantasia From Wagneriana, Part 1** (Wagner-arr. Herman Hand)
CVE 41691-4   **Grand Fantasia From Wagneriana, Part 2** (Wagner-arr. Herman Hand)

50: February 15, 1928   VICTOR (LH, NY)

PAUL WHITEMAN AND HIS ORCHESTRA
Henry Busse, Charles Margulis, Eddie Pinder (tp); Bix Beiderbecke (c); Boyce Cullen, Wilbur Hall, Bill Rank (tb); Frank Trumbauer, Chester Hazlett, Irving Friedman, Rube Crozier, Roy Maier, Charles Strickfaden (reeds); Kurt Dieterle, Mischa Russell, Matty Malneck, Mario Perry (vln); Roy Bargy (p); Mike Pingitore (bj); Mike Trafficante (sb); Hal McDonald (dm/slide whistle); Jack Fulton and Austin Young (voc)

CVE 41682-5   **A Shady Tree** (Donaldson-arr. Ferde Grofé)
solos: Busse (30)—Fulton, voc (30)—Young, recitation (32)—Fulton, voc (16)

Test pressing that was not released by Victor. Austin Young recites "Trees," a poem by Joyce Kilmer.

51: February 16, 1928   10:15–12:45 / 14:40–16:00   VICTOR (LH, NY)

PAUL WHITEMAN AND HIS ORCHESTRA
Henry Busse, Charles Margulis, Eddie Pinder (tp); Bix Beiderbecke (c); Boyce Cullen, Wilbur Hall, Bill Rank, Jack Fulton (tb); Chester Hazlett, Rube Crozier, Roy Maier, Harold McLean, Charles Strickfaden (reeds); Kurt Dieterle, Mischa Russell, Matty Malneck, Mario Perry, Charles Gaylord, John Bouman (vln); Roy Bargy (p); Mike Pingitore (bj); Mike Trafficante (sb); Min Leibrook (bsx); Hal McDonald (dm); Frank Trumbauer & Irving Friedman (reeds) on Part 2 only

CVE 41693-2   **Three Shades of Blue, Part 1: Indigo** (Ferde Grofé-arr. Grofé)
CVE 41692-3   **Three Shades of Blue, Part 2: Alice Blue & Heliotrope** (Ferde Grofé-arr. Grofé)

52: February 18, 1928   11:30–12:40   VICTOR (LH, NY)

PAUL WHITEMAN AND HIS ORCHESTRA
Bix Beiderbecke (c); Eddie Pinder (tp); Bill Rank (tb); Frank Trumbauer, Chester Hazlett (as); Irving Friedman (cl); Charles Strickfaden (ts); Roy Bargy (p); Min Leibrook (tu); Mike Pingitore (bj); Mike Trafficante (sb); Hal McDonald (dm); unknown (ukulele); Irene Taylor (voc); Bing Crosby, Harry Barris, Al Rinker (Rhythm Boys) and Jack Fulton, Charles Gaylord, Austin Young (Sweet Trio) (voc).

BVE 41696-2   **Mississippi Mud** (Barris-arr. Tom Satterfield)
BVE 41696-3   **Mississippi Mud**
solos: Rhythm Boys (6)—Bix, leads (22+16)—Friedman (22)—Taylor, voc & Sweet Trio (22)—Crosby (4) & Young & Rhythm Boys (4)—Crosby (4) + Young & Rhythm Boys (4)—Taylor, voc & Sweet Trio (12)—Bix, leads (8)—Tram (2)—Bix, leads (16)—Taylor & Sweet trio (4)

53: February 27, 1928   12:00–15:15   **VICTOR (LH, NY)**

PAUL WHITEMAN AND HIS ORCHESTRA
Henry Busse, Charles Margulis, Eddie Pinder (tp); Bix Beiderbecke (c); Boyce Cullen, Wilbur Hall, Bill Rank, Jack Fulton (tb); Frank Trumbauer (Cms, bassoon); Rube Crozier (flute, bassoon); Chester Hazlett, Irving Friedman, Roy Maier, Charles Strickfaden (reeds); Kurt Dieterle, Mischa Russell, Matty Malneck, Mario Perry (vln); Roy Bargy (p); Mike Pingitore (bj); Mike Trafficante (sb); Min Leibrook (tu); Hal McDonald (dm); Austin Young (voc)

CVE 43116-3   **Chloe** (Kahn-Moret-arr. Grofé)
solos: Crozier, flute & Hazlett, cl (intro)—
Young, voc—Dieterle, vln

54: February 28, 1928   11:00–14:30 / 14:30–15:45   **VICTOR (LH, NY)**

PAUL WHITEMAN AND HIS ORCHESTRA
Henry Busse, Charles Margulis (tp); Boyce Cullen, Wilbur Hall (tb); Frank Trumbauer (Cms, bassoon); Chester Hazlett, Irving Friedman, Rube Crozier, Roy Maier, Charles Strickfaden (reeds); Kurt Dieterle, Mischa Russell, Matty Malneck, Mario Perry (vln); Roy Bargy (p); Mike Pingitore (bj); Mike Trafficante (sb); Min Leibrook (tu); Hal McDonald (dm); Bing Crosby (voc)

CVE 43117-3   **High Water, a Spiritual** (Brennan-McCardy-
arr. Satterfield)
solos: Crosby, voc & Tram, bassoon—Crosby,
voc & Friedman, cl

Bix was previously listed on this recording. However, Don Rayno specifies that the original score/arrangement for this number gives the two trumpet parts to Busse and Margulis. This is confirmed, as Bix is not audible.

PAUL WHITEMAN AND HIS ORCHESTRA
Charles Margulis (tp); Bix Beiderbecke (c); Bill Rank (tb); Frank Trumbauer (?), Chester Hazlett, Irving Friedman, Roy Maier, Charles Strickfaden (reeds); Kurt Dieterle, Mischa Russell, Matty Malneck (vln); Harry Barris (p); Mike Pingitore (bj); Mike Trafficante (tu); Min Leibrook (bsx); Hal McDonald (dm); Bing Crosby, Al Rinker; Charles Gaylord, Austin Young, Jack Fulton (Sweet Trio) (voc)

BVE 41689-4   **From Monday On** (Barris-Crosby-arr.
Malneck)

BVE 41689-6   **From Monday On**
solos: Sweet Trio (4)—Fulton (2)—Crosby &
Rinker (6)—Bix (32)—Crosby & vocal acc.
(31)—Bix & orch (30+6+14+4)

Don Rayno specifies that the Victor files for this session list only five reeds (including Leibrook on bsx), and that Trumbauer should be omitted.

PAUL WHITEMAN AND HIS ORCHESTRA
Henry Busse, Charles Margulis, Eddie Pinder (tp); Bix Beiderbecke (c); Boyce Cullen, Wilbur Hall, Bill Rank, Jack Fulton (tb); Frank Trumbauer, Chester Hazlett, Irving Friedman, Rube Crozier, Roy Maier, Charles Strickfaden (reeds); Kurt Dieterle, Mischa Russell, Matty Malneck, Mario Perry (vln); Roy Bargy (p); Mike Pingitore (bj); Mike Trafficante (sb); Min Leibrook (tu); Hal McDonald (dm)

BVE 43118-1   **Sugar** (Pinkard-arr. Bill Challis)
BVE 43118-2   *Sugar*
solos: Bix & Strickfaden, bar (16)—Rank (8)—
Bix, straight mute & Strickfaden, bar (8)—
Tram, as (8)—Bix (8)

55: February 29, 1928   9:30–12:00   **VICTOR (LH, NY)**

PAUL WHITEMAN AND HIS ORCHESTRA
Henry Busse, Charles Margulis, Eddie Pinder (tp); Bix Beiderbecke (c); Boyce Cullen, Wilbur Hall, Bill Rank, Jack Fulton (tb); Chester Hazlett, Rube Crozier, Roy Maier, Charles Strickfaden (reeds); Kurt Dieterle, Mischa Russell, Matty Malneck, Mario Perry, Charles Gaylord (vln); Roy Bargy (p); Mike Pingitore (bj); Mike Trafficante (sb); Min Leibrook (tu); Hal McDonald (dm)

CVE 43119-1   **Sea Burial** (Eastwood Lane-arr. Ferde Grofé)

PAUL WHITEMAN AND HIS ORCHESTRA
Henry Busse, Charles Margulis (tp); Bix Beiderbecke (c); Boyce Cullen, Wilbur Hall, Bill Rank (tb); Frank Trumbauer, Chester Hazlett, Irving Friedman, Roy Maier, Charles Strickfaden (reeds); Kurt Dieterle, Mischa Russell, Matty Malneck (vln); Roy Bargy (p); Mike Pingitore (bj); Mike Trafficante (sb); Min Leibrook (tu); Hal McDonald (dm)

BVE 43120-1   **When You're with Somebody Else**
(Baer-Gilbert-arr. Bill Challis)
BVE 43120-2   **When You're with Somebody Else**

solos: Bix (2)—Strickfaden, bar (15)—Hazlett, as (1+7)—Strickfaden, bar (1+6)—Tram or Friedman, as (8)

56: March 1, 1928   10:15–12:00 / 14:00–15:30   **VICTOR (LH, NY)**

PAUL WHITEMAN AND HIS ORCHESTRA
Henry Busse, Charles Margulis (tp); Bix Beiderbecke (c); Boyce Cullen, Wilbur Hall (tb); Frank Trumbauer, Chester Hazlett, Irving Friedman, Rube Crozier, Roy Maier, Charles Strickfaden (reeds); Kurt Dieterle, Mischa Russell, Matty Malneck, Mario Perry (vln); Roy Bargy (p); Mike Pingitore (bj); Mike Trafficante (sb); Hal McDonald (dm); chorus: Olive Kline, D. Baker, V. Hold, R. Rogers (sopranos); E. Baker, H. Clark, E. Indermauer (altos); Lambert Murphy, C. Harrison, L. James, J. Hause (tenors); W. Glen, E. Shaw, F. Croxton, Kinsley (basses)

CVE 43123-2   **Selections from** *Show Boat* (Hammerstein-Kern-arr. Satterfield)
CVE 43123-4   **Selections from** *Show Boat*
solos: on "Why Do I Love You?": Kline, voc (31), Tram, bassoon (3); on "Can't Help Lovin' Dat Man": Margulis, tp (12)—Bix (12)—choir, voc; on "You Are Love": Murphy, voc (48); on "Make Believe": Murphy, voc (8)—Kline, voc (6)—Murphy & Kline, voc duet (2+8)—duet & choir (8)

57: March 2, 1928   10:30–12:10 / 13:15–15:50   **VICTOR (LH, NY)**

PAUL WHITEMAN AND HIS ORCHESTRA
Henry Busse, Charles Margulis, Eddie Pinder (tp); Bix Beiderbecke (c); Boyce Cullen, Wilbur Hall, Bill Rank, Jack Fulton (tb); Frank Trumbauer, Chester Hazlett, Charles Strickfaden, Rube Crozier (as); Roy Maier (ts); Irving Friedman (bar); Kurt Dieterle, Mischa Russell, Matty Malneck, Mario Perry (vln); Roy Bargy, Tom Satterfield (p); Mike Pingitore (bj); Mike Trafficante (sb); Min Leibrook (tu); Hal McDonald (dm)

CVE 43124-3   **A Study in Blue** (Domenico Savino-arr. Savino)

PAUL WHITEMAN AND HIS ORCHESTRA
Henry Busse, Charles Margulis, Eddie Pinder (tp); Bix Beiderbecke (c); Boyce Cullen, Wilbur Hall, Bill Rank (tb); Chester Hazlett, Charles Strickfaden, Rube Crozier, Roy Maier, Irving Friedman (reeds); Kurt Dieterle, Mischa Russell, Matty Mal-

neck (vln); Roy Bargy (p); Mike Trafficante (sb); Mike Pingitore (bj); Min Leibrook (tu); Hal McDonald (dm)

BVE 43125-1   **Coquette** (Kahn-Green-Lombardo-arr. Bill Challis)
BVE 43125-3   **Coquette**
solos: Margulis, tp & Hazlett, bcl (32)—Bix & brass trio (16)—Rank (8)

58: March 3, 1928   **HARMONY (NY)**

LOU RADERMAN & HIS PELHAM HEATH INN ORCHESTRA
Bix Beiderbecke? (c); Mannie Klein (tp); ? (tb); ? (cl); ? 2 (as); ? (ss); ? (ts); ? (p); ? (bj); ? (tu); ? (dm); Irving Kaufman on 145720 & 145721, Harry Donahey on 145722 (voc)

145720-2   **Oh Gee! Oh Joy!** (Romberg-Gershwin, George & Ira-P.G. Wodehouse)
solos: Kaufman, voc (32)—?, as (16+8)
145721-2   **Why Do I Love You?** (Hammersten-Kern)
solos: Kaufman, voc (32)—Bix ? (16)—?, cl (8)
145722-2   **Ol' Man River** (Hammerstein-Kern)
solos: ?, as (16)—Klein, tp (8)—?, as (8)—Donahey, voc (32)—Bix ? (16)—?, tb (8)

Confirmed by bandleader Lou Raderman, Bix's presence on these sides was questioned by different people—such as Mannie Klein, who claimed to have played all the recorded trumpet or cornet solos.

59: March 12, 1928   9:30–12:00 / 14:00–15:00   **VICTOR (LH, NY)**

PAUL WHITEMAN AND HIS ORCHESTRA
Charles Margulis, Eddie Pinder (tp); Bix Beiderbecke (c); Boyce Cullen, Bill Rank (tb); Frank Trumbauer, Chester Hazlett, Irving Friedman, Charles Strickfaden, Rube Crozier, Roy Maier (reeds); Roy Bargy (p); Mike Pingitore (bj); Mike Trafficante (sb); Min Leibrook (tu); Hal McDonald (dm); Jack Fulton, Charles Gaylord, Austin Young, Al Rinker, Harry Barris (voc)

BVE 43138-2   **When** (Razaf-Schafer-Johnson-arr. Satterfield)
BVE 43138-3   **When**
solos: Friedman, cl (8)—Tram (12)—Fulton, Gaylord, Young, voc (30)—Barris, scat & vocal quartet (8)—Bix & vocal quartet (6)—Barris, scat & vocal quartet (2+8)—Bix & vocal quartet (7)

60: March 13, 1928   9:30–13:00 / 14:30–16:00   **VICTOR (LH, NY)**

PAUL WHITEMAN AND HIS ORCHESTRA
Henry Busse, Charles Margulis, Eddie Pinder (tp); Bix Bei-derbecke (c); Boyce Cullen, Wilbur Hall, Bill Rank, Jack Fulton (tb); Frank Trumbauer, Chester Hazlett, Irving Fried-man, Charles Strickfaden, Rube Crozier, Roy Maier (reeds); Kurt Dieterle, Mischa Russell, Matty Malneck, Mario Perry, Charles Gaylord (vln); Roy Bargy (p); Mike Pingitore (bj); Mike Trafficante (sb); Min Leibrook (tu); Hal McDonald (dm)

| CVE 43142-4 | **Metropolis, Part 1** (Ferde Grofé-arr. Grofé) |
| CVE 43141-4 | **Metropolis, Part 2** (Ferde Grofé-arr. Grofé) |

> On Part 2, Bix can be heard on over six bars, at (6:19–6:26) on BXCD7 (Volume 3 of *Bix Restored*), and Bill Rank imme-diately after, at (6:31–6:41).

61: March 14, 1928   **VICTOR (LH, NY)**

PAUL WHITEMAN AND HIS ORCHESTRA
Same personnel as previous session (60) with the addition of Bing Crosby, Jack Fulton, Al Rinker, Austin Young, Boyce Cullen (voc)

CVE 43143-3	**Metropolis, Part 3** (Ferde Grofé-arr. Grofé)
CVE 43143-4	**Metropolis, Part 3**
	solos: humming by the vocal group (16)

> Bix and Irving Friedman on the last eight bars of the synco-pated moment ("Fugue," 11:04–11:14 on BXCD 7, Volume 3 of *Bix Restored*).

62: March 15, 1928   9:30–12:00   **VICTOR (LH, NY)**

PAUL WHITEMAN AND HIS ORCHESTRA
Charles Margulis, Eddie Pinder (tp); Bix Beiderbecke (c); Boyce Cullen, Wilbur Hall (tb); Frank Trumbauer, Chester Hazlett, Roy Maier, Charles Strickfaden, Rube Crozier (reeds); Kurt Dieterle, Mischa Russell, Matty Malneck (vln); Roy Bargy (p); Mike Pingitore (bj); Min Leibrook (bsx); Hal McDonald (dm); Bing Crosby (voc)

| BVE 43145-1 | **Lovable** (Holmes-Simons-Whiting-arr. Bill Challis) |
| | solos: Strickfaden, bar (8)—Bix (4+4)—Friedman, as (32)—Crosby, voc (32)—Bix (8) |

63: March 17, 1928   **VICTOR (LH, NY)**

PAUL WHITEMAN AND HIS ORCHESTRA
Same personnel as session (60)

| CVE 43149-3 | **Metropolis, Part 4** (Ferde Grofé-arr. Grofé) |

64: April 3, 1928   **OKEH (NY)**

FRANK TRUMBAUER AND HIS ORCHESTRA
Bix Beiderbecke (c), Charlie Margulis (tp), Bill Rank (tb), Frank Trumbauer (Cms), Irving Friedman (cl/as), Chet Ha-zlett (as), Matty Malneck (vln), Lennie Hayton (p), Eddie Lang (g), Min Leibrook (bsx), Hal McDonald (dm); Irving Kaufman, under the name of Noel Taylor (voc)

W 400188-A	**Our Bungalow of Dreams** (Malie-Newman-Verges)
	solos: Bix (8+20)—Kaufman, voc, with reeds acc (32)—Tram (16)—Bix (8)
W 400189-B	**Lila** (Gottler-Tobias-Pinkard)
	solos: Bix (2)—Kaufman, voc (32)—Bix (4+8) (leads 8)—Tram (1)—Bix (8)

65: April 10, 1928   **OKEH (NY)**

FRANK TRUMBAUER AND HIS ORCHESTRA
Same personnel as previous session (64), Harold "Scrappy" Lambert replaces Irving Kaufman (voc)

W 400603-B	**Borneo** (Donaldson-arr. Bill Challis)
	solos : Lambert, voc (31)—Bix & Tram, chase chorus 2/2 (30)
W 400604-B	**My Pet** (Yellen-Ager-arr. Bill Challis)
W 400604-C	**My Pet**
	solos: Leibrook (2)—Rank (16)—Friedman, cl (16)—Bix (6)—Lambert, voc & Lang, g (31)—Leibrook (2)—Bix (last 2 notes)

66: April 17, 1928   **OKEH (NY)**

BIX BEIDERBECKE AND HIS GANG
Bix Beiderbecke (c), Bill Rank (tb), Irving Friedman (cl), Roy Bargy (p), Min Leibrook (bsx), Hal McDonald (dm), harpophone)

W 400616-B	**Somebody Stole My Gal** (Wood)
	solos: Friedman (16)—Bargy (16)—Bix (24)—Rank (16)
W 400617-A	**Thou Swell**

9-second test groove; Bargy: "Damn"—"I got it";
Bix (possibly): "Take it from the last four"; Bargy
plays; Bix: "About time!"; laughs

W 400617-A **Thou Swell** (Rodgers-Hart)
W 400617-C **Thou Swell**
solos: Friedman (6)—Bargy (2+24)—Leibrook
(8)—Friedman (8)—Leibrook (8)—Friedman (8)

67: April 21, 1928   10:00–13:25 / 14:25–16:00   **VICTOR**
                                                      (LH, NY)

PAUL WHITEMAN AND HIS ORCHESTRA
Henry Busse, Charles Margulis, Eddie Pinder (tp); Bix Beider-
becke (c); Boyce Cullen, Wilbur Hall, Bill Rank, Jack Fulton
(tb); Frank Trumbauer, Chester Hazlett, Irving Friedman,
Charles Strickfaden, Rube Crozier, Roy Maier (reeds); Kurt
Dieterle, Mischa Russell, Matty Malneck, Mario Perry, John
Bouman, Charles Gaylord (vln); Roy Bargy, Lennie Hayton
(p); Mike Pingitore (bj); Mike Trafficante (sb); Min Leibrook
(tu); Hal McDonald (dm); Austin Young, Charles Gaylord, Al
Rinker, Jack Fulton (voc)

BVE 43659-1 **In My Bouquet of Memories** (Lewis-Young-
Akst-arr. Satterfield)
BVE 43659-3 **In My Bouquet of Memories**
solos: Hazlett, cl (16+8) (2)—Fulton & vocal
trio & Hazlett (32)

According to Phil Evans, Chester Hazlett got his sub-tone effect "by placing his tongue against the reed; this dampened
the sound and it also lowered the pitch. To compensate, he
equipped his clarinet with a short barrel of his own design"
(*The Leon Bix Beiderbecke Story*, p. 351).

Same personnel with the addition of Bing Crosby (voc)

BVE 43660-3 **I'm Afraid of You** (Davis-Daly-Gottler-arr.
Satterfield)
BVE 43660-4 **I'm Afraid of You**
solo: Crosby, voc (32)

Same personnel; Jack Fulton, Charles Gaylord, Al Rinker
(voc) replace Bing Crosby

BVE 43661-1 **My Angel** (Pollack-Rapee-arr. Satterfield)
BVE 43661-2 **My Angel**
solo: Fulton & vocal trio (32)

68: April 22, 1928   10:00–12:05 / 13:05–15:00   **VICTOR**
                                                      (LH, NY)

PAUL WHITEMAN AND HIS ORCHESTRA
Henry Busse, Charles Margulis, Eddie Pinder (tp); Bix Beiderbecke (c); Boyce Cullen, Wilbur Hall, Bill Rank, Jack
Fulton (tb); Frank Trumbauer, Chester Hazlett, Irving Friedman, Charles Strickfaden, Rube Crozier, Roy Maier
(reeds); Kurt Dieterle, Mischa Russell, Matty Malneck,
Mario Perry, John Bouman, Charles Gaylord (vln); Roy
Bargy, Lennie Hayton, Ferde Grofé (p); Mike Pingitore (bj);
Mike Trafficante (sb); Min Leibrook (tu/bsx); Hal McDonald (dm); Bing Crosby, Al Rinker, Jack Fulton, Charles Gaylord, Austin Young (voc)

BVE 43662-1 **My Pet** (Yellen-Ager-arr. Bill Challis)
BVE 43662-2 **My Pet**
BVE 43662-3 **My Pet**
solos: Bix, leads (8)—Strickfaden, bar (8)—Bix
& orch (16)—vocal quartet (16)—Crosby &
vocal quartet (15)—Bix & orch (16)—Tram
(8)—Friedman, cl & orch (8)

Same personnel; Jack Fulton (voc) omitted

BVE 43663-1 **It Was the Dawn of Love** (Coots-Davis—arr.
Satterfield)
BVE 43663-2 **It Was the Dawn of Love**
BVE 43663-3 **It Was the Dawn of Love**
solos: Bargy (1+1+2)—Tram (4+4+2)—Bargy
(16+8)—Crosby (16)—vocal quartet (8)—
Crosby (8)—Crosby (4, whistle + 2, voc)—
Bargy (4)
BVE 43664-1 **Dancing Shadows** (Golden-arr. Satterfield)
solos: Tram & humming vocal by the group
(8+7)—Rank (8+8)

Same personnel; Ferde Grofé (p) omitted and with Jack
Fulton (voc)

BVE 43665-2 **Forget-Me-Not** (Leslie-Wendling-Hoffman-arr.
Challis)
BVE 43665-3 **Forget-Me-Not**
solos: Bix, leads (16)—Busse (32)—Fulton,
voc (32)—Bix, straight or Harmon mute (16)—
Strickfaden (8)

69: April 23, 1928   10:00–12:05 / 13:05–16:00   **VICTOR (LH, NY)**

PAUL WHITEMAN AND HIS ORCHESTRA
Henry Busse, Charles Margulis, Eddie Pinder (tp); Bix Beiderbecke (c); Boyce Cullen, Wilbur Hall, Bill Rank, Jack Fulton (tb); Frank Trumbauer, Chester Hazlett, Irving Friedman, Charles Strickfaden, Rube Crozier, Roy Maier (reeds); Kurt Dieterle, Mischa Russell, Matty Malneck, Mario Perry, John Bouman, Charles Gaylord (vln); Roy Bargy (p); Lennie Hayton (cel); Mike Pingitore (bj); Mike Trafficante (sb); Min Leibrook (tu/bsx); Hal McDonald (dm); Austin Young (voc)

BVE 43666-1   **Dixie Dawn** (Trent-DeRose-arr. Ferde Grofé)
BVE 43666-2   **Dixie Dawn**
BVE 43666-3   **Dixie Dawn**
              solos: Young, voc (32)—Pingitore (7+7)

Same personnel; with Bing Crosby, Jack Fulton, Austin Young, Charles Gaylord (voc)

BVE 43667-1   **Louisiana** (Razaf-Schafer-Johnson-arr. Bill Challis)
BVE 43667-3   **Louisiana**
              solos: Bix, derby mute (4)—Friedman, cl (16)—Bix, leads (4)—Crosby & Sweet Trio, voc (32)—Bix, derby mute (16)—Friedman, cl (4)

70: April 24, 1928   10:00–11:45 / 13:00–14:30   **VICTOR (LH, NY)**

PAUL WHITEMAN AND HIS ORCHESTRA
Henry Busse, Charles Margulis, Eddie Pinder (tp); Bix Beiderbecke (c); Boyce Cullen, Wilbur Hall, Bill Rank, Jack Fulton (tb); Frank Trumbauer, Chester Hazlett, Irving Friedman, Charles Strickfaden, Rube Crozier, Roy Maier (reeds); Kurt Dieterle, Mischa Russell, Matty Malneck, Mario Perry, John Bouman, Charles Gaylord (vln); Roy Bargy, Lennie Hayton (p/cel); Mike Pingitore (bj); Mike Trafficante (sb); Min Leibrook (tu/bsx); Hal McDonald (dm); Bing Crosby, Jack Fulton, Charles Gaylord, Al Rinker (voc)

BVE 43668-2   **Grieving** (Axtell-arr. Satterfield)
              solo: Hazlett (16+6)—Gaylord, voc (32)—vocal quartet (8)

Same personnel, without Jack Fulton (voc)

BVE 43669-2   **Do I Hear You Saying "I Love You?"**
              (Rodgers-Hart-arr. Satterfield)
              solo: vocal trio (32)—Tram (32)

71: April 25, 1928   10:00–11:30   **VICTOR (LH, NY)**

PAUL WHITEMAN AND HIS ORCHESTRA
Henry Busse, Charles Margulis, Eddie Pinder (tp); Bix Beiderbecke (c); Boyce Cullen, Wilbur Hall, Bill Rank, Jack Fulton (tb); Frank Trumbauer, Chester Hazlett, Irving Friedman, Charles Strickfaden, Rube Crozier, Roy Maier (reeds); Kurt Dieterle, Mischa Russell, Matty Malneck, Mario Perry, John Bouman, Charles Gaylord (vln); Roy Bargy, Lennie Hayton (p); Mike Pingitore (bj); Mike Trafficante (sb); Min Leibrook (tu/bsx); George Marsh (dm); Bing Crosby, Austin Young, Jack Fulton, Charles Gaylord (voc)

BVE 43760-1   **You Took Advantage of Me** (Rodgers-Hart-arr. Satterfield)
              solos: Hazlett (2)—Bix, straight mute & Tram, chase chorus (32)—Crosby & Sweet Trio, voc (32)

72: May 12, 1928   **COLUMBIA (US, NY)**

PAUL WHITEMAN AND HIS ORCHESTRA
Henry Busse, Charles Margulis, Eddie Pinder (tp); Bix Beiderbecke (c); Boyce Cullen, Bill Rank, Jack Fulton (tb); Wilbur Hall (tb/g); Frank Trumbauer, Chester Hazlett, Irving Friedman, Charles Strickfaden, Rube Crozier, Roy Maier (reeds); Kurt Dieterle, Mischa Russell, Matty Malneck (vln); Roy Bargy (p); Lennie Hayton (cel); Mike Pingitore (bj); Mike Trafficante (sb); Min Leibrook (tu); Wilbur Hall (g); George Marsh (dm); unknown string guitar; Jack Fulton, Charles Gaylord, Austin Young (voc)

W 98533-2   **La Paloma (The Dove)** (Yradier-Kautner-arr. Ferde Grofé)

Same personnel with the addition of Mario Perry and Charles Gaylord (vln)

W 98534-3   **La Golondrina (The Swallow)** (Gilbert-Serradell-arr. Grofé)
              solos: Tram (16)—Hall, g & unknown-stg (16)

73: May 15, 1928　　　　　COLUMBIA (US, NY)

PAUL WHITEMAN AND HIS ORCHESTRA
Charles Margulis, Harry Goldfield, Eddie Pinder (tp); Bix Beiderbecke (c); Boyce Cullen, Wilbur Hall, Bill Rank, Jack Fulton (tb); Frank Trumbauer, Chester Hazlett, Irving Friedman, Charles Strickfaden, Rube Crozier, Roy Maier (reeds); Kurt Dieterle, Mischa Russell, Matty Malneck, Charles Gaylord, Mario Perry, John Bouman (vln); Roy Bargy (p); Lennie Hayton (cel); Mike Pingitore (bj); Mike Trafficante (sb); Min Leibrook (tu); George Marsh (dm) ; Austin Young (voc)

W 98537-4　　**My Melancholy Baby** (Burnett-Norton-arr.
　　　　　　　Satterfield)
　　　　　　　solos: Hazlett (intro)—Hayton (2)—Bargy (2)—
　　　　　　　Margulis (30)—Bargy (4)—muted trombone
　　　　　　　quartet (32)—Young, voc & Bix, straight mute
　　　　　　　(32)—Bargy (4)—Hazlett (8)

Same personnel in an evening session

-　　　　　　**My Ohio Home** (Kahn-Donaldson)

　　Soundtrack of a film made by Fox Movietone news; one third (which is actually 1 minute and 43 seconds) has been unearthed. In the beginning, at the left rear, Bing Crosby calls for Harry Barris and Austin Young—Paul Whiteman tears up his Victor contract, with George Marsh on vibes behind him—Whiteman conducts the band—Whiteman in profile; Mario Perry, John Bouman, and Charles Gaylord on violins; Charles Strickfaden, Roy Maier, and Rube Crozier on reeds; Bix stands up on the left rear and plays. These 200 feet of newsreel are available on the DVD Yazoo 514, *At the Jazz Band Ball*, Shanachie Entertainment Corp., 2000.

74: May 16, 1928　　　　　COLUMBIA (US, NY)

PAUL WHITEMAN AND HIS ORCHESTRA
Same personnel as previous session (73); Vaughn De Leath (voc) replaces Austin Young

W 98538-2　　**The Man I Love** (George & Ira Gershwin-arr.
　　　　　　　Ferde Grofé)
W 98538-4　　**The Man I Love**
　　　　　　　solos: Bargy (4)—Margulis & Hazlett, cl (16)—
　　　　　　　Dieterle (8)—Margulis & Hazlett, cl (8)—De
　　　　　　　Leath, voc (32)—Bargy (12)—Tram (16)—De
　　　　　　　Leath, voc (4)

75: May 17, 1928　　　　　COLUMBIA (US, NY)

PAUL WHITEMAN AND HIS ORCHESTRA
Charles Margulis, Harry Goldfield, Eddie Pinder (tp); Bix Beiderbecke (c); Boyce Cullen, Wilbur Hall, Bill Rank (tb); Frank Trumbauer, Chester Hazlett, Irving Friedman, Charles Strickfaden, Rube Crozier (reeds); Kurt Dieterle, Mischa Russell, Matty Malneck, Mario Perry (vln); Roy Bargy (p); Mike Pingitore (bj); Mike Trafficante (sb); Min Leibrook (tu); George Marsh (dm); Bing Crosby?, Al Rinker, Harry Barris, Austin Young, Jack Fulton, Charles Gaylord (voc)

W 146291-2　　**C-O-N-S-T-A-N-T-I-N-O-P-L-E** (Carlton-arr.
　　　　　　　Satterfield)
W 146291-3　　**C-O-N-S-T-A-N-T-I-N-O-P-L-E**
　　　　　　　number made of vocal parts (solos and choral
　　　　　　　parts) with orchestral accompaniment; Bing
　　　　　　　Crosby's voice cannot be identified

76: May 21, 1928　　　　　COLUMBIA (US, NY)

PAUL WHITEMAN AND HIS ORCHESTRA
Henry Busse, Charles Margulis, Eddie Pinder (tp); Bix Beiderbecke (c); Boyce Cullen, Bill Rank, Jack Fulton (tb); Wilbur Hall (tb/g); Frank Trumbauer, Chester Hazlett, Irving Friedman, Charles Strickfaden, Rube Crozier, Roy Maier (reeds); Kurt Dieterle, Mischa Russell, Matty Malneck (vln); Roy Bargy, Lennie Hayton (p); Mike Pingitore (bj); Mike Trafficante (sb); Min Leibrook (tu); George Marsh (dm); unknown string guitar; Jack Fulton, Charles Gaylord, Austin Young (voc)

W 98533-6　　**La Paloma (The Dove)** (Yradier-Kautner-arr.
　　　　　　　Ferde Grofé)

　　Final and master take of the title recorded on May 12.

77: May 22, 1928　　　　　COLUMBIA (US, NY)

PAUL WHITEMAN AND HIS ORCHESTRA
Henry Busse, Charles Margulis (tp); Bix Beiderbecke (c); Boyce Cullen, Wilbur Hall, Bill Rank (tb); Frank Trumbauer, Chester Hazlett, Irving Friedman, Charles Strickfaden, Rube Crozier, Roy Maier (reeds); Kurt Dieterle, Mischa Russell, Matty Malneck, Mario Perry (vln); Roy Bargy (p); Mike Pingitore (bj); Mike Trafficante (sb); Min Leibrook (tu); George Marsh (dm)

W 146317-3　　**Is It Gonna Be Long?** (Cowan-Abbot-
　　　　　　　Whiting-arr. Bill Challis)

solos: Busse (30)—Bix (4)—Bix & orch (16)—
Friedman, ts (16+8)—Bix (4)—Bix, Friedman
& orch (16)—Busse (8)—Bix, Friedman &
orch (16)

78: May 23, 1928   COLUMBIA (NY)

PAUL WHITEMAN AND HIS ORCHESTRA

Charles Margulis, Eddie Pinder (tp); Bix Beiderbecke (c);
Boyce Cullen, Wilbur Hall, Bill Rank (tb); Frank Trumbauer,
Chester Hazlett, Irving Friedman, Charles Strickfaden, Rube
Crozier, or Roy Maier (reeds); Kurt Dieterle, Mischa Russell,
Matty Malneck, Mario Perry (vln); Roy Bargy (p); Mike Pin-
gitore (bj); Mike Trafficante (sb); Min Leibrook (tu); George
Marsh (dm)

W 146327-2   **Oh! You Have No Idea** (Ponce-Dougherty-arr.
Bill Challis)
solos: Rank, tb with megaphone (32)—Bix,
leads (16)—Leibrook (8)—Bix, leads (8)—
Friedman, cl (4+12+4)—Bix, leads (16)—Tram
(6)—Bix, leads (12)

79: May 24, 1928   COLUMBIA (NY)

PAUL WHITEMAN AND HIS ORCHESTRA

Henry Busse, Charles Margulis (tp); Bix Beiderbecke (c);
Boyce Cullen, Wilbur Hall (tb); Frank Trumbauer, Chester
Hazlett, Charles Strickfaden, Roy Maier (reeds); Kurt Di-
eterle, Mischa Russell, Matty Malneck (vln); Roy Bargy (p);
Mike Pingitore (bj); Mike Trafficante (sb); Min Leibrook (tu);
George Marsh (dm); Jack Fulton (voc)

W 146329-3   **Blue Night** (Rollins-Mahoney-arr. Satterfield)
solos: Hazlett (16+8)—Fulton, voc (32)

80: May 25, 1928   COLUMBIA (NY)

PAUL WHITEMAN AND HIS ORCHESTRA

Charles Margulis, Eddie Pinder (tp); Bix Beiderbecke (c);
Boyce Cullen, Bill Rank, Wilbur Hall (tb); Chester Hazlett,
Roy Maier (as); Rube Crozier (ts); Frank Trumbauer (Cms);
Charles Strickfaden (bar); Kurt Dieterle, Mischa Russell,
Matty Malneck, Mario Perry (vln); Roy Bargy (p); Mike Pin-
gitore (bj); Mike Trafficante (sb); Min Leibrook (tu); George
Marsh (dm); Austin Young (voc, orchestral sounds)

W 146334-4   **Felix The Cat** (Kortlander-Wendling-arr.
Satterfield)
solos: Bix (8+6)—Young, voc (32)—Tram (14)

81: June 10, 1928   COLUMBIA (NY)

PAUL WHITEMAN AND HIS ORCHESTRA

Charles Margulis, Eddie Pinder (tp); Bix Beiderbecke (c);
Boyce Cullen, Bill Rank, Wilbur Hall (tb); Frank Trumbauer,
Chester Hazlett, Irving Friedman, Rube Crozier, Roy Maier,
Charles Strickfaden (reeds); Kurt Dieterle, Mischa Russell,
Matty Malneck, Mario Perry (vln); Roy Bargy (p); Mike Pin-
gitore (bj); Mike Trafficante (sb); Min Leibrook (tu); George
Marsh (dm); Bing Crosby (voc)

W 146316-9   **'Tain't So, Honey, 'Tain't So** (Robison-arr.
Challis)
solos: Crosby, voc (20+31)—Bix (4 open)
(8 straight mute) (16 open)—Tram, Crozier &
Mayer, bassoons (16)—Bix, straight mute (4)

PAUL WHITEMAN AND HIS ORCHESTRA

Charles Margulis, Harry Goldfield, Eddie Pinder (tp); Bix Bei-
derbecke (c); Boyce Cullen, Bill Rank, Wilbur Hall (tb); Frank
Trumbauer, Chester Hazlett, Irving Friedman, Rube Crozier,
Roy Maier, Charles Strickfaden (reeds); Kurt Dieterle, Mischa
Russell, Matty Malneck (vln); Roy Bargy, Lennie Hayton (p);
Mike Pingitore (bj); Mike Trafficante (sb); Min Leibrook (tu);
George Marsh (dm); Austin Young & Charles Gaylord, Jack
Fulton, Bing Crosby, Al Rinker (voc)

W 146318-6   **Japanese Mammy** (Donaldson-Kahn-arr. Grofé)
solos: Young, voc (16)—Young + vocal quartet
(32)—Bargy (16)—Goldfield (32)—
Strickfaden, bar (8+8)

Composition of vocal quartet is not certain.

PAUL WHITEMAN AND HIS ORCHESTRA

Charles Margulis, Harry Goldfield, Eddie Pinder (tp); Bix
Beiderbecke (c); Boyce Cullen, Bill Rank, Wilbur Hall, Jack
Fulton (tb); Frank Trumbauer, Chester Hazlett, Irving Fried-
man, Rube Crozier, Roy Maier, Charles Strickfaden (reeds);
Kurt Dieterle, Matty Malneck, Mischa Russell, Mario Perry,
John Bouman (vln); Roy Bargy (p); Mike Pingitore (bj);
Mike Trafficante (sb); Min Leibrook (tu); George Marsh
(dm/cel); Bing Crosby, Al Rinker, Harry Barris, Charles Gay-
lord, Jack Fulton, Austin Young (voc)

W 146320-5   **I'd Rather Cry Over You** (Dougherty-Ponce-
arr. Challis)
solos: Gaylord, Fulton, Young, voc (16)—
Crosby, Rinker & Barris, voc (32)—Bix (4)—
Bix, leads (8)—Tram (8)—Friedman, cl (4)

Same personnel, with Wilbur Hall (tb/g) and unknown string guitar; add Lennie Hayton (p); Jack Fulton (voc) replaces vocal group

W 146335-6   **Chiquita** (Gilbert-Wayne-arr. Grofé)
             solos: Fulton & Marsh, cel (intro)—Fulton &
             Hall, g (32)—Hazlett (32) (8)

82: June 17, 1928   COLUMBIA (NY)

PAUL WHITEMAN AND HIS ORCHESTRA
Charles Margulis, Harry Goldfield (tp); Eddie Pinder or Bix Beiderbecke (c); Boyce Cullen, Bill Rank, Wilbur Hall, Jack Fulton (tb); Frank Trumbauer, Chester Hazlett, Irving Friedman, Rube Crozier, Roy Maier, Charles Strickfaden (reeds); Kurt Dieterle, Matty Malneck, Mischa Russell (vln); Roy Bargy, Lennie Hayton (p); Mike Pingitore (bj); Mike Trafficante (sb); George Marsh (dm); Bing Crosby, Charles Gaylord, Jack Fulton, Austin Young (voc)

W 146541-3   **I'm On a Crest of a Wave** (DeSylva-Brown-
             Henderson-arr. Grofé)
             solos: Hazlett (intro)—Crosby & Sweet Trio
             (32+16)—vocal quartet (8)—Friedman, ts (8)

PAUL WHITEMAN AND HIS ORCHESTRA
Bix Beiderbecke (c); Charles Margulis (tp); Boyce Cullen, Bill Rank (tb); Frank Trumbauer, Chester Hazlett, Irving Friedman, Charles Strickfaden (reeds); Kurt Dieterle, Matty Malneck, Mischa Russell, Mario Perry (vln); Roy Bargy (p); Mike Pingitore (bj); Mike Trafficante (sb); Min Leibrook (tu); George Marsh (dm); Bing Crosby, Harry Barris, Al Rinker (Rhythm Boys) (voc)

W 146542-3   **That's My Weakness Now** (Green-Stept-arr.
             Satterfield)
             solos: Bix (1+1+1+1)—Rank (4)—[Rhythm
             Boys (2)—Bix (2)—Tram (4)]—[repeated
             sequence]—Rhythm Boys (32)—[Rhythm Boys
             & Friedman,cl (1+1+1+1+1+2)]—[Rhythm
             Boys & Bix (1+1+1+1+1+2)]—Rank (8)—
             [Rhythm Boys & Tram (1+1+1+1+1+2)]—Bix,
             leads (16)—Rhythm Boys (4)

PAUL WHITEMAN AND HIS ORCHESTRA
Charles Margulis, Harry Goldfield (tp); Bix Beiderbecke (c); Boyce Cullen, Bill Rank, (tb); Chester Hazlett (as); Irving Friedman, Charles Strickfaden (ts); Frank Trumbauer (Cms/as); Kurt Dieterle, Matty Malneck, Mischa Russell,

Mario Perry (vln); Roy Bargy (p); Mike Pingitore (bj); Mike Trafficante (sb); Min Leibrook (tu); George Marsh (dm); Jack Fulton, Charles Gaylord, Austin Young (Sweet Trio) (voc)

W 146543-3   **Georgie Porgie** (Mayerl-Paul-arr. Challis)
             solos: Sweet Trio, voc (32)—Tram (8)—Bix (4)

83: June 18, 1928   COLUMBIA (NY)

PAUL WHITEMAN AND HIS ORCHESTRA
Charles Margulis, Eddie Pinder (tp); Bix Beiderbecke (c); Boyce Cullen, Wilbur Hall (tb); Chester Hazlett, Frank Trumbauer (as); Irving Friedman (ts/cl); Charles Strickfaden (bar); Kurt Dieterle, Matty Malneck, Mischa Russell (vln); Roy Bargy (p); Mike Pingitore (bj); Mike Trafficante (sb); Min Leibrook (tu); George Marsh (dm); Bing Crosby & Jack Fulton, Charles Gaylord, Austin Young (Sweet Trio) (voc)

W 146549-2   **Because My Baby Don't Mean "Maybe"
             Now** (Donaldson-arr. Challis)
             solos: Dieterle (4)—Margulis (4+ leads, 16)
             (8)—Bix (16+8)—Strickfaden (16)—Crosby &
             Sweet Trio, voc (32)—Friedman & orch (6)—
             Dieterle (4)—Margulis (3)

PAUL WHITEMAN AND HIS ORCHESTRA
Same personnel; Bing Crosby, Harry Barris, Al Rinker (voc)

W 146550-3   **Out Of Town Gal** (Donaldson-arr. Challis)
             solos: Bix & orch (4+2)—Strickfaden (8)—
             Margulis (4)—Rhythm Boys (16+32)—
             Friedman, ts (4)—Rank (4+4)—Bix (8)

84: June 19, 1928   COLUMBIA (US, NY)

PAUL WHITEMAN AND HIS ORCHESTRA
Charles Margulis, Harry Goldfield, Eddie Pinder (tp); Bix Beiderbecke (c); Boyce Cullen, Wilbur Hall, Bill Rank, Jack Fulton (tb); Frank Trumbauer, Chester Hazlett, Irving Friedman, Rube Crozier, Roy Maier, Charles Strickfaden (reeds); Kurt Dieterle, Matty Malneck, Mischa Russell, John Bouman, Charles Gaylord, Mario Perry (vln); Roy Bargy, Lennie Hayton (p); Mike Pingitore (bj); Mike Trafficante (sb); Min Leibrook (tu); George Marsh (dm); Austin Young (voc)

W 146551-2   **American Tune** (DeSylva-Brown-Henderson-
             arr. Grofé)
             solo: Young, voc (52)

A patriotic tune, which includes quotes from "Yankee Doodle," "Columbia the Gem of the Ocean," "National Emblem March," and "The Star-Spangled Banner."

85: June 20, 1928   COLUMBIA (US, NY)

PAUL WHITEMAN AND HIS ORCHESTRA

Instrumental; same personnel as previous session (84) with Lennie Hayton (cel) and George Marsh (percussions)

| W 98556-3 | **Tchaikowskiana** (Fantasy of Tchaikowsky Themes)—**Part 1** |
| W 98557-4 | **Tchaikowskiana** (Fantasy of Tchaikowsky Themes)—**Part 2** (arr: Herman Hand) |

86: July 5, 1928   OKEH (CHI)

FRANK TRUMBAUER AND HIS ORCHESTRA

Bix Beiderbekce (c), Bill Rank (tb), Irving Friedman (cl/as), Frank Trumbauer (Cms/as), Chester Hazlett (as), Min Leibrook (bsx), Roy Bargy or Lennie Hayton (p), George Rose (bj/g), Harry Gale (dm); Frank Trumbauer, Dee Orr, Harry Barris, Marlin Hurt (voc)

| W 400989-C | **Bless You! Sister** (Dubin-Robinson) solos: Bix (intro:1+3)—Bix (16)—Tram (8)—Bix (8)—Tram, voc & vocal trio & g (35)—Leibrook (4)—?, voc (4)—Tram, voc (4)—Bix (2)—?, p (4)—Bix (false start)—Friedman, cl (8)—Bix (4) |
| W 400990-B | **Dusky Stevedore** (Razaf-Johnson) solos: Tram, voc (2)—Bix (1)—Tram, as (1)—Bix (leads 34+8)—Friedman (4)—Bix (4)—?, voc (16) & vocal quartet (32)—Tram (16) |

87: July 7, 1928   OKEH (CHI)

BIX BEIDERBECKE AND HIS GANG

Bix Beiderbekce (c), Bill Rank (tb), Irving Friedman (cl), Min Leibrook (bsx), Roy Bargy (p), Harry Gale (dm)

| W 400994-A | **Ol' Man River** (Kern-Hammerstein) solos: Bix (32)—Rank (24)—Bargy (16)—Bix (4)—Friedman (4)—Bargy (16) |
| W 400995-A | **Wa-Da-Da (Everybody's Doing It Now)** (Barris-Cavanaugh) solos: Bargy (16)—Leibrook (8)—Friedman (8)—Leibrook (8)—Bix (8) |

88: September 4, 1928   COLUMBIA (US, NY)

PAUL WHITEMAN AND HIS ORCHESTRA

Charles Margulis, Harry Goldfield, Eddie Pinder (tp); Bix Beiderbecke (c); Boyce Cullen, Wilbur Hall, Bill Rank, Jack Fulton (tb); Frank Trumbauer, Chester Hazlett, Irving Friedman, Roy Maier, Charles Strickfaden (reeds); Kurt Dieterle, Matty Malneck, Mischa Russell, Mario Perry (vln); Roy Bargy (p); Lennie Hayton (cel); Mike Pingitore (bj); Mike Trafficante (sb); Min Leibrook (tu); George Marsh (dm); Austin Young (voc)

| W 146947-3 | **Roses of Yesterday** (Irving Berlin-arr. Ferde Grofé) solos: Hazlett & orch (32)—Young, voc (16+32) |

89: September 14, 1928   COLUMBIA (US, NY)

PAUL WHITEMAN AND HIS ORCHESTRA

Charles Margulis, Eddie Pinder (tp); Bix Beiderbecke (c); Boyce Cullen, Wilbur Hall, Bill Rank (tb); Frank Trumbauer, Chester Hazlett, Irving Friedman, Roy Maier, Charles Strickfaden (reeds); Kurt Dieterle, Matty Malneck, Mischa Russell, Mario Perry (vln); Roy Bargy (p); Lennie Hayton (cel); Mike Pingitore (bj); Mike Trafficante (sb); Min Leibrook (tu); George Marsh (dm/vib); Jack Fulton, Charles Gaylord, Austin Young, Boyce Cullen (voc)

| W 146945-5 | **In the Good Old Summertime** (Waltz-medley-arr. Bill Challis) |

Waltz medley including the following titles: "In the Good Old Summertime," "Little Annie Rooney," "Comrades," "Rosie O'Grady," and "Yip I Addy I Ay."

PAUL WHITEMAN AND HIS ORCHESTRA

Charles Margulis (tp); Bix Beiderbecke (c); Bill Rank, Wilbur Hall (tb); Frank Trumbauer, Chester Hazlett, Roy Maier, Charles Strickfaden (reeds); Kurt Dieterle, Matty Malneck, Mischa Russell, Mario Perry (vln); Roy Bargy (p); Lennie Hayton (cel); Mike Pingitore (bj); Mike Trafficante (sb); Min Leibrook (tu); George Marsh (dm); Jack Fulton, Charles Gaylord, Austin Young, Boyce Cullen (voc)

| W 146946-6 | **The Sidewalks of New York** (Waltz medley-arr. Bill Challis) |

Medley including the following titles: "The Sidewalks of New York," "The Bowery," and "Hail, Hail, the Gang."

90: September 15, 1928 COLUMBIA (US, NY)

PAUL WHITEMAN AND HIS ORCHESTRA

Charles Margulis, Harry Goldfield, Eddie Pinder (tp); Bix Beiderbecke (c); Boyce Cullen, Wilbur Hall, Bill Rank, Jack Fulton (tb); Frank Trumbauer, Chester Hazlett, Irving Friedman, Rube Crozier, Roy Maier, Charles Strickfaden (reeds); Kurt Dieterle, Matty Malneck, Mischa Russell, John Bouman, Charles Gaylord, Mario Perry (vln); Roy Bargy (p); Mike Pingitore (bj); Mike Trafficante (sb); Min Leibrook (tu); George Marsh (perc); Lennie Hayton (cel) on 98569 only

W 98568-8	**Concerto in F** (Gershwin-arr. Grofé)
	Part 1: First Movement: *Allegro*
W 98569-5	**Concerto in F** (Gershwin-arr. Grofé)
	Part 2: First Movement: *Allegro*
	(continuation)
W 98570-5	**Concerto in F** (Gershwin-arr. Grofé)
	Part 3: First Movement: *Allegro* (end)
W 98576-2	**Concerto in F** (Gershwin-arr. Grofé)
	Part 4: Second Movement: *Andante con Moto*.
	solos at the beginning of part 4: Margulis, tp (15)—Bix, Harmon mute (10)—Margulis (11)

Middle muted solo has also been attributed to Harry Goldfield (Don Rayno).

91: September 17, 1928 COLUMBIA (US, NY)

PAUL WHITEMAN AND HIS ORCHESTRA

Charles Margulis, Harry Goldfield, Eddie Pinder (tp); Bix Beiderbecke (c); Boyce Cullen, Wilbur Hall, Bill Rank, Jack Fulton (tb); Frank Trumbauer, Chester Hazlett, Irving Friedman, Rube Crozier, Roy Maier, Charles Strickfaden (reeds); Kurt Dieterle, Matty Malneck, Mischa Russell, Mario Perry (vln); Roy Bargy (p); Lennie Hayton (cel); Mike Pingitore (bj); Mike Trafficante (sb); Min Leibrook (tu); George Marsh (dm); Jack Fulton (voc)

| W 98577-3 | **Jeannine, I Dream of Lilac Time** (Gilbert-Shilkret-arr. Grofé) |
| | solos: Fulton, voc (32)—Bargy (8+8) |

PAUL WHITEMAN AND HIS ORCHESTRA

Same personnel as previous session (90)

| W 98578-4 | **Concerto in F** (Gershwin-arr. Grofé) |
| | **Part 5: Second Movement: *Andante con Moto*** (continuation) |

| W 98575-3 | **Concerto in F** (Gershwin-arr. Grofé) |
| | **Part 6: Finale: *Allegro con Brio*** |

92: September 18, 1928 COLUMBIA (US, NY)

PAUL WHITEMAN AND HIS ORCHESTRA

Charles Margulis, Harry Goldfield, Eddie Pinder (tp); Bix Beiderbecke (c); Boyce Cullen, Wilbur Hall, Bill Rank, Jack Fulton (tb); Frank Trumbauer, Chester Hazlett, Irving Friedman, Rube Crozier, Roy Maier, Charles Strickfaden (reeds); Kurt Dieterle, Matty Malneck, Mischa Russell, John Bouman, Charles Gaylord (vln); Mario Perry (vln/accordion); Roy Bargy, Lennie Hayton (p); Mike Pingitore (bj); Mike Trafficante (sb); Min Leibrook (tu); George Marsh (perc); unknown (cimbalom); Austin Young (voc)

| W 98579-5 | **Gypsy** (Malneck-Signorelli-Gilbert-arr. Ferde Grofé) |
| | solos: ? cimbalom (intro)—Young, voc (24+32)—? cimbalom (interlude)—Perry, acc (8)—Dieterle, vln (interlude+10)—Bix, straight mute (8)—Bix & Hazlett (8+8) |

PAUL WHITEMAN AND HIS ORCHESTRA

Charles Margulis, Harry Goldfield, Eddie Pinder (tp); Bix Beiderbecke (c); Boyce Cullen, Wilbur Hall, Bill Rank, Jack Fulton (tb); Frank Trumbauer, Chester Hazlett, Irving Friedman, Roy Maier, Charles Strickfaden (reeds); Kurt Dieterle, Matty Malneck, Mischa Russell, Mario Perry, Charles Gaylord, John Bouman (vln); Roy Bargy (p); Lennie Hayton (cel); Mike Pingitore (bj); Mike Trafficante (sb); Min Leibrook (tu); George Marsh (dm); Jack Fulton (voc)

| W 98584-1 | **Sweet Sue** (Harris-Young-arr. Bill Challis) |
| | solos: Fulton, voc (32)—Bix, derby mute (32) |

93: September 19, 1928 COLUMBIA (US, NY)

PAUL WHITEMAN AND HIS ORCHESTRA

Charles Margulis, Harry Goldfield, Eddie Pinder (tp); Bix Beiderbecke (c); Boyce Cullen, Wilbur Hall, Bill Rank, Jack Fulton (tb); Frank Trumbauer, Chester Hazlett, Irving Friedman, Roy Maier, Rube Crozier, Charles Strickfaden (reeds); Kurt Dieterle, Matty Malneck, Mischa Russell, Mario Perry (vln); Roy Bargy (p); Lennie Hayton (cel); Mike Pingitore (bj); Mike Trafficante (sb); Min Leibrook (tu); George Marsh (dm); Eddie King (sleigh bells); unknown (harp); Jack Fulton, Charles Gaylord, Austin Young, Boyce Cullen (voc)

W 98586-3   **Christmas Melodies (O Holy Night, Adeste Fideles)**
(traditional-arr. Grofé)

94: September 20, 1928   OKEH (NY)

FRANK TRUMBAUER AND HIS ORCHESTRA

Bix Beiderbecke (c), Bill Rank (tb), Irving Friedman (cl/ts), Frank Trumbauer (Cms/as/voc), Min Leibrook (bsx), Roy Bargy (p), Wilbur Hall (g), Lennie Hayton (dm), Harold "Scrappy" Lambert (voc)

W 401133-B   **Take Your Tomorrow (And Give Me Today)**
(Razaf-Johnson-arr. Hayton)
solos: Tram (16)—Tram & Lambert, spoken vocal (14)—Tram & Lambert & Bix, Harmon mute? (32)—Bix / Rank / Friedman / Leibrook (1+1+1+1)

W 401134-C   **Love Affairs** (Dubin-Robinson-arr. Hayton)
solos: Bix, leads (16)—Rank, leads (8)—Bix, leads (8)—Bargy (6)—Bix & orch (16)—Lambert, voc & g (31)—Tram, Cms (5)—Rank (16)—Bargy (15)—Bix (2)

95: September 21, 1928   COLUMBIA (US, NY)

PAUL WHITEMAN AND HIS ORCHESTRA

Charles Margulis, Harry Goldfield, Eddie Pinder (tp); Bix Beiderbecke (c); Boyce Cullen, Wilbur Hall, Bill Rank, Jack Fulton (tb); Frank Trumbauer, Chester Hazlett, Irving Friedman, Roy Maier, Rube Crozier, Charles Strickfaden (reeds); Kurt Dieterle, Matty Malneck, Mischa Russell, Mario Perry, John Bouman, Charles Gaylord (vln); Roy Bargy (p); Lennie Hayton (cel); Mike Pingitore (bj); Mike Trafficante (sb); Min Leibrook (tu); George Marsh (dm); Jack Fulton (voc)

W 98589-3   **I Can't Give You Anything But Love**
(Fields-McHugh-arr. Grofé)
solos: Bargy (intro)—Fulton (32)—Tram (8)

96: September 21, 1928   OKEH (NY)

BIX BEIDERBECKE AND HIS GANG

Bix Beiderbecke (c), Bill Rank (tb), Irving Friedman (cl), Min Leibrook (bsx), Roy Bargy (p), Lennie Hayton (dm/p/harmonium)

W 401138-B   **Rhythm King** (Joe Hoover)
solos: Bix (32)—Bargy (16)—Friedman (16)

W 401139-A   **Louisiana** (Razaf-Schafer-Johnson)
solos: Bix (intro, 4)—Bargy & Hayton, p (14)—Leibrook (2)—Rank (16)—Hayton, harm (2)

W 401140-A   **Margie** (Davis-Conrad-Robinson)
solos: Bargy (30)—Friedman (2+16)—Bix (16)

97: October 5, 1928 (I)   COLUMBIA (US, NY)

PAUL WHITEMAN AND HIS ORCHESTRA

Charles Margulis, Harry Goldfield, Eddie Pinder (tp); Bix Beiderbecke (c); Boyce Cullen, Wilbur Hall, Bill Rank, Jack Fulton (tb); Frank Trumbauer, Chester Hazlett, Irving Friedman, Rube Crozier, Roy Maier, Charles Strickfaden (reeds); Kurt Dieterle, Matty Malneck, Mischa Russell, John Bouman, Charles Gaylord, Mario Perry (vln); Roy Bargy (p); Mike Pingitore (bj); Mike Trafficante (sb); Min Leibrook (tu); George Marsh (perc)

W 98575-7   **Concerto in F** (Gershwin-arr. Grofé)
Part 6: Finale: *Allegro con Brio*

Orchestra conducted by William Daly; recording made in the presence of George Gershwin.

98: October 5, 1928 (II)   OKEH (NY)

FRANK TRUMBAUER AND HIS ORCHESTRA

Bix Beiderbecke (c); Charles Margulis (tp); Bill Rank (tb); Irving Friedman (cl/ts); Frank Trumbauer (Cms/voc); Lennie Hayton (p); Wilbur Hall (g); ? (dm); Rube Crozier (bassoon), not on the first title; Charles Gaylord (voc), except on 401196

W 401195-B   **The Love Nest** (Harbach-Hirsch)
solos: Friedman (8)—Rank (4)—Gaylord, voc (32)—Bix (16)

W 401196-C   **The Japanese Sandman** (Egan-Whiting)
solos: Tram, Cms (32)—Margulis (16)—Tram, voc (32)—Bix & orch (15)—Margulis (3)

W 401197-A   **High Up On A Hilltop** (Baer-Whiting-Campbell)
solos: Margulis (15)—Rank (1+7)—Margulis (6)—Friedman (2)—Tram (2)—Rank (2)—Friedman & orch (5)—Gaylord, voc (31)—Tram (16)—Bix (8)—Margulis (8)

W 40119-A   **Sentimental Baby** (Jack Palmer)
solos: Rank, leads (35)—Gaylord, voc & Tram, Cms (31)—Bix, derby mute (20)—Rank (8)

99: October 6, 1928   COLUMBIA (US, NY)

PAUL WHITEMAN AND HIS ORCHESTRA
Charles Margulis, Harry Goldfield (tp); Eddie Pinder or Bix Beiderbecke (c); Boyce Cullen, Wilbur Hall, Bill Rank (tb); Frank Trumbauer, Chester Hazlett (as); Irving Friedman, Roy Maier (ts); Charles Strickfaden (bar); Kurt Dieterle, Matty Malneck, Mischa Russell, Charles Gaylord (vln); Roy Bargy (p); Lennie Hayton (cel); Mike Pingitore (bj); Mike Trafficante (sb); Min Leibrook (tu); George Marsh (dm); Jack Fulton (voc)

W 147032-8   **Where Is the Song of Songs for Me?** (Berlin-arr. Ferde Grofé)
              solos: Fulton, voc (32+4)

Third trumpet part is most probably played by Eddie Pinder.

from December 11, 1928 through January 10, 1929

The dates over which Bix Beiderbecke was in and out of the River Crest Sanitarium still remain unknown. No evidence—aural perception, written documents, witnesses—could be found to confirm Bix's presence on any of the titles recorded by the Paul Whiteman Orchestra during that period. The following recordings were released:

PAUL WHITEMAN AND HIS ORCHESTRA   COLUMBIA (US, NY)
December 13, 1928:

W 98610-2   **Liebestraum** (Liszt-arr. Bargy)

December 19, 1928:

W 147534   **I'm Bringing a Red, Red Rose** (Donaldson-Kahn-arr. Grofé)

December 22, 1928:

W 147540   **Makin' Whoopee** (Donaldson-arr. Grofé)
W 147536   **Let's Do It, Let's Fall in Love** (Porter-arr. Challis).

It is certain that Bix was not in the recording-studio on December 22, as "his" solo on "Makin' Whoopee" was played by Mannie Klein.

100: January 10, 1929   COLUMBIA (US, NY)

PAUL WHITEMAN AND HIS ORCHESTRA
Charles Margulis, Harry Goldfield, Eddie Pinder (tp); Bix Beiderbecke? (c); Boyce Cullen, Wilbur Hall, Bill Rank, Jack Fulton (tb); Frank Trumbauer, Chester Hazlett, Irving Friedman, Roy Maier, Rube Crozier, Charles Strickfaden (reeds); Kurt Dieterle, Matty Malneck, Mischa Russell, Charles Gaylord, John Bouman, Mario Perry (vln); Roy Bargy (p); Lennie Hayton (cel); Mike Pingitore (bj); Mike Trafficante (sb); Min Leibrook (tu); George Marsh (dm)

W 147750-2   **Chinese Lullaby** (Bowers-arr. Grofé)
              solo: Cullen, muted tb (28)

PAUL WHITEMAN PRESENTS: BEE PALMER WITH THE FRANK TRUMBAUER ORCHESTRA
Unknown (tp) or Bix Beiderbecke (c); Bill Rank (tb); Frank Trumbauer (Cms); Charles Strickfaden? (as); Irving Friedman (cl/ts); Lennie Hayton (p); Edwin "Snoozer" Quinn (g); George Marsh (dm); Beatrice "Bee" Palmer (voc)

W 147770-2   **Don't Leave Me, Daddy** (Verges-arr. Challis-Hayton)
              sung by Bee Palmer (16+64), with one Tram solo (32)
W 147771-1   **Singin' the Blues** (Robinson-Conrad-lyrics by Ted Koehler-arr. Hayton-Challis)
W 147771-3   **Singin' the Blues**
              solo: Bee Palmer, voc (48)

The orchestra plays an arrangement built on the saxophone solo created by Tram on February 4, 1927; this part is followed by Bee Palmer singing on the same melody as Tram's solo, then scat-singing on the solo played by Bix on the original Okeh recording.

Snoozer Quinn emphasized that Bix was attending this session, but the few cornet (or trumpet) notes played on "Singin' the Blues" make identification impossible.

101: January 24, 1929   BRUNSWICK (CHI)

RAY MILLER AND HIS ORCHESTRA
Muggsy Spanier, Bix Beiderbecke? (c); Lloyd Wallen, Jules Fasthoff (tb); Jim Cannon, Maurice Morse, Lyle Smith (reeds); Paul Lyman (vln); Art Gronwall (p); Al Carsella (pac); Leo Kaplan (bj/g); Jules Cassard (tu, sb); Bill Paley (dm); Bob Nolan (voc), replaced by unknown accordion on take C

C 2857-A?   **Cradle of Love** (Wayne-Gilbert)
C 2857-B?   **Cradle of Love**
C 2857-C?   **Cradle of Love**

solos: Spanier (16)—Nolan, voc, or accordion (32)—Wallen or Fasthoff, tb (4)—Bix, derby mute? (16)—Wallen or Fasthoff, tb (8)

The third take, discovered in 2005, has no vocal: such alternate takes were recorded by Brunswick for exclusive release in the German market.

102: March 8, 1929   OKEH (NY)

FRANK TRUMBAUER AND HIS ORCHESTRA
Bix Beiderbecke, Andy Secrest (c); Bill Rank (tb); Frank Trumbauer (Cms/voc); Irving Friedman (cl/ts); Chester Hazlett (as); Matty Malneck (vln); Lennie Hayton (p); Snoozer Quinn (g); Min Leibrook (bsx); Stan King (dm); Smith Ballew (voc) on the second title

W 401703-A   **Futuristic Rhythm** (McHugh-arr. Matty Malneck)
W 401703-B   **Futuristic Rhythm**
        solos: Rank (intro 2)—Hayton (5)—Tram, voc (32)—Hayton (2)—Bix (16)—Rank (8)—Bix (8)—Friedman / Tram / Rank / Leibrook (1+1+1+1)
W 401704-A   **Raisin' the Roof** (McHugh-arr. Matty Malneck)
W 401704-D   **Raisin' the Roof**
        solos: Secrest? (8)—Malneck (4)—Malneck & Quinn (16)—Tram (16)—Friedman (8)—Tram (7)—Secrest? (8)—Tram (1)—Malneck (1)

Alternate takes "A" of "Futuristic Rhythm" and "Raisin' the Roof" were discovered in 2004, and released in 2005 on the fifth and last volume of *Bix Restored*. Bix sounds more confident on the first take (A) of "Futuristic Rhythm," and his two solos offer significant differences. The cornet solos on the two takes of "Raisin' the Roof" are identical, confirming thus that they are probably played by Andy Secrest.

103: March 15, 1929   COLUMBIA (US, NY)

PAUL WHITEMAN AND HIS ORCHESTRA
Charles Margulis, Harry Goldfield (tp); Bix Beiderbecke, Andy Secrest (c); Boyce Cullen, Bill Rank, Jack Fulton (tb); Wilbur Hall (tb/g); Frank Trumbauer, Chester Hazlett, Irving Friedman, Roy Maier, Rube Crozier, Charles Strickfaden (reeds); Kurt Dieterle, Matty Malneck, Mischa Russell, John Bouman (vln); Roy Bargy (p); Lennie Hayton (cel); Mike Pingitore (bj); Mike Trafficante (sb); Min Leibrook (tu);

George Marsh (perc); unknown string guitar; Charles Gaylord, Jack Fulton (voc)

W 148085-4   **Blue Hawaii** (Baer-Caesar-Schuster-arr. Grofé)
        solos: Gaylord, Fulton (32)—Hall, g & ? string g (16+8)

Same personnel, but Bing Crosby (voc) replaces Gaylord and Fulton

W 148086-3   **Louise** (Robin-Whiting-arr. Bargy)
        solos: Crosby, voc (32)—Cullen (8)—Tram (4)

Bix has often been omitted on this number. His presence on this title, however, sounds highly probable because of the drive from the brass ensemble.

104: April 5, 1929   COLUMBIA (US, NY)

PAUL WHITEMAN AND HIS ORCHESTRA
Charles Margulis, Harry Goldfield (tp); Bix Beiderbecke, Andy Secrest (c); Boyce Cullen, Bill Rank, Wilbur Hall (tb); Frank Trumbauer, Chester Hazlett, Irving Friedman, Roy Maier, Bernie Daly, Charles Strickfaden (reeds); Kurt Dieterle, Matty Malneck, Mischa Russell (vln); Roy Bargy, Lennie Hayton (p); Mike Pingitore (bj); Mike Trafficante (sb); Min Leibrook (tu); George Marsh (dm); Bing Crosby, Al Rinker, Harry Barris (voc)

W 148183-3   **I'm in Seventh Heaven** (DeSylva-Brown-Henderson-arr. Bill Challis)
        solos: Bix, straight mute & Strickfaden, bar (16)—Hazlett, as (8+4)—Bix, straight mute & Strickfaden, bar (8)—vocal trio (32)—Bargy & Hayton, p (16)—Dieterle (8)

105: April 17, 1929   OKEH (NY)

FRANK TRUMBAUER AND HIS ORCHESTRA
Bix Beiderbecke, Andy Secrest (c); Bill Rank (tb); Frank Trumbauer (Cms/voc); Irving Friedman (cl/ts); Chester Hazlett or Charles Strickfaden (as); Matty Malneck (vln); Roy Bargy (p); Snoozer Quinn (g); Min Leibrook (bsx); Stan King (dm); Smith Ballew (voc) on the two first titles

W 401809-B   **Louise** (Robin-Whiting-arr. Malneck)
        solos: Secrest & orch (8)—Ballew, voc (32)—Tram (16)—Friedman (8)—Secrest, leads (8) & Bix, high notes (4)

W 401810-C   **Wait Till You See "Ma Chérie"** (Robin-Whiting-arr. Malneck)
solos: Friedman (intro 4)—Malneck & Quinn (16)—Tram, Cms (16)—Rank (8)—Tram (8)—Ballew, voc & vln (32)—Bix, derby mute (4+4)—Friedman (8)

W 401811-C   **Baby, Won't You Please Come Home?** (Warfield-Williams-arr. Malneck)
solos: Secrest (16)—Tram, voc & Bix, derby mute (16)—Tram, Cms (16)—Bix, derby mute (16)—Secrest, leads (16)

106: April 25, 1929   COLUMBIA (US, NY)

PAUL WHITEMAN AND HIS ORCHESTRA

Charles Margulis, Harry Goldfield (tp); Bix Beiderbecke, Andy Secrest (c); Boyce Cullen, Bill Rank, Wilbur Hall, Jack Fulton (tb); Frank Trumbauer, Chester Hazlett, Irving Friedman, Roy Maier, Bernie Daly, Charles Strickfaden (reeds); Kurt Dieterle, Mischa Russell, Matty Malneck, John Bouman, (vln); Roy Bargy (p); Lennie Hayton (cel); Mike Pingitore (bj); Mike Trafficante (sb); Min Leibrook (tu); George Marsh (perc); Bing Crosby (voc)

W 148184-8   **Little Pal** (DeSylva-Brown-Henderson-arr. Grofé)
solos: Crosby, voc (32)—Hazlett (24)

Same personnel, without John Bouman (vln) and Lennie Hayton (cel)

W 98653-4   **Song of India** (Rimsky-Korsakov-arr. Bargy).
solo: Hazlett, cl (12)

107: April 30, 1929   OKEH (NY)

FRANK TRUMBAUER AND HIS ORCHESTRA

Bix Beiderbecke, Andy Secrest (c); Bill Rank (tb); Frank Trumbauer (Cms/as); Irving Friedman (cl/ts); Charles Strickfaden (cl, as, oboe); Matty Malneck, Mischa Russell, Kurt Dieterle (vln); Lennie Hayton (p); Eddie Lang (g); Min Leibrook (bsx); Stan King (dm); Smith Ballew (voc)

W 401840-B   **No One Can Take Your Place** (Gilbert-Malneck-Signorelli-arr. Malneck)
solos: Tram (8)—Ballew, voc (32)—Bix, derby mute (8)

Bix Beiderbecke, Andy Secrest (c); Charles Margulis (tp); Bill Rank (tb); Frank Trumbauer (Cms/as); Irving Friedman (cl/ts); Charles Strickfaden (cl, as, oboe); Matty Malneck (vln); Lennie Hayton (p); Eddie Lang (g); Min Leibrook (bsx); Stan King (dm)

W 401841-C   **I Like That** (Hayton-Trumbauer-Kohler-arr. Hayton)
solos: Bix (8)—Hayton (5)—Tram (16)—Bix, derby mute (16)—Friedman (8)—Bix, derby mute (7)—Rank (4+4)

108: May 3, 1929   COLUMBIA (US, NY)

PAUL WHITEMAN AND HIS ORCHESTRA

Charles Margulis, Harry Goldfield (tp); Bix Beiderbecke, Andy Secrest (c); Boyce Cullen, Bill Rank, Wilbur Hall, Jack Fulton (tb); Frank Trumbauer, Chester Hazlett, Irving Friedman, Roy Maier, Bernie Daly, Charles Strickfaden (reeds); Kurt Dieterle, Mischa Russell, John Bouman, Charles Gaylord (vln); Roy Bargy (p); Lennie Hayton (cel); Mike Pingitore (bj); Mike Trafficante (sb); Min Leibrook (tu); George Marsh (dm); Jack Fulton (voc)

W 148407-4   **When My Dreams Come True** (Irving Berlin-arr. Bargy)
solos: Margulis (16)—Tram, as (8)—Secrest (8)—Bargy (4)—Strickfaden, bar (4)—Bargy (4)—Strickfaden (4)—Fulton, voc (32)—Hazlett, bcl (16)—Tram, as (8)

Same personnel, but without Lennie Hayton (cel); Bing Crosby (voc) replaces Jack Fulton

W 148408-4   **Reachin' for Someone** (Donaldson-Leslie—arr. Challis)
solos: Rank, tb (8)—Tram (16+8)—Crosby, voc (32)—Bix (8)

Bix Beiderbecke, Andy Secrest (c); Charles Margulis (tp); Bill Rank (tb); Frank Trumbauer (Cms); Chester Hazlett, Bernie Daly (as); Irving Friedman (cl/ts); Charles Strickfaden (ts); Kurt Dieterle, Mischa Russell, Charles Gaylord (vln); Roy Bargy (p); Mike Pingitore (bj); Mike Trafficante (sb); Min Leibrook (tu); George Marsh (dm)

W 148409-4   **China Boy** (Winfree-Boutelje-arr. Hayton)
solos: Friedman, cl (16+8)—Tram (16+2)—Secrest (4)—Bix, derby mute (16)—Margulis (4)

109: May 4, 1929   COLUMBIA (US, NY)

PAUL WHITEMAN AND HIS ORCHESTRA

Charles Margulis, Harry Goldfield (tp); Bix Beiderbecke, Andy Secrest (c); Boyce Cullen, Bill Rank, Wilbur Hall, Jack Fulton (tb); Frank Trumbauer, Chester Hazlett, Irving Friedman, Roy Maier, Bernie Daly, Charles Strickfaden (reeds); Kurt Dieterle, Mischa Russell, John Bouman, Charles Gaylord (vln); Roy Bargy (p); Lennie Hayton (cel); Mike Pingitore (bj); Mike Trafficante (sb); Min Leibrook (tu); George Marsh (dm); Bing Crosby (voc)

W 148421-4 **Oh! Miss Hannah** (Deppen-Hollingsworth-arr. Challis)
      solos: Strickfaden (16)—Margulis (4)—Tram (16)—Crosby, voc (16)—Bix, Harmon mute (16)—Margulis (20)
W 148423-4 **Orange Blossom Time** (Goodwin-Edwards-arr. Grofé)
      solos: Strickfaden (32)—Crosby, voc (32)—Hazlett (8)

110: May 16, 1929   COLUMBIA (US, NY)

PAUL WHITEMAN AND HIS ORCHESTRA

Same personnel as previous session (109); Bing Crosby, Jack Fulton, Al Rinker (voc)

W 148422-8 **Your Mother and Mine** (Goodwin-Edwards-arr. Bargy)
      solos: Strickfaden (8) (8)—vocal trio (8)—Crosby, voc (8)—vocal trio (8)—Crosby (4)—vocal trio (4)—Tram (2)—Rank (8)—Hazlett (8)—Rank (8)—Hazlett (8)—vocal trio (12)

111: September 6, 1929   COLUMBIA (US, NY)

PAUL WHITEMAN AND HIS ORCHESTRA

Charles Margulis, Harry Goldfield (tp); Bix Beiderbecke, Andy Secrest (c); Boyce Cullen, Bill Rank, Wilbur Hall, Jack Fulton (tb); Frank Trumbauer, Chester Hazlett, Irving Friedman, Roy Maier, Bernie Daly, Charles Strickfaden (reeds); Kurt Dieterle, Mischa Russell, Matty Malneck, Otto Landau (vln); Roy Bargy (p); Lennie Hayton (cel); Mike Pingitore (bj); Mike Trafficante (sb); Eddie Lang (g); Min Leibrook (tu); George Marsh (dm); Bing Crosby, Al Rinker, Jack Fulton (voc)

W 148985-3 **At Twilight** (Tracy-Pinkard-arr. Grofé)
      solos: vocal trio (32)—Tram (8)

112: September 13, 1929 COLUMBIA (US, NY)

PAUL WHITEMAN AND HIS ORCHESTRA

Charles Margulis, Harry Goldfield (tp); Bix Beiderbecke, Andy Secrest (c); Boyce Cullen, Bill Rank, Wilbur Hall, Jack Fulton (tb); Frank Trumbauer, Chester Hazlett, Irving Friedman, Roy Maier, Bernie Daly, Charles Strickfaden (reeds); Kurt Dieterle, Mischa Russell, Matty Malneck, Otto Landau, John Bouman, Ted Bacon (vln); Roy Bargy (p); Lennie Hayton (cel); Mike Pingitore (bj); Mike Trafficante (sb); Eddie Lang (g); Min Leibrook (tu); George Marsh (dm); Bing Crosby (voc)

W 148986-8 **Waiting at the End of the Road** (Irving Berlin-arr. Grofé)
      solos: Margulis (4)—Crosby, voc (32)—Margulis (12)—Bix (8)

Same personnel; without Bouman and Bacon (vln); and without Bix Beiderbecke (c) on the edited take; with Bing Crosby, Al Rinker, Jack Fulton (voc)

W 149005-3 **When You're Counting the Stars Alone** (Russell-Rose-Murray-arr. Challis)
      solos: Tram, as (16+8)—vocal trio (32)—Secrest (8)

113: January 21 or 22, 1930 BRUNSWICK (NY)

ROGER WOLFE KAHN & HIS ORCHESTRA

Bix Beiderbecke? (c); Muggsy Spanier? (c); 2? (tp); ? (tb); 4? (reeds); 2? (vln); ? (p); ? (bj); ? (tu); ? (dm); Libby Holman (voc)

E31960 **Cooking Breakfast for the One I Love** (Billy Rose-Henry Tobias)
      solos: ?, tb (16)—Holman, voc (32)—? tp (4+4)—Spanier? (16)
E31961-G **Cooking Breakfast for the One I Love** (issued in Germany, no vocal?)
E31962 **When a Woman Loves a Man** (Billy Rose-Ralph Rainger)
E3196? **When a Woman Loves a Man**
      solos: Holman, voc (32)—Bix, muted? (16)
E31963-G **When a Woman Loves a Man** (issued in Germany, no vocal?)

Neither of the two cornet soloists is one of the trumpet players listed for the date in discographies: Tony Gianelli and John O. Egan. Eddie Lang, Joe Venuti, Joe Tarto (tu), and

Chauncey Morehouse (dm) are also listed for this session: Lang and Venuti were in Los Angeles, filming *The King of Jazz*, and they can be ruled out; Tarto and Morehouse have stated they were not on the recording. The second take (E3196?) of "When a Woman Loves a Man" was played in the 1970s on Rich Conaty's weekly *Big Broadcast* on WFUV. This alternate has not been clearly identified, but it may have been used, together with the first take, on the same Brunswick record 4699. (Thanks to Vito Ciccone for pointing out this extremely interesting recording session.)

114: May 21, 1930　　　　　RCA-VICTOR (LH, NY)

HOAGY CARMICHAEL AND HIS ORCHESTRA
Bix Beiderbecke (c); James "Bubber" Miley (tp); Tommy Dorsey (tb); Benny Goodman (cl); Arnold Brilhart (as); Lawrence "Bud" Freeman, Larry Binyon (ts); Irving Brodsky (p); Joe Venuti (vln); Eddie Lang (g); Harry Goodman (tu); Gene Krupa (dm); Hoagy Carmichael (pipe-organ, voc)

BVE 59800-2　　**Rockin' Chair** (Carmichael-arr. Carmichael)
　　　　　　　solos: Freeman (4)—Miley (16)—Dorsey (8)—
　　　　　　　Miley (8) [Bix growls on second bar]—Venuti
　　　　　　　(16)—Freeman (4)—Carmichael, vocal on a
　　　　　　　double register (32)—Venuti & Lang (4)—Bix,
　　　　　　　derby mute (8)—Miley (4)—Bix (3)

Same personnel with Carmichael (p), and Hoagy Carmichael, Carson Robison (voc)

BVE 62301-1　　**Barnacle Bill, the Sailor** (Luther-Robison-arr.
　　　　　　　Carmichael)
　　　　　　　solos: Carmichael, voc (8)—Robison, voc &
　　　　　　　choir (8)—Bix, derby mute (4+16)—
　　　　　　　Carmichael, voc (8)—Robison, voc & choir
　　　　　　　(8)—Goodman (16)—Freeman (8)—Venuti (2)

115: June 6, 1930　　　　　　BRUNSWICK (NY)

IRVING MILLS AND HIS HOTSY-TOTSY GANG
Bix Beiderbecke (c); prob. Charlie Margulis (tp); Jack Teagarden (tb); Benny Goodman (cl/as); Larry Binyon (ts); Joe Venuti & unknown player (vln); Min Leibrook (bsx); Frank Signorelli (p); Lew Green (g); Gene Krupa (dm); Dick Robertson (voc) on the last title

E 32948-A　　**Loved One** (Trumbauer-Hayton-Mills)
E 32948-B　　**Loved One**

　　　　　　　solos: Bix (8)—Teagarden (16)—Marguilis
　　　　　　　(8)—Teagarden (6)—Goodman (4)—Bix
　　　　　　　(16)—Goodman (8)
E 32949-B　　**Deep Harlem** (Mills-Signorelli-Malneck)
　　　　　　　solos: Bix (16)—Goodman (16)—Teagarden
　　　　　　　(1)—Bix (2+2)—Venuti & Goodman (16)
E 32950-B　　**Strut Miss Lizzie** (Creamer-Layton)
　　　　　　　solos: Venuti? (4)—Roberson, voc & Venuti,
　　　　　　　vln (20+16)—Bix (12)—Leibrook (4)—Bix
　　　　　　　(4)—Goodman (20)—Teagarden (12)—Venuti
　　　　　　　(4)—Teagarden (4)—Venuti, fart chorus (4)

Ray Lodwig was listed on former discographies, but we believe Frank van Nus is right to hear Charlie Margulis on trumpet. The names of Nat Brusiloff and Matty Malneck have been suggested for the second violinist.

116: September 8, 1930　　10:00–13:30 / 14:30–16:30
　　　　　　　　　　　　　RCA-VICTOR (Studio # 2)

BIX BEIDERBECKE AND HIS ORCHESTRA
Bix Beiderbecke (c); Ray Lodwig (tp); Boyce Cullen (tb); Benny Goodman, Jimmy Dorsey, Charles "Pee Wee" Russell (cl/as); Bud Freeman (ts); Min Leibrook (bsx); Irving Brodsky (p); Joe Venuti (vln); Eddie Lang (g); Gene Krupa (dm); Wes Vaughan (voc)

BVE 63630-1　　**Deep Down South** (Collins-Green)
BVE 63630-2　**Deep Down South**
　　　　　　　solos: Leibrook (2)—Vaughan, voc (32)—
　　　　　　　Goodman (4)—Bix (16)—Goodman (8)—Bix (4)
BVE 63631-1　　**I Don't Mind Walkin' in the Rain** (Rich-
　　　　　　　Hoffman)
　　　　　　　solos: Bix (8)—Vaughan, voc (32)—Russell, cl
　　　　　　　& orch (4)—Venuti & Russell, cl (16)—Brodsky
　　　　　　　(8)—Venuti & Russell, cl (6)—Lodwig (2+6)

Bix Beiderbecke (c); Ray Lodwig (tp); Boyce Cullen (tb); Benny Goodman, Jimmy Dorsey, Charles "Pee Wee" Russell (cl/as); Bud Freeman (ts); Min Leibrook (sb); Irving Brodsky (p); Gene Krupa (dm); Wes Vaughan (voc)

BVE 63632-2　　**I'll Be a Friend with Pleasure** (Pinkard)
BVE 63632-3　**I'll Be a Friend with Pleasure**
　　　　　　　solos: Intro, Cullen / Dorsey / Bix / Freeman
　　　　　　　(1+1+1+1); Lodwig (16)—Cullen (8)—Lodwig
　　　　　　　(6)—Vaughan, voc (30)—Bix, derby mute
　　　　　　　(2+16)—Dorsey (16)—Vaughan, voc (4)

117: September 15, 1930   13:15–17:10   **RCA-VICTOR**
(Studio #2)

HOAGY CARMICHAEL AND HIS ORCHESTRA
Bix Beiderbecke (c); Ray Lodwig (tp); Jack Teagarden, Boyce Cullen (tb); Jimmy Dorsey (cl/as); Bud Freeman (ts); Pee Wee Russell (as); Irving Brodsky (p); Joe Venuti (vln); Eddie Lang (g); Min Leibrook (bsx); Chauncey Morehouse (dm); Hoagy Carmichael (voc) on 63653 and 63655

BVE 63653-1   **Georgia on My Mind** (Carmichael-Gorrell-arr. Carmichael)
solos: Carmichael, voc (30)—Venuti (2)—Lodwig (16)—Venuti (8)—Teagarden (6)—Bix, derby mute (10)

Bix didn't participate in the recording of the following title:

BVE 63654-1   **One Night in Havana**
(Carmichael-Porter-arr. Carmichael)

Same personnel as for "Georgia on My Mind"

BVE 63655-1   **Bessie Couldn't Help It** (Warner-Richmond-Bayha-arr. Carmichael)
BVE 63655-2   **Bessie Couldn't Help It**
solos: Bix (8)—Teagarden (32)—Venuti (8)—Freeman (16)—Carmichael, voc (32)—Dorsey (24)

ADDRESSES OF RECORDING STUDIOS

Whenever possible, record companies used the top floor of their buildings for studios. The floors were made of wood, and any noise coming from upstairs would have spoiled the recordings.

GENNETT (IN)	Gennett Recording Company South First and A Streets Richmond, Indiana
GENNETT (NY)	Starr Piano Co. 9–11 East 37th Street New York, NY
VICTOR (Detroit)	Victor Talking Machine Co. Detroit Athletic Club Detroit, Michigan
VICTOR (NY)	Victor Talking Machine Co. 28 West 44th Street (Lab)
	16 West 46th Street (Studio) New York, New York

The studio at 28 West 44th Street was the older of the two; the second appears to have been constructed for the Western Electric recording system, somewhere around 1925 or 1926. However, most of the post 1925 recordings were made at the older studio.

VICTOR (Church Studio, Camden)	Victor Talking Machine Co. Trinity Baptist Church 114 North 5th Street Camden, New Jersey
VICTOR (LH, NY)	Victor Talking Machine Co. Liederkranz Hall 111–119 East 58th Street New York, NY

Starting in April 1927, Victor leased the Grand Ballroom of the Liederkranz Hall for some of their recording sessions.

VICTOR (CHI)	Victor Talking Machine Co. 952 North Michigan Avenue Chicago, IL
RCA-VICTOR (LH, NY) a division of Radio Corp. of America	Liederkranz Hall, New York
RCA-VICTOR (Studio #2) a division of Radio Corp. of America	Studio # 2 145–155 East 24th Street, New York, NY

This location was the former New Gramercy movie studios, where the Bessie Smith movie was shot. Studios were at 145 East 24th Street, and offices at 155.

OKEH (NY)	Okeh Phonograph Corp. 25 West 45th Street (main office) 145 West 45th Street (Tom Rockwell's office in January 1927) 11 Union Square (studio opened at beginning of 1927) New York, NY

The New York Okeh studios recorded the best sounds of the 1920s. Unfortunately, the exact location for each session could not clearly be identified. A change in recording room acoustics is obvious between the February 4, 1927, session ("Singin' the Blues") and the following one, recorded on May 9, 1927 ("Riverboat Shuffle"). This move is confirmed by an article published in the April 1927 issue of *Talking Machine World*: "The Okeh recording laboratory is moving to new and larger quarters on April 1, in the old Tiffany building at 14th Street and Union Square." This building was on the right side of the Spingler Building, and it was Tiffany's jewelry store between 1870 and 1905.

OKEH (CHI)   Okeh Phonograph Corp.
                       Consolidated Talking Machine Co.
                       Building
                       227–229 West Washington Street
                       Chicago, IL

PERFECT (NY)   recorded by Pathé Phonograph &
                       Radio Corp.
                       150 East 53rd Street
                       New York, NY

COLUMBIA (NY)   Columbia Phonograph Co.
                       Gotham National Bank Building
                       1819 Broadway at
                       Columbus Circle
                       New York, NY
                       Columbia Phonograph Co.
                       55 Fifth Avenue
                       New York, NY

This second studio was opened in 1926. It was located between 12th and 13th Streets, very close to the Okeh studios at 11 Union Square.

COLUMBIA (US, NY) Columbia Phonograph Co.
                       Union Square (?)
                       New York, NY

According to Don Rayno, most of the Columbia files for the Whiteman sessions indicate in 1928 and 1929: "Union Square studios." On October 15, 1926, the Okeh and Odeon record divisions were sold to the Columbia Phonograph Company. Did Columbia use part of the Okeh studios at Union Square (see: OKEH NY) for these Whiteman recording sessions?

HARMONY (NY)   recorded by Columbia
                       Phonograph Co.
                       see possible addresses
                       for Columbia

BRUNSWICK (NY)   Brunswick-Balke-Collender
                       Company
                       799 Seventh Avenue
                       (at 52nd Street)
                       New York, NY

BRUNSWICK (CHI)   Brunswick-Balke-Collender
                       Company
                       Brunswick Building, 6th floor
                       623–633 South Wabash Ave.
                       Chicago, IL

Many thanks to James Kidd and Allan Sutton for their effective help and information. An article by Bernhard H. Behncke, related to Liederkranz Hall, was published in issue 134 (summer 2004) of *VJM'S Jazz & Bluesmart* (www.vjm.biz), and an article by Steven Lasker, "What Made That Great Okeh Sound?" was published in the autumn 2004 issue of the same magazine.

SOUND SOURCES (CD)

All the titles listed in the present discography are available in four volumes containing three CDs each, and one single CD for the fifth volume:

Bix Restored, The Complete Recordings and Alternates,
    Volume 1 (2000) to 5 (2005), released by
        Sunbeam Records/Origin Jazz Library
        1534 North Moorpark Road, PMB #333
        Thousand Oaks, CA 91360 USA
        www.originjazz.com

This remarkable and respectful remastering, carried out by John R. T. Davies and Michael Kieffer, is an invaluable reference. These CD box sets can be ordered from Origin Jazz Library.

The only titles or recording sessions not included in the *Bix Restored* sets are as follows:

—*(25) September 17, 1927*: the test-take of "Wringin' an' Twistin'" is included in the Mosaic Set MD7-211, **The Complete Okeh and Brunswick Bix Beiderbecke, Frank Trumbauer and Jack Teagarden ses-**

sions (1924–36), www.mosaicrecords.com, released in 2001. This 7-CD set includes the titles recorded by Bix and Tram in small groups. The sound restoration by Doug Pomeroy is splendid.

—*(58) March 3, 1928*: **Lou Raderman & His Pelham Heath Inn Orchestra**: the three sides recorded in this session are included in Columbia CK 46175 (CD), **Bix Beiderbecke Volume 2, *At the Jazz Band Ball.***

—*(100) January 10, 1929*: **Bee Palmer with the Frank Trumbauer Orchestra**: three takes of this session are included in the third CD of the above mentioned set Mosaic MD7-211.

—*(101) January 24, 1929*: **Ray Miller and His Orchestra:** *Cradle of Love*: 2 takes of this recording, unearthed by American musican and researcher Brad Kay, is included, with his comments, in the CD issued by the excellent Dutch label Timeless Records, www.timeless-records.com, under reference CBC 1-066: ***Ray Miller and his Brunswick Orchestra (1924–1929)***, with sound restoration by Hans Eekhoff.

—*(103) March 15, 1929*: **Paul Whiteman and His Orchestra: "Louise"**: this side can be found in the complete Bing Crosby series: **The Chronological Bing Crosby, Volume 6:** *January 26–September 6, 1929*, a JZCD-6 CD issued by Jonzo Records, PO Box 212, Harrow, Middlesex, HA3 7LD, England.

—*(113) January 21–22, 1930:* **Roger Wolfe Kahn and His Orchestra:** the first take of "When a Woman Loves a Man" (E31962) was issued, together with "Cooking Breakfast for the One I Love," on the Jazz Oracle CD BDW 8013: **Roger Wolfe Kahn, Recorded in New York, 1925–1932,** www.jazzoracle.com. The second can be heard on Norman Field's Web site: http://www.normanfield.com/jeanpierrelion.htm.

Bix Beiderbecke's compositions have been the subject of numerous interpretations, a selection of which follow, in chronological order:

—**"In a Mist": Red Norvo and Benny Goodman**, November 21, 1933 (on *Bix Beiderbecke Complete Edition, Volume 8, Masters of Jazz*) [Red Norvo recorded "In a Mist" for Brunswick as early as October 1929, but this take was not released.]

—**"Flashes" / "In the Dark"—"Candlelights": Jess Stacy** (p), November 15 or 16, 1935, January 18, 1939 (on *Bix Restored, volume 1*).

—**"In a Mist"—"Flashes"—"Davenport Blues"— "Candlelights"—"In the Dark": Bunny Berigan and His Men,** November 30 and December 1, 1938 (on *Bunny Berigan and his Orchestra, 1938,* Classics 815 and 844).

—**"In the Dark"—"Flashes"—"Candlelights"—"In a Mist": Ralph Sutton** (p), March 13, 1950, *The Bix Beiderbecke Suite* (on Mosaic MR20-134, *The Complete Commodore Jazz Recordings—Volume III*).

—**"Flashes"—"In a Mist"—"Candlelights"—"In the Dark"—"Davenport Blues": Dill Jones** (p), 1972 (on *Davenport Blues*, LP Chiaroscuro CR112; on this record, Dill Jones gives an interpretation of "I'd Climb the Highest Mountain," which was the basis for Bix's sixth composition: "For No Reason at All in C").

—**"Davenport Blues"—"Candlelights"—"Flashes"— "In the Dark"—"In a Mist": Bucky Pizzarelli Guitar Quintet**, February 4 and 5, 1974, *The Piano Music of Bix Beiderbecke*, arr. Bill Challis (on CD Audiophile DAPCD238).

—**"In a Mist"—"Flashes"—"Davenport Blues": Ry Cooder**, May 1978 (on *Jazz*, a CD released by Warner Bros.).

—**"In a Mist"—"Flashes"—"Candlelight"** [*sic*]—"In the Dark": **Joseph Smith** (p), 1993 (on *American Piano, Volume 4: Rhythmic Moments*, Premier Recordings PRCD 1028).

—**"In a Mist"—"Candlelights"—"Flashes"—"In the Dark"—"Davenport Blues": Mike Polad** (p), 1994 (on *Piano Deco, Volume 1*, Polecat Records CD 101; this record also includes "Adirondack Sketches," "Five American Dances," and "Sea Burial" by Eastwood Lane).

—"In a Mist"—"Candlelights"—"Flashes"—"In the Dark"—"Davenport Blues": **Patrick Artero** (tp & arr.), 2004 (on *2 Bix But Not Too Bix*, Nocturne NTCD 352, Paris).

Two recordings related to Bix are also of interest: one cut on June 24, 1999, **Randy Sandke and The New York All-stars**, with seven numbers associated with Bix Beiderbecke (*The Re-Discovered Louis and Bix*, Nagel-Heyer CD 058). The titles selected are:

—"**No One Knows What It's All About**" (Rose-Wood): recorded on January 26, 1925, in Richmond by **Bix and His Rhythm Jugglers**, and destroyed by Gennett

—"**Play It Red**" (Barris): recorded in Camden on May 23, 1927, by **Jean Goldkette and His Orchestra**, and rejected by Victor

—"**Lily**" (McDonald-Warren-Broones): also recorded in Camden by the **Goldkette Orchestra**, on May 16, 1927, all four takes were destroyed

—"**Did You Mean It?**" (Baker-Silvers-Lyman): recorded by the **Frank Trumbauer Orchestra** on October 26, 1927, during the session that produced the controversial "Sugar"; all three takes were destroyed

—"**Stampede**" (Fletcher Henderson): recorded on February 1, 1927, by the **Goldkette Orchestra**, follow-ing "My Pretty Girl"; neither of the two takes has been found

—"**Betcha I Getcha**" (Beiderbecke?-Venuti): Joe Venuti asserted to have composed this title with Bix: pianist Dick Hyman recorded Venuti's version and transcribed it

—"**Cloudy**" (Beiderbecke?): piece played by Charlie Davis in Brigitte Berman's documentary film *Bix, Ain't None of Them Played Like Him Yet*; Charlie Davis said that Bix had played this tune for him, and had entitled it "Cloudy"

and that recorded in January and March 2003 by **Tom Pletcher-Dick Hyman and their Gang,** *If Bix Played Gershwin:* the CD includes sixteen George Gershwin compositions that Bix never recorded, one title written by Ira Gershwin—"**Sunny Disposish**"—which was recorded by the Goldkette Orchestra, and Bix's composition, "In a Mist" (ARCD 19283, by Arbors Records, Inc.).

FILMOGRAPHY

A DVD of the Goldkette film (see p124n23) is available from the Louisiana State Museum, P.O. Box 2448, New Orleans, LA 70176, USA; contact Mr. Tom Lanham, tlanham@crt.state.la.us.

The Fox Movietone newsreel, filmed on May 15, 1928, is included in part on the Yazoo 514 DVD, *At the Jazz Band Ball*, Shanachie Entertainment Corp, 2000; and also on Brigitte Berman's *Bix, Ain't None of Them Play Like Him Yet*, a Playboy Jazz DVD, Playboy Entertainment Group, 1994.

Index